ADMINISTRATIVE PROCEDURE AND PRACTICE

PROBLEMS AND CASES

Second Edition

By

William F. Funk
Professor of Law
Lewis and Clark Law School

Sidney A. Shapiro
John M. Rounds Professor of Law
University of Kansas
School of Law

Russell L. Weaver
Professor of Law
University of Louisville
School of Law

AMERICAN CASEBOOK SERIES®

WEST GROUP

A THOMSON COMPANY

ST. PAUL, MINN., 2001

American Casebook Series, and the West Group symbol
are registered trademarks used herein under license.

COPYRIGHT © 1997 WEST GROUP
COPYRIGHT © 2001 By WEST GROUP
        610 Opperman Drive
        P.O. Box 64526
        St. Paul, MN 55164–0526
        1–800–328–9352

ISBN 0–314–24650–9

 TEXT IS PRINTED ON 10% POST CONSUMER RECYCLED PAPER

2nd Reprint — 2004

For Renate,
for Jeremy and Sarah,
and for Ben and Kate

*

Preface to the First Edition

Most law students will practice administrative law sometime in their careers. Some students will work for the government as attorneys or in other capacities. Most other students will end up with administrative law issues because their clients will inevitably be involved in some governmental activity. Clients cannot avoid such entanglements because government is so intertwined in our lives. Indeed, it is difficult to think of any commercial or social activity that is not impacted (at least indirectly) by some local, state, or federal administrative agency.

The main goal of this book is to prepare you for the practice of administrative law. Our approach has three parts. First, we rely on a problem method, which simulates the day-to-day problem solving and advocacy in which practitioners of administrative law are involved. The problems are drawn from actual administrative law issues and you will be asked to perform the same functions as the administrative lawyers involved in these issues. As in real life, where most administrative law practice occurs in the agencies, rather than the courts, many problems are not structured as judicial appeals. For example, there is significant treatment of lobbying and the use of the political process as part of the administrative process. In addition, problems involving ethical issues peculiar to administrative law practice, which are almost never covered in professional responsibility courses, are included as an integral part of the book. The final chapter even deals with how lawyers get paid in administrative law practice, an important practice issue for many lawyers.

Second, our coverage of the two basic procedural approaches in administrative law, rulemaking (Chapter 2) and adjudication (Chapter 3), is presented in chronological order. Coverage begins with the first event in each process and continues step-by-step until the completion of the process. Thus, you will experience each process in the same manner as if you were participating in it from its inception to its completion.

Finally, as you become acquainted with the day-to-day realities of administrative law practice, we ask you to consider some of the theoretical issues presented by administrative law. Lawyers in administrative practice quickly realize that unelected administrators exercise significant power, and that administrative law is intended to make the exercise of such authority more accountable. As citizens and lawyers, how well administrative law accomplishes this purpose is worthy of consideration. The theory of administrative law may be even more important to its practice. A lawyer is more effective if he or she understands the connection between an administrative law rule and the goal or purpose that rule is supposed to serve.

Our approach affects the way that teachers teach and students study. Each section begins with a narrative description of the law, much like a hornbook, which may also include short excerpts from leading cases. This material, including the cases, is intended to acquaint you with the legal rules that govern an area. If those principles of law are well settled, the problems use the rules to explore the area beyond where the law is clear. Of course, where the basic law is not clear, it becomes a fertile source for the problems itself. Problem materials, which can include cases, statutes, regulations, and other materials, are provided as resources to aid the student in addressing the problems. These materials are the type of documents that you would consult in practice to resolve the issues presented by a problem. You will need to read the problem materials closely because they are used to resolve the problem presented in the text. Unlike in other casebooks, however, understanding these materials, particularly the cases, is not an end in itself, it is only a means to the end of trying to answer the problem, as in real life.

Although this book is different from other administrative law casebooks in its presentation and practice orientation, it is also traditional in several ways. First, all of the subject matter of traditional administrative law courses is included. The addition of more practice-oriented materials has not been at the sacrifice of traditional administrative law subjects. Second, the focus of the book is federal administrative law, although state administrative law issues and differences are not ignored. Each of the authors has substantial state administrative law experience and expertise, so that the secondary place of state administrative law is not due to any belief in its lack of importance, especially as a practice area. Nevertheless, learning basic administrative law in a semester course is difficult enough, without attempting to play too many variations on a theme. Finally, we include the important questions of administrative law theory, although they receive less emphasis than in other books because of our practice orientation. Nevertheless, we anticipate that students may gain a better understanding of such issues. As mentioned, our approach is to raise a theoretical issue after students are acquainted with the area of administrative law practice in which the issue arises, which should assist students in thinking about the issue.

W.F.F.
S.A.S
R.L.W.

January, 1997

Preface to the Second Edition

The first edition of this casebook arose out of the authors' interest in focusing the administrative law course on administrative law practice. To accomplish this goal, we organized the book around using problems as the primary teaching method, rather than the presentation of traditional cases for analysis and synthesis by students. We presented students with cases, statutes, federal register notices, legislative history, and the like as tools to solve the problems, just as students might use these materials as lawyers. We also organize the book to introduce students to all stages of the administrative process, from lobbying, internal agency deliberations, client counseling, and ethical problems to the more traditional judicial review. Finally, the first edition reversed the traditional orientation of many administrative law casebooks which start with administrative law theory. While theory was not ignored, our coverage arose out of the crucible of the reality-based problems, providing students a basis to understand the theory.

We were pleased with the reception that our innovations received. Our aim in this edition is to retain and strengthen the approach of the first edition. Thus, we have retained most of the problems and materials of the first edition, but, based on the feedback of users, we have fine-tuned some of the existing problems and replaced others. We have also rearranged material in two of the chapters for better clarity, and, of course, updated the book in light of judicial and legislative developments that have occurred since the first edition.

We will continue to maintain an online web-based supplement to keep the book up to date with the latest administrative law developments. Its address is: http://www.lclark.edu/~funk/adlaw/.

As with the first edition, we view the casebook as a collaborative effort. We appreciate the feedback that we received from our colleagues at other law schools who used the casebook, and we look forward to collaboration with them on this edition.

W.F.F.
S.A.S.
R.L.W.

March, 2001

*

Supplement

_____

A web-based supplement can be found at:
http://www.lclark.edu/~funk/adlaw/.

*

Acknowledgments

As those who have done so know, preparing a "casebook" is an arduous process, requiring the assistance of many persons. Not the least of those are the students who had to suffer through prior drafts. Preparing a "cases and problems book" is even harder on students, because problems, like exam questions, are not easy to write. Often, struggling with a problem in class demonstrates unforeseen difficulties. So, we are very grateful, if not a little apologetic, to the several classes of students at Lewis and Clark, Kansas, and Louisville that have helped to hone the problems in this book. If they work, it is largely due to the students' feedback; if they do not, it is probably because we did not pay enough attention to the student comments. In addition, we would like to thank in particular Tom McMann at Louisville for his research assistance and Audie Huber, Maureen Flanagan, and Jennifer Reibman at Lewis and Clark for their proofreading. Of course, we retain all responsibility for any errors.

We acknowledge with appreciation the following authors, publishers, and journals which have graciously granted permission to reprint excerpts from their publications:

Administrative & Regulatory Law News: Daniel E. Troy, *New Congressional Review Procedures of Agency Rules,* 21 ADMIN. & REG.LAW NEWS 4 (Summer, 1996). Daniel Troy is a partner at Wiley, Rein and Fielding and an associate scholar at the American Enterprise Institute.

Administrative Law Journal: *Initiating Agency Action: Comments of Patricia Bailey,* 5 ADMIN. L. J. OF AM. U. 24 (1991).

Administrative Law Journal: *Initiating Agency Action: Comments of Cornish Hitchcock,* 5 ADMIN. L. J. OF AM. U. 53 (1991).

Administrative Law Review: Roger C. Cramton, *Administrative Procedure Reform: The Effects of S. 1663 on the Conduct of Federal Rate Proceedings,* 16 ADMIN. L. REV. 108 (1964).

Administrative Law Review: Thomas M. Susman, *A Perspective on the Washington Lawyer Today and Charles Horsky's Washington Lawyer of 1952,* 44 ADMIN. L. REV. 1 (1991).

Administrative Law Review: Richard M. Thomas, *Prosecutorial Discretion and Agency Self-Regulation: CNI v. Young and the Aflatoxin Dance,* 44 ADMIN. L. REV. 131 (1992).

American Bar Association: ABA MODEL RULES OF PROFESSIONAL CONDUCT (1995); ABA MODEL CODE OF PROFESSIONAL RESPONSIBILITY (1981). Copies of the ABA *Model Rules of Professional Conduct* (1995) and the ABA *Model Code of Professional Responsibility* (1981) are available from Member Services, American Bar Association, 750 North Lake Shore Drive, Chicago, IL. 60611.

Aspen Law and Business: K. DAVIS & R. PIERCE, JR., ADMINISTRATIVE LAW TREATISE, §9.2, at 7 (1994). Copyright © 1994 Little, Brown and Company, assigned to Aspen Law & Business, a division of Aspen Publishers, Inc.

District of Columbia Bar: Report By The District of Columbia Bar Special Committee On Governmental Lawyers and the Model Rules of Professional Conduct.

Duke Law Journal: William V. Luneburg, *Retroactivity And Administrative Rulemaking,* 1991 DUKE L.J. 106.

Duke Law Journal: Antonin Scalia, *Judicial Deference to Administrative Interpretations of Law,* 1989 DUKE L.J. 511.

Duke Law Journal: Sidney A. Shapiro & Robert L. Glicksman, *Congress, the Supreme Court, and the Quiet Revolution in Administrative Law,* 1988 DUKE L.J. 819.

Duke Law Journal: Sidney A. Shapiro & Thomas O. McGarity, *Not So Paradoxical: The Rationale For Technology-Based Regulation,* 1991 DUKE L.J. 729.

Duke Law Journal: Peter L. Strauss, *The Rulemaking Continuum,* 41 DUKE L.J. 1463 (1992).

Environmental Law: William Funk, *When Smoke Gets in Your Eyes: Regulatory Negotiation and the Public Interest—EPA's Woodstove Standards,* 18 ENVL. L. 55 (1987).

Federal Bar News and Journal: Bruce Fein, *Promoting the President's Policies Through Legal Advocacy: An Ethical Imperative of the Government Attorney,* FEDERAL BAR NEWS & JOURNAL, September/October 1983, Volume 30, No. 9–10, 6–10.

George Washington Law Review: Douglas Letter, *Lawyering and Judging on Behalf of the United States: All I Ask for Is a Little Respect,* 61 GEO. WASH. L. REV. 1295 (1993).

Harvard Law Review: Richard H. Fallon, Jr., *Of Legislative Courts, Administrative Agencies, and Article III,* 101 HARV. L. REV. 915 (1988). © By The Harvard Law Review Association.

Kansas Law Review: Russell Weaver, Chevron: Martin, *Anthony, and Format Requirements,* 40 KAN. L. REV. 587 (1992).

Law and Contemporary Problems: Thomas O. McGarity, *The Internal Structure of EPA Rulemaking,* 54 Law & Contemp. Probs., Autumn 1991, at 57.

Minnesota Law Review: Ronald M. Levin, *Understanding Unreviewability in Administrative Law,* 74 MINN. L. REV. 689 (1990).

New York Law Publishing Company: George Van Cleve, *Deciding When to Contest an EPA Rule,* NATIONAL LAW JOURNAL, May 31, 1993, at 25.

Reprinted with the permission of *The National Law Journal.* 1993, The New York Law Publishing Company, and of George Van Cleve, Attorney At Law, Washington, D.C. (former Deputy Assistant Attorney General, Environmental and Natural Resources, U.S. Department of Justice).

Notre Dame Law Review: Russell L. Weaver, *Retroactive Regulatory Interpretations: An Analysis of Judicial Responses,* 1 NOTRE DAME L. REV. 167 (1986). Volume 61, Issue 5, the *Notre Dame Law Review* (1986) 167–219. Reprinted with permission. Copyright © by *Notre Dame Law Review,* University of Notre Dame. The Notre Dame Law Review does not bear any responsibility for any errors which have occurred in reprinting or editing.

Seton Hall Law Review: William Funk, *Close Enough for Government Work?—Using Informal Procedures for Imposing Administrative Penalties,* 24 SETON HALL L. REV. 1 (1993).

University of Pennsylvania Law Review: Harold Leventhal, *Environmental Decisionmaking And The Role of The Courts,* 122 U. Pa. L. Rev. 509 (1974).

Yale Journal on Regulation: Robert A. Anthony, *Which Agency Interpretations Should Bind Citizens and the Courts?,* 7 YALE J. REG. 1 (1990). Copyright © 1990 by the YALE JOURNAL ON REGULATION, P.O. Box 20815, New Haven, CT. 06520–8215. Reprinted from Volume 7:1 by permission. All rights reserved.

Yale Journal on Regulation: Lawrence Susskind & Gerard McMahon, *The Theory and Practice of Negotiated Rulemaking,* 3 YALE J. ON REG. 133 (1985). Copyright © 1985 by the YALE JOURNAL ON REGULATION, P.O. Box 20815, New Haven, CT. 06520–8215. Reprinted from Volume 3:1 by permission. All rights reserved.

*

Summary of Contents

Table of Contents

*

Table of Cases

The principal cases are in bold type. Cases cited or discussed in the text are roman type. References are to pages. Cases cited in principal cases and within other quoted materials are not included.

*

ADMINISTRATIVE PROCEDURE AND PRACTICE

PROBLEMS AND CASES

Second Edition

*

Chapter 1

ADMINISTRATIVE LAW PRACTICE

This book is about administrative law and, in particular, about administrative law practice. The following is a typical example of a case involving administrative law and administrative law practice.

FUND FOR ANIMALS, INC. v. RICE
85 F.3d 535 (11th Cir.1996).

DUBINA, CIRCUIT JUDGE:

The Plaintiffs–Appellants ("the Plaintiffs"), seek to prevent the construction of a municipal landfill on a site in Sarasota County, Florida, that the Plaintiffs claim is an indispensable habitat for the highly endangered Florida Panther and also home to the threatened Eastern Indigo Snake. . . .

I. BACKGROUND

The Florida Panther (Felis concolor coryi) was listed as endangered [by the Fish and Wildlife Service (FWS)] in 1967. See 32 Fed.Reg. 4001. This panther, which is a subspecies of the cougar, "is a large, slender cat, tawny above and whitish below." According to the FWS, the Florida Panther is "one of the most endangered large mammals in the world." Although the Florida Panther once ranged throughout the Southeastern United States, it has been reduced to a single population in south Florida. The "geographic isolation, habitat loss, small population size, and associated inbreeding" of the remaining population have resulted in a significant loss of health and genetic variability in Florida Panthers. According to current estimates, there are only thirty to fifty adult Florida Panthers left in the wild. However, the record in this case indicates that there have been no confirmed sightings of the Florida Panther in the area in which the landfill is to be built.

The Eastern Indigo Snake (Drymarchon corais couperi) was listed as threatened in 1978. Measuring up to 8½ feet, this docile, nonpoisonous snake is the longest found in North America. Although this iridescent black snake once ranged throughout Florida, Georgia, southeastern

1

South Carolina, southern Alabama, and southern Mississippi, its known populations are now restricted to certain areas in Florida and Georgia.

On November 22, 1989, the United States Army Corps of Engineers ("the Corps") received an application from Sarasota County, Florida ("Sarasota County" or "the County") for a permit under Section 404 of the Clean Water Act ("CWA"). [That Act prohibits the discharge of dredged or fill material into the waters of the United States without a permit from the Corps of Engineers. Waters of the United States include wetlands. The Corps can grant a permit only if the proposed discharge is consistent with the Section 404(b)(1) guidelines promulgated by the Environmental Protection Agency (EPA). EPA may review proposed permit issuances for consistency with the guidelines. In addition, if a government action may adversely affect an endangered species, the Endangered Species Act (ESA) requires the FWS to review the action and issue a "Biological Opinion" assessing whether the adverse effect would "jeopardize" the species. Agencies are prohibited from taking an action that would jeopardize a species. Finally, the National Environmental Policy Act (NEPA) requires all agencies, if their actions may have a significant effect on the environment, to create Environmental Impact Statements (EIS). Agencies conduct Environmental Assessments to determine whether an EIS is required.] The proposed project for which Sarasota County sought a permit consists of constructing an 895–acre landfill and required ancillary structures on a 6,150–acre site known as the "Walton Tract." . . . According to current projections, the fill material for the landfill will impact approximately seventy-four acres of isolated wetlands. . . .

During June of 1990, the Corps dispersed notice of Sarasota County's application to government agencies, private organizations, and other interested persons. The notice invited public comment on the landfill proposal. Two months later, the FWS issued a Biological Opinion consenting to the project, [although it did not consider the effect on the Florida Panther or the Eastern Indigo Snake.] However, the EPA recommended denial of the permit under Section 404(b)(1) of the guidelines promulgated pursuant to the Clean Water Act. At that time, Sarasota County projected that the landfill would affect 120 acres of wetlands.

The following year, Sarasota County submitted an alternative analysis, which included modifications of the project calculated to reduce the prospective effect on wetlands . . . from 120 acres to approximately seventy-four acres. In February of 1994, the EPA notified the Corps that it no longer objected to the issuance of the permit.

At the end of May 1994, the Corps completed an Environmental Assessment and Statement of Findings, determining that no environmental impact statement was required. In addition, the Corps announced that a public hearing would not benefit the decision-making process. After nearly five years of administrative review, the Corps approved the requested permit on June 3, 1994. . . . [Two weeks later the plaintiffs notified defendants of their intent to sue.] Two months later, the FWS requested resumption of [consultation] under the ESA to allow consideration of any potential effect on the Florida Panther and the Eastern Indigo Snake.

In October of 1994, the FWS issued its first Biological Opinion addressing concerns regarding the Florida Panther and the Eastern Indigo Snake. The Opinion concluded that the project was unlikely to jeopardize further the existence of either the Florida Panther or the Eastern Indigo Snake. However, it did include . . . recommendations for Florida Panther conservation, wetland preservation, and a monitoring program. The Corps incorporated the FWS's recommendations and modified Sarasota County's permit on November 14, 1994. Two weeks later, the Plaintiffs commenced an action in federal district court against the Corps, the FWS, the EPA, and the Sarasota County Administrator. . . .

In response to the suit, the FWS requested that the Corps resume . . . consultation on the permit. The Corps suspended Sarasota County's permit the next day. . . . In April of 1995, the FWS issued to the Corps its second Biological Opinion addressing concerns regarding the Florida Panther and the Eastern Indigo Snake. The Opinion included [more] conservation recommendations for the Florida Panther. This Opinion, which superseded the FWS's previous Biological Opinion, again concluded that the proposed project was unlikely to jeopardize the continued existence of either the Florida Panther or the Eastern Indigo Snake.

On April 12, 1995, the Plaintiffs submitted comments to the Corps on the FWS's new Biological Opinion. The next day, the Corps determined, based on the FWS's Biological Opinion and the Corps' independent environmental assessment, that reinstatement of the permit to dredge and fill seventy-four acres of wetlands with additional modifications was in the public interest. Thus, the modified permit was reinstated on April 13, 1995.

Following final issuance of the permit, the Plaintiffs filed their Second Amended Complaint. . . . The complaint requested declaratory and injunctive relief. . . .

II. Statement of the Issues

(1) Whether the district court erred in finding that the Corps did not act arbitrarily or capriciously in making the following three decisions: A. to grant a permit to fill seventy-four acres of wetland on the Walton Tract for a county landfill; B. not to hold its own public hearing on the project; and C. not to prepare an Environmental Impact Statement under NEPA. (2) Whether the district court erred in finding that the FWS did not violate the ESA by issuing "no jeopardy" Biological Opinions and in finding that the Corps did not act arbitrarily or capriciously in relying on those Opinions. . . .

IV. Discussion

[The court found against the plaintiff on all the issues and so affirmed the district court which had denied relief to the plaintiffs.]

Notes and Questions

1. One of the ways that this case is a typical administrative law case is that it involves private persons, regulated entities, and government agencies. It is usual in administrative law cases to have three different perspectives on a problem—the government agency that has done something; a person or group outside the agency that approves of what the agency has done; and a person or group outside the agency that disapproves of what the agency has done. Here there are several government agencies—the Corps of Engineers, the Environmental Protection Agency, and the Fish and Wildlife Service—and each has its particular role. The regulated entity is Sarasota County; it is a regulated entity because it wants to fill a wetland, and the Clean Water Act forbids persons from filling a wetland without a permit issued by the Corps of Engineers under standards derived from the Act. In addition, there are members of the public (who belong to the Fund for the Animals), who are not subject to the regulation, but who we might say are among the intended beneficiaries of the Act.

2. The case is also typical because it involves an agency doing something to or for someone. Here the Corps of Engineers has granted a permit to Sarasota County. The environmental group is unhappy that the permit was granted, and although the Corps has not done anything to it, the environmental group goes to court because it believes the Corps has not acted lawfully in granting the permit. If the Corps had instead denied the permit as inconsistent with the Act, Sarasota County might have brought this suit, instead of the environmental group, asserting that the Corps acted unlawfully.

3. Another way this case is typical is that the plaintiffs bring their suit under the Administrative Procedure Act arguing, among other things, that the Corps acted unlawfully by not complying with required procedures applicable to granting these permits. Recall that the plaintiffs argue the agency did not hold a required hearing and failed to prepare a required Environmental Impact Statement. Administrative law, we will find, is full of required procedures that agencies must follow. Failure to follow those procedures is likely to result in reversal of the agency action. Here, however, the court rejected the plaintiffs' arguments that the agency did not comply with applicable procedures.

4. Still another way this case is typical is that the lawsuit is similar to the visible portion of the iceberg. Most of the lawyering in this case occurred in the administrative process prior to the lawsuit being heard. Both Sarasota County and the environmental group were actively pursuing their administrative avenues of influencing the agency's decision, by filing comments, briefs, evidence, letters not only with the Corps, but also with EPA and the FWS, because of their participation in the permit decision under the CWA and the ESA. Both the time and effort expended in the administrative process dwarf the time and effort spent in litigation, and the threat of litigation is useful to influence the administrative

process. Finally and typically, while the party that won in the administrative process (Sarasota County) was the ultimately successful party, as the case describes, the environmental groups' efforts were not for naught. Ultimately, the Corps issued a permit that contained numerous conservation, mitigation, and monitoring requirements to protect the endangered species which would not have been included but for the group's participation in the administrative process.

A. WHAT IS ADMINISTRATIVE LAW AND WHY SHOULD WE STUDY IT?

American government, whether federal, state, or local, is characterized by administrative agencies. Federal administrative agencies decide what percentage of peanut butter by weight must come from peanuts, how many and what type of emissions can come from woodstoves and automobiles, the extent of workplace safety, and a host of other things. Agencies range from the well-known, such as the Environmental Protection Agency (EPA), to the obscure, such as the Occupational Safety and Health Review Commission (OSHRC). State administrative agencies can regulate air and water pollution in their states, set rates that utility companies can charge their customers, license admission to the practice of professions—from beauticians to lawyers, from barbers to doctors—and, of course, much more. State agencies are not usually as well-known as federal agencies, and what is more, they differ from state to state, even if they perform much the same functions.

Administrative law, broadly conceived, includes two different facets: the law that governs agencies and the law that agencies make. The latter you generally study in courses on the substantive law, such as labor law, securities law, environmental law, or tax law. The former you study in administrative law. Why you might study the substantive law that agencies make is self-evident. As lawyers, your clients will be subject to or have to deal with that law. It may be less clear why you should study the administrative law that governs agencies. The answer is several-fold. First, you might work as a lawyer for a government agency, in which case administrative law will govern many of your agency's activities in the same way that substantive law governs private actors. Second, as a lawyer in private practice, you may be faced with an agency taking some action that may be beneficial or detrimental to your client. This is equally true for a lawyer who works for a "public interest" group, where the agency action may further or hinder the goals of your group. Administrative law may provide you with the means to influence the agency's decision, or, if you are dissatisfied with it, the basis for challenging that decision. Third, and most broadly, studying the law that governs agencies is like an extension of Constitutional Law; you learn about how the legal system as a whole operates, the interrelationship at the federal level between Congress, the President, agencies, and the courts. This in turn will make you a better lawyer.

In beginning this enterprise, it would be nice to meet the objects of administrative law: the agencies. As indicated above, there is a wide range of federal agencies, so many, that any list of them is bound to be incomplete. Chart 1–1 provides a rough introduction to the most important agencies. You should note that agencies, besides having different areas of administration, come in different shapes and sizes.

1. WHAT IS AN AGENCY?

This is a good time to expose yourself to the Administrative Procedure Act (APA), which is the foundation of any administrative law course. Section 551, the definitions section of the Act, defines "agency" in subsection (1).

"Departments" are agencies, and they have the highest status. This explains initiatives to make agencies into departments to give them greater importance, such as President Clinton's early attempt to have the Environmental Protection Agency made into the Department of the Environment, and vice-versa to downgrade their importance, such as attempts in 1995–96 to de-departmentalize the Departments of Commerce, Education, and Energy. As Chart 1–1 indicates, departments invariably have various sub-entities with specialized responsibilities. Before there were so many departments, Presidents tended to utilize their heads collectively as a group, called the Cabinet, for advice and counsel. While the term is still used to refer collectively to the department heads, recent Presidents have created new entities for advice and counsel.

Chart 1–1
FEDERAL AGENCIES

Departments Some Subentities	Description	Regional Offices	Number of employees	Number of Lawyers
Agriculture (Office of General Counsel)				235
Forest Service	Manages and regulates the national forests	9	40606	
Food and Nutrition Service	Runs food stamp, school lunch, food donation, and emergency food assistance programs	7	2794	
Food Safety and Inspection Service	Sets standards for food processing plants and for food with meat in it	5	14171	
Natural Resources Conservation Service	Promotes the conservation of soil, water, and related resources			
Commerce Department (Office of General Counsel)				120
Bureau of Export Administration	Oversees export licensing, technology and policy analysis and foreign availabili-	7		13

Departments Some Subentities	Description	Regional Offices	Number of employees	Number of Lawyers
	ty, enforces export control laws			
National Oceanic and Atmospheric Administration	Explores, maps, and charts the global ocean and its living resources and manages, uses, and conserves those resources; implements the Coastal Zone Management Act	11		61
National Marine Fisheries Service *	Regulates fishery limits; administers Endangered Species Act with respect to marine species			
International Trade Administration	Expands exports, improves enforcement of U.S. laws, upgrades government activities	52		41
Defense (Office of General Counsel)				29
Army Corps of Engineers	Regulates all construction of projects in the navigable waters of the United States; administers the Clean Water Act's § 404 program	12		490
Education (Office of General Counsel)				65
Office of Civil Rights	Protects the rights of students in education programs or activities that receive financial assistance from the Dept. of Education	10		96
Energy (Office of General Counsel)				248
Federal Energy Regulatory Commission **	Regulates transmission, prices, pipelines and services of oil and natural gas; regulates interstate sales of electricity; licenses hydroelectric facilities	5	1643	220
Energy Information Administration	Gathers statistical data on energy production and consumption			
Health and Human Services (Office of General Counsel)				415
Office for Civil Rights	Ensures that HHS financial aid beneficiaries receive benefits without discrimination	10	1,479	
Administration for Families and Children	Responsible for federal programs that promote the			

* NMFS is actually a subentity of NOAA.

** Although a subentity within the Department of Energy, the Federal Energy Regulatory Commission is also an independent regulatory agency, meaning that it is part of the Department of Energy for administrative purposes only, and otherwise is not subject to the supervision or control of the Department.

Departments Some Subentities	Description	Regional Offices	Number of employees	Number of Lawyers
	economic and social well-being of families, children, individuals, and communities			
Public Health Service	Promotes standards that assure the highest level of health care is available for all U.S. citizens and cooperates with other nations on health projects	10		
Food and Drug Administration	Assures safety, effectiveness, and proper labeling of foods, drugs, cosmetics, and medical devices	6	8,383	40
Health Care Financing Administration	Oversees medicare and medicaid programs, and related federal medical care quality control staffs	N/A		
Housing and Urban Development (Office of General Counsel)				150
Office of Equal Opportunity and Fair Housing	Administers the fair housing program. Advises the HUD secretary on civil rights issues	10	113	
Office of Housing	Insures mortgages on single family homes, multi-family rental homes, condominiums, land purchased for residential development, nursing homes, hospitals, etc.	10		
Office of Public and Indian Housing	Directs HUD's low-income housing program and coordinates all departmental housing and community development programs for Indians and Alaskan natives	6		
Interior (Office of the Solicitor)				275
U.S. Fish and Wildlife Service	Conservation of fish and wildlife resources and their habitats; administers the Endangered Species Act for terrestrial species	7	7,672	
Bureau of Indian Affairs	Promotes Indian economic development and assists tribes in preserving their natural resources	12		
National Park Service	Conserves scenery, natural and historic objects, and wildlife in the nation's parks	10	13,934	
Bureau of Reclamation	Responsible for water and power resource development protection and management in the 17 western states	5		
Bureau of Land Management	Administers 270 million acres of public lands, develops mineral resources on 582 million more acres	4	9,655	

Departments Some Subentities	Description	Regional Offices	Number of employees	Number of Lawyers
Justice				
Drug Enforcement Administration	Coordinates the drug enforcement activities of other federal agencies and works with them to control the supply of illicit drugs in the United States	21		27
Immigration and Naturalization Service	Responsible for enforcing the laws regulating the admission of foreign-born persons (aliens) to the United States	3		
Labor (Office of General Counsel)				700
Occupational Safety and Health Administration	Sets and enforces standards to achieve safe and healthy work environments and conditions	94	3,002	20
Pension and Welfare Benefits Administration	Regulates pension and benefit plans, ensures compliance with ERISA		478	N/A
State (Office of Legal Advisor)				100
Transportation (Office of General Counsel)				70
United States Coast Guard	Regulates vessels, sets and enforces safety standards, and prescribes license requirements for merchant marine personnel	17		20
Federal Aviation Administration	Establishes and enforces rules and regulations for safety standards covering all aspects of civil aviation	11	56,393	185
Federal Highway Administration	Sets functional safety standards for design, construction, and maintenance of the nation's highways	10		45
National Highway Transportation Safety Administration	Sets and enforces motor vehicle safety standards and determines when recalls are warranted	10	913	22
Treasury (Office of General Counsel)				2,100
Bureau of Alcohol, Tobacco, and Firearms	Combines functions involving enforcement, industry regulation, and tax collection	29		50
United States Customs Service	Assesses and collects duties on imports and enforces customs laws	7	16,003	105
Internal Revenue Service	Collects income and social security taxes	7	84,522	1,400
Veterans Affairs (Office of General Counsel)	Administers programs to assist the nation's veterans, their families, and dependents			100

Independent Executive Branch Agencies	Description	Regional Offices	Number of employees	Number of Lawyers
Equal Employment Opportunity Commission	Enforces employment discrimination laws	50	3622	144
Social Security Administration	Administers the social security system	10	84774	519
Environmental Protection Agency	Establishes and enforces air and water quality standards, implements federal environmental statutes	10	12,891	360

Independent Regulatory Agencies	Description	Regional Offices	Number of employees	Number of Lawyers	# & Tenure of Members
Federal Communications Commission	Regulates interstate and foreign communications by radio, cable, television, wire, and satellite	5	2233	250	5 members 5 yrs.
Federal Deposit Insurance Corp.	Protects bank depositors and the nation's money supply by insuring deposits	12	3544	900	5 members 6 yrs.
Consumer Product Safety Commission	Protects the public against risks caused by, and develops standards for, consumer products	3	927	13	5 members 7 yrs.
Federal Trade Commission	Combats business monopolies, trade restraints, and fraud and deception in the marketplace	10	2032	311	5 members 7 yrs.
National Labor Relations Board	Enforces the federal labor-management laws, adjudicates disputes over unfair labor practices	34	3032	650	5 members 5 yrs.
Securities and Exchange Commission	Implements and enforces federal securities laws	9	2155	710	5 members 5 yrs.
Commodity Futures Trading Commission	Regulates the trade in commodities futures	4	447	130	5 members 5 yrs.
Federal Election Commission	Administers compliance with laws governing election campaigns		270	42	6 members 6 yrs.
Nuclear Regulatory Commission	Regulates civilian uses of nuclear power	5	3078	65	5 members 5 yrs.
Federal Reserve System Board of Governors	Conducts the federal government's monetary policy	37		40	7 members 14 yrs.
Occupational Safety and Health Review Commission	Adjudicates and hears appeals from adjudications of enforcement actions under the Occupational Safety and Health Act			10	3 members 6 yrs.
Federal Mine Safety and Health Review Commission	Adjudicates and hears appeals from adjudications of enforcement actions under the Federal Mine Safety and Health Act				5 members 6 yrs.

Sources: CONGRESSIONAL QUARTERLY, FEDERAL REGULATORY DIRECTORY (Carolyn Goldinger, ed. 1990); AMERICAN BAR ASSOCIATION, NOW HIRING: GOVERNMENT JOBS FOR LAWYERS (Abbie Thorner, ed. 1988); UNITED STATES SENATE COMMITTEE OF GOVERNMENT AFFAIRS, ORGANIZATION OF FEDERAL EXECUTIVE DEPARTMENTS AND AGENCIES (1980); FEDERAL REPORTS, INC., FEDERAL CAREERS FOR ATTORNEYS (Richard L. Herman, Linda P. Sutherland, Beth Fishkin, eds. 1991)

With the exception of the Department of Justice, headed by the Attorney General, departments are headed by a "Secretary." The President appoints these heads with the advice and consent of the Senate, and by tradition (the laws creating the departments being silent on the question) they hold their offices at the pleasure of the President, which means he can fire them for any reason. Departments invariably have a General Counsel or its equivalent (*e.g.*, the Department of Interior's chief lawyer is called the Solicitor) who is in charge of the department's lawyers.

Departments always contain a host of subentities, each of which is an agency for legal purposes. For example, the Forest Service is an agency within the Department of Agriculture, the Corps of Engineers is an agency within the Department of the Army, and the Food and Drug Administration (FDA) is an agency within the Department of Health and Human Services (HHS). The individuals who head most of these agencies within departments, such as the Internal Revenue Service (IRS) within the Treasury Department, the Federal Bureau of Investigation (FBI) within the Justice Department, and the Fish and Wildlife Service within the Department of Interior, likewise are appointed by the President with the advice and consent of the Senate, and serve at the President's pleasure. The titles for these agency heads vary greatly and do not have independent significance. Some are Assistant Secretaries within the department; others may be Administrators, Directors, or Chiefs. Many of the agencies within departments have their own legal staff to advise the agency and its head. Thus, the IRS, the Corps of Engineers, and the FBI each has its own lawyers. However, the general counsel's office in many departments also serves as counsel for some or all of the agencies within that department. For example, the Solicitor's office in Interior acts as counsel for the Fish and Wildlife Service.

Many agencies are freestanding agencies, which means that they are not part of a department. Many, if not most, of these freestanding agencies are known as "**independent agencies**," to distinguish them from what are known as "**executive agencies**." Examples of independent agencies are the National Labor Relations Board (NLRB), the Securities and Exchange Commission (SEC), the Federal Reserve Board (FRB), and the Federal Trade Commission (FTC). All departments and almost all the agencies within departments are executive agencies. EPA and the Social Security Administration (SSA) are two very important free-standing executive agencies. There is one anomalous independent agency within a department. For administrative support, the Federal Energy Regulatory Commission (FERC) is located in the Department of Energy, but for all policy purposes, it is independent.

The full ramifications of the distinctions between independent agencies and executive agencies are put off until Chapter 6, but we can say that independent agencies tend to be slightly more independent from the President's influence than executive agencies. This relative independence derives from several characteristics generally shared by independent agencies. First, unlike executive agencies, the independent agencies are headed not by a single person but by a multimember group (*e.g.*, a commission, board, council, or conference), who reach decisions by majority vote. Typically, there are 5 or 7 members who make up the governing body of the agency. Second, unlike executive agencies whose heads generally serve at the pleasure of the President, members of the group heading the independent agency normally can only be removed for cause. Thus, mere political disagreement with the President would not be grounds for removing one of these independent agency members. Third, unlike heads of executive agencies who serve until they resign or are fired, members of the independent agency serve for a term of years (generally 5 years) on a staggered basis, so that a President in a single term could not replace the entire governing group. Fourth, unlike executive agency heads, who almost invariably are members of the President's political party, the statutes creating independent agencies normally require that no more than a simple majority of the agency can come from a single party. In other words, in a commission of five members, no more than three could be from one party.

The foregoing describes federal agencies, but the pattern is reproduced with variations at the state level. Thus, most states have departments, which have agencies as subunits. Most states have both executive and independent agencies, with the independent agencies similarly composed of multi-members who can be removed only for cause and who serve for a fixed term.

The definition of "agency" in the APA is broadly inclusive, "each authority of the Government of the United States, whether or not it is within or subject to review by another agency," with specific exceptions. What are "authorities" of the United States besides the entities we have described? For example, do you think the President is himself an authority of the United States? Congress and the courts are among the specific exceptions, but the President is not mentioned. Surprisingly, the issue was not decided until 1992, when the Supreme Court in *Franklin v. Massachusetts*, 505 U.S. 788, 112 S.Ct. 2767, 120 L.Ed.2d 636, held that the President is not an "agency" under the APA. Despite the language of the APA, the Court reached this conclusion in light of separation-of-powers concerns and historical practice—no President since the APA was enacted ever considered himself subject to it or acted pursuant to it. It is unusual in the administrative law context for the President to be the person charged by a statute for its implementation. More typically, the statute charges the head of the agency with that responsibility. Thus, in the statutory scheme involved in *Fund for Animals*, the Clean Water Act charges the Secretary of the Army with the responsibility for issuing individual fill permits. He, in turn, has delegated that authority to the Chief Engineer of the Corps, who has further delegated the authority to the District Engineers. The Endangered Species Act charges the Secretary of Interior with the responsibility for listing endangered species and engaging in the consultations with other agencies whose actions may affect those species. The Secretary has delegated his functions to the Fish and Wildlife Service.

Government corporations are another authority of government that may or may not be agencies under the APA. For some, the statutes creating them explicitly declare them to be agencies, *e.g.*, the Overseas Private Investment Corporation, and for others, their statutes explicitly declare them not to be agencies, *e.g.*, Amtrak, Comsat, the Corporation for Public Broadcasting, and the Legal Services Corporation. Generally, when Congress wishes to utilize the corporate form for conducting what otherwise would be government business, it does not intend the entity to be subjected to the procedures applicable to the government form ("agency").

2. WHAT DO AGENCIES DO?

Agencies execute the laws of the United States. Functionally, we can lump agencies into different categories according to the type of laws they execute.

a. *Regulate Private Conduct*

We call agencies that are primarily engaged in regulating private conduct **regulatory agencies**. At the federal level, there are dozens of regulatory agencies enforcing hundreds of laws that address consumer protection, preservation of the environment, individual health and safety, economic welfare, and other social and economic goals. Between 1969 and 1979 alone, Congress enacted 120 regulatory programs, and by 1980, there were 56 major federal regulatory agencies. Sidney Shapiro & Joseph Tomain, Regulatory Law & Policy 32 (1993). The EPA was established in this period (to regulate how people affect the environment), as was the Occupational Safety and Health Administration (OSHA) (to regulate workplace health and safety practices). Existing agencies, such as the FTC (which regulates trade practices by commercial entities), were given new regulatory powers.

There are also a large number of regulatory programs and agencies at the state level. A listing of state agencies prepared by the National Council on State Governments lists 143 different regulatory functions undertaken by state government. Council of State Governments, State Administrative Officials Classified By Function (1989). Chart 1–2 describes some of these functions and gives examples of state agencies that implement them.

Local government also executes many regulatory functions. The local government unit, such as a city council, serves as an administrative agency when it promulgates zoning regulations or issues licenses for such functions as bars and liquor stores. Local administrators include city building inspectors, fire marshals who enforce safety codes, and police who issue citations for non-criminal violations. *See* Charles Rhyne, The Law of Local Government Operations (1980).

Chart 1–2: STATE AGENCIES

FUNCTION	DESCRIPTION	EXAMPLES
Agriculture	Enforces agricultural laws and administers agricultural programs in the state.	Department of Agriculture (CO) Department of Agriculture, Trade & Consumer Protection (WI) Agriculture & Horticulture Commission (AZ)
Air Quality	Administers the state's clean air laws.	Department of Environmental Quality (AZ) Bureau of Air Quality Control (ME) Department of Natural Resources & Community Development (NC)
Alcoholic Beverage Control	Administers and enforces the laws governing the manufacturing, distribution, and dispensing of alcoholic beverages.	Liquor Licenses & Control (AZ) Division of Alcoholic Beverages & Tobacco (FL) Department of Alcoholic Beverage Control (VA)
Banking	Administers laws regulating banking institutions.	Department of Banking & Finance (GA) Department of Economic Development (LA) Financial Institutions Department (TN)
Civil Rights	Has overall responsibility for preventing and redressing discrimination due to race, color, sex, age, national origin, religion or handicap in employment, education, housing, public accommodations, and credit.	Department of Fair Employment & Housing (CA) Commission on Human Rights & Opportunities (CT) Commission Against Discrimination (MA)
Consumer Affairs	Investigates and mediates consumer complaints of deceptive and fraudulent business practices.	Bureau of Consumer Credit & Protection (ME) Trade & Consumer Protection Division (WI) Department of Consumer & Regulatory Affairs (DC)
Education	Official with overall responsibility for public elementary and secondary school systems.	Department of Education (AL) Department of Public Instruction (IN)
Environmental Protection	Seeks to improve the quality of the environment by coordinating and managing the state's pollution control programs and planning granting permits, and regulating standards.	Department of Health & Welfare (ID) Department of Natural Resources (DE) Environmental Protection & Health Services (HI)
Equal Employment Opportunity	Enforces the laws protecting equal employment opportunity.	Department of Labor & Industry (MT) Division of Anti–Discrimination & Labor (UT) Industrial Labor & Human Relations (WI)
Fish and Wildlife	Protects, manages, and enhances fish and wildlife resources and enforces the state's fish and game laws.	Department of Natural Resources (CO) Game & Parks Commission (NE) Department of Environmental Conservation (NY)

Two general justifications exist for this extensive regulation of private conduct. First, the country has a private market system, but markets are subject to imperfections that the government can remedy or at least mitigate. Second, the operation of unregulated markets may also produce results or consequences that a majority of the citizens consider unacceptable, even if they are efficient from an economic perspective. Thus, regulation is also used to conform market outcomes to social values, such as fairness or equity, or to other social aspirations.

In economic theory, the unfettered forces of supply and demand maximize consumer welfare by delivering the exact mix of goods and services that consumers desire at the lowest possible price. A market will not operate in this "efficient" manner, however, if there is inadequate information about goods or services, insufficient competition, or spillover costs. Regulation can make markets more efficient when the government reduces or eliminates such market failures.

Regulation, as noted, addresses inadequate consumer information. For example, some sellers, like itinerant roofers, are free to mislead consumers because they do not depend significantly on repeat sales. Agencies such as the FTC address this problem by prohibiting sellers from "false or deceptive acts or practices" in the sale of their products or services. 15 U.S.C.A. §§ 45, 52 (1982). In other markets, sellers can exploit consumers because buyers are unlikely to undertake the costly testing that is necessary to develop product information. Congress protects the buyers of pharmaceutical drugs, for example, by requiring sellers to test drugs before they are sold, and the Food and Drug Administration (FDA) reviews test results to ensure that drugs are safe and efficacious. 21 U.S.C.A. §§ 351–360ee. Similarly, the states engage in occupational licensing to ensure that consumers do not purchase services from incompetent practitioners in architecture, engineering, law, medicine, and many other occupations. *See* Jonathan Rose, *Occupational Licensing: A Framework for Analysis*, 1979 ARIZ. L.J. 189.

Other justifications concern insufficient competition. Utility markets may only have one seller, for instance, and by virtue of its monopoly position, the utility can charge higher than competitive prices. Government regulation is used in such cases to set prices at competitive levels, *see* Richard Posner, *Natural Monopoly and Its Regulation*, 21 STAN. L. REV. 548 (1969), or to find methods to introduce more competition into the market, *see* SHAPIRO & TOMAIN, *supra*, at 236–252. A competitive problem also exists when persons in contract negotiations do not have equal bargaining power. For example, the National Labor Relations Board (NLRB) regulates employers to prevent them from exploiting any superior bargaining power to prevent employees from collective bargaining. *See* National Labor Relations Act, 29 U.S.C.A. §§ 157–58.

Regulation is also used for spillover costs which exist when the activity of an individual or company harms other persons or the environment. The harm is a "spillover cost" because the responsible person or company will not pay for the damage it has caused in an unregulated market. State tort law can to some degree "internalize" these spillover costs, but Congress has reached the judgment in many areas that federal regulation is also necessary. Agencies such as the EPA and OSHA have the authority to order manufacturers to lessen pollution and other dangerous conditions. *See* Richard Pierce, *Encouraging Safety: The Limits of Tort Law and Government Regulation*, 33 VAND. L. REV. 1281, 1289 (1980).

Economic theory posits that regulation is unnecessary in the absence of market defects, but, as noted earlier, legislators may adopt regulatory programs for noneconomic reasons. *See* CASS SUNSTEIN, AFTER THE RIGHTS REVOLUTION: RECONCEIVING THE REGULATORY STATE 57–58 (1990); Richard Stewart, *Regulation in a Liberal State: The Role of Noncommodity Values*, 92 YALE L.J. 1537 (1983). Thus, the government seeks to prevent discrimination on the basis of racial or other characteristics that society considers unacceptable. Other regulatory programs reject or regulate commercial activity because market transactions are inconsistent with social values. For example, the adoption of children is regulated by the states and in many localities the decision concerning who is entitled to adopt is made by an administrative agency. *See* J. Robert Prichard, *A Market for Babies?*, 34 U. TORONTO L.J. 341 (1984).

b. Administer Entitlements Programs

As important as regulatory agencies are, their functions do not hold a candle, in terms of impact on state and federal budgets, to the agencies that administer the so-called **entitlements programs**, such as Social Security, Medicare, Medicaid, welfare, and food stamps. Here the focus is not on regulating private conduct but on dispensing federal and state funds for specified purposes to the proper recipients. That is, the focus is on assuring that the recipients qualify for the program and that persons who qualify will in fact receive the benefits.

There are economic justifications for most entitlement programs. Social Security and Medicare in theory are insurance programs that the federal government created because the market would not. Medicaid, welfare, and food stamps, as welfare programs, can be described as increasing the general welfare of society because of the crime and social upheaval that would occur in the absence of these programs. In economic terms, these programs are "public goods" because their benefits spill over to the entire public including persons who have not paid for the program. Private markets will not produce public goods, or will underproduce them, because sellers cannot charge most beneficiaries for the benefit they receive, while government can use the tax system to overcome this hurdle. SHAPIRO & TOMAIN, *supra*, at 46.

Entitlement programs, however, can also be described as government charity, done for altruistic, rather than utilitarian, motives. Even an efficient market system can produce a distribution of wealth that a majority of citizens find unsatisfactory because some people are too poor to live a humane existence. Welfare programs thus reflect a collective judgment that a just society does not relegate the poorest of its citizens to conditions of degradation and despair. MICKEY KAUS, THE END OF EQUALITY 14–16 (1992).

While entitlements programs, and the administrative law relevant to them, focus on delivering funds to the proper persons for the proper purposes, there can also be a subsidiary or related regulatory effect. For example, Medicare reimburses hospitals and doctors for medical treatment to covered persons according to payment schedules adopted by the Health Care Finance Administration (HCFA), an agency within the Department of Health and Human Services (HHS). Because Medicare is such a large purchaser of medical services, these payment schedules take on some of the practical effects of price controls, regulating (or at least substantially affecting) the delivery of health care in the nation. Similarly, most plans for welfare reform include tying welfare payments to certain kinds of behavior by the recipients, so that the welfare payments are an incentive to persons to change their conduct. In both situations, government is not *forcing* persons by law to change their conduct, as regulatory programs would; rather, government is inducing persons to change their conduct in specified ways by offering benefits under certain conditions. Thus, administrative law becomes concerned not only with the accuracy of the agency decision as to whether a particular recipient qualifies for the benefits, but also with the appropriateness of the agency decision as to the qualifications for receiving benefits.

c. *Everything Else*

Needless to say, not everything agencies do can be characterized neatly into one or the other of the above categories. The Internal Revenue Service's collection of taxes does not easily fit into either regulatory or entitlements concepts, but its impact on persons and the economy is pervasive. The Immigration and Naturalization Service (INS) within the Department of Justice admits and deports aliens. The Customs Service in the Department of Treasury clears goods imported into the United States. The Department of State issues passports. The Department of Defense and other agencies issue and revoke security clearances. The Forest Service sells timber in the national forests; the Bureau of Land Management (BLM) in the Department of Interior issues mining and grazing permits on public lands administered by the agency. The National Park Service in the Department of Interior runs the national parks, and the National Aeronautics and Space Administration runs the space program. All, to a greater or lesser extent, have impacts on the welfare of persons and companies, impacts that give rise to a natural concern about the government action.

Notes and Questions

1. The substantive reasons for regulation are part and parcel of the practice of regulatory lawyers. For example, lawyers who represent regulated entities must be able to articulate public policy reasons why their client should not be regulated or should be regulated less stringently. A regulated entity is normally unhappy about being regulated because it increases costs. Yet, if regulation serves a public purpose, the cost to the client is not a sufficient objection to being regulated. Regulatory lawyers must therefore convince an administrator that regulation is unwise or unnecessary from the public's point of view. Understanding the purposes of regulation is the first step in constructing such argu-

ments. If you take any substantive public law courses, such as Banking Law, Consumer Law, Environmental Law, Food and Drug Law, Health Law, Labor Law, Land Use Regulation, Public Lands Law, Securities Regulation, or Tax Law, you will learn more about the policy arguments that underlie such regulatory areas. Your school might also offer a survey course, such as Regulatory Law & Policy, which presents an overview of the substantive arguments for and against government regulation.

2.   This course, by comparison, concerns the *process* of regulation and is focussed on the procedures used by regulatory agencies to reach regulatory decisions. Administrative law and the procedures it requires are, at least in part, intended to make regulatory decisions "better" decisions in the sense that the costs and benefits of regulation will be taken into account. As we will see, this is a particular focus of recent administrative law legislation. Because improving regulatory decisions is one of the purposes of administrative procedures, it is necessary to pay some attention to the purposes of regulation.

3.   TYPES OF AGENCY ACTION

However an agency is structured, Congress or a state legislature can authorize it to undertake three different types of actions that are the subject of administrative law: Rulemaking, Adjudicating, and Investigating. These types of actions roughly correspond to types of actions performed by the three branches of government.

Rulemaking corresponds to legislative action. When an agency engages in rulemaking, it promulgates a regulation that has the same force and effect of law as if it had been passed by Congress or a state legislature. Most agencies have rulemaking power. Nevertheless, some important agencies do not have rulemaking power with respect to their programs—for example, the Equal Employment Opportunity Commission and the Administrator of the Wage and Hour Division of the Department of Labor (responsible for enforcing the maximum hours, minimum wage laws). Moreover, an agency's rulemaking authority is limited to what it has been delegated. For example, EPA has delegated rulemaking authority with respect to how hazardous waste sites are to be cleaned up, but it does not have delegated rulemaking authority with respect to who is liable to pay for those clean ups. *See Kelley v. EPA*, 25 F.3d 1088 (D.C.Cir.1994).

Adjudication corresponds to the judicial function of the courts. When an agency engages in adjudication, it applies an existing rule or statute to a set of facts to determine what outcome is required by the rule or statute. An agency can use adjudication to determine whether a regulated entity has violated an agency rule or a provision of a statute that the agency enforces. Adjudication can also be used to determine whether a person or entity qualifies for some government permit, benefit, or entitlement.

Many agencies have not been granted the authority to adjudicate alleged violations of statutes or regulations which those agencies enforce. These agencies, having investigated possible violations, must bring actions in a federal court to enforce the statutes or regulations. For example, the Antitrust Division of the Department of Justice is responsible for enforcing the Sherman Antitrust Act. It does this by bringing actions in federal court alleging that persons have violated the Act. In the course of such lawsuits, the agency can argue for a certain interpretation of its statute, but it is up to a court whether to adopt that interpretation. The more modern approach is to authorize agencies to proceed administratively both for compliance orders (the equivalent of court injunctions) and penalty orders (the equivalent of judicially imposed civil fines). In 1987, for example, amendments to the Clean Water Act permitted EPA to issue orders and obtain penalties administratively, rather than having to go to court.

Finally, **investigation** is part of the executive branch function of law enforcement; agencies determine whether someone may be in violation of an agency rule or the agency's legislative mandate. For this purpose, some agencies have the power to compel persons to turn over to them information in their possession or to inspect the premises where those persons work or reside.

While the following discussion focuses on federal agency activities, the activities of state agencies likewise fall within the same three categories of rulemaking, adjudication, and investigation.

a. *Rulemaking*

When Congress or a state legislature creates an agency, it establishes a legislative mandate for the agency. As part of that mandate, the legislature can empower the agency to make rules. Using this power, the agency can specify further regulations in addition to the rules created in its statutory mandate. In other words, the legislature gives the agency the "power to fill up the details." *United States v. Grimaud*, 220 U.S. 506, 31 S.Ct. 480, 55 L.Ed. 563 (1911).

Federal agencies initially publish their regulations in the Federal Register. The Federal Register is a document that the federal government publishes daily for the purpose of providing notice to the public concerning proposed and final rules and other agency actions. Annually, the government collects all the agencies' regulations and publishes them in the Code of Federal Regulations (CFR). This is organized by subject matter in titles, much like the United States Code is for statutes. Thus, 40 CFR §§ 1500 *et seq.* contains the Council on Environmental Quality's regulations interpreting the National Environmental Policy Act.

Although both legislatures and agencies can regulate, an agency's rulemaking power is only "quasi-legislative." Unlike Congress, the agency does not have the power to regulate concerning any subject permitted by the Constitution, because its authority to act is limited to the powers specified in its legislative mandate. Moreover, agency rules are subject to judicial review to ensure that a rule does not exceed an agency's statutory authority. Another difference between a legislature and an agency is that the agency must have adequate reasons why a regulation has been adopted. *Motor Vehicle Manufacturers Assoc. v. State Farm Mutual Auto. Insurance Co.*, 463 U.S. 29, 103 S.Ct. 2856, 77 L.Ed.2d 443 (1983). A final difference is that regulations promulgated by an agency are valid only if the agency follows the procedural requirements applicable to rulemaking. 5 U.S.C.A. § 706(2)(D).

An agency lawyer serves three general functions in the rulemaking process. First, the lawyer ensures that the agency complies with the applicable rulemaking procedures and he or she helps other agency staff to write the legal documents that those procedures require. Second, the lawyer may be asked to give a legal opinion whether certain regulatory options are within the agency's statutory authority. Finally, agency lawyers help defend the agency in court if a rule is appealed. In most cases, however, the Civil Division of the Department of Justice is responsible for the litigation; lawyers in the agency suing or being sued normally only assist the Department of Justice lawyers. This arrangement permits the Justice Department to coordinate the overall litigation strategy of the government and to ensure that agencies take a consistent position concerning common procedural issues. The arrangement can also be a source of tension between agencies and the Justice Department when they disagree concerning litigation strategy.

b. Adjudication

In addition to rulemaking authority, many agencies have adjudicatory powers. For example, the FTC uses adjudication to decide whether a party has violated the FTC Act or one of the Commission's rules. 15 U.S.C.A. § 45(b). Other agencies, such as the Social Security Administration, use adjudication to determine the eligibility of an applicant for governmental benefits, such as monetary assistance to persons who are disabled and cannot work. 42 U.S.C.A. § 421. Finally, still other agencies, like the Department of Transportation, use adjudication to determine whether state and local governments are eligible for highway funding under applicable laws and regulations. *See Citizens to Preserve Overton Park, Inc. v. Volpe*, 401 U.S. 402, 91 S.Ct. 814, 28 L.Ed.2d 136 (1971).

The power to adjudicate means that an agency decision concerning how a law or regulation applies in a specific circumstance has the same force of law as if it had been made by a court. Although both courts and agencies issue adjudicatory decisions, an agency's power is only "quasi-adjudicatory" because its power to adjudicate is limited to the functions specified in its enabling act. Moreover, an agency's decision is generally subject to judicial review to ensure that it is consistent with the enabling act and that the agency has obeyed applicable procedures in reaching its decision.

When agencies engage in adjudication, lawyers serve a variety of functions. At the FTC, for example, some agency lawyers serve as prosecutors and others advise the FTC Commissioners who make the final agency determination whether a law or rule has been violated. As will be explained in more detail below, the case is tried before an Administrative Law Judge (ALJ), who is a lawyer with powers similar to a judge. At the Department of Transportation, grant decisions are reviewed by agency lawyers to ensure that the agency is in compliance with its statutory mandates. Finally, if the agency's adjudicatory decision is challenged in court, agency lawyers will assist the Department of Justice in defending the decision.

c. *Investigations*

Some agencies have neither rulemaking nor adjudicatory powers. Their function is usually to bring enforcement actions in federal court. Moreover, even agencies with rulemaking or adjudicatory powers may need to go to federal court to enforce the agency's rules or orders.

Whether agencies engage in rulemaking, adjudication, or judicial enforcement actions, they will usually need to obtain information from outside the agency in order to support its actions. Unless Congress or a state legislature has authorized an agency to compel the production of information, however, the agency must rely on interested parties to provide the information voluntarily. If the legislature perceives that such cooperation may not be forthcoming, it can authorize an agency to compel the production of information in several ways.

Subpoena power is historically the most common investigatory tool. A legislature can authorize an agency to compel the production of documents and to compel the testimony of persons with information relevant to an investigation. The FTC, for example, can order the production of documentary evidence and the testimony of witnesses. 15 U.S.C.A. § 49. The agency can use this information to determine whether someone has violated the FTC Act which prohibits unfair and deceptive acts and practices or to gather information to support a rule.

The legislature can also authorize an agency to compel regulated entities to file periodic or special reports with the agency. For example, OSHA is authorized to require employers to report the death of a worker to the agency. 29 U.S.C.A. § 657(c)(2). This information alerts the agency to determine whether the employer violated any OSHA regulation. The power to order reports is different from subpoena power because an agency can require an entity to compile information that otherwise would not exist. An agency's subpoena power can only be used to recover existing documents.

Finally, the legislature can authorize an agency to inspect the premises of a regulated entity to determine if it is in compliance with regulations promulgated by the agency or the legislature. OSHA, for example, regularly conducts inspections of workplaces and if an employer refuses to admit an inspector, the agency will use its inspection power to compel the employer to admit the inspector. 29 U.S.C.A. § 657(a)(1). Likewise, FDA has the authority to conduct inspections to ensure that a regulated entity is using color additives only for the purposes the agency has approved. 21 U.S.C.A. § 374.

An agency's power to compel the production of information, witnesses and records or to conduct inspections is subject to judicial review. A court will ensure that the agency's action is within its statutory authority and that it complies with applicable constitutional protections such as Fourth Amendment constraints on searches. U.S. CONST., amend. IV.

Agency lawyers play a role concerning all of these investigatory tools. They draft agency subpoenas and negotiate with regulated entities concerning compliance. If an agency has the authority to compel testimony, lawyers question witnesses in a proceeding that is similar to a deposition. The lawyers also advise the agency concerning its authority to compel reports and conduct inspections. Finally, the lawyers defend the agency when a regulated entity challenges the compulsion of information or an inspection in court.

d. Separation of Powers

Central to American constitutional concepts is the doctrine of Separation of Powers—the idea that legislative, executive, and judicial functions should be separated to safeguard liberty. Within agencies, however, we see that these functions can be combined to a great degree, so that an agency may make law (by rulemaking) and enforce it against persons in agency adjudications. Similarly, democratic accountability of the legislative and executive branches is also fundamental to American constitutionalism, but agencies, sometimes characterized as a "headless Fourth Branch" of government, are not directly accountable to the electorate. One of the large themes of administrative law is how to protect persons and limit agencies in ways that substitute for the lack of democratic accountability and a separation of powers.

We put off to Chapter 6 detailed consideration of how separation of powers doctrine intersects with administrative law. At this point, you should understand that, as well established as agencies are in our governmental system, there remains a constitutional tension involved in their functions. The Administrative Procedure Act in part is a response to that tension, reflecting the belief that, by subjecting agencies to particular kinds of procedures and judicial review, the excesses of concentrations of power can be avoided. While the APA is intended to regularize and proceduralize agency action, another means of trying to control agencies is by accepting a degree of political influence on agencies, thereby affording some democratic accountability. One of the issues to be addressed in Chapter 6 is the means by which this political influence can be exercised.

B. A WALK THROUGH THE APA

Federal administrative law revolves around the Administrative Procedure Act (APA) which defines the procedural rights of persons outside of government and structures the manner in which persons inside of government make decisions. This section introduces you to the basic concepts of the federal Administrative Procedure Act and other administrative procedure. Your "walk through the APA" covers three topics. First, what is the difference between adjudication and rulemaking? Second, what procedures does the APA require for each process? Third, what does the APA say about judicial review? This walk through is an introduction and an opportunity to become acquainted with the statute around which this course largely revolves. We will deal with each of these topics in much more detail in the chapters ahead.

1. DEFINITION OF ADJUDICATION AND RULEMAKING

The nature of an agency's decisionmaking procedures depends on whether it is engaged in "adjudication" or "rulemaking." "Adjudication" is the "agency process for the formulation of an order," 5 U.S.C.A. § 551(7),* and an "order" is the "whole or part of a final disposition . . . other than rule making but including licensing." *Id.* § 551(6). In other words, adjudication is any final agency disposition except dispositions produced by rulemaking. "Rulemaking" is the "agency process for formulating, amending, or repealing a rule," *id.* § 551(5), and a "rule" is "an agency statement of . . . future effect designed to implement, interpret, or prescribe law or policy. . . ." *Id.* § 551(4).

The key distinction is that a "rule" is an agency statement of "future effect." In this sense, the rulemaking process resembles the legislative process. New law is being made and it is binding only concerning future conduct. When an agency engages in adjudication, by comparison, it applies an existing rule or statute to a set of facts to determine what outcome is required by the rule or statute. As noted earlier, when an agency determines whether a regulated entity has violated an agency rule, or a provision of a statute that the agency enforces, it is engaged in adjudication.

2. RULEMAKING

Section 553 of the APA indicates what procedures an agency must follow when it is engaged in rulemaking. These procedures apply unless the rule concerns (1) military or foreign affairs or (2) matters relating to

---

* When the APA was originally passed, it had 12 sections, with Section 2 definitions, Section 4 rulemaking, Section 5 adjudication, Section 7 hearings, Section 8 decisions, and Section 10 judicial review. In 1966 Congress repealed the original act and reenacted it with different section numbers as part of a general codification of Title 5 of the United States Code. It is not technically accurate to refer to the original section numbers (except when referring to them as originally enacted), but some judges and commentators continue to use the original section numbers out of habit, and of course some of the older cases may use the original section numbers.

agency management or personnel or to public property, loans, grants, benefits or contracts. *Id*. § 553(a).

The APA implicitly recognizes two types of rulemaking: informal and formal. As the names imply, informal rulemaking involves fewer procedures and thus less procedural formality. Section 553 first defines what procedures an agency must use in informal rulemaking. It then indicates when formal rulemaking is to be used and what procedures it involves.

Informal Rulemaking: Section 553 establishes a three-step process for informal rulemaking. First, an agency is required to publish a notice of the proposed rule in the Federal Register with two exceptions. *Id*. § 553(b). One exception is for "interpretive rules, general statements of policy, or rules of agency organization, procedure, and practice." *Id*. § 553(A). The other is for when the agency has "good cause" for bypassing the notice stage of rulemaking. *Id*. § 553(B).

Second, the agency must give "interested persons an opportunity to participate in the rule making through submission of written data, views, or arguments with or without opportunity for oral presentation." *Id*. § 553(c). Note that although the agency must give interested persons the opportunity to submit written material, it is the agency's option whether to permit oral presentations. Most agencies do not permit oral presentations. The written comments are kept in a document room at the agency and may be viewed by other interested persons who might wish to respond to the submissions. Agencies are currently in the process of establishing ways to make such comments available electronically through the Internet.

Last, the agency must "incorporate in the rules adopted a concise general statement of their basis and purpose." *Id*. This statement appears in the Federal Register along with the final version of the rule. For reasons discussed later in the course, many statements of basis and purpose are anything but concise. A justification of a controversial rule is often more than 100 pages.

Formal Rulemaking: In "formal" rulemaking, an agency follows the procedures specified in sections 556–57 instead of steps two and three above. *Id*. Sections 556 and 557 are discussed in more detail below with respect to adjudications (where they are more often used), but in short if an agency is required to use formal rulemaking, it must undertake the same type of trial that it would use for formal adjudication. These procedures replace the comment period and the statement of basis and purpose.

Section 553(c) provides the test for when an agency must use formal rulemaking. Formal rulemaking is required when "rules are required by statute to be made on the record after an opportunity for agency hearing." *Id*. § 553(c). The statute to which section 553(c) refers is the agency's mandate (sometimes referred to as the agency's organic statute). If the agency's mandate requires it to adopt a rule "on the record after an opportunity for agency hearing,'' it must then use the procedures specified in sections 556–57.

Since only a few agencies have mandates that require formal rulemaking, informal rulemaking is used for most rulemaking activity. As you might have inferred, informal rulemaking is generally quicker than formal rulemaking because the agency can avoid undertaking a trial-like hearing.

Hybrid Rulemaking: Under the APA itself, there are only the two models of rulemaking—formal and informal—but Congress has created numerous new programs and agencies in the years since the APA was passed, often imposing particular rulemaking procedures on those programs or agencies. We refer to these particular procedures as ''hybrid'' rulemaking procedures—hybrid, because they invariably add some additional procedures to section 553's requirements, while not going so far as to mandate the procedures of sections 556–57. The process the Federal Trade Commission (FTC) uses to promulgate trade regulation rules may be the most prominent example of hybrid rulemaking. Among other additional procedures, the FTC must include an informal hearing at which interested parties can make oral presentations and, with some limitations, present and cross-examine witnesses. 15 U.S.C.A. § 57a. Other hybrid rulemaking schemes include the Clean Air Act, which contains specific procedures for EPA to follow in adopting rules implementing the Clean Air Act, *see* 42 U.S.C.A. § 7607(d), and the Department of Energy Organization Act, which requires the department to supplement the procedures of section 553 with additional requirements, including a public hearing unless the Secretary determines that no substantial issue of law or fact exists with respect to a rule and that the rule is unlikely to have a substantial impact on the Nation's economy or large numbers of businesses or individuals. *See* 42 U.S.C.A. § 7191(c)(1).

The casebook covers rulemaking in Chapters 2 and 4. Chapter 2 covers the fundamental procedural issues that arise in rulemaking, while Chapter 4 covers issues that add additional complexity to the rulemaking process.

3. ADJUDICATION

There are also two types of adjudicatory processes implicitly recognized by the APA: formal and informal. If an agency is required to engage in ''formal adjudication,'' the APA requires the agency to use procedures that resemble a trial. By comparison, the APA does not mandate any procedures for ''informal'' adjudication.

Section 554(a) controls whether an agency must use formal adjudication. This section states that the procedures listed in section 554 apply ''in every case of adjudication required by statute to be determined on the record after opportunity for agency hearing.'' *Id*. § 554(a). The ''statute'' to which section 554(a) refers is the agency's mandate. If the agency's mandate requires it to reach adjudicatory decisions ''on the record after opportunity for agency hearing," the agency must then use the procedures required in sections 554, 556 and 557.

Formal Adjudication: Section 554 requires several procedures generally used in trials. The agency must give notice to the parties of its hearing, *id.* § 554(b), and offer an opportunity to reach a settlement. *Id.* § 554(c)(1). In addition, the person who presides at the hearing is prohibited from receiving *ex parte* contacts, or communications from the parties including employees of the agency. Finally, the agency must conduct the hearing in accordance with sections 556 and 557 of the APA. *Id.* § 554(c)(2).

Section 556 addresses the hearing procedures. It authorizes the use of an Administrative Law Judge (ALJ) and specifies the judge's authority, *id.* § 556(b)–(c), places the burden of proof on the agency, provides that oral and written evidence can be received, permits cross-examination of witnesses, and mandates that any decision must be based on the entire record, which is defined to include the hearing transcript and all documentary evidence. *Id.* § 556(d).

ALJs are technically agency employees who are appointed to serve as judges in agency adjudications and other processes. 5 U.S.C.A. § 3105. Two features of the appointment process give ALJs independence from the agencies for which they work. The ALJs' pay is determined by a separate agency, the Office of Personnel Management, *id.* § 5372, and ALJs may not be subjected to removal, suspension, or have their pay reduced, except after a hearing before the Merit Systems Protection Board, another separate agency. *Id.* § 7521.

Section 557 addresses appeal procedures. It provides that the ALJ shall "initially decide the case," although the agency can bypass this step. *Id.* § 557(b). If the ALJ makes an initial decision, either the staff or any party can appeal the decision to the agency administrator, or if the agency is a commission, to the commission members, and the parties have the right to submit briefs. *Id.* Although this process is similar to an appellate review in the courts, there is an important difference. An appellate judge gives deference to a district court's fact finding, but section 557 provides that "[o]n appeal from or review of the initial decision, the agency has all the power which it would have in making the initial decision." *Id.* This means that the administrator or commissioners are not required to give deference to the factual conclusions of the ALJ. The agency's final decision must be justified in a written opinion on the basis of the entire record. *Id.* § 556(c). Finally, any person who makes the final decision is prohibited from receiving *ex parte* contacts from any interested person outside of the agency and from any agency employee except their law clerks. *Id.* § 556(d).

Informal Adjudication: If an agency is not required by its mandate to conduct adjudication "on the record after opportunity for an agency hearing," *id.* § 554(a), the APA does not prescribe any procedures for adjudication. Nevertheless, two circumstances may require an agency to follow certain hearing procedures. First, although the agency's mandate may not require it to use formal adjudication, the statute might still require that the agency use some hearing procedures. For example, Congress has required that a state or locality hold a public meeting to obtain citizen input about the location of any highway to be financed by Department of Transportation. *See Citizens to Preserve Overton Park, Inc. v. Volpe,* 401 U.S. 402, 91 S.Ct. 814, 28 L.Ed.2d 136 (1971); Peter Strauss, *Revisiting Overton Park: Political and Judicial Controls Over Administrative Actions Affecting The Community,* 39 U.C.L.A. L.Rev. 1251 (1992).

Second, if the due process clause applies to the agency's action, it may be obligated to follow some type of hearing process. The obligation of due process applies if the agency's action will deprive a person of "liberty" or "property," U.S. Const. amend. V, XIV, as those terms have been defined by the United States Supreme Court. The Court has also determined what types of procedures must be used when property or liberty is affected. A full trial-like hearing is not generally required to satisfy due process; instead, what is required is "some kind of hearing." Richard Pierce, Sidney Shapiro & Paul Verkuil, Administrative Law & Process § 6.3 (1992).

The casebook covers adjudication in Chapters 3 and 4. Chapter 3 covers the fundamental procedural issues that arise in adjudication, while Chapter 4 covers issues that add additional complexity to the adjudication process.

4. JUDICIAL REVIEW

Both adjudicatory and rulemaking decisions are generally subject to judicial review. As briefly described below, however, the APA has several important rules that may limit if or when judicial review may be obtained.

First, although most agency actions can be appealed, the APA recognizes that not all decisions are subject to judicial review. Section 701 establishes that a person is not entitled to review if "statutes preclude review" or if "agency action is committed to agency discretion by law." *Id*. § 701. The first clause refers to the circumstance when Congress has prohibited judicial review in an agency's mandate. Until recently, the Veteran's Administration was the most prominent example of a prohibition on review. Congress originally prohibited review of VA decisions concerning eligibility for veterans' benefits with the intention of preserving an informal system that did not involve lawyers. In 1988, Congress established a new adjudicatory system for veteran's cases and provided for some limited review. 38 U.S.C.A. § 7251 *et seq.* (1991). The second clause refers to circumstances in which Congress has delegated the final decisionmaking authority to an agency in a manner other than by an express declaration. *See Webster v. Doe,* 486 U.S. 592, 108 S.Ct. 2047, 100 L.Ed.2d 632 (1988); *Citizens to Preserve Overton Park v. Volpe,* 401 U.S. 402, 91 S.Ct. 814, 28 L.Ed.2d 136 (1971).

Second, the APA and federal common law have imposed limitations as to when a person may seek review of agency action. One requirement is that the agency action be "final." 5 U.S.C.A. § 704. Another requirement can be that the person seeking review has exhausted any administrative remedies that the agency has provided. *Id.* Finally, the courts have imposed a requirement that the agency action be "ripe" for review, meaning in essence that it is appropriate for judicial consideration at the time the law suit is filed.

Third, the Constitution itself imposes a requirement that the person challenging agency action have "standing." In short, this means that the person has suffered (or is about to suffer) injury as a result of the government action and that a favorable court decision can redress (or prevent) the injury. The APA imposes an additional statutory requirement on this general requirement when a person is challenging agency action under the APA. The APA creates a legal right to review for persons "suffering legal wrong because of agency action, or adversely affected or aggrieved by agency action within the meaning of a relevant statute," *id.* § 702. Thus, the person suing must either be suffering a "legal wrong" or be adversely affected "within the meaning of a relevant statute." Chapter 5 discusses in detail the doctrines that restrict access to the courts to obtain judicial review of agency action.

If a court undertakes judicial review, it must determine what scope of review to apply. The APA contains three standards of review of agency action that establish a continuum ranging from no deference to almost complete deference. The "de novo" standard instructs a court to substitute its judgment for that of the agency. Under this test, the court must agree with the agency decision in order to uphold it. The "substantial evidence" standard instructs a court to uphold a decision if it is "reasonable." Under this test, the court need not agree with the agency's conclusion to affirm it; it only needs to find that the agency's conclusions are reasonable ones. Finally, the "arbitrary and capricious" or "abuse of discretion" standards instruct a court to affirm a decision unless the judges can say that the decision is "arbitrary." The last standard historically has been considered the most deferential, although most courts no longer find any practical difference between the last two standards in light of intervening judicial decisions. Chapters 2 and 3 discuss the application of these standards in relationship to rulemaking and adjudication respectively.

Notes and Questions

1. Passage of the APA was the result of a decade long political battle between the friends and foes of the New Deal. From the perspective of today's highly regulated society, it is difficult to understand the threat that the Roosevelt administration posed for the business and legal communities. Because the New Deal was extraordinary for its time in the degree of intrusion on private autonomy and in its premise that the capitalistic market system was fundamentally flawed, many business and

legal leaders were extremely hostile. JEROLD AUERBACH, UNEQUAL JUSTICE: LAWYERS & SOCIAL CHANGE IN AMERICA (1976); Robert Rabin, *Federal Regulation In Perspective*, 38 STAN. L. REV. 1189, 1252–53 (1986). Their criticisms made little impression on a public still reeling from the worst depression in the history of the country, but as economic conditions slowly improved, the momentum for procedural reform picked up steam. In 1939, Congress passed the Walter–Logan Bill, which was based on an American Bar Association proposal. Paul Verkuil, *The Emerging Concept of Administrative Procedure*, 78 COLUM. L. REV. 258, 271 (1978). Denounced as "so rigid, so needlessly interfering, as to bring about a crippling of the administrative process," *id.* at 272, the bill was vetoed by President Roosevelt. The political tide was turned by an influential report issued by the Attorney General which endorsed a more flexible administrative procedure act. *See* FINAL REPORT OF THE ATTORNEY GENERAL'S COMMITTEE ON ADMINISTRATIVE PROCEDURE (1941). After a war-induced delay, Congress passed the Administrative Procedure Act in 1946.

2. Professor Martin Shapiro argues that the APA was a compromise between supporters and opponents of the New Deal. He explains that the adjudicatory procedures were "weighted heavily" in favor of the opponents, but rulemaking "constituted an almost total victory for the liberal New Deal forces." Martin Shapiro, *APA: Past, Present, & Future*, 72 VA. L. REV. 447, 453 (1986). Can you explain the basis of Professor Shapiro's conclusion in light of your walk through the APA?

3. As you read, Congress has required some agencies to engage in "hybrid" rulemaking, which obligates an agency to comply with procedures in addition to those required for informal rulemaking. Such additional procedures have been criticized as unnecessary and too slow. *See, e.g.*, Barry Boyer, *Trade Regulation Procedures of the Federal Trade Commission*, *in* 1980 ADMINISTRATIVE CONFERENCE OF THE UNITED STATES: RECOMMENDATIONS AND REPORTS 33, 124–27.* How should we evaluate whether additional procedures are valuable?

4. Professor Cramton has proposed the following criteria for evaluating proposed changes in administrative procedure:

> There are no fixed and immutable criteria by which the operation of procedural systems, existing or proposed, may be judged. For the most part, procedure is a means to an end—the accomplishment of social purposes—but to a certain extent procedural forms in themselves may create or destroy important human values. The usual statement of these values, in terms of "fairness," "due process," and the like, suffers from undue generality, since the content of these value-laden words shifts from time to time and from person

* The Administrative Conference of the United States (ACUS) was a unique agency that existed from 1968 to 1995. It was composed of between 75 and 101 individuals drawn from agencies, academia, and the private sector who were expert in administrative law, who volunteered their time. The primary function of the Conference was to study administrative processes with an eye to recommending improvements to Congress and the agencies. Many, if not most, of its recommendations became the basis for much of what is standard administrative law today.

to person. The basic notion, in a society committed to a representative form of government by and for the citizens, is that private persons should have a meaningful opportunity to participate in government decisions which directly affect their property and activities. This becomes especially important when the governmental action is based on individual rather than on general considerations.

Beyond the fundamental principle of meaningful party participation, any evaluation of administrative procedures must rest on a judgment which balances the advantages and disadvantages of each proposal. In striking this balance, I believe that the following formulation of competing considerations is more helpful than "fairness" or "due process": (1) the extent to which the procedure furthers the accurate selection and determination of relevant facts and issues; (2) the extent to which it furthers the efficient disposition of business; and (3) the extent to which the procedure, when viewed in the light of the statutory objectives, is acceptable to the agency, the participants, and the general public.

The first consideration, accuracy, serves as a reminder that the ascertainment of truth, or, more realistically, as close an approximation of reality as human frailty permits, is the major goal of most contested proceedings. There are better and worse ways, in various contexts, of getting at the truth. The second consideration, efficiency, emphasizes the time, effort, and expense of elaborate procedures. The work of the world must go on, and endless nit-picking, while it may produce a more nearly ideal solution, imposes huge costs and impairs other important values. The final consideration, acceptability, emphasizes the indispensable virtues of procedures that are considered fair by those whom they affect, as well as by the general public. The authority of decisions in a society resting on the consent of the governed is based on their general acceptability. Moreover, if procedures are deemed fair by those most immediately affected, their cooperation and assistance can be obtained, with the result that administrative action will be better informed and thought-out.

Roger Cramton, *Administrative Procedure Reform: The Effects of S. 1663 on the Conduct of Federal Rate Proceedings*, 16 ADMIN. L. REV. 108, 111–112 (1964).

5. As Professor Cramton suggests, procedures imposed on agencies are supposed to serve one of two purposes: increased accuracy of the agency determinations and increased opportunity for persons interested in the agency action to participate in its determinations. Procedures, however, are not cost free. They increase the time and resources necessary to complete the government action. Throughout this course you will see the tension between the goals of accuracy and public participation and accountability on the one hand and of efficient and expeditious government action on the other.

6. Opponents and supporters of regulation are not oblivious to the tactical advantages and disadvantages of procedures. Recall the history

of the APA described in notes 1 and 2. Should we be suspicious of arguments by a regulated industry that more procedures are necessary? Sometimes, in the political give-and-take associated with creating an agency's mandate, those who oppose the agency's substantive mission, but who do not have the votes to defeat it, bargain for procedural "safeguards" to assure the agency only acts "properly." In reality, these supporters of procedural safeguards are hoping that the burdens imposed by the procedures will minimize agency activity. Terry Moe, *Political Institutions: The Neglected Side of the Story*, 6 J.L. ECON. & ORG. 213, 230 (1990). For example, the burdens associated with the FTC's hybrid rulemaking procedures have had that effect. At the same time, many agencies have learned to live with their hybrid procedural requirements without significantly affecting their regulatory output. EPA, for example, is subject to hybrid procedures for adopting rules under the Clean Air Act, and it actively regulates under that Act.

7. Will a regulated industry always favor the use of more procedures as a way of slowing down the imposition of more regulation? What if the regulation consists of licensing and the regulated firms cannot enter a market until they obtain a license? Will public interest groups always favor the use of more procedures to assure public participation? What if such participation would aid private interests in delaying government action the public interest group favors?

C. ADMINISTRATIVE LAW PRACTICE

Problem 1–1

Imagine for a moment that Helen is a lawyer with a private law firm. A friend of Helen's parents calls her with a problem. He had planned to build a retirement home on some unimproved land he had owned for twenty years. His contractor, however, had raised a question about part of the land being wetlands and whether a permit would be required from the Army Corps of Engineers. He spoke to the other persons who lived in the vicinity, and none of them had obtained any Corps permit, but he contacted the Corps because the contractor was not willing to go forward without some assurance. The Corps person he spoke to on the phone confirmed that wetlands could not be filled without a permit, and the person indicated that it would be difficult to obtain a permit for a retirement home. Helen's parents' friend is very upset.

Helen does a little research and discovers that section 404 of the Clean Water Act and implementing regulations do require a permit for filling certain kinds of wetlands. Nevertheless, Helen finds that the regulations are not explicit about what wetlands are subject to the regulation. Specifically, the regulation includes: interstate wetlands, wetlands adjacent to other covered waters, and wetlands "whose use, degradation, or destruction could affect interstate or foreign commerce." Helen's parents' friend's property certainly does not involve either interstate wetlands or wetlands adjacent to other covered waters, and it is not clear to Helen how their use, degradation, or destruction could possibly affect interstate commerce.

Helen contacts the local office of the Corps and seeks an appointment to talk with their local counsel, Jay.

(a) Should Jay meet with Helen?

(b) If Jay agrees to meet with Helen, what should Helen's strategy for this meeting be? Why doesn't she just sue the Corps?

Problem 1–2

Jay confers with another lawyer in the office about the situation. Jay knows that until January 2001 the Corps had interpreted the language in the regulation to reach any wetlands used by migratory fowl, because migratory fowl affect interstate commerce by being the object of attention of birdwatchers and hunters who spend billions of dollars on their activities. However, in January 2001, the Supreme Court decided a case holding that the Clean Water Act does not regulate nonnavigable, isolated, intrastate waters and wetlands based solely on their use by migratory birds. The Corps Chief Counsel issued a memorandum to all Division and District Counsels explaining the effect of that decision on the Corps' regulations. It stated that the Court had not decided whether a nonnavigable, isolated, intrastate water or wetland was covered by the Clean Water Act if the degradation or destruction of the water or wetland would otherwise affect interstate commerce. Accordingly, the memo concluded, if polluting or filling a nonnavigable, isolated, intrastate water or wetland would interfere with recreational activity like boating, fishing, or swimming in that water or wetland (or in waters or wetlands hydrologically connected to the polluted or filled water or wetland), the Corps should still exercise jurisdiction under the Clean Water Act. This memo was never the subject of notice and comment, and indeed was never published for the public, but Headquarters intends that field offices follow it. Jay has no idea if Helen's wetland is in fact connected to waters used for recreation, but he thinks it is likely.

If you were Jay, what weight would you give to this memorandum in deciding what to do? How should the memo be characterized in administrative law?

Problem 1–3

Assume that after the meeting, Jay responds by letter to Helen, saying that in his opinion the wetlands in question are subject to the regulation because their degradation could affect recreational use of nearby waters. What should Helen do? What is Jay's letter in administrative law?

Problem 1–4

Assume, instead, he responds to Helen by saying that, absent positive indications that filling the wetlands would affect interstate commerce, the wetlands are not subject to the Corps jurisdiction. What should the local chapter of the National Wildlife Federation do?

D. PROFESSIONAL ETHICS AND THE AGENCY LAWYER

1. BAR DISCIPLINARY RULES

A lawyer in private practice, whether for a private law firm, a public interest group, or a corporation, is subject to the disciplinary rules of the bar of which he or she is a member. These rules have evolved over time in light of the ethical problems that private lawyers confront. The American Bar Association and state bars, however, have generally ignored the particular issues involving government lawyers, and whether particular rules should be adopted for them, if only because government lawyers were only a small minority of their members. In the 1980s, the District of Columbia Bar, a bar with a peculiarly large number of government lawyers, took up the issue, in part as a response to a claim by the Department of Justice that state bars could not constitutionally regulate the practice of federal government lawyers. The Bar's Board of Governors voted to transmit the report to the District of Columbia Court of Appeals, stating that the report reflected the views only of the committee and not of the Board.

REPORT BY THE DISTRICT OF COLUMBIA BAR SPECIAL COMMITTEE ON GOVERNMENTAL LAWYERS AND THE MODEL RULES OF PROFESSIONAL CONDUCT

PREFACE

The Board of Governors has determined that all members of the District of Columbia Bar are subject to its disciplinary rules, no matter how employed. It would, however, be grossly unfair to seek to apply the Bar's disciplinary rules in the inherently ambiguous context of the ethical responsibilities of government employment without sufficient guidance to enable the conscientious lawyer to understand and abide by those rules. . . .

I. THE ROLE OF THE GOVERNMENT LAWYER

. . . The government lawyer must address ethical issues in a different environment from the lawyer in private practice. Because of their status as government employees, government lawyers are subject to a wide range of statutes and regulations governing their conduct that are not applicable to lawyers in private practice. In addition, the private lawyer, whether employed by a single employer or by a multitude of clients, generally has a clear understanding of who his or her client is and what his or her obligations are to that client. . . .

The government lawyer faces a more complex environment. Many people believe that government service—*public* service—requires a recognition of a duty to the "public interest," however that may be defined. Since elected and appointed officials are generally transients reflecting the flux of political administrations, some believe there is a higher obligation than to the individual who currently commands a government agency or department. Who really is the client of the government lawyer? This question, generally a given in private practice, is a critical first step in understanding the ethical obligations of every lawyer employed by a governmental body, for the identity of the client will determine the outcome of conflict questions, the appropriateness of disclosure of confidential information, and even the amount of discretion the government lawyer can exercise in handling litigation.

Based on its review and discussion, the Special Committee concluded that the critical ethical issue facing the government lawyer was determining the identity of his or her client. If, as Judge Charles Fahy concluded in a 1950 lecture at Columbia University School of Law, "the Government is a composite of the people and Government counsel therefore has as a client the people as a whole," significant confidentiality and conflict issues may arise. If, on the other hand, the "client of the [government] lawyer, using the term in the sense of where lies his immediate professional obligation and responsibility, is the agency where he is employed . . .," . . . different confidentiality and conflict issues may be presented.

II. THE AGENCY AS CLIENT: THE CRITICAL BUILDING BLOCK OF THE PROPOSED RULES

The ultimate source of authority for government under our constitutional system is, as the Constitution recognizes: "We, the people. . . ." For any governmental employee, therefore, there must be some sense of obligation to the public interest, however abstract that concept may be. There are some who argue strenuously that a government lawyer's ultimate obligation must be to the public interest as he or she sees it. . . .

As a general proposition, however, the notion of the "public interest" as the ultimate standard of performance, professional or otherwise, is an anarchic one, and is not the model upon which our governmental bodies function today. While there are various procedural and substantive limitations throughout the range of governmental entities in this country, all are organized to allow command and response employment structures, and all have one or more individuals (generally elected) who have ultimate responsibility for governmental action. Government in this country is consensual, but the form of government is hierarchical.

This fact permeates our government structures. Notwithstanding the fact that government is the people's business, all governmental bodies make and implement policy decisions, where necessary, through direction of employees who may or may not agree with the particular policy they are asked to implement. Thus, a budget analyst or a legislative aide must respond to instructions by superiors or face dismissal, even if that individual's conception of the "public interest" differs from that of his superiors.

It could be argued that government *lawyers* should be different. To some, government lawyers represent the independent conscience of government. Because of the lawyer's duty to serve his client's interests above all others, save for extraordinary circumstances, some believe the government lawyer is *required* to look beyond the individuals who are his superiors and the agency he serves and address the interest of his ultimate client—the public. . . .

The Special Committee recognized the importance of this concept as an abstract principle. Most, if not all, government lawyers are drawn to government service by a sincere desire to serve the public interest. The Special Committee concluded, however, that "the public interest" was an unworkable ethical guideline, and indeed was inconsistent with the underlying rationale of many significant ethical concepts. If a lawyer is to function effectively as counselor and adviser to elected and appointed officials, those officials must not view the lawyer as some independent actor, liable at any time to arrive at some individualistic perception of the "public interest" and act accordingly. The governmental client, to be encouraged to use lawyers, must believe that the lawyer will represent the legitimate interests the governmental client seeks to advance, and not be influenced by some unique and personal vision of the "public interest." Just like a private client, the governmental client must have a reasonable belief in the confidentiality of his or her communications to a lawyer in order to encourage free and full communications. In the governmental context, in short, a lawyer must be the same kind of professional servant of the client that is required by ethical rules in the private sector.

Taking these factors into account, the Special Committee concluded that the "public interest" was too amorphous a standard to have practical utility in regulating lawyer conduct or in providing ethical guidance. The Special Committee then considered, as an alternative, that the particular government as a whole (*e.g.,* the United States government or the District of Columbia) should appropriately be considered the government lawyer's client. Three possible justifications were raised in support of this proposition. First, it could be argued that the attorney-client relationship in the context of the government lawyer is too complicated to make more specific rules that can be effectively applied. By defining the client as the government as a whole, government lawyers are effectively removed from the strictures of many of the ethical rules. This is not a problem, arguably, because there are sufficient internal controls within the government, such as statutes, regulations, and agency or departmental codes of ethics, to regulate the conduct of the government lawyer. Finally this definition would recognize the external regulation of government lawyers may be preempted in some situations by the government's internal controls.

Notwithstanding the provocative issue raised by these arguments, the Special Committee concluded that the "entire government as client" standard was also not an appropriate decisional foundation for ethical rules.... The identification of one's client as the entire government would raise serious questions regarding client control and confidentiality. For example, without some focus of responsibility, each government lawyer would be free to perform as he or she saw fit, subject only to the practical constraint of internal agency discipline.... The Special Committee concluded that defining the client of the government lawyer as the government as a whole, or even as the particular branch of government in which the lawyer functions, suffered from the same essential deficiencies as the public interest approach.

This analysis inevitably led to the conclusion that the employing agency should normally be regarded as the client of the government lawyer. In most cases, the employing agency will be a discrete entity, clearly definable and the source of identifiable lines of authority. The lawyer's duties typically will be directed by the head of the agency or his delegate; the lawyer's explicit responsibilities will be limited to those assigned by the agency; and agency regulations provide a clear benchmark of assessing attorney conduct. These factors provide bounds and give concrete meaning to the lawyer-client relationship in the government context.

This identification of the client with the employing agency permits a lawyer seeking guidance from the Rules, in the vast majority of situations, to determine clearly his or her duties and obligations, both in advancing the interests of the client and protecting its confidences and secrets. It permits those in the agency to rely on the lawyer in the same way that a private client can rely on its private lawyer. And finally, the rules so interpreted can be effectively enforced by a disciplinary body....

Obviously, the conclusion that the government lawyer's client is the lawyer's employing agency does not answer every ethical question. After all, there are many situations in government where lawyers are asked to represent diverse client interests: several different agencies, for example, or perhaps individuals and agencies simultaneously. In these situations, a careful analysis will be required to determine the lawyer's obligations. But these problems are inherent in the legal profession, and are faced by nongovernmental lawyers every day....

Establishing a definitional benchmark for government lawyers employed in the judicial and legislative branches of government may appear somewhat more complicated but, after due consideration, the Special Committee concluded that those who are in fact employed and functioning as lawyers in the judicial and legislative branches should be governed by the same Rules as executive branch lawyers....

2. ABA MODEL RULES OF PROFESSIONAL CONDUCT

As the D.C. Bar's Report indicates, lawyers in private practice often face thorny questions as to who is the client when they represent an organization, like a corporation. The ABA Model Rules of Professional Conduct directly address this issue. In addition, they include a comment directly addressed to the situation of government lawyers.

Rule 1.13 Organization as Client

(a) A lawyer employed or retained by an organization represents the organization acting through its duly authorized constituents.

(b) If a lawyer for an organization knows that an officer, employee or other person associated with the organization is engaged in action, intends to act or refuses to act in a matter related to the representation that is a violation of a legal obligation to the organization, and is likely to result in substantial injury to the organization, the lawyer shall proceed as is reasonably necessary in the best interest of the organization. In determining how to proceed, the lawyer shall give due consideration to the seriousness of the violation and its consequences, the scope and nature of the lawyer's representation, the responsibility in the organization and the apparent motivation of the person involved, the policies of the organization concerning such matters and any other relevant considerations. Any measures taken shall be designed to minimize disruption of the organization and the risk of revealing information relating to the representation to persons outside the organization. Such measures may include among others:

(1) asking reconsideration of the matter;

(2) advising that a separate legal opinion on the matter be sought for presentation to appropriate authority in the organization; and

(3) referring the matter to higher authority in the organization, including, if warranted by the seriousness of the matter, referral to the highest authority that can act in behalf of the organization as determined by applicable law.

(c) If, despite the lawyer's efforts in accordance with paragraph (b), the highest authority that can act on behalf of the organization insists upon such action, or a refusal to act, that is clearly a violation of law and is likely to result in substantial injury to the organization, the lawyer may resign. . . .

Comment

. . . .**Government Agency**

The duty defined in this Rule applies to governmental organizations. However, when the client is a governmental organization, a different balance may be appropriate between maintaining confidentiality and assuring that the wrongful official act is prevented or rectified, for public business is involved. In addition, duties of lawyers employed by the government . . . may be defined by statutes and regulation. Therefore, defining precisely the identity of the client and prescribing the resulting obligations of such lawyers may be more difficult in the government context. Although in some circumstances the client may be a specific agency, it is generally the government as a whole. For example, if the action or failure to act involves the head of a bureau, either the department of which the bureau is a part or the government as a whole may be the client for purpose of this Rule. Moreover, in a matter involving the conduct of government officials, a government lawyer may have authority to question such conduct more extensively than that of a lawyer for a private organization in similar circumstances. This Rule does not limit that authority.

3.   A HIGHER DUTY?

Many government lawyers, who chose working for the federal government because of a belief that government could do good, were not enthusiastic supporters of Presidential candidate Ronald Reagan's campaign pledge to roll back the federal government. Thus, when President Reagan was elected, many of his political appointees were doubtful as to the loyalty and commitment that the career bureaucracy, including the lawyers, would demonstrate to fulfilling that pledge. From affirmative action to environmental laws, from public land laws to workplace safety rules, Reagan appointees attempted to forge new paths. Government lawyers often raised legal objections. The following excerpt, written by the then General Counsel of the Federal Communications Commission, appointed by Ronald Reagan, proposed an ethical obligation to do the President's bidding.

BRUCE FEIN, PROMOTING THE PRESIDENT'S POLICIES THROUGH LEGAL ADVOCACY: AN ETHICAL IMPERATIVE OF THE GOVERNMENT ATTORNEY

Federal Bar News & Journal, September/October
1983, Volume 30, No. 9–10, 6–10.

The Watergate scandal a decade ago precipitated a widespread examination of the ethical norms of government attorneys. . . .

Generally rejected from these omnibus discussions over the ethics of lawyers, however, has been an exploration of the duty a government attorney in the Executive Branch owes to his client, the incumbent President. I submit that ethical imperatives derived from our constitutional system of representative government and separation of powers obligate the government attorney to devote virtually unreservedly his legal talents and insights towards advancing the policies of the President through legal advocacy.

The Executive Branch employs thousands of attorneys most of whom are insulated from removal after a change of Administration because of constitutional or statutory protections and because of practical limits on recruitment of new attorneys. I do not deplore the impressive array of rights afforded government attorneys against discharge, transfer, or demotion. But these rights create a corollary responsibility to provide unremitting assistance through legitimate legal argument to the incumbent Administration in furtherance of the policies championed by the President. This ethical canon echoes one applicable to the private attorney, which instructs a lawyer to advocate any construction of the law favorable to his client that is not frivolous. If the ethical obligation of the government attorney is not faithfully discharged, then the electoral system is mocked, the President's ability to implement his policies could be stymied, and unelected lawyers in the Executive Branch will be censurable for disdaining the will of the people. . . .

De Tocqueville observed over 150 years ago, that in America, virtually every political question is ultimately transformed into a legal one. That canonical utterance has withstood the test of time, and perhaps should be crowned as an eternal verity of American political science. . . . A President must be successful in litigation defending his actions or initiatives if he is to have a significant role in shaping and implementing public policy. . . .

At times, prevailing legal doctrines must be modified, distinguished, or even overruled to accommodate or facilitate many of a President's policy objectives. When Franklin Roosevelt acceded to the Presidency in March of 1933, the cornucopia of New Deal legislation and programs that he trumpeted could be effectuated only by a radical alteration of established constitutional jurisprudence lionizing freedom of contract, property rights, and State sovereignty. . . . Many of Roosevelt's major policy initiatives were initially denounced by the Supreme Court as unconstitutional. . . .

Roosevelt, the Attorney General, and government attorneys, however, did not renounce the New Deal policy goals despite these resounding judicial rebuffs. The Executive Branch collaborated in marshalling legal arguments distinguishing or urging modification or overruling of Supreme Court precedents in a quest to obtain a jurisprudence that would countenance New Deal programs. . . . In sum, President Roosevelt's New Deal would have been stillborn if government attorneys refused to advocate with skill and imagination a dramatic change in prevailing constitutional doctrines. . . .

The President and his subordinates, of course, cannot defy court decrees. Moreover, the President should not insist on undertaking initiatives where there is no plausible likelihood of surmounting judicial review within the reasonably foreseeable future. But such occasions seldom, if ever, arise. . . .

4. A VIEW FROM THE TRENCHES

The following excerpt was written by a career litigator in the Department of Justice.

DOUGLAS LETTER, LAWYERING AND JUDGING ON BEHALF OF THE UNITED STATES: ALL I ASK FOR IS A LITTLE RESPECT

61 Geo. Wash. L. Rev. 1295 (1993).

I. The Unique Role of Government Attorneys

There is an inescapable fact that differentiates Department of Justice and other federal government lawyers from the overwhelming number of litigators in private practice. Government lawyers are paid a salary set and appropriated by Congress and the Executive *solely* in order to carry out their duties and responsibilities as employees of a democratically elected government. Business development is not one of their concerns. For virtually all purposes, these public service attorneys are *no* different from doctors in the Public Health Service, economists in the Bureau of Labor Statistics, field operatives in the CIA, air traffic controllers in the FAA, housing rehabilitation specialists at HUD, veterinarians in the Department of Agriculture, or foreign service officers at the State Department. We are all salaried professionals carrying out a public service under the ultimate direction of appointees of a popularly elected President and pursuant to the rules established by Congress in public laws. In theory, federal public servants have a single master: the people of the United States. In reality, however, they sometimes serve that master through loyalty not to the people directly but to institutions created by them, such as the Presidency, Congress, their agency employers, or the federal courts. . . .

By contrast, a private legal practitioner serves almost exclusively an individual private client and that client's interests, regardless of what these interests might be and whether, in any particular instance, they might be antithetical to the established law or current government policy. . . .

Unlike public servants, most private lawyers operate much like any other business enterprise; their primary purpose is to make a profit by selling their services to the public. . . . Like most other people in the business, private lawyers generally provide a valuable and necessary service for our society. . . .

One of the clearest demonstrations of the difference between the role of the Department of Justice lawyer and that of a private practitioner is revealed by words written on one wall of the Department of Justice headquarters, near the office of the Attorney General: "The United States wins its point whenever justice is done its citizens in Court." This means that, if a government attorney litigates a case on behalf of the United States and loses in a just way, the client served has won regardless of the seemingly unfavorable result. This maxim is not true for a private practitioner, who rarely will be able to convince a client that it has actually prevailed if judgment is rendered against it. . . .

For example, I was assigned to a case some years ago in the D.C. Circuit in which an attorney from one of the most prominent firms in

Washington, D.C. represented the other side—a major newspaper. That firm had made a technical error in perfecting an appeal from an adverse judgment. While assessing the case, I realized that I could have made a respectable argument that the appeal should be dismissed. Despite the harshness of that result, I thought there was a possibility that the court would grant the dismissal.

One of the opposing counsel, having realized the error, called me to say that she assumed that the United States would not attempt to take advantage of such a technical argument to dismiss an appeal involving an issue of substantive importance. As I spoke to her, I knew that if I were representing a private party, she would not have made the telephone call. Moreover, I would have committed gross malpractice through violation of my duty of loyalty to the client in such a situation if I had decided not to attempt to gain a dismissal under those circumstances.

In this instance, however, neither she nor I viewed her plea to me as improper or futile. Nevertheless, because her firm is notorious for its hardball litigation tactics, I could not resist asking her what she would have done had I been the one who had made the technical error on behalf of the government. I am sure that we both knew the answer, and that we both understood that each of us worked under a different obligation. . . .

This type of scene replays often in Department of Justice work. One of my duties in the Department is to provide orientation for attorneys joining the office. This includes both new attorneys fresh from law school or clerkships and experienced lawyers from private firms. During the sessions that I conduct, I emphasize that Justice Department attorneys serve a special role because we litigate on behalf of the United States. In particular, we are in an odd situation because we almost always litigate against the people of the United States, who are the very people that we ultimately serve. Thus, if we prevail, it is usually only because one of the citizens of the United States, or their corporations or associations, has lost. This fact can and should be sobering. . . .

Because of the interest that government attorneys must serve, it is not surprising that the D.C. Circuit and other federal courts impose special obligations on government lawyers. D.C. Circuit judges quite reasonably assume that government lawyers bear responsibilities—of fair dealing, full disclosure, and allegiance to the court system—that are not shared by private practitioners.

In the recent opinion in *Freeport–McMoRan Oil & Gas Co. v. FERC,* 962 F.2d 45 (D.C.Cir.1992), Chief Judge Mikva, writing for the D.C. Circuit, "address[ed] FERC counsel's remarkable assertion at oral argument that government attorneys ought not be held to higher standards than attorneys for private litigants." Chief Judge Mikva explained that "[t]he notion that government lawyers have obligations beyond those of private lawyers did not originate in oral argument in this case." Rather, he noted that the Supreme Court has instructed that a government lawyer " 'is the representative not of an ordinary party to a controversy,

... but of a sovereign whose obligation ... is not that it shall win a case, but that justice shall be done.' " Chief Judge Mikva also pointed out that the American Bar Association's Model Code of Professional Responsibility expressly holds government lawyers, whether acting in a civil or criminal capacity, "to higher standards than private lawyers."

Courts and the public in general would be horrified—and properly so—if government attorneys engaged in the types of sharp practices that regularly are overlooked when used by private practitioners and that are even praised and admired by members of the bar when utilized by legends in the private legal profession....

Problem 1–5

Consider the decision by Letter not to assert a probably winning procedural defense against the major newspaper. Assume the lawsuit was brought by the Department of Justice against the newspaper alleging violations of the Sherman Antitrust Act. Who would Letter's client be? Would Letter need the permission of his client before waiving a winning procedural point in order to reach the merits? Would it make a difference if the lawsuit involved an attempt by the Internal Revenue Service to obtain payments for taxes allegedly due?

Problem 1–6

Recall Problems 1–1 through 1–4. Assume that slightly before Helen's visit, a new President was inaugurated. As one of his first acts, he directs the Corps of Engineers to grant all permits for filling wetlands unless the particular fill would have a direct, immediate, substantial, and irreparable harm to interstate commerce. If Jay believes this order is inconsistent with the agency's authority, what is his responsibility? How should this affect his decision with regard to Helen's problem?

What is Jay's ethical obligation if his boss insists on granting the permit because Helen's client has been a major contributor to the President's party?

Notes and Questions

1. The D.C. Bar Report concludes that the agency is the government lawyer's client, but Fein argues that the government lawyer should serve the interests of the President. Are these two positions in tension with one another? Or are they harmonious? The D.C. Bar Report rejects the notion that the government as a whole is the government lawyer's client, but the ABA Model Rules Comment seems to say that it is. Is there a way to harmonize these two provisions? If not, which do you think is right?

2. Even if one concludes that a government lawyer's client is the agency, this hardly settles all the problems. Is the agency itself the client

the lawyer serves, or is the client the head of the agency? This is no academic question if the head of the agency proposes to take action that is not in the best interest of the agency. During the Reagan Revolution many government lawyers believed this was the situation. Does it make a difference if the agency head (or President) has expressly targeted the agency for extinction, as President Reagan had for the Department of Energy? How would the ABA Model Rules handle this problem?

3.   One of the reasons that government lawyers worked so hard to find legal justifications and arguments for the New Deal was because they believed in it. Fein is writing to government lawyers who do not believe in what the President is doing. Why do you suppose government lawyers believed in the New Deal, but not in the Reagan Revolution?

4.   Letter's article addresses government litigators. Can his counsel be applied outside of the litigation context? Even in the litigation context, is his advice consistent with the D.C. Bar's determination that a government lawyer's client is the agency? If Letter is zealously representing his client (the Department of Justice), can he give away claims or arguments that might win the case, to further the "public interest"? How would you reconcile Letter's advice with the D.C. Bar's determination? *See* James R. Harvey, III, *Loyalty in Government Litigation: Department of Justice Representation of Agency Clients,* 37 WM. & MARY L.REV. 1569 (1996).

5.   As you read, the Department of Justice had taken the position that state bars cannot impose their disciplinary rules on federal government lawyers. The Department argued that under the Constitution states cannot regulate federal entities unless Congress so authorizes it, because that would violate the Supremacy Clause. While this Constitutional issue was a real one for a number of years, Congress largely settled the matter by legislation in 1998. In the "Citizens Protection Act of 1998," 28 U.S.C. § 530B, Congress provided that Department of Justice attorneys shall be subject to "State laws and rules, and local Federal court rules, governing attorneys in each State where such attorney engages in that attorney's duties, to the same extent and in the same manner as other attorneys in that State." Attorneys employed by other agencies, however, are not covered by the terms of the Act. Are they subject to state disciplinary rules?

6.   A lawyer, whether employed by government or a private firm, can be a litigator or a counselor (or both, but usually not at the same time). A lawyer in private practice understands that when he counsels a client as to the law, the client is free to take or reject his legal advice in light of other factors important to the client. The "law" may be just one factor in the client's calculus. Things are different in government. Government officials swear to uphold the law; the law must be followed. There may be sufficient ambiguity in the law to allow for a range of options, but if the law precludes an action, government officials are not free to ignore legal advice. Even Fein at the end of his article recognizes this. The lawyer may be under substantial pressure not to take a

particular opinion because of this dynamic; the government official may suggest strongly that the law must be ambiguous enough to allow the proposed action. It is in these situations that a government lawyer can literally be a hero by upholding the rule of law, and, not incidentally, perhaps saving the official from serious problems. This is not to say that the official is likely to thank the lawyer for thwarting his plans.

7. Because of the effective ability to veto a proposed government action as illegal, a government lawyer possesses a great deal of power, and this power can be abused. When a government lawyer opposes an action on the merits or believes the best legal arguments are against it, it is an easy step to let the personal preferences drive the legal conclusion that the action is illegal. One is unlikely to do this consciously, but the desire to stop the action may cloud the legal judgement. It is some consolation to know that a lawyer, whether government or private, is not limited to counseling on the law. Rule 2.1 of the ABA Model Rules states:

> In representing a client, a lawyer shall exercise independent professional judgment and render candid advice. In rendering advice, a lawyer may refer not only to law but to other considerations such as moral, economic, social and political factors, that may be relevant to the client's situation.

Thus, one is free to advise the official as to the merits of what should be done, but here only the lawyer's persuasive ability carries weight.

8. For a discussion of who is the client, see Jeffrey Rosenthal, *Who is the Client of Government Lawyers?*, in ETHICAL STANDARDS IN THE PUBLIC SECTOR: A GUIDE FOR GOVERNMENT LAWYERS, CLIENTS, AND PUBLIC OFFICIALS (Patricia E. Salkin ed. 1999). An excellent symposium on "Government Lawyering" was published in 61 LAW & CONTEMP. PROBS. 1 (1998). It has different sections dealing with government lawyers shaping law and policy, government lawyers litigating on behalf of the United States, government lawyers for Congress, and government lawyers for the Executive Branch.

Problem 1–7

Assume Jay had participated in the Corps of Engineers' comments on a draft of the President's proposed order in which the Corps had advised the White House Counsel's Office that in its opinion the order was inconsistent with the Corps' statutory duty. Jay would like to "leak" a copy of this memo to the Washington Post; what are his ethical obligations? Would they differ if he wanted to "leak" a copy to the Senate Environment Committee?

Rule 1.6 of the ABA Model Rules of Professional Conduct has this to say about confidentiality:

> (a) A lawyer shall not reveal information relating to representation of a client unless the client consents after consultation, except for disclosures that are impliedly authorized in order to carry out the representation, and except as stated in paragraph (b).

(b) A lawyer may reveal such information to the extent the lawyer reasonably believes necessary:

(1) to prevent the client from committing a criminal act that the lawyer believes is likely to result in imminent death or substantial bodily harm; or

(2) to establish a claim or defense on behalf of the lawyer in a controversy between the lawyer and the client, to establish a defense to a criminal charge or civil claim against the lawyer based upon conduct in which the client was involved, or to respond to allegations in any proceeding concerning the lawyer's representation of the client.

One of the comments elaborates:

[5]   The principle of confidentiality is given effect in two related bodies of law, the attorney-client privilege (which includes the work product doctrine) in the law of evidence and the rule of confidentiality established in professional ethics. The attorney-client privilege applies in judicial and other proceedings in which a lawyer may be called as a witness or otherwise required to produce evidence concerning a client. The rule of client-lawyer confidentiality applies in situations other than those where evidence is sought from the lawyer through compulsion of law. The confidentiality rule applies not merely to matters communicated in confidence by the client but also to all information relating to the representation, whatever its source. A lawyer may not disclose such information except as authorized or required by the Rules of Professional Conduct or other law.

Notes and Questions

1.   As Comment 5 to Rule 1.6 notes, the principle of confidentiality is given effect in the attorney-client privilege (which includes the work product doctrine) in the law of evidence and in the rule of confidentiality established in professional ethics. When a government attorney asserts an attorney-client privilege to refuse to divulge information, there can be an issue of who is the client. Consider *In re Grand Jury Subpoena Duces Tecum*, 112 F.3d 910 (8th Cir.1997), in which the "Whitewater" Independent Counsel subpoenaed the notes "created during meetings attended by any attorney from the Office of Counsel to the President and Hillary Rodham Clinton." The White House invoked the attorney-client privilege for two sets of notes created in meetings during breaks in and following Mrs. Clinton's testimony before a grand jury investigating the discovery of certain law firm billing records in the White House residence area. Present at the meetings were Mrs. Clinton, her private lawyers, an associate counsel to the President, and a special counsel to the President, the latter two being government employees. The court ordered the attorneys to comply with the subpoena.

In the course of its decision, the court made clear that the client of the White House lawyers was the Office of the President, not the person who happened to be President or his wife. In addition, the Court also distinguished between the ethical obligations of lawyers under the Rules of Professional Conduct (in the District of Columbia) and the scope of the attorney-client privilege—an evidentiary privilege. The court expressly stated that the ethical obligations of lawyers, which might prohibit disclosure, do not govern the scope of the attorney-client privilege.

After identifying the White House as the client, the court considered whether the White House, as the client, was entitled to protect the information sought by the Independent Counsel from disclosure. The court noted that the White House was unable to identify *any* cases refusing to enforce a grand jury subpoena in this context. It was also impressed by the fact that a Federal statute requires executive branch employees, including attorneys, to report to the Attorney General any criminal activity by other government employees. Finally, because a government entity, as opposed to individuals within it, cannot be subject to criminal prosecution, the court concluded that the lack of protection of attorney-client communications is unlikely to result in diminished adequacy of legal representation of government entities in the future. In short, the court concluded that even if there were an attorney-client privilege for government entities in some circumstances, there was no such privilege with respect to grand jury subpoenas.

2.   The District of Columbia Circuit Court of Appeals reached a similar conclusion in *In re Lindsey (Grand Jury Testimony)*, 158 F.3d 1263 (1998). In this case, the Independent Counsel sought the testimony of a Deputy White House Counsel, Bruce Lindsey, concerning communications with the President about the President's testimony in the Paula Jones case and his relations with Monica Lewinsky. The court acknowledged that there is a government attorney-client privilege, but it also indicated that the client is the agency, not an individual, so here the client would be the Office of the President, not William Clinton. Having recognized a privilege, the court concluded that it is a limited privilege, which did not protect against disclosure to a federal grand jury investigating federal crimes.

The court noted several distinctions between the government attorney-client privilege and the ordinary private attorney-client privilege. First, government attorneys are bound to comply with the provision of federal law which requires that "information ... received in a department or agency of the executive branch of the Government relating to violations of [federal criminal law] involving Government officers and employees shall be expeditiously reported to the Attorney General." Second, the duty of government attorneys is not to defend clients against criminal charges, but to take care that the laws are faithfully executed, including the investigation and prosecution of federal crimes. Third, the government attorney's representation of his client is not for the benefit of the client, but for the public's benefit. If those interests are not coincident, as when the client's private interests are in conflict with the government's investigation of a crime, the public's interests must prevail. Finally, the court concluded that the absence of a privilege against a grand jury demand was not likely to decrease substantially the candor and availability of government attorneys' advice.

3. For a discussion of the issues raised by the previous cases, see Michael K. Forde, *The White House Counsel and Whitewater: Government Lawyers and the Scope of Privileged Communications*, 16 YALE L. & POL'Y REV. 109 (1997); Lance Cole, *The Government–Client Privilege after Office of the President v. Office of the Independent Counsel*, 22 J. LEGAL PROF. 15 (1997–98).

4. If the District of Columbia's Rules of Professional Conduct prohibit a lawyer from disclosing certain information, but a court enforces a subpoena requiring the lawyer to disclose that information, what should the lawyer do? If the lawyer discloses the information pursuant to the subpoena, can the local bar discipline the person?

Chapter 2

RULEMAKING

Most descriptions of rulemaking procedure begin with the publication of a notice of proposed rulemaking and end with the publication of the final rule. In reality, however, the rulemaking process really begins when an agency considers whether to propose a rule, and it may not end until there has been judicial review of the promulgated rule. This chapter explains each of the steps of the rulemaking process in chronological order. It covers the initiation of rulemaking, writing the rule, advocacy by interested parties, the notice and comment period, and judicial review.

Most agencies are engaged in informal rulemaking, which, as the last chapter discussed, involves giving notice, inviting written comments, and justifying the rule in a statement of basis and purpose. 5 U.S.C.A. § 553. The rulemaking process, however, is more complex than reference to section 553 would suggest. First, there has been judicial interpretation of section 553, which has imposed additional procedural obligations on agencies. Second, an agency may have to utilize procedures imposed by sources other than the APA. The agency's mandate may impose additional procedures, such as a required oral hearing or the opportunity to cross-examine persons submitting information. In addition, statutes like the National Environmental Policy Act (NEPA), the Paperwork Reduction Act, and the Regulatory Flexibility Act may impose additional procedures if the rule will have certain effects. Third, the agency may wish to take advantage of certain mechanisms for developing rules, which entail special procedures. For example, an agency may desire to develop a rule through consensus-building among interested parties. A procedure for this exists called "regulatory negotiation." Or an agency may want to obtain the advice of outside persons before proposing a rule. If an agency utilizes an advisory committee, for example, it must comply with the Federal Advisory Committee Act (FACA), which regulates the formation and operation of such committees. 5 U.S.C. App. II. Fourth, executive branch agencies must comply with executive orders issued by the President, such as E.O. 12,866, which required agencies to prepare a "regulatory impact analysis" for any significant regulatory action. Finally, the rulemaking process is impacted by the nature of the internal procedures, incentives, and management methods used by an agency. *See* Thomas O. McGarity, *Some Thoughts On Deossifying The Rulemaking Process*, 41 DUKE L.J. 1385 (1992) (describing the complications of the rulemaking).

The following text, problems, and secondary materials will introduce you to some of the complexity of the rulemaking process. Although this complexity makes the rulemaking process more difficult to understand, the complexity is unavoidable for those who practice administrative law. Indeed, it is what makes rulemaking a particularly interesting area of administrative law in which to practice.

A. RULEMAKING INITIATION

A number of events can prompt an agency to propose a rule. The agency may act pursuant to a statutory command, in response to staff recommendations, as a result of a rulemaking petition from an interested person, or from political pressure from the legislative or the executive branches. This section considers how an agency initiates the rulemaking process and how members of the public can influence an agency's rulemaking agenda.

1. SOURCES OF PROPOSED REGULATIONS

Probably the most common source of proposed regulations is legislation requiring specific regulations, often by a particular time or upon the occurrence of certain events. For example, the Clean Air Act Amendments of 1990 created the acid deposition control program to attack the problem of acid rain. Part of that law required EPA to "promulgate, not later than 18 months after November 15, 1990, a system for issuing, recording, and tracking [the] allowances [that authorize emissions of acid rain precursors], which shall specify all necessary procedures and requirements for an orderly and competitive functioning of the allowance system." 42 U.S.C.A. § 7615b(d). *See* Gregory L. Ogden, *Reducing Administrative Delay: Timeliness Standards, Judicial Review of Agency Procedures, Procedural Reform, and Legislative Oversight*, 4 U. DAYTON L. REV. 71 (1979). Often, however, a statute mandating regulations merely requires the agency to adopt rules generally to protect safety (such as the Occupational Safety and Health Act and the National Highway Traffic Safety Act) or to adopt rules in the public interest, convenience, and necessity (such as the Federal Communications Act). These broad requirements provide substantial discretion to agencies to determine what, if anything, needs to be regulated, and when regulation is appropriate.

The question then becomes what influences the agency in the exercise of that discretion? Rules often begin with a staff recommendation. Staff recommendations can arise in several ways. First, staff members may suggest that a rule is necessary when they identify problems that the agency should address. In a health and safety agency, for example, regulatory proposals may be based on new scientific research, regulatory developments in other countries, or recommendations by private standard-setting organizations. In addition, the agency's enforcement efforts will produce information that can be used to determine how well existing regulations are being met and what aspects of the regulations are not working or are unrealistic. Finally, the agency might have a formal system of priority-setting that identifies potential rulemaking subjects and ranks them according to their importance. This process would identify candidates for rulemaking on an on-going basis. One might call this a bottom-up approach.

Political pressure is another conventional source of a decision to undertake a rulemaking. An agency may propose a rule to avoid a critical legislative investigation prompted by complaints from statutory beneficiaries. Most administrators wish to avoid answering hostile questions before the television cameras in a congressional hearing concerning the failure to respond to a problem considered important by a legislative committee. As further motivation to act, Congress can threaten to reduce the agency's budget or to attach an appropriations amendment that limits future agency action. Richard J. Pierce & Sidney A. Shapiro, *Political & Judicial Review of Agency Action*, 59 TEX. L. REV. 1175, 1198 (1981). Legislatures are not the only source of political pressure. Presidents and governors, like legislators, are sensitive to political constituencies, and like legislative pressure, executive pressure can be highly motivating. For example, the Reagan administration sent to several agencies a "hit list" of regulations to be modified or withdrawn in 1981. Agencies responded by devoting substantial resources over the next few years to determining whether such regulations should be weakened or repealed. JONATHAN LASH, KATHERINE GILLMAN, & DAVID SHERIDAN, A SEASON OF SPOILS: THE STORY OF THE REAGAN ADMINISTRATION'S CONTROVERSIAL ATTACK ON THE ENVIRONMENT 29–45 (1984). One might call these sources of rulemakings the top-down approach.

The public can also become a source for proposed regulations. Acting indirectly through legislators or executive officials, lobbyists representing a segment of the "public" can generate political heat that triggers the top-down approach. Lobbying can also be done at the staff level to create interest in a possible rule. Both these types of lobbying are done by industry and business groups as well as public interest and environmental groups. In addition, the public can trigger rulemaking by filing rulemaking petitions. The APA provides that "[e]ach agency shall give an interested person the right to petition for issuance, amendment, or repeal of a rule." 5 U.S.C.A. § 553(e). Further, the APA mandates that "[p]rompt notice shall be given of the denial in whole or in part of a written application, petition, or other request of an interested person made in connection with any agency proceeding" and "the notice shall be accompanied by a brief statement of the grounds for denial." *Id.* § 555(e). As will be discussed in more detail below, the petitioner can seek judicial review of an agency's decision not to proceed with rulemaking.

The APA does not require any further procedures concerning a rulemaking petition, but an agency's own mandate might do so. The Toxic Substances Control Act (TSCA), for example, requires that EPA make a decision concerning a petition within 90 days. If EPA grants the petition, it must promptly commence rulemaking, and if EPA denies the petition, it must publish the reasons in the Federal Register. 15 U.S.C.A. § 2620.

Notes and Questions

EPA, OSHA, and other health and safety regulators have been criticized for relying on ad hoc staff recommendations for proposed rules instead of employing a priority-setting process that ranks different regulatory proposals, particularly concerning environmental, health, and safety risks, by their significance. *E.g.*, STEPHEN BREYER, BREAKING THE VICIOUS CIRCLE: TOWARD EFFECTIVE RISK REGULATION 1–29 (1993); Sidney A. Shapiro & Thomas O. McGarity, *Reorienting OSHA: Regulatory Alternatives and Legislative Reform*, 6 YALE J. ON REG. 1, 15–18 (1989). Agencies have been slow to adopt priority setting, in part because regulatory problems are difficult to rank. Administrators often have limited information about such problems, and for that reason, it is difficult to know which risks are the most significant. Moreover, administrators are reluctant for political reasons to admit that some problem is less important than other problems. Regulatory beneficiaries will dislike an agency's decision to ignore their problem, and legislators who represent such persons are likely to make this displeasure known to the agency. Shapiro & McGarity, *supra*, at 18–20. Can you think of other reasons why an agency would be reluctant to adopt a priority setting process?

2. LOBBYING

Problem 2–1: Lobbying the Agency

The following problem is based on EPA's regulation of pesticides manufactured by biotechnology. Agricultural researchers using biotechnology have the potential to create biodegradable microbial pesticides derivable from bacteria, viruses, and fungi that can synthesize toxins poisonous to specific insects. Biotechnology can also be used to transfer a pesticide-producing gene into a plant to improve its natural defense mechanism.

Before new "pesticides" can be sold, the Federal Insecticide, Fungicide, and Rodenticide Act (FIFRA) requires that the manufacturer obtain a "registration" or a license from EPA. FIFRA defines the term "pesticide" very broadly to include any substance "intended for preventing, destroying, repelling, or mitigating any pest," or "intended for use as a plant regulator, defoliant, or desiccant." To register a pesticide product, a manufacturer must demonstrate, among other requirements, that the pesticide will "perform its intended function without unreasonable adverse effects on the environment." To support the registration, a manufacturer must generally conduct field tests and experiments. For this purpose, FIFRA authorizes EPA to issue an "Experimental Use Permit (EUP)." As you might imagine, obtaining one of these permits can be expensive and time consuming.

EPA has promulgated a rule that exempts small-scale (10 acres or less) field tests of chemical pesticides from this requirement. The agency has refused to broaden the rule to exempt from the EUP requirements small scale field tests of pesticides produced by biotechnology, because not enough is known about the environmental hazards of such products.

Imagine that you work for a law firm that represents a biotech company. The company foresees that it will wish to engage in a number of small scale tests of bio-engineered pesticides, and it believes that the stringent requirements for EUPs, however appropriate in the beginning of biotechnology, are no longer necessary or called for. Armed with studies showing no environmental injuries and only one uncontrolled environmental release (with no untoward effects) out of hundreds of field tests, the company asks your firm to get EPA to amend its rule. What should your firm do?

Problem Materials

The materials that follow are three different articles. The first, by Professor Tom McGarity of the University of Texas Law School, describes the players involved and internal procedures used at EPA in rulemaking. The organizational table of EPA in Chart 2–1 will help you understand Professor McGarity's description. The second and third are two perspectives on how to lobby agencies. The first of these is by Patricia Bailey, a partner in a Washington law firm and previously a Commissioner of the Federal Trade Commission (FTC). The second is by Cornish Hitchcock, who is an attorney for the Public Citizen Litigation Center.

EPA ORGANIZATIONAL CHART

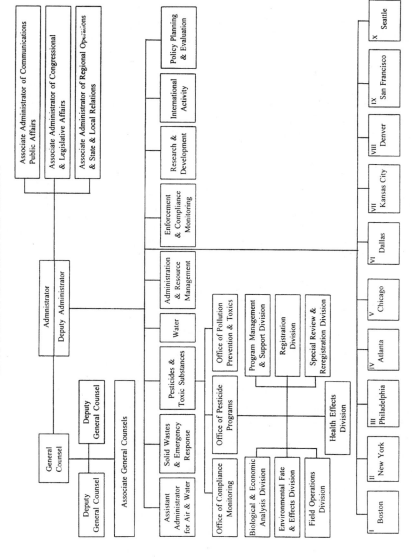

Chart 2-1

THOMAS O. McGARITY, THE INTERNAL STRUCTURE OF EPA RULEMAKING

54 Law & Contemp. Probs., Autumn 1991, at 57, 65–90.

III. INTRODUCTION TO THE MAJOR INSTITUTIONAL ACTORS

An examination of EPA's current decisionmaking processes must begin with a description of the agency hierarchy and an introduction to the major institutional players. The administrator stands at the top of the hierarchy and is the most important institutional actor. He or she is the final decisionmaker on agency rules, the ultimate judge in agency adjudications, and the court of last resort in intra-agency turf battles. With the final say over the allocation of resources within the agency, the administrator determines agency priorities and decides which offices play what roles in the decisionmaking process. Finally, the administrator is the principal spokesperson for the agency and the primary focal point in interactions between the agency, the White House, Congress, and the public.

The deputy administrator is the second in command but (like the vice president) has only such institutional power as the administrator cares to delegate. . . .

The next level in the formal hierarchy consists of the nine politically appointed assistant administrators. At this level of the hierarchy, the historical dual structure of the agency becomes most apparent. The agency is divided into both programmatic and functional areas. Each important regulatory program within the agency reports to a particular assistant administrator with programmatic responsibilities, but there are also assistant administrators for broad functions, such as resource management, research and development, enforcement, and policy management. . . . The current list of assistant administrators consists of the assistant administrators with programmatic responsibilities (the Assistant Administrators for Air and Radiation, for Pesticides and Toxic Substances, for Solid Waste and Emergency Response, and for Water) and those with overall functional responsibilities that cut across programmatic areas (the Assistant Administrators for Administration and Resource Management, for Enforcement and Compliance Monitoring, for International Activities, for Policy, Planning, and Evaluation, and for Research and Development).

The Assistant Administrator for Enforcement and Compliance Monitoring has the primary responsibility for enforcing EPA rules. Together with attorneys from the Justice Department, the lawyers for the Office of Enforcement and Compliance Monitoring investigate potential violations, prepare enforcement actions, negotiate with polluters, and prosecute civil and criminal actions in court. The office also has the responsibility for ensuring that the rules the agency drafts are easily enforced.

Although most of the program offices have economists on staff, the agency's principal regulatory analysts work in the Office of Policy and

Compliance Monitoring Analysis under the Assistant Administrator for Policy, Planning, and Evaluation. . . .

The general counsel is the agency's chief attorney. The Office of General Counsel ("OGC") is divided programmatically and functionally, reflecting the dual organization of the agency. Under the general counsel and two deputy general counsels, there are seven associate general counsels with their associated staffs. OGC is responsible for legal interpretations underlying agency rules and for defending those rules in court. Its duty to ensure that rules survive "arbitrary and capricious" review justifies the office in taking positions on the substantive merits of proposals and on the technical and economic validity of the support documents. . . .

The next level in the agency hierarchy (the highest level nonpolitical appointee) is the office director. Each of the assistant administrators is responsible for several offices, and each office director is typically responsible for one important program. The office directors are the actual managers of agency regulatory programs, and they are the officials primarily responsible for the substance of agency rules. They are also the officials most easily accessible to regulatees and important citizen groups. Typically an office director in one of the program offices assumes responsibility for all of the agency's substantive rules under a particular statute.

The offices in turn are subdivided into divisions, each of which has programmatic or functional responsibilities. For example, the Office of Air Quality Planning and Standards contains the Air Quality Management Division (responsible for promulgating and overseeing the implementation of the National Ambient Air Quality Standards), the Emissions Standards Division (responsible for promulgating new source performance standards and national emission standards for hazardous air pollutants), the Stationary Source Compliance Division (responsible for compliance monitoring and technical support for enforcement), and the Technical Support Division (responsible for technical support for rulemaking and enforcement activities and for assembling national databases). Each office director is a senior civil service employee and is aided by a deputy director of almost equal status.

The staff sergeants of the agency are the branch chiefs, who are located just below the office directors in the agency hierarchy. Each branch chief supervises a staff of agency professionals who do the actual work of writing and compiling the technical support for agency rules. The branches are populated by scientists, engineers, and other professionals with training or experience in environmental management. . . .

Superimposed upon this entire structure are ten regional offices, each of which has a politically appointed regional administrator and a staff that reports to the regional administrator but is organized roughly along the lines of the headquarters staff. The primary functions of the regional offices are to oversee state and federal permitting processes, approve state implementation plans and delegations, conduct monitoring and enforcement efforts, and serve as representatives of the agency to the general citizenry.

The primary collective decisionmaking entity at EPA is the "Steering Committee," which is a standing group composed of high level representatives of each assistant administrator and the general counsel. The Steering Committee concept has been in use at the agency since its inception, and although its importance has waxed and waned through the years, it has proven remarkably durable. Its purpose is to coordinate and integrate the agency's regulation development activities. . . .

IV.   The Decisionmaking Process

A. *The Origin of EPA Rules*

Under the existing highly formalized internal procedures, the first step in a rulemaking initiative is the start action request that the lead office submits to the Steering Committee. The primary purposes of the start action request are to alert other agency officials to the lead office's intention to develop a rule and to provide the Steering Committee with an opportunity to discuss and plan for any inter-office and cross-media aspects of the rule. The request can also avoid duplication. If one office is aware that another office is working on a regulatory problem of interest to both offices, they can coordinate their efforts. Finally, the start action request provides the occasion for specifying and preparing for subsequent stages of the rulemaking process for the particular rule. . . .

B. *The Workgroup*

1. The Role of the Workgroup. Shortly after the Steering Committee approves a start action request, the project officer in the lead office must convene a workgroup. The workgroup is chaired by the project officer from the lead office, and it contains the lead analyst from the Office of Policy Analysis, a staff attorney from OGC, and usually staff representatives of the Office of Research and Development, the Office of Enforcement and Compliance Monitoring, and a regional office. Other offices may send representatives when the workgroup will be addressing issues that concern them. . . .

Workgroup meetings, which occur regularly throughout the life cycle of a rule, are intended to "provide a forum for sharing expertise" and to help "resolve conflicts at the start, thus enhancing the quality of Steering Committee review." Another unarticulated, but very real function of the workgroup is to bring together professionals with different perspectives to focus their attention on a regulatory problem and debate the appropriate ways to address that problem. Ideally, the interchange of perspectives helps achieve a synthesis that goes beyond the outlook or observations of any individual group member. Obviously, the likelihood that creative synergy will occur depends upon the level of energy that the workgroup members put into the effort. . . .

The workgroup's final product is a rulemaking package that is composed of the workgroup's suggested draft of the proposed rule, the draft preliminary regulatory impact analysis, other required documents, and a decision memorandum outlining the options, detailing the pros and cons of each option, and explaining why and when each was rejected. The package must also estimate the resources required for implementing the rule, including enforcement plans and anticipated regional resource requirements. . . .

C. Steering Committee Review

The rulemaking packages for major and significant rules are sent to the Steering Committee for final review. The Steering Committee reviews all major rules and many significant rules at a regular meeting. Members of the Steering Committee rarely suggest options that have not already been identified at the workgroup level. The Steering Committee is more a reviewing body than an institution for developing innovative solutions to regulatory problems. The Steering Committee meeting on a rulemaking package can be a forum for debating issues that have not been resolved in the workgroup. In addition, one of the committee's responsibilities is to identify significant issues for upper-level management, whether or not the workgroup has reached consensus on those issues. The closure memorandum drafted by the Steering Committee chairman documents the committee's resolution of outstanding issues. . . .

D. Red Border Review

After the Steering Committee has concluded its deliberations, the package is cleared for "Red Border Review." This process is the formal review procedure whereby senior management (usually assistant and regional administrators and the general counsel) reviews and approves regulatory packages for all rules (including minor rules) before they are presented to the administrator. The review always includes the general counsel and the Assistant Administrator for Policy, Planning and Evaluation, and other assistant administrators for offices that were represented on the workgroup. . . .

E. Final Rules

The agency procedures for responding to public comments on a proposed rule and for preparing the final rule and its accompanying regulatory package are virtually identical to the procedures governing the preparation of the initial rulemaking and regulatory analysis documents. The project officer in the lead office is responsible for assembling the public comments and breaking them down by issue as far as possible. The agency sometimes hires contractors to read and separate the comments. The comments are then distributed to the personnel who drafted the portions of the documents that the comments addressed. After the various offices have had a sufficient opportunity to respond individually, the project officer calls a workgroup meeting to discuss how the agency as a whole should respond to the comments. The workgroup again attempts to reach consensus on the changes that should be made in light of the public comments. The workgroup's recommendations and dissenting opinions are then forwarded to the Steering Committee and from there sent to Red Border Review.

INITIATING AGENCY ACTION: COMMENTS OF PATRICIA BAILEY

5 Admin. L. J. of Am. U. 24–30 (1991).

The first thing to do is to think about what you're trying to do. Agency actions are taken pursuant to statutes and regulations or congressional oversight indictments. And in that respect, they are making legal decisions. But that is the only respect in which you can call a lot of these decisions legal. While regulations and statutes are at the foundation of agency action, decisions that are being made are what government should do, not really so much what the government is compelled to do by the statute. And so you have to remember, I think, when you go forward to do battle with the government agency, that an agency is not a courtroom. . . .

These people are making policy decisions. . . .

Getting the agency to act in a certain way requires certain policy advocacy skills. And in no particular order, I would say that those skills are an ability to understand the agency's problem, to have a fairly firm grip on the legislative process, the ability to deal with the political environment that the agency finds itself in, and an understanding of basic policy analysis tools that most all agencies use. The final skill would be, of course, to know when none of these other skills would work, and to know what to do then.

Let me elaborate a little bit. Let's say that you are dealing with an agency where a decision is going to be made and a proposal has already been made about it. I think that there is no need to come whining to the agency that some policy or decision that they make is going to harm your client or harm consumers or do harm to someone. Because almost any decision that an agency makes is going to harm someone. Allegation without more does not surprise them and does not cause them to change course.

You have to know what the agency's mission is, what its purpose is, what its causes are. And that may enable you to argue that whatever action it is that they are proposing to take will damage their own interests. This is often a good tactic to take, because, hopefully, you can get them to see that whatever it is you want them to do is in their own best interests, based on your understanding of what they have been told to do and what they are trying to do. And at the same time, don't ever try to conceal your own self-interest, because your reasons from the outside are inherently suspect.

If you understand an agency's position, you may discover that what is primary for the agency is really secondary or even unimportant to you. But what may be crucial to you is only secondary for the agency. If you can look at it that way, you may be able to get something that is very important to you eliminated or added, whatever your interest is, in a way that will enable the agency to deal with the problem without compromising its own case. A 100% win is not attainable. It is probably a waste of money to pursue, and unwise in the end. . . .

Now, regardless of how serious and significant the issue may be, the decision reached will be based largely on the material generated at the staff level by the staff. To be most effective, input of data and arguments from outsiders must be made at that level. It will make less and less of an impact as a matter for decision moves up the chain.

I cannot tell you the number of people I know who want to come in and talk to the Secretary of Commerce about a matter that somebody has said in the regulatory agenda he's going to make a decision on this week. The problem, however, is that it is too late, it is just too late to do that. . . .

You have to educate yourselves about the agency's normal procedures. And all government agencies have the same kind of modus operandi. They have these lengthy in-depth analyses by the stack, but somewhere—and you should find out where—somebody is responsible for making an overall synthesis of these arguments so that it tells a story that makes sense to somebody. And then there's going to be a summary at the top for the people at the highest levels of the decision chain. So you should prepare your papers in the same format.

Understand that once the papers leave the staff unit, the decisions made in that unit will not be reversed. The lawyers are not going to reverse anything that the economists have written. And that's true all across this spectrum. In the end, the arguments of the unit may be rejected, but they're not going to be reversed by anyone. So you have to get in on the ground floor. You cannot risk missing out at that level. . . .

I would say, partly because of the foregoing, do not gratuitously insult the staff of an agency. What will happen is that most likely the agency will close ranks against you, freeze you out. That is going to be true even if you have a pretty good case or an argument. I have seen it happen a lot. I call it the "New York lawyers' syndrome." It is sort of, you know, "These people are really not very bright. They're not very something." They have an animosity toward my client, born surely of their ignorance. And it could as well be called "the Chicago's economist syndrome" or "the cumulus single-minded public advocate approach." There is a way not to deal with these things. In court you can go in and make light of somebody else's argument. But to try that in an agency; you're on your way out.

Now I would say, try to understand the political environment that the agency is involved in. Don't talk about unelected bureaucrats with arbitrary unchecked power; that is not how it seems to them. With OMB (The Office of Management and Budget) on one shoulder and the White House on another and congressional oversight investigative appropriations committees, agency constituents—whomever they may be—labor, agriculture, business, and the media. [T]he media is always there, disclosing things, commenting on things, criticizing them and subjecting them to ridicule. It doesn't seem to [the agencies] like they have unchecked power. So you should keep in mind when you're urging an agency to take a certain kind of action how it is going to appear to the significant others that surround that agency. Because that is the way that agency will be looking at it.

I would also say that if your views are an anathema to some of those people that you are trying to persuade, if you represent Exxon and you're trying to deal with the EPA on oil spill regulation or something, what you might try to do is to form a coalition and get someone else to make your argument. . . .

It is helpful if you know the rudiments of policy analysis—cost/benefit analysis, risk assessment, knowledge of market forces and all that stuff. All agencies talk a lot about that now. And actually these are useful tools. . . .

INITIATING AGENCY ACTION: COMMENTS OF CORNISH HITCHCOCK

5 Admin. L. J. of Am. U. 53–62 (1991).

[I have] six observations and rules of thumb on how to influence agencies. . . .

The first one is, knock on every door. What that means is look for various supporters when people might be interested in whatever form. People in Congress might be interested to the extent that they are willing to introduce legislation. People at the agencies may be interested in the subject matter. People in the news media may be interested if it is a good story. Whatever door may be open, try it.

The second rule of thumb is look for allies. That is important for several reasons. One is political. The more friends you have, the more people you have saying, "This is a good idea," the more likely you are to achieve the goals. The second reason that this rule is important, particularly if you represent groups like ours, is that it provides a way to get empirical data to bolster your case. . . .

The third rule of thumb is read the newspapers. Now why do you do that? The reason is because it is important in terms of learning what signals the administration, the agency, and political higher-ups are sending. What are they looking for? What is the policy? How does your particular proposal comport with the overall regulatory policy? How does it fit in? What are the signals that are being sent? What are the things that the agency, the staff is going to be asked when they come forward with the recommendation?

The fourth rule of thumb (which is sort of related to the last rule of thumb) is know your audience. This operates at several levels. . . . It also deals with something that lawyers seem to have trouble getting the knack of, and I think it reflects on legal training, which tries to teach you how to be a litigator but not necessarily how to influence agencies or Congress. One thing you have to know is that in the agencies, the Bureau of Economics gets the economic issue, the General Counsel's office looks at the legal issue, things get farmed out, and you have to make sure that the comments are structured so that they will be considered by professionals with different backgrounds, not all of whom respond to legal points. . . .

The other principle in terms of knowing your audience involves comments in rulemakings, that is, sounding the themes that the Secretary or the Administrator or the administration generally is interested in sounding. As your policy proposal works its way into the system, you can put in arguments that this will achieve the following three goals in the state of the union message or whatever else you want to use as your jumping off point. And that needs to be reflected in your writing.

You also need to keep in mind a broader audience: Congress, the press, the public at large. You get calls from the Hill or from the news media. What are you people doing? What are you saying? If you have a ten or twenty page statement with all of the material in there, readily understandable, you are going to accomplish a lot.

The point I made a moment ago about lawyer-training is that a lot of time lawyers think of doing comments pretty much as if they were writing a brief to a court. However, it is a different exercise. Agency practice is much more like congressional practice. Your focus really has to be to persuade the agency, whoever may be reading it, why the world would be a better place if your proposal is enacted. And that is a different exercise than trying to persuade an appellate court that case A is really distinguishable from case B, or that the court is compelled to rule in your favor on the basis of case C. That is what litigation is about.

Point number five is read the rules. You need to know to what extent you can talk to the staff. When do the *ex parte* rules drop like an iron curtain across your ability to communicate and provide additional information? What are the chances for expediting it? . . .

And finally a point on style in terms of writing comments. I have expressed it in the outline this way: If you can't think of something nice to say, say it anyway. What that means is there will be times when there is a proposal that comes from an agency that you think is truly dreadful; there is the temptation to say it is truly dreadful. And that may be good if you're talking to the news media who want to understand whether something is good or bad—nuanced distinctions don't always get into the coverage.

Notes and Questions

1. The above problem posited that you represented a biotech company. If someone in EPA told someone in the National Wildlife Federation (NWF) what that law firm was doing, what should the NWF do?

2. As the last two excerpts mention, a lawyer's advocacy role is not limited to talking with agency personnel; advocates will reach out to elected officials and seek their assistance. Tom Susman, a former chair of the Administrative Law and Regulatory Practice Section of the American Bar Association, has noted that such political contacts have become an important aspect of agency practice:

> Politics defines relationships among people—and among institutions—especially governmental institutions. Politics is thus irrelevant, or peripheral, only in the most focused, structured, and formalized proceeding—like a hearing room without a jury....
>
> Joseph Goulden, in *The Superlawyers*, saw this as the dark side of Washington law practice and characterized the exercise of the lawyer's art of influencing government decisionmaking a violation of the public interest. Goulden sold a lot of books but missed the point. Our system of checks and balances—which includes in Washington many cross-checks and counter-balances—works on many levels, in many ways.
>
> Politics provides both the board and the rules for the game of government, the game many Washington Lawyers play for their livelihood. Whether personal or partisan, issue-development or fundraising, endorsements or referrals, grass-roots or national or international, politics touches ... most aspects of Washington lawyering. Politics has become an integral part of the regular practice of law for the Washington Lawyer.

Thomas M. Susman, *A Perspective on the Washington Lawyer Today and Charles Horsky's Washington Lawyer of 1952*, 44 ADMIN. L. REV. 1, 6–7 (1992).

Do you agree with Mr. Susman that lobbying is a normal and expected, even desirable, part of public law practice, or with Joseph Goulden, that such activities are nothing more than influence peddling? Is state administrative law practice different?

3. For a detailed and informative description of the rulemaking process, including lobbying, see CORNELIUS M. KERWIN, HOW GOVERNMENT AGENCIES WRITE LAW AND MAKE POLICY (1994). Professor Kerwin asserts, "Rulemaking is the single most important function performed by agencies of government." He explains why this is so and how it relates to the "politics" of the rulemaking process:

> Rulemaking refines, and in some instances defines, the mission of every government agency. In so doing, it provides direction and content for budgeting, program implementation, procurement, personnel management, dispute resolution, and other important governmental activities. Rules provide specific, authoritative statements of the obligations the government has assumed and the benefits it must provide. It is to rules, not statutes or other containers of law, that we turn most often for an understanding of what is expected of us and what can expect from government. As a result, intense

political activity surrounds the contemporary rulemaking process and effective political action in America is no longer possible without serious attention to rulemaking.

Id. at xi. How does Kerwin's claim help explain Tom Susman's assertion that "politics touches ... most aspects of Washington lawyering"?

4. The problem involved someone trying to initiate agency action, but lobbying also goes on with respect to matters the agency is presently considering or thinking about considering. There are formal means by which agencies are supposed to inform the public about their regulatory proposals, even before they publish their notices of proposed rulemaking. One of these is the semi-annual Regulatory Agenda that Presidents have required agencies to publish. *See* Executive Order 12866, 58 Fed. Reg. 51735 (1993). Twice a year agencies publish a description of each of the regulatory initiatives they intend to take during the next six months, as well as provide a status report on previously described initiatives. The White House makes the agenda available to the public on the Internet: http://ciir.cs.umass.edu/ua/. Nevertheless, knowing what agencies are doing is part of what Washington, D.C., law firms market as their expertise. One of the ways that law firms keep abreast of what agencies are doing is by hiring persons who have worked in the agencies and who still have friends there.

3. PETITIONS FOR RULEMAKING

As indicated earlier, one of the ways the public can initiate rulemaking is through a petition for rulemaking. One should not think of this as an alternative to lobbying, however. Rather, filing such a petition may be part of a total lobbying strategy.

Under section 553 of the APA, agencies are required "to give an interested person the right to petition for the issuance, amendment, or repeal of a rule." This might lead you to expect that agencies would have procedural rules governing the filing of petitions for rulemaking, but such rules are rare. The Administrative Conference of the United States (ACUS) recommended that agencies adopt basic procedures for the receipt, consideration, and prompt disposition of petitions for rulemaking, including procedures for publicizing the address for filing petitions and what should be included in their contents, the maintenance of a public petition file, and a commitment to prompt notice of a petition's disposition. Recommendation No. 86–6, "Petitions for Rulemaking," 1 C.F.R. § 305.86–6. Because an agency may have procedures for petitions, you must ascertain whether there are any applicable rules, or else your petition may not qualify for consideration. Under section 555, an agency cannot ignore a petition for rulemaking; that section requires the agency to give "prompt notice ... of the denial" and to accompany the notice with "a brief statement of the grounds for the denial." Thus, filing a petition is a way to force some action out of the agency if it is otherwise reluctant.

If the agency grants the petition and proceeds to rulemaking, no issue for judicial review arises, but if the agency does not respond to the petition within a reasonable time, or if the agency rejects the petition, the petitioner can seek judicial review under the APA.

a. *Agency Inaction*

Section 551(13) of the APA defines "agency action" to include "failure to act," and this definition of agency action applies to the judicial review chapter of the APA. 5 U.S.C.A. § 701(b)(2). Moreover, section 706, which addresses the scope of judicial review of agency action, specifically provides that "[t]he reviewing court shall compel agency action unlawfully withheld or unreasonably delayed." 5 U.S.C.A. § 706(1).

As you will see later in this course, when courts review agency action, the court usually has an agency decision to review, and the court can assess whether that decision meets various legal criteria. When, however, the very problem is the absence of an agency decision, it is much harder for courts to review what the agency has (not) done. Usually the agency's reason or excuse for not making a decision is that, in light of existing responsibilities and priorities, a decision on whether to begin the petitioned for rulemaking has not yet been made. In other words, the agency asserts that because of limited resources and other commitments, it simply cannot make an informed decision yet whether to begin a rulemaking. What is a court to do? It could order the agency to change its relative priorities and to make a decision on the rulemaking within a prescribed period. The difficulty with this solution is that the court is in no position to assess the relative priorities of all the things the agency does. Perhaps the agency's explanation is in good faith.

While we address the issue of agency inaction here with respect to petitions for rulemaking, this issue can also arise once a rulemaking has begun but the agency does not conclude it. This issue also arises in adjudications when complaints have been made to an agency and it has failed to institute the adjudication, or where the adjudication has begun but the agency takes a long time to render a decision. Thus, how courts address the issue of delay in these additional contexts may be relevant to judicial review of agency inaction on petitions for rulemaking.

Problem 2–2: *Agency Delay*

In Problem 2–1, the law firm undertook to lobby EPA to change its rule. Let us suppose that at some point the firm filed a petition for rulemaking with EPA to amend its EUP rule to allow small-scale field tests without having to obtain an EUP. Imagine now that two years have passed, and EPA has not responded to the petition. When asked informally, EPA has answered orally and in writing that the petition is pending, but that matters of higher priority—the large backlog of existing pesticides that FIFRA requires EPA to screen for safety—have precluded the agency from determining whether rulemaking is justified for amending the EUP regulation.

How do you assess the likelihood of success of bringing a lawsuit under the APA to force EPA to engage in the rulemaking or at least to respond to your petition?

Problem Materials

TELECOMMUNICATIONS RESEARCH & ACTION CENTER v. FEDERAL COMMUNICATIONS COMMISSION

750 F.2d 70 (D.C.Cir.1984).

HARRY T. EDWARDS, CIRCUIT JUDGE:

[The Telecommunications Research & Action Center (TRAC) sought judicial review of the FCC's failure to decide whether the American Telephone and Telegraph Company should reimburse ratepayers for certain allegedly unlawful overcharges. These overcharges allegedly occurred in 1978, and TRAC filed a petition with the FCC in 1979 indicating its belief that the overcharges had occurred and seeking FCC enforcement. The FCC issued a Notice of Inquiry seeking public comment on the issue, preliminary to deciding whether or not to take action. Thereafter, over the almost next five years, the FCC took no action.]

Representative Timothy Wirth, Chairman of the Subcommittee on Telecommunications, Consumer Protection and Finance of the House Committee on Energy and Commerce, has twice written to the FCC to inquire about the unexplained delay in agency action. In 1981, FCC officials responded that they expected a staff recommendation that fall. However, no such recommendation was produced. In the spring of 1984, agency officials modified their response and estimated that a staff recommendation would be issued that summer. The agency failed on this commitment, too. Now, in the face of this court action, the Commission has recently indicated that it plans to resolve the matter on or before November 30, 1984.

III.   MERITS OF THE UNREASONABLE DELAY CLAIM

[G]iven the clear legislative preference for review of final action, we must be circumspect in exercising jurisdiction over interlocutory petitions. Postponing review until relevant agency proceedings have been concluded "permits an administrative agency to develop a factual record, to apply its expertise to that record, and to avoid piecemeal appeals." ...

Claims of unreasonable agency delay clearly fall into that narrow class of interlocutory appeals from agency action over which we appropriately should exercise our jurisdiction. It is obvious that the benefits of agency expertise and creation of a record will not be realized if the agency never takes action. Agency delay claims also meet [the] criteria for our interlocutory intervention—not only is there an outright violation of 5 U.S.C.A. § 555(b)'s mandate that agencies decide matters in a reasonable time, there also is no need for the court to consider the merits of the issue before the agency. Finally and most significantly, Congress has instructed statutory review courts to compel agency action that has been unreasonably delayed. 5 U.S.C.A. § 706(1).

In the context of a claim of unreasonable delay, the first stage of judicial inquiry is to consider whether the agency's delay is so egregious as to warrant mandamus. Although this court has decided several cases involving claims of unreasonable delay, we have not articulated a single test for when the writ should issue. On reading these cases together, however, one can discern the hexagonal contours of a standard. Although the standard is hardly ironclad, and sometimes suffers from vagueness, it nevertheless provides useful guidance in assessing claims of agency delay: (1) the time agencies take to make decisions must be governed by a "rule of reason"; (2) where Congress has provided a timetable or other indication of the speed with which it expects the agency to proceed in the enabling statute, that statutory scheme may supply content for this rule of reason; (3) delays that might be reasonable in the sphere of economic regulation are less tolerable when human health and welfare are at stake; (4) the court should consider the effect of expediting delayed action on agency activities of a higher or competing priority; (5) the court should also take into account the nature and extent of the interests prejudiced by delay; and (6) the court need not "find any impropriety lurking behind agency lassitude in order to hold that agency action is 'unreasonably delayed.' "

Because, in the instant case, the FCC has assured us that it is moving expeditiously on both overcharge claims, we need not test the delay here against the above standard to determine if it is egregious enough to warrant mandamus. But in light of the Commission's failure to meet its self-declared prior deadlines for these proceedings, we believe these delays are serious enough for us to retain jurisdiction over this case until final agency disposition.

In [an earlier case] we announced that: the entire ratemaking procedure in the 1934 Communications Act revolves around a "rule of reason".... It assumes that rates will be finally decided within a reasonable time encompassing months, occasionally a year or two, but not several years or a decade.... Complex regulation must still be credible regulation; the delay at issue here threatens the FCC's credibility.... Many of the same considerations that impel judicial protection of the right to a "speedy trial" in criminal cases or implementation of civil decrees with all deliberate speed are not inapposite in agency deliberations. Those situations generally involve protection of constitutional rights, but delay in the resolution of administrative proceedings can also deprive regulated entities, their competitors or the public of rights and economic opportunities without the due process the Constitution requires. In that case we found a four year delay to be unreasonable. In the instant case, the FCC has delayed almost five years on the rate of return inquiry.... Even the agency recognizes, at least with regard to the rate of return delay, that "an unfortunately long time has elapsed since [this] matter first appeared." Whether or not these delays would justify mandamus, we believe they clearly warrant retaining jurisdiction. . . .

Notes and Questions

1. As the case indicates, courts are reluctant to engage in any review when an agency has not issued a final decision. In some circumstances, courts may not even engage in review. This subject is treated in Chapter 5.

2. Why do you suppose the court included the history of congressional interest in the issue? How do you think that history affects the court's judgment?

3. If the court agreed there was unreasonable delay, what sort of remedy should it use? What is the purpose of the court deciding to retain jurisdiction in *TRAC*?

4. If the likelihood of success of a lawsuit is minimal, are there good reasons to bring the suit anyway? Would it be ethical conduct?

5. Note that *TRAC* is decided by the United States Court of Appeals for the D.C. Circuit. Among courts of appeals, the D.C. Circuit has traditionally been recognized as having relative expertise in administrative law, because it hears so many administrative law cases. There are two principal reasons why so many cases are brought there. First, several statutes require persons seeking judicial review of agency action to bring suit in the District of Columbia. The justification for this requirement is that if only one court will hear cases under that statute, there will not be a possibility of a split among the circuits, which would create confusion as to the agency's mandate in different parts of the country. Second, even when laws do not require that suits be brought in the District of Columbia, plaintiffs know that they *can* bring suit there, because it is the principal place of business for the agency.

6. As noted earlier, Congress sometimes sets deadlines for the completion of certain rules and if an agency does not comply, it can be sued by statutory beneficiaries. Although the courts are less reluctant to enforce such deadlines than to hold that an agency has violated the APA's prohibition against "unreasonable delay," the deadlines do not always work, as the following analysis indicates:

> The Court of Appeals for the District of Columbia Circuit has [said that] a court must consider the context of the statutory scheme authorizing the agency to act. If the statute includes a deadline for agency action, the agency has no regulatory discretion at all; it must act according to the legislative timetable. Judicial relief to redress action "unreasonably delayed" is therefore more likely in a case involving a statutory deadline. . . .
>
> When agencies have ignored statutory deadlines, . . . courts are less likely to accept justifications [for the delay]. Equitable discretion

allows courts to refrain from ordering agencies to comply with statutory deadlines when compliance is impossible, but courts impose a heavy burden of justifying impossibility claims, and regularly require agencies to comply with statutory deadlines despite such claims.

Although courts recognize the need for judicially enforceable deadlines as a remedy for unreasonable delay, they frequently seem uncomfortable enforcing such deadlines. Some courts believe that they must solicit a revised timetable from the agency and must accept it if the agency proceeds in good faith. While other courts deny any obligation to solicit the agency's views in drafting a timetable, most nevertheless do so. And judicial ire is greatest when an agency misses its own timetable. Thus, coercive statutes authorizing agencies to set initial deadlines are more likely to be strictly enforced than those imposing statutory deadlines on the agency.

Sidney A. Shapiro & Robert L. Glicksman, *Congress, the Supreme Court, & the Quiet Revolution in Administrative Law*, 1988 Duke L.J. 819, 832–36.

7. In some cases, the courts have interpreted statutory deadlines as being non-binding. The Occupational Safety and Health Act (OSH Act), for example, provides that "[w]ithin sixty days after" completion of a rulemaking hearing, the administrator of the Occupational Safety and Health Agency (OSHA) "shall issue a rule promulgating, modifying or revoking an occupational safety or health standard or make a determination that a rule shall not issue." 29 U.S.C. § 655(b)(4). Despite the apparently mandatory "shall issue" language, the courts have held that OSHA may rationally delay development of a standard on the basis of competing priorities. *National Congress of Hispanic Am. Citizens (El Congresso) v. Marshall*, 626 F.2d 882, 888 (D.C.Cir.1979); *accord National Congress of Hispanic Citizens v. Usery*, 554 F.2d 1196, 1199–1200 (D.C.Cir.1977). In *El Congresso*, the court determined the 60 day deadline was not mandatory because other sections of the OSH Act give OSHA considerable latitude to determine when, and in what areas, it should establish health and safety standards. In *Action on Smoking and Health v. Department of Labor*, 100 F.3d 991, 994 (D.C.Cir.1996), the court noted that, even if the statutory language established a mandatory deadline, the deadline was only one of the factors in *TRAC* that judges consider in deciding whether to intervene. In *Forest Guardians v. Babbitt*, 164 F.3d 1261 (10th Cir.1998), modified 174 F.3d 1178 (10th Cir.1999), however, the court declined to apply *TRAC* because Congress had established a specific, non-discretionary time within which an agency was required to act.

8. Why are the courts reluctant to enforce statutory deadlines? Should courts give an agency more time after it has missed a statutory deadline? Other than statutory deadlines, what other mechanisms might

Congress use to ensure that agencies adopt regulations in an expeditious manner? Is the only alternative leaving it up to courts to determine what is unreasonable delay? *See* Shapiro & McGarity, *supra,* at 53–57 ("Congress should require OSHA to set rulemaking deadlines and then should make those deadlines judicially enforceable. This would permit the Agency to set realistic deadlines, while still holding the Agency accountable. Congress could further assure accountability by providing that Agency-set deadlines could be extended only for good cause and only for congressionally determined intervals. Finally, Congress should provide for judicial review of Agency-set deadlines to prevent OSHA from setting unreasonably long deadlines.").

b. *Denial of a Petition*

Once an agency has denied a petition for rulemaking, one of the obstacles to judicial review is eliminated. The agency has made a decision that can be reviewed. And now there is a new legal issue: is the denial lawful? Answering this question depends upon what laws are applicable and on what basis the agency denied the petition. For example, if the agency denies the petition because, conceding the facts in the petition, the agency does not have the legal authority to adopt the rule requested, the issue is purely legal—does the agency have the authority or not? On the other hand, if the agency denies the petition because its view of the facts is different from the petitioners' view, then the issue is factual, or perhaps judgmental. A common basis for denial of a petition could be that the issue is simply not important enough, given the agency's resources and priorities, to justify rulemaking at this time. Courts are likely to respond differently to these different kinds of justifications.

Problem 2–3: Agency Denial of a Petition

Imagine that EPA, badgered by your law firm, has finally responded to your requests and petition for rulemaking to amend the EUP rule; it has denied the petition. It rejects the petition on the following grounds. The current rule requiring individual permits for biological pesticide small-scale field tests has worked well. The lack of injuries and uncontrolled releases are evidence of the current system's effectiveness. Whatever economic efficiencies might be achieved by exempting small-scale field tests from the EUP requirements would be relatively minor, and the cost to EPA of determining whether such an exemption would adequately protect against uncontrolled releases or injuries would be substantial. Moreover, at the current time (and for the foreseeable future), EPA lacks the resources to undertake such a rulemaking, in light of the resources it is using to assess the safety and effectiveness of the backlog of currently permitted pesticides.

What is the likelihood of getting a court to overturn this decision?

Problem Materials

ARKANSAS POWER & LIGHT CO. v. INTERSTATE COMMERCE COMMISSION

725 F.2d 716 (D.C.Cir.1984).

HARRY T. EDWARDS, CIRCUIT JUDGE:

[Arkansas P & L and other coal burning utilities petitioned the ICC to institute rulemaking to collect certain data to implement its responsibilities for approving the rates railroads may charge to so-called "captive" shippers. At the time of the case, the ICC regulated the rates that railroads could charge for the interstate shipment of goods and commodities. The ICC rejected the petition for rulemaking.]

Addressing rulemaking, the ICC observed at the outset that Congress had not evinced any intent to require a rulemaking proceeding.... In addition, the ICC observed that annual carrier-by-carrier or commodity-by-commodity elasticity studies—used to determine whether a carrier could improve its profitability on a given route by altering its pricing structure—would be inconsistent with the design of the ... Act to minimize the need for regulatory control. Rules and guidelines for gathering and applying a nationwide data base would also be difficult to develop, and the amount of information necessary to develop an avoidable loss data base would be "enormous and enormously difficult to gather." Along with these negative ramifications of a rulemaking proceeding, the agency considered the positive aspects of case-by-case evolution of standards to apply in implementing the [Act]. It concluded,

> making this assessment in individual cases is more productive and efficient than a rulemaking because it will avoid applying a massive reporting burden on carriers which are efficient....

> [W]e affirm the Commission's decision not to engage in rulemaking....

Initially, it is not unreasonable for the ICC to conclude that development of a nationwide data base is unnecessarily cumbersome—because it would require numerous railroads, operating both efficiently and inefficiently, to produce data that might never be used—and to conclude that case-by-case evolution of standards is most productive and efficient.... Finally, the ICC indicates that it will follow adequate procedures in the individual adjudications to enable petitioners, through discovery and otherwise, to obtain the kind of data they seek through rulemaking. Thus, the ICC has explained why rulemaking would be unnecessarily burdensome and how individual adjudications can and will accomplish the same result. Taking the ICC at its word, we perceive no necessity for rulemaking....

Second. As a general proposition, this court will compel an agency to institute rulemaking proceedings only in extremely rare instances. The law in this Circuit makes clear that the scope of review under the

Administrative Procedure Act ("APA") of an agency decision to deny a rulemaking petition is very narrow. Such review is limited to ensuring that the agency has adequately explained the facts and policy concerns it relied on, and that the facts have some basis in the record. Given this very narrow standard of review, there is absolutely no basis on this record to compel rulemaking.

NORTHERN SPOTTED OWL v. HODEL

716 F.Supp. 479 (W.D.Wash.1988).

ZILLY, DISTRICT JUDGE:

A number of environmental organizations bring this action against the United States Fish & Wildlife Service ("Service") and others, alleging that the Service's decision not to list the northern spotted owl as endangered or threatened under the Endangered Species Act of 1973 ("ESA" or "the Act") was arbitrary and capricious or contrary to law.

Since the 1970s the northern spotted owl has received much scientific attention, beginning with comprehensive studies of its natural history by Dr. Eric Forsman, whose most significant discovery was the close association between spotted owls and old-growth forests. This discovery raised concerns because the majority of remaining old-growth owl habitat is on public land available for harvest.

In January 1987, plaintiff Greenworld . . . petitioned the Service to list the northern spotted owl as endangered. . . .

The ESA directs the Secretary of the Interior to determine whether any species have become endangered or threatened due to habitat destruction, overutilization, disease or predation, or other natural or manmade factors. . . .

The Service's role in deciding whether to list the northern spotted owl as endangered or threatened is to assess the technical and scientific data in the administrative record against the relevant listing criteria in [the Act] and then to exercise its own expert discretion in reaching its decision.

In July 1987, the Service announced that it would initiate a status review of the spotted owl and requested public comment. The Service assembled a group of Service biologists, including Dr. Mark Shaffer, its staff expert on population viability, to conduct the review. The Service charged Dr. Shaffer with analyzing current scientific information on the owl. Dr. Shaffer concluded that: the most reasonable interpretation of current data and knowledge indicate continued old growth harvesting is likely to lead to the extinction of the subspecies in the foreseeable future which argues strongly for listing the subspecies as threatened or endangered at this time.

The Service invited a peer review of Dr. Shaffer's analysis by a number of U.S. experts on population viability, all of whom agreed with

Dr. Shaffer's prognosis for the owl, although each had some criticisms of his work.

The Service's decision is contained in its 1987 Status Review of the owl ("Status Review") and summarized in its Finding on Greenworld's petition. The Status Review was completed on December 14, 1987, and on December 17 the Service announced that listing the owl as endangered under the Act was not warranted at that time. This suit followed. Both sides now move for summary judgment on the administrative record before the Court. . . .

This Court reviews the Service's action under the "arbitrary and capricious" standard of the Administrative Procedure Act ("APA"). This standard is narrow and presumes the agency action is valid, but it does not shield agency action from a "thorough, probing, in-depth review." Courts must not "rubber-stamp the agency decision as correct." Rather, the reviewing court must assure itself that the agency decision was "based on a consideration of the relevant factors. . . ." Moreover, it must engage in a "substantial inquiry" into the facts, one that is "searching and careful." This is particularly true in highly technical cases. . . . Agency action is arbitrary and capricious where the agency has failed to "articulate a satisfactory explanation for its action including a 'rational connection between the facts found and the choice made.' "

The Status Review and the Finding to the listing petition offer little insight into how the Service found that the owl currently has a viable population. Although the Status Review cites extensive empirical data and lists various conclusions, it fails to provide any analysis. The Service asserts that it is entitled to make its own decision, yet it provides no explanation for its findings. An agency must set forth clearly the grounds on which it acted. Judicial deference to agency expertise is proper, but the Court will not do so blindly. The Court finds that the Service has not set forth the grounds for its decision against listing the owl.

The Service's documents also lack any expert analysis supporting its conclusion. Rather, the expert opinion is entirely to the contrary. The only reference in the Status Review to an actual opinion that the owl does not face a significant likelihood of extinction is a mischaracterization of a conclusion of Dr. Mark Boyce:

> Boyce (1987) in his analysis of the draft preferred alternative concluded that there is a low probability that the spotted owls will go extinct. He does point out that population fragmentation appears to impose the greatest risks to extinction.

Dr. Boyce responded to the Service:

> I did not conclude that the Spotted Owl enjoys a low probability of extinction, and I would be very disappointed if efforts to preserve the Spotted Owl were in any way thwarted by a misinterpretation of something I wrote.

Numerous other experts on population viability contributed to or reviewed drafts of the Status Review, or otherwise assessed spotted owl viability. Some were employed by the Service; others were independent. None concluded that the northern spotted owl is not at risk of extinction. . . .

The Court will reject conclusory assertions of agency "expertise" where the agency spurns unrebutted expert opinions without itself offering a credible alternative explanation. Here, the Service disregarded all the expert opinion on population viability, including that of its own expert, that the owl is facing extinction, and instead merely asserted its expertise in support of its conclusions.

The Service has failed to provide its own or other expert analysis supporting its conclusions. Such analysis is necessary to establish a rational connection between the evidence presented and the Service's decision. Accordingly, the United States Fish and Wildlife Service's decision not to list at this time the northern spotted owl as endangered or threatened under the Endangered Species Act was arbitrary and capricious and contrary to law. . . .

In deference to the Service's expertise and its role under the Endangered Species Act, the Court remands this matter to the Service, which has 90 days from the date of this order to provide an analysis for its decision that listing the northern spotted owl as threatened or endangered is not currently warranted. Further, the Service is ordered to supplement its Status Review and petition Finding consistent with this Court's ruling.

Notes and Questions

1. The *Northern Spotted Owl* case contains a good summary of the "arbitrary, capricious, abuse of discretion" standard of judicial review. *See* 5 U.S.C.A. § 706(2)(a). You will find that this standard is a basis for review of agency action under a number of different circumstances, in particular of agency rulemaking.

2. What do you think of the court's remedy in *Northern Spotted Owl*? For what reasons did the court refuse to order the agency to undertake the rulemaking to list the owl? After all, at the end of that rulemaking, the agency could decide not to list the owl if the record supported that conclusion. In *American Horse Protection Association, Inc. v. Lyng*, 812 F.2d 1 (D.C.Cir.1987), the court also found that the agency's explanation for not instituting a rulemaking was arbitrary and capricious—not a product of reasoned decisionmaking—and it gave this explanation for not ordering a rulemaking.

> The Association seeks an order directing the Secretary to institute rulemaking proceedings. Our cases make clear, however, that such a remedy is appropriate "only in the rarest and most compelling circumstances." [In another case, we] merely remanded to the agency to inquire into whether changed circumstances called for amendment of the earlier rule, leaving it to the agency to choose the

form of inquiry. This remedy is particularly appropriate when the agency has failed to provide an adequate explanation of its denial.

3. What if EPA does institute a rulemaking to consider amending the EUP rule but at the end of the rulemaking concludes that no rule is appropriate? If challenged, how would judicial review differ from judicial review of the denial of the petition for rulemaking? In *Williams Natural Gas Co. v. FERC*, 872 F.2d 438 (D.C.Cir.1989), which involved a decision not to promulgate a final rule by the Federal Energy Regulatory Commission, the court noted that there is a distinction between

> an agency's refusal to undertake a rulemaking (reviewable, if at all, under an exceedingly narrow standard), and its decision to terminate a docket after a substantial record has been compiled. In the present case, [t]he agency has issued a lengthy [Notice of Proposed Rulemaking (NOPR)] expressing its tentative conclusions that a change in the regulation is warranted, and it has received numerous comments on the issue from interested parties. Under these circumstances, a court will have a sufficient evidentiary base for determining whether the Commission's ultimate decision was arbitrary and capricious or in contravention of the statute.

How is this different from what the court did in *Northern Spotted Owl*?

B. APA RULEMAKING PROCEDURES

1. THE EXCEPTIONS

Before we turn in detail to the APA procedures applicable to rulemaking, we want to address the exceptions to these requirements. The first step for an agency lawyer is to determine whether the procedures apply at all, and an important step for any lawyer thinking about challenging a rule adopted without notice and comment is to determine whether notice and comment were required.

a. General exceptions

As mentioned in Chapter 1, section 553 of the APA is the section governing rulemaking. It contains the "notice and comment" procedures applicable to "informal rulemaking," and it directs persons to sections 556 and 557 if "formal rulemaking" is triggered. However, none of section 553 applies to certain kinds of rules: rules involving military or foreign affairs functions and rules involving agency management or personnel, or involving public property, loans, grants, benefits, or contracts. 5 U.S.C.A. § 553(a). The idea that military and foreign affairs matters should not be subject to notice and comment rulemaking is readily understandable, although the scope of the exception may be broader than necessary. *See generally* ACUS, Recommendation 73–5, Elimination of the "Military or Foreign Affairs Function" Exemption from APA Rulemaking Requirements, 1 C.F.R. § 305.73–5. And not involving the public in rules relating only to an agency's internal management or personnel likewise seems efficient. The APA, however, also exempts *all* rules involving public property. This includes rules concerning public lands (*i.e.,* Forest Service, Bureau of Land Management, and National Park Service regulations), loans (*i.e.,* rules about student loans, small business loans, and housing loans), grants, benefits (*i.e.,* Social Security, Medicare, Medicaid, welfare rules), and contracts (*i.e.,* procurement regulations and regulations governing government sales, such as Bonneville Power Administration electricity sales). Why these functions should be exempt from the APA's procedural requirements is less clear, but it explains a lot about the origins of the APA.

Recall that the explosion of new regulatory programs and agencies during the New Deal, largely in response to the Great Depression, was the motivating force behind the APA. The American Bar Association, representing the businesses affected by the new regulations and agencies, was concerned about government acting on private persons (including businesses) by restricting their ability to do what they wanted. Thus, the focus of the APA and its procedures was from the perspective of the private person who is restricted from doing what he or she wishes. The exceptions from the rulemaking procedures reflect this focus, because when government regulates its own property, or makes grants, loans, or benefits available to persons, or enters into contracts with persons, it is not restricting or imposing its will on the liberty of private persons.

Subsequent history has undermined this focus of the APA, although it has not entirely eliminated it. More recently, the APA has been viewed not only as a source of protection *from* government action, but also a source of protection *for* statutory rights. Thus, a Consumer Product Safety Commission rule not only imposes burdens on the regulated businesses, but it also creates protections for consumers. The CPSC, by not fulfilling its legal requirements or by regulating inappropriately, can harm either (or both) groups. The APA, and other procedural laws, should protect both groups. *See* Richard B. Stewart, *The Reformation of American Administrative Law*, 88 HARV. L. REV. 1669 (1975). The idea that the APA should also protect beneficiary groups undermines the public property, grants, loans, benefits, and contracts exception in section 553. Some commentators and the Administrative Conference of the United States have called for the elimination of the exemption. *See* ACUS, Recommendation 69–8, Elimination of Certain Exemptions from the APA Rulemaking Requirements, 1 C.F.R. § 305.69–8; Arthur E. Bonfield, *Public Participation in Federal Rulemaking Relating to Public Property, Loans, Grants, Benefits, or Contracts*, 118 U. PA. L. REV. 540 (1970).

Responsive to, or reflective of, the changed attitudes, many agencies by regulation have voluntarily waived these exceptions and subjected themselves to section 553's requirements. For example, the Department of Health and Human Services (then Health, Education, and Welfare) waived the exemption in 1971, *see* 36 Fed. Reg. 2532 (1971), as did the Department of Agriculture, *see* 36 Fed. Reg. 13804 (1971). While these agencies could always repeal these regulations, until they do so, they must comply with them. *See Morton v. Ruiz*, 415 U.S. 199, 94 S.Ct. 1055,

39 L.Ed.2d 270 (1974). Congress by statute has also eliminated the exemption for some agencies and programs. For example, the Department of Energy Organization Act eliminated the exemption for that Department and its subdivisions, *see* 42 U.S.C.A. § 7191(b)(3). Thus, the applicability of the APA's section 553 may turn on laws outside of the APA itself.

Although some rules may be exempt from section 553, they are not exempt from section 552. While section 552 is often referred to as the Freedom of Information Act (FOIA), which is dealt with in Chapter 8, it contains a general requirement that "substantive rules of general applicability adopted as authorized by law" and "each amendment, revision, or repeal of the foregoing" be published in the Federal Register "for the guidance of the public." If an agency fails to publish the rule in the Federal Register, section 552 provides that, unless persons have actual notice of the rule, they may not be adversely affected by it.

b. Exceptions From Notice and Comment

In addition to the above exemptions from all of section 553, section 553 also contains specific exemptions from the notice and comment requirements for (1) rules of agency organization, procedure, or practice, (2) interpretive rules, (3) general statements of policy, and (4) other rules for which notice and public procedure are impracticable, unnecessary, or contrary to the public interest. This last exception, unlike the previous three, requires the agency to find good cause for invoking this exception and to publish that finding and the reasons therefor with the rule. Each of these exceptions has its own body of law defining the exception, but as a general matter it has been said that exemptions are "narrowly construed and only reluctantly countenanced." *American Fed. Govt. Employees v. Block*, 655 F.2d 1153 (D.C.Cir.1981). For reasons that hopefully will become clearer later, we will put off the "law" dealing with interpretive rules and statements of policy until Chapter 4. We will deal with the other exceptions now.

Problem 2–4: Exceptions From Notice and Comment

Imagine that the Administrator of EPA was called up to the House Agriculture Committee to explain why EPA was deliberately imposing higher food costs on consumers by requiring unnecessary and burdensome paperwork on biotech companies with respect to their pesticides as opposed to chemical companies and their pesticides. When asked, the Administrator was unable to estimate when, if ever, the agency would be able to address the rulemaking requested by the biotech companies. By the end of the hearing, the Administrator, to avoid worse problems, had agreed to address the biotech company's rulemaking request in an expedited fashion. Back at EPA, the Administrator wants to be rid of this problem. It is not important enough to consume her time or that of other persons at the agency. She directs that the matter be disposed of as quickly as possible.

The program office, on the basis of the materials submitted by the biotech company, remains reluctant to exempt small-scale field tests of biologically engineered pesticides from the EUP requirement altogether, but it believes that EPA could substantially decrease the regulatory burdens for permitting such tests. The present application procedure requires the permit applicant to submit an elaborate application form (together with a $4500 fee) to EPA, which then is reviewed by EPA, and EPA makes an initial decision within four months, usually imposing specific conditions. In place of this system, the program office suggests adopting a regulation specific to small-scale field tests of biologically engineered pesticides that would include a number of generic conditions to ensure safety. Then, the permit application would merely identify the applicant and the pesticide to be tested, and the applicant would certify that it would follow the regulatory conditions. This application would be deemed granted seven days after receipt unless EPA specifically took action to require an individually tailored permit.

The Assistant Administrator asks the General Counsel whether this regulation could be adopted immediately, without prior notice and comment, under one or more of the APA exceptions to the requirement of notice-and-comment procedures. As an attorney in EPA's General Counsel's office, what do you advise?

Problem Materials

AMERICAN HOSPITAL ASSN. v. BOWEN

834 F.2d 1037 (D.C.Cir.1987).

WALD, CHIEF JUDGE:

[In 1982, Congress amended the Medicare system to create a method for cost control administered by Peer Review Organizations (PROs), private organizations of doctors that would monitor "some or all of the professional activities" of the providers of Medicare services in their areas. In passing the 1982 amendments, Congress painted with a broad brush, leaving HHS to fill in many important details of the workings of peer review. The principal function of a PRO is to review for conformance with the substantive standards of the Medicare Act the professional activities of physicians, hospitals, and other providers of health care. The standard of review is whether the services and items provided by the doctor or hospital "are or were reasonable and medically necessary," and thus whether these activities satisfy the standards for federal government reimbursement under Medicare. HHS promulgated a number of regulations after notice and comment to implement the PRO system. In addition to these regulations, HHS issued, without notice or comment, a series of directives and transmittals governing the PRO program. These transmittals contain a wide variety of instructions, guidelines and procedures covering aspects of the PRO program.]

On October 10, 1984, complaining of ... "the small and incomplete selection of regulations" HHS had published implementing the PRO program and the large number of procedures set forth in documents not published as regulations, AHA filed with HHS a petition for rulemaking.... In it, AHA requested HHS to promulgate a complete set of regulations governing all aspects of the PRO program.... AHA sent another letter on January 8, 1985, requesting a date for HHS' response. No response to this letter was ever received.

On January 29, 1985, AHA brought suit against HHS in the District Court for the District of Columbia. Its complaint argued that HHS had circumvented the notice and comment requirements of § 553 of the APA, and asked that the court declare the transmittals and directives ... invalid for failure to comply with § 553.

... The distinctive purpose of § 553's [exemption] for "rules of agency organization, procedure or practice" is to ensure "that agencies retain latitude in organizing their internal operations." A useful articulation of the exemption's critical feature is that it covers agency actions that do not themselves alter the rights or interests of parties, although it may alter the manner in which parties present themselves or their viewpoints to the agency.

Over time, our circuit in applying the § 553 exemption for procedural rules has gradually shifted focus from asking whether a given procedure has a "substantial impact" on parties to inquiring more broadly whether the agency action also encodes a substantive value judgment or puts a stamp of approval or disapproval on a given type of behavior. The gradual move away from looking solely into the substantiality of the impact reflects a candid recognition that even unambiguously procedural measures affect parties to some degree.

While the range of cases applying this exemption may appear idiosyncratic, a few recent decisions of this and other circuits illustrate the scope and limits of the procedural exemption. In *Neighborhood TV Co., Inc. v. FCC*, we held that a FCC decision to freeze applications for television licenses on some frequencies affected an applicant's interest "only incidentally," and thus was procedural. In *Guardian Federal Savings & Loan Association*, we held that a directive specifying that requisite audits be performed by nonagency accountants was exempt as a procedural measure. And in *United States Department of Labor v. Kast Metals Corp.*, ... the Fifth Circuit held that the agency's rules governing the selection of employers for workplace safety investigations was a procedural rule. By contrast, we have struck down as nonprocedural an agency rule foreclosing home health agencies from the right to deal with the Secretary of HHS in order to gain reimbursement for Medicare, and we have held that a parole board's selection of parole eligibility guidelines had the intent and effect of changing substantive outcomes.

[One of the contested directives is PRO Manual IM85–2]. A broadbrush description of IM85–2 is that it maps out an enforcement strategy for the PROs with whom HHS contracts. As the district court observed, the statutes and preexisting regulations that deal with PRO review are relatively sketchy, and thus IM85–2 makes a significant contribution towards describing the daily functions of PROs. It requires, for instance, that the PRO review at least 5% of all hospital admissions, selected at random. Where a "significant pattern" of unnecessary admissions appears in a particular subcategory of medicine, the PRO is instructed to step up its review to 100% of hospital admissions in the area.

... The requirements set forth in the transmittal are classic procedural rules, exempt under that distinctive prong of § 553. The bulk of the regulations in the transmittal set forth an enforcement plan for HHS's agents in monitoring the quality of and necessity for various operations. They essentially establish a frequency and focus of PRO review, urging its enforcement agents to concentrate their limited resources on particular areas where HHS evidently believes PRO attention will prove most fruitful.

As we have previously observed, enforcement plans developed by agencies to direct their enforcement activity warrant considerable deference.

The Fifth Circuit's decision in *United States Department of Labor v. Kast Metals Corp.*, 744 F.2d 1145 (5th Cir.1984), is particularly instructive with regard to this manual. In *Kast Metals*, the court of appeals held that the Occupational Safety and Health Administration ("OSHA") had validly developed a calculus to target employers for inspection, despite the fact that this calculus had been adopted without notice and comment rulemaking. The court reasoned that OSHA's inspection plan, known as CPL 2.25B, fell far short of the sort of investigative activity likely to have the intent or effect of substantially altering party behavior. "The creation and use of CPL 2.25B to select employers for inspection did not of itself constitute investigation; rather, the plan sets forth procedural steps to guide the agency in exercise of its statutory authority to conduct investigations." In classifying OSHA's rule as procedural under § 553, the Fifth Circuit wrote, "[t]he Secretary used CPL 2.25B to concentrate OSHA's inspection resources in industries with the highest potential for safety and health violations.... The plan is procedural on its face." Like OSHA rule CPL 2.25B, HHS Manual IM85–2 operates to concentrate agency inspection resources in areas (here, medical procedures) with the highest potential for statutory violations (here, violations of Medicare's reimbursement standards), and like CPL 2.25B, HHS' manual is procedural on its face....

The manual imposes no new burdens on hospitals that warrant notice and comment review. This is not a case in which HHS has urged its reviewing agents to utilize a different standard of review in specified medical areas; rather, it asks only that they examine a greater share of operations in given medical areas. Were HHS to have inserted a new standard of review governing PRO scrutiny of a given procedure, or to have inserted a presumption of invalidity when reviewing certain operations, its measures would surely require notice and comment, as well as close scrutiny to insure that it was consistent with the agency's statutory mandate. But that is not this case.

At worst, Manual IM85–2 burdens hospitals by (1) making it more likely that their transgressions from Medicare's standards will not go unnoticed and (2) imposing on them the incidental inconveniences of complying with an enforcement scheme. The former concern is patently illegitimate: Congress' very purpose in instituting peer review was to crack down on reimbursements for medical activity not covered by Medicare. As for the second burden, case law clearly establishes that such derivative burdens hardly dictate notice and comment review. Accordingly, we hold that PRO Manual IM85–2 is a procedural rule exempt from § 553's notice and comment requirements. . . .

AIR TRANSPORT ASSOCIATION OF AMERICA v. DEPARTMENT OF TRANSPORTATION

900 F.2d 369 (D.C.Cir.1990).

HARRY T. EDWARDS, CIRCUIT JUDGE:

The issue in this case is whether respondent governmental agencies (collectively "Federal Aviation Administration" or "FAA") were obliged to engage in notice and comment procedures before promulgating a body of regulations ("Penalty Rules" or "Rules") governing the adjudication of administrative civil penalty actions. . . . The FAA maintains that it was justified in dispensing with notice and comment under the "rules of agency organization, procedure, or practice," and "good cause" exceptions to section 553.

We grant the petition for review. It is well established that the exemption under section 553(b)(A), for "rules of agency organization, procedure, or practice," does not apply to agency action that "substantially alter[s] the rights or interests of regulated" parties. *American Hosp. Ass'n v. Bowen*. The Penalty Rules fall outside the scope of the exception because they substantially affect civil penalty defendants' "right to avail [themselves] of an administrative adjudication." Moreover, because we find that the time constraints of the enabling statute did not impose an insurmountable obstacle to complying with the applicable notice and comment requirements of the APA, we also reject the FAA's reliance on the "good cause" exception under section 553(b)(B). Consequently, we hold that the Penalty Rules are invalid and that the FAA may not initiate new prosecutions until it has complied with the procedural requirements of the APA.

In December of 1987, Congress enacted a series of amendments to the Federal Aviation Act relating to civil penalties. Among other things, these amendments raised to $10,000 the maximum penalty for a single violation of aviation safety standards and established a "demonstration program" authorizing the FAA to prosecute and adjudicate administrative penalty actions involving less than $50,000. . . .

Approximately nine months after enactment of [these amendments], the FAA promulgated the Penalty Rules. Effective immediately upon their issuance, the Penalty Rules established a schedule of civil penalties, including fines of up to $10,000 for violations of the safety standards of the Federal Aviation Act and related regulations. The Penalty Rules also established a comprehensive adjudicatory scheme providing for formal notice, settlement procedures, discovery, an adversary hearing before an ALJ and an administrative appeal. In explaining why it dispensed with prepromulgation notice and comment, the FAA emphasized the procedural character of the Penalty Rules. The FAA did respond to post promulgation comments but declined to make any amendments to the Rules. . . .

Section 553's notice and comment requirements are essential to the scheme of administrative governance established by the APA. These procedures reflect Congress' "judgment that . . . informed administrative decisionmaking require[s] that agency decisions be made only after affording interested persons" an opportunity to communicate their views to the agency. Equally important, by mandating "openness, explanation, and participatory democracy" in the rulemaking process, these procedures assure the legitimacy of administrative norms. For these reasons, we have consistently afforded a narrow cast to the exceptions to section 553, permitting an agency to forgo notice and comment only when the subject matter or the circumstances of the rulemaking divest the public of any legitimate stake in influencing the outcome. In the instant case, because the Penalty Rules substantially affected civil penalty defendants' right to avail themselves of an administrative adjudication, we cannot accept the FAA's contention that the Rules could be promulgated without notice and comment.

The FAA argues that the Penalty Rules are exempt as "rules of agency organization, procedure, or practice" because they establish "procedures" for adjudicating civil penalty actions. According to the FAA, it would have been obliged to permit public participation in the rulemaking process only if the Penalty Rules affected aviators' "substantive" obligations under the Federal Aviation Act. We find this analysis unpersuasive.

Our cases construing section 553(b)(A) have long emphasized that a rule does not fall within the scope of the exception merely because it is capable of bearing the label "procedural." . . .

Rather than focus on whether a particular rule is "procedural" or "substantive," [our] decisions employ a functional analysis. Section 553(b)(A) has been described as essentially a "housekeeping" measure, "[t]he distinctive purpose of . . . [which] is to ensure 'that agencies retain latitude in organizing their internal operations,' " Where nominally "procedural" rules "encode[ ] a substantive value judgment" or "substantially alter the rights or interests of regulated" parties, however, the rules must be preceded by notice and comment.

The Penalty Rules fall outside the scope of section 553(b)(A) because they substantially affect a civil penalty defendant's right to an administrative adjudication. Under both the due process clause and the APA, a party has a right to notice and a hearing before being forced to pay a monetary penalty. Congress expressly directed the FAA to incorporate these rights into its civil penalty program. In implementing this mandate, the FAA made discretionary—indeed, in many cases, highly contentious—choices concerning what process civil penalty defendants are due. Each one of these choices "encode[d] a substantive value judgment," on the appropriate balance between a defendant's rights to adjudicatory procedures and the agency's interest in efficient prosecution. The FAA was no less obliged to engage in notice and comment before taking action affecting these adjudicatory rights than it would have been had it taken action affecting aviators' "substantive" obligations under the Federal Aviation Act.

The cases cited by the FAA do not suggest a contrary conclusion. The FAA puts its primary emphasis on *American Hospital Association*.... Nothing in *American Hospital Association* detracts from the principle that the public does have a legitimate interest in participating in agency decisions affecting statutory and constitutional rights "to avail oneself of an administrative adjudication."

Also inapposite are various decisions in which we have applied section 553(b)(A) to rules that regulate such matters as the timing of applications for benefits or the timing of the agency's processing of such applications. The rules at issue in these cases did affect "the manner in which the parties present themselves or their viewpoints to the agency," but they did not affect any component of a party's statutory or constitutional right to avail himself of an administrative adjudication. They were all cases, in short, in which "the need for public participation" in the rulemaking process was "too small to warrant it." The Penalty Rules, in contrast, affect the entire range of adjudicatory rights guaranteed by the due process clause, the APA and section 1475(d)(1)—matters far too important to be withdrawn from public deliberation....

The dissent ... contends that we have "obliterated" the distinction between substance and procedure. But, as the case law clearly illustrates, there is no such "distinction" to obliterate for purposes of section 553(b)(A). The dissent refuses to come to terms with the precedent characterizing this exception to notice and comment rulemaking as a mere "housekeeping" measure applicable to rules " 'organizing [agencies'] internal operations.' " The dissent's infusion of a rigid "procedure"—"substance" distinction is not only inconsistent with our precedent but is also inconsistent with the statutory text. Section 553(b)(A) does not exempt "rules of procedure" per se, but rather "rules of agency organization, procedure, or practice." The dissent's exclusive focus on the word "procedure" thus violates the well established principle of construction "that 'words grouped in a list should be given related meaning.' "

In sum, the FAA's contention that it did not affect the "substantive" obligations of aviators under the Federal Aviation Act is irrelevant. "The characterizations 'substantive' and 'procedural'—no more here than elsewhere in the law—do not guide inexorably to the right result, nor do they really advance the inquiry very far." In using the terms "rules of agency organization, procedure, or practice," Congress intended to distinguish not between rules affecting different classes of rights— "substantive" and "procedural"—but rather to distinguish between rules affecting different subject matters—"the rights or interests of regulated" parties and agencies' " 'internal operations.' " Because the Penalty Rules substantially affect civil penalty defendants' "right to avail [themselves] of an administrative adjudication," members of the aviation community had a legitimate interest in participating in the rulemaking process.

We also disagree that the two-year duration of section 1475's demonstration program furnished the FAA with "good cause" to dispense with notice and comment procedures. Like the other exceptions, the good cause exception is to "be narrowly construed and only reluctantly countenanced." In particular, we have explained that statutory time limits do not ordinarily excuse compliance with the APA's procedural requirements. . . . Adopting the reasoning of two of our sister circuits, we held that the statutory deadline did not constitute good cause to forgo notice and comment absent " 'any express indication' " by Congress to this effect.

. . . Congress did not express an intention to relieve the FAA of the legal obligation to engage in notice and comment procedures before promulgation of the Penalty Rules. Indeed, section 1475 did not even set a formal deadline for implementation of the agency's authority to assess civil penalties. It is true that the two-year duration of the "demonstration program," along with the associated eighteen-month reporting deadline, encouraged the FAA to act with reasonable dispatch. But we believe that the FAA, using expedited notice and comment procedures if necessary, could have realized this objective short of disregarding its obligations under the APA.

Finally, the FAA is foreclosed from relying on the good cause exception by its own delay in promulgating the Penalty Rules. The agency waited almost nine months before taking action to implement its authority under section 1475. At oral argument, counsel for the FAA conceded that the delay was largely a product of the agency's decision to attend to other obligations. We are hardly in a position to second guess the FAA's choices in determining institutional priorities. But insofar as the FAA's own failure to act materially contributed to its perceived deadline pressure, the agency cannot now invoke the need for expeditious action as "good cause" to avoid the obligations of section 553(b).

Finally, we reject the FAA's contention that its response to comments after promulgation of the Penalty Rules cured any noncompliance with section 553. Section 553 provides "that notice and an opportunity for comment are to precede rule-making." We strictly enforce this requirement because we recognize that an agency is not likely to be receptive to suggested changes once the agency "put[s] its credibility on the line in the form of 'final' rules. People naturally tend to be more close-minded and defensive once they have made a 'final' determination."

SILBERMAN, CIRCUIT JUDGE, dissenting:

I [believe] the rules fall, by ample measure, within the "procedural" exemption of section 553(b)(A), which exempts from notice and comment "rules of agency organization, procedure, or practice." To be sure, the rules in this case could as well be described as rules of "practice" (covering the practice of the parties and attorneys before the FAA) and also in some respects rules of "agency organization" (dealing with the interrelationship between the administrative law judges and the Administrator). I use the term "procedure" here to cover all three concepts.

Lines between substance and procedure in various areas of the law are difficult to draw and therefore often perplex scholars and judges. But Congress, when it passed the Administrative Procedure Act, made that difference critical, and we are therefore obliged to implement a viable distinction between "procedural" rules and those that are substantive. . . .

If we assume a spectrum of rules running from the most substantive to the most procedural, I would describe the former as those that regulate "primary conduct," . . . and the latter are those furthest away from primary conduct. In other words, if a given regulation purports to direct, control, or condition the behavior of those institutions or individuals subject to regulation by the authorizing statute it is not procedural, it is substantive. At the other end of the spectrum are those rules, such as the ones before us in this case, which deal with enforcement or adjudication of claims of violations of the substantive norm but which do not purport to affect the substantive norm. These kinds of rules are, in my view, clearly procedural.

Rules are no less procedural because they are thought to be important or affect outcomes. Congress did not state, when it passed the APA, that all but insignificant rules must be put out for notice and comment. . . .

Admittedly, not all our cases fit precisely along the continuum I described above. When an agency, rather than publishing rules which define a substantive norm to which regulated groups must conform or which flesh out enforcement procedures to effectuate such compliance, instead adopts rules dealing with the award of benefits, a slightly different but similar analysis is used to distinguish substantive from procedural rules. Sometimes the Government's prospective award of benefits is actually designed, in part, to affect primary conduct—such as the standards used to determine whether to renew a broadcast license or the criteria employed to determine eligibility for unemployment insurance. But typically, benefits are bestowed in accordance with preexisting qualifications or status. In those circumstances, it cannot be said that the rules seek to condition primary conduct. We still think of such rules as substantive because defining eligibility for a benefit program is the very essence of the program. It is in this context that we said that substantive rules are those that affect the "rights and interests of parties." . . .

Of course, procedure impacts on outcomes and thus can virtually always be described as affecting substance, but to pursue that line of analysis results in the obliteration of the distinction that Congress demanded. We avoided that snare only recently in *American Hosp. Ass'n v. Bowen*, where we held, over a strong dissent in many respects redolent of the majority opinion here, that HHS rules that set forth the enforcement priorities for peer review organizations (acting as agents to ensure medically reasonable and necessary hospital health care), as well as some adjudicatory procedures similar to those contained in the rules before us, did not have to be published for comment. . . .

It might be thought that there is something vaguely underhanded about an agency publishing important rules without an opportunity for those affected to comment. And lawyers and judges tend to prefer, on the margin, added procedure. But . . . we have been admonished somewhat dramatically by *Vermont Yankee* to not add more procedure to the APA than Congress required. I am afraid the majority opinion by obliterating the distinction between substance and procedure in section 553 does just that.

JEM BROADCASTING COMPANY, INC. v. FEDERAL COMMUNICATIONS COMMISSION

22 F.3d 320 (D.C.Cir.1994).

HARRY T. EDWARDS, CIRCUIT JUDGE:

In July 1988, appellant JEM Broadcasting Company, Inc. ("JEM") submitted a license application for a new FM station in Bella Vista, Arkansas. The Federal Communications Commission ("FCC" or "Commission") accepted JEM's application for filing, but determined upon further review that JEM had provided inconsistent geographic coordinates for its proposed transmitter site. Unable to resolve the inconsistency from the application papers, the FCC, acting pursuant to its "hard look" processing rules, dismissed JEM's application without providing JEM an opportunity to correct its error.

[In 1985, in anticipation of a flood of new FM license applications, the FCC adopted its so-called "hard look" regulations, designed to weed out incomplete applications.] The "hard look" rules established a fixed filing period—known as a "window"—for all applications requesting use of a particular channel. Applications filed within the window period would be evaluated for "substantial completeness"; those meeting this standard would be accepted for tender. . . .

Applications that did not include the prescribed information by the close of the window were considered "unacceptable for tender" and were returned without opportunity for filing a curative amendment. Moreover, if any data were incorrect or inconsistent, and the [sic] "the critical data [could not] be derived or the inconsistency resolved within the confines of the application and with a high degree of confidence," the application was deemed unacceptable for tender and would be dismissed with no opportunity to cure the defect. . . . JEM's application met this latter fate.

. . . JEM contends that the so-called "hard look" rules cannot be applied against it because the rules were promulgated without notice and comment in violation of the Administrative Procedure. . . .

The APA provides that "rules of agency organization, procedure, or practice" are exempt from the general notice and comment requirements of section 553. Although in applying this provision we have struggled with the distinction between "substantive" and "procedural" rules, we find the instant application to be straightforward. Our oft-cited formulation holds that the "critical feature" of the procedural exception "is that it covers agency actions that do not themselves alter the rights or interests of parties, although it may alter the manner in which the parties present themselves or their viewpoints to the agency." "Of course, procedure impacts on outcomes and thus can virtually always be described as affecting substance, but to pursue that line of analysis results in the obliteration of the distinction that Congress demanded." *Air Transport Ass'n of Am. v. Department of Transp.* (Silberman, J., dissenting). The issue, therefore, "is one of degree," and our task is to identify which substantive effects are "sufficiently grave so that notice and comment are needed to safeguard the policies underlying the APA."

In this case, JEM challenges so much of the "hard look" rules as deprives license applicants of the opportunity to correct errors or defects in their filings and submit the applications nunc pro tunc. JEM cannot deny, of course, that the Commission always has required applications to be complete in all critical respects by some date or suffer dismissal; and the Commission argues that its new rules simply "shift[ed] to the beginning of the process some of the application checks previously made later in the process." Although we do not think the instant rule change can be dismissed quite so glibly—after all, the previous regime gave applicants notice of errors and a window for redress—we conclude that a license applicant's right to a free shot at amending its application is not so significant as to have required the FCC to conduct notice and comment rulemaking, particularly in light of the Commission's weighty efficiency interests. The APA's procedural exception embraces cases, such as this one, in which the interests "promoted by public participation in rulemaking are outweighed by the countervailing considerations of effectiveness, efficiency, expedition and reduction in expense."

. . . The critical fact here, however, is that the "hard look" rules did not change the substantive standards by which the FCC evaluates license applications, e.g., financial qualifications, proposed programming, and transmitter location. This fact is fatal to JEM's claim.

We think the "hard look" rules fall comfortably within the realm of the "procedural" as we have defined it in other cases. . . .

Finally, seizing on another aspect of our law in this area, JEM argues that we cannot find the instant rule to be procedural because it encodes the substantive value judgment that applications containing minor errors should be sacrificed to promote efficient application processing. We have indeed held that the procedural exception to notice and comment "does not apply where the agency 'encodes a substantive value judgment.' " However, JEM's attempt to force the "hard look" rules into this rubric is unavailing. JEM's reasoning threatens to swallow the procedural exception to notice and comment, for agency housekeeping rules often embody a judgment about what mechanics and processes are most efficient. In *Air Transport Association of America v. Department of Transportation*, a divided panel of this court held that the Department of Transportation's adoption of a comprehensive scheme for adjudicating civil penalty actions required notice and comment, in part because the rules encoded a substantive value judgment "on the appropriate balance between a defendant's rights to adjudicatory procedures and the agency's interest in efficient prosecution." [Because after the Supreme Court remanded that case with a suggestion that it was moot, we vacated that judgment,] *Air Transport* is no longer binding precedent, [and] we recognize that our opinion there extended the "value judgment" rationale further than any other case of this circuit of which we are aware; and to the extent that it suggests a different result here, we disavow its reasoning.

Notes and Questions

1. What difference would it make to your analysis if you knew that the Sierra Club stringently opposes any environmental releases of biologically engineered pesticides and would likely view this regulation negatively? What difference would it make if from your experience you were pretty sure that no organized group would oppose the regulation?

2. If EPA did adopt the rule without notice and comment, and a court found that no exception applied, what might be the proper remedy? Should requiring after-the-fact comment suffice? Would it make a difference if some biotech companies were already running small-scale field tests pursuant to the new procedures?

3. Why should courts be skeptical of statutory deadlines for rulemaking as grounds for avoiding notice and comment, assuming that the deadline is so short as to make meaningful notice and comment impossible? What do you suppose Congress intended in such a circumstance? Should courts do other than give effect to congressional will?

What if the statutory deadline provided enough time for notice and comment, but the agency through oversight or lack of planning waits until the last moment and then claims "good cause" for avoiding notice and comment? The agency certainly should not be rewarded for its failure to provide enough time, but should "teaching the agency a lesson" be done at the expense of meeting the statutory deadline? Courts have routinely held rules invalid under these circumstances.

4. In 1998, the Government Accounting Office (GAO) completed a study for Congress estimating the number of final rules for which agencies did not publish a notice of proposed rulemaking (NPRM). The report made the following estimates:

> During calendar year 1997, federal agencies published 4,658 final regulatory actions in the Federal Register. Analysis of our sample of 250 of these actions indicated that about 51 percent, or 2,360, were published without NPRMs. Therefore, . . . we estimated that there were no associated proposed rules for between 44 and 58 percent of the final regulatory actions published during 1997. . . .

> Although most of the regulatory actions without NPRMs in the sample appeared to involve routine or minor issues, our previous work indicated that some of the most significant regulatory actions that agencies have published in recent years also did not have NPRMs. . . . [W]e examined the subset of 61 major rules that were published during calendar year 1997. Of these, 11 did not have NPRMs. Although the APA permits agencies to issue rules, including major rules, without NPRMs in appropriate circumstances, it is nonetheless notable that nearly one-fifth of the major rules published during 1997 did not have notices. . . .

U.S. General Accounting Office, Federal Rulemaking: Agencies Often Published Final Actions Without Proposed Rules 11, 13 (August 1998).

GAO also investigated how agencies justified their failure to utilize a notice-and-comment process:

> As previously noted, agencies can publish final regulatory actions without NPRMs using either good cause, categorical, or statute-specific exceptions to the APA's notice and comment requirements. Our review indicated that, in 1997, agencies most commonly used the good cause exception. Agencies also used the categorical and, to a much lesser extent, statute-specific NPRM exceptions.

> Our analysis of the sample cases indicated that federal agencies cited the good cause exception to the APA's notice requirement in about 59 . . . percent, or about 1,400, of the final regulatory actions published without NPRMs in 1997. . . .

> In our review, . . . the agencies most frequently indicated that NPRMs were impracticable because of the time-sensitive nature of the regulatory actions being taken. For example, in eight of the actions, the agencies indicated that some kind of emergency made issuance of an NPRM impracticable or contrary to the public interest. In one such case, the Administrator of USDA's Animal and Plant Health Inspection Service determined that an emergency existed after a trapping survey revealed that the Oriental fruit fly had moved into parts of Los Angeles County. . . . In seven of the sample actions, the agencies cited statutory deadlines that required the prompt promulgation of the action at issue. For example, the Department of Veterans Affairs said that it published a final rule on

guidelines for furnishing veterans with "sensori-neural aids" (e.g., eyeglasses, contact lenses, and hearing aids) without an NPRM because a provision in the Veteran's Health Care Eligibility Reform Act of 1996 required that the guidelines be established "(n)ot later than 30 days after the date of the enactment of this Act." In eight of the cases in our sample, the agencies indicated that they used the good cause exception because the regulatory actions being taken were matters of public safety. For example, the Coast Guard published a final rule without an NPRM that established a temporary safety zone near the mouth of the Severn River in Annapolis, Maryland, to protect marine traffic and spectators from potential hazards during an event involving the U.S. Navy's Blue Angels....

We estimated that 30 ... percent, or about 710, of the final actions that federal agencies published without NPRMs in 1997 did not have a notice because the agencies indicated that the actions were covered by broad categorical exceptions permitted in the APA—e.g., actions involving military or foreign affairs; agency management or personnel; or public property, loans, grants, benefits, or contracts.

Id. at 16–18.

Are you surprised by the frequency with which agencies attempt to avoid notice and comment rulemaking? Even if this procedure is not required, agencies are still free voluntarily to use it. Why do you suppose agencies are not tempted to do so? Put another way, why is it that the burdens of notice-and-comment rulemaking appear to agencies to outweigh the benefits? You may wish to return to this question after you learn more about these burdens in subsequent sections of this chapter.

5.   As you read, the "good cause" exception requires an agency to find that notice and public procedure are "impracticable, unnecessary, or contrary to the public interest." 5 U.S.C. § 553(b)(B). The APA's legislative history offers the following definition of the key terms:

"Impracticable" means a situation in which the due and required execution of the agency functions would be unavoidably prevented by its undertaking public rule-making proceedings. "Unnecessary" means unnecessary so far as the public is concerned, as would be the case if a minor or merely technical amendment in which the public is not particularly interested were involved. "Public interest" supplements the terms "impracticable" or "unnecessary"; it requires that public rulemaking procedures shall not prevent an agency from operating and that, on the other hand, lack of public interest in rulemaking warrants an agency to dispense with public procedure.

ADMINISTRATIVE PROCEDURE ACT: LEGISLATIVE HISTORY, S. DOC. NO. 248 (1946), at 200. Thus, "situations potentially covered by the 'good cause' exception are those in which advance notice would defeat the agency's regulatory objective; immediate action is necessary to reduce or avoid health hazards or other imminent harm to persons or property; or inaction will lead to serious dislocation in government programs or the marketplace." JEFFREY S. LUBBERS, A GUIDE TO FEDERAL AGENCY RULEMAK-ING 78 (3d ed. 1998).

Can you think of any reasons why providing notice and comment on the EUP rule amendment would be unnecessary, impractical, or contrary to the public interest?

6. Sometimes an agency adopts a rule without notice and comment, invoking one of the "good cause" exceptions, but invites the public to make comments on the rule, saying that the agency will consider them and, if appropriate, make changes in the rule. This is usually called an "interim final rule." In a few situations, Congress has authorized the use of interim final rules. *See, e.g.*, 42 U.S.C.A. § 1395hh (authorizing the use of interim-final regulations for some aspects of the Social Security program). If Congress has not authorized interim rules, should courts be less strict in policing the "good cause" exception when agencies use this process? Some courts have not been. *See, e.g., NRDC v. U.S. EPA*, 683 F.2d 752 (3d Cir.1982); *American Fed. of Gov't Employees v. Block*, 655 F.2d 1153 (D.C.Cir.1981). Why not? The Administrative Conference of the United States issued a recommendation that whenever agencies adopt rules without notice and comment (other than when the agency finds notice and comment "unnecessary"), they simultaneously ask for comments on the rule and respond to the comments received. If agencies do respond to these adverse comments and ratify or modify the rule as appropriate, the Administrative Conference recommends that courts consider the initial failure to provide notice and comment, even if in error, to be harmless error. Recommendation 95–4, 60 Fed. Reg. 43108 (1995).

7. Although some rules are noncontroversial, an agency may hesitate to invoke the good cause exemption on this basis, even though it is unlikely to receive any comments in response to a rulemaking notice. The Environmental Protection Agency (EPA) invented the concept of "direct-final rulemaking" to address this situation. To use this procedure, an agency publishes a final rule in the Federal Register with a statement that the rule will become effective on a particular date unless an adverse comment is received before that date. If an adverse comment is received, the agency withdraws the rule, and it then publishes it as a proposed rule under notice and comment procedures. The concept of direct final rulemaking has been endorsed by the Administrative Conference, Recommendation 95–4, 60 Fed. Reg. 43108 (1995), and by the National Performance Review, a series of reports by the Clinton administration identifying ways to reinvent government processes to be more effective. OFFICE OF THE VICE–PRESIDENT, CREATING A GOVERNMENT THAT WORKS BETTER AND COSTS LESS, IMPROVING REGULATORY SYSTEMS, NATIONAL PERFORMANCE REVIEW 42–44 (1993). For arguments that this process is consistent with the APA, see Ronald Levin, *Direct Final Rulemaking*, 64 GEO. WASH. L. REV. 1 (1995).

8. If there was an emergency justifying an exception from prior notice and comment, the APA does not require later notice and com-

ment, nor does it limit the time the rule may remain in effect. The Model State Administrative Procedure Act, which generally requires notice-and-comment rulemaking as well, has a parallel "unnecessary, impracticable, or contrary to the public interest" exception. MSAPA § 3–108. It, however, provides a mechanism whereby the agency may be required to undertake a notice and comment rulemaking proceeding with respect to the rule within two years of the promulgation of the rule. MSAPA § 3–108(c). If the new rulemaking proceeding requirement is triggered, the rule adopted without notice and comment goes out of effect in 180 days. *Id.* The Endangered Species Act has a similar provision, allowing for listing of a threatened or endangered species without notice and comment in an emergency, but limiting the effect of that listing for 240 days, presumably enough time to undertake a rulemaking proceeding. 16 U.S.C.A. § 1533(b)(7).

2. FORMAL, INFORMAL, OR HYBRID RULEMAKING

As you read in Chapter 1, there are three types of rulemaking procedures: informal, formal, and hybrid. The APA itself only recognizes the first two; hybrid rulemaking is what we call it when Congress has imposed additional procedures, or substituted different procedures, beyond those required by the APA. Probably most rules are made by informal rulemaking. These rules are only subject to the notice-and-comment procedures required by section 553 and must be accompanied by a statement of basis and purpose when they are promulgated. 5 U.S.C.A. § 553. Congress has required the use of "formal" rulemaking in a few circumstances. In these circumstances, agencies must follow the procedures specified in sections 556–57, which essentially require a trial-type proceeding, to promulgate a rule. Finally, Congress has required many agencies to use "hybrid" rulemaking in a number of situations. The nature of the additional or substitute procedures required differs from statute to statute, but they are more burdensome to the agency than those required for informal rulemaking, while less burdensome than the procedures required in formal rulemaking.

Because formal rulemaking is so rare, and because its procedures are virtually indistinguishable from the procedures for formal adjudication, discussed in Chapter 3, those procedures will be discussed there. We will deal with hybrid rulemaking after we consider basic APA informal rulemaking.

In a trilogy of cases in the 1970s, the Supreme Court clarified three key issues concerning rulemaking procedures. In *United States v. Allegheny–Ludlum Steel Corp.*, 406 U.S. 742, 92 S.Ct. 1941, 32 L.Ed.2d 453 (1972), the Court interpreted when section 553 triggers the requirement of formal rulemaking. *United States v. Florida East Coast Railroad Co.*, 410 U.S. 224, 93 S.Ct. 810, 35 L.Ed.2d 223 (1973), reiterated that decision and clarified when a "hearing" requirement triggers the need for a trial-type proceeding in a rulemaking, even if formal rulemaking is not required. Finally, *Vermont Yankee Nuclear Power Corp. v. Natural Resources Defense Council, Inc.*, 435 U.S. 519, 98 S.Ct. 1197, 55 L.Ed.2d

460 (1978), considered whether the courts can impose hybrid rulemaking procedures on an agency.

UNITED STATES v. ALLEGHENY–LUDLUM STEEL CORP.

406 U.S. 742, 92 S.Ct. 1941, 32 L.Ed.2d 453 (1972).

REHNQUIST, JUSTICE:

[The Interstate Commerce Commission (ICC), which has been abolished, once regulated various aspects of railroad transportation including the rates that railroads could charge. Disappointed with a rule promulgated by the ICC using informal rulemaking, some shippers, including Allegheny Ludlum Steel Corporation, sought judicial review. They argued, among other contentions, that the Esch Act, quoted below, required the ICC to hold a hearing before promulgating any rule, which the agency did not do.]

. . . Appellees claim that the Commission's procedure here departed from the provisions of 5 U.S.C. §§ 556 and 557 of the Act. Those sections, however, govern a rulemaking proceeding only when 5 U.S.C. § 553 so requires. The latter section, dealing generally with rulemaking, makes applicable the provisions of §§ 556 and 557 only "[w]hen rules are required by statute to be made on the record after opportunity for an agency hearing. . . ." The Esch Act, authorizing the Commission "after hearing, on a complaint or upon its own initiative without complaint, (to) establish reasonable rules, regulations, and practices with respect to car service . . . ," does not require that such rules "be made on the record." 5 U.S.C. § 553. That distinction is determinative for this case. "A good deal of significance lies in the fact that some statutes do expressly require determinations on the record." Sections 556 and 557 need be applied only where the agency statute, in addition to providing a hearing, prescribes explicitly that it be "on the record." We do not suggest that only the precise words "on the record" in the applicable statute will suffice to make §§ 556 and 557 applicable to rulemaking proceedings, but we do hold that the language of the Esch Car Service Act is insufficient to invoke these sections. . . .

UNITED STATES v. FLORIDA EAST COAST RAILROAD CO.

410 U.S. 224, 93 S.Ct. 810, 35 L.Ed.2d 223 (1973).

REHNQUIST, JUSTICE:

Appellees, two railroad companies, . . . challenged the order of the Commission on both substantive and procedural grounds. The District Court held that the language of § 1(14)(a)[1] of the Interstate Commerce

---

1. Section 1(14)(a) provides: "The Commission may, after hearing, on a complaint or upon its own initiative without complaint, establish reasonable rules, regulations, and practices with respect to car service by common carriers by railroad subject

Act, required the Commission in a proceeding such as this to act in accordance with the Administrative Procedure Act, 5 U.S.C. § 556(d), and that the Commission's determination to receive submissions from the appellees only in written form was a violation of that section because the respondents were "prejudiced" by that determination within the meaning of that section.

Following our decision last Term in *United States v. Allegheny–Ludlum Steel Corp.*, we noted probable jurisdiction, and requested the parties to brief the question of whether the Commission's proceeding was governed by 5 U.S.C. § 553, or by §§ 556 and 557, of the Administrative Procedure Act. We here decide that the Commission's proceeding was governed only by § 553 of that Act, and that appellees received the "hearing" required by § 1(14)(a) of the Interstate Commerce Act....

II. APPLICABILITY OF ADMINISTRATIVE PROCEDURE ACT

In *United States v. Allegheny–Ludlum Steel Corp.*, we held that the language of § 1(14)(a) of the Interstate Commerce Act authorizing the Commission to act "after hearing" was not the equivalent of a requirement that a rule be made "on the record after opportunity for an agency hearing" as the latter term is used in § 553(c) of the Administrative Procedure Act....

Both of the district courts that reviewed this order of the Commission concluded that its proceedings were governed by the stricter requirements of §§ 556 and 557 of the Administrative Procedure Act, rather than by the provisions of § 553 alone. The conclusion of the District Court for the Middle District of Florida, which we here review, was based on the assumption that the language in § 1(14)(a) of the Interstate Commerce Act requiring rulemaking under that section to be done "after hearing" was the equivalent of a statutory requirement that the rule "be made on the record after opportunity for an agency hearing." Such an assumption is inconsistent with our decision in *Allegheny-Ludlum.* ...

III. "HEARING" REQUIREMENT OF § 1(14)(a) OF THE INTERSTATE COMMERCE ACT

Inextricably intertwined with the hearing requirement of the Administrative Procedure Act in this case is the meaning to be given to the language "after hearing" in § 1(14)(a) of the Interstate Commerce Act. Appellees, both here and in the court below, contend that the Commission procedure here fell short of that mandated by the "hearing" requirement of § 1(14)(a), even though it may have satisfied § 553 of the Administrative Procedure Act. The Administrative Procedure Act states that none of its provisions "limit or repeal additional requirements

to this chapter, including the compensation to be paid and other terms of any contract, agreement, or arrangement for the use of any locomotive, car, or other vehicle not owned by the carrier using it (and whether or not owned by another carrier), and the penalties or other sanctions for nonobservance of such rules, regulations, or practices." ...

imposed by statute or otherwise recognized by law." 5 U.S.C. § 559. Thus, even though the Commission was not required to comply with §§ 556 and 557 of that Act, it was required to accord the "hearing" specified in § 1(14)(a) of the Interstate Commerce Act....

The term "hearing" in its legal context undoubtedly has a host of meanings. Its meaning undoubtedly will vary, depending on whether it is used in the context of a rulemaking-type proceeding or in the context of a proceeding devoted to the adjudication of particular disputed facts. It is by no means apparent what the drafters of the Esch Car Service Act of 1917, which became the first part of § 1(14)(a) of the Interstate Commerce Act, meant by the term.... What is apparent, though, is that the term was used in granting authority to the Commission to make rules and regulations of a prospective nature....

Here, the incentive payments proposed by the Commission in its tentative order, and later adopted in its final order, were applicable across the board to all of the common carriers by railroad subject to the Interstate Commerce Act. No effort was made to single out any particular railroad for special consideration based on its own peculiar circumstances.... Though the Commission obviously relied on factual inferences as a basis for its order, ... [t]he factual inferences were used in the formulation of a basically legislative-type judgment, for prospective application only, rather than in adjudicating a particular set of disputed facts. [Accordingly, the Court held that here the word "hearing" in the Interstate Commerce Act did "not necessarily embrace either the right to present evidence orally and to cross-examine opposing witnesses, or the right to present oral argument to the agency's decisionmaker."]

VERMONT YANKEE NUCLEAR POWER CORP. v. NATURAL RESOURCES DEFENSE COUNCIL, INC.

435 U.S. 519, 98 S.Ct. 1197, 55 L.Ed.2d 460 (1978).

Rehnquist, Justice:

[The Natural Resources Defense Council (NRDC) challenged a rule promulgated by the Atomic Energy Commission (AEC). The NRDC contended that the absence of discovery or cross-examination denied it a meaningful opportunity to participate in the rulemaking proceedings. The District of Columbia Circuit Court of Appeals remanded the rule to the AEC. According to the Supreme Court, the "ineluctable mandate" of the circuit court's decision was that "the procedures followed during the hearings were inadequate." The Court stated that "[a]gencies are free to grant additional procedural rights in the exercise of their discretion, but reviewing courts are generally not free to impose them if the agencies have not chosen to grant them." Thus, "[a]bsent constitutional constraints or extremely compelling circumstances," administrative agencies " 'should be free to fashion their own rules of procedure and to pursue methods of inquiry capable of permitting them to discharge their multitudinous duties.' '' The Court cited several "compelling" reasons for its holding:]

In the first place, if courts continually review agency proceedings to determine whether the agency employed procedures which were, in the court's opinion, perfectly tailored to reach what the court perceives to be the "best" or "correct" result, judicial review would be totally unpredictable. And the agencies, operating under this vague injunction to employ the "best" procedures and facing the threat of reversal if they did not, would undoubtedly adopt full adjudicatory procedures in every instance. Not only would this totally disrupt the statutory scheme, through which Congress enacted "a formula upon which opposing social and political forces have come to rest," but all the inherent advantages of informal rulemaking would be totally lost.

Secondly, it is obvious that the court in these cases reviewed the agency's choice of procedures on the basis of the record actually produced at the hearing, and not on the basis of the information available to the agency when it made the decision to structure the proceedings in a certain way. This sort of Monday morning quarterbacking not only encourages but almost compels the agency to conduct all rulemaking proceedings with the full panoply of procedural devices normally associated only with adjudicatory hearings.

Finally, and perhaps most importantly, this sort of review fundamentally misconceives the nature of the standard for judicial review of an agency rule. The court below uncritically assumed that additional procedures will automatically result in a more adequate record because it will give interested parties more of an opportunity to participate in and contribute to the proceedings. But informal rulemaking need not be based solely on the transcript of a hearing held before an agency. Indeed, the agency need not even hold a formal hearing. Thus, the adequacy of the "record" in this type of proceeding is not correlated directly to the type of procedural devices employed, but rather turns on whether the agency has followed the statutory mandate of the Administrative Procedure Act or other relevant statutes. If the agency is compelled to support the rule which it ultimately adopts with the type of record produced only after a full adjudicatory hearing, it simply will have no choice but to conduct a full adjudicatory hearing prior to promulgating every rule. In sum, this sort of unwarranted judicial examination of perceived procedural shortcomings of a rulemaking proceeding can do nothing but seriously interfere with that process prescribed by Congress.

Notes and Questions

1.   The hostility against formal rulemaking reflected in *Allegheny–Ludlum* and *Florida East Coast Railway* turns on the trial-like procedure involved in formal rulemaking (as well as in formal adjudication). *Vermont Yankee* similarly reflects a skepticism about trial-like procedures in informal rulemaking. Why is it that the Court discounts the

value of trial-like procedures for determining facts in rulemakings when, as we will see, it continues to recognize the value of those procedures in adjudications? Professor Kenneth Culp Davis's answer is that adjudication and rulemaking involve different types of facts and that adjudicatory procedures are unnecessary to resolve factual disputes that typically come up in rulemaking. Kenneth Culp Davis, *An Approach To The Problems of Evidence*, 55 HARV. L. REV. 364, 402–416 (1942). Professors Richard Pierce and Davis explain:

> All government actions necessarily are based on a large number of findings or assumptions concerning many facts. The factual underpinnings of government actions frequently are disputed. The nature of the disputed facts vary widely, however. A determination that an individual committed a crime must be based on findings of historical fact unique to an individual. A legislative decision to subsidize a particular type of housing is based at least implicitly, and usually explicitly, on factual determinations that the type of housing to be subsidized is particularly valuable to society and that it would not be available in sufficient quantity in the absence of a subsidy. Similarly, the Court based its landmark decision in *Brown v. Board of Education*, 347 U.S. 483 (1954), on factual determinations concerning the effects of educational segregation on members of racial minorities.

> . . . Courts refer to [facts concerning the individual] as adjudicative facts, which usually answer the questions of who did what, where, when, how, why, with what motive or intent; adjudicative facts are roughly the kind of facts that go to a jury in a jury case.

> Facts related to an individual are intrinsically the kinds of facts that should not be resolved to the individual's detriment without giving the individual an opportunity to be heard with respect to those facts. An individual knows more about the facts concerning herself and her activities than anyone else is likely to know. Thus, an individual is uniquely well-positioned to rebut or explain evidence that bears upon an adjudicative fact concerning her past conduct.

> The second type of fact—illustrated by the Court's decision in *Brown* and the hypothetical legislative decision to subsidize a particular type of housing—is a legislative fact. Legislative facts do not describe the individual who is uniquely affected by the government action or that individual's past conduct. Rather, legislative facts are the general facts that help a government institution decide questions of law, policy, and discretion. An individual adversely affected by a government action is not uniquely well-positioned to contribute to the resolution of a dispute with respect to a legislative fact. The Constitution permits the institutions of government to resolve disputed legislative facts by relying on sources other than the individuals who are affected by resolution of those facts. The most useful sources of data for resolution of disputes concerning legislative facts

often are contained in the published literature of the social or natural science disciplines relevant to the legislative fact at issue. K. DAVIS & R. PIERCE, JR., ADMINISTRATIVE LAW TREATISE § 9.2, at 7 (1994). Can you think of examples of the two types of facts?

2.   Besides theoretical reasons for hostility towards formal rulemaking, the Court was aware of egregious examples where formal rulemaking had taken time and resources wholly out of proportion to any value gained from the procedures. The most famous case involved the Food and Drug Administration's nine-year formal rulemaking proceeding to determine the percentage of weight in peanut butter that must come from peanuts. *See* Robert W. Hamilton, *Rulemaking on a Record by the Food and Drug Administration*, 50 TEX. L. REV. 1132, 1150 (1972).

3.   INFORMAL RULEMAKING REQUIREMENTS

a.   *Notice*

The APA requires that a "general notice of proposed rulemaking shall be published in the Federal Register." 5 U.S.C.A. § 553(b). These notices are variously abbreviated as NPRMs or NOPRs. Although a Federal Register notice is not required if persons subject to the rule "are named or either personally served or otherwise have actual notice [of the rulemaking] in accordance with law," *id.*, agencies seldom, if ever, rely on actual notice. Moreover, publication in the Federal Register is "constructive" notice of a rule and is legally sufficient even if an affected or interested party is unaware of the notice. For this reason, one responsibility of regulatory lawyers in places like trade associations, interest groups, corporations, or lawyers with on-going clients, is to look at the Federal Register each day to determine if an agency has proposed a rule, or issued some other notice, about which their client or organization should be aware. Publications such as loose-leaf reporter services and trade publications also follow the Federal Register and include stories about proposed rulemakings, and often include the actual notices as well, concerning issues of interest to their readers.

The NPRM must include the "time, place, and nature" of the public proceedings. *Id.* § 553(b)(1). Providing the time, place, and nature of the proceedings enables interested persons to participate in those proceedings by indicating the type of rule involved, the time during which the agency will receive written comments, and instructions concerning where to file the comments. An agency must also indicate the legal authority under which the rule is proposed and "either the terms or substance of the proposed rule or a description of the subjects and issues involved." *Id.* Agencies, however, normally publish much more than what the APA requires. Virtually all agencies today publish the actual text of the proposed rule. Moreover, agencies also publish something known as a "preamble" to the actual rule text, which, in addition to what is required by the APA, gives a background to the rulemaking and describes what the rule is intended to do. Partially, this is a result of statutes that have added additional requirements to what the APA

ncies to provide. Partially, this is a reaction by agencies to
possibility that a court will decide that the agency's notice
＿ent.

ᵣrior to *Vermont Yankee Nuclear Power Corp. v. NRDC*, 435 U.S.
519, 98 S.Ct. 1197, 55 L.Ed.2d 460 (1978), which held that courts could
not impose additional rulemaking procedures on agencies, a number of
courts had enforced the notice requirement of section 553, not according
to its terms, but according to the purposes perceived to be behind that
requirement. For example, the legislative history of the APA stated that
notice must be "sufficient to fairly apprise interested persons of the
issues involved, so that they may present responsive data or argument."
Legislative History of the Administrative Procedure Act, S. Doc. No. 248,
79th Cong., 2d Sess. 200 (1946). Giving effect to this idea, rather than
the text of section 553, a number of courts, for example, required that
agencies must identify in the NPRM the data and methodology of any
scientific evidence on which they relied. *Portland Cement Association v.
Ruckelshaus*, 486 F.2d 375 (D.C.Cir.1973), *cert. denied* 417 U.S. 921, 94
S.Ct. 2628, 41 L.Ed.2d 226 (1974), is often cited as the source of this
trend. EPA had promulgated a final rule which adopted new source
performance standards for Portland cement plants based on test results
that had not been made available for public comment. The court found a
"critical defect in the decision-making process ... in the initial inability
of petitioners to obtain—in timely fashion—the test results and procedures used ...," because "[i]t is not consonant with the purpose of a
rule-making proceeding to promulgate rules on the basis of inadequate
data, or on data that, [in] critical degree, is known only to the agency."
See also United States v. Nova Scotia Food Products Corp., 568 F.2d 240
(2d Cir.1977). When an agency fails to make the necessary disclosures, a
court will remand a final rule to an agency for a new notice and
comment period.

Despite *Vermont Yankee*, this body of case law is still given effect.
See, e.g., Lloyd Noland Hospital & Clinic v. Heckler, 762 F.2d 1561 (11th
Cir.1985). A common "hybrid" requirement added by Congress is for
agencies to include different types of background data (or summaries or
notices thereof) in the NPRM. *See, e.g.,* 42 U.S.C. § 7191(b)(1) (Department of Energy NPRMs must include "a statement of the research,
analysis, and other available information in support of, the need for, and
the probable effect of, any proposed rule....."); 42 U.S.C.A. § 7607(d)(3)
(proposed rules under the Clean Air Act must include "a summary of the
factual data on which the proposed rule is based; the methodology used
in obtaining the data and in analyzing the data; and the major legal
interpretations and policy considerations underlying the proposed
rule.").

The adequacy of the notice in a proposed rule is a common procedural challenge to a rule. Whenever the agency adopts as a final rule text
that is different from what was in the proposed rule, someone may
complain that the NPRM did not provide adequate notice. Obviously,
where the change is minor this complaint is unavailing. Moreover, an

agency may have flagged an issue in its preamble as something that might change in the course of the rulemaking, so that persons would be fairly on notice of a particular change. Nevertheless, it is not uncommon, either because the agency merely changes its mind or because of some information that arises in the course of the rulemaking, for the agency to decide that the final rule should differ in a material fashion from the proposed rule, even where the agency has not specifically flagged the issue.

The courts have struggled concerning to what extent an agency can change a final rule without the necessity of giving new notice and holding a second comment period. On the one hand, a rule that obligates agencies to give new notice each time that they make a change in a proposed rule would discourage agencies from making any changes. This result would defeat the purpose of the comment period which is to educate the agency concerning what constitutes an appropriate rule. On the other hand, if agencies can change a rule in fundamental ways without giving new notice, interested persons are denied a fair opportunity to influence the nature of the final rule.

To protect the interest of parties in commenting on proposed rules, the courts have consistently held that the notice of proposed rulemaking must "fairly apprise interested persons" of the issues in the rulemaking. *United Steelworkers v. Marshall*, 647 F.2d 1189, 1221 (D.C.Cir.1980). Interested persons are fairly apprised if the final rule is a "logical outgrowth" of the rulemaking proceeding. *United Steelworkers*, 647 F.2d at 1191; *Taylor Diving & Salvage Co. v. U.S. Dept. of Labor*, 599 F.2d 622, 626 (5th Cir.1979); *BASF Wyandotte Corp. v. Costle*, 598 F.2d 637, 642 (1st Cir.1979), *cert. denied* 444 U.S. 1096, 100 S.Ct. 1063, 62 L.Ed.2d 784 (1980).

Problem 2–5: Lack of Notice

Most secondary schools in the United States offer a lunch program that subsidizes the cost of meals for students from families with poverty level incomes. The program is administered by the Department of Agriculture (USDA) which establishes the requirements that schools must meet to be eligible for the program. These conditions include minimum dietary standards. Schools normally follow the same dietary standards for students who are not eligible for subsidized lunches.

The USDA dietary requirements, which were adopted shortly after Congress passed the National School Lunch Act in 1946, have never been updated to reflect new scientific knowledge concerning nutrition. Because the standards are out of date, lunches served by most school districts do not follow the 1990 Dietary Guidelines For Americans, exposing students to levels of fat and sodium, for example, that are often double or triple the recommended amounts. The 1990 guidelines are based on scientific evidence that has identified certain eating patterns as increasing the risk of chronic diseases such as coronary heart disease, stroke, diabetes, and certain types of cancer.

USDA proposed a rule that would require schools to serve lunches that complied with the 1990 dietary guidelines. Specifically, USDA proposed that lunches must meet the following conditions:

(a) A limit on the percent of calories from total fat to 30 percent based on the actual number of calories offered;

(b) A limit on the percent of calories from saturated fat to less than 10 percent based on the actual number of calories offered;

(c) a reduction of the levels of sodium and cholesterol; and

(d) an increase in dietary fiber.

Assume that USDA has received comments from the Vegetarian Energy Group Institute (VEGI) which advocated that schools should be required to serve a minimum of five vegetarian meals per month. VEGI made two arguments for its position. First, it noted that the standards proposed by USDA were based on the assumption that individuals comply with the 1990 guidelines for other meals. VEGI presented survey evidence that indicated many families, however, do not comply with the guidelines at home. For this reason, it argued that more restrictive standards were necessary if the health of children was to be protected. Second, VEGI argued that having vegetarian lunches would serve an educational function because it would acquaint students about the possibility of vegetarian diets.

Assume that USDA accepted the argument put forward by VEGI and required that schools serve a minimum of five vegetarian lunches a month. A vegetarian lunch was defined as food that does not include any type of meat, fish, or eggs.

If you are a lawyer for:

(a) the National Association of Beef Producers, which opposes the change because it will reduce the amount of meat that schools will be able to serve, what arguments would you make that USDA has not complied with the requirements of section 553? How would you rate the Association's chances of convincing an appellate court to remand the rule?

(b) USDA, what arguments would you make that USDA has complied with the requirements of section 553?

Problem Materials

CHAPTER 13, SCHOOL LUNCH PROGRAMS, 42 U.S.C.A.

§ 1751. Congressional Declaration of Policy

It is declared to be the policy of Congress, as a measure of national security, to safeguard the health and well-being of the Nation's children and to encourage the domestic consumption of nutritious agricultural commodities and other food, by assisting the States, through grants-in-aid and other means, in providing an adequate supply of foods and other facilities for the establishment, maintenance, operation, and expansion of nonprofit school lunch programs.

§ 1752.   Authorization of Appropriations; "Secretary" Defined

For each fiscal year there is authorized to be appropriated, out of money in the Treasury not otherwise appropriated, such sums as may be necessary to enable the Secretary of Agriculture (hereinafter referred to as the "Secretary") to carry out the provisions of this chapter, other than sections 1761 and 1766 of this title. Appropriations to carry out the provisions of this chapter and of the Child Nutrition Act of 1966 for any fiscal year are authorized to be made a year in advance of the beginning of the fiscal year in which the funds will become available for disbursement to the States. Notwithstanding any other provision of law, any funds appropriated to carry out the provisions of this chapter and the Child Nutrition Act of 1966 shall remain available for the purposes of the Act for which appropriated until expended.

§ 1753.   Apportionments to States

(a) The sums appropriated for any fiscal year pursuant to the authorizations contained in section 1752 of this title, shall be available to the Secretary for supplying agricultural commodities and other food for the program in accordance with the provisions of this chapter....

§ 1756.   Payments to States

(a)(1) Funds appropriated to carry out section 1753 of this title during any fiscal year shall be available for payment to the States for disbursement by State educational agencies in accordance with such agreements, not inconsistent with the provisions of this chapter, as may be entered into by the Secretary and such State educational agencies for the purpose of assisting schools within the States in obtaining agricultural commodities and other foods for consumption by children in furtherance of the school lunch program authorized under this chapter....

§ 1757.   State Disbursement to Schools; Purpose; Child and Children Defined; Food Costs; Limitation

Funds paid to any State during any fiscal year pursuant to section 1753 of this title shall be disbursed by the State educational agency, in accordance with such agreements approved by the Secretary as may be entered into by such State agency and the schools in the State, to those schools in the State which the State educational agency, taking into account need and attendance, determines are eligible to participate in the school lunch program....

§ 1758.   Program Requirements

(a) Nutritional standards; medical and special dietary needs of individual students; whole milk as beverage; diminution of food waste; acceptance of offered foods.

(1) Lunches served by schools participating in the school lunch program under this chapter shall meet minimum nutritional requirements prescribed by the Secretary on the basis of tested nutritional research; . . .

DEPARTMENT OF AGRICULTURE, PROPOSED RULE NATIONAL SCHOOL LUNCH PROGRAM AND SCHOOL BREAKFAST PROGRAM: NUTRITION OBJECTIVES FOR SCHOOL MEALS

59 Fed. Reg. 30218 (1994).

SUMMARY: This rule proposes to amend the regulations outlining the nutrition standards for the National School Lunch and School Breakfast Programs. It is part of an integrated, comprehensive plan for promoting the health of children. Specifically, this proposal would update the current nutrition standards to incorporate the Dietary Guidelines for Americans, which reflect medical and scientific consensus on proper nutrition as a vital element in disease prevention and long-term health promotion. This proposal would also adopt meal planning based on analysis of key nutrients (Nutrient Standard Menu Planning) in lieu of the current meal pattern. . . .

BACKGROUND

Nutrition Standards in the School Meal Programs

The primary purpose of the National School Lunch Program (NSLP), as originally stated by Congress in 1946 in section 2 of the National School Lunch Act (NSLA), is "to safeguard the health and well-being of the Nation's children. . . ." At that time, nutritional concerns in the United States centered on nutrient deficiencies and issues of under-consumption. Over time, meal requirements for the NSLP, 7 CFR 210.10, were designed to provide foods sufficient to approximate one-third of the National Academy of Sciences' Recommended Dietary Allowances (RDA). Participating schools were required to offer meals that complied with general patterns established by the Department. These patterns were developed to provide a balanced meal by focusing on minimum amounts of specific components (meat/meat alternate, bread/bread alternate, vegetables, fruits and dairy products) rather than on the nutrient content of the entire meal. Over the years, virtually no substantive changes have been made to these patterns.

An array of scientific data now augments our knowledge by documenting that excesses in consumption are a major concern because of their relationship to the incidence of chronic disease. The typical diet in the United States is high in fat, saturated fat and sodium and low in complex carbohydrates and fiber. The meal requirements for the NSLP have not kept pace with the growing consensus of the need to modify eating habits. Given the importance of school meals to the nation's children, especially needy children, the Department is committed to meeting its health responsibilities by updating the nutrition standards for school meals to ensure that children have access to a healthful diet as well as an adequate one. To accomplish this task, the Department is proposing to have school meals conform to the 1990 Dietary Guidelines for Americans (hereinafter referred to as the Dietary Guidelines) as well as provide proper levels of nutrients and calories. . . .

School Meals' Lack of Compliance With Current Dietary Guidelines

The current Dietary Guidelines recommend that people eat a variety of foods; maintain a healthy weight; choose a diet with plenty of vegetables, fruits, and grain products; and use sugar and sodium in moderation. The Dietary Guidelines also recommend diets low in fat, saturated fat, and cholesterol so that over time, fat comprises 30 per cent or less of caloric intake, and saturated fat less than 10 per cent of total calories, for persons two years of age and older.

However, information available to the Department consistently shows that children's diets, including meals served in schools, do not conform to the recommendations of the Dietary Guidelines. . . .

PROPOSED REGULATORY CHANGES

Expanding and Updating Nutrition Requirements

The Department's mission continues to be to carry out the declared policy of Congress to "safeguard the health and well-being of the Nation's children." In order to meet this goal, school meals must change to reflect the scientific consensus that is articulated in the Dietary Guidelines. Therefore, the Department believes that current nutrition standards must be expanded to incorporate the Dietary Guidelines in the NSLP and SBP regulations and is proposing to amend §§ 210.10 and 220.8 to require that school meals meet the applicable recommendations of the Dietary Guidelines including the quantified standards established for fat and saturated fat. Proposed regulations would also require schools to make an effort to reduce sodium and cholesterol, increase dietary fiber and serve a variety of foods. . . .

Accordingly, 7 CFR parts 210 and 220 are proposed to be amended as follows:

PART 210—NATIONAL SCHOOL LUNCH PROGRAM

8. A new section 210.10 is added to read as follows:

§ 210.10 Nutrition standards for lunches and menu planning systems

(a) Nutrition standards for reimbursable lunches. School food authorities shall ensure that participating schools provide nutritious and well-balanced meals to children based on the nutrition standards provided in this section. . . . For the purposes of this section, the nutrition standards are:

(1) Provision of one-third of the Recommended Dietary Allowances (RDA) of protein, calcium, iron, vitamin A and vitamin C to the applicable age groups in accordance with the Minimum Nutrient Levels for School Lunches in paragraph (e)(4)(i) of this section;

(2) Provision of the lunchtime energy allowances for children based on the four age groups provided for in the Minimum Nutrient Levels for School Lunches in paragraph (e)(4) of this section;

(3) The applicable 1990 Dietary Guidelines for Americans which are:

(i) Eat a variety of foods;

(ii) Limit total fat to 30 percent of calories;

(iii) Limit saturated fat to less than 10 percent of calories;

(iv) Choose a diet low in cholesterol;

(v) Choose a diet with plenty of vegetables, fruits, and grain products; and

(vi) Use salt and sodium in moderation; and

(4) The following measures of compliance with the 1990 Dietary Guidelines for Americans:

(i) A limit on the percent of calories from total fat to 30 percent based on the actual number of calories offered;

(ii) A limit on the percent of calories from saturated fat to less than 10 percent based on the actual number of calories offered;

(iii) A reduction of the levels of sodium and cholesterol; and

(iv) An increase in the level of dietary fiber.

CHOCOLATE MANUFACTURERS ASSOCIATION v. BLOCK

755 F.2d 1098 (4th Cir.1985).

SPROUSE, CIRCUIT JUDGE:

Chocolate Manufacturers Association (CMA) appeals from the decision of the district court denying it relief from a rule promulgated by the Food and Nutrition Service (FNS) of the United States Department of Agriculture (USDA or Department). CMA protests that part of the rule that prohibits the use of chocolate flavored milk in the federally funded Special Supplemental Food Program for Women, Infants and Children (WIC Program). Holding that the Department's proposed rulemaking did not provide adequate notice that the elimination of flavored milk would be considered in the rulemaking procedure, we reverse.

I

. . . The WIC Program was established by Congress in 1972 to assist pregnant, postpartum, and breastfeeding women, infants and young children from families with inadequate income whose physical and mental health is in danger because of inadequate nutrition or health care. Under the program, the Department designs food packages reflecting the different nutritional needs of women, infants, and children and provides cash grants to state or local agencies, which distribute cash or vouchers to qualifying individuals in accordance with Departmental regulations as to the type and quantity of food.

[T]he Department in November 1979 published for comment the proposed rule at issue in this case. Along with the proposed rule, the Department published a preamble discussing the general purpose of the rule and acknowledging the congressional directive that the Department design food packages containing the requisite nutritional value and appropriate levels of fat, sugar, and salt. Discussing the issue of sugar at length, it noted, for example, that continued inclusion of high sugar cereals may be "contrary to nutrition education principles and may lead to unsound eating practices." It also noted that high sugar foods are more expensive than foods with lower sugar content, and that allowing them would be "inconsistent with the goal of teaching participants economical food buying patterns."

The rule proposed a maximum sugar content specifically for authorized cereals. The preamble also contained a discussion of the sugar content in juice, but the Department did not propose to reduce the allowable amount of sugar in juice because of technical problems involved in any reduction. Neither the rule nor the preamble discussed sugar in relation to flavoring in milk. Under the proposed rule, the food packages for women and children without special dietary needs included milk that could be "flavored or unflavored."

The notice allowed sixty days for comment and specifically invited comment on the entire scope of the proposed rules: "The public is invited to submit written comments in favor of or in objection to the proposed regulations or to make recommendations for alternatives not considered in the proposed regulations." Over 1,000 comments were received from state and local agencies, congressional offices, interest groups, and WIC Program participants and others. Seventy-eight commenters, mostly local WIC administrators, recommended that the agency delete flavored milk from the list of approved supplemental foods.

In promulgating the final rule, the Department, responding to these public comments, deleted flavored milk from the list, explaining:

> In the previous regulations, women and children were allowed to receive flavored or unflavored milk. No change in this provision was proposed by the Department. However, 78 commenters requested the deletion of flavored milk from the food packages since flavored milk has a higher sugar content than unflavored milk. They indicated that providing flavored milk contradicts nutrition education and the Department's proposal to limit sugar in the food packages. Furthermore, flavored milk is more expensive than unflavored milk. The Department agrees with these concerns. . . .

Therefore, to reinforce nutrition education, for consistency with the Department's philosophy about sugar in the food packages, and to maintain food package costs at economic levels, the Department is deleting flavored milk from the food packages for women and children. Although the deletion of flavored milk was not proposed, the comments and the Department's policy on sugar validate this change. . . .

On this appeal, CMA contends first that the Department did not provide notice that the disallowance of flavored milk would be considered, and second that the Department gave no reasoned justification for changing its position about the nutritional value of chocolate in the food distributed under its authority. The Department responds to the first contention by arguing that its notice advised the public of its general concern about high sugar content in the proposed food packages and that this should have alerted potentially interested commenters that it would consider eliminating any food with high sugar content. It also argues in effect that the inclusion of flavored milk in the proposed rule carried with it the implication that both inclusion and exclusion would be considered in the rulemaking process. Because we agree with CMA that the Department provided inadequate notice and, therefore, that it must reopen the comment period on the rule, we do not reach the issue of the reasonable justification for its change of position.

II

The requirement of notice and a fair opportunity to be heard is basic to administrative law. Our single chore is to determine if the Department's notice provided interested persons, including CMA, with that opportunity. We must decide whether inclusion of flavored milk in the allowable food packages under the proposed rule should have alerted interested persons that the Department might reverse its position and exclude flavored milk if adverse comments recommended its deletion from the program.

Section 4 of the Administrative Procedure Act (APA) requires that the notice in the Federal Register of a proposed rulemaking contain "either the terms or substance of the proposed rule or a description of the subjects and issues involved." The purpose of the notice-and-comment procedure is both "to allow the agency to benefit from the experience and input of the parties who file comments . . . and to see to it that the agency maintains a flexible and open-minded attitude towards its own rules." The notice-and-comment procedure encourages public participation in the administrative process and educates the agency, thereby helping to ensure informed agency decisionmaking.

The Department's published notice here consisted of the proposed rule and a preamble discussing the negative effect of high sugar content in general and specifically in relation to some foods such as cereals and juices, but it did not mention high sugar content in flavored milk. The proposed rule eliminated certain foods with high sugar content but specifically authorized flavored milk as part of the permissible diet. In a discussion characterized by pointed identification of foods with high sugar content, flavored milk was conspicuous by its exclusion. If after comments the agency had adopted without change the proposed rule as its final rule, there could have been no possible objection to the adequacy of notice. The public was fully notified as to what the Department considered to be a healthy and adequate diet for its target group. The final rule, however, dramatically altered the proposed rule, changing for the first time the milk content of the diet by deleting flavored milk. The agency concedes that the elimination of flavored milk by the final rule is a complete reversal from its treatment in the proposed rule, but it explains that the reversal was caused by the comments received from 78 interested parties—primarily professional administrators of the WIC Program.

This presents then not the simple question of whether the notice of a proposed rule adequately informs the public of its intent, but rather the question of how to judge the adequacy of the notice when the proposal it describes is replaced by a final rule which reaches a conclusion exactly opposite to that proposed, on the basis of comments received from parties representing only a single view of a controversy. In reviewing the propriety of such agency action, we are not constrained by the same degree of deference we afford most agency determinations. "Though our review of an agency's final decision is relatively narrow, we must be strict in reviewing an agency's compliance with procedural rules." "The question of adequacy of notice where a proposed rule is changed after comment . . . requires careful consideration on a case-by-case basis."

There is no question that an agency may promulgate a final rule that differs in some particulars from its proposal. Otherwise the agency "can learn from the comments on its proposals only at the peril of starting a new procedural round of commentary." An agency, however, does not have carte blanche to establish a rule contrary to its original proposal simply because it receives suggestions to alter it during the comment period. An interested party must have been alerted by the notice to the possibility of the changes eventually adopted from the comments. Although an agency, in its notice of proposed rulemaking, need not identify precisely every potential regulatory change, the notice must be sufficiently descriptive to provide interested parties with a fair opportunity to comment and to participate in the rulemaking. . . .

The test devised by the First Circuit for determining adequacy of notice of a change in a proposed rule occurring after comments appears to us to be sound: notice is adequate if the changes in the original plan "are in character with the original scheme," and the final rule is a "logical outgrowth" of the notice and comments already given. Other circuits also have adopted some form of the "logical outgrowth" test. Stated differently, if the final rule materially alters the issues involved in the rulemaking or, if the final rule "substantially departs from the terms or substance of the proposed rule," the notice is inadequate.

There can be no doubt that the final rule in the instant case was the "outgrowth" of the original rule proposed by the agency, but the question of whether the change in it was in character with the original scheme and whether it was a "logical outgrowth" is not easy to answer. In resolving this difficult issue, we recognize that, although helpful, verbal formulations are not omnipotent talismans, and we agree that in the final analysis each case "must turn on how well the notice that the agency gave serves the policies underlying the notice requirement." Under either view, we do not feel that CMA was fairly treated or that the administrative rulemaking process was well served by the drastic alteration of the rule without an opportunity for CMA to be heard.

It is apparent that for many years the Department of Agriculture has permitted the use of chocolate in some form in the food distribution programs that it administers.... Chocolate flavored milk has been a permissible part of the WIC Program diet since its inception and there have been no proposals for its removal until the present controversy....

The published preamble to the proposed rule consisted of twelve pages in the Federal Register discussing in detail factors that would be considered in making the final rule. Two pages were devoted to a general discussion of nutrients, including protein, iron, calcium, vitamin A, vitamin C, folic acid, zinc, and fiber, and the dangers of overconsumption of sugar, fat, and salt. The preamble discussed some foods containing these ingredients and foods posing specific problems. It did not discuss flavored milk.

In the next eight pages of the preamble, the nutrition content of food packages was discussed—under the general headings of "cereal" and "juice" for infants; and "eggs," "milk," "cheese," "peanut butter and mature dried beans and peas," "juice," "additional foods," "cereals," "iron," "sugar," "whole grain cereals," "highly fortified cereals," and "artificial flavors and colors" for women and children. The only reference to milk concerned the correct quantity to be provided to children, i.e., 24 quarts per month instead of 28 quarts. Although there was considerable discussion of the sugar content of juice and cereal, there was none concerning flavored milk. Likewise, there was considerable discussion of artificial flavor and color in cereal but none concerning flavored milk. The only reference to flavored milk was in the two-page discussion of the individual food packages, which noted that the proposed rule would permit the milk to be flavored or unflavored. The proposed rule which followed the preamble expressly noted that flavored or unflavored milk was permitted in the individual food packages for women and children without special dietary needs.

At the time the proposed rulemaking was published, neither CMA nor the public in general could have had any indication from the history of either the WIC Program or any other food distribution programs that flavored milk was not part of the acceptable diet for women and children without special dietary needs. The discussion in the preamble to the proposed rule was very detailed and identified specific foods which the agency was examining for excess sugar. This specificity, together with total silence concerning any suggestion of eliminating flavored milk, strongly indicated that flavored milk was not at issue. The proposed rule positively and unqualifiedly approved the continued use of flavored milk. Under the specific circumstances of this case, it cannot be said that the ultimate changes in the proposed rule were in character with the original scheme or a logical outgrowth of the notice. We can well accept that, in general, an approval of a practice in a proposed rule may properly alert interested parties that the practice may be disapproved in the final rule in the event of adverse comments. The total effect of the history of the use of flavored milk, the preamble discussion, and the proposed rule, however, could have led interested persons only to conclude that a change in flavored milk would not be considered. Although ultimately their comments may well have been futile, CMA and other interested persons at least should have had the opportunity to make them. We believe that there was insufficient notice that the deletion of flavored milk from the WIC Program would be considered if adverse comments were received, and, therefore, that affected parties did not receive a fair opportunity to contribute to the administrative rulemaking process. That process was ill-served by the misleading or inadequate notice concerning the permissibility of chocolate flavored milk in the WIC Program and "does not serve the policy underlying the notice requirement."

The judgment of the district court is therefore reversed, and the case is remanded to the administrative agency with instructions to reopen the comment period and thereby afford interested parties a fair opportunity to comment on the proposed changes in the rule.

Notes and Questions

1. To make the logical outgrowth test more concrete, the Seventh Circuit articulated the following principles to determine the adequacy of a NPRM:

> ... The adequacy of notice in any case must be determined by a close examination of the facts of the particular proceeding which produced a challenged rule. However, without reciting in detail the facts of other cases, we note that courts have upheld final rules which differed from proposals in the following significant respects: outright reversal of the agency's initial position; elimination of compliance options contained in an NPR; collapsing, or further subdividing, distinct categories of regulated entities established in a proposed rule; exempting certain entities from the coverage of final rules; or altering the method of calculating or measuring a quantity relevant to a party's obligations under the rule.

> On the other hand, a rule will be invalidated if no notice was given of an issue addressed by the final rules. Moreover, courts have held on numerous occasions that notice is inadequate where an issue was only addressed in the most general terms in the initial proposal, or where a final rule changes a pre-existing agency practice which

was only mentioned in an NPR in order to place unrelated changes in the overall regulatory scheme into their proper context.

The crucial issue, then, is whether parties affected by a final rule were put on notice that "their interests [were] 'at stake' "; in other words, the relevant inquiry is whether or not potential commentators would have known that an issue in which they were interested was "on the table" and was to be addressed by a final rule. From this perspective it is irrelevant whether the proposal contained in the NPR was favorable to a particular party's interests; the obligation to comment is not limited to those adversely affected by a proposal. "[A]pproval of a practice in a proposed rule may properly alert interested parties that the practice may be disapproved in the final rule in the event of adverse comments."

American Medical Association v. United States, 887 F.2d 760, 767–68 (7th Cir.1989).

2. If some parties comment on an issue, is this sufficient evidence that the original notice was adequate to provide interested parties with a fair opportunity to comment on that issue? Compare *United Steelworkers of America v. Schuyekill Metal Corp.*, 828 F.2d 314, 318 (5th Cir.1987) (rejecting claim that the notice was not adequate to raise an issue because other parties had commented on the issue) with *AFL–CIO v. Donovan*, 757 F.2d 330 (D.C.Cir.1985) (existence of comments on an issue is evidence of the adequacy of the original notice, but the adequacy of the notice cannot be established based on such comments alone). Why might courts be reluctant to accept the existence of comments as adequate proof of the adequacy of the original notice?

3. If the National Association of Beef Producers wins its lawsuit, USDA will have to undertake another round of notice and comment rulemaking, assuming that it still wants to promulgate new nutritional guidelines. Have the beef producers won a Pyrrhic victory? How likely is it that USDA will adopt the same rule that was struck down? What do the beef producers gain if USDA adopts an identical rule?

4. One administrative law expert has offered the following advice to agency attorneys who are responsible for drafting a notice of proposed rulemaking that is adequate to sustain changes in a proposed rule:

Although specific proposals are valuable in focusing comment, they may ultimately place the agency at a disadvantage, in that the proposal's very specificity might limit the options available in the final rule. On the other hand, although a generally worded proposal may well avoid some of the restrictions of a too-specific proposal, an agency must be careful that such a proposal is not so general that it affords inadequate notice of particular issues in the proceeding. . . .

One way an agency can both set forth specific proposals in an NRPM and retain flexibility in fashioning the final rule is to include in the NPRM several alternatives that are under considerations. . . .

A related approach would be for the agency, in addition to its specific proposal, to pose a series of questions going beyond the terms of the proposal on which it seeks comment.

JEFFREY S. LUBBERS, A GUIDE TO FEDERAL AGENCY RULEMAKING 190–91(3d ed. 1998).

If you were the attorney for USDA who wrote the notice for the new nutrition guidelines, how could you employ these techniques? Is there any disadvantage to using them?

b. *Opportunity for Comment*

As the previous materials make clear, the purpose of the NPRM is to enable interested persons to comment on the proposed rule. Accordingly, section 553(c) requires agencies to provide interested persons an opportunity to comment "through submission of written data, views, or arguments." There is no requirement for an oral presentation or hearing. Moreover, the APA does not mandate any specific time period for this opportunity. It does have a requirement that final rules must be published 30 days prior to their effective date, *id.* § 553(d), which is sometimes misinterpreted as mandating a 30 day comment period. Again, this is an area that Congress has often chosen to add "hybrid" requirements, specifying a minimum time period for comments in some statutes. The Safe Drinking Water Act, for example, requires a minimum 60 day comment period for certain rules. 42 U.S.C.A. § 300g–1(b)(2)(B). Even without a requirement of this type, most agencies will provide for 60 or more days for complex or controversial rules, and they will often extend the time for comments if requested to do so. An agency will announce a time extension in the Federal Register.

A question that arises in informal rulemaking is what constraints exist with respect to how these comments might be made. The NPRM indicates where comments should be sent and by what date, but may interested persons make comments through other means as well? In other words, can they continue lobbying? In *formal rulemaking* the APA places specific prohibition on ex parte communications—that is, communications made to decisionmakers in the agency outside of the prescribed (and public) procedures. *See* 5 U.S.C.A. § 557(d). Section 553, by comparison, does not prohibit such contacts in informal rulemaking. Congress can, and sometime does, prohibit or limit such contacts in an agency's mandate. Moreover, an agency can adopt prohibitions or limitations on its own. For example, the FTC at one time prohibited all ex parte contacts between Commissioners and outside persons or staff assistants during a rulemaking. 42 Fed. Reg. 43973–74 (1977). In 1980, Congress established statutory ex parte limitations applicable to certain FTC rulemakings. 15 U.S.C.A. § 57(a)–(j).

Finally, *Sangamon Valley Television Corp. v. United States*, 269 F.2d 221 (D.C.Cir.1959), held that due process prohibits ex parte contacts when rulemaking involves "conflicting claims to a valuable privilege." The case involved a rule promulgated by the Federal Communications

Commission (FCC). One of the FCC's functions is to allocate the radio spectrum to different uses, such as radio, television, cellular telephones, and other uses. The FCC rule determined that a VHF channel, used by a television station in Springfield, Illinois, should be transferred to St. Louis, and two UHF channels, used by St. Louis stations, should be transferred to Springfield. The VHF channel was more valuable because it reached more viewers with better reception. While the rule was under consideration, representatives of a St. Louis UHF station that was interested in having a new VHF channel assigned to St. Louis, and representatives of two Springfield business interests, which were interested in retaining the VHF channel, made ex parte presentations to various FCC commissioners with respect to the merits of the rulemaking proceeding.

The court held that such contacts were not permissible and offered this brief explanation:

> The Commissioner and the intervenor contend that because the proceeding now on review was "rule-making," ex parte attempts to influence the Commissioners did not invalidate it. The Department of Justice disagrees. On behalf of the United States, the Department urges that whatever the proceeding may be called it involved not only allocation of TV channels among communities but also resolution of conflicting claims to a valuable privilege, and that basic fairness requires such a proceeding to be carried out in the open. We agree with the Department of Justice. Accordingly, private approaches to members of the Commission vitiated its action and the proceeding must be reopened.

269 F.2d at 224.

Problem 2–6: Ex Parte Communications

In the previous problem, the Department of Agriculture had proposed a rule to update the nutrition standards for school lunches and, last we heard, on the basis of the comments received, it seem disposed to adopt the arguments of VEGI to require at least five vegetarian meals a month. Imagine that the National Association of Beef Producers (NABP) learns that USDA is in the process of trying to write a preamble justifying this decision, and it wants to engage in a concerted effort to try to demonstrate to the Secretary of Agriculture that such a requirement would impose additional costs while actually harming students' health. Students will discard the vegetables and not eat lunch at all, probably substituting snacks and candy instead of a nutritious, filling, and tasty meat main course. NABP contacts senators and congresspersons from Iowa, Kansas, Texas, and Florida to tell them about USDA's expected action. In addition, NABP contacts the Office of Management and Budget, in the Executive Office of the President, to present its case that USDA is about to make a terrible mistake. Finally, NABP writes and phones the Secretary of Agriculture, asking for an appointment to speak to him about the depressed state of cattle prices and the school lunch program. The Secretary has already had calls from Capitol Hill "requesting" him to come visit with a group of members of Congress from cattle states. His secretary has given him a message that the President's domestic policy adviser has asked him to prepare a briefing for the President on the School Lunch regulations.

Assume you are a lawyer with the General Counsel's office in the Department of Agriculture. The Secretary wants to know what he can and cannot do in response to this onslaught. As someone who answers to the President, who must deal with Congress every day, and who is supposed to look out for the interests of agricultural interests (as well as run the school lunch program), he would like to meet with these people and hear them out, but he does not want to do anything illegal or anything that would jeopardize whatever rule USDA adopts.

Problem Materials

HOME BOX OFFICE v. FEDERAL COMMUNICATIONS COMMISSION

567 F.2d 9 (D.C.Cir.1977).

PER CURIAM:

[In the early days of cable television, the FCC strictly regulated what cable programmers could provide, for fear that cable would destroy the broadcast TV industry, to the ultimate detriment of the public interest. In this rulemaking, the FCC had proposed to loosen those restrictions somewhat. After the comment period, however, the FCC met with many of the interested parties, trying to negotiate an outcome acceptable to all. After the rule was adopted, however, it was challenged by a number of the parties. One of the issues was the ex parte communications the FCC had engaged in.]

... It is apparently uncontested that a number of participants before the Commission sought out individual commissioners or Commission employees for the purpose of discussing *ex parte* and in confidence the merits of the rules under review here. In fact, the Commission itself solicited such communications in its notices of proposed rulemaking.... In an attempt to clarify the facts this court *sua sponte* ordered the Commission to provide "a list of all of the *ex parte* presentations, together with the details of each, made to it, or to any of its members or representatives, during the rulemaking proceedings." In response to this order the Commission filed a document over 60 pages long which revealed, albeit imprecisely, widespread *ex parte* communications involving virtually every party before this court....

Unfortunately, the document filed with this court does not allow an assessment of what was said to the Commission by the various persons who engaged in ex parte contacts. To give a flavor of the effect of these contacts, however, we think it useful to quote at length from the brief of amicus Geller:

> [*Ex parte*] presentations have in fact been made at crucial stages of the proceeding. Thus, in early 1974, then-Chairman Burch sought to complete action in this proceeding. Because the Commission was "leaning" in its deliberations towards relaxing the existing rules "with 'wildcard' rights for 'blockbuster' movies," American Broadcasting Company's representatives contacted "key members of Congress," who in turn successfully pressured the Commission not to take such action. Further, in the final crucial decisional period, the tentative course to be taken by the Commission would leak after each non-public meeting, and industry representatives would rush to make ex parte presentations to the Commissioners and staff. . . .

It is important to note that many contacts occurred in the crucial period between the close of oral argument on October 25, 1974 and the adoption of the *First Report and Order* on March 20, 1975, when the rulemaking record should have been closed while the Commission was deciding what rules to promulgate. The information submitted to this court by the Commission indicates that during this period broadcast interests met some 18 times with Commission personnel, cable interests some nine times, motion picture and sports interests five times each, and "public interest" intervenors not at all.

Although it is impossible to draw any firm conclusions about the effect of ex parte presentations upon the ultimate shape of the pay cable rules, the evidence is certainly consistent with often-voiced claims of undue industry influence over Commission proceedings, and we are particularly concerned that the final shaping of the rules we are reviewing here may have been by compromise among the contending industry forces, rather than by exercise of the independent discretion in the public interest the Communications Act vests in individual commissioners. Our concern is heightened by the submission of the Commission's Broadcast Bureau to this court which states that in December 1974 broadcast representatives "described the kind of pay cable regulation that, in their view, broadcasters 'could live with.' " If actual positions were not revealed in public comments, as this statement would suggest, and, further, if the Commission relied on these apparently more candid private discussions in framing the final pay cable rules, then the elaborate public discussion in these dockets has been reduced to a sham.

Even the possibility that there is here one administrative record for the public and this court and another for the Commission and those "in the know" is intolerable. Whatever the law may have been in the past, there can now be no doubt that implicit in the decision to treat the promulgation of rules as a "final" event in an ongoing process of administration is an assumption that an act of reasoned judgment has occurred, an assumption which further contemplates the existence of a body of material documents, comments, transcripts, and statements in various forms declaring agency expertise or policy with reference to which such judgment was exercised. Against this material, "the full administrative record that was before (an agency official) at the time he made his decision," it is the obligation of this court to test the actions of the Commission for arbitrariness or inconsistency with delegated authority. Yet here agency secrecy stands between us and fulfillment of our obligation. . . .

The failure of the public record in this proceeding to disclose all the information made available to the Commission is not the only inadequacy we find here. Even if the Commission had disclosed to this court the substance of what was said to it *ex parte*, it would still be difficult to judge the truth of what the Commission asserted it knew about the television industry because we would not have the benefit of an adversarial discussion among the parties. The importance of such discussion to the proper functioning of the agency decisionmaking and judicial review processes is evident in our cases. We have insisted, for example, that information in agency files or consultants' reports which the agency has identified as relevant to the proceeding be disclosed to the parties for adversarial comment. Similarly, we have required agencies to set out their thinking in notices of proposed rulemaking. This requirement not only allows adversarial critique of the agency but is perhaps one of the few ways that the public may be apprised of what the agency thinks it knows in its capacity as a repository of expert opinion. From a functional standpoint, we see no difference between assertions of fact and expert opinion tendered by the public, as here, and that generated internally in an agency: each may be biased, inaccurate, or incomplete—failings which adversary comment may illuminate. . . .

From what has been said above, it should be clear that information gathered *ex parte* from the public which becomes relevant to a rulemaking will have to be disclosed at some time. On the other hand, we recognize that informal contacts between agencies and the public are the "bread and butter" of the process of administration and are completely appropriate so long as they do not frustrate judicial review or raise serious questions of fairness. Reconciliation of these considerations in a manner which will reduce procedural uncertainty leads us to conclude that communications which are received prior to issuance of a formal notice of rulemaking do not, in general, have to be put in a public file. Of course, if the information contained in such a communication forms the basis for agency action, then, under well established principles, that information must be disclosed to the public in some form. Once a notice of proposed rulemaking has been issued, however, any agency official or employee who is or may reasonably be expected to be involved in the decisional process of the rulemaking proceeding, should "refus[e] to discuss matters relating to the disposition of a [rulemaking proceeding] with any interested private party, or an attorney or agent for any such party, prior to the [agency's] decision * * *." If ex parte contacts nonetheless occur, we think that any written document or a summary of any oral communication must be placed in the public file established for each rulemaking docket immediately after the communication is received so that interested parties may comment thereon.

SIERRA CLUB v. COSTLE

657 F.2d 298 (D.C.Cir.1981).

WALD, CIRCUIT JUDGE:

[This case involved EPA's adoption of a rule pursuant to the 1977 Amendments to the Clean Air Act to govern emissions from coal burning power plants. During the pendency of the rulemaking, EPA was the subject of ex parte contacts by interested parties, legislators, and the President's staff.]

V. THE 1.2 LBS./MBTU EMISSION CEILING

[The Environmental Defense Fund (EDF)] challenges this part of the final regulation on procedural grounds, contending that although there may be evidence supporting the 1.2 lbs./MBtu standard, EPA should have and would have adopted a stricter standard if it had not engaged in post-comment period irregularities and succumbed to political pressures. . . .

B. *EDF's Procedural Attack*

EDF alleges that as a result of an "ex parte blitz" by coal industry advocates conducted after the close of the comment period, EPA backed away from adopting the .55 lbs./MBtu limit, and instead adopted the higher 1.2 lbs./MBtu restriction. . . . "Scores" of pro-industry "ex parte" comments were received by EPA in the post-comment period, states EDF, and various meetings with coal industry advocates including Senator Robert Byrd of West Virginia took place during that period. These communications, EDF asserts, were unlawful and prejudicial to its position.

In order for this court to assess these claims, we must identify the particular actions and incidents which gave rise to EDF's complaints. Aside from a passing reference to a telephone call from an EPA official to the Chief Executive Officer of the National Coal Association, EDF's procedural objections stem from either (1) comments filed after the close of the official comment period, or (2) meetings between EPA officials and various government and private parties interested in the outcome of the final rule, all of which took place after the close of the comment period.

1. *Late Comments*

The comment period for the [regulation] began on September 19, 1978, and closed on January 15, 1979. After January 15, EPA received almost 300 written submissions on the proposed rule from a broad range of interests. EPA accepted these comments and entered them all on its administrative docket. EPA did not, however, officially reopen the comment period, nor did it notify the public through the Federal Register or by other means that it had received and was entering the "late" comments. . . .

2. Meetings

EDF objects to nine different meetings. . . .

EDF believes that the communications just outlined, when taken as a whole, were so extensive and had such a serious impact on the NSPS rulemaking, that they violated EDF's rights to due process in the proceeding, and that these "ex parte" contacts were procedural errors of such magnitude that this court must reverse. EDF does not specify which particular features in each of the above-enumerated communications violated due process or constituted errors under the statute; indeed, EDF nowhere lists the communications in a form designed to clarify why any particular communication was unlawful. Instead, EDF labels all post-comment communications with EPA from whatever source and in whatever form as "ex parte," and claims that "this court has repeatedly stated that ex parte contacts of substance violate due process."

At the outset, we decline to begin our task of reviewing EPA's procedures by labeling all post-comment communications with the agency as "ex parte." Such an approach essentially begs the question whether these particular communications in an informal rulemaking proceeding were unlawful. Instead of beginning with a conclusion that these communications were "ex parte," we must evaluate the various communications in terms of their timing, source, mode, content, and the extent of their disclosure on the docket, in order to discover whether any of them violated the procedural requirements of the Clean Air Act, or of due process.

C. Standard for Judicial Review of EPA Procedures

This court's scope of review is delimited by the special procedural provisions of the Clean Air Act, which declare that we may reverse the Administrator's decision for procedural error only if (i) his failure to observe procedural requirements was arbitrary and capricious, (ii) an objection was raised during the comment period, or the grounds for such objection arose only after the comment period and the objection is "of central relevance to the outcome of the rule," and (iii) "the errors were so serious and related to matters of such central relevance to the rule that there is a substantial likelihood that the rule would have been significantly changed if such errors had not been made." The essential message of so rigorous a standard is that Congress was concerned that EPA's rulemaking not be casually overturned for procedural reasons, and we of course must respect that judgment.

Our authority to reverse informal administrative rulemaking for procedural reasons is also informed by *Vermont Yankee Nuclear Power Corp. v. Natural Resources Defense Council, Inc.* In its unanimous opinion, the Supreme Court unambiguously cautioned this court against imposing its own notions of proper procedures upon an administrative agency entrusted with substantive functions by Congress....

D.   Statutory Provisions Concerning Procedure

[T]he 1977 Amendments required the agency to establish a "rule-making docket" for each proposed rule which would form the basis of the record for judicial review. [Section 307 of the Act requires the docket to] contain, inter alia, (1) "notice of the proposed rulemaking ... accompanied by a statement of its basis and purpose," and a specification of the public comment period; (2) "all written comments and documentary information on the proposed rule received from any person ... during the comment period(;) (t)he transcript of public hearings, if any(;) and (a)ll documents ... which become available after the proposed rule has been published and which the Administrator determines are of central relevance to the rulemaking...."; (3) drafts of proposed rules submitted for interagency review, and all documents accompanying them and responding to them; and (4) the promulgated rule and the various accompanying agency documents which explain and justify it.

In contrast to other recent statutes, there is no mention of any restrictions upon "ex parte" contacts. However, the statute apparently did envision that participants would normally submit comments, documentary material, and oral presentations during a prescribed comment period. Only two provisions in the statute touch upon the post-comment period, one of which, as noted immediately supra, states that "(a)ll documents which become available after the proposed rule has been published and which the Administrator determines are of central relevance to the rulemaking shall be placed in the docket as soon as possible after their availability." But since all the post-comment period written submissions which EDF complains of were in fact entered upon the docket, EDF cannot complain that this provision has been violated.

[S]ince this court can reverse an agency on procedural grounds only if it finds a failure to observe procedures "required by law," we must first decide whether the procedures followed by EPA between January 15 and June 1, 1979 were unlawful. Only if we so find would we then face the second issue whether the unlawful errors were "of such central relevance to the rule that there is a substantial likelihood that the rule would have been significantly changed if such errors had not been made." We now hold that EPA's procedures during the post-comment period were lawful, and therefore do not face the issue whether any alleged errors were of "central relevance" to the outcome.

E.   Validity of EPA's Procedures During the Post–Comment Period

The post-comment period communications about which EDF complains vary widely in their content and mode; some are written documents or letters, others are oral conversations and briefings, while still others are meetings where alleged political arm-twisting took place. For analytical purposes we have grouped the communications into categories and shall discuss each of them separately. As a general matter, however, we note at the outset that nothing in the statute prohibits EPA from admitting all post-comment communications into the record; nothing expressly requires it, either. Most likely the drafters envisioned promulgation of a rule soon after the close of the public comment period, and did not envision a months-long hiatus where continued outside communications with the agency would continue unabated. We must therefore attempt to glean the law for this case by inference from the procedural framework provided in the statute.

1. Written Comments Submitted During Post–Comment Period

Although no express authority to admit post-comment documents exists, the statute does provide that: All documents which become available after the proposed rule has been published and which the Administrator determines are of central relevance to the rulemaking shall be placed in the docket as soon as possible after their availability.

This provision, in contrast to others in the same subparagraph, is not limited to the comment period. Apparently it allows EPA not only to put documents into the record after the comment period is over, but also to define which documents are "of central relevance" so as to require that they be placed in the docket. The principal purpose of the drafters was to define in advance, for the benefit of reviewing courts, the record upon which EPA would rely in defending the rule it finally adopted; it was not their purpose to guarantee that every piece of paper or phone call related to the rule which was received by EPA during the post-comment period be included in the docket. EPA thus has authority to place post-comment documents into the docket, but it need not do so in all instances.

Such a reading of the statute accords well with the realities of Washington administrative policymaking, where rumors, leaks, and over-reactions by concerned groups abound, particularly as the time for promulgation draws near. In a proceeding such as this, one of vital concern to so many interests, industry, environmental groups, as well as Congress and the Administration it would be unrealistic to think there would not naturally be attempts on all sides to stay in contact with EPA right up to the moment the final rule is promulgated. The drafters of the 1977 Amendments were practical people, well versed in such activity, and we decline now to infer from their silence that they intended to prohibit the lodging of documents with the agency at any time prior to promulgation. Common sense, after all, must play a part in our interpretation of these statutory procedures.

EPA of course could have extended, or reopened, the comment period after January 15 in order formally to accommodate the flood of new documents; it has done so in other cases. But under the circumstances of this case, we do not find that it was necessary for EPA to reopen the formal comment period. In the first place, the comment period lasted over four months, and although the length of the comment period was not specified in the 1977 Amendments, the statute did put a premium on speedy decisionmaking by setting a one year deadline from the Amendments' enactment to the rules' promulgation. . . .

If, however, documents of central importance upon which EPA intended to rely had been entered on the docket too late for any meaningful public comment prior to promulgation, then both the structure and spirit of section 307 would have been violated. The Congressional drafters, after all, intended to provide "thorough and careful procedural safeguards . . . (to) insure an effective opportunity for public participation in the rulemaking process." . . .

The case before us, however, does not present an instance where documents vital to EPA's support for its rule were submitted so late as to preclude any effective public comment, [and] EDF itself has failed to show us any particular document or documents to which it lacked an opportunity to respond, and which also were vital to EPA's support for the rule.

2. Meetings Held With Individuals Outside EPA

The statute does not explicitly treat the issue of post-comment period meetings with individuals outside EPA. Oral face-to-face discussions are not prohibited anywhere, anytime, in the Act. The absence of such prohibition may have arisen from the nature of the informal rulemaking procedures Congress had in mind. Where agency action resembles judicial action, where it involves formal rulemaking, adjudication, or quasi-adjudication among "conflicting private claims to a valuable privilege," the insulation of the decisionmaker from ex parte contacts is justified by basic notions of due process to the parties involved. But where agency action involves informal rulemaking of a policymaking sort, the concept of ex parte contacts is of more questionable utility.

Under our system of government, the very legitimacy of general policymaking performed by unelected administrators depends in no small part upon the openness, accessibility, and amenability of these officials to the needs and ideas of the public from whom their ultimate authority derives, and upon whom their commands must fall. As judges we are insulated from these pressures because of the nature of the judicial process in which we participate; but we must refrain from the easy temptation to look askance at all face-to-face lobbying efforts, regardless of the forum in which they occur, merely because we see them as inappropriate in the judicial context. Furthermore, the importance to effective regulation of continuing contact with a regulated industry, other affected groups, and the public cannot be underestimated. Informal contacts may enable the agency to win needed support for its program, reduce future enforcement requirements by helping those regulated to anticipate and shape their plans for the future, and spur the provision of information which the agency needs. The possibility of course exists that in permitting ex parte communications with rulemakers we create the danger of "one administrative record for the public and this court and another for the Commission." Under the Clean Air Act procedures, however, "(t)he promulgated rule may not be based (in part or whole) on any information or data which has not been placed in the docket. . . ." Thus EPA must justify its rulemaking solely on the basis of the record it compiles and makes public.

Regardless of this court's views on the need to restrict all post-comment contacts in the informal rulemaking context, however, it is clear to us that Congress has decided not to do so in the statute which controls this case. . . .

Lacking a statutory basis for its position, EDF would have us extend our decision in *Home Box Office, Inc. v. FCC* to cover all meetings with individuals outside EPA during the post-comment period. Later decisions of this court, however, have declined to apply *Home Box Office* to informal rulemaking of the general policymaking sort involved here, and there is no precedent for applying it to the procedures found in the Clean Air Act Amendments of 1977.

It still can be argued, however, that if oral communications are to be freely permitted after the close of the comment period, then at least some adequate summary of them must be made in order to preserve the integrity of the rulemaking docket, which under the statute must be the sole repository of material upon which EPA intends to rely. The statute does not require the docketing of all post-comment period conversations and meetings, but we believe that a fair inference can be drawn that in some instances such docketing may be needed in order to give practical effect to section 307['s requirement] that all documents "of central relevance to the rulemaking" shall be placed in the docket as soon as possible after their availability. This is so because unless oral communications of central relevance to the rulemaking are also docketed in some fashion or other, information central to the justification of the rule could be obtained without ever appearing on the docket, simply by communicating it by voice rather than by pen, thereby frustrating the command of section 307 that the final rule not be "based (in part or whole) on any information or data which has not been placed in the docket. . . ."

EDF is understandably wary of a rule which permits the agency to decide for itself when oral communications are of such central relevance that a docket entry for them is required. Yet the statute itself vests EPA with discretion to decide whether "documents" are of central relevance and therefore must be placed in the docket; surely EPA can be given no less discretion in docketing oral communications, concerning which the statute has no explicit requirements whatsoever. Furthermore, this court has already recognized that the relative significance of various communications to the outcome of the rule is a factor in determining whether their disclosure is required. A judicially imposed blanket requirement that all post-comment period oral communications be docketed would, on the other hand, contravene our limited powers of review, would stifle desirable experimentation in the area by Congress and the agencies, and is unnecessary for achieving the goal of an established, procedure-defined docket, viz., to enable reviewing courts to fully evaluate the stated justification given by the agency for its final rule.

Turning to the particular oral communications in this case, we find that only two of the nine contested meetings were undocketed by EPA. The agency has maintained that, as to the May 1 meeting where Senate staff people were briefed on EPA's analysis concerning the impact of alternative emissions ceilings upon coal reserves, its failure to place a summary of the briefing in the docket was an oversight. We find no evidence that this oversight was anything but an honest inadvertence; furthermore, a briefing of this sort by EPA which simply provides background information about an upcoming rule is not the type of oral communication which would require a docket entry under the statute.

The other undocketed meeting occurred at the White House and involved the President and his White House staff. . . .

(a) Intra–Executive Branch Meetings

We have already held that a blanket prohibition against meetings during the post-comment period with individuals outside EPA is unwarranted, and this perforce applies to meetings with White House officials. We have not yet addressed, however, the issue whether such oral communications with White House staff, or the President himself, must be docketed on the rulemaking record, and we now turn to that issue. The facts, as noted earlier, present us with a single undocketed meeting held on April 30, 1979, at 10:00 a. m., attended by the President, White House staff, other high ranking members of the Executive Branch, as well as EPA officials, and which concerned the issues and options presented by the rulemaking.

We note initially that section 307 makes specific provision for including in the rulemaking docket the "written comments" of other executive agencies along with accompanying documents on any proposed draft rules circulated in advance of the rulemaking proceeding. . . . This specific requirement does not mention informal meetings or conversations concerning the rule . . . , nor does it refer to oral comments of any sort. Yet it is hard to believe Congress was unaware that intra-executive meetings and oral comments would occur throughout the rulemaking process. We assume, therefore, that unless expressly forbidden by Congress, such intra-executive contacts may take place, both during and after the public comment period; the only real issue is whether they must be noted and summarized in the docket.

The court recognizes the basic need of the President and his White House staff to monitor the consistency of executive agency regulations with Administration policy. He and his White House advisers surely must be briefed fully and frequently about rules in the making, and their contributions to policymaking considered. The executive power under our Constitution, after all, is not shared it rests exclusively with the President. . . .

We recognize, however, that there may be instances where the docketing of conversations between the President or his staff and other Executive Branch officers or rulemakers may be necessary to ensure due process. This may be true, for example, where such conversations directly concern the outcome of adjudications or quasi-adjudicatory proceedings; there is no inherent executive power to control the rights of individuals in such settings. Docketing may also be necessary in some circumstances where a statute like this one specifically requires that essential "information or data" upon which a rule is based be docketed. But in the absence of any further Congressional requirements, we hold that it was not unlawful in this case for EPA not to docket a face-to-face policy session involving the President and EPA officials during the post-comment period, since EPA makes no effort to base the rule on any "information or data" arising from that meeting. Where the President himself is directly involved in oral communications with Executive Branch officials, Article II considerations combined with the strictures of *Vermont Yankee* require that courts tread with extraordinary caution in mandating disclosure beyond that already required by statute.

The purposes of full-record review which underlie the need for disclosing ex parte conversations in some settings do not require that courts know the details of every White House contact, including a Presidential one, in this informal rulemaking setting. After all, any rule issued here with or without White House assistance must have the requisite factual support in the rulemaking record, and under this particular statute the Administrator may not base the rule in whole or in part on any "information or data" which is not in the record, no matter what the source. The courts will monitor all this, but they need not be omniscient to perform their role effectively. Of course, it is always possible that undisclosed Presidential prodding may direct an outcome that is factually based on the record, but different from the outcome that would have obtained in the absence of Presidential involvement. In such a case, it would be true that the political process did affect the outcome in a way the courts could not police. But we do not believe that Congress intended that the courts convert informal rulemaking into a rarified technocratic process, unaffected by political considerations or the presence of Presidential power. In sum, we find that the existence of intra-Executive Branch meetings during the post-comment period, and the failure to docket one such meeting involving the President, violated neither the procedures mandated by the Clean Air Act nor due process.

Notes and Questions

1. The D.C. Circuit's attitude toward ex parte communications seems to have changed between *Home Box Office* and *Sierra Club*. Can you think of any reason for the switch, such as an intervening Supreme Court case? *Home Box Office* itself seems to have been a fragile opinion; one of the three judges on the panel concurred specially to disagree with the majority's *ex parte* analysis, and in less than a year a different panel of the D.C. Circuit refused to apply *Home Box Office*'s *ex parte* analysis to another FCC case. Although that panel technically held that it would not apply *Home Box Office*'s analysis to activity occurring before the decision was rendered, the full opinion of the panel clearly indicated its

belief that *Home Box Office*'s strict *ex parte* rules were inappropriate in ordinary notice-and-comment rulemaking. *See Action for Children's Television v. FCC*, 564 F.2d 458 (D.C.Cir.1977). Even if *Home Box Office* is not "good law," can you think of any reasons why agencies might wish to follow it anyway?

2. Note that *Sierra Club* did not involve a challenge to EPA's procedures under Section 553 of the APA or under the APA at all, but rather involved a challenge under the Clean Air Act's own procedural requirements applicable to rulemaking. These requirements are much more specific than the comparable requirements of the APA. Is this a basis for distinction from the APA? See *Board of Regents v. Environmental Protection Agency*, 86 F.3d 1214, 1222 (D.C.Cir.1996) (distinguishing *Sierra Club* on the ground that, unlike the Clean Air Act, § 553 of the APA does not contain language requiring an agency to place all documents of "central relevance" to the rulemaking "proceeding" in the rulemaking docket).

3. In *Home Box Office* it seemed that an important part of the offense to the court was the fact that the information provided to the Commission had not been subjected to comment by opposing parties. In *Sierra Club*, the court specifically determined that EDF had adequate opportunity to respond to all the important new information provided EPA after the close of the comment period. Courts do continue to police agencies' use of information either received or generated by the agency and not made available for public comment. *See, e.g., Ober v. U.S. EPA*, 84 F.3d 304 (9th Cir.1996) (overturning EPA's approval of a state's Clean Air Act state implementation plan because EPA had invited and received over 300 pages of information from the state after the close of the public comment period, when EPA relied on that information to approve the state plan) and *Idaho Farm Bureau Fed. v. Babbitt*, 58 F.3d 1392 (9th Cir.1995) (finding an APA violation when the FWS relied on a United States Geological Survey draft study in order to justify a rule listing Bruneau Hot Springs Snail as an endangered species without making that draft available to the public). *But see Solite Corp. v. U.S. EPA*, 952 F.2d 473 (D.C.Cir.1991) (an agency may use supplementary data, unavailable during the notice and comment period, that expands on and confirms information contained in the proposed rulemaking and addresses alleged deficiencies in the pre-existing data, so long as no prejudice is shown); *Rybachek v. U.S. EPA*, 904 F.2d 1276 (9th Cir.1990) (permissible for EPA to rely on over 6000 pages of material added to record after the close of the comment period because material was EPA's response to comments).

4. Another issue in *Sierra Club* was whether members of Congress had unlawfully pressured EPA to adopt the rules that it did. No statute imposes any particular limitation on congressional "pressure," but an earlier D.C. Circuit case, *D.C. Federation of Civic Associations v. Volpe*, 459 F.2d 1231 (D.C.Cir.1971), had found improper pressure. The court distinguished the case as follows:

In *D.C. Federation* the Secretary of Transportation, pursuant to applicable federal statutes, made certain safety and environmental findings in designating a proposed bridge as part of the interstate highway system. Civic associations sought to have these determinations set aside for their failure to meet certain statutory standards, and because of possible tainting by reason of improper Congressional influence. Such influence chiefly included public statements by the Chairman of the House Subcommittee on the District of Columbia, Representative Natcher, indicating in no uncertain terms that money earmarked for the construction of the District of Columbia's subway system would be withheld unless the Secretary approved the bridge. [A] majority did agree on the controlling principle of law: "that the decision (of the Secretary) would be invalid if based in whole or in part on the pressures emanating from Representative Natcher." ... The court remanded simply so that the Secretary could make this decision strictly and solely on the basis of considerations made relevant by Congress in the applicable statute.

D.C. Federation thus requires that two conditions be met before an administrative rulemaking may be overturned simply on the grounds of Congressional pressure. First, the content of the pressure upon the Secretary is designed to force him to decide upon factors not made relevant by Congress in the applicable statute. Representative Natcher's threats were of precisely that character, since deciding to approve the bridge in order to free the "hostage" mass transit appropriation was not among the decisionmaking factors Congress had in mind when it enacted the highway approval provisions of Title 23 of the United States Code. Second, the Secretary's determination must be affected by those extraneous considerations.

In the case before us, there is no persuasive evidence that either criterion is satisfied. Senator Byrd requested a meeting in order to express "strongly" his already well-known views that the SO 2 standards' impact on coal reserves was a matter of concern to him. EPA initiated a second responsive meeting to report its reaction to the reserve data submitted by the NCA. In neither meeting is there any allegation that EPA made any commitments to Senator Byrd. The meetings did underscore Senator Byrd's deep concerns for EPA, but there is no evidence he attempted actively to use "extraneous" pressures to further his position. Americans rightly expect their elected representatives to voice their grievances and preferences concerning the administration of our laws. We believe it entirely proper for Congressional representatives vigorously to represent the interests of their constituents before administrative agencies engaged in informal, general policy rulemaking, so long as individual Congressmen do not frustrate the intent of Congress as a whole as expressed in statute, nor undermine applicable rules of procedure. Where Congressmen keep their comments focused on the substance of the proposed rule, and we have no substantial evidence to cause us to believe Senator Byrd did not do so here, administrative agencies are expected to balance Congressional pressure with the pressures emanating from all other sources. To hold otherwise would deprive the agencies of legitimate sources of information and call into question the validity of nearly every controversial rulemaking.

c. *Statement of Basis and Purpose*

After receiving comments from interested persons, Section 553(c) requires agencies "after consideration of the relevant matter presented, ... [to] incorporate in the rules adopted a concise general statement of their basis and purpose." This preamble to the final rule was intended "to enable the public to obtain a general idea of the purpose of, and a statement of the basis and justification for, the rules," rather than "an elaborate analysis of rules or of the detailed considerations upon which they are based." Legislative History of the Administrative Procedure Act, *supra*, at 225.

As in the case of notice, however, this original practice has changed notably. Today, the preamble to a complicated or controversial rule can easily exceed 100 pages of the double-columned, small type Federal Register. As noted earlier, there are two reasons for this development. In part, extensive preambles are the result of statutes that require agencies to do more in their final preambles. *See, e.g.,* 42 U.S.C.A. § 7191(d) (DOE must accompany rule with "an explanation responding to the major comments, criticisms, and alternatives offered during the comment period"); 42 U.S.C.A. § 7607(d)(6) (EPA under Clean Air Act must include in statement of basis and purpose "an explanation of the reasons for any major changes in the promulgated rule from the proposed rule" and "a response to each of the significant comments, criticisms, and new data submitted in written or oral presentations during the comment period"). *See also* 40 CFR § 1503.4 (agencies in their final Environmental Impact Statements must respond to comments submitted during the comment period). The more detailed and expansive statements of basis and purpose are also the result of court decisions that either set aside or remanded to the agency rules which the courts found inadequately justified. As we will see later, the agency's contemporaneous explanation for its action, supported by information in the rulemaking record, is the basis upon which courts review the substantive rationality of the rule. To skimp on the statement of basis and purpose, therefore, effectively limits the ability of the agency later to justify the rule if it is challenged in court. We will address this issue later in this chapter when we consider judicial review.

4. HYBRID RULEMAKING PROCEDURES

The discussion concerning the procedures applicable to informal rulemaking has made clear that many statutes have added various requirements to the basic APA informal rulemaking procedures. In addition, beginning with President Nixon, every president has issued an Executive Order that imposes requirements that agencies often must complete before a rule can be promulgated. Since it is probably a rare rule today that is subject only to the APA's procedures, lawyers must be attuned to these other sources of procedural requirements.

The **National Environmental Policy Act**, which dates back to 1970, contains the oldest analytical requirement. Agencies are required to make Environmental Impact Statements before engaging in activities (including rulemaking) that may have a significant effect on the human environment. *See* 42 U.S.C.A. § 4332(2)(c); *see generally* NEPA DESK-BOOK (1989). These EIS's describe in some detail the effect the proposed action will have on the environment and the effects that alternatives to the proposed action would have. Because NEPA does not require agencies to take, or not take, some particular action on the basis of the EIS, NEPA is known as imposing procedural, rather than substantive requirements. Like the procedures of the APA, however, agencies are subject to judicial review concerning compliance with NEPA's procedural requirements. NEPA's concept of an impact statement has subsequently been copied by a number of other statutes, as well as Executive Orders, all designed, as NEPA was, to improve agency decisionmaking.

The **Regulatory Flexibility Act**, originally passed in 1980 and significantly amended in 1996, requires agencies to create a Regulatory Flexibility Analysis (RFA) whenever they propose a rule that may have a significant economic impact on a substantial number of small businesses, organizations, or governments. 5 U.S.C.A. § 601 *et seq. See generally* Paul R. Verkuil, *A Critical Guide to the Regulatory Flexibility Act*, 1982 DUKE L.J. 213 (1981). Despite the language of the Act, courts have consistently interpreted it to require an RFA only when the significant economic effect is on a substantial number of small entities that actually would be subject to the proposed rule, as opposed to merely affected by it. *See, e.g., Motor & Equip. Mfrs. Ass'n. v. Nichols*, 142 F.3d 449, 467 & n. 18 (D.C.Cir.1998). The initial analysis accompanies the proposed rule and includes the reasons why the agency is proposing the action, a statement of the objectives and legal basis for the proposed rule, a description of the affected small entities, the reporting and recordkeeping requirements, an identification of other federal rules that may overlap or conflict with the proposed rule, and a description of any significant regulatory alternatives that would accomplish the stated objectives but minimize the impact on small entities. After an opportunity for comment on the proposed rule and initial analysis, the Act requires the agency to accompany the final rule with a final RFA that summarizes the comments received, the agency's response to them, and an explanation why any alternative was not adopted that would have reduced the impact on small entities. Persons familiar with NEPA's EIS requirement should recognize the similarity between the EIS and the RFA. Unlike NEPA, however, as originally passed, the Regulatory Flexibility Act prohibited any judicial review of an agency's compliance with the Act. Rather, the Chief Counsel for Advocacy of the Small Business Administration (a free-standing executive agency) was given responsibility for monitoring agency compliance. Nevertheless, affected entities could not enforce the Act's requirements, and many thought the Act a paper tiger, routinely ignored by agencies because of the lack of consequences attendant to its violation.

Acting on complaints about the ineffective nature of the Regulatory Flexibility Act, Congress authorized judicial review of agency compliance in 1996. Small Business Regulatory Enforcement Fairness Act, Pub. L. No. 104–121, § 242, 110 Stat. 847 (1996) (codified at 5 U.S.C.A. § 611). If an agency fails to comply with required procedures, a court may remand a rule back to an agency and defer enforcement of the rule against small entities. The RFA becomes part of the rulemaking record when there is judicial review of a rule. In other words, a court cannot directly review the substance of an RFA, but it can consider the RFA in determining whether a rule is arbitrary and capricious under section 706. In addition, the amendments created special procedural requirements for rules adopted by EPA and OSHA that affect small entities. In essence, they require those agencies to create special advisory committees composed of members of small entities to review proposed rules, apparently before they are published for public comment.

Congress also established the **Paperwork Reduction Act** in 1980. 44 U.S.C.A. §§ 3501 *et seq. See generally* William Funk, *The Paperwork Reduction Act: Paperwork Reduction Meets Administrative Law*, 24 HARV. J. LEGIS. 1 (1987). This Act requires agencies to engage in a notice and comment procedure prior to imposing any reporting or recordkeeping requirement on persons. As a result of amendments in 1995, these reporting and recordkeeping requirements include both situations where the information is to be reported to a federal agency and where the information is only to be reported to the public, such as in labelling. The agency must determine that the collection of information is necessary for the proper performance of the functions of the agency, is not unnecessarily duplicative of information otherwise available to the agency, takes account of the particular problems of small entities, is written in plain language, and uses information technology to reduce burden. The agency must also send its proposed requirement to the Office of Information and Regulatory Affairs (OIRA), which Congress created to approve or disapprove these rules. OIRA is part of the Office of Management and Budget (OMB), which is located organizationally in the Executive Office of the President. As OMB's names implies, it is responsible for management and budget functions for the President, and because of its presence in the Executive Office of the President, among agencies it is often viewed as being more closely connected to the policies of the President. If OIRA approves a paperwork requirement, it assigns it a control number. The act prohibits the government from penalizing a person for failing to comply with an information requirement "if the information collection does not display a valid control number." 42 U.S.C.A. § 3512.

President Reagan also acted in 1980 to obligate agencies to conduct regulatory analyses. He required executive agencies to assess the benefits and costs of proposed and final "major" rules, and he assigned to OIRA the responsibility to oversee agency compliance. Exec. Order No.

12,291, 3 C.F.R. § 127 (1982), *reprinted in* 5 U.S.C.A. § 601 (1988). A "major" rule was one with an annual economic impact of $100 million or more on the economy or one with other significant effects on individuals, businesses, governments, or the economy. OIRA was empowered to comment on an agency's proposed and final rules, but it could not disapprove a rule. The order also had a substantive component: executive agencies were forbidden from promulgating any regulation whose benefits did not exceed its costs unless this restriction was contrary to an agency's statutory mandate. After his initial order, President Reagan also issued executive orders to require executive agencies to assess the impacts of their actions on the family, federalism, property and trade.

Presidents Bush and Clinton continued and expanded the approach of the Reagan administration to regulatory oversight. President Bush kept the previous executive orders and added a requirement that agencies assess the impact of regulations on civil litigation. After President Clinton took office, he issued **Executive Order 12866**, which replaced Executive Order 12291 issued by President Reagan. The order, however, imposed most of the same requirements for analysis of proposed and final "major" rules, although it changed the term from "major rule" to "significant action," and it likewise appointed OIRA to be responsible for agency compliance.

This oversight continued a long tradition of presidential review. President Nixon had required EPA and OSHA to prepare a summary of the costs of proposed regulations and their alternatives, and he created an interagency taskforce to review the summaries. President Ford expanded the review process by requiring all executive agencies to prepare an "Inflation Impact Statement" for proposed rules, which included a quantitative assessment of the benefits and costs of a proposed rule. President Carter likewise required a regulatory analysis for proposed "major" rules, and he created an interagency taskforce, the Regulatory Analysis Review Group, to monitor agency compliance. *See* McGarity, *supra*, at 18–21.

All of these executive orders commonly provided that they were intended "only to improve the internal management of the Federal government, and [are] not intended to create any right or benefit, substantive or procedural, enforceable at law by a party against the United States...." The intent was to preclude judicial review of agency compliance with the requirements of the orders, and the courts have respected this intent. As a result, neither regulated entities nor regulatory beneficiaries can obtain judicial enforcement of the orders. OMB, however, has a number of means by which to ensure compliance with the orders, and its power in no small part derives from the commitment of each of the various Presidents to reform and improve the regulatory process. Because of OMB's power, it is lobbied by interested parties who wish it to seek changes in proposed agency rules.

All of these laws and orders provide a backdrop for the regulatory reform legislation considered since 1995. In March, 1995, the House of

Representatives passed the Job Creation and Wage Enhancement Act, which contained detailed analytical and substantive requirements for agency rulemaking. H.R. 9, 104th Cong., 1st Sess. (1995). This legislation was part of the effort to implement the "Contract with America" proposed by House Republicans elected in 1994. The Senate took up its own version of general regulatory reform in the Comprehensive Regulatory Reform Act of 1995, which was also known as the "Dole bill," after its primary sponsor, Senator Dole. S. 343, 104th Cong., 1st Sess. (1995). Republicans failed to end a filibuster that blocked consideration of this legislation in the Senate by two votes. In May 1999, the Senate Governmental Affairs Committee voted to send S. 746, a descendent of the earlier "Dole" bill, to the floor for consideration by the entire Senate. S. 746, 106th Congress, 1st Sess. (1999). S. 746 had been amended in 1998 to adopt specific differences that President Clinton favored. Nevertheless, the Senate did not vote on the legislation during the 106th Congress, which ended in December, 2000.

The legislation that has been proposed since 1995 addresses three procedural aspects of rulemaking: what events will trigger an agency's obligation to engage in rulemaking analyses, what analyses must an agency undertake, and to what extent will there be judicial review of agency compliance with the legislation. In addition, some reformers have sought to establish substantive decisional criteria applicable to rulemaking at all agencies.

Triggers: Following the pattern of the executive orders, the proposed legislation has mandated rulemaking analyses for all "major" rules, but there have been two proposed changes. First, reformers have sought to require all agencies to comply with the procedures mandated by the legislation, while the executive orders have generally applied only to executive agencies. Second, some of the earlier versions of the legislation defined a "major" rule as one with an annual economic impact of $50 million or more, as compared to the executive orders' threshold of $100 million or more.

In earlier versions of the legislation, the requirement for rulemaking analyses was not limited to new rules. Agencies would have been required to schedule reviews of selected existing rules and to establish priorities for review among the rules selected. The reviews of "major" rules would have required new rulemaking analyses. If an agency did not include a "major" rule in its schedule, any person subject to the rule was authorized to petition an agency to include that rule in its review schedule, and the courts were empowered to review the denial of such a petition by an agency. Some legislators favored a "sunset" provision to terminate any "major" rule that was not reviewed by an agency within a prescribed number of years. The periodic review or sunset requirements would lead to rulemaking if an agency decided that a regulation should be modified or rescinded based on the results of its analysis.

Analysis: For proposed and final "major" rules, the legislation would require agencies to prepare an analysis of a rule's potential benefits and costs, and, if the benefits of a rule included the reduction of a health or safety risk, the legislation also required separate analysis of the risk the agency proposed to regulate. The various versions of the legislation specify detailed procedures concerning the scope of these analyses, although later versions have been less detailed and prescriptive. The latest version, S. 746, contains the following directions concerning analysis of a proposed rule:

Sec. 623. Regulatory Analysis . . .

(b)(2) Each initial regulatory analysis shall contain—

(A) a cost-benefit analysis of the proposed rule that shall contain—

(i) an analysis of the benefits of the proposed rule, including any benefits that cannot be quantified, and an explanation of how the agency anticipates that such benefits will be achieved by the proposed rule, including a description of the persons or classes of persons likely to receive such benefits;

(ii) an analysis of the costs of the proposed rule, including any costs that cannot be quantified, and an explanation of how the agency anticipates that such costs will result from the proposed rule, including a description of the persons or classes of persons likely to bear such costs;

(iii) an evaluation of the relationship of the benefits of the proposed rule to its costs, including the determinations required under subsection (d) [mandating procedures for risk analysis], taking into account the results of any risk assessment;

(iv) an evaluation of the benefits and costs of a reasonable number of reasonable alternatives reflecting the range of regulatory options that would achieve the objective of the statute as addressed by the rule making, including, where feasible, alternatives that—

(I) require no government action or utilize voluntary programs;

(II) provide flexibility for small entities under subchapter I and for State, local, or tribal government agencies delegated to administer a Federal program;

(III) employ flexible regulatory options; and

(IV) assure protection of sensitive subpopulations, or populations exposed to multiple and cumulative risks; and

(V) a description of the scientific or economic evaluations or information upon which the agency substantially relied in the cost-benefit analysis and risk assessment required under this subchapter, and an explanation of how the agency reached the determinations under subsection ;

(B) if required, the risk assessment in accordance with section 624 [mandating procedures for risk analysis]; and

(C) when scientific information on substitution risks to health, safety, or the environment is reasonably available to the agency, an identification and evaluation of such risks. . . .

(d)(1)(A) The agency shall include in the statement of basis and purpose for a proposed or final major rule a reasonable determination, based upon the rule making record as a whole—

(i) whether the rule is likely to provide benefits that justify the costs of the rule:

(ii) whether the rule is likely to substantially achieve the rule making objective in a more cost-effective manner, or with greater net benefits, than the other reasonable alternatives considered by the agency; and

(iii) whether the rule adopts a flexible regulatory option.

S. 746, §§ 623(b)(2), (d)(1)(A).

Judicial Review: Congress has considered three approaches to judicial review. The most limited approach, like the original Regulatory Flexibility Act and the executive orders, would preclude judicial enforcement of the analysis requirements themselves, although any analyses conducted would become part of the rulemaking record. A second approach followed the judicial review provisions later adopted in the Unfunded Mandates Reform Act, *see infra*. Here, courts could review agencies' compliance with the rulemaking analysis procedural requirements, but if the agency had not adequately complied, the court could only order the agency after-the-fact to comply; it could not enjoin the rule as to which the procedural requirements had been violated. The final and most intrusive approach treated the rulemaking analysis requirements in the same manner as NEPA's EIS requirements, fully subject to judicial review. If the agency violates the requirements, the court can prohibit the agency from promulgating or enforcing the rule.

Under S. 746, the latest legislative proposal, any cost-benefit analysis, cost-effectiveness determination, and risk analysis becomes part of the rulemaking record. This information, as part of the rulemaking record, may be considered by a court in determining whether a rule is arbitrary and capricious under § 706(2) of the APA, which you will study in the last portion of this chapter. In addition, a court can remand or invalidate a rule, giving due regard to prejudicial error, if an agency fails to perform any required cost-benefit analysis, cost-effectiveness determination, or risk analysis. A court, however, would not be authorized to invalidate or remand a rule based on the agency's compliance with other requirements of the legislation concerning such studies. *See id.* §§ 627(d)-(e).

Substantive Provisions: Some reformers also sought substantive changes in addition to new procedural requirements. As noted earlier, executive orders have forbidden executive agencies from promulgating any regulation whose benefits did not exceed its costs unless this restriction was contrary to an agency's statutory mandate. Some reformers wanted to codify this provision and extend it to all agencies. Other reformers wanted a more radical change. They supported a provision (called the "super-mandate") that prohibited all agencies, without exception, from promulgating any regulation whose benefits did not exceed its costs. Since current laws authorize EPA and OSHA, among other agencies, to issue regulations without meeting a cost-benefit standard, this change might have had significant substantive ramifications for health and safety regulation.

While Congress has been unsuccessful at enacting general procedural reform in the last few years, it has enacted several laws that affect the procedural requirements applicable to agency rulemaking. One is the **Unfunded Mandates Reform Act of 1995**, Pub. L. No. 104–4, 109 Stat. 48. Title I of the Act provides various parliamentary restrictions on legislative bills that would impose unfunded mandates—federally imposed enforceable duties on *either* state, local, or tribal governments *or* the private sector. Title II, however, entitled "Regulatory Accountability and Reform," requires federal agencies, before promulgating either a proposed or final regulation that would include a "mandate" resulting in costs over $100 million annually on state, local, or tribal governments or the private sector, to prepare a statement assessing the effect of the regulation. *See* 2 U.S.C.A. § 1532(a). The agency must include a summary of the statement in the proposed and final rules. Whenever the agency is required to prepare such a statement, the agency must "identify and consider a reasonable number of regulatory alternatives." 2 U.S.C.A. § 1535(a). Moreover, from among these alternatives, the agency must "select the least costly, most cost-effective or least burdensome alternative that achieves the objectives of the rule." *Id.* The cost and burden referred to are the costs and burdens to state, local, and tribal governments, and the private sector, not the costs and burdens to the federal government. This substantive requirement applies unless it is inconsistent with provisions of another law, or the head of the agency explains why the least costly, most cost-effective, or least burdensome rule was not adopted. 2 U.S.C.A. § 1535(b). Title II also imposes special coordination requirements on agencies promulgating regulations with effects on state, local, or tribal governments. *See* 2 U.S.C.A. §§ 1533–34. Title IV of the Act provides for judicial review of the compliance or noncompliance by agencies with some of the regulatory reform requirements. 2 U.S.C.A. § 1571. As indicated above, however, a court may not enjoin an agency rule if the agency violates the requirements. The court may only order the agency to comply with those requirements after the fact.

As noted above, Congress also made significant amendments to the Regulatory Flexibility Act, primarily in subjecting its requirements to full judicial review and in imposing special requirements on EPA and OSHA rulemaking. In addition, Congress also reauthorized the Paperwork Reduction Act. The only notable change made was to overrule the

Supreme Court's decision in *Dole v. United Steelworkers of America*, 494 U.S. 26, 110 S.Ct. 929, 108 L.Ed.2d 23 (1990), in which the Supreme Court had held that the act's requirements did not apply to government demands on private persons to supply information to the public. The amendments make clear that government requirements for persons to gather and disclose information to the public, as in product labeling requirements or workplace safety notices, are fully subject to the Paperwork Reduction Act's requirements. Finally, Congress created wholly new requirements for agencies to submit new final rules to Congress for review. *See* 5 U.S.C.A. §§ 801–808. The statute requires agencies to delay the effective date of the rule for 60 days, except in certain circumstances. Recall that under Section 553 of the APA agencies were already required to delay the effective date for most rules for 30 days. We will deal with these new requirements in more detail in Chapter 6.

Problem 2–7: Hybrid Requirements

Imagine that you are a lawyer in the General Counsel's office in the Department of Agriculture. Before the Department adopts any regulation in Problem 2–5, relating to nutrition standards for school lunches, it wants to know what additional requirements are imposed by the Unfunded Mandates Reform Act, the Regulatory Flexibility Act, and E.O. 12866. The Department considers the rule a significant regulatory action and has treated it accordingly. Consider in particular:

(a) Does the Unfunded Mandates Reform Act apply at all? If so, what, if anything, would it require that the agency does not already do under E.O. 12866?

(b) Does the Regulatory Flexibility Act apply at all? If so, what, if anything, would it require that the agency does not already do under E.O. 12866?

(c) How would the regulatory impact analysis prepared under the Unfunded Mandates Reform Act differ from the analyses required by the Regulatory Flexibility Act and the Executive Order?

Notes and Questions

1. Executive orders, as noted, require agencies to engage in various impact analyses, including the impact on the family, federalism, private property, and civil litigation. If all of these requirements were taken as seriously as NEPA or E.O. 12866, the time and resources necessary for agencies to engage in rulemaking would be increased substantially. In a time of concern about excessive governmental expenditures, one may question the benefit (given the costs) of engaging in such studies. As a matter of fact, however, because the orders are not judicially enforced, and because the White House has not seen fit to ensure full compliance with these orders, they are routinely ignored or given short shrift.

2. Although presidential rulemaking review has become routine, it was controversial at the time that President Reagan adopted E.O. 12291.

There was controversy because of the predictable hostility of a Congress dominated by Democrats who had their own views of what regulatory action agencies should take. Presidential oversight was also controversial because it was conducted in secrecy which invited charges that OMB officials were delaying or weakening regulations at the behest of industry lobbyists. These suspicions were fed by President Reagan's decision to create a Task Force on Regulatory Relief chaired by then Vice–President George Bush. *See* Sidney A. Shapiro, *Political Oversight and the Deterioration of Regulatory Policy*, 46 ADMIN. L. REV. 1, 11–13, 21–23 (1994). President Clinton's E.O. 12866 makes presidential oversight public in three ways. After a regulatory action is published in the *Federal Register*, OIRA will make available all documents exchanged between it and the relevant agency. OIRA also maintains a public list of rules that it has under review and it identifies persons from outside of the government from whom it has received written and oral communications concerning such rules. Finally, agencies will publicize the substantive changes between the version of a rule that was submitted to OIRA and the version that the agency adopted, and it will indicate which changes resulted from OIRA's recommendations. *Id.* at 37–38. S. 746, discussed earlier, would codify a similar group of procedures aimed at public disclosure of key aspects of OIRA oversight.

If you represented a regulated entity, would you prefer that you not be subject to the disclosure provisions adopted by President Clinton? In what ways, if any, would such disclosure provisions change how you would approach OIRA?

3. Much of the debate concerning regulatory reform during the summer of 1995 involved competing claims by the Republicans that the reforms were necessary to bring government regulation into line with common sense and by Democrats that the effect of such reforms would be to prevent the adoption of important health and safety regulations because agencies were tied up in doing studies. The debate crystallizes a continuing conundrum in administrative law described in Professor Crampton's comments in Chapter 1—to the extent that one increases procedural requirements to make agency action more accountable or rational, the less efficient agency action is.

There is a considerable academic literature debating whether the increased accountability attributable to the various analytical obligations imposed by Congress and the President have greater costs, in terms of slowing down the rulemaking process, than benefits, in terms of making agencies smarter about the rules that they promulgate. (Besides these analytical requirements, judicial review doctrines are also blamed for slowing the rulemaking process, as you will read later in this chapter.) The slow-down is referred to as the "ossification" of rulemaking, and as Professor McGarity explains, many observers think it has fundamentally changed the nature of the process:

As the "rulemaking era" dawned in the early 1970s, the courts, commentators, and most federal agencies agreed that informal rulemaking under section 553 of the Administrative Procedure Act (APA) offered an ideal vehicle for making regulatory policy.... Twenty years later, the bloom is off the rose.... During the last fifteen years the rulemaking process has become increasingly rigid and burdensome. An assortment of analytical requirements have been imposed on the simple rulemaking model, and evolving judicial review doctrines have obligated agencies to take greater pains to ensure that the technical basis for rules are capable of withstanding judicial scrutiny. Professor Donald Elliot, former General Counsel of the Environmental Protection Agency, refers to this troublesome phenomenon as the "ossification" of the rulemaking process, and many observers from across the political spectrum agree with him that it is one of the most serious problems current facing regulatory agencies.

Thomas O. McGarity, *Some Thoughts on "Deossifying" the Rulemaking Process*, 41 DUKE L.J. 1385, 1385 (1992); *see also* Richard J. Pierce, Jr., *Seven Ways to Deossify Agency Rulemaking*, 47 ADMIN. L. REV. 59 (1995).

How does one go about assessing the benefits of these analytical requirements and the loss of efficiency they entail? How can legislators or the President determine whether there is too much, too little, or the right number of analytical requirements? After all, how one feels about this tradeoff may depend on its impact on the person. Accordingly, it is not surprising that environmentalists favor the impact statements required by NEPA, with judicial review thereof, when the government might take action adverse to the environment, but they adamantly object to imposing similar requirements when the government's proposed action might protect the environment. Of course, the same can be said of commercial and industrial interests, which oppose procedural roadblocks to government action that is necessary or useful to do business, such as government licensing or the sale of government property, but which support procedural protections when the government action would raise their costs, such as the imposition of safety or health regulations.

4. Is the absolute number of separate analytical requirements an indication that Congress and the President have contributed unnecessarily to ossification? Professor Seidenfeld has identified 110 separate procedural steps that an agency might have to complete if every analytical requirement contained in statutes and executive orders applied to a proposed rule. Mark Seidenfeld, *A Table of Requirements for Federal Administrative Rulemaking*, 27 F.S.U. L. REV. 533, 536–37 (2000). Not every requirement would apply to every rule, and most rules may trigger only a few requirements. Nevertheless, agency lawyers still need to determine which of these 110 steps apply when they are preparing to propose a rule. Should Congress and the President simplify and reconcile these various hybrid rulemaking requirements? Professor Seidenfeld notes, "Even if one believes that analysis of regulatory impacts is salutary, the patchwork of statutes and executive orders by which these analysis requirements have been imposed and the interrelations between

these various statutes have created a confusing labyrinth through which agencies seeking to adopt rules must grope." *Id.* at 535.

5. Generally, rulemaking in the states imitates the basic notice-and-comment rulemaking under the APA. *See generally* A. Bonfield, STATE ADMINISTRATIVE RULE MAKING (1986). Some states, however, have hybrid systems. California is notable in having a highly developed system, including a separate agency, the Office of Administrative Law, operating somewhat in the same status as OIRA, but with the power to disapprove other agencies' rules for failure to meet substantive and procedural requirements. *See generally* Marsha Cohen, *Regulatory Reform: Assessing the California Plan*, 1983 DUKE L. J. 231.

5. NEGOTIATED RULEMAKING

The previous section related how dissatisfaction with existing rulemaking resulted in various procedural changes designed to improve the process. At the same time, the growing interest in Alternative Dispute Resolution (ADR) in the judicial context led some to consider its use in the rulemaking context as a response to many of the perceived problems with rulemaking. *See generally* Philip J. Harter, *Negotiating Regulations: A Cure for the Malaise*, 71 GEO. L.J. 1 (1982). For a comprehensive compilation of materials dealing with this subject, *see* A.C.U.S., NEGOTIATED RULEMAKING SOURCEBOOK (1990). Three selections follow. The first, by two proponents of negotiated rulemaking, explains how it is a form of regulatory reform. The second, a recommendation by the Administrative Conference of the United States, provides both a justification and a means by which agencies might utilize this new procedure. The last selection provides a critique of the theory of negotiated rulemaking.

LAWRENCE SUSSKIND & GERARD McMAHON, THE THEORY AND PRACTICE OF NEGOTIATED RULEMAKING

3 Yale J. on Reg. 133 (1985).

I. NEGOTIATED RULEMAKING AS A REGULATORY REFORM

Almost all the parties involved in federal rulemaking—business associations, public interest groups, and many government officials—complain about the time and expense involved in developing and implementing regulations. Businesses assert that delays are costly and increase the uncertainty surrounding investment decisions. Advocacy groups complain that litigation delays implementation of important rules. Each party tends to think that the agency favors the others. Agency officials, on the other hand, feel that their autonomy has been unreasonably limited by procedural requirements mandated by Congress and the courts. Courts, however, are inappropriate as final arbitrators of technically complex regulatory disputes. Many judges fear "government by the judiciary" and admit their inability to cope with complex technical issues.

These groups would certainly be less troubled if they believed that the conventional rulemaking process generated rules responsive to their interests, but few are satisfied with the time it takes to enact rules, the cost involved, or the quality of the rules produced. . . .

How did this situation develop? The roots of the problem can be found in the evolution of the regulatory process and in the changing nature of the issues that the process has been forced to address during the past several decades. Agency rulemaking from the New Deal to the early 1960's was characterized by broad deference to agency expertise and discretion. By the late 1960's, however, the groups being regulated, the newly emergent environmental advocacy organizations, and the courts had become unwilling to let such discretion go unchallenged.

Federal regulations typically are developed under procedures defined by the Administrative Procedure Act of 1946. Using in-house expertise and informal individual meetings with stakeholders (parties who are interested in or will be affected by the rule), an agency such as EPA first develops a Notice of Proposed Rulemaking, which is published in the *Federal Register*. Non-agency stakeholders, such as businesses or environmental organizations, are then able to respond by adding to a rulemaking record through a formal public comment process. Oral hearings are permissible but not required. The agency must base the final rulemaking on a consideration of the record, although in addressing ambiguities and uncertainties in the record it may make policy choices where necessary.

Many of the regulations promulgated over the past two decades have involved the resolution of complex factual questions. More importantly, they have required difficult policy decisions that, at times, have lacked an operable political consensus. If all regulations had a clearly determinable factual basis, arguments about the exercise of agency discretion would be moot. Agencies, however, must also make policy choices in situations where either the desired facts are not available or the available "facts" are contested. In such situations, the agency exercises considerable discretion as it interprets inconsistent facts, balances various and often competing interests, and ultimately makes subjective policy choices with very real economic and political ramifications. In this context, an agency can expect opposition to almost every rule it develops.

Congress, the White House, and the courts have explored a variety of strategies to forestall concerns about the exercise of agency discretion and to increase agency accountability. However, the government's efforts to limit discretion have increased the time and cost involved in rulemaking. Congress has enacted the Federal Advisory Committee Act (FACA), the Sunshine Act, the *ex parte* prohibitions of the Administrative Procedure Act, and the Freedom of Information Act. In issuing Executive Orders 12,291 and 12,498 [the Reagan administration's regulatory reform executive orders], the White House has given the Office of Management and Budget (OMB) greatly expanded responsibility for reviewing the probable cost-effectiveness of proposed regulations. Since 1970, the courts have expanded judicial supervision of agencies by broadening the rules of standing, issuing more specific criteria regarding the development and use of a factual record, expanding notice and comment requirements, and expressing a willingness to take a "hard look" at the reasonableness of proposed regulations. These changes have produced "hybrid rulemaking," so-called because it is intermediate between the informal notice and comment rulemaking and formal procedures which include evidentiary hearings.

While these developments have increased agency accountability, they have not fully responded to concerns about the legitimacy of regulatory actions. Limiting the role of non-agency participants to adversarial challenges to the rulemaking record has been an ineffective means of building support for the policy choices that agencies have had to make. The current rulemaking process is bound to generate dissatisfaction as long as regulatory agencies retain the exclusive responsibility for making the technical judgments and political compromises needed to develop a rule. By encouraging and empowering regulatees to challenge agency decisionmaking in an effort to enhance the political legitimacy of the rulemaking process, Congress and the courts have simply increased the complexity, cost, and time it takes to generate rules that can be implemented.

A number of scholars have suggested negotiated rulemaking as a response to these problems of delay, increased cost, and loss of political legitimacy. In negotiated rulemaking, an agency and other parties with a significant stake in a rule participate in facilitated face-to-face interactions designed to produce a consensus. Together the parties explore their shared interests as well as differences of opinion, collaborate in gathering and analyzing technical information, generate options, and bargain and trade across these options according to their differing priorities. If a consensus is reached, it is published in the *Federal Register* as the agency's notice of proposed rulemaking, and then the conventional review and comment process takes over. Because most of the parties likely to comment have already agreed on the notice of proposed rulemaking, the review period should be uneventful. The prospects of subsequent litigation should be all but eliminated.

A.C.U.S., Recommendation 82–4, 1 CFR § 305.82–4

§ 305.82–4 Procedures for Negotiating Proposed Regulations (Recommendation No. 8–24)

The complexity of government regulation has increased greatly compared to that which existed when the Administrative Procedure Act was enacted, and this complexity has been accompanied by a formalization of the rulemaking process beyond the brief, expeditious notice and comment procedures envisioned by section 553 of the APA. Procedures in addition to notice and comment may, in some instances, provide important safeguards against arbitrary or capricious decisions by agencies and help ensure that agencies develop sound factual bases for the exercise of the discretion entrusted them by Congress, but the increased formalization of the rulemaking process has also had adverse consequences. The participants, including the agency, tend to develop adversarial relationships with each other causing them to take extreme positions, to withhold information from one another, and to attack the legitimacy of opposing positions. Because of the adversarial relationships, participants often do not focus on creative solutions to problems, ranking of the issues involved in a rulemaking, or the important details involved in a rule. Extensive factual records are often developed beyond what is necessary. Long periods of delay result, and participation in rulemaking proceedings can become needlessly expensive. Moreover, many participants perceive their roles in the rulemaking proceeding more as positioning themselves for the subsequent judicial review than as contributing to a solution on the merits at the administrative level. Finally, many participants remain dissatisfied with the policy judgments made at the outcome of rulemaking proceedings.

Participants in rulemaking rarely meet as a group with each other and with the agency to communicate their respective views so that each can react directly to the concerns and positions of the others in an effort to resolve conflicts. Experience indicates that if the parties in interest were to work together to negotiate the text of a proposed rule, they might be able in some circumstances to identify the major issues, gauge their importance to the respective parties, identify the information and data necessary to resolve the issues, and develop a rule that is acceptable to the respective interests, all within the contours of the substantive statute. For example, highly technical standards are negotiated that have extensive health, safety, and economic effects; lawsuits challenging rules are regularly settled by agreement on a negotiated rule; public law litigation involves sensitive negotiation over rule-like issues; and many environmental disputes and policies have been successfully negotiated. These experiences can be drawn upon in certain rulemaking contexts to provide procedures by which affected interests and the agency might participate directly in the development of the text of a proposed rule through negotiation and mediation. . . .

The suggested procedures provide a mechanism by which the benefits of negotiation could be achieved while providing appropriate safeguards to ensure that affected interests have the opportunity to participate, that the resulting rule is within the discretion delegated by Congress, and that it is not arbitrary or capricious. The premise of the recommendation is that provision of opportunities and incentives to resolve issues during rulemaking, through negotiations, will result in an improved process and better rules. Such rules would likely be more acceptable to affected interests because of their participation in the negotiations. The purpose of this recommendation is to establish a supplemental rulemaking procedure that can be used in appropriate circumstances to permit the direct participation of affected interests in the development of proposed rules. This procedure should be viewed as experimental, and should be reviewed after it has been used a reasonable number of times.

RECOMMENDATION

1. Agencies should consider using regulatory negotiation, as described in this recommendation, as a means of drafting for agency consideration the text of a proposed regulation. . . .

4. An agency considering use of regulatory negotiation should select and consult with a convener at the earliest practicable time about the feasibility of its use. The convener should conduct a preliminary inquiry to determine whether a regulatory negotiating group should be empaneled to develop a proposed rule relating to the particular topic. . . . Other factors bearing on this decision include the following:

(a) The issues to be raised in the proceeding should be mature and ripe for decision. Ideally, there should be some deadline for issuing the rule, so that a decision on a rule is inevitable within a relatively fixed time frame. The agency may also impose a deadline on the negotiations.

(b) The resolution of issues should not be such as to require participants in negotiations to compromise their fundamental tenets, since it is unlikely that agreement will be reached in such circumstances. Rather, issues involving such fundamental tenets should already have been determined, or not be crucial to the resolution of the issues involved in writing the proposed regulation.

(c) The interests significantly affected should be such that individuals can be selected who will adequately represent those interests. Since negotiations cannot generally be conducted with a large number of participants, there should be a limited number of interests that will be significantly affected by the rule and therefore represented in the negotiations. A rule of thumb might be that negotiations should ordinarily involve no more than 15 participants.

(d) There should be a number of diverse issues that the participants can rank according to their own priorities and on which they might reach agreement by attempting to optimize the return to all the participants.

(e) No single interest should be able to dominate the negotiations. The agency's representative in the negotiations will not be deemed to possess this power solely by virtue of the agency's ultimate power to promulgate the final rule.

(f) The participants in the negotiations should be willing to negotiate in good faith to draft a proposed rule.

(g) The agency should be willing to designate an appropriate staff member to participate as the agency's representative, but the representative should make clear to the other participants that he or she cannot bind the agency.

5. If the convener determines that regulatory negotiation would be appropriate, it would recommend this procedure to the agency. If the agency and the convener agree that regulatory negotiation is appropriate, the convener should be responsible for determining preliminarily the interests that will likely be substantially affected by a proposed rule, the individuals that will represent those interests in negotiations, the scope of issues to be addressed, and a schedule for completing the work.... Reasonable efforts should be made to secure a balanced group in which no interest has more than a third of the members and each representative is technically qualified to address the issues presented, or has access to qualified individuals....

7. To ensure that the appropriate interests have been identified and have had the opportunity to be represented in the negotiating group, the agency should publish in the *Federal Register* a notice that it is contemplating developing a rule by negotiation and indicate in the notice the issues involved and the participants and interests already identified....

8. The agency should designate a senior official to represent it in the negotiations and should identify that official in the FEDERAL REGISTER notice.

9. It may be that, in particular proceedings, certain affected interests will require reimbursement for direct expenses to be able to participate at a level that will foster broadly-based successful negotiations....

10. The convener and the agency might consider whether selection of a mediator is likely to facilitate the negotiation process....

11. The goal of the negotiating group should be to arrive at a consensus on a proposed rule. Consensus in this context means that each interest represented in the negotiating group concurs in the result, unless all members of the group agree at the outset on another definition. Following consensus, the negotiating group should prepare a report to the agency containing its proposed rule and a concise general statement of its basis and purpose. The report should also describe the factual material on which the group relied in preparing its proposed regulation, for inclusion in the agency's record of the proceeding. The participants may, of course, be unable to reach a consensus on a proposed rule, and, in that event, they should identify in the report both the areas in which they are agreed and the areas in which consensus could not be achieved. This could serve to narrow the issues in dispute, identify information necessary to resolve issues, rank priorities, and identify potentially acceptable solutions.

12. The negotiating group should be authorized to close its meeting to the public only when necessary to protect confidential data or when, in the judgment of the participants, the likelihood of achieving consensus would be significantly enhanced.

13. The agency should publish the negotiated text of the proposed rule in its notice of proposed rulemaking. If the agency does not publish

the negotiated text as a proposed rule, it should explain its reasons. The agency may wish to propose amendments or modifications to the negotiated proposed rule, but it should do so in such a manner that the public at large can identify the work of the agency and of the negotiating group.

14.   The negotiating group should be afforded an opportunity to review any comments that are received in response to the notice of proposed rulemaking so that the participants can determine whether their recommendations should be modified. The final responsibility for issuing the rule would remain with the agency.

WILLIAM FUNK, WHEN SMOKE GETS IN YOUR EYES: REGULATORY NEGOTIATION AND THE PUBLIC INTEREST—EPA'S WOODSTOVE STANDARDS
18 Env. L. 55 (1987).

V.   REGULATORY NEGOTIATION AND ADMINISTRATIVE LAW

... It is my thesis that the theory and principles of regulatory negotiation are at war with the theory and principles of American administrative law applicable to rulemaking, which Kenneth Culp Davis has described as "one of the greatest inventions of modern government."

Modern American administrative law begins with the New Deal, and James Landis provided the best contemporary justification and explanation for the administrative state in his now classic book, THE ADMINISTRATIVE PROCESS. According to his analysis, Congress creates administrative agencies because modern society requires government regulation to a degree simply beyond the resources and expertise of Congress. These agencies are empowered to make law because they are or will become expert in their fields. Not articulated, but implicit in his analysis, was a belief that these agencies faced problems capable of objective solution, that politically neutral administrators could determine finite and correct answers to the problems of modern industrial society.

Not all shared his optimistic belief in neutral bureaucrats finding objectively verifiable answers to clearly understood problems. The response, however, was not to eliminate the administrative agencies, or even to reduce their powers, but rather it was to subject their actions to procedural restraints and judicial review. The Administrative Procedure Act (APA) was the result, a compromise piece of legislation designed to constrain the discretion of agencies while legitimating their remaining discretion through procedural regularity and judicial oversight. While the APA perhaps reflects a loss of the naive faith in the natural ability of expert bureaucrats to scientifically discover objectively correct solutions to society's problems, it does not indicate a lessened determination to use agencies and rulemaking to solve politically perceived problems. In this, the APA is much like the Constitution; it does not indicate a rejection of the need for strong government for the proper functioning of modern society, but rather a healthy disrespect for the motives and abilities of men placed in power. And like much of the Constitution, the

APA uses procedural mechanisms to check the power granted, while not denying the need for the power.

The continuing belief in the importance and legitimacy of agencies as regulators of private conduct, despite a distrust of the regulators, was confirmed by the great period of agency creation during the 1960's and 1970's. Now the focus was more on health and safety regulation, perhaps reflecting a once again naive belief in the existence of scientifically and objectively determinable solutions to problems, but now there was even more concern about the necessity of procedures to constrain the discretion of agencies. Both courts and Congress combined to establish procedures aimed at fostering the rationality of agency decision making. Thus, these procedures, which have come to be known as "hybrid rulemaking," focus on maximizing the information available to the agency, ensuring its critical assessment, and most importantly, requiring that the ultimate decision be objectively reasonable in light of the information obtained. Most recently, the executive branch's contribution has been to require cost/benefit analyses, again to foster rationality in agency decision making.

Today the emphasis is on deregulation, reflecting a reassessment of whether certain problems exist at all or, if they exist, are best addressed by public law solutions. Nevertheless, where a problem is still perceived to require government action, today's answer to that problem remains agency action. We have come a long way from the simple faith of James Landis, but for the most part we have not rejected his solution where there is agreement as to the need for government action. In place of his faith we have substituted procedural requirements to foster rationality, but we have not abandoned the goal of reasoned decision making to achieve the public interest.

Defining the public interest may be a different undertaking from achieving an agreed-upon public interest. In the Clean Air Act, for instance, a number of provisions ... requires the weighing of various factors, at least some of which are difficult if not impossible to quantify. The statute implies that this weighing process defines the public interest. In this realm, information and data, logic and science, are only of limited help. Here, values and philosophies may be more pertinent. Yet, here too Congress has delegated to agencies the power to make this definition....

Of course, agencies are not to make their determinations in a vacuum. Procedural requirements assure input from interested parties, and recent executive orders institute a supervisory executive branch oversight of executive agencies' determinations. Moreover, this supervisory oversight can properly have a policy component; it need not be politically sterile. Nevertheless, the ultimate responsibility for the determination continues to rest with the agency. Not only is the final responsibility to be the agency's, but in the oft-quoted words of *Scenic Hudson Preservation Conference v. FPC*, an agency's role as representative of the public interest "does not permit it to act as an umpire blandly calling balls and strikes for adversaries appearing before it; the right of the public must receive active and affirmative protection at the hands of the [agency]."

The concept of regulatory negotiation stands this role on its head, first, by reducing the agency to the level of a mere participant in the formulation of the rule, and second, by essentially denying that the agency has any responsibility beyond giving effect to the consensus achieved by the group. In addition, regulatory negotiation finds its legitimacy in the agreement between the parties, rather than in the determination under the law of the public interest; in other words, regulatory negotiation substitutes a private law remedy for a public law remedy. . . .

This fundamental change in the role of the agency in the rulemaking process is mirrored by the fundamental change in the underlying theoretical justification for the eventual rule. As Harter admits: "Under the traditional hybrid process, the legitimacy of the rule rests on a resolution of complex factual materials and rational extrapolation from those facts, guided by the criteria of the statute. Under regulatory negotiation, however, the regulation's legitimacy would lie in the overall agreement of the parties." Stated another way, the parties to the rule are happy with it; therefore, it matters not whether the rule is rational or lawful. Discretion delegated to the agency by Congress is effectively exercised by the group of interested parties, constrained only by the need to obtain consensus. The law no longer directs or even necessarily constrains the outcome but has become merely a factor in the give-and-take necessary to achieve consensus. . . .

The tendency of alternative dispute resolution to focus on the interests of the specific parties to the dispute without regard to broader values has been noted in the literature related to alternatives to litigation. As Judge Edwards has noted, there are important differences between alternative dispute resolution where only private interests and values are at stake and where public values and interests are involved. "[I]f ADR is extended to resolve difficult issues of constitutional or public law—making use of nonlegal values to resolve important social issues or allowing those the law seeks to regulate to delimit public rights and duties—there is real reason for concern." Regulatory negotiation, by reducing disputes over what is in the public interest to disputes between various private interests, and by substituting private agreement for public determinations made according to legal norms, transforms administrative rulemaking into an area of private law, and this is a fundamental alteration.

Problem 2–8: Negotiated Rulemaking

In Problem 2–1, a biotech company lobbied EPA to adopt a regulation that would exempt small-scale field tests of pesticides produced by biotechnology from certain licensing provisions. The Administrator of EPA is interested in the possibility of adopting such a regulation, and she asks the General Counsel to recommend whether the agency should use negotiated rulemaking for this purpose. As a lawyer who works for the General Counsel, would you recommend that the proposed regulation is a good candidate for negotiated rulemaking? Assuming that negotiated rulemaking is feasible, are there reasons why EPA should not rely on it? Would you recommend the procedure despite these reasons?

Notes and Questions

1. Both Congress and the President are supportive of negotiated rulemaking. In 1990 Congress passed the Negotiated Rulemaking Act, 5 U.S.C.A. §§ 561 *et seq.*, which essentially codified the Administrative Conference's recommendations. It did, however, exempt from judicial review any agency action creating, assisting, or terminating a negotiated rulemaking committee. Executive Order 12866 on regulatory planning and review directed each agency "to explore and, where appropriate, use consensual mechanisms for developing regulations, including negotiated rulemaking." The same day that he issued the executive order, President Clinton also issued a memorandum to all departments and selected agencies directing them to identify to OMB within 90 days at least one rulemaking that the agency would develop through negotiated rulemaking during 1994 or explain why it would not be feasible to use negotiated rulemaking during 1994.

2. The Administrative Conference's study of negotiated rulemaking indicated that the Federal Advisory Committee Act (FACA) was a hurdle that impeded agencies using negotiated rulemaking. Its recommendation asked Congress to amend the Act to facilitate the use of negotiated rulemaking. The Negotiated Rulemaking Act, however, generally requires that a negotiated rulemaking committee comply with the requirements of FACA. These requirements will be addressed in Chapter 8, but generally they require notice of meetings, public access to meetings, and public access to the committee materials. These are not insuperable barriers to negotiating rules, but they do stifle spontaneity and tend to formalize a process that may work most efficiently through less formal procedures.

3. To date, the success of negotiated rulemaking is widely heralded. Although not all negotiations have resulted in consensus and a negotiated proposed rule, many have, and almost without exception no one has challenged these rules in court. Nevertheless, there are some skeptics. *Compare* Cary Coglianese, *Assessing Consensus: The Promise and Performance of Negotiated Rulemaking*, 46 DUKE L.J. 1255, 1335 (1997) ("Negotiated rulemaking does not appear any more capable of limiting regulatory time or avoiding litigation than do the rulemaking procedures ordinarily used by agencies.") *with* Philip J. Harter, *Fear of Commitment: An Affliction of Adolescents*, 46 DUKE L.J. 1389, 1423 (1997) (disputing Coglianese's conclusions and supporting the efficacy of consultation and negotiation). Assuming that negotiated rulemaking has been successful most of the time it has been tried, why do you suppose that

the overall number or percentage of rules adopted through negotiated rulemaking remains small?

C. JUDICIAL REVIEW

The procedural requirements of the APA and other statutes, as well as the substantive requirements for rulemaking in agency mandates, are law, binding on agencies, whether or not they are enforceable by courts. After all, all federal officers are bound by the Constitution to follow the laws of the United States. Nevertheless, as a practical matter, as experience under the Regulatory Flexibility Act has shown, absent judicial enforcement of the law, agencies are less likely to comply with it. We have already seen how courts enforce the APA's procedural requirements, but we have yet to address how courts enforce other legal requirements. In this portion of the chapter we will consider how courts review agency actions alleged to be substantively unlawful, either because the agency has incorrectly interpreted the governing statute or because the agency's decision is arbitrary and capricious.

1. STATUTORY INTERPRETATION

Agencies frequently must interpret statutes in determining what type of rule to adopt, and these interpretations are subject to judicial review under section 706 of the APA. Section 706 directs the reviewing court to hold unlawful agency action "not in accordance with law," 5 U.S.C.A. § 706(2)(A), and agency action "in excess of statutory jurisdiction, authority, limitations, or short of statutory right," *id.* § 706(2)(C). Sometimes the agency is interpreting a statute that applies to many agencies, such as Title VII of the Civil Rights Act of 1964, which prohibits discrimination in employment on the basis of race, religion, national origin, or gender. More often the agency is interpreting its statutory mandate, such as the Clean Air Act for EPA, the Endangered Species Act for the Fish and Wildlife Service, or the Federal Trade Commission Act for the Federal Trade Commission.

Since *Marbury v. Madison*, 5 U.S. (1 Cranch) 137, 2 L.Ed. 60 (1803), it has been black letter law that: "It is emphatically the province and duty of the judicial department to say what the law is." At the same time, when agencies act pursuant to statutory mandates, they are acting under a delegation from Congress, have a day-to-day familiarity with the law and its effects, and presumably have some substantive expertise with respect to the subject matter of the mandate. Thus, there may be a reason for courts to act somewhat differently when they deal with agencies' interpretations of their statutory mandates. This issue is often phrased in terms of whether courts should give "deference" to agency interpretations. In 1984 the Supreme Court decided *Chevron v. Natural Resources Defense Council, Inc.*, 467 U.S. 837, 104 S.Ct. 2778, 81 L.Ed.2d 694 (1984), addressing this issue, perhaps the most cited Supreme Court administrative law decision.

CHEVRON v. NATURAL RESOURCES DEFENSE COUNCIL, INC.

467 U.S. 837, 104 S.Ct. 2778, 81 L.Ed.2d 694 (1984).

[The issue in *Chevron* concerned a section in the 1977 Amendments to the Clean Air Act (CAA) which required polluters in certain areas of the country to obtain a permit from a state regulator before the construction of any "new or modified stationary sources" of air pollution. 42 U.S.C. § 7502(b)(6). The state regulator could not grant the permit unless the polluter met stringent conditions concerning abatement of the new pollution. EPA had promulgated a rule which interpreted the words "stationary source" to include what the agency called a "bubble policy." According to this policy, an existing plant that contained several pollution-emitting devices could install or modify one piece of equipment without obtaining a permit if the alteration did not increase the total emissions from the plant. In other words, EPA defined the words "stationary source" to include all of the pollution-emitting devices within the same industrial group as though the plant was encased within a single "bubble."

EPA's interpretation was challenged by the Natural Resource Defense Council (NRDC) which argued that the word "source" meant each individual pollution-emitting piece of equipment. Under NRDC's interpretation, a plant would have to obtain a permit any time it created a new source of pollution or modified an existing source if the effect were to increase the pollution from that source. Under EPA's interpretation, no permit was necessary if the increase in pollution from the new or modified source were offset by decreases in pollution from other pollution-emitting sources within the plant. The Court of Appeals agreed with the NRDC position because the court believed this interpretation better served the goals of the Clean Air Act than the EPA interpretation.]

STEVENS, JUSTICE:

... The basic legal error of the Court of Appeals was to adopt a static judicial definition of the term "stationary source" when it had decided that Congress itself had not commanded that definition....

When a court reviews an agency's construction of the statute which it administers, it is confronted with two questions. First, always, is the question whether Congress has directly spoken to the precise question at issue. If the intent of Congress is clear, that is the end of the matter; for the court, as well as the agency, must give effect to the unambiguously expressed intent of Congress.[9] If, however, the court determines Congress has not directly addressed the precise question at issue, the court

9. The judiciary is the final authority on issues of statutory construction and must reject administrative constructions which are contrary to clear congressional intent. If a court, employing traditional tools of statutory construction, ascertains that Congress had an intention on the precise question at issue, that intention is the law and must be given effect.

does not simply impose its own construction on the statute, as would be necessary in the absence of an administrative interpretation. Rather, if the statute is silent or ambiguous with respect to the specific issue, the question for the court is whether the agency's answer is based on a permissible construction of the statute.[11]

"The power of an administrative agency to administer a congressionally created ... program necessarily requires the formulation of policy and the making of rules to fill any gap left, implicitly or explicitly, by Congress." If Congress has explicitly left a gap for the agency to fill, there is an express delegation of authority to the agency to elucidate a specific provision of the statute by regulation. Such legislative regulations are given controlling weight unless they are arbitrary, capricious, or manifestly contrary to the statute. Sometimes the legislative delegation to an agency on a particular question is implicit rather than explicit. In such a case, a court may not substitute its own construction of a statutory provision for a reasonable interpretation made by the administrator of an agency.

We have long recognized that considerable weight should be accorded to an executive department's construction of a statutory scheme it is entrusted to administer, and the principle of deference to administrative interpretations "has been consistently followed by this Court whenever decision as to the meaning or reach of a statute has involved reconciling conflicting policies, and a full understanding of the force of the statutory policy in the given situation has depended upon more than ordinary knowledge respecting the matters subjected to agency regulations.... If this choice represents a reasonable accommodation of conflicting policies that were committed to the agency's care by the statute, we should not disturb it unless it appears from the statute or its legislative history that the accommodation is not one that Congress would have sanctioned."

In light of these well-settled principles it is clear that the Court of Appeals misconceived the nature of its role in reviewing the regulations at issue. Once it determined, after its own examination of the legislation, that Congress did not actually have an intent regarding the applicability of the bubble concept to the permit program, the question before it was not whether in its view the concept is "inappropriate" in the general context of a program designed to improve air quality, but whether the Administrator's view that it is appropriate in the context of this particular program is a reasonable one. Based on the examination of the legislation and its history which follows, we agree with the Court of Appeals that Congress did not have a specific intention on the applicability of the bubble concept in these cases, and conclude that the EPA's use of that concept here is a reasonable policy choice for the agency to make.

[Using this framework, the Court assessed the statutory language and found it ambiguous on the point at issue; the legislative history, the Court said, was "unilluminating."]

---

11. The court need not conclude that the agency construction was the only one it permissibly could have adopted to uphold the construction, or even the reading the court would have reached if the question initially had arisen in a judicial proceeding.

The arguments over policy that are advanced in the parties' briefs create the impression that respondents are now waging in a judicial forum a specific policy battle which they ultimately lost in the agency and in the 32 jurisdictions opting for the "bubble concept," but one which was never waged in the Congress. Such policy arguments are more properly addressed to legislators or administrators, not to judges.

In these cases, the Administrator's interpretation represents a reasonable accommodation of manifestly competing interests and is entitled to deference: the regulatory scheme is technical and complex, the agency considered the matter in a detailed and reasoned fashion, and the decision involves reconciling conflicting policies. Congress intended to accommodate both interests, but did not do so itself on the level of specificity presented by these cases. Perhaps that body consciously desired the Administrator to strike the balance at this level, thinking that those with great expertise and charged with responsibility for administering the provision would be in a better position to do so; perhaps it simply did not consider the question at this level; and perhaps Congress was unable to forge a coalition on either side of the question, and those on each side decided to take their chances with the scheme devised by the agency. For judicial purposes, it matters not which of these things occurred.

Judges are not experts in the field, and are not part of either political branch of the Government. Courts must, in some cases, reconcile competing political interests, but not on the basis of the judges' personal policy preferences. In contrast, an agency to which Congress has delegated policy-making responsibilities may, within the limits of that delegation, properly rely upon the incumbent administration's views of wise policy to inform its judgments. While agencies are not directly accountable to the people, the Chief Executive is, and it is entirely appropriate for this political branch of the Government to make such policy choices—resolving the competing interests which Congress itself either inadvertently did not resolve, or intentionally left to be resolved by the agency charged with the administration of the statute in light of everyday realities.

When a challenge to an agency construction of a statutory provision, fairly conceptualized, really centers on the wisdom of the agency's policy, rather than whether it is a reasonable choice within a gap left open by Congress, the challenge must fail. In such a case, federal judges—who have no constituency—have a duty to respect legitimate policy choices made by those who do. The responsibilities for assessing the wisdom of such policy choices and resolving the struggle between competing views of the public interest are not judicial ones: "Our Constitution vests such responsibilities in the political branches."

We hold that the EPA's definition of the term "source" is a permissible construction of the statute which seeks to accommodate progress in reducing air pollution with economic growth. . . .

Notes and Questions

1.   The Court's approach in *Chevron* has been called the "*Chevron* two-step." In the first step, the court determines whether the statute clearly requires or forbids the agency's interpretation. If the statute does not clearly answer the question, or in other words the statute is ambiguous, the court proceeds to the second step, determining whether the agency's interpretation is reasonable or permissible. Step one involves the independent judgement of the court, consistent with *Marbury*; step two is highly deferential to the agency's interpretation.

2.   One might expect from the two-step approach dictated by *Chevron* that agencies would generally win at step two, but would have more difficulty prevailing at step one. A study of the impact of *Chevron* in the courts of appeals during 1995 and 1996 found that agencies prevailed 42 percent of the time at step one and 89 percent of the time at step two, giving agencies an over-all 71 percent success rate. Orin S. Kerr, *Shedding Light on* Chevron: *An Empirical Study of the* Chevron *Doctrine in the U.S. Courts of Appeals*, 15 YALE J. REG. 1, 31 (1998). As of 1991, the Supreme Court had never found that an agency's interpretation failed step two. *See* Thomas W. Merrill, *Judicial Deference to Executive Precedent*, 101 YALE L. J. 969, 980 (1992). The Supreme Court continues to defer at step two, although sometimes an agency does not prevail. *See, e.g., AT & T Corporation v. Iowa Utilities Board*, 525 U.S. 366, 392, 119 S.Ct. 721, 142 L.Ed.2d 835 (1999) (invalidating an FCC regulation because the Commission had not interpreted the terms of the statute in a "reasonable fashion").

3.   Because of the extreme deference that courts show agencies in *Chevron*'s step two, application of step one becomes critical. Agencies want to show that a statute is ambiguous; persons challenging the agency interpretation want to show that it is not. The Court has given mixed signals as to what it will look to determine ambiguity. In some cases, the Court determines whether a statute is ambiguous under a "plain meaning" test that forgoes the use of such tools of statutory construction such as legislative history or inferring legislative intent from the statute's animating principles. In other cases, the court will move to step two only if it cannot resolve an ambiguity by applying such tools of statutory construction.

Using the first approach, the Court has described the analysis at step one as follows:

> In ascertaining the plain meaning of the statute, the court must look to the particular statutory language at issue, as well as the language and design of the statute as a whole. If the statute is silent or ambiguous with respect to the specific issue addressed by the regulation, the question becomes whether the regulation is a permissible construction of the statute. If the agency regulation is not in conflict with the plain meaning of the statute, a reviewing court must give deference to the agency's interpretation of the statute.

K Mart Corp. v. Cartier, Inc. 486 U.S. 281, 291–92, 108 S.Ct. 1811, 1817–18, 100 L.Ed.2d 313 (1988).

Using the second approach, the Court has described the analysis at step one as " 'determin[ing] congressional intent using traditional tools of statutory construction.' " The starting point is "the language of the statute," but "in expounding a statute," a court is "not guided by a single sentence, but look[s] to the provisions of the whole law, and to its object and policy." *Dole v. United Steelworkers of America*, 494 U.S. 26, 35, 110 S.Ct. 929, 934, 108 L.Ed.2d 23 (1990). In *Chemical Manufacturers Assoc.* v. *Natural Resources Defense Council, Inc.*, 470 U.S. 116, 126, 105 S.Ct. 1102, 1108, 84 L.Ed.2d 90 (1985), for instance, the Court announced it would defer to the agency's interpretation "unless the legislative history or the purpose or structure reveal a contrary intent on the part of Congress."

4.   The Court's two approaches to step one are in part a product of its assessment of the value of legislative history. Some members of the Supreme Court, such as Justices Scalia and Thomas, have expressed displeasure with judicial reliance on legislative history to interpret statutes in any circumstances, not just when *Chevron* might be applicable because an agency's interpretation of its mandate is in question. In essence, their position is two-fold: legislative history as evidence of congressional intent is a fiction, not reality, and the meaning of laws should be available to all—that is, apparent on the face of the statute, not hidden in historical materials which only lawyers (and historians) may be able to find. The majority of the Court, however, reflects what is now the traditional view, that legislative history is a tool to aid in determining the meaning of legislative language. *See* Michael Sherman, *The Use of Legislative History: A Debate Between Justice Scalia and Judge Breyer*, 16 ADMIN. L. NEWS 1 (Summer 1991).

Nevertheless, the majority view does not include agreement on the particular weight to be assigned to legislative history or when it is to be used. For example, one view is that a person looks to legislative history only when the statutory language is ambiguous. In the *Chevron* context, however, that might mean you would *not* look to legislative history at all, because if the statute is ambiguous, the court is to proceed to step two—to ask whether the agency's interpretation is reasonable. Or, it might mean that the court would look to legislative history if the language is ambiguous, and only if the law is still ambiguous after looking at the legislative history, would one go to *Chevron* step two. The Court has not definitively answered these questions.

5.   Just as there is question about the use of legislative history to resolve (or find) ambiguity, there is question about the use of canons of construction to resolve textual ambiguity. *See* Eben Moglen & Richard J. Pierce, *Sunstein's New Canons: Choosing the Fictions of Statutory Interpretation*, 57 U.CHI. L.REV. 1203 (1990). Although the Court has not directly addressed the issue, it appears that courts are willing to use

canons, as traditional means of statutory construction, to resolve ambiguity.

6. Some believe that a plain language approach is more likely to result in a finding of ambiguity. Intuitively, it would seem that a court will reach *Chevron's* step two more easily if it will not look to the legislative history and legislative purpose to resolve ambiguity. Nevertheless, as Justice Scalia, the primary advocate against use of legislative history, has observed

> where one stands on this last point—how clear is clear—may have much to do with where one stands on the earlier points of what *Chevron* means and whether *Chevron* is desirable. In my experience, there is a fairly close correlation between the degree to which a person is (for want of a better word) a "strict constructionist" of statutes, and the degree to which that person favors *Chevron* and is willing to give it broad scope. The reason is obvious. One who finds more often (as I do) that the meaning of a statute is apparent from its text and from its relationship with other laws, thereby finds less often that the triggering requirement for *Chevron* deference exists. It is thus relatively rare that *Chevron* will require me to accept an interpretation which, though reasonable, I would not personally adopt. Contrariwise, one who abhors a "plain meaning" rule, and is willing to permit the apparent meaning of a statute to be impeached by the legislative history, will more frequently find agency-liberating ambiguity, and will discern a much broader range of "reasonable" interpretation that the agency may adopt and to which the courts must pay deference. The frequency with which *Chevron* will require that judge to accept an interpretation he thinks wrong is infinitely greater.

Antonin Scalia, *Judicial Deference to Administrative Interpretations of Law,* 1989 DUKE L.J. 511.

7. Consistent with Justice Scalia's prediction, Professor Pierce argues that increasing reliance by the Supreme Court on the plain meaning rule has decreased the Court's deference to agency statutory interpretations:

> The Court now rarely defers to an agency's construction of ambiguous statutory language because a majority of justices have now begun to use textualist methods of construction that routinely allow them to attribute "plain meaning" to statutory language that most observers would characterize as ambiguous or internally inconsistent.... Indeed, the Court's new approach accords significantly less deference to agency construction that was the case before *Chevron*.

Richard J. Pierce, *The Supreme Court's New Hypertextualism: An Invitation to Cacophony and Incoherence in the Administrative State*, 95 COLUM. L. REV. 749, 752 (1995). Professor Merrill explains, "In effect, the textualist interpreter does not *find* the meaning of the statute so much as *construct* the meaning. Such a person will very likely experience some difficulty in deferring to the meaning that other institutions have developed." Thomas W. Merrill, *Textualism and the Future of the* Chevron *Doctrine*, 72 Wash. U.L.Q. 351, 372 (1994) (emphasis in the original).

Not everyone agrees with Professor Pierce that a majority of the Supreme Court primarily relies on a plain meaning approach, as our previous note indicated. There is little doubt, however, that the plain meaning approach has decreased the Court's reliance on other forms of statutory interpretation, particularly legislative history. Why, according to Professor Merrill, is the plain meaning approach more likely to lead judges to reject agency statutory interpretations? What does he mean when he says that a textualist approach "constructs" the meaning of a statute, rather than "interprets" it? Should a judge assume that Congress meant the same meaning for a word that is the preferred meaning in a dictionary?

As the title of Professor Pierce's article reveals, he believes strict reliance on the plain meaning approach is more likely to lead to cacophony and incoherence in government regulation. If the Supreme Court is likely to defer to agency statutory interpretations, why might this choice increase the coherence of national regulatory and benefit programs? *See* Pierce, *supra*, at 753 n. 22.

8.   An interesting question regarding what can eliminate ambiguity is what effect prior judicial opinions have on what would otherwise be ambiguous statutes. In three cases, the Court has made clear that *its* prior decisions regarding the meaning of ambiguous laws eliminate *Chevron* ambiguity. *See Neal v. United States*, 516 U.S. 284, 116 S.Ct. 763, 133 L.Ed.2d 709 (1996); *Lechmere, Inc. v. NLRB.*, 502 U.S. 527, 112 S.Ct. 841, 117 L.Ed.2d 79 (1992); *Maislin Industries, U.S., Inc. v. Primary Steel, Inc.*, 497 U.S. 116, 110 S.Ct. 2759, 111 L.Ed.2d 94 (1990). The Court has not addressed what effect lower court decisions should have, but decisions in lower courts on the issue have generally held that lower court decisions do not eliminate ambiguity. *See, e.g., Satellite Broadcasting and Communications Assn. of America v. Oman*, 17 F.3d 344 (11th Cir.1994); *but see Bankers Trust New York Corp. v. United States*, 225 F.3d 1368 (Fed.Cir.2000) (agency regulation cannot trump a court's established precedent).

9.   Another recurring issue in applying *Chevron* is the question of whether it applies to all agency interpretations of its statutory mandate, or whether various types of interpretations escape *Chevron* deference. In *Food and Drug Administration v. Brown & Williamson Tobacco Corporation*, 529 U.S. 120, 120 S.Ct. 1291, 146 L.Ed.2d 121 (2000), the Court found *Chevron* inapplicable because it had doubts that Congress actually intended to delegate interpretive authority to FDA, notwithstanding the presence of a statutory ambiguity. Thus, there may be cases where, although statutory language is ambiguous, a court will not defer to a reasonable interpretation of that language by an agency under step 2 of *Chevron*.

10.   *Chevron* involved a legislative rule, adopted after notice and comment rulemaking. Does *Chevron* also apply to an interpretative rule

adopted without notice and comment? We will take up this issue in Chapter Five.

Problem 2–9: Applying Chevron

The Food Safety and Inspection Service (FSIS), located in the Department of Agriculture (USDA), is responsible for "the inspection of poultry and poultry products ... to prevent the movement or sale in interstate or foreign commerce ... of poultry products which are adulterated or misbranded." Poultry is adulterated when "it bears or contains any poisonous or deleterious substance which may render it injurious to health...."

FSIS has an important public health mandate. About 7 billion chickens and turkeys are processed annually in the United States. Proper handling during processing is important because about 40 percent of raw poultry is contaminated with salmonella, a bacterium that cause various diseases in humans and animals. Although FSIS inspects poultry processors, at least 40,000 salmonella infections are reported each year to the Centers for Disease Control and Prevention (CDC), a federal agency that tracks infectious diseases. CDC estimates that each year between 40,000 and 4 million people become ill from salmonella and about 500 of these persons die of salmonellosis, an illness that causes fever and intestinal disorders.

Congress has required that "[E]ach official establishment slaughtering poultry or processing poultry products ... shall have premises, facilities, and equipment, and shall be operated in accordance with such sanitary practices as are required by regulations promulgated by the Secretary for the purposes of preventing the entry into ... commerce ... of poultry products which are adulterated." Accordingly, USDA has published detailed regulations specifying how chicken and turkeys are to be processed to kill harmful bacteria.

Congress has also required that USDA protect the public from unsafe poultry or poultry products that are imported into the United States. For poultry that is imported from countries other than Canada and Mexico, USDA is to ensure that the poultry is "subject to the *same* inspection, sanitary, quality, species verification, and residue standards applied to products produced in the United States," and has "been processed in facilities and under conditions that are the *same* as those under which similar products are processed in the United States." (Emphasis added). For poultry that is imported from Canada and Mexico, USDA is to ensure that the poultry is "subject to the inspection, sanitary, quality, species verification, and residue standards that are *equivalent to* United States standards" and has "been processed in facilities and conditions that meet standards that are *equivalent to* United States standards." (Emphasis added).

USDA has promulgated a regulation concerning poultry imported from all other countries that reads as follows:

Whenever it shall be determined by the Administrator that the system of poultry inspection maintained by any foreign country, with respect to establishments preparing products in such country for export to the United States, ensures compliance of such establishments and their poultry products, with requirements *at least equal to* all the provisions of the Act and the regulations in this part which are applied to official establishments in the United States and their poultry products, and that reliance can be placed upon certificates required under this subpart from authorities of such foreign country, . . . Thereafter, poultry products processed in such establishments which are certified and approved . . . shall be eligible, so far as the regulations in this part are concerned, for importation into the United States from such foreign country after applicable requirements of this part have been met.

(Emphasis added).

(a) As a lawyer for the National Broiler Council (NBC), a non-profit trade association formed by domestic poultry producers, how would you advise your client with respect to seeking judicial review of this rule? What is the likelihood for success and what relief would you get if you are successful? Are there other options to litigation?

(b) Assume NBC files a lawsuit in the Southern District of Mississippi arguing that the regulation's requirement that foreign poultry producers be subject to procedures "at least equal to" United States procedures violated the Act, which requires that foreign producers, except those in Canada and Mexico, be subject to procedures that are the "same" as domestic procedures. USDA is the defendant. As a lawyer for the Australian Trade Association (ATA), what are your options? The ATA is interested in the outcome because Australian poultry producers use radiation to kill bacteria on poultry. This process, which is widely used in Europe and Australia, is acknowledged to be more protective of consumers than the procedures used in the United States. It has not been used in the United States, however, because of consumer reluctance to purchase foods that have been radiated. USDA does not currently require domestic poultry processors to use radiation although it acknowledges that this process is the equivalent to any process used in the United States in terms of protecting consumers from salmonella. ATA believes that consumers in the United States can be convinced to purchase radiated poultry if it can be sold in this country.

(c) What arguments should NBC and USDA (and ATA) make to the court?

Problem Materials

TITLE 21. FOOD AND DRUGS AND POULTRY PRODUCTS INSPECTION

§ 452. Congressional declaration of policy

It is hereby declared to be the policy of the Congress to provide for the inspection of poultry and poultry products and otherwise regulate the processing and distribution of such articles as hereinafter prescribed to prevent the movement or sale in interstate or foreign commerce of, or the burdening of such commerce by, poultry products which are adulterated or misbranded. It is the intent of Congress that when poultry and poultry products are condemned because of disease, the reason for condemnation in such instances shall be supported by scientific fact, information, or criteria, and such condemnation under this chapter shall be achieved through uniform inspection standards and uniform applications thereof.

UNITED STATES DEPARTMENT OF AGRICULTURE, FOOD SAFETY AND INSPECTION SERVICE, FINAL RULE: REQUIREMENTS FOR IMPORTED POULTRY PRODUCTS

54 Fed. Reg. 43948 (1989).

SUMMARY: This rule implements the provisions of the Food Security Act of 1985, Public Law 99–198, that amended the Poultry Products Inspection Act (PPIA). The rule amends the poultry products inspection regulations to specifically require foreign countries to implement a residue sampling and testing program at the point of slaughter for poultry and poultry products offered for importation into the United States. The rule also amends the regulations to make clear that all inspection, sanitation, quality, species verification, and residue standards that are applied to imported poultry products must meet the same standards as those applied to poultry and poultry products produced in the United States. . . .

BACKGROUND

Section 17 of the Poultry Products Inspection Act (PPIA) (21 U.S.C. § 466) prohibits the importation into the United States of slaughtered poultry, or parts thereof, unless they are healthful, wholesome, fit for human food, not adulterated, and contain no dye, chemical, preservative, or ingredient which renders them unhealthful, unwholesome, adulterated, or unfit for human food, and unless they also comply with rules and regulations made by the Secretary to assure that imported poultry and poultry products comply with the standards provided for in the Act. The regulations addressing imported poultry or poultry products are contained in 9 CFR part 381. In these regulations the Administrator has established procedures by which foreign countries desiring to export poultry or poultry products to the United States may become eligible to do so.

Section 381.196 of the poultry products inspection regulations provides that a poultry inspection system maintained by a foreign country, with respect to establishments preparing products in that country for export to the United States, must ensure compliance of such establishments and their poultry products with requirements at least equal to all of the provisions of the PPIA and the regulations that are applied to official establishments in the United States and their poultry products. In addition, these regulations provide for certain other system requirements as a means for FSIS to assure that eligible foreign countries are complying with on-going conditions of eligibility. . . .

EXPORT ELIGIBILITY REQUIREMENTS

The Foreign Programs Division, International Programs, of FSIS has primary responsibility for determining that countries producing poultry or poultry products for export to the United States have inspection programs that are designed to assure that all such exports are safe, wholesome, unadulterated and not misbranded and comply with all other provisions of the PPIA and regulations thereunder (9 CFR part 381 et seq.).

To determine eligibility, FSIS conducts a complete evaluation of the country's inspection system. The evaluation consists of two major parts: A review of foreign system documents, and an on-site review of the country's inspection system operations. . . .

CONTINUING OVERSIGHT OF ELIGIBLE COUNTRIES

Once the poultry inspection system of a foreign country has been certified by the Agency as eligible to export products to the United States, the individual establishments operating within that country desiring to export products to the United States must apply to their national inspection authorities for certification. The chief inspection official of the foreign country must in turn certify to FSIS that each establishment authorized to export products to the United States meets all the applicable standards. . . .

FSIS personnel conduct periodic on-site reviews of foreign inspection systems. The reviews focus on the full spectrum of risks to the production and processing of acceptable poultry products and how the foreign inspection system controls these risks. The on-site system review provides FSIS with continued assurance that the foreign country is maintaining an inspection system that is at least equal to the inspection system of the United States. . . .

THE FOOD SECURITY ACT OF 1985

On December 23, 1985, Public Law 99–198, The Food Security Act of 1985, was enacted (hereinafter referred to as the 1985 Farm Bill).

Section 1701 of Public Law 99–198 amended section 17 of the Poultry Products Inspection Act (PPIA) (21 U.S.C. § 466) to require residue testing and species verification of imported poultry or parts or products. This legislation is comparable to an amendment to the Federal Meat Inspection Act (FMIA) provided by the Agriculture and Food Act of 1981 (Pub. L. 97–98) that mandated residue and species verification for imported meat products.

Section 1701 of the 1985 Farm Bill adds a new subparagraph (d) to section 17 of the PPIA as follows:

(d)(1) Notwithstanding any other provision of law, all poultry, or parts or products thereof, capable of use as human food offered for importation into the United States shall:

(A) be subject to the same inspection, sanitary, quality, species verification, and residue standards applied to products produced in the United States; and

(B) have been processed in facilities and under conditions that are the same as those under which similar products are processed in the United States.

(2) Any such imported poultry article that does not meet such standards shall not be permitted entry into the United States.

(3) The Secretary shall enforce this subsection through:

(A) random inspection for such species verification and for residues; and

(B) random sampling and testing of internal organs and fat of carcasses for residues at the point of slaughter by the exporting country, in accordance with methods approved by the Secretary.

The primary purpose of the legislation was to add a provision to the PPIA that would require foreign countries currently exporting or desiring to export poultry or poultry products to the United States to develop and implement a program for the sampling and testing of residues. This new requirement would apply the requirements for residue testing that were specified in the Food and Agriculture Act of 1981 for imported meat products to imported poultry products.

COMMENTS ON THE PROPOSED RULE

Therefore, on May 1, 1987, FSIS published a proposed rule to implement the provisions of the 1985 Farm Bill with regard to requirements for poultry products intended for export to the United States. FSIS received 31 comments in response to the proposed rule: 7 in favor and 24 not in favor. Those commenters in support of the proposed rule included 2 industry members, 3 trade associations, 1 government agency and 1 foreign government agency. Those commenters not in support of the proposed rule included 14 industry members, 8 Members of Congress, on behalf of one or more of the 14 industry members, and 2 trade associations. The following are the issues raised by the commenters and FSIS's response to each.

Comment: All of the opposing commenters objected to FSIS's interpretation of the language in the Farm Bill which states that a foreign inspection system be "the same as" the United States inspection system before product can be imported. These commenters felt that the phrase should be distinguished from "at least equal to" because the latter phrase would allow for subjective evaluation of foreign country requirements, would permit standards less than those of the United States, would create an unfair competitive advantage for foreign poultry products and would result in inferior products entering the United States.

Response: As a result of the legislation, the PPIA does provide that imported poultry and poultry products must comply with certain standards which are "the same as" those applicable to products produced in the United States. However, this does not mean that all the regulations of a foreign country must be precisely, word for word, "the same as" those in the United States. In our view, the Act does not prohibit a foreign country from having requirements more stringent than those applicable to products produced in the United States. If a requirement is narrow and specific (e.g., a product standard, maximum water intake level), it can be relatively easy to determine whether the foreign country's requirement is "the same as" ours. However, if our requirement is general and is applied on a case-by-case basis (e.g., facility requirements to preclude adulteration), the requirement can be met by a similarly general requirement. A general requirement permits variations within an established framework. FSIS applies "the same as" requirement by assessing whether the alternative procedures, even if they employ different inspectional techniques, are at least equal to the requirements applicable to domestically produced product. That is, the means of achieving products the same as ours in a foreign country will, in some respects, vary from the means employed in the United States. Interpretation of the law in this way provides the only reasonable basis for comparing inspection systems, since literal application of the term "the same as" would prohibit all imports of poultry products from foreign countries and would be nothing more than a non-tariff trade barrier. The USDA presently recognizes the poultry inspection systems in five countries (Canada, France, Israel, Great Britain and Hong Kong). Again, literal application of the term "the same as" would require the USDA to withdraw its recognition of those countries' eligibility to ship poultry and poultry products to the United States. USDA does not believe it was the intent of Congress that such action be taken.

These foreign inspection systems have evolved in widely varying cultural and political environments under various animal health, public health and food production circumstances. This has resulted in a variety of specific procedures and processes used in maintaining national inspection controls. The quality of the finished product is what is important and decisive. Nonetheless, there are certain features that any system must have to be considered "the same as" ours. These basic requirements are currently in FSIS regulations (9 CFR 381.196).

131 CONGRESSIONAL RECORD 33358
(Nov. 22, 1985).

Mr. HELMS. On behalf of Senator ZORINSKY and myself, I send [a] purely technical amendment[ ] to the desk and ask that [it] be immediately considered.

The PRESIDING OFFICER. The amendment will be stated.

The assistant legislative clerk read as follows:

The Senator from North Carolina <Mr. HELMS> for himself and Mr. ZORINSKY, proposes an amendment numbered 1163.

On page 455, line 18, strike out "at least equal to" and insert in lieu thereof "the same as".

Mr. HELMS. Mr. President, this amendment . . . changes the provision relating to inspection of imported poultry products to provide that imported poultry must have been processed in facilities and under conditions that are the same as those under which similar products are processed in the United States. This change clarifies the provision to reflect the original intent of the provision as adopted by the committee in markup.

The PRESIDING OFFICER. Is there further debate? The Chair hears none. The question is on agreeing to the amendment.

The amendment (No. 1163) was agreed to.

S. REP. NO. 99–145, at 516, 3 U.S.C.C.A.N. 2182
(1985).

[The Agriculture Committee in markup amended the 1985 Farm Bill to adopt an equivalency requirement. The Committee report explained that the change would:]

(7) amend the Poultry Products Inspection Act to require all poultry and poultry products, capable of use as human food that are imported into the United States, to be subject to inspection, sanitary, quality, species verification, and residue standards applied to poultry products produced in the United States. The Amendment also would require that such products be produced in facilities and under conditions at least equal to those under which similar products are processed in the United States. Any imported poultry article that does not meet the standards would not be permitted entry into the Untied States. . . .

BLACKS LAW DICTIONARY 1340
(6th ed. 1990).

Same: Identical, equal, equivalent. The word "same," however, does not always mean "identical." It frequently means of the kind or species, not the specific thing. . . .

RANDOM HOUSE COLLEGE DICTIONARY 1164
(1973).

same . . . *adj.* 1. Identical with what is about to be or has just been mentioned. . . . 2. being one or identical though having different names, aspects, etc. . . . 3. agreeing in kind, amount, etc.; corresponding . . .

2. SUBSTANTIVE DECISIONS

When an agency promulgates a rule, it reaches two types of substantive decisions. First, it determines on the basis of the evidence available to it, what are the relevant facts. Next, it decides what type of rule, if any, is appropriate in light of those facts, choosing the regulatory option that will best further its statutory mandate. Section 706 authorizes courts to review both types of conclusions when it mandates that the "reviewing court shall . . . hold unlawful and set aside agency action, findings, and conclusions found to be—(A) arbitrary, capricious, an abuse of discretion or not otherwise in accordance with law; . . . [and] (E) unsupported by substantial evidence in a case subject to sections 556 and 557 of this title. . . ." 5 U.S.C.A. § 6706.

Judicial review of the agency's substantive decisions under section 706 involves three issues: (1) What is the scope of review: "arbitrary & capricious" or "substantial evidence"?; (2) What constitutes the rulemaking record to be reviewed by the court? ; (3) What obligation does the scope of review impose on an agency to explain its decision?

a. Scope of review

As section 706 states, the "substantial evidence" standard applies when an agency must comply with sections 556–557, which involves "formal" rulemaking (and adjudication, which will be addressed in the next chapter). Thus, in informal rulemaking, the "arbitrary and capricious" scope of review will normally apply. In the agency's statutory mandate, however, Congress sometimes requires the use of a "substantial evidence" standard for judicial review of informal or hybrid rulemaking. *See* Note, *Convergence of the Substantial Evidence and Arbitrary and Capricious Standards of Review During Informal Rulemaking*, 54 GEO. WASH. 541, 542 N. 5 (1986) (list of agencies subject to substantial evidence scope of review for informal or hybrid rulemaking). For example, OSHA uses informal rulemaking to promulgate workplace health and safety standards, but it is subject to a "substantial evidence" scope of review. 29 U.S.C.A. § 655(f). A litigant must therefore check an agency's statutory mandate to determine whether it imposes a different scope of review on the agency's rulemaking.

Because so little agency rulemaking is formal rulemaking, the judicial decisions explaining "substantial evidence" review have developed almost entirely in the context of formal adjudication, covered in the next chapter. For purposes here, it suffices to say that the "substantial evidence" standard instructs the court to uphold a rule if it finds the agency's decision to be "reasonable," or the record contains "such evidence as a reasonable mind might accept as adequate to support a conclusion." *Consolidated Edison v. NLRB*, 305 U.S. 197, 229, 59 S.Ct. 206, 216, 83 L.Ed. 126 (1938). The standard does not require that the court agree with the agency's conclusions; it only requires that the agency's choice is a reasonable one, even if the court would have made another choice.

Historically, the "arbitrary and capricious" standard was viewed as very deferential, essentially the equivalent of judicial review of economic regulation under substantive due process. *See, e.g., Pacific States Box & Basket Co. v. White*, 296 U.S. 176, 56 S.Ct. 159, 80 L.Ed. 138 (1935). Unlike "substantial evidence" review, which required the decision to be supported by evidence in a record developed in a trial-like proceeding, "arbitrary and capricious" review required no record or decision to justify the agency's action. Rather, a challenger had to prove the negative—that there were no facts or good reasons to support the agency action. This all changed in the early 1970s, beginning with *Citizens to Preserve Overton Park v. Volpe*, 401 U.S. 402, 91 S.Ct. 814, 28 L.Ed.2d 136 (1971), which some have called the first modern administrative law case. There, the Supreme Court said that the arbitrary and capricious standard "require[s] the reviewing court to engage in a substantial inquiry...., a thorough, probing in-depth review.... [To] find arbitrariness, the court must consider whether the decision was based on a consideration of relevant factors and whether there has been a clear error of judgment.... Although this inquiry into the facts is to be searching and careful, the ultimate standard of review is a narrow one." Precisely what this means is the subject of much writing, both scholarly and judicial. One question has been how does this modern "arbitrary and capricious" standard compare to the "substantial evidence" standard. Although the Supreme Court once suggested that the arbitrary and capricious standard was "more lenient" than the substantial evidence standard, *American Paper Institute v. American Electric Power Service Corp.*, 461 U.S. 402, 405 n. 1, 103 S.Ct. 1921, 1924 n. 1, 76 L.Ed.2d 22 (1983), it has never defined the difference between the two standards or explained why one standard would be more lenient than the other. Appellate courts tend to treat the two standards as functionally identical, observing that the two standards tend to "converge" or that any distinction between the two is "largely semantic." *E.g., Association of Data Processing Service Organizations, Inc. v. Board of Governors*, 745 F.2d 677 (D.C.Cir.1984) (Scalia, J.).

There are two reasons why the two standards have converged. Prior to *Overton Park*, informal actions neither had "records" nor contemporaneous agency explanations to justify why the agency reached its decision, whereas formal proceedings under sections 556 and 557 had both. *Overton Park* initiated the concept of a "record" for an informal agency proceeding. Therefore, while the means by which the record is created (and what may be in it) may differ between formal and informal proceedings, both will have records by which to assess the reasonableness of the agency decision. *Overton Park* is also the origin of the need for an agency to explain its decision in informal proceedings. Consequently, this contemporaneous explanation was similarly subject to judicial review.

Which standard applies, however, might make some difference. Professor Roy Schotland has described the scope of review as a "mood point" which sets the critical attitude with which a court should approach an administrative decision. Thus, a court might be less tolerant of a possible error by an agency in an informal or hybrid rulemaking under a substantial evidence standard contained in the agency's statutory mandate, compared to section 706's otherwise applicable arbitrary and capricious standard, if the court perceived Congress's intent in using the substantial evidence standard was to increase judicial scrutiny.

b. *Rulemaking Record*

Section 706 requires that a court "review the whole record" when determining whether to affirm a rule. This obligation raises the issue of what constitutes the "whole record" in formal and informal rulemaking.

In formal rulemaking, the APA's drafters envisioned that the "substantial evidence" standard would apply to the evidentiary record created by the hearing procedures specified in sections 556–57. The testimony and documents in the record are "evidence," and a court can evaluate this information to determine if the agency's conclusions are supported by "such relevant evidence as a reasonable mind might accept as adequate to support a conclusion." *Consolidated Edison*, 305 U.S. at 229, 59 S.Ct. at 216.

There is no similar record required by the APA for informal rulemaking, however. As discussed earlier in the chapter, an agency is not limited to the comments submitted in choosing what type of rule to adopt, but rather it can rely on any relevant information that comes to its attention. For this reason, the Supreme Court in *Overton Park* defined the "record" for informal proceedings to be the information that the agency actually considered in making the decision. After *Overton Park*, the record for informal rulemaking normally is composed of the Federal Register notices for the proposed and final rule, the comments that were submitted, and any studies or data created or used by the agency that were not published in the notices.

One of the differences between judicial review of a trial-like proceeding and a rulemaking is the nature of the factual determinations an agency is making. In a formal agency adjudication, as well in court trials, the nature of the facts in issue usually relate to what happened in the past. In rulemaking, however, often the "facts" in issue relate to what will happen in the future (thereby justifying a regulation to prevent it). As Judge McGowan noted with respect to an OSHA standard rulemaking,

> From extensive and often conflicting evidence, the Secretary [of Labor] in this case made numerous factual determinations. With respect to some of those questions, the evidence was such that the task consisted primarily of evaluating the data and drawing conclusions from it. The court can review the data in the record and determine whether it reflects substantial support for the Secretary's position. But some of the questions involved in the promulgation of these standards are on the frontiers of scientific knowledge, and consequently as to them insufficient data is presently available to make a fully informed factual determination. Decision making must in that circumstance depend to a greater extent upon policy judgments and less upon purely factual analysis.
>
> . . . [P]olicy choices of this sort are not susceptible to the same type of verification by reference to the record as are some factual questions.

Industrial Union Department v. Hodgson, 499 F.2d 467, 474–75 (D.C.Cir. 1974).

When unknowable facts are being reviewed, the Supreme Court has emphasized that courts should be highly deferential. In *Baltimore Gas & Electric Co.* v. *Natural Resources Defense Council*, 462 U.S. 87, 103 S.Ct. 2246, 76 L.Ed.2d 437 (1983), the Court affirmed a rule stating that licensing boards of the Nuclear Regulatory Commission (NRC) should assume that permanent storage of nuclear waste would have no adverse effect on the environment for purposes of granting a license to nuclear power plants. The Court unanimously reversed a decision of the D.C. Circuit that the NRC did not have sufficient evidence to support this finding. The Court found that because the agency had explored the uncertain risks associated with permanent storage of nuclear waste, the D.C. Circuit should have deferred to the agency's policy judgment concerning the impact of those risks:

> Resolution of these fundamental policy issues lies . . . with Congress and the agencies to which Congress has delegated authority.
>
> . . .
>
> [A] reviewing court must remember that the commission is making predictions, within its area of special expertise, at the frontiers of science. When examining this kind of scientific determination, as opposed to simple findings of fact, a court must generally be at its most deferential.

Id. at 103, 103 S.Ct. at 2255.

c. *Adequate Explanation*

In recent years, judicial review has focussed on the requirement that agencies provide "adequate reasons" for adoption of the rule. *See* Sidney A. Shapiro & Richard E. Levy, *Heightened Scrutiny of the Fourth Branch: Separation of Powers and The Requirement of Adequate Reasons For Agency Decisions*, 1987 Duke L.J. 387. When an agency lacks "adequate reasons," its action is "arbitrary and capricious." Nevertheless, a court will normally remand a rule to an agency rather than declaring it to be invalid. Although the agency has not offered an adequate explanation for its rules, the remand recognizes that it might be able to do so if given another opportunity to defend its rule.

The definition of "arbitrary and capricious" as requiring "adequate reasons" started in the 1970s. In *Overton Park*, the Court refused to require agencies to produce written findings *as a procedural matter*. However, in order for it to determine whether the agency decision was arbitrary or capricious, and absent a contemporaneous explanation by the agency, the Court remanded the case back to the district court to take testimony from the head of the agency as to the reasons behind his decision. Moreover, the Court indicated that because these reasons would be given after the fact, they would have to be subject to a certain skepticism. As you might imagine, agency heads do not want to be examined or cross-examined in court as to their reasons for adopting a rule. Consequently, agencies have developed the practice of providing their explanations in writing as part of the final rule. In addition, as a contemporaneous statement, this explanation does not trigger the courts' heightened scrutiny of a *post hoc* rationalization. If the written statement is inadequate, current practice is to remand the rule to the agency for further explanation, rather than take oral testimony in court on the issue.

The circuit courts quickly applied *Overton Park* in reviewing informal rulemaking even though *Overton Park* itself involved review of informal adjudication. Judge Harold Leventhal of the District of Columbia Court of Appeals gave the name "hard look" to the scrutiny mandated by *Overton Park*. He explained:

> In the exercise of the court's supervisory function, full allowance must be given for the reality that agency matters typically involve a kind of expertise—sometimes technical in a scientific sense, sometimes more a matter of specialization in kinds of regulatory programs. Nevertheless, the court must ... ensure that the agency "has given reasoned discretion to all of the material facts and issues." The court exercises this ... role with particular vigilance if it becomes aware, especially from a combination of danger signals, that the agency has not really taken a *hard look* at the salient problems, and has not genuinely engaged in reasoned decisionmaking.

Harold Leventhal, *Environmental Decisionmaking And The Role Of The Courts*, 122 U. Pa. L. Rev. 509, 511 (1974) (emphasis in original).

In *Motor Vehicle Manufacturers Assoc. v. State Farm Mutual Automobile Ins. Co.*, 463 U.S. 29, 103 S.Ct. 2856, 77 L.Ed.2d 443 (1983), which is included in the problem materials below, the Court confirmed that an agency must give adequate reasons for a rule. As the Court explained, "the agency must examine the relevant data and articulate a satisfactory explanation for its action including a 'rational connection between the facts found and the choice made.'" *Id.* at 43. Moreover, the Court indicated when an agency fails to meet this obligation: "Normally, an agency rule would be arbitrary and capricious if the agency has relied on factors which Congress has not intended it to consider, entirely failed to consider an important aspect of the problem, offered an explanation for its decision that runs counter to the evidence, or is so implausible that it could not be ascribed to a difference in view or the product of agency expertise." *Id.*

When an agency has not provided an adequate explanation, even if the court itself could discern an adequate explanation from the record, the court should remand the case back to the agency. The leading case for this proposition is *SEC v. Chenery Corp.*, 318 U.S. 80, 63 S.Ct. 454, 87 L.Ed. 626 (1943). There the Securities and Exchange Commission had disapproved the Chenery Corporation's reorganization plan on the theory that the officers had violated a common law fiduciary duty by trading in the stock during the reorganization, thereby rendering the reorganization not "fair and equitable" as required by the statute. The Supreme Court held that the SEC erred in its determination that the officers had violated a common law fiduciary duty, so the SEC's decision could not stand, even though the Court went on to suggest that the SEC could exercise its own policy making authority to declare such trading not fair and equitable. The Court said, "[t]he Commission's action cannot be upheld merely because findings might have been made and considerations disclosed which would justify its order...." The Court noted that Congress had entrusted the agency, not the courts, with the exercise of discretion in implementing the statute, so a court can only review the justification made by the agency, not supply its own.

Problem 2–10: Judicial Review of Substantive Decisions

In 1975, Congress enacted the Magnuson–Moss Warranty—Federal Trade Commission Improvement Act. The Act clarified that the Federal Trade Commission (FTC) had rulemaking authority, required the FTC to use hybrid rulemaking, and mandated that the Commission promulgate a rule regulating "warranties and warranty practices in connection with the sale of used motor vehicles."

In 1981, just before the Carter administration left office, the FTC promulgated a rule that required used car dealers to post on a window a standard sticker that contained several consumer warnings. The two most important warnings were:

    (a) *Warranty Disclosure:* The dealer was required to disclose to a buyer whether the car was being sold without any warranty ("As

Is"/No Warranty), with a "Limited Warranty," or with a "Full Warranty" by checking the appropriate box on the window sticker.

(b) *Mechanical Defects Disclosure*: The window sticker contained a list of potential major mechanical defects and the dealer was required to check off those defects of which the dealer had knowledge. The dealer, however, was not required to inspect any automobile it was selling.

In 1983, before completion of judicial review of the rule, the FTC announced that it would reconsider its regulation, and the court remanded the rule back to the Commission. After soliciting further comments, the FTC adopted the same rule as previously with some minor changes, but without the known-defects disclosure requirement.

Consumers Union, which opposed deletion of the known-defects provision, sought judicial review of the revised rule in the D.C. Circuit Court of Appeals. Two trade associations, the National Automobile Dealers Association (NADA) and the National Independent Automobile Dealers Association (NIADA), intervened to support the FTC's decision to drop the known-defects requirement.

(1) If you are a lawyer representing:

(a) Consumers Union, what arguments would you make that the court should reverse the Commission concerning the known-defect rule; or

(b) NADA or NIADA, what arguments would you make that the court should affirm the Commission concerning the known-defect rule.

(2) As you consider what arguments that you can raise on behalf of the parties, please identify the "scope of review" that the court should apply and explain your choice.

Problem Materials

UNITED STATES CODE ANNOTATED TITLE 15. COMMERCE AND TRADE

§ 45. Unfair methods competition unlawful; prevention by Commission

(a) Declaration of unlawfulness; power to prohibit unfair practices; inapplicability to foreign trade

(1) Unfair methods of competition in or affecting commerce, and unfair or deceptive acts or practices, in or affecting commerce, are declared unlawful.

§ 57a. Unfair or deceptive acts or practices rulemaking proceedings

(a) Authority of Commission to prescribe rules and general statements of policy

(1) Except as provided in subsection (i) of this section, the Commission may prescribe—

. . .

(B) rules which define with specificity acts or practices which are unfair or deceptive acts or practices in or affecting commerce (within the meaning of section 45(a)(1) of this title), except that the Commission shall not develop or promulgate any trade rule or regulation with regard to the regulation of the development and utilization of the standards and certification activities pursuant to this section. Rules under this subparagraph may include requirements prescribed for the purpose of preventing such acts or practices. . . .

(e) Judicial review; petition; jurisdiction and venue; rulemaking record; additional submissions and presentations; scope of review and relief; review by Supreme Court; additional remedies

(1)(A) Not later than 60 days after a rule is promulgated under subsection (a)(1)(B) of this section by the Commission, any interested person (including a consumer or consumer organization) may file a petition, in the United States Court of Appeals for the District of Columbia circuit or for the circuit in which such person resides or has his principal place of business, for judicial review of such rule. . . .

(B) For purpose of this section, the term "rulemaking record" means the rule, its statement of basis and purpose, the transcript required by subsection (c)(5) of this section, any written submissions, and any other information which the Commission considers relevant to such rule. . . .

(3) Upon the filing of the petition under paragraph (1) of this subsection, the court shall have jurisdiction to review the rule in accordance with chapter 7 of Title 5 and to grant appropriate relief, including interim relief, as provided in such chapter. The court shall hold unlawful and set aside the rule on any ground specified in subparagraphs (A), (B), (C), or (D) of section 706(2) of Title 5 (taking due account of the rule of prejudicial error), or if—

(A) the court finds that the Commission's action is not supported by substantial evidence in the rulemaking record (as defined in paragraph (1) (B) of this subsection) taken as a whole, . . .

The term "evidence," as used in this paragraph, means any matter in the rulemaking record.

(4) The judgment of the court affirming or setting aside, in whole or in part, any such rule shall be final, subject to review by the Supreme Court of the United States upon certiorari or certification, as provided in section 1254 of Title 28. . . .

FEDERAL TRADE COMMISSION, FINAL RULE: SALE OF USED MOTOR VEHICLES

46 Fed. Reg. 41328 (1981).

II.   Basis for a Rule

A.   Deceptive Practices in the Industry. The record in this proceeding provides substantial evidence of deceptive acts and practices by used car dealers. The principal abuses recorded relate to oral misrepresentations by dealers regarding: (1) warranty responsibilities for after-sale repairs and (2) mechanical condition at the time of sale. Such oral statements are often inconsistent with the warranty terms, or disclaimers thereof, provided in the written sales contract and with the dealer's actual knowledge of the car's mechanical condition at the time of sale. Consumer injury occurs because consumers make purchasing decisions based on dealer deception and not only fail to get the car they bargained for but face unexpected expensive repair bills. . . .

2.   Mechanical Condition Practices—a. Materiality of Mechanical Condition Information. The utility of a vehicle as a means of transportation is directly affected by mechanical condition. Therefore, it is not surprising that consumer research indicates a consistent concern about mechanical condition. In fact, mechanical condition at the time of sale is reported by consumers as the most important factor in reaching a purchasing decision. Consumers who are aware of defects prior to purchase are able to use that information in pricing and selecting vehicles, as well as in budgeting for repair expenses. For example, record surveys indicate that consumers who had potential used car purchases inspected prior to purchase made significant use of inspection results in subsequent bargaining for repairs and price reductions or in making purchasing decisions.

Defect information is also important because repairs resulting from hidden defects are costly to consumers. . . .

The great bulk of repair cost is borne by the purchaser. Moreover, out-of-pocket costs caused by defects often go beyond the cost of repairs. . . .

Therefore, the Commission finds that mechanical condition information is material to the used car transaction. Dealer misrepresentations regarding mechanical condition and failures to disclose known defect information are therefore deceptive acts and practices. Record evidence regarding such deceptive acts and practices is set forth below.

b.   Deception Concerning the Mechanical Condition of Used Cars. The record contains significant evidence demonstrating oral misrepresentations by used car dealers of material facts concerning the mechanical condition of vehicles offered for sale. These deceptions include failures to disclose known defects, oral misrepresentations of sound mechanical condition and unsubstantiated claims about the car's mechanical condition.

One record study presented survey evidence demonstrating that dealers fail to disclose known defects. The California Public Interest Research Group (CALPIRG) undertook a survey which tested for the degree of known mechanical defect disclosure by dealers to consumers. The survey used trained test shoppers who participated in actual sales transactions up to the point of determining what disclosures were made. After a test car was taken from the dealer's lot to a diagnostic center for inspection, the test shopper returned the car with a copy of the diagnostic report and discussed the report with the salesperson. The test shoppers then broke off negotiations. A second test shopper returned on a follow-up visit to determine whether the defect results of the diagnosis were being disclosed to the new prospective buyers. CALPIRG reports that, in 75 of the 101 completed tests, the follow-up purchaser did not receive defect information that had been provided to the dealer. In 47 of these 75 cases of non-disclosure, the second test shopper dealt with the same salesman who had been given the diagnostic results by the first test shopper.

In addition to the CALPIRG Study, the record is replete with testimony and documentary evidence citing dealer failure to disclose known defects. . . .

Closely linked to the failure to disclose known defects is the dealer practice of orally representing a car's mechanical condition as sound when such is not the case. Record testimony and documentary evidence regarding such misrepresentations are supported by data reported in several studies. . . .

c. Dealers Know That Defects Are Present in Used Cars at the Time of Sale. The record demonstrates not only that many used cars have serious defects at the time of sale but also that dealers often know that these defects are present at the time of sale. This knowledge is obtained through inspections and evaluations that are made before the car is placed on the lot for sale.

The record shows that dealers routinely inspect vehicles for defects. Those dealers who purchase cars at auctions can and do inspect for defects after purchase and have an option to rescind or renegotiate the sale if they find sufficient problems with the vehicle. Moreover, many auction facilities have rules requiring disclosure of known defects by the selling dealer so that the buying dealer obtains knowledge of defects at the auction.

Even when not purchasing at auction, the industry practice is to appraise a vehicle before purchase. The appraiser typically takes the vehicle for a road test, visually inspects the body and mechanical condition of the car, and estimates the extent of repairs needed to make it saleable. After dealers obtain vehicles, there is still further opportunity to inspect and evaluate in more detail, in order to determine what level of warranty coverage will be appropriate for the particular car. If the inspection uncovers problems that are sufficiently great, a dealer may decide to wholesale the vehicle to another dealer, or to sell it "as is" rather than with a warranty. . . .

D. Remedies.

. . .

2. Disclosure of Known Defects. The record shows that dealers go to great lengths to learn the mechanical condition of the cars they sell. They obtain knowledge of defects from various sources. The record reflects that, at auctions, dealers may inspect after purchase and, in fact, may rescind or renegotiate if problems found are severe. After purchase by dealers, additional defects are discovered during further inspections, appearance reconditioning and repairs. In addition, dealers also become aware of defects through third-party service contract company inspectors (who examine cars for defects when deciding which cars qualify for the service contract), through sellers, and through selling or servicing the car previously.

Despite their knowledge of defects, many dealers do not disclose defects to prospective purchasers. However, the record also shows that, when dealers are faced with an obligation to disclose known defects, they are likely to comply rather than evade the requirement. Although Wisconsin's mandatory inspection and disclosure law is not a perfect analogue to the Commission's Rule[254] it is worthy of note that under the Wisconsin law more buyers received pre-purchase defect information from dealers.[255] This increase in disclosure of defects is even more significant in light of the fact that costs of dealer inspections did not increase substantially;[256] from this we conclude that dealers did not simply begin to find more defects but instead began to disclose more defects. . . .

FEDERAL TRADE COMMISSION, FINAL RULE: SALE OF USED MOTOR VEHICLES
49 Fed. Reg. 45692 (1984).

2. MECHANICAL CONDITION PRACTICES

a. Materiality of Mechanical Condition Information. The utility of a vehicle as a means of transportation is directly affected by its

254. There are important differences between the Commission's Rule and the Wisconsin law. Under the Wisconsin law, dealers must inspect and check either "OK" or "Not OK" for each system and subsystem listed on a disclosure statement. It could be argued that dealers in Wisconsin have some incentive to check "Not OK", thereby disclosing known defects, since an "OK" check may carry post-sale repair responsibilities for the dealer.

255. The Wisconsin Study indicates that 28.1 percent of pre-law used car buyers who bought from dealers were aware of defects prior to purchase. This percentage increased to 38.7 percent among those who purchased from dealers following passage of the mandatory inspection law. This increase

in defect awareness was accompanied by an increase in the number of buyers who stated that their knowledge of defects came from information supplied by the dealer. In the Wisconsin Study, one percent of pre-law respondents said that they learned of defects before purchase from dealers. In the post-law sample, 9 percent said they learned of defects before purchase from dealers.

256. The record shows that, after implementation of the Wisconsin law, two-thirds of the dealers reported that they incurred no additional costs to inspect in order to comply with the mandatory disclosure scheme.

mechanical condition. Therefore, it is not surprising that consumer research indicates consumers' consistent concern about mechanical condition. In fact, mechanical condition at the time of sale is reported by consumers as the most important factor in reaching a purchasing decision....

Mechanical condition information is also important because needed repairs resulting from hidden defects are costly to consumers.... Therefore, the Commission finds that mechanical condition information is material to the used car transaction. Dealer misrepresentations regarding mechanical condition are therefore deceptive acts and practices.

b. Deception Concerning the Mechanical Condition of Used Cars. The record demonstrates that misrepresenting a car's mechanical condition is a common dealer practice....

c. Consumer Reliance on Dealer Representations and Injury. The record clearly demonstrates the existence of a substantial information disparity between the buyer and seller in the used car market relating to the mechanical condition of used cars....

Based on the evidence in the rulemaking record, the Commission finds that many used car dealers have knowingly misrepresented the mechanical condition of the cars they sell and thereby cause substantial injury to consumers....

A. *Disclosure of Known Defects*

The 1981 Rule contained provisions requiring dealers to disclose certain material defects, if known at the time of sale.... [T]he Commission has decided not to include a known defect disclosure requirement in the Rule, to make the warranty and "as is" disclosures on the Buyers Guide more prominent, and to make other minor adjustments to the Buyers Guide.

In reaching its decision, the Commission carefully analyzed the rulemaking record including the comments submitted during the recent comment and rebuttal periods to determine the potential effects of the known defects disclosure requirement, both intended and unintended. The Commission has concluded that the known defects disclosure requirement will not provide used car buyers with a reliable source of information concerning a car's mechanical condition and that the provision would be exceedingly difficult to enforce....

1. THE RELIABILITY OF INFORMATION DISCLOSED UNDER A KNOWN DEFECTS DISCLOSURE REQUIREMENT

Any benefits from a known defects disclosure requirement depend on the extent to which dealers have detailed knowledge about the mechanical condition of the vehicles they sell and whether the dealer's knowledge of defects can be communicated in a way that will not be confusing to potential used car buyers.

a. Dealer Knowledge of Defects. In order to provide useful disclosures under the known defects disclosure requirement, dealers must have knowledge of specific defects. If dealers do not ordinarily possess knowledge about specific defects, they would only be able to discover such information through additional inspections. Inspections will be costly and will ultimately raise the price of used cars. Therefore, in determining the costs and benefits of the known defect disclosure requirement, the issue of whether dealers ordinarily have knowledge about specific defects is an important one.

Despite the importance of this question, there is relatively little direct evidence that addresses it. The record does indicate that most experts and commenters agree that all dealers assess the general condition of the cars they sell and that individual dealers may examine cars thoroughly. However, even during the initial rulemaking proceeding there was disagreement concerning what the record reveals about the extent of the average dealer's knowledge of the condition of specific systems in his or her cars at the time of sale. . . .

The Commission's current review of both the preexisting rulemaking record and the additional comments submitted during the present proceeding indicates that the conclusion that dealers ordinarily know about specific defects may well be incorrect and, in any event, is not supported by a preponderance of substantial reliable evidence.

First, careful inspections do not always reveal or predict mechanical problems that may occur shortly after the sale. Thus, there is little basis for inferring knowledge from the mere fact that failures occur after purchase. In Wisconsin, where dealers are required to inspect their cars and disclose the results of the inspection, one record study indicates that 51 percent of Wisconsin used car buyers ultimately repaired problems not known when they bought their cars. These data are consistent with another record study which indicates 52.1 percent of Wisconsin consumers, who purchased cars after the Wisconsin law went into effect, discovered defects after the sale. Moreover, in a comment supporting the "known defects" provision, Detroit II, a company currently providing warranties for used cars, points out that even after cars are inspected for inclusion in their warranty program and all "known defects" are repaired, a survey of their buyers revealed that "slightly over 50% of them have some sort of mechanical problem within 45 days of the sale." The Detroit II figures are within the range of the incidence of mechanical problems experienced by used car buyers generally.

Second, dealer knowledge about general condition of a car does not necessarily mean that the dealer has knowledge of specific defects. Although there is evidence that dealers have a high degree of confidence in their ability to assess the general condition of a car through a walk-around examination and a test drive, this general assessment of overall condition is probably sufficient to protect the dealer's interest only because most buyers are likely to perform no more than a similarly superficial examination. Moreover, the dealer's evaluation is likely to focus on the cost of appearance reconditioning or detailing because, as the record indicates, many consumers believe that a "good looking" car is also mechanically sound. There is, however, no evidence that such measures are ordinarily adequate to reveal specific mechanical defects.

Third, although the record contains anecdotal evidence indicating that dealers know about specific defects, other record evidence supports the conclusion that most dealers do not have knowledge of specific defects. Indeed, the record contains extensive testimony from dealers and vocational educational instructors that the inspection process is uncertain and imperfect.

Even though the utility of a "known defects" disclosure depends on dealers having system-by-system information about the cars they sell, the provision gives dealers little incentive to inspect their cars. Under the provision, honest dealers who learn of defects must reveal their knowledge on the disclosure portion of the window sticker, whereas dealers who avoid gaining this knowledge may honestly leave the sticker blank. Disclosing "known defects" calls attention to the car's problems, but does not reward the dealer's integrity for revealing these problems. Thus, a dealer who regularly inspects and honestly discloses all "known defects" may be put at a competitive disadvantage relative to dealers who do not inspect. This factor may then have the unintended and perverse effect of discouraging, rather than encouraging, inspections and disclosure of defects.

b. Buyer Knowledge Under the Defects Disclosure Provision. When the Commission promulgated the Rule in 1981, it cited data from the Wisconsin Study suggesting that the Wisconsin law increased overall consumer awareness of defects prior to purchase and that the law made it more likely that consumers would receive defect information from the dealer. However, contradictions in the data presented in the Wisconsin Study become apparent upon close review. On the one hand, the data show some increase in the percentage of post-law buyers who knew about defects before the sale and those who received pre-purchase defect information from dealers. On the other hand, data from the study shows that more consumers in Minnesota (a state with no defect disclosure requirement) reported awareness of defects prior to sale than consumers in post-law Wisconsin.

Finally, the data in the Wisconsin Study do not show that the Wisconsin defect disclosure requirement made it more likely that consumers would receive the information they felt they needed concerning the car's mechanical condition. Approximately 32 percent of pre-law consumers reported that they lacked needed information on the car's mechanical condition. This percentage decreased only slightly for post-law consumers (28.52 percent). Moreover, there was essentially no difference in the percentage of pre-law and post-law consumers reporting that the dealer gave them accurate information on the mechanical condition of the car they purchased (62.6 percent vs 62.8 percent). . . .

In addition to our serious questions concerning the effectiveness of a defect disclosure provision in making consumers aware of defects prior to purchase, we are equally concerned that the defect disclosure provision included in the 1981 Rule may confuse consumers and cause them to make inaccurate assumptions about the condition of a car after reading the defect disclosure. . . . Thus, buyers may not only be getting no useful information about a car's condition, but may be affirmatively harmed by mistakenly inferring that the dealer's lack of knowledge about defects means that no defects exist.[301] Unscrupulous dealers or salespersons could easily exploit the likelihood that consumers will mistake the absence of a disclosure for a claim that the car is of high quality. For example, dealers might highlight that there are no "known defects" in the car or argue that the requirement to disclose known defects makes an independent inspection unnecessary—"If we knew of any problems, we'd have to tell you about them." . . .

MOTOR VEHICLE MANUFACTURERS ASSOC. v. STATE FARM MUTUAL AUTOMOBILE INS. CO.

463 U.S. 29, 103 S.Ct. 2856, 77 L.Ed.2d 443 (1983).

WHITE, JUSTICE:

. . . Within months of assuming office, Secretary Brock Adams . . . issued a new mandatory passive restraint regulation, known as Modified Standard 208. The Modified Standard mandated the phasing in of passive restraints beginning with large cars in model year 1982 and extending to all cars by model year 1984. The two principal systems that would satisfy the Standard were airbags and passive belts; the choice of which system to install was left to the manufacturers. . . .

In February 1981, however, Secretary of Transportation Andrew Lewis reopened the rulemaking due to changed economic circumstances and, in particular, the difficulties of the automobile industry. Two months later, the agency ordered a one-year delay in the application of the standard to large cars, extending the deadline to September 1982, and at the same time, proposed the possible rescission of the entire standard. After receiving written comments and holding public hearings, NHTSA issued a final rule (Notice 25) that rescinded the passive restraint requirement contained in Modified Standard 208.

---

301. The "known defects" disclosure in the 1981 Rule contained a warning that the absence of a disclosed defect does not necessarily mean that the car is free from defects. However, there is no evidence that this warning would be effective. For example, a consumer comparing a car with a disclosed defect and car with an undisclosed defect may find the inference that the car with no disclosed defect was in better condition irresistible despite the warning.

II

In a statement explaining the rescission, NHTSA maintained that it was no longer able to find, as it had in 1977, that the automatic restraint requirement would produce significant safety benefits. This judgment reflected not a change of opinion on the effectiveness of the technology, but a change in plans by the automobile industry. In 1977, the agency had assumed that airbags would be installed in 60% of all new cars and automatic seatbelts in 40%. By 1981 it became apparent that automobile manufacturers planned to install the automatic seatbelts in approximately 99% of the new cars. For this reason, the life-saving potential of airbags would not be realized. Moreover, it now appeared that the overwhelming majority of passive belts planned to be installed by manufacturers could be detached easily and left that way permanently. Passive belts, once detached, then required "the same type of affirmative action that is the stumbling block to obtaining high usage levels of manual belts." For this reason, the agency concluded that there was no longer a basis for reliably predicting that the standard would lead to any significant increased usage of restraints at all. . . .

III

. . . Both the Motor Vehicle Safety Act and the 1974 Amendments concerning occupant crash protection standards indicate that motor vehicle safety standards are to be promulgated under the informal rulemaking procedures of § 553 of the Administrative Procedure Act. The agency's action in promulgating such standards therefore may be set aside if found to be "arbitrary, capricious, an abuse of discretion, or otherwise not in accordance with law." We believe that the rescission or modification of an occupant protection standard is subject to the same test. . . .

Petitioner Motor Vehicle Manufacturers Association (MVMA) disagrees, contending that the rescission of an agency rule should be judged by the same standard a court would use to judge an agency's refusal to promulgate a rule in the first place—a standard Petitioner believes considerably narrower than the traditional arbitrary and capricious test and "close to the borderline of nonreviewability." We reject this view. The Motor Vehicle Safety Act expressly equates orders "revoking" and "establishing" safety standards; neither that Act nor the APA suggests that revocations are to be treated as refusals to promulgate standards. . . .

The Department of Transportation accepts the applicability of the "arbitrary and capricious" standard. It argues that under this standard, a reviewing court may not set aside an agency rule that is rational, based on consideration of the relevant factors and within the scope of the authority delegated to the agency by the statute. We do not disagree with this formulation.[9] The scope of review under the "arbitrary and

9. The Department of Transportation suggests that the arbitrary and capricious standard requires no more than the minimum rationality a statute must bear in

capricious" standard is narrow and a court is not to substitute its judgment for that of the agency. Nevertheless, the agency must examine the relevant data and articulate a satisfactory explanation for its action including a "rational connection between the facts found and the choice made." In reviewing that explanation, we must "consider whether the decision was based on a consideration of the relevant factors and whether there has been a clear error of judgment." Normally, an agency rule would be arbitrary and capricious if the agency has relied on factors which Congress has not intended it to consider, entirely failed to consider an important aspect of the problem, offered an explanation for its decision that runs counter to the evidence before the agency, or is so implausible that it could not be ascribed to a difference in view or the product of agency expertise. The reviewing court should not attempt itself to make up for such deficiencies: "We may not supply a reasoned basis for the agency's action that the agency itself has not given." We will, however, "uphold a decision of less than ideal clarity if the agency's path may reasonably be discerned." For purposes of this case, it is also relevant that Congress required a record of the rulemaking proceedings to be compiled and submitted to a reviewing court, and intended that agency findings under the Motor Vehicle Safety Act would be supported by "substantial evidence on the record considered as a whole." . . .

V

The ultimate question before us is whether NHTSA's rescission of the passive restraint requirement of Standard 208 was arbitrary and capricious. We conclude, as did the Court of Appeals, that it was. We also conclude, but for somewhat different reasons, that further consideration of the issue by the agency is therefore required. We deal separately with the rescission as it applies to airbags and as it applies to seatbelts.

A

The first and most obvious reason for finding the rescission arbitrary and capricious is that NHTSA apparently gave no consideration whatever to modifying the Standard to require that airbag technology be utilized. . . .

The agency has now determined that the detachable automatic belts will not attain anticipated safety benefits because so many individuals will detach the mechanism. Even if this conclusion were acceptable in its entirety, standing alone it would not justify any more than an amendment of Standard 208 to disallow compliance by means of the one technology which will not provide effective passenger protection. It does not cast doubt on the need for a passive restraint standard or upon the efficacy of airbag technology. . . .

order to withstand analysis under the Due Process Clause. We do not view as equivalent the presumption of constitutionality afforded legislation drafted by Congress and the presumption of regularity afforded an agency in fulfilling its statutory mandate.

B

Although the issue is closer, we also find that the agency was too quick to dismiss the safety benefits of automatic seatbelts. NHTSA's critical finding was that, in light of the industry's plans to install readily detachable passive belts, it could not reliably predict "even a 5 percentage point increase as the minimum level of expected usage increase." The Court of Appeals rejected this finding because there is "not one iota" of evidence that Modified Standard 208 will fail to increase nationwide seatbelt use by at least 13 percentage points, the level of increased usage necessary for the standard to justify its cost. Given the lack of probative evidence, the court held that "only a well-justified refusal to seek more evidence could render rescission non-arbitrary."

Petitioners object to this conclusion. In their view, "substantial uncertainty" that a regulation will accomplish its intended purpose is sufficient reason, without more, to rescind a regulation. We agree with petitioners that just as an agency reasonably may decline to issue a safety standard if it is uncertain about its efficacy, an agency may also revoke a standard on the basis of serious uncertainties if supported by the record and reasonably explained. Rescission of the passive restraint requirement would not be arbitrary and capricious simply because there was no evidence in direct support of the agency's conclusion. It is not infrequent that the available data does not settle a regulatory issue and the agency must then exercise its judgment in moving from the facts and probabilities on the record to a policy conclusion. Recognizing that policymaking in a complex society must account for uncertainty, however, does not imply that it is sufficient for an agency to merely recite the terms "substantial uncertainty" as a justification for its actions. The agency must explain the evidence which is available, and must offer a "rational connection between the facts found and the choice made." Generally, one aspect of that explanation would be a justification for rescinding the regulation before engaging in a search for further evidence.

In this case, the agency's explanation for rescission of the passive restraint requirement is not sufficient to enable us to conclude that the rescission was the product of reasoned decisionmaking. To reach this conclusion, we do not upset the agency's view of the facts, but we do appreciate the limitations of this record in supporting the agency's decision. We start with the accepted ground that if used, seatbelts unquestionably would save many thousands of lives and would prevent tens of thousands of crippling injuries. . . . We move next to the fact that there is no direct evidence in support of the agency's finding that detachable automatic belts cannot be predicted to yield a substantial increase in usage. The empirical evidence on the record, consisting of surveys of drivers of automobiles equipped with passive belts, reveals more than a doubling of the usage rate experienced with manual belts.[16]

16. Between 1975 and 1980, Volkswagen sold approximately 350,000 Rabbits equipped with detachable passive seatbelts that were guarded by an ignition interlock.

Much of the agency's rulemaking statement—and much of the controversy in this case—centers on the conclusions that should be drawn from these studies. The agency maintained that the doubling of seatbelt usage in these studies could not be extrapolated to an across-the-board mandatory standard because the passive seatbelts were guarded by ignition interlocks and purchasers of the tested cars are somewhat atypical.[17] Respondents insist these studies demonstrate that Modified Standard 208 will substantially increase seatbelt usage. We believe that it is within the agency's discretion to pass upon the generalizability of these field studies. This is precisely the type of issue which rests within the expertise of NHTSA, and upon which a reviewing court must be most hesitant to intrude.

But accepting the agency's view of the field tests on passive restraints indicates only that there is no reliable real-world experience that usage rates will substantially increase. To be sure, NHTSA opines that "it cannot reliably predict even a 5 percentage point increase as the minimum level of increased usage." But this and other statements that passive belts will not yield substantial increases in seatbelt usage apparently take no account of the critical difference between detachable automatic belts and current manual belts. A detached passive belt does require an affirmative act to reconnect it, but—unlike a manual seat belt—the passive belt, once reattached, will continue to function automatically unless again disconnected. Thus, inertia—a factor which the agency's own studies have found significant in explaining the current low usage rates for seatbelts[18]—works in favor of, not against, use of the protective device. Since 20 to 50% of motorists currently wear seatbelts on some occasions,[19] there would seem to be grounds to believe that seatbelt use by occasional users will be substantially increased by the detachable passive belts. Whether this is in fact the case is a matter for the agency to decide, but it must bring its expertise to bear on the question. . . .

General Motors sold 8,000 1978 and 1979 Chevettes with a similar system, but eliminated the ignition interlock on the 13,000 Chevettes sold in 1980. NHTSA found that belt usage in the Rabbits averaged 34% for manual belts and 84% for passive belts. For the 1978–1979 Chevettes, NHTSA calculated 34% usage for manual belts and 71% for passive belts. On 1980 Chevettes, the agency found these figures to be 31% for manual belts and 70% for passive belts.

17. "NHTSA believes that the usage of automatic belts in Rabbits and Chevettes would have been substantially lower if the automatic belts in those cars were not equipped with a use-inducing device inhibiting detachment."

18. NHTSA commissioned a number of surveys of public attitudes in an effort to better understand why people were not using manual belts and to determine how they would react to passive restraints. The surveys reveal that while 20% to 40% of the public is opposed to wearing manual belts, the larger proportion of the population does not wear belts because they forgot or found manual belts inconvenient or bothersome. In another survey, 38% of the surveyed group responded that they would welcome automatic belts, and 25% would "tolerate" them. NHTSA did not comment upon these attitude surveys in its explanation accompanying the rescission of the passive restraint requirement.

19. Four surveys of manual belt usage were conducted for NHTSA between 1978 and 1980, leading the agency to report that 40% to 50% of the people use their belts at least some of the time.

The agency also failed to articulate a basis for not requiring nondetachable belts under Standard 208. It is argued that the concern of the agency with the easy detachability of the currently favored design would be readily solved by a continuous passive belt, which allows the occupant to "spool out" the belt and create the necessary slack for easy extrication from the vehicle. The agency did not separately consider the continuous belt option, but treated it together with the ignition interlock device in a category it titled "option of use-compelling features." The agency was concerned that use-compelling devices would "complicate extrication of [a]n occupant from his or her car." "To require that passive belts contain use-compelling features," the agency observed, "could be counterproductive [given] . . . widespread, latent and irrational fear in many members of the public that they could be trapped by the seat belt after a crash." In addition, based on the experience with the ignition interlock, the agency feared that use-compelling features might trigger adverse public reaction.

By failing to analyze the continuous seatbelts in its own right, the agency has failed to offer the rational connection between facts and judgment required to pass muster under the arbitrary and capricious standard. We agree with the Court of Appeals that NHTSA did not suggest that the emergency release mechanisms used in nondetachable belts are any less effective for emergency egress than the buckle release system used in detachable belts. In 1978, when General Motors obtained the agency's approval to install a continuous passive belt, it assured the agency that nondetachable belts with spool releases were as safe as detachable belts with buckle releases. NHTSA was satisfied that this belt design assured easy extricability: "the agency does not believe that the use of [such] release mechanisms will cause serious occupant egress problems . . ." While the agency is entitled to change its view on the acceptability of continuous passive belts, it is obligated to explain its reasons for doing so. . . .

JUSTICE REHNQUIST, with whom THE CHIEF JUSTICE, JUSTICE POWELL, and JUSTICE O'CONNOR join, concurring in part and dissenting in part.

I join parts I, II, III, IV, and V–A of the Court's opinion. In particular, I agree that, since the airbag and continuous spool automatic seatbelt were explicitly approved in the standard the agency was rescinding, the agency should explain why it declined to leave those requirements intact. In this case, the agency gave no explanation at all. Of course, if the agency can provide a rational explanation, it may adhere to its decision to rescind the entire standard.

I do not believe, however, that NHTSA's view of detachable automatic seatbelts was arbitrary and capricious. The agency adequately explained its decision to rescind the standard insofar as it was satisfied by detachable belts. . . .

The agency's changed view of the standard seems to be related to the election of a new President of a different political party. It is readily apparent that the responsible members of one administration may consider public resistance and uncertainties to be more important than do their counterparts in a previous administration. A change in administration brought about by the people casting their votes is a perfectly reasonable basis for an executive agency's reappraisal of the costs and benefits of its programs and regulations. As long as the agency remains within the bounds established by Congress, it is entitled to assess administrative records and evaluate priorities in light of the philosophy of the administration.

Notes and Questions

1. The requirement of adequate reasons, or hard look review, has been controversial. Supporters defend it as necessary and appropriate to ensure agency accountability. Professor Seidenfeld, for example, writes:

The [hard look] doctrine helps to ensure that agency decisions are determined neither by accommodation of purely private interests nor by surreptitious commandeering of the decisionmaking apparatus to serve an agency idiosyncratic view of the public interest. . . . Essentially, under the hard look test, the reviewing court scrutinizes the agency's reasoning to make certain that the agency carefully deliberated about the issues raised by its decision.

In short, hard look review performs a valuable function by encouraging agencies to think through the full implications of their policies. Abandoning meaningful judicial review altogether, in contrast, encourages policies that react to short term political preferences of powerful interest groups. . . .

Mark Seidenfeld, *Demystifying Deossification: Rethinking Recent Proposals to Modify Judicial Review of Notice and Comment Rulemaking*, 75 Tex. L. Rev. 483, 491, 514 (1997); *see also* William H. Rodgers, Jr., *A Hard Look at* Vermont Yankee: *Environmental Law Under Close Scrutiny*, 67 Geo. L.J. 699 (1979).

Critics blame hard look review, along with rulemaking analysis requirements, for rulemaking ossification. Professor McGarity sees the following linkage between judicial review and ossification:

Fully aware of the consequences of a judicial remand, the agencies are constantly "looking over their shoulders" at the reviewing courts in preparing supporting documents, in writing preambles, in responding to public comments, and in assembling the rulemaking "records." Because they can never know what issues dissatisfied litigants will raise on appeal, they must attempt to prepare responses to all contentions that may prove credible to an appellate court, no matter how ridiculous they may appear to agency staff. . . .

The predictable result of stringent "hard look" judicial review of complex rulemaking is ossification. Because the agencies perceive that the reviewing courts are inconsistent in the degree to which they are deferential, they are constrained to prepare for the worst-case scenario on judicial review. This can be extremely resource-intensive and time-consuming.

Thomas O. McGarity, *Some Thoughts on "Deossifying" the Rulemaking Process*, 41 DUKE L.J. 1385, 1412, 1419 (1992); *see, also* Stephen Breyer, Vermont Yankee *and the Court's Role in the Nuclear Energy Controversy*, 91 HARV. L.REV. 1804 (1978).

2. In assessing the adequacy of the reasons that an agency gives to justify a rule, how strict should a court be? Professor McGarity supports judicial review of the agency reasoning process, but he opposes "stringent" hard look review. McGarity, *supra*, at 1551–53. Professor Seidenfeld recognizes that hard look review can cause ossification, but he warns that an increase in "overall deference to agency rulemaking will forfeit many of the benefits of hard look review." Seidenfeld, *surpa*, at 524. At the time that the "hard look" doctrine was introduced, some judges described the courts as a "partner" in the development of regulatory policy. Later, Judge Patricia Wald, one of the most thoughtful students of administrative law on the District of Columbia Circuit, has suggested that a more appropriate metaphor might assign the courts the role of "nursemaid" for regulatory programs. Patricia M. Wald, *Making Informed Decisions on the District of Columbia Circuit*, 50 GEO. WASH. L.REV. 135, 138 (1982). This metaphor suggests that the courts should assist an agency in providing reasons that would justify its actions. Professors McGarity and Shapiro propose that a "pass-fail" test be used:

> A better metaphor might be a "pass-fail" test for adequacy. According to this metaphor, the judge is like a professor who is vaguely familiar with the subject matter of a paper and must determine whether the paper meets minimum standards for passable work. The professor's disagreement with the paper's conclusion is not a reason for the student to "flunk." Moreover, a check of the citations may reveal that the student could have more sources or that the student may have mischaracterized one of the cited sources, and still the paper may pass. Only where there is some inexcusable gap in the analysis, an obvious misquote, or evidence of intellectual dishonesty will the professor put an "F" on the paper and send it back to the student. . . .

THOMAS O. MCGARITY & SIDNEY A. SHAPIRO, WORKERS AT RISK: THE FAILED PROMISE OF THE OCCUPATIONAL SAFETY AND HEALTH ADMINISTRATION 260 (1993).

Which metaphor best describes the Supreme Court's decision in *State Farm*? Do you need two metaphors to describe the Court's decision? Which metaphor do you favor and why?

3. As footnote 9 of the Court's opinion indicates, the government asked the Court to define "arbitrary and capricious" review in terms of the minimal rationality requirement associated with substantive due process review of economic regulation. An old Supreme Court case, *Pacific States Box & Basket Co. v. White*, 296 U.S. 176, 56 S.Ct. 159, 80 L.Ed. 138 (1935), had stated in a due process case challenging a state

agency regulation, "With the wisdom of such a regulation we have, of course, no concern. We may inquire only whether it is arbitrary or capricious." That level of minimal rationality may have been what the drafters of the APA originally had in mind, but such review would have been inconsistent with *Overton Park* and its progeny. In *State Farm*, however, the government hoped that because *Vermont Yankee* had limited judicial activism in procedural review of agency action, the Court might take the next step and limit judicial activism in substantive review of agency action. While the government was not successful here, recall that in *Chevron* a year later the Court restricted judicial review of agency interpretations of law.

4. If *Vermont Yankee* says that courts are not to impose additional procedures on agencies not otherwise required by law, where is the source of authority for requiring the kind of agency explanation the Supreme Court demands in *State Farm*? In *Pension Benefit Guaranty Corp. v. LTV Corp.*, 496 U.S. 633, 110 S.Ct. 2668, 110 L.Ed.2d 579 (1990), the Supreme Court had this to say in response to a claim that a demand for a reasoned explanation in *Overton Park* was inconsistent with *Vermont Yankee*: "[A]lthough one initially might feel that there is some tension between *Vermont Yankee* and *Overton Park*, the two cases are not necessarily inconsistent. *Vermont Yankee* stands for the general proposition that courts are not free to impose upon agencies specific procedural requirements that have no basis in the APA. At most, *Overton Park* suggests that § 706(2)(A), which directs a court to ensure that an agency action is not arbitrary and capricious or otherwise contrary to law, imposes a general 'procedural' requirement of sorts by mandating that an agency take whatever steps it needs to provide an explanation that will enable the court to evaluate the agency's rationale at the time of decision."

5. What is the relationship between step two of *Chevron* and the traditional "arbitrary and capricious" test prescribed in § 706(2)(A) of the APA? The Supreme Court has sometimes referred to the adequate reasons requirement of *State Farm* in applying step two. *E.g., Rust v. Sullivan*, 500 U.S. 173, 186, 111 S.Ct. 1759, 1769, 114 L.Ed.2d 233 (1991) ("We find that the Secretary amply justified his change of interpretation with a 'reasoned analysis.'"). Professor Sunstein proposes that the inquiry whether an agency's decision is arbitrary and capricious and the test at step two of *Chevron* should be similar. Cass Sunstein, *Law & Administration After* Chevron, 90 COLUM. L. REV. 2072, 2104 (1990). Professor Levin proposes that the two inquiries should be identical. Ronald B. Levin, *The Anatomy of* Chevron: *Step Two Reconsidered*, 72 CHI. KENT. L. REV. 1253, 1254 (1997). Do you approve of either of these recommendations?

6. In *State Farm*, the Court (and even the concurring Justices who would have upheld part of the rule) seemed concerned that the agency had changed its position. The reference in the concurrence to a "change in administration" reflected the recognition that the passive restraint rule was highly politicized. Although the Supreme Court did not explicit-

ly alter its standard of review because of that concern, the court of appeals below, in an opinion by then-judge Mikva, a former politician, specifically held that it would apply a *higher* standard of review to a change in agency position. In *Chevron*, however, the agency had also shifted its position as a result of a change of administrations, and the Supreme Court seemed unperturbed, stating that "the fact that the agency has adopted different definitions in different contexts adds force to the argument that the definition itself is flexible." Does this difference suggest that the Court does *not* equate step two of *Chevron* with the assessment of whether an action is arbitrary and capricious? Or is the difference more bound up in the facts of the particular cases? In *Rust v. Sullivan*, 500 U.S. 173, 111 S.Ct. 1759, 114 L.Ed.2d 233 (1991), the Court cited to both *State Farm* and *Chevron* in upholding HHS's interpretation of certain family planning grant statutes, despite the agency's change in interpretation.

7. If the exact content of "arbitrary and capricious" review seems a bit fuzzy in the federal system, generalizing among the states is near to impossible. Some states employ the equivalent of a "hard look" doctrine; others eschew any review of the rationality of rulemaking. *See generally* William Funk, *Rationality Review of State Administrative Rulemaking*, 43 ADMIN. L. REV. 147 (1991). Funk is highly critical of states that do not allow any judicial review of the rationality of rulemaking. Probably the leading academic proponent of no review (albeit also a state Attorney General and state legislator) is Professor David Frohnmayer. *See especially* David Frohnmayer, *National Trends in Court Review of Agency Action: Some Reflections on the Model State Administrative Procedure Act and New Utah Administrative Procedure Act*, 3 B.Y.U. J. OF PUB. LAW 1 (1989). His primary argument is that because legislatures have delegated policymaking by rulemaking to agencies, judicial review of that policymaking should be limited to the review courts would make of legislation. The judicial review provision of the Model State Administrative Procedure Act, which few states have adopted, is ambivalent on the subject, including arbitrary and capricious review as an "optional" provision. Professor Bonfield, the reporter for the Act, explained this outcome as the result of concern that some state courts had "substitute[d] their judgment for that of the Agency." ARTHUR BONFIELD, STATE ADMINISTRATIVE RULE MAKING 574 (1986). At the same time, the MSAPA provides for "substantial evidence" review of factual issues in rulemaking, including legislative facts. Bonfield concludes that the practical effect of the MSAPA's standard is the same as under the federal APA.

3. CHALLENGING THE AGENCY RULE

Problem 2–11: Do You Always Appeal?

Recall Problem 2–4, in which EPA was considering whether to adopt without notice and comment a rule exempting small scale field tests of biologically engineered pesticides from the normal Experimental Use

Permit requirement. Assume it decided to do so and has issued an immediately effective rule. You represent an environmental group that believes the rule is ill advised and seeks your counsel as to whether it should challenge the rule. What factors should the attorney take into account when giving such advice to a client?

Problem Materials

VAN CLEVE, "DECIDING WHEN TO CONTEST AN EPA RULE"

National Law Journal, May 31, 1993, at 25.

These days, corporate counsel with environmental responsibilities face a real bind. Environmental regulation is increasing steadily, and government is backing it up with tougher enforcement, extending even to criminal sanctions. At the same time, there is increased management pressure to control legal costs.

Thus, even though effective challenges to complex environmental regulations can limit their adverse effects, such challenges can be expensive and difficult to sell to management. Because both of these trends—regulation and cost-consciousness—are likely to accelerate during the Clinton administration, environmental counsel need to focus on specific, critical factors in evaluating environmental challenges in order to spend scarce legal dollars efficiently.

Some Environmental Protection Agency rules are a necessary part of the cost of doing business in an industrialized society and should be accepted rather than challenged. But when a rule has an adverse impact on a company's business, several steps can be taken to limit or avoid the costs of a judicial challenge.

First and foremost is effective advocacy during the legislative and rule-making processes. To be effective, advocacy must be based on carefully marshaled facts presented clearly, at the right time and in cognizance of the full context of agency action, including constituency pressures. Effective advocacy also includes knowing when to compromise if the results of legislation or rule-making would be preferable to results that could be obtained through judicial review.

If court review nevertheless appears necessary, four basic questions should be considered before deciding to undertake a challenge. They are:

— Are there alternatives to litigation?

— Is the rule vulnerable to challenge?

— What results would be obtained by a successful challenge?

— What will a challenge cost, both in financial terms and in terms of the company's overall relationship with the EPA?

The first issue is whether the company has alternatives other than a court challenge that may be less expensive, more effective or both.

One option is to ask the EPA to interpret the rule so that its impact on the company is lessened to a point at which it becomes acceptable. Like other federal agencies, the EPA usually strives to adopt generally applicable rules and, like other federal agencies, the EPA sometimes fails to achieve this goal. A company that can demonstrate persuasively that it is differently situated than other similarly regulated entities may be able to convince the EPA that a rule should be modified or limited in application. This process usually is less visible, and often is less expensive, than more formal challenges to the rule.

Alternatively, it may be possible to convince the EPA or the White House to reconsider the rule. There are times when the full impact of a rule becomes clear only after it has been proposed by the EPA. In such cases, the administration may conclude it would be preferable to revise the rule rather than face the prospect of either congressional revision or judicial invalidation. Again, it is often relatively inexpensive to determine preliminarily whether or not the administration is willing to consider revisiting a rule, and corporate counsel should consider this option before deciding on a judicial challenge.

It also may be possible to persuade Congress to revise the rule legislatively. Obviously, this course presents a significant challenge and will have its costs. Lobbying a bill through Congress can be expensive and involves many uncertainties. But often it is relatively inexpensive to determine whether there is a reasonable prospect that Congress would be willing to revise an EPA rule or block its implementation.

If Congress is willing to intervene, its intervention sometimes can be more focused and effective than court intervention. Furthermore, Congress' willingness to act sometimes can prompt agency reconsideration designed to avoid legislation.

The second issue to be considered in deciding on the advisability of a court challenge is the vulnerability of the rule. An EPA rule may be vulnerable for any of five major reasons: It exceeds the agency's statutory authority, it is unconstitutional, it is unreasonable, it is not supported in the agency's record, or it is otherwise procedurally inadequate or improper.

EPA rules are invalid if they are "in excess of statutory . . . authority." In many cases, however, Congress is deliberately general about what it expects the EPA to do and does not dictate to the EPA the permissible scope of a given rule. Although it is always tempting to challenge EPA rules on the ground that they conflict with a congressional delegation of authority or misinterpret an ambiguous statute, this is often a trap for the unwary, and one should approach such an action with caution.

Courts generally are reluctant to overrule otherwise rational EPA decisions on the basis that there is some implicit inconsistency between the proposed regulation and the language or legislative history of a given statute. If, however, the conflict between the statutory language and the EPA rule is substantial, or if the rule sweeps beyond the statutory purpose or scope, it may be possible to persuade a court that the EPA has exceeded the authority Congress granted. . . .

Assuming they meet other requirements discussed in this article, the EPA's rules are considered legally valid unless they are "arbitrary, capricious [or] an abuse of discretion." The courts have interpreted this test to mean that the EPA's rules should be upheld if they represent "reasoned decisionmaking."

At a minimum, this standard means that the agency decision must be supported by facts in the record, provide reasons and consider clearly viable alternatives. In addition, although courts sometimes are precluded by statute from weighing the costs and benefits of environmental rules, it is evident from court decisions that the relationship between costs and benefits is often not far from the surface of the judicial review process. . . .

In developing a realistic assessment of the costs and benefits of an EPA rule, corporate counsel should consider the following points. Often, affected groups exaggerate the cost of a regulation to them, or underestimate the benefits that may accrue to others. The costs and benefits are likely to become reasonably clear in the adversarial give-and-take of the judicial review process. It is error to appraise the merits of a challenge based on an unrealistic appraisal of a rule's costs or benefits because it skews the results in favor of a challenge-risking wasted expense and needlessly alienating the EPA.

Therefore, in evaluating a rule's validity, one must determine whether it is adequately explained, fairly considers alternatives and has costs and benefits that are reasonably proportionate. If these criteria are not met, the rule may be vulnerable.

The EPA's administrative decisions—unlike adjudicatory processes often employed by other administrative agencies—usually are made by writing rules that need not meet a statutorily prescribed evidentiary standard to pass muster. The courts have developed a set of relatively informal criteria by which to judge the sufficiency of the administrative record to support EPA decisions.

The first informal evidentiary criterion is the scope of the EPA's competence in promulgating the rule at issue. Courts clearly regard the EPA as more competent in some circumstances than others. It is important, therefore, to determine whether the potentially vulnerable portions of a rule fall within an area in which the court regards the EPA's technical or policy competence as substantial, or whether the EPA is operating at the boundaries of its statutory competence. . . .

A related consideration is whether the EPA's decision relies on data that are reasonably solid. Clearly, some EPA rules have better evidentiary support than others, and there are circumstances in which the EPA relies on fairly limited data to support its conclusions. As mentioned, there are certainly circumstances in which a court will defer to the EPA notwithstanding a lack of data. If the EPA has ignored substantial conflicting data, however, a court may be willing to force the EPA to revisit the issues involved in a particular rule.

The validity of the procedure employed by the agency in its rule-making should be considered as well. The EPA has substantial procedural flexibility in establishing many of its rules, and can usually engage at its discretion in a variety of public hearings or adversarial proceedings in addition to taking written comments. Yet it is still important to look at whether the EPA followed its own regulations and the basic notice-and-comment procedures required by the Administrative Procedure Act. It is also worth asking whether the EPA's process was adequate to meet the decision-making task presented by a particular rule. . . .

It is relatively rare that a court will strike down an EPA rule permanently. The normal course is to remand the rule to the agency for further consideration.

Superficially, this might suggest that it is difficult to obtain significant results from challenges to EPA rules. In many cases, however, nothing could be further from the truth. In fact, the most significant victories over EPA rules are those in which the agency is forced to rewrite a rule after a remand by a court that was clearly unhappy with the rule's fundamental thrust. In such cases, the EPA may be unable to rewrite the rule in a manner that will satisfy the court. . . .

Certain initial costs will be incurred in any serious challenge or evaluation of a challenge. The significance of these costs will depend on the rule, the EPA's commitment to the rule, the rule's perceived importance and its importance to the company. Beyond that, the ultimate cost of a judicial challenge is principally a function of two factors: the size of the regulatory record on a given issue, and whether a further appeal will be necessary to resolve the issue.

The regulatory record can play a key role because frequently the heart of a judicial challenge to an EPA rule is the creation of a persuasive argument that the EPA has not successfully meshed the "real-world facts" related to the rule with the abstract, general command of Congress. Marshaling complex facts can be as critical in defeating a rule as constructing a legal argument that the rule has violated broad statutory standards. If there is an extensive rule-making record that must be reviewed, preparing a challenge to a regulation will be more time-consuming and expensive.

In some cases, the issue addressed by the rule is so significant that the losing party will be likely—or certain—to seek to appeal the initial reviewing court's decision. Sometimes this cannot be anticipated, but often it can, and the added costs and risks should be considered.

Whether it makes sense to spend several hundred thousand dollars or more to challenge an EPA rule in court will depend on the circumstances. If an industry has lobbied a particular regulatory issue heavily before Congress and the executive branch, the expense of a judicial challenge may be viewed as the marginal cost of attacking the EPA rule in another forum. On the other hand, if the industry already has spent large sums to oppose the rule and believes the rule's vulnerability is limited, attacking the rule in court probably would not be financially justifiable. . . .

Notes and Questions

1. Very few significant agency regulations go uncontested in the courts. Does this mean that every significant regulation is worth an appeal? Consider the following analysis concerning OSHA regulations:

> OSHA estimated that the average annual cost of complying with each of the 376 PELS in the air contaminants standard was about $2 million. Because judicial review "delay[s] the implementation of OSHA standards by an average of two years," a company or trade association could save its industry $320,000, by filing an appeal, assuming an eight percent annual interest rate. Therefore, even if the trade association discounted the prospects of victory, it would justify an appeal to its members as long as the appeal cost less than $320,000. If the association's lawyers spent 500 hours on the appeal (which seems more than sufficient to appeal even a complicated standard), the association could afford legal fees of up to $640 an hour and still save its members money compared to the costs of immediate compliance with the OSHA standard. Investment in an appeal becomes more attractive when the trade association can purchase legal services at less than $640 an hour (a likely possibility), when the industry can place the money into investments that earn a higher return than eight percent, or when the standard is likely to cost the industry more than $2 million.

Sidney A. Shapiro & Thomas O. McGarity, *Not So Paradoxical: The Rationale For Technology–Based Regulation*, 1991 DUKE L.J. 729, 737–38.

Problem 2–12: Appeal for Purposes of Delay?

Recall Problem 2–5, in which USDA adopted a dietary guideline that would require five vegetarian school lunches each month. You represent the National Association of Beef Producers. Imagine that your assessment of the likelihood of success is very, very small. Your client, however, notes that if the regulation were delayed even a short while, it would delay the effect of the new guidelines for another entire school year, because the agency has indicated it would not impose the regulation in the middle of a school year. The financial benefit to meat producers of a year's delay is significant. If you challenge the rule and either the agency on its own or the court by motion stays the rule, your client would derive substantial benefit, even if you ultimately lose on the merits.

What are your ethical considerations in bringing the lawsuit? Can you weigh the benefits of delay at all? Would it be improper to bring the lawsuit solely (or primarily) to obtain delay?

Problem Materials

Model Code of Professional Responsibility

Canon 7

A Lawyer Should Represent a Client Zealously Within the Bounds of the Law

ETHICAL CONSIDERATIONS

EC 7–1 The duty of a lawyer, both to his client and to the legal system, is to represent his client zealously within the bounds of the law, which includes Disciplinary Rules and enforceable professional regulations. . . .

EC 7–3 Where the bounds of law are uncertain, the action of a lawyer may depend on whether he is serving as advocate or adviser. A lawyer may serve simultaneously as both advocate and adviser, but the two roles are essentially different. In asserting a position on behalf of his client, an advocate for the most part deals with past conduct and must take the facts as he finds them. By contrast, a lawyer serving as adviser primarily assists his client in determining the course of future conduct and relationships. While serving as advocate, a lawyer should resolve in favor of his client doubts as to the bounds of the law. In serving a client as adviser, a lawyer in appropriate circumstances should give his professional opinion as to what the ultimate decisions of the courts would likely be as to the applicable law.

Duty of the Lawyer to a Client

EC 7–4 The advocate may urge any permissible construction of the law favorable to his client, without regard to his professional opinion as to the likelihood that the construction will ultimately prevail. His conduct is within the bounds of the law, and therefore permissible, if the position taken is supported by the law or is supportable by a good faith argument for an extension, modification, or reversal of the law. However, a lawyer is not justified in asserting a position in litigation that is frivolous.

EC 7–5 A lawyer as adviser furthers the interest of his client by giving his professional opinion as to what he believes would likely be the ultimate decision of the courts on the matter at hand and by informing his client of the practical effect of such decision. He may continue in the representation of his client even though his client has elected to pursue a course of conduct contrary to the advice of the lawyer so long as he does not thereby knowingly assist the client to engage in illegal conduct or to take a frivolous legal position. . . .

EC 7–7 In certain areas of legal representation not affecting the merits of the cause or substantially prejudicing the rights of a client, a lawyer is entitled to make decisions on his own. But otherwise the authority to make decisions is exclusively that of the client and, if made within the framework of the law, such decisions are binding on his lawyer. . . .

American Bar Association Model Rules of Professional Conduct

Rule 3.1 Meritorious Claims and Contentions

A lawyer shall not bring or defend a proceeding, or assert or controvert an issue therein, unless there is a basis for doing so that is not frivolous, which includes a good faith argument for an extension, modification or reversal of existing law....

COMMENT:

The advocate has a duty to use legal procedure for the fullest benefit of the client's cause, but also a duty not to abuse legal procedure....

The filing of an action or defense or similar action taken for a client is not frivolous ... even though the lawyer believes that the client's position ultimately will not prevail. The action is frivolous, however, if the client desires to have the action taken primarily for the purpose of harassing or maliciously injuring a person or if the lawyer is unable either to make a good faith argument on the merits of the action taken or to support the action taken by a good faith argument for an an extension, modification or reversal of existing law.

Rule 3.2 Expediting Litigation

A lawyer shall make reasonable efforts to expedite litigation consistent with the interests of the client.

Comment

Dilatory practices bring the administration of justice into disrepute. Delay should not be indulged merely for the convenience of the advocates, or for the purpose of frustrating an opposing party's attempt to obtain rightful redress or repose. It is not a justification that similar conduct is often tolerated by the bench and bar. The question is whether a competent lawyer acting in good faith would regard the course of action as having some substantial purpose other than delay. Realizing financial or other benefit from otherwise improper delay in litigation is not a legitimate interest of the client.

Notes and Questions

1. Section 705 of the APA provides that an agency may postpone the effective date of an action pending judicial review. An agency might voluntarily stay a rule pending review in light of the costs industry might incur unnecessarily if the rule is overturned. In Problem 2–5, for example, perhaps USDA would not want local school districts (perhaps small entities under the Regulatory Flexibility Act) to have to change once for the rule and perhaps change back if the rule were invalidated and then perhaps change again if the rule were repromulgated. If the agency does not voluntarily delay the effective date, Section 705 authorizes courts to stay agency actions pending judicial review "to the extent

necessary to prevent irreparable injury'' or ''to preserve status or rights pending conclusion of the proceedings.'' Do you think a court would grant a stay to the beef producers in Problem 2–5? How about to an environmental group challenging an EPA rule, adopted without notice and comment, to exempt small-scale field tests of biologically engineered pesticides from the burdensome registration requirements?

2. Ethical obligations are enforced by a state's licensing agency for lawyers. Often this is a function of the state bar or of the state judiciary. Typically, someone files a complaint to the proper agency alleging an ethical violation. Depending on the violation, sanctions can range from a reprimand to disbarment. Increasingly, attorneys in the federal system have come to use Rule 11 of the Federal Rules of Civil Procedure as an enforcement mechanism. While its standards for abusive pleading are not directly related to the ethical Rules or Code, both may be said to address similar kinds of problems.

3. Dean Anthony Kronman attributes the public's low regard for lawyers to a ''demise of an older set of values that until quite recently played a vital role in defining the aspiration of American lawyers.'' ''At the very center of these values,'' Kronman explains, ''was the belief that the outstanding lawyer—the one who serves as a model for the rest—is not simply an accomplished technician but a person of prudence or practical wisdom as well.'' Because what counts is ''the quality of judgment, not expertise,'' Kronman describes this idea as ''the ideal of the lawyer-statesman.'' ANTHONY T. KRONMAN, THE LOST LAWYER: FAILING IDEALS OF THE LEGAL PROFESSION 2–3 (1993). A lawyer-statesman is one to whom clients look for guidance and advice that is ''not just instrumental,'' but is ''advice about ends.'' The lawyer-statesman's role is to help clients ''come to a better understanding of their own ambitions, interests, and ideals and to guide their choice among alternative goals.'' *Id.* at 15. Thus, the lawyer-statesman ''deliberate[s], for and with ... clients, about the wisdom of the client's ends, as opposed simply to supply them with the legal means for realizing their desires.'' *Id.* at 133.

What does Kronman's concept of the lawyer-statesman suggest about the role of the lawyer who is asked by a client to delay a regulation that is most likely legal? Does a lawyer have a professional or ethical obligation to deliberate with the client concerning the wisdom of this course of action? Is it your impression that practicing lawyers engage in such conversations with their clients? Are clients likely to engage in such deliberations, or will they simply hire another, less deliberative lawyer?

Chapter 3

ADJUDICATION

A. INTRODUCTION

The Administrative Procedure Act identifies only three types of agency proceedings: rulemaking (§ 551(5)); adjudication (§ 551(7)); and licensing (§ 551(9)). The last chapter dealt with rulemaking and this chapter addresses adjudication.

Under the APA's definitions, an "order" is a "final disposition . . . of an agency in a matter other than rule making but including licensing." 5 U.S.C.A. § 551(6). In other words, the APA's definition seems to say that, except for rulemaking, an agency's final disposition is necessarily an order. Because the APA defines "adjudication" as the process for formulating an "order," any agency process that results in a final disposition, which is not rulemaking, is necessarily adjudication. While this may overstate the case somewhat, the universe of agency process can be divided into rulemaking and adjudication for administrative law purposes.

The one major caveat on the previous statement relates to investigations or information gathering. An investigation or information gathering may be incidental to an adjudication or rulemaking. For example, the Federal Trade Commission (FTC) might undertake a wide ranging investigation into an industry's trade practices to determine whether to bring individual cases against a firm or whether to propose a trade regulation rule. Investigations or information gathering, however, can be totally independent of any adjudication or rulemaking. For example, the Department of Energy (DOE) has an entire agency within it, the Energy Information Administration, whose sole purpose is to gather and analyze information and data relating to energy sources, use, etc. Similarly, the Census Bureau in the Department of Commerce is devoted to gathering and analyzing data. Investigations and information gathering may involve rulemaking or adjudication, but this is not always the case. An agency can use rulemaking to gather information by adopting a rule that requires persons to report information to the agency. An agency may also seek to gather information as part of an adjudication when it seeks discovery or utilizes its subpoena power as part of the trial process.

Often, however, agencies pursue information gathering or investigations separately from any rulemaking or adjudication, if only because rulemaking and adjudication usually involve procedural requirements that the agency can avoid by using other information gathering techniques, such as report orders or subpoenas. Chapter 7 covers the subject of agency information gathering.

Because adjudication can generally be considered as everything that is not rulemaking, it necessarily covers a very wide range of activity. On the one hand, adjudication includes administrative proceedings that are hardly distinguishable from judicial proceedings, with an agency attorney who prosecutes a person for violating the law and who seeks an administrative order that is the equivalent of an injunction and penalties. On the other hand, an adjudication can include a determination that a law student qualifies for a federal student loan, a determination made without any hearing, attorneys, or other trappings of the judicial process. And between these two endpoints is an infinite variety of other types of agency actions that qualify as adjudications. Given this wide range of activities that qualify as adjudication, there are some types of adjudication that must process literally millions of cases a year, while others may only process a handful.

Just as adjudication can include a wide variety of actions using different procedures, agency adjudication can, like judicial actions, include actions that are mundane and routine (such as Social Security Disability and Medicare reimbursement claims) as well as actions that are policy-making and precedential (e.g., deciding whether a particular kind of employer action with respect to a union is an unfair labor practice). Because the mundane, routine actions tend to occur in great numbers, a central administrative law issue is how to achieve "mass justice"; that is, how do you retain justice while administering huge numbers of claims in an efficient, low-cost manner? The central administrative law issue in precedent-setting, policy-making cases, by comparison, is how to preserve agency discretion to set policy and yet safeguard the individual targets of the agency action from agency overreaching and abuse.

This chapter introduces you to the procedures used in adjudication and asks you to consider both the previous issues and some additional issues that complicate the design of appropriate adjudicative procedures. As in the previous chapter, the coverage proceeds through the various steps of the adjudicatory process. The starting point is the issue of whether an agency is required to use "formal" or "informal" adjudication. Although there are a variety of types of adjudication, as noted above, the APA recognizes only the categories usually referred to as formal and informal adjudication. These terms, however, can be misleading, because informal adjudication can be very formal (that is, highly proceduralized). It would be more accurate to refer to them as APA adjudication and non-APA adjudication, meaning that the former is governed by the procedures specified in the APA and the latter is not. The APA procedures for formal adjudication are found at 5 U.S.C.A.

§§ 554, 556, and 557. In many ways these procedures reproduce the procedures applicable to a trial without a jury, with an Administrative Law Judge (ALJ) presiding.

By comparison, the APA contains no requirements applicable specifically to informal adjudication. The minimal requirements of section 555 are applicable to all agency proceedings: the right in any proceeding to be represented by counsel or, if allowed by the agency, by an other-qualified representative; the right of interested persons (as opposed to parties) to appear before an agency in any proceeding "so far as the orderly conduct of public business permits"; the right to have an agency conclude a matter presented to it within a "reasonable time"; the right to retain (or obtain) copies of materials required to be submitted to an agency; the right to utilize agency subpoena power upon a showing of general relevance and reasonable scope of the evidence sought; and the right to receive prompt notice of a denial of a request, application, or petition, as well as a "brief statement of the grounds for the denial." In addition, section 558 generally requires that license suspensions, revocations, or annulments can only occur after reasonable notice and an opportunity to demonstrate or achieve compliance with all lawful requirements for the license. It further provides that a timely application for a renewal of a license for a continuing activity tolls the expiration date until the agency has made a final action on the application.

Normally, an agency will develop procedures applicable to particular types of informal adjudications and publish them in the Code of Federal Regulations. In addition to the minimal requirements of the APA, the content of these procedures may be governed by requirements in the agency's mandate or in the statute governing the particular activity. For example, the Clean Water Act requires EPA to follow certain procedures when imposing administrative penalties. *See* 33 U.S.C.A. § 1319(g)(2)(A), (4). EPA has embellished on the spare statutory requirements and published the applicable procedures at 40 CFR Part 28.

The content of the procedures applicable to informal adjudication can also be affected by the requirements of the Due Process Clause of the Fifth Amendment (and the 14th Amendment in state agencies). For example, an agency might be required by its own statutory mandate to use certain limited procedures, such as permitting persons to appear in a legislative type hearing, in which they can make a presentation but cannot present witnesses. A person adversely affected by the agency's action might attack it on the grounds that the person was deprived of property or liberty without due process. Assuming that the person's property or liberty is at stake, the court will have to determine whether the due process clause obligates the agency to use more procedures than the agency used. A due process challenge is unlikely to arise when an agency uses formal adjudication because this process already includes nearly all of the procedural protections that are associated with a formal trial.

After an agency has made its adjudication, a person adversely affected by the decision almost invariably has an opportunity for judicial review. As in the case of rulemaking, a key issue is what scope of review the court should apply. The chapter ends by exploring this issue in the context of the review of an agency's fact finding and its legal conclusions.

B. FORMAL OR INFORMAL ADJUDICATION

Section 554 of the APA, which contains some of the procedures required in formal adjudication, states that it applies "in every case of adjudication required by statute to be determined on the record after an opportunity for an agency hearing," with certain exceptions. If section 554 applies, it invokes sections 556 and 557 as well, which contain the other procedural requirements of formal APA adjudication. If, however, section 554 does not apply, the agency may provide for an adjudication governed only by the minimal APA requirements of sections 555 and 558, whatever due process might require, and whatever some other statute might require. Invariably these procedural protections are less than would be available in a formal APA adjudication. Accordingly, it is important for lawyers to determine whether an APA adjudication is required.

Early in the history of the APA, the Supreme Court read the triggering language in section 554 relatively broadly in *Wong Yang Sung v. McGrath*, 339 U.S. 33, 70 S.Ct. 445, 94 L.Ed. 616 (1950). There the question was whether a deportation hearing could be held before an "immigrant inspector," a person involved in the investigation and prosecution of deportable aliens, instead of before an ALJ, as would be required under the APA. (At the time, the APA provided for "examiners" rather than ALJs. The new title for this position was adopted in 1978.) The Supreme Court concluded that because the Due Process Clause of the Fifth Amendment required a hearing on the record prior to deportation, the statute providing for deportation should be read to require such a hearing, triggering the requirements of the APA concerning adjudication. The Court stated that the APA "represents a long period of study and strife; it settles long-continued and hard-fought contentions, and enacts a formula upon which opposing social and political forces have come to rest." In other words, the Court believed it appropriate to read the APA's provisions as the presumed solution to questions concerning the extent of administrative procedure. With the passage of time, however, the notion that one should, when in doubt, invoke the APA's procedures has waned.

The following problem concerns when an agency is required to use formal adjudication. Since *Wong Yang Sung*, the United States Supreme Court has not established a controlling test. Thus, you are asked to resolve the issue based on leading appellate cases.

Problem 3–1: The NEA Hearing Process

Congress recently amended the law governing the National Endowment for the Arts to require the Endowment to recover any federal funds expended to produce "obscene" art. Part of the amendment provides:

> Upon petition by an interested person or on its own motion, the Endowment shall hold a hearing to determine whether any work or activity funded in whole or in part by the Endowment is obscene. "Obscene" means that the work or activity depicts or describes sexual activities or sexual organs in a patently offensive manner and, viewed as a whole, appeals primarily to a prurient interest rather than to a serious artistic interest. If the Endowment determines that the work or activity is obscene, whoever received funds from the Endowment attributable to that work or activity shall be liable to the Endowment for the amount of those funds. Any person who received funds from the Endowment attributable to the allegedly obscene work or activity shall be afforded the opportunity to participate in the hearing, and if adversely affected by the Endowment's decision, the opportunity for judicial review of the Endowment's decision.

The NEA has adopted procedural regulations providing for the hearings mentioned in the recent amendment. The regulations specify that the hearings are not subject to §§ 554, 556, or 557. The preamble to the regulations explain that, because the most likely issue to be addressed in the hearings is the question whether or not a work or activity is obscene as defined in the amendment, the hearings are likely to focus on persons' perceptions and experts' opinions, so that techniques designed to determine disputed facts, especially whether persons are telling the truth, are unnecessary.

Your law firm represents the Boston Museum of Fine Arts, which is the recipient of several NEA grants. Your firm is preparing a legal memo for the museum to inform it about the new law, and you are asked to assess whether the regulations are lawful. The legislative history of the amendment is totally silent as to the issue.

Problem Materials

SEACOAST ANTI–POLLUTION LEAGUE v. COSTLE

572 F.2d 872 (1st Cir.1978).

COFFIN, CHIEF JUDGE.

This case is before us on a petition by the Seacoast Anti–Pollution League and the Audubon Society of New Hampshire (petitioners) to review a decision by the Administrator of the Environmental Protection Agency (EPA)....

The Public Service Company of New Hampshire (PSCO) filed an application with the EPA for permission to discharge heated water into the Hampton–Seabrook Estuary which runs into the Gulf of Maine. The water would be taken from the Gulf of Maine, be run through the condenser of PSCO's proposed nuclear steam electric generating station at Seabrook, and then be directly discharged back into the Gulf at a temperature 39° higher than at intake. The water is needed to remove waste heat, some 16 billion BTU per hour, generated by the nuclear reactor but not converted into electrical energy by the turbine....

Section 301(a) of the Federal Water Pollution Control Act (FWPCA) prohibits the discharge of any pollutant unless the discharger, the point source operator, has obtained an EPA permit. Heat is a pollutant.... The parties agree that the cooling system PSCO has proposed does not meet the EPA standards because PSCO would utilize a once-through open cycle system—the water would not undergo any cooling process before being returned to the sea. Therefore, PSCO applied not only for a discharge permit under § 402 of the FWPCA but also an exemption from the EPA standards pursuant to § 316 of the FWPCA. Under § 316(a) a point source operator who "after opportunity for public hearing, can demonstrate to the satisfaction of the Administrator" that the EPA's standards are "more stringent than necessary to assure the projection (sic) and propagation of a balanced, indigenous population of shellfish, fish, and wildlife in and on the body of water" may be allowed to meet a lower standard. Moreover, under § 316(b) the cooling water intake structure must "reflect the best technology available for minimizing adverse environmental impact." ...

Petitioners assert that the proceedings by which the EPA decided this case contravened certain provisions of the APA governing adjudicatory hearings. Respondents answer that the APA does not apply to proceedings held pursuant to § 316 or § 402 of the FWPCA ....[4]

The dispute centers on the meaning of the introductory phrases of § 554(a) of the APA:

> "This section applies ... in every case of adjudication required by statute to be determined on the record after opportunity for an agency hearing...."

Both § 316(a) and § 402(a)(1) of the FWPCA provide for public hearings, but neither states that the hearing must be "on the record." We are now the third court of appeals to face this issue. The Ninth Circuit and the Seventh Circuit have each found that the APA does apply to proceedings pursuant to § 402. *Marathon Oil Co. v. EPA*, 564 F.2d 1253

---

4. The determination that the EPA must make under § 316 of the FWPCA is not a rule because it is not "designed to implement, interpret, or prescribe law or policy." 5 U.S.C. § 551(4). Rather the EPA must decide a specific factual question already prescribed by statute. Since the determination is not a rule, it is an order. 5 U.S.C. § 551(6). The agency process for for-

mulating an order is an adjudication. 5 U.S.C. § 551(7). Therefore, § 554 rather than § 553 of the APA is the relevant section. The same result is dictated because § 316(a) of the FWPCA is a licensing, 5 U.S.C. § 551(9), since it results in the granting or denial of a form of permission. *See* 5 U.S.C. § 551(8). A license is an order. 5 U.S.C. § 551(6).

(9th Cir.1977); *United States Steel Corp. v. Train*, 556 F.2d 822 (7th Cir.1977). We agree.

At the outset we reject the position of intervenor PSCO that the precise words "on the record" must be used to trigger the APA. The Supreme Court has clearly rejected such an extreme reading even in the context of rule making under § 553 of the APA. See *United States v. Florida East Coast Ry. Co.*, 410 U.S. 224, 245, 93 S.Ct. 810, 35 L.Ed. 2d 223 (1973); *United States v. Allegheny–Ludlum Steel Corp.*, 406 U.S. 742, 757, 92 S.Ct. 1941, 32 L.Ed.2d 453 (1972). Rather, we think that the resolution of this issue turns on the substantive nature of the hearing Congress intended to provide.[6]

We begin with the nature of the decision at issue. The EPA Administrator must make specific factual findings about the effects of discharges from a specific point source. On the basis of these findings the Administrator must determine whether to grant a discharge permit to a specific applicant. Though general policy considerations may influence the decision, the decision will not make general policy. Only the rights of the specific applicant will be affected. "As the instant proceeding well demonstrates, the factual questions involved in the issuance of section 402 permits will frequently be sharply disputed. Adversarial hearings will be helpful, therefore, in guaranteeing both reasoned decisionmaking and meaningful judicial review. In summary, the proceedings below were conducted in order 'to adjudicate disputed facts in particular cases,' not 'for the purposes of promulgating policy-type rules or standards.'"

This is exactly the kind of quasi-judicial proceeding for which the adjudicatory procedures of the APA were intended. As the Supreme Court has said, "Determination of questions of (the Administrative Procedure Act's) coverage may well be approached through consideration of its purposes as disclosed by its background." *Wong Yang Sung v. McGrath*. One of the developments that prompted the APA was the "[m]ultiplication of federal administrative agencies and expansion of their functions to include adjudications which have serious impact on private rights." This is just such an adjudication. The panoply of procedural protections provided by the APA is necessary not only to protect the rights of an applicant for less stringent pollutant discharge limits, but is also needed to protect the public for whose benefit the very strict limitations have been enacted. If determinations such as the one at issue here are not made on the record, then the fate of the Hampton–Seabrook Estuary could be decided on the basis of evidence that a court would never see or, what is worse, that a court could not be sure existed. We cannot believe that Congress would intend such a result.

---

6. Like the Ninth Circuit we consider it significant that § 509 of the FWPCA provides for judicial review of the EPA determination.... Certainly that is an indication that the agency must be careful to provide some basis for appellate court review. But we are unable to agree that § 509, standing alone, satisfies an "on the record" requirement. The APA makes it clear that in some cases review of agency action can be had though the action was not on the record....

Our holding does not render the opening phrases of § 554 of the APA meaningless. We are persuaded that their purpose was to exclude "governmental functions, such as the administration of loan programs, which traditionally have never been regarded as adjudicative in nature and as a rule have never been exercised through other than business procedures." Attorney General's Manual on the Administrative Procedure Act 40 (1947). Without some kind of limiting language, the broad sweep of the definition of "adjudication," defined principally as that which is not rule making would include such ordinary procedures that do not require any kind of hearing at all. In short, we view the crucial part of the limiting language to be the requirement of a statutorily imposed hearing. We are willing to presume that, unless a statute otherwise specifies, an adjudicatory hearing subject to judicial review must be on the record. The legislative history of the APA and its treatment in the courts bear us out.

. . . The presumption in rule making cases is that formal, adjudicatory procedures are not necessary. A hearing serves a very different function in the rule making context. Witnesses may bring in new information or different points of view, but the agency's final decision need not reflect the public input. The witnesses are not the only source of the evidence on which the Administrator may base his factual findings. For these reasons, we place less importance on the absence of the words "on the record" in the adjudicatory context.

"It is believed that with respect to adjudication the specific statutory requirement of a hearing, without anything more, carries with it the further requirement of decision on the basis of the evidence adduced at the hearing. With respect to rule making, it was concluded that a statutory provision that rules be issued after a hearing, without more, should not be construed as requiring agency action 'on the record', but rather as merely requiring an opportunity for the expression of views. That conclusion was based on the legislative nature of rule making, from which it was inferred, unless a statute requires otherwise, that an agency hearing on proposed rules would be similar to a hearing before a legislative committee, with neither the legislature nor the agency being limited to the material adduced at the hearing. No such rationale applies to administrative adjudication. In fact, it is assumed that where a statute specifically provides for administrative adjudication (such as the suspension or revocation of a license) after opportunity for an agency hearing, such specific requirement for a hearing ordinarily implies the further requirement of decision in accordance with evidence adduced at the hearing. Of course, the foregoing discussion is inapplicable to any situation in which the legislative history or the context of the pertinent statute indicates a contrary congressional intent." Attorney General's Manual, supra, 42–43 (footnote and citation to statutory history omitted).

Here the statute certainly does not indicate that the determination need not be on the record, and we find no indication of a contrary congressional intent. Therefore, we will judge the proceedings below according to the standards set forth in §§ 554, 556, and 557 of the APA....

CITY OF WEST CHICAGO v. U.S. NUCLEAR REGULATORY COMMISSION

701 F.2d 632 (7th Cir.1983).

CUMMINGS, CHIEF JUDGE....

Kerr–McGee (KM) operated a milling facility in West Chicago for the production of thorium and thorium compounds from 1967 to 1973. Although the plant closed in 1973, there is presently on site approximately 5 million cubic feet of contaminated waste material consisting of building rubble, contaminated soil, and tailings from the milling of thorium ore....

The current NRC license for the West Chicago site is a "source material" license ... authorizing KM to possess and store thorium ores. In March 1980 and March 1981 KM submitted emergency requests to demolish Buildings Nos. 1 and 3 at the West Chicago site. On April 24, 1981, the NRC staff granted these requests as Amendment No. 1 to KM's existing license. Amendment No. 3, which is the focus of the City's suit challenging the NRC order, was issued in September 1981 and allowed demolition of six additional buildings on site in a non-emergency situation. Amendment No. 3 also authorized receipt and storage on site of contaminated material that was formerly taken from the site for use as landfill.

On October 14, 1981, the City brought suit challenging the issuance of Amendment No. 3.... Judge McGarr temporarily enjoined KM's activities under the amendment and ordered the NRC to give notice to the City and consider any request for hearing that the City might make. NRC did so, and on February 11, 1982, issued its order denying the City's request for a formal, trial-type hearing, addressing the contentions raised by the City in the written materials it submitted, and reissuing Amendment No. 3....

The Atomic Energy Act of 1954 (AEA) clearly requires NRC to grant a "hearing" if requested "[i]n any proceeding under this chapter, for the granting, suspending, revoking, or amending of any license or construction permit * * *." The parties in this case are arguing about the kind of "hearing" the NRC is required to conduct when issuing an amendment to a source materials license. The City argues that NRC must hold a formal, adversarial, trial-type hearing.... NRC and intervenor KM argue that the NRC may hold an informal hearing in which it requests and considers written materials without providing for traditional trial-type procedures such as oral testimony and cross-examination. We shall refer to this kind of hearing as an "informal hearing." In the circumstances of this case, we find that an informal hearing suffices....

The City claims that a materials licensing hearing under Section 189(a) of the AEA must be in accordance with Section 554 of the

Administrative Procedure Act (APA). Section 554 does not by its terms dictate the type of hearing to which a party is entitled; rather it triggers the formal hearing provisions of Sections 556 and 557 of the APA if the adjudication in question is required by the agency's governing statute to be "determined on the record after opportunity for an agency hearing * * *." The City argues that Section 189(a) of the AEA triggers the formal hearing provisions of the APA because it provides that the "Commission shall grant a hearing upon the request of any person whose interest may be affected by the proceeding, and shall admit any such person as a party to such proceeding."

Although Section 554 specifies that the governing statute must satisfy the "on the record" requirement, those three magic words need not appear for a court to determine that formal hearings are required. However, . . . in the absence of these magic words, Congress must clearly indicate its intent to trigger the formal, on-the-record hearing provisions of the APA. *See also United States v. Florida East Coast Ry.,* 410 U.S. 224, 234–238, 93 S.Ct. 810, 815–818, 35 L.Ed.2d 223; *United States v. Allegheny–Ludlum Steel Corp.,* 406 U.S. 742, 756–758, 92 S.Ct. 1941, 1950, 32 L.Ed.2d 453. We find no such clear intention in the legislative history of the AEA, and therefore conclude that formal hearings are not statutorily required for amendments to materials licenses. . . .

In adopting rules to carry out the AEA, however, the Atomic Energy Commission (AEC) [the predecessor agency to the NRC] did provide by regulation for formal hearings on request in all licensing cases. The agency did not indicate whether the formal hearings were a matter of discretion or statutory mandate. In 1957, the Act was amended to add the second sentence of Section 189(a), mandating a hearing on certain applications for construction permits even when uncontested. Again, the type of hearing to be held was left undefined. After the 1957 amendment took effect, there was a significant amount of criticism of the AEC for overformalizing the licensing process. The staff of the Joint Committee on Atomic Energy published a report criticizing the AEC for going "further in some respects than the law required, particularly in regard to the number of hearings required and the formality of procedures." With respect to materials licenses, the Joint Committee staff suggested registration rather than licensing of materials, though it did recommend hearings before a hearing examiner in contested materials licensing cases. The Joint Committee then held hearings to explore legislative improvements to the AEC regulatory process. Although witnesses debated whether Section 189(a) of the AEA required formal procedures in licensing cases, the Joint Committee did not resolve the issue. . . .

The AEC continued to hold formal hearings in all contested reactor cases, as well as in materials licensing cases. However, based on the threadbare legislative history concerning materials licenses, we are unable to conclude that the AEC's procedures were mandated by statute. . . .

The City argues that under the APA, agency action is classified either as rulemaking or adjudication, and since licensing is adjudication, NRC is obliged to provide a formal hearing in this case. The "on the record" requirement of APA Section 554, according to the City has been relevant primarily in cases involving rulemaking, not adjudication; in adjudication, the City claims the absence of the "on the record" requirement is not decisive. For example, Section 402 of the Federal Water Pollution Control Act (FWPCA), 33 U.S.C. § 1342(a)(1), which provides for a "public hearing," has been held by three courts including this one to require a formal hearing pursuant to Section 554. The First Circuit relied principally on the adjudicative nature of the decision at issue— issuance of a permit to allow discharge of a pollutant—finding that primarily the rights of the particular applicant would be affected, and that resolution of the issues required specific factual findings by the EPA Administrator. *Seacoast Anti–Pollution League v. Costle*. The court also mentioned the judicial review provision of Section 509 of the FWPCA, which provides for review of a determination required under the FWPCA to be made "on the record." . . . Unlike the "on the record" requirement of Section 509 of the FWPCA, there is no indication even in the judicial review Section of the AEA, the governing statute, that Congress intended to require formal hearings under the APA.

Thus even in adjudication, the "on the record" requirement is significant at least as an indication of congressional intent. We agree with the courts and commentators who recognize that adjudication may be either informal or formal. Formal adjudications are those required by statute to be conducted through on-the-record proceedings. Informal adjudications constitute a residual category including "all agency actions that are not rulemaking and that need not be conducted through 'on the record' hearings." . . .

Despite the fact that licensing is adjudication under the APA, there is no evidence that Congress intended to require formal hearings for all Section 189(a) activities. In light of the above analysis, we conclude that NRC did not violate the AEA when it denied the City's request for a formal hearing. . . .

CHEMICAL WASTE MANAGEMENT, INC. v. U.S. ENVIRONMENTAL PROTECTION AGENCY
873 F.2d 1477 (D.C.Cir.1989).

D.H. GINSBURG, CIRCUIT JUDGE:

Petitioners Chemical Waste Management, Inc. and Waste Management of North America seek review of Environmental Protection Agency regulations that establish informal procedures for administrative hearings concerning the issuance of corrective action orders under § 3008(h) of the Resource Conservation and Recovery Act (RCRA). We conclude that the regulations represent a reasonable interpretation of an ambiguous statutory provision and are not, on their face, inconsistent with the requirement of due process. Accordingly, we deny the petition for review.

Subsection (a) of RCRA § 3008 authorizes EPA to enter orders assessing civil penalties, including suspension or revocation of permits, for violation of RCRA regulations. Subsection (b) provides that, upon request made within thirty days of the issuance of a subsection (a) order, EPA "shall promptly conduct a public hearing."

In 1978, EPA promulgated procedural regulations to implement the "public hearing" provision of subsection (a). 40 C.F.R. Part 22. These procedures conform to the provisions of the Administrative Procedure Act for formal adjudication. . . .

In the Hazardous and Solid Waste Amendments of 1984, Congress added to § 3008 a new subsection (h), authorizing the Administrator of EPA to issue "an order requiring corrective action" whenever he "determines that there is or has been a release of hazardous waste into the environment" from an interim facility. Such orders must indicate "the nature of the required corrective action or other response measure, and . . . specify a time for compliance," and may include suspension or revocation of the facility's authorization to operate as an interim facility. The Administrator may assess a civil penalty of up to $25,000 per day for noncompliance with a corrective action order. The 1984 Amendments also modified subsection (b) to make it clear that those subject to corrective action orders under the new subsection (h) have the right to a "public hearing."

To govern subsection (h) hearings, EPA promulgated the procedural regulations here under review, 40 C.F.R. Part 24. Those rules specifically provide that the formal adjudicatory procedures of Part 22 shall be applicable only to challenges to subsection (h) corrective action orders that include a suspension or revocation of interim status or an assessment of civil penalties for noncompliance. . . . [All other corrective action orders are subject to] informal rather than formal adjudicatory procedures. . . .

Petitioners argue initially that the informal procedures of Part 24 are inconsistent with the intent of Congress in enacting and amending § 3008. To this end, petitioners[, among other arguments, contend] that precedent in this circuit erects a presumption that when Congress refers to an adjudication as a "hearing," it intends that formal procedures be used.

We approach petitioners' arguments within the framework that the Supreme Court decreed in *Chevron U.S.A. v. Natural Resources Defense Council*, 467 U.S. 837 (1984), for judicial review of an agency's interpretation of a statute under its administration. At the outset, we ask whether "Congress has directly spoken to the precise question at issue"; if so, then we "must give effect to the unambiguously expressed intent of Congress" and may not defer to a contrary agency interpretation. If the statute is "silent or ambiguous with respect to the specific issue," however, we proceed to ask "whether the agency's answer is based on a permissible construction of the statute"; if so, then we must defer to the agency's construction.

Petitioners point to our statement in a footnote in *Union of Concerned Scientists v. U.S. NRC*, 735 F.2d 1437, 1444 n. 12 (D.C.Cir.1984) (UCS), that "when a statute calls for a hearing in an adjudication the hearing is presumptively governed by 'on the record' procedures," notwithstanding omission of the phrase "on the record" in the statute. *See also Seacoast Anti–Pollution League v. Costle*, 572 F.2d 872, 877 (1st Cir.1978); *Marathon Oil v. EPA*, 564 F.2d 1253, 1264 (9th Cir.1977). For the reasons set out below, however, we decline to adhere any longer to the presumption raised in *UCS*. . . .

. . . *UCS* and its kin, *Seacoast* and *Marathon*, all predate the Supreme Court's decision in *Chevron*. Under that decision, it is not our office to presume that a statutory reference to a "hearing," without more specific guidance from Congress, evinces an intention to require formal adjudicatory procedures, since such a presumption would arrogate to the court what is now clearly the prerogative of the agency, viz., to bring its own expertise to bear upon the resolution of ambiguities in the statute that Congress has charged it to administer. In effect, the presumption in *UCS* truncates the *Chevron* inquiry at the first step by treating a facially ambiguous statutory reference to a "hearing" as though it were an unambiguous constraint upon the agency. We will henceforth make no presumption that a statutory "hearing" requirement does or does not compel the agency to undertake a formal "hearing on the record," thereby leaving it to the agency, as an initial matter, to resolve the ambiguity.

While an agency might not be able reasonably to read a requirement that it conduct a "hearing on the record" to permit informal procedures in the converse situation to that presented here, an agency that reasonably reads a simple requirement that it hold a "hearing" to allow for informal hearing procedures must prevail under the second step of *Chevron*. As usual in cases involving *Chevron*'s second step, the court will evaluate the reasonableness of the agency's interpretation using the normal tools of statutory interpretation—such as legislative history, structural inferences, or exceptional circumstances of the type presented in *UCS*.

In the alternative, petitioners contend that EPA failed to provide a reasoned explanation, as required under the "arbitrary or capricious" standard of APA § 706 to support its conclusion that corrective action orders under subsection (h) are amenable to informal adjudicatory procedures. Since it would clearly be unreasonable for the agency to resolve a statutory ambiguity to support an arbitrary result, petitioners' position is functionally a *Chevron* step two contention that EPA's interpretation of the statute is unreasonable. This is the issue joined.

Specifically, petitioners attack EPA's claims that subsection (h) orders will pose fewer factual issues than do subsection (a) orders; that any factual issues that do arise can be resolved by considering documents and oral statements without need of trial-type examination of witnesses; and that informal procedures will allow the agency to respond more quickly to releases of hazardous waste.

In its preamble accompanying the Part 24 regulations, EPA predicts that "[subsection] (h) cases will present fewer factual issues than the typical case involving an RCRA [subsection] (a) compliance order," since "questions as to whether certain events or violations occurred, the timing of certain events/violations, the seriousness of the violation, [and] the economic benefit to respondent of the violation" will arise less frequently. In addition, EPA said that those factual issues that do arise "will relate almost entirely to technical (or policy) matters" that create "little need to establish witness veracity or credibility through observation of a witness's demeanor on cross-examination" and therefore "can just as easily (perhaps more effectively) be resolved through analysis of the administrative record and the written submissions and oral statements of the parties."

The preamble to the notice promulgating Part 24 also refers to the seemingly obvious "need to respond quickly to releases of hazardous waste." ... [Nevertheless, because the legislative history indicates otherwise,] EPA cannot rely upon the need for swift adjudication to justify its use of informal hearing procedures.

Nonetheless, we conclude that the agency has provided a reasonable explanation for its choice of informal procedures in Part 24, based on the number and nature of factual issues expected in a typical subsection (h) proceeding....

Notes and Questions

1.   The problem cases are the leading cases on when a formal, APA adjudication is required. The Supreme Court has not settled the issue.

2.   Two years after *Wong Yang Sung* was decided, Congress amended the immigration law to state specifically that deportation hearings would not be subject to the APA. This change was challenged in *Marcello v. Bonds*, 349 U.S. 302, 75 S.Ct. 757, 99 L.Ed. 1107 (1955), but the Court confirmed that its decision in *Wong Yang Sung* had been one of statutory construction, construing the immigration law to trigger an APA adjudication. While due process still required a hearing on the record in deportation hearings, the content of that due process hearing would no longer be the APA. Although *Marcello* held that deportation hearings were not longer subject to APA procedures, it did not reject the analysis of *Wong Yang Sung* that applied when a statute was silent concerning the nature of hearing procedures. Recall that *Wong Yang Sung* held that a statute requires a formal, APA hearing when it is silent concerning the nature of the hearing procedures that an agency is required to use and when due process requires a hearing on the record. Later Supreme Court cases, however, have in effect overruled this aspect of *Wong Yang Sung*. *See Mathews v. Eldridge*, 424 U.S. 319, 96 S.Ct. 893, 47 L.Ed.2d 18

(1976) (despite applicability of due process clause, APA formal adjudication not required).

3.   Subsequent to and consistent with the First Circuit's decision in *Seacoast Anti–Pollution League v. Costle*, EPA provided in its procedural regulations that permits for the discharge of pollutants under the Clean Water Act would be issued under APA adjudication procedures. In 1996, citing *Chevron v. NRDC* and *Chemical Waste Management*, EPA proposed to amend its procedural regulations to provide that these permits would be issued using informal, non-APA procedures. *See* 61 FR 65268 (1996). Do you see any legal grounds to object to this change? How do you think a district court in the First Circuit would deal with the conflict between *Chemical Waste* and *Seacoast* if a challenge was brought to a discharge permit under the new regulations?

4.   Because of the potentially significant differences in procedural protections afforded persons under formal and informal adjudications, one might hope that there was a principled or logical basis for when Congress requires formal adjudication and when it does not. Unfortunately, this does not generally seem to be the case. In some situations Congress has tailored the formality of the proceedings to the relative harshness of the consequences of the adjudication, *e.g.,* allowing informal adjudication of penalties under \$25,000, but requiring formal adjudication of penalties totaling more than that, 33 U.S.C.A. § 1319(g)(2). *See also* 42 U.S.C. § 9609 (administrative penalties under the Comprehensive Environmental Response, Compensation and Liability Act). More frequently, however, there is little objective justification for when formal and informal adjudication is required. *Compare* 42 U.S.C.A. § 300h–2(c) (up to \$125,000 penalty can be assessed in informal adjudication under Safe Drinking Water Act). Agencies lobby Congress for informal adjudication, rather than formal adjudication authority, because agencies believe that the adjudications will be faster, simpler, and easier if the requirements of the APA need not be followed. Sometimes Congress accedes to the agency wishes. Sometimes Congress is moved by concerns with persons who may be involved in these adjudications, or elements of Congress who are not sympathetic to the agency's mandate wish to burden its exercise, and Congress requires formal adjudication. And as the problem cases suggest, often Congress simply is not clear. As a result, there is little rhyme or reason behind which proceedings must be formal and which may be informal. For example, the decision to build a highway through a park is an informal adjudication; the decision that a Social Security Disability Benefit recipient is no longer eligible is a formal adjudication; the decision to deport a person from the United States is an informal adjudication; the decision that an employer wrongfully discharged an employee for union activities is a formal adjudication; the decision to order a company to undertake a multimillion dollar hazardous waste cleanup is an informal adjudication; and the decision to suspend temporarily the registration of a particular pesticide is a formal adjudication.

C. ADJUDICATORY PROCEDURES

The APA addresses in some detail the procedures for adjudications under the APA. This section describes these procedures and contains a problem that involves some of the issues that arise in formal adjudication.

1. NOTICE

The APA requires that the proceeding begin with notice that includes the time, place and manner of the hearing; the legal authority for the hearing, and the matters of fact and law asserted by whoever is bringing the proceeding, 5 U.S.C.A. § 554(b). If there is a defendant, the party usually is required to reply to the notice with issues controverted in fact or law. *Id.*

It is worth noting here that APA adjudications run the gamut from cases where the government is the initiating party charging someone with a violation of some law or regulation (for example, EPA enforcing environmental regulations or the Secretary of Labor enforcing occupational safety regulations), to cases where two private parties are proceeding against each other before an agency decisionmaking body (for example, a person seeking workers compensation under various federal workers compensation statutes), to cases where a person seeks a benefit from the government and there is no adverse party (for example, in social security disability cases).

The specific way an adjudication begins depends on the particular activity involved. For example, under OSHA, an inspector can issue a citation to an employer in the course of an inspection. Issuing the citation is itself a form of adjudication (very informal)—the inspector is making a determination that the employer is violating applicable health or safety regulations and assesses a penalty. If the employer wishes to contest the citation, it seeks a formal adjudication of the matter before an ALJ of the Occupational Safety and Health Review Commission. Under the Clean Water Act, on the other hand, EPA issues a complaint to a person it believes is violating the Act or its regulations. The person then files an answer, much like the beginning of a case under the Federal Rules of Civil Procedure. The National Labor Relations Act, which protects employees and unions from unfair management practices and management from unfair labor practices, utilizes a rather unique system. A person who thinks he has been the victim of an unfair practice reports it to the Regional Counsel of the NLRB. The Regional Counsel in consultation with the General Counsel in Washington, D.C., decides whether to bring an action alleging an unfair practice on behalf of the charging party. If an action is brought, the Regional Counsel files a complaint with the defendant to begin the adjudication. This action is brought in the name of the NLRB, not in the name of the victim, who, as in a criminal case, may be a witness but is not a party to the action.

2. INTERVENORS

Many adjudications are of major consequence, setting precedents for future cases and for all practical purposes establishing agency "rules." As a result, it is not uncommon for persons who are not parties to want to participate in the proceeding to affect its outcome. Even where the subject matter is not of national import, the actual effect of the adjudication may affect non-parties significantly. This is particularly true of licensing decisions, where typically only the license applicant or holder is a party initially. Persons who might be affected by the grant of the license (e.g., to construct or operate a nuclear reactor, or to operate a broadcast television station) may want to influence the agency as to the standards employed in or the outcome of the proceeding. The APA states that, "as far as orderly conduct of public business permits, an interested person may appear before an agency" in a proceeding. 5 U.S.C.A. § 555(b). This provision is not limited to formal, APA adjudications, but by its terms applies to all agency proceedings—formal or informal, rulemaking or adjudication. This is a very permissive standard, but it is not clear what it means to be allowed to "appear" before the agency. Thinking in judicial terms, one could interpret the right to "appear" as a right to intervene or a right to be an amicus. The primary effect of the difference would be that if the phrase means intervention, the person can appeal an adverse decision, whereas if it constitutes merely an amicus presentation, the person cannot appeal.

The Supreme Court has not declared a standard to control when a person can intervene as a party. A decision by the D.C. Circuit, however, has been widely followed concerning this issue. In *Office of Communication of United Church of Christ v. FCC*, 359 F.2d 994 (D.C.Cir.1966), the court held that if a person has standing to appeal the decision of the agency, as a matter of the case and controversy requirements of the Constitution, the person has a right to intervene. (The issue of standing to appeal the decision of an agency is covered in Chapter 5.) Later cases have suggested that limited intervention may be justified (*i.e.*, the agency cannot deny it) in particular circumstances even where the person would not have standing to appeal the agency's decision. *See Koniag, Inc. v. Andrus*, 580 F.2d 601 (D.C.Cir.1978).

The D.C. Circuit, however, has recently held that standing and the right to intervene in an agency proceeding are not controlled by the same standard when intervention is sought under an agency's statutory mandate. In *Envirocare of Utah v. Nuclear Regulatory Commission*, 194 F.3d 72 (D.C.Cir.1999), the court interpreted a provision of the Atomic Energy Act that required the NRC to admit any person as a party in a hearing "whose interests may be affected by the proceeding." Applying *Chevron*, the court determined first that Congress' intent concerning who was entitled to intervene was unclear and second that the NRC's decision that Envirocare was not entitled to be an intervenor was a reasonable interpretation of the statute. The NRC had refused to grant existing market participants, such as Envirocare, intervenor status because nothing indicated Congress meant the licensing requirement to protect market participants from new competition. The court conceded that Envirocase might have standing to appeal the NRC's decision to grant the license, but it held that standing law was not applicable because it concerns the constitutional authority of the judiciary to hear an appeal. The court distinguished *Church of Christ* on the ground that the agency in that case had equated the right to intervene with standing law, which meant the court had no occasion to decide whether the two concepts might be different. The court also noted that Envirocare did not invoke the APA's intervenor provision, § 555(b), and it expressed no view whether § 555(b) might require a different result.

3. SETTLEMENT

The APA has always provided that there should be an opportunity before a hearing for the parties to settle or adjust their dispute, 5 U.S.C.A. §§ 554(c), 556(c)(6). In addition, Congress enacted the Administrative Dispute Resolution Act in 1990 to amend the APA to give special emphasis to alternative dispute resolution or ADR. 5 U.S.C. §§ 571–583. The amendments authorize agencies to use a number of different ADR techniques, including settlement, mini-trial, conciliation, mediation, and arbitration. ADR is never required, nor can it be forced on any party; it is a voluntary process. The amendments contain provisions that enable arbitration to be enforced (and reviewed) in the same manner as arbitration under the Federal Arbitration Act, 9 U.S.C.A. §§ 1 et seq.

4. ADMINISTRATIVE LAW JUDGES

If there is a hearing, the APA states that one of three entities must oversee the taking of evidence: the agency, one or more members of the body that comprises the agency, or one or more Administrative Law Judges (ALJs). 5 U.S.C.A. § 556(b). When the APA refers to the agency or a member of the agency having some function in an adjudication, it means the person or persons who are in charge of the agency. For example, if the hearing were before EPA, the "agency" would be the Administrator; if, however, the hearing were before an independent regulatory agency like the NLRB or FCC, then the "agency" would be the entire board or commission, while a "member" of the agency would be a Board member or Commissioner.

As a practical matter, an ALJ virtually always is the person who presides at an APA hearing. The presiding officer (hereafter referred to as the ALJ) has the same types of authorities and responsibilities as a federal judge in a trial without a jury. The ALJ can administer oaths, issue subpoenas authorized by law, rule on offers of proof and receive relevant evidence, take depositions or have depositions taken, regulate the course of the hearing, hold conferences for settlement, dispose of procedural requests, and take other action authorized by agency rule. 5 U.S.C.A. § 556(c). Almost invariably agencies will have published procedural regulations (like mini-Federal Rules of Civil Procedure) spelling out the procedures applicable to their APA hearings. Like trial court judges, ALJs (and agencies) may take official notice ("judicial notice") of facts. If, however, a decision rests on official notice, a party is entitled to an opportunity to try to disprove it. Finally, agencies can decide whether the ALJ will initially decide the case or merely make a recommended decision to the agency. 5 U.S.C.A. § 557(b). If the case involves an application for an initial license, the agency may limit the ALJ to merely presiding over the preceding and assembling the record.

Who is an ALJ? When the APA was passed, they were called Hearing Examiners. The original name reflected the view that their primary role was to preside at a hearing and assemble the record that would be the basis for decision by the agency. Their name was changed in 1978 to Administrative Law Judges, but neither their powers nor responsibilities were changed. As of October 1996, there were 1381 federal ALJs working in about 30 different agencies, which is more than twice the number of federal district court judges. Over 1100 of the ALJs work for just one agency, the Social Security Administration. The nature of the cases that ALJs hear vary greatly in different agencies. In SSA, for example, the ALJs almost invariably hear routine benefits cases, while ALJs in the Nuclear Regulatory Commission or the Federal Energy Regulatory Commission deal with some of the most complex technical scientific and economic issues.

The role of the ALJ is problematical. The ALJ functions much like a judge, but the ALJ is not independent like a judge. ALJs are employees of the agency for which they act as judges. 5 U.S.C.A. § 3105. Because in most cases the agency is a party before the ALJ, the fact that the ALJ is an employee of the agency is in tension with our notion of a neutral decisionmaker. The APA has several provisions to try to mitigate this tension. Most importantly, agencies are not allowed to rate, evaluate, discipline, reward, punish, or remove the ALJs who work for them. Adverse personnel actions can only be made by the Merit Systems Protection Board after a formal APA adjudication. 5 U.S.C.A. § 7521. Whether as a result of this insulation or other reasons, as a practical matter, ALJs do not in fact feel allegiance to the agency they work for and for all meaningful purposes are independent and neutral.

In recent years, there has been an increasing literature questioning the current status and organization of ALJs. *See* Joseph J. Simeone, *The Function, Flexibility, and Future of United States Judges of the Executive Department*, 44 ADMIN. L. REV. 159 (1992); Paul R. Verkuil, *Reflections upon the Federal Administrative Judiciary*, 39 UCLA L. REV. 1341 (1992); Charles H. Koch, Jr., *Administrative Presiding Officials Today*, 46 ADMIN. L. REV. 271 (1994). The Administrative Conference of the United States (ACUS), in an attempt to suggest substantial (but less than radical) changes, adopted a report and recommendations that were perceived as very controversial. ACUS acknowledged that the role of ALJs as independent fact finders requires that they be protected from agency pressure in making their decisions, but it also recognized that agencies have a legitimate interest in being able to manage their employees, including ALJs, to ensure that the adjudicatory system is efficient and fair. ACUS therefore recommended that ALJs in each agency be subject to review by the chief ALJ, who would develop case processing guidelines in conjunction with other agency ALJs, agency managers, and others. The Chief ALJ would then evaluate an ALJ's performance based on compliance with the guidelines and other factors, such as judicial comportment and demeanor, and provide appropriate professional guidance, including reprimands if necessary, to ALJs. *See* ADMINISTRATIVE CONFERENCE OF THE UNITED STATES, 1992 RECOMMENDATIONS AND REPORTS 35–37, 41.

To further assure the independence of the ALJ, the APA prohibits an agency employee engaged in investigation or prosecution of a case from participating or advising in the ALJ's decision, recommended decision, or agency review of that decision except as witness or counsel in the public proceedings. 5 U.S.C.A. § 554(d). This prohibition is known as the separation of functions—separating the prosecution from the adjudicative functions within the agency. There are three exceptions to this prohibition. 5 U.S.C.A. § 554(d)(A)–(C). Again, initial licensing is excepted, as are proceedings involving the validity or application of rates or practices of public utilities or common carriers. Both of these exceptions are premised on the idea that in such cases there is *no* prosecuting or investigating function in the agency.

The third exception is for "the agency or a member or members of the body comprising the agency." That is, the head of the agency or the members of commissions and boards are not forbidden from both engaging in the prosecuting function and the adjudicative function. This exception reflects the basic combination of functions that characterize administrative agencies. Thus, the head of the agency (or the board or commission in an independent regulatory agency) first decides to investigate a potential violator, then decides whether the evidence justifies bringing a case against the person, and ultimately, either in review of an ALJ's initial decision or in making the final decision after the ALJ's recommended decision, decides whether the evidence supports a finding against the person. Thus, at the ALJ level there is a separation of functions, but at the top level a combination of functions is acceptable. Why this combination is acceptable is covered later in the chapter.

The APA also provides that ALJs are subject to disqualification for personal bias or other reason from hearing a case, but it does not specify a standard. 5 U.S.C.A. § 556(b). Generally, it is fair to say that the standards applicable to ALJs are equivalent to those applicable to federal judges, a product of a mix of common law and procedural due process.

Even if the ALJ is neutral and independent, the ALJ cannot second-guess, ignore, or invalidate the formally adopted legal positions of the agency, because the ALJ is an employee of the agency. For example, the agency may be trying to assess a civil penalty against a person who violated the agency's regulations. The person may wish to defend on the basis that the regulation is unconstitutional, beyond statutory authority, and adopted in violation of procedural requirements, but none of these arguments can be considered by the ALJ. The agency adopted the rule, and it is conclusively presumed to be valid for purposes of the proceeding before the ALJ. This obviously makes the ALJ considerably different than a federal judge, or even a magistrate, who pursuant to *Marbury v. Madison*, 5 U.S. (1 Cranch) 137, 2 L.Ed. 60 (1803), must be able to determine the validity of the underlying regulation being enforced.

5. THE "SPLIT–ENFORCEMENT" ARRANGEMENT

As noted, the APA permits the "head" of an agency to engage in both prosecutorial and adjudicative functions. In two instances, however, Congress has separated these functions by adopting a "split enforcement" model. The Occupational Safety and Health Administration (OSHA) and the Mine Safety and Health Administration (MSHA) are the two agencies that operate under this arrangement. Both agencies are located in the Department of Labor and they police workplace safety and health in workplaces and mines respectively. The adjudication of OSHA cases indicates how this arrangement works. The Occupational Safety and Health Act (OSHA Act) created the Occupational Safety and Health Review Commission (OSHRC), an independent, three person board appointed by the President and confirmed by the Senate, to adjudicate whether an employer has violated the OSH Act or a regulation promulgated by OSHA. Accordingly, the ALJ is an employee of OSHRC, rather than OSHA, and appeals from the ALJ are made to OSHRC. OSHRC, therefore, stands in the position of the "agency" under sections 554, 556, and 557 of the APA and rules *de novo* on cases appealed from the ALJ. The rationale of the split enforcement arrangement is to protect employers from any possible bias that the Department of Labor might have regarding the adjudication of safety or health violations in workplaces or mines. *See* Benjamin W. Mintz, *Administrative Separation of Functions at OSHA and NLRB*, 47 CATH. U.L. REV. 877 (1998).

Because of this split enforcement approach, the courts were divided concerning to which agency, OSHA or OSHRC, they should defer concerning the resolution of any ambiguity in a regulation. An agency's construction of its own regulations is normally entitled to deference when that construction is subject to review. The deference reflects the assumption that Congress delegated to an agency the primary responsibility to clarify its regulations. This arrangement recognizes the agency's expertise and permits it to develop consistent policies. (This subject is discussed further in Chapter 4). In *Martin v. OSHRC*, 499 U.S. 144, 111 S.Ct. 1171, 113 L.Ed.2d 117 (1991), the Supreme Court clarified that OSHA was to receive deference for any interpretation of its regulations. Thus, the Court rejected the idea that OSHRC was to have a policy role in determining what OSHA's regulations meant.

6. BURDEN OF PROOF

The APA specifies that the proponent has the burden of proof, 5 U.S.C.A. § 556(d), but it was not until 1994, in *Director, Office of Workers' Compensation Programs v. Greenwich Collieries*, 512 U.S. 267, 114 S.Ct. 2251, 129 L.Ed.2d 221 (1994), that the Court clarified that this means "burden of persuasion," rather than the "burden of production." The Court reviewed a Department of Labor regulation that provided when the evidence was evenly balanced in a case involving an application for a disability because of black lung disease, the benefits claimant wins. The Court held that the regulation violated the APA requirement that the proponent of a rule or order has the burden of proof because that person has the burden of persuasion. In other words, the claimant did not establish eligibility by a preponderance of the evidence.

The APA requires that an agency's decision "be supported by and in accordance with the reliable, probative, and substantial evidence." 5 U.S.C.A. § 556(d). The use of the term "substantial evidence" in this context is confusing. As will be discussed later, this term has a long history as a standard of judicial review of agency fact-finding, but here the term seems to relate to the evidence as perceived by the factfinder, not by a reviewing court. It is further confusing because of the expectation that the minimum necessary evidence to support a finding would be a preponderance of the evidence. Indeed, as noted, the Supreme Court's recent decision in *Greenwich Collieries* assumes that the burden of persuasion requires at least a preponderance of the evidence. The explanation probably is that the term "substantial evidence" here does not refer to the amount of evidence, but to the quality of the evidence. For example, certain evidence is by its nature less substantial than other evidence. In *Consolidated Edison Co. v. NLRB*, 305 U.S. 197, 230, 59 S.Ct. 206, 217, 83 L.Ed. 126 (1938), the Court said that "[m]ere uncorroborated hearsay or rumor does not constitute substantial evidence."

The APA, nevertheless, following the practice at the time of its adoption, clearly authorized the admission of hearsay evidence and other evidence that might be excluded under the Federal Rules of Evidence, as long as the evidence is not irrelevant, immaterial, or unduly repetitious. 5 U.S.C.A. § 556(d). It 1946, however, it was not clear whether a decision could rely solely upon hearsay evidence. Many states followed what was called the Residuum Rule. It prohibited a decision from being rendered based solely upon hearsay evidence. The Supreme Court has never directly addressed this issue, but it is generally conceded that the Court's decision in *Richardson v. Perales*, 402 U.S. 389, 91 S.Ct. 1420, 28 L.Ed.2d 842 (1971), signaled the rule's federal death knell. The Court affirmed a finding by the Social Security Administration that a claimant was not entitled to a disability benefit on the basis of the reports of physicians who had examined the claimant, but who was not present to testify in a hearing before the ALJ. The Court said:

> We conclude that a written report by a licensed physician who has examined the claimant and who sets forth in his report his medical findings in his area of competence may be received as evidence in a disability hearing and, despite its hearsay character and an absence of cross-examination, and despite the presence of opposing direct medical testimony and testimony by the claimant himself, may constitute substantial evidence supportive of a finding

by the hearing examiner adverse to the claimant, when the claimant has not exercised his right to subpoena the reporting physician and thereby provide himself with the opportunity for cross-examination of the physician.

402 U.S. at 402. To say that hearsay evidence can form the sole basis of a decision in some situations, where the nature of the hearsay is relatively "reliable, probative, and substantial," such as a doctor's report, is not to say that all hearsay could support a decision.

7. TESTIMONY AND DOCUMENTS

Ordinarily, the APA entitles parties to present their case by oral or documentary evidence, to submit rebuttal evidence, and to conduct cross examination. 5 U.S.C.A. § 556(d). However, in adjudications involving claims for money or benefits or applications for initial licenses, the agency is allowed to provide for the submission of evidence in written form, rather than orally. *Id.* The reason for the exception is the notion that in those types of cases there are not normally adverse parties involved in the adjudication; it is only a party submitting evidence in its support without any other party contesting it.

8. THE RECORD AND EX PARTE COMMUNICATIONS

As is true in judicial trials, the transcript of testimony and exhibits, together with any papers filed in the proceeding, constitutes the exclusive record for decision. 5 U.S.C.A. § 556(e). This exclusivity of the record created in the proceeding is what marks "formal" adjudication and rulemaking under the APA. While "informal" proceedings also have records (whatever was before the decisionmaker at the time of the decision), those records were not necessarily compiled in a "proceeding."

To protect the exclusivity of the record as the basis of decision, the APA prohibits ex parte communications during APA adjudications. Ex parte communications are communications to someone involved in the decisional process (the ALJ or the head of the agency or a member of the board or commission) from an interested person outside the agency (or from the agency person to the interested person) with respect to the merits of a particular case that are not made on the public record as to which all parties had notice. 5 U.S.C.A. §§ 551(14), 557(d). Violations of this prohibition are to be cured by placing the communications on the public record with notice to all parties, with the possibility of sanctions against the violator. 5 U.S.C.A. § 557(d)(1)(C) & (D). It should be noted, however, that this prohibition only reaches ex parte communications with persons *outside the agency*. There is a comparable, but not completely equivalent, provision that prohibits an ALJ from "consult[ing] a person or party on a fact in issue, unless on notice and opportunity for all parties to participate." 5 U.S.C.A. § 554(d)(1). This would appear to allow an agency employee to advise an ALJ on a point of law (as opposed to a fact in issue) in secret, so long as that employee was not engaged in prosecuting or investigating functions with respect to that or a related case.

9. APPEALS

As indicated above, the ALJ makes either a recommended or initial decision for the agency, although most ALJ decisions are initial decisions. Before the ALJ takes this step, the parties have an opportunity to submit proposed findings and conclusions with supporting reasons. 5 U.S.C.A. § 557(c). The initial or recommended decision includes findings of fact and conclusions of law, the reasons or basis for those findings and conclusions, and the appropriate order. *Id.* This decision itself becomes part of the record of the proceeding. *Id.* After the ALJ makes the initial decision, it becomes the final decision of the agency unless a party appeals the decision or an agency official (or officials) with the discretion to review the decision decides to do so.

Agencies employ different types of appeals procedures. Some agencies, such as the Social Security Administration (SSA), employ review boards, which have the final authority to reach a decision for the agency. At SSA, an appeal is assigned to one of the appellate judges of the "Appeals Council (AC)", who has the authority to dispose of a case if it does not disturb the ALJ's decision (*i.e.*, if the appeals judge denies or dismisses the appeal). If the original appellate judge rejects the ALJ's decision, by a reversal or remand, a second appeals judge also reviews the case. If the two judges concur, they can dispose of the case, but if they disagree, a third judge reviews the case, and the two judges who agree dispose of it. In other agencies, the review board's decision is subject to further discretionary review by the agency head (or some high-level political appointee designated by the head). For example, the Federal Communications Commission has delegated most of its review authority to an appellate board, but it has reserved to itself the right to review decisions involving the revocation and renewal of licenses. At a few agencies, the agency head directly reviews an ALJ's decision, but with assistance from law clerks or other subordinates. The Federal Trade Commission (FTC) follows this approach. After a decision by the ALJ, an appeal is taken directly to the Commission where it is reviewed by the commissioners who sit en banc. *See* Russell Weaver, *Appellate Review in Executive Departments and Agencies*, 48 AD. L. REV. 251 (1996).

Unlike appeals of trial court judges' decisions, appeals within an agency are not in the nature of appellate review. Instead, the APA states that "the agency has all the powers which it would have in making the initial decision." In other words, the appeals board or agency head decides the case *de novo*. Otherwise, however, these appeals are similar to appellate practice, with briefing and oral argument typical.

The previous paragraphs describe the requirements of the APA, but as is generally true in administrative law, a lawyer must always look more widely than just the APA. Even where the APA normally would apply, other statutes may add, change, or delete requirements. Nevertheless, the APA's formal adjudication requirements are the model for trial-type adjudication, even where the APA's formal adjudication requirements do not apply by their terms.

10. STATE ADJUDICATION

Adjudication in most states mirrors the federal mode—agencies hire their own ALJs and retain the authority to make final adjudicatory decisions. In about one-fifth of the states, which employ "central panels" of ALJs, the ALJs are not even technically employees of the agency for which they are judges. Instead, they are employees of some central personnel agency which is responsible for the judges' assignments, promotion, and discipline. Legislation to create a central panel system for the federal government has been considered for years, but agencies have resisted the idea. As noted earlier, agencies have an interest in managing ALJs to ensure that the adjudicatory system is efficient and fair.

Some states deny agencies the authority to make final decisions in at least some cases. In these states, the ALJ's decision is appealed directly to a state court or to a separate "administrative court" and its decisions can be appealed directly to the state courts. *See* Jim Rossi, *ALJ Final Orders on Appeal: Balancing Independence With Accountability*, 19 J. Nat'l Assoc. of Admin. Law Judges 1, 6–9 (Fall, 1999) (listing states with such finality provisions); *see also* Arthur E. Bonfield & Michael Asimow, State and Federal Administrative Law 176 (1989).

11. APPLYING ADJUDICATORY PROCEDURES

The following problem asks you to analyze compliance with APA hearing procedures in the context of an enforcement action brought under the Occupational Safety and Health Act (OSH Act). It involves the "split enforcement" approach, discussed earlier in the text, that OSHA is required to use to engage in enforcement of its regulations.

Problem 3–2: OSHA Hearing Procedures

Under the OSH Act, the Secretary of Labor is responsible for setting and enforcing workplace health and safety standards. The Secretary has delegated that authority to the Assistant Secretary for OSHA, who also is the head of OSHA, an agency within the Department of Labor. OSHA inspectors inspect workplaces, and if they find violations, they issue citations. An employer may contest the citation in a formal adjudication before an ALJ, who is an employee of OSHRC. As explained earlier, the OSH Act differs from most regulatory statutes by creating "split enforcement" model and by establishing OSHRC as the body that adjudicates OSHA citations.

Lane's Autobody was inspected by an OSHA inspector, who issued a citation with a $10,000 penalty because Lane's employees working in the paint shop were not wearing respirators. The citation described the facts and then charged Lane's with violation of 29 CFR § 1910.1029(g)(4). This regulatory provision, however, relates to the standards for respirators, not to the requirement for wearing respirators, which is found in an entirely separate regulation.

Lane's sought a hearing before an ALJ. Prior to the hearing, Lane's moved to dismiss the citation on the grounds that the facts contained in it did not support a finding of a violation of the cited regulatory provision. The ALJ denied the motion.

In the hearing, OSHA introduced an affidavit from the inspector that he had inspected the Lane facility and that the persons in the paint shop were not wearing respirators. Lane's presented two witnesses who testified that the inspector had not actually been present when painting was being done, and that at the time the inspector went in the paint shop no one was painting. Lane's argued that even assuming the workers were not wearing respirators while painting, those facts did not support a finding of a violation of the cited regulatory section. In addition, Lane's argued that the requirement for wearing respirators in OSHA's regulations only applied when the workers were engaged in painting, not to anytime they were in the paint shop. Finally, Lane's argued that OSHA had failed to carry its burden of persuasion because its evidence was based entirely upon hearsay—the affidavit of the inspector.

OSHA responded that the citation to 29 CFR § 1910.1029(g)(4) was an administrative error and the citation should be amended to reflect the proper citation, but that Lane's was not prejudiced by the error. Further, OSHA admitted that its regulation mandating that respirators be worn was ambiguous, but it interpreted the regulation to require the wearing of respirators whenever an employee is in a dedicated paint shop, not just when painting is going on. Even when painting is not going on, OSHA indicated, paint fumes may linger in the air in concentrations that would be unhealthy. Finally, OSHA argued that the inspector's affidavit constituted substantial, reliable and probative evidence, because Lane's had never denied the fact that the workers in the paint shop were not wearing respirators at the time the inspector was there, and that Lane's could have subpoenaed the inspector if it had wished to cross-examine him.

The ALJ adopted all of OSHA's arguments, and Lane's appealed to OSHRC. You are a law clerk to one of the members of OSHRC, who asks you to prepare a bench memorandum on the issues raised in the case.

Problem Materials

NATIONAL LABOR RELATIONS BOARD v. LOCAL UNION NO. 25, INTERNATIONAL BROTHERHOOD OF ELECTRICAL WORKERS

586 F.2d 959 (2d Cir.1978).

LUMBARD, CIRCUIT JUDGE:

The National Labor Relations Board ... petitions for enforcement of its ... order, which invalidates part of Local 25's collective-bargaining agreement....

... Ernesto Flores, an American citizen of Puerto Rican ancestry, filed a complaint with the NLRB alleging that the union had engaged in unfair labor practices by failing to provide him with job referrals because he was not a member of the union.... Administrative Law Judge Samuel Ross found that the union had referred union members to jobs to which Flores ... had equal or superior claims, and that the union had done so not for lawful reasons, but solely in order to favor union members over non-members and to encourage union membership, thereby engaging in unfair labor practices.

Although this ruling disposed of the issues raised by the NLRB complaint, Judge Ross went beyond the complaint to consider the legality of Article XI of the collective-bargaining agreement, which provides that an applicant

> who has registered for referral but who thereafter is employed in the building and construction trade in Nassau and Suffolk Counties as an electrician for an employer who does not pay the wage rates and fringe benefits contained in this Collective Bargaining Agreement, shall be ineligible for referrals ... for a period of one year following the termination of such employment.

The question of Article XI's legality was not raised in the amended complaint, in the briefs, or in oral argument, and no evidence was presented concerning this issue. Judge Ross nevertheless concluded, *sua sponte*, that Article XI is illegal on its face ... because it unlawfully encourages unionism. The NLRB contends that this court should enforce its order embodying the findings and conclusions of Judge Ross invalidating Clause XI.

In their original statement of exceptions to Judge Ross's decision, respondents objected to his holding with respect to Article XI not because they had been denied a fair hearing with respect to that provision, but because they believed that his decision was legally incorrect. At oral argument before this court, however, respondents for the first time argued that his decision with respect to Article XI violated the Administrative Procedure Act, 5 U.S.C. § 554.... Since the question of Article XI's legality was not raised in the amended complaint, in the briefs, or in oral argument, and no evidence was presented concerning that issue, we agree with respondents that they did not receive the notice required by the APA and that the decision of the Administrative Law Judge, as well as the order of the NLRB adopting that decision, cannot stand.

SOUTHWEST SUNSITES, INC. v. FEDERAL TRADE COMMISSION

785 F.2d 1431 (9th Cir.1986).

BEEZER, CIRCUIT JUDGE:

Petitioners ... appeal the Federal Trade Commission's finding that their representations and failures to disclose, in connection with the sale of rural, undeveloped land, violated the Federal Trade Commission Act. Petitioners contend that application of a new deception standard violates . . . the Administrative Procedures Act. . . .

. . . Petitioners are engaged in the sale of undeveloped rural land in west Texas for use as farms, ranches, homesites, and commercial uses. Sales are primarily to out-of-state purchasers. . . .

The FTC lodged a three count complaint contending that petitioners engaged in unfair and deceptive practices in violation of § 5 of the Federal Trade Commission Act. The complaint alleged that petitioners (1) misrepresented that the parcels were a good investment involving little or no financial risk and deceptively failed to disclose material information regarding their financial risk, (2) misrepresented that the land was suitable for residential use, farming, and ranching, and deceptively failed to disclose material information regarding the suitability of the properties for these purposes, and (3) sold land that was of little or no value for the represented purposes and unfairly retained proceeds from the sales. An administrative law judge (ALJ) dismissed the complaint, the Commission reversed and issued a cease and desist order, from which petitioners timely appeal. . . .

The ALJ dismissed the complaint under the deception standard that "any advertising representation that has the *tendency and capacity* to mislead or deceive a prospective purchaser is an unfair and deceptive practice." The Commission applied a "new" standard: "[T]he Commission will find deception if there is a representation, omission or practice that is *likely* to mislead the consumer acting *reasonably* in the circumstances, to the consumer's *detriment*."

Petitioners contend that application of the new deception standard violated the Administrative Procedures Act (APA), 5 U.S.C. § 554(b) which requires that they be "timely informed of the matters of fact and law asserted." . . .

The purpose of the notice requirement in the Administrative Procedures Act is satisfied, . . . if the party proceeded against "understood the issue" and "was afforded full opportunity" to justify his conduct.

Each of the three elements of the new standard challenged by petitioner imposes a greater burden of proof on the FTC to show a violation of Section 5. First, the FTC must show probable, not possible, deception (*"likely* to mislead," not *"tendency and capacity* to mislead"). Second, the FTC must show potential deception of "consumers acting reasonably in the circumstances," not just any consumers. Third, the new standard considers as material only deceptions that are likely to cause injury to a reasonable relying consumer, whereas the old standard reached deceptions that a consumer might have considered important, whether or not there was reliance.

The Commission reversed the ALJ's findings on a theory more narrow than, but completely subsumed in, the prior theory. All evidence relevant to the old theory was necessarily relevant to the new. We

cannot accept petitioners' argument that a "substantially different standard was applied, to which [they] had no opportunity to respond." . . .
The Commission did not violate the APA. . . .

JOHN D. COPANOS AND SONS, INC. v. FOOD AND DRUG ADMINISTRATION

854 F.2d 510 (D.C.Cir.1988).

D.H. GINSBURG, CIRCUIT JUDGE:

John D. Copanos & Sons, Inc., and Kanasco, Ltd., affiliated enterprises owned by John D. Copanos (hereinafter referred to collectively as Kanasco), manufacture and distribute human and veterinary drugs, including, until recently, a number of sterile injectable products. These injectable drugs were produced pursuant to a number of New Drug Applications (NDAs) and New Animal Drug Applications (NADAs) approved by the respondent Food and Drug Administration (FDA). On March 10, 1987, the FDA published a Notice of Opportunity for a Hearing (NOOH) in the Federal Register, proposing to withdraw Kanasco's NDAs and NADAs for sterile injectable products on the ground that the methods, facilities, and controls used to produce these drugs were inadequate to assure their identity, strength, quality, and purity. Kanasco responded to this Notice, and requested a hearing, but on August 6, 1987, the agency denied the hearing and summarily withdrew its approval of the company's applications, effectively barring Kanasco from producing the subject drugs.

Upon the company's petition for review, we conclude that Kanasco received adequate notice of the basis for the FDA's action, and that the agency did not err in proceeding by summary judgment to withdraw its approvals of Kanasco's applications. Accordingly, we deny the petition for review.

I. STATUTORY BACKGROUND

The Federal Food Drug and Cosmetic Act (FDCA) prohibits the introduction into interstate commerce of any new drug, or any new animal drug, unless an NDA or an NADA for that drug has been approved by the FDA. Each application must include, among other things, reports of all investigations of the safety and efficacy of the drug, and "a full description of the methods used in, and the facilities and controls used for, the manufacture, processing, and packing of such drug."

The Act also establishes procedures whereby the FDA, "after due notice and opportunity for hearing to the applicant," can withdraw its prior approval. One of the statutory grounds for such withdrawal is that:

the Secretary finds . . . that on the basis of new information before him, evaluated together with the evidence before him when the application was approved, the methods used in, or the facilities and controls used for, the manufacture, processing and packing of such drug are inadequate to assure and preserve its identity, strength, quality, and purity and were not made adequate within a reasonable time after receipt of written notice from the Secretary specifying the matter complained of.

The standards for determining whether a manufacturer's "methods[,] ... facilities and controls" are adequate "to assure and preserve [the] identity, strength, quality and purity" of its drugs are set forth in the FDA's "Current Good Manufacturing Practice" (CGMP) regulations.... Drugs produced in violation of these CGMP regulations are deemed to be adulterated without the agency having to show that they are actually contaminated....

II. FACTS

[Over a three year period, FDA inspected Kanasco's facilities on numerous occasions. On each occasion numerous and widespread violations of the CGMP were found. Each inspection resulted in the issuance of a FDA–483 form, which specifies the nature of the violations. On each occasion Kanasco promised to come into compliance, which promise soon proved to be false. In addition, Kanasco violated agreements not to distribute its products until it was in compliance, and Kanasco kept false records to cover up its violations].

Its patience finally exhausted, the FDA published a notice in the Federal Register on March 10, 1987, proposing to withdraw Kanasco's NDAs and NADAs for sterile injectable products. Seven of the NOOH's eight pages consisted of a "Regulatory History of Kanasco," recounting the above-stated chronology in greater detail. At the end of this recitation of deficiencies, which was organized around the various Forms FDA–483 left at the firm starting in 1976, the FDA concluded, in accordance with the terms of the statute that:

> on the basis of new information before [it], evaluated together with the evidence before [it] when the application was approved, the methods used in, and the facilities and controls for, the manufacture, processing, and packing of [sterile injectable] drugs are inadequate to assure and preserve their identity, strength, quality, and purity and were not made adequate within a reasonable time after receipt of written notice from the FDA specifying the matters complained of.

The NOOH required Kanasco, if it wanted a hearing, to submit "the data, information, and analyses relied on to justify a hearing...." The notice also warned that "[a] request for a hearing may not rest upon mere allegations or denials, but must present specific facts showing that there is a genuine and substantial issue of fact that requires a hearing." Failing that, "the Commissioner of Food and Drugs will enter summary judgment against the person(s) who request the hearing, making findings and conclusions, and denying a hearing."

Kanasco both requested a hearing and moved for summary judgment. The hearing request included a number of declarations and other exhibits that, according to the company, demonstrated that it was in compliance with CGMP and that it was committed to maintaining such compliance. The motion for summary judgment was based on the argument that the agency had not complied with the requirements . . . that it provide Kanasco with proper written notice "specifying the matter complained of" and "a reasonable time after receipt of written notice" within which to make adequate any deficiencies.

By a Notice published August 6, 1987, the FDA denied both the hearing request and the motion for summary judgment, and ordered that Kanasco's NDAs and NADAs be withdrawn from the market. . . .

Kanasco filed this petition for review. . . .

Thus, the issues before us on this petition [are] the following: (1) whether the FDA's NOOH gave the petitioners sufficient notice to serve as the basis for administrative summary judgment. . . .

III. Notice

Section 355(e) of 21 U.S.C., which governs the withdrawal of NDA approvals, requires the FDA to provide "due notice and opportunity for hearing to the applicant." It is well settled that this provision does not guarantee the applicant a hearing in all circumstances; the agency may by regulation provide for summary withdrawal of approvals when there is no "genuine and substantial issue of fact that requires a hearing."

The possibility of summary action makes the requirement of "due notice" especially important. . . . When the FDA issues a Notice of Opportunity for Hearing, its summary judgment procedures are available if the requesting party fails to raise material issues of fact. For that reason, the contents of the response are of critical importance, and the need for and importance of the response in turn enhances the significance of the notice given the adverse party. In order to be adequate, such notice given by the agency to an adverse party must contain enough information to provide the respondent a genuine opportunity to identify material issues of fact. Test

Kanasco claims that it was denied such an opportunity because the agency failed to give it notice of the "type of information that is required to be submitted to justify a hearing." The company notes that while the FDA regulation governing hearing requests specifically advises companies of the information they must submit to justify a hearing on the issues of safety and efficacy, no comparable provisions address withdrawals based on CGMP violations. According to Kanasco, this omission precluded it from making an effective response to the NOOH and thereby denied it the "due notice" to which it was entitled by statute. . . .

We have not read [the case law] to hold, however, that precise regulations specifying the type of evidence necessary to justify a hearing are a prerequisite to due notice whenever the agency is contemplating summary action. The requirements of "due notice" must depend upon the context of the agency's action. In [one case], for example, the 1962 amendments to the Act placed on applicants the burden of producing "adequate and well-controlled investigations" demonstrating efficacy in order to retain their FDA approval. The success, *vel non,* of the applicant's submission therefore turned upon the types of evidence that would satisfy the statutory standard of "adequate and well-controlled." The agency's notice indicating its intent to withdraw approval, however, generally failed to explain why the information provided to the NAS–NRC panel did not meet this standard. Under those circumstances, particularized regulations were necessary to provide the applicant with notice of what its submission must contain in order to warrant continued authorization to market a drug.

By contrast, the petitioners here were not confronted with any significant ambiguity regarding the type of information that would warrant a hearing before the agency. The NOOH discussed in detail the facts and evidence that formed the basis for the agency's proposed withdrawal of approval. Read in conjunction with the record of prior proceedings and the CGMP regulations, this document provided adequate notice of the type of information that Kanasco would have to submit in order to command a hearing. To take but one example, the NOOH alleged that Kanasco manufactured a drug product for human use that was required to be penicillin free in the same area and with the same equipment used to make products containing penicillin. Due notice of the basis for the agency's action would hardly require the FDA to specify, in regulations or in the NOOH, what types of evidence Kanasco needed to submit to raise a material issue of fact about this allegation. The answer is self-evident: any competent evidence (e.g., affidavits or documentary exhibits) to the effect that (1) Kanasco did not in fact manufacture penicillin products using equipment also used for non-penicillin products; or (2) that the deficiency had been remedied within a reasonable time after receipt of written notice of the violation from the Secretary or his designee. We do not mean to suggest, of course, that an action withdrawing an NDA on CGMP grounds can never raise a genuine issue regarding the type of evidence that would be responsive. When the sorts of evidence that would be responsive appear to be obvious, however, as in this case, we think it is incumbent upon the petitioner to demonstrate how it was prejudiced by the lack of specific instructions telling it what to produce. Because Kanasco has failed to identify any evidence, or type of evidence, that it might have presented but for lack of notice as to its relevance, we reject the company's claim to any more specific notice than it received.

Nonetheless, we observe in the NOOH a more substantial notice problem that warrants discussion even though it does not feature prominently among petitioners' arguments. As we mentioned earlier, the NOOH consists largely of a highly detailed "Regulatory History of Kanasco" that proceeds in chronological order and is centered around the various Forms FDA–483 presented to Kanasco over the years. Both preceding and following this regulatory history are conclusory allegations that the facts stated in it satisfy the relevant statutory standard.... The NOOH failed, however, to organize the relevant facts in any way that would show how they met this statutory standard. Thus, both petitioners and this court were required to sift through an undifferentiated mass of "facts," and to rearrange them in a way that indicated whether the agency had made out its case. This manner of proceeding comes perilously close to obscuring the "basis" for the agency's action, and thus denying the applicant a meaningful opportunity to respond. We stop short of so holding because we are hesitant to reverse the agency on what is essentially a matter of form, especially in view of the novelty of this proceeding. In future cases, however, the agency would be well advised to adopt a format for its notice that would clearly reveal (1) each CGMP violation that forms a basis for the withdrawal action, the specific regulation governing this violation, and the date or dates on which it was observed; (2) the date or dates on which the applicant received proper written notice of the violation; and (3) the date on which the violation was corrected or later observed to be still uncorrected. Such a format would make it easier for the petitioner to identify material issues in dispute and for the Court to ascertain if summary withdrawal of the approval was appropriate. While we do not intend to dictate any particular format for presenting this information, the agency may be assured that neither will we tolerate again its effectively shifting to this court its responsibility to organize in a sensible fashion the facts upon which it relies....

WALLACE v. BOWEN

869 F.2d 187 (3d Cir.1989).

SLOVITER, CIRCUIT JUDGE.

The Secretary of the Department of Health and Human Services (HHS), after a hearing before an administrative law judge (ALJ) and review by the Appeals Council, found appellant John R. Wallace not disabled and therefore not entitled to social security disability insurance benefits or to supplemental security income benefits.... Wallace sought review before the district court, which upheld the Secretary's decision and granted his motion for summary judgment.

Wallace appeals on two grounds. First, he argues that the ALJ's reliance upon medical expert reports obtained after the hearing without an opportunity for cross-examination by Wallace denied him both his statutory right to have a decision on his claim based on "evidence adduced at the hearing," and his due process rights under the Constitution. Second, he maintains that the ALJ's decision is not supported by substantial evidence.

Because we agree with Wallace that the ALJ's reliance upon post-hearing reports in the circumstances of this case without the opportunity for cross-examination denied him his statutory right to a decision based on "evidence adduced at the hearing," we will not consider Wallace's contention that the Secretary's decision is not supported by substantial evidence.

II.

In February 1985, Wallace, while working as a steelworker, suffered a heart attack. One month later he suffered a stroke which may have caused a loss of vision in the right eye, ...

In May 1985, Wallace applied for disability insurance benefits and supplemental security income on the ground of his heart condition and visual impairments. After his claims were denied, Wallace was granted a hearing before an administrative law judge pursuant to 42 U.S.C. § 405(b)(1). At that hearing, Wallace testified and introduced reports from his examining physicians detailing his cardiological and visual impairments. . . .

After the hearing, the ALJ sent Wallace's medical records to two "consultative physicians," Dr. Oberhoff, a Board-certified ophthalmologist, and Dr. Shugoll, a Board-certified cardiologist, who were both under contract with the HHS to render their medical opinions when requested. Dr. Oberhoff was asked whether Wallace's "visual difficulties" met or equaled one of the Listings for visual impairments contained in 20 C.F.R. pt. 404, subpt. P, App. 1, §§ 2.03–.05. Dr. Shugoll was asked whether Wallace's "cardiovascular disease" met or equaled the Listing for "[h]ypertensive vascular disease" in section 4.03 of the Listings. Each physician concluded that the claimant's impairments did not meet the relevant listing. . . .

The ALJ then rendered his decision, finding Wallace not disabled under the terms of the Social Security Act. In reaching this conclusion, the ALJ first found that "claimant's impairments do not meet or equal the criteria of any . . . Listing." In so finding the ALJ relied, in the ALJ's own words, "in particular [on] the medical advisor's [consultative physician's] observations." . . .

III.

Wallace's argument begins with the Social Security Act's provision for a hearing and for a determination based on evidence adduced at the hearing. Section 205(b) of the Act provides in relevant part:

> Upon request by any such individual [who receives an unfavorable determination of his claim] . . . [the Secretary] shall give such applicant . . . reasonable notice and opportunity for a hearing with respect to such decision, and, if a hearing is held, shall, *on the basis of evidence adduced at the hearing*, affirm, modify, or reverse his findings of fact and such decision.

. . . We believe, however, that it is unmistakable under the statute that the Secretary may not rely on post-hearing reports without giving the claimant an opportunity to cross-examine the authors of such reports, when such cross-examination may be required for a full and true disclosure of the facts.

In *Richardson v. Perales*, 402 U.S. 389, (1971), the Supreme Court, in considering the hearing and review procedures under the Social Security Act, "accept[ed] the proposition[ ] ... that procedural due process is applicable to the adjudicative administrative proceeding involving 'the differing rules of fair play, which through the years, have become associated with differing types of proceedings.'" The Court equated the Social Security Act procedures with those of the Administrative Procedure Act, which expressly entitles a party, *inter alia*, "to conduct such cross-examination as may be required for a full and true disclosure of the facts." 5 U.S.C. § 556(d) (1982), *quoted in Richardson*, 402 U.S. at 409.

Although the Court held that examining physician reports adverse to claimant supplied before the hearing could be used as "substantial evidence" even though the reports were hearsay and the physicians were not present at the hearing, the Court carefully qualified its holding by approving such admission "when the claimant has not exercised his right to subpoena the reporting physician and thereby provide himself with the opportunity for cross-examination of the physician." ... We construe *Richardson* as holding that an opportunity for cross-examination is an element of fundamental fairness of the hearing to which a claimant is entitled under section 205(b) of the Social Security Act, 42 U.S.C. § 405(b).

The Secretary argues that it is sufficient under the statute to give a claimant an opportunity to comment on and present additional evidence in response to post-hearing reports. He maintains that cross-examination is not necessary in cases such as this where a medical opinion is obtained post-hearing, in that the issue is "wholly medical" and can be "addressed with great probity by a physician who has reviewed the medical record." In the Secretary's view, the opportunity to provide written comment is an adequate substitute for cross-examination since "the only real possible objection" is that it is not supported by the medical record, an objection which can be equally well-made by written comment.

We disagree with the Secretary's evaluation of the utility of cross-examination in such a situation. Effective cross-examination could reveal what evidence the physician considered or failed to consider in formulating his or her conclusions, how firmly the physician holds to those conclusions, and whether there are any qualifications to the physician's conclusions....

We thus hold that when an administrative law judge chooses to go outside the testimony adduced at the hearing in making a determination on a social security claim, the ALJ must afford the claimant not only an opportunity to comment and present evidence but also an opportunity to cross-examine the authors of any post-hearing reports when such cross-examination is necessary to the full presentation of the case, and must reopen the hearing for that purpose if requested. The necessary consequence of our opinion requires modification of the form letter to give notice that the claimant may request a supplementary hearing at which the claimant may cross-examine the authors of any post-hearing reports submitted by the Secretary. . . .

IV.

Ordinarily, whether cross-examination of the author of a report is necessary for a full and true disclosure of the facts, is a question entrusted to the ALJ in the first instance. *See* 5 U.S.C. § 556(d); 20 C.F.R. § 404.950(d)(1) (subpoena to issue "[w]hen it is reasonably necessary for the full presentation of a case"). It may be that different considerations apply to cross-examination with respect to post-hearing evidence than pre-hearing evidence because the applicant may find it more difficult to respond effectively to post-hearing reports in the absence of an opportunity to present live rebuttal evidence. In any event, in this case, it is apparent that the requisite standard governing the need for cross-examination has been met.

The consultative physician reports were substantially relied on by the ALJ both in his determination that Wallace's impairments, particularly his visual impairments, did not meet or equal the Listings and for his determination that Wallace was not so impaired that he could not do sedentary work. Although one of Wallace's examining physicians, Dr. Barnett, had found Wallace's visual impairments to equal the Listing in section 2.05, the ALJ stated that he relied "in particular" upon the report of Dr. Oberhoff, the consultative physician, to find that this impairment did not meet the Listing. Similarly, Dr. Oberhoff's report was given "greater weight" than that of an examining physician in determining Wallace's capacity to do sedentary work. Under these circumstances, we conclude the reliance upon evidence adduced outside of a hearing without the opportunity for cross-examination could have unfairly affected the ultimate result.

V.

We will therefore vacate the judgment of the district court and remand with directions for it to remand the case to the Secretary who should afford Wallace, at a minimum, the right to cross-examine the physicians.

Notes and Questions

1.   The previous section indicated that there are many different types of adjudications that are not formal adjudications under the APA, but informal adjudications. The range of procedural protections afforded in those informal adjudications varies greatly. Consider, for example, the corrective action order proceedings at issue in *Chemical Waste Management*, one of the cases you studied earlier concerning when formal adjudication is required. The procedures afforded defendants in such hearings cover twenty sections of the Code of Federal Regulations and provide most of the procedures available in formal adjudication other than true cross examination. The fact that such adjudications often have

a high degree of procedural formality has led some commentators to prefer the denomination non-APA adjudication, rather than informal adjudication. Nevertheless, one feature all non-APA adjudications lack is the presence of an ALJ. The avoidance of ALJs appears to be one of motivations for agencies to seek non-APA adjudicatory authority rather than APA adjudicatory authority. In *Chemical Waste Management*, EPA successfully sought to preserve its interpretation that RCRA did not require it to engage in "formal adjudication," which would have required it to use an ALJ for this type of hearing.

Professor Funk, in a study for the Administrative Conference of informal adjudication of administrative penalties reached this conclusion:

> The assumption underlying the creation of these [informal adjudications] must be that APA adjudication, which was created as a more expeditious, less formal proceeding than its alternative—a judicial proceeding—is itself so cumbersome and immune to expedition that a new type of proceeding is required. . . .

> The perception that formal, APA adjudication is complex, costly, and slow is widespread. . . . Yet, if this perception is true, it is not necessarily due to the procedural requirements of the APA. Sections 554, 556, and 557 do not mandate long, drawn-out proceedings. Indeed, they allow [for a number of techniques to expedite hearings.] Nevertheless, the history of agencies attempting to expedite APA adjudications is not one to instill confidence in an agency proposing such an undertaking. This history is fraught with conflicts between agencies and ALJs over ALJ independence.

William Funk, *Close Enough for Government Work?—Using Informal Procedures for Imposing Administrative Penalties*, 24 SETON HALL L.REV. 1, 64–65 (1993).

Professor Funk went on to explain that these conflicts resulted from agency attempts to achieve expedition by review, evaluation, and criticism of individual judges, rather than by making procedural rules of general applicability providing or mandating time-and resource-saving trial techniques. This, he suggests, would likely be more successful, but deep-seated agency distrust of ALJs stands in the way of agencies providing the discretion to ALJs that they are willing to provide to non-ALJ presiding officers. *Id.*

2. There are approximately 3000 non-ALJ presiding officers (or simply Administrative Judges (AJs)), more than twice as many as ALJs, engaged in adjudicatory activity for a variety of agencies. *See generally* John H. Frye, III, *Survey of Non–ALJ Hearing Programs in the Federal Government*, 44 ADMIN. L. REV. 261 (1992). Unlike ALJs, AJs have no statutory protection of their independence. Agencies typically attempt to insulate them from the agency participants in the adjudications, but it is entirely possible for them to be a judge one day and an agency prosecutor the next, or to be subject to supervision and rating by the same personnel who supervise the agency litigants. Surprisingly, perhaps, AJs

do not perceive as much threat to their independence as ALJs. *See* Charles H. Koch, Jr., *Administrative Presiding Officials Today*, 46 ADMIN. L. REV. 271, 278–281 (1994). This study, however, did not assess whether litigants before AJs perceive AJs to be less independent.

D. EX PARTE COMMUNICATIONS

You may recall that the APA prohibits ex parte communications during formal rulemaking, but that there is no similar ban concerning ex parte contacts in informal rulemaking. The same conclusion applies to formal and informal adjudication. Since informal adjudication is not subject to sections 556 and 557 of the APA, the ex parte prohibitions contained in section 557 are not applicable. Of course, section 557 does apply to formal adjudication and ex parte communications are accordingly prohibited in such proceedings.

The prohibition of ex parte communications applies to "any interested party outside the agency." Agency staff members, who investigate or prosecute a matter, are also prohibited from communicating with a decisionmaker in a formal adjudication, although this requirement springs from Congress' intent to ensure a separation of the agency's enforcement and judicial functions. When agencies are engaged in formal adjudication, section 554(d) prohibits an "employee or agent engaged in the performance of investigative or prosecuting functions" in a case (or a factually related case) from participating or advising in any aspect of the agency's decision in that matter. Thus, section 554(d) bars communications between an employee and the ALJ, an administrator, or any member of a Commission or Board, who is responsible for making a decision in a matter in which the employee has served as an investigator or prosecutor.

The following problem and materials expand on the subjects of ex parte communications and separation of functions. The problem, which arises out of an actual incident, concerns whether a representative of the President can discuss the merits of a pending case with adjudicators. The problem materials consist of an appellate case that addresses when the APA ex parte contact ban applies.

Problem 3–3: White House Contacts

The Northern Spotted Owl is a small grayish-brown owl that lives in the so-called old growth forests of the Pacific Northwest. Due to substantial logging in the area, the habitat of the owl has decreased significantly and the Fish and Wildlife Service responded (with some prodding from environmental groups and the courts) by listing the owl as a threatened species under the Endangered Species Act. The Bureau of Land Management wished to make a number of timber sales on land within its jurisdiction, but it was determined that logging those areas would "jeopardize" the owl. The Endangered Species Act prohibits Federal agencies from taking any action that would jeopardize a listed species unless they obtain an exemption from the Endangered Species Committee (ESC) (popularly known as the "God Squad" because it decides whether a species lives or dies).

The Committee is composed of seven members: the Secretary of the Interior, the Secretary of Agriculture, the Secretary of the Army, the Chair of the Council of Economic Advisors, the Administrator of the EPA, the Administrator of the National Oceanic and Atmospheric Administration (NOAA), and one person appointed by the President to represent the affected State. The procedure for the exemption is somewhat confusing and cumbersome. Initially, the Secretary of Interior, who is chair of the Committee, determines whether an application for exemption meets certain statutory criteria. If it does, the Secretary holds a formal adjudication and prepares a report to the Committee. The Act then requires the Committee to make a final determination within 30 days of receiving the Secretary's report. Specifically, it provides that "[t]he Committee shall grant an exemption ... if, by a vote of not less than five of its members voting in person—it determines on the record, based upon the report of the Secretary, the record of the hearing held ..., and on such other testimony or evidence as it may receive, that [the statutory requirements have been satisfied]." This language is interpreted as requiring a formal adjudication under the APA.

The Bureau of Land Management petitioned for an exemption from the God Squad, and the Secretary made his initial finding, held the formal adjudication, and reported to the Committee. The Committee by a 5–2 vote granted the exemption.

An environmental group, which was allowed to participate in the adjudication, appeals the committee's decision to the Court of Appeals, alleging that some members of the Committee were subject to ex parte communications concerning the petition. The allegation was based upon wire service reports and an affidavit by the lead counsel for the environmental group.

The AP report, in pertinent part, reads as follows:

> The Bush administration is pressuring "God Squad" members to exempt 44 Northwest timber sales from the Endangered Species Act's protection of the northern spotted owl, sources said Tuesday. Two administration sources, speaking on condition of anonymity, said that at least three members of the panel have been summoned to White House meetings to discuss coming decisions on the owl....
> But a spokesman for Interior Secretary Manuel Lujan Jr. said the conversations pertain to general environmental policy and that no political pressure is being placed on the Endangered Species Committee. According to the sources, each of the meetings was attended by Lujan, the chairman of the committee, and Clayton Yeutter, President Bush's domestic policy adviser. William K. Reilly, head of the Environmental Protection Agency and a committee member, joined Lujan and Yeutter in a meeting Tuesday, one source said.

John Knauss, head of the National Oceanic and Atmospheric Administration and a committee member, attended a similar meeting within the last two weeks, the source said. Frances Hunt, a forestry specialist for the National Wildlife Federation, said other administration sources had told her that Knauss was pressured at the meeting to vote for the exemption to the Endangered Species Act. "My understanding is that it was all-out arm-twisting," she said Tuesday. "Lujan is portraying this as something the administration needs." ... Steve Goldstein, Lujan's chief spokesman, confirmed that Lujan and Reilly met Tuesday with Yeutter. "Clayton Yeutter is the environmental policy coordinator for the administration. We are part of the administration. But no one from the administration will dictate to any committee member how they should vote," Goldstein said.

The Reuters report contained similar information.

The affidavit filed by the environmental group said:

> Since the ESC's final decision ..., I have spoken with several sources within the Administration, including federal staff and employees close to some of the decisionmakers on the ESC. These individuals hold positions in which I would expect them either to have direct access to ESC decisionmakers themselves, or to other individuals with such access, and I would therefore expect them to be familiar with the events surrounding the ESC's ... decision to exempt 13 timber sales from the provision of ... [the Endangered Species Act]. In fact, these sources have indicated to me that they are familiar with these events in considerable detail. In particular, my conversations with these individuals have revealed both that the media reports of pre-decisional pressure from the White House on ESC members were accurate (despite denials from a spokesman for the Department of the Interior). Moreover, they reveal that at least in one instance, such pressure may have succeeded in influencing (and, ultimately, changing) the vote of at least one decisionmaker. Such a changed vote would have led directly to the ESC's granting of the exemption, instead of denying it. (Given that an exemption application must receive five votes to prevail, and that the ESC voted 5–2 in favor of the exemption in this case, even a single vote change would have meant a denial of the exemption.) Based on these conversations, I have good cause to believe at least the following facts regarding contacts between the White House and the ESC:

> a. The press reports of White House pressure on ESC decisionmakers to vote in favor of an exemption—particularly, on Administrator John Knauss ... and Administrator William Reilly ...—during the period preceding the ESC's vote ... are accurate. Administrator Knauss met with Clayton Yeutter and other members of the White House staff on April 28, 1992, and several times thereafter. Administrator Knauss and his staff also had substantial on-going contacts with White House staff concerning the substance of his

decision on the application for exemption by telephone and facsimile, as well as through staff intermediaries.

   b.   Administrator Reilly also met with Clayton Yeutter and other White House staff, on May 5, 1992, and again on May 13, 1992.

   c.   ESC members were told by White House staff that the Bush Administration viewed an ESC decision to grant an exemption as extremely important politically. White House staff sought to persuade ESC members, including both Administrator Knauss and Administrator Reilly, to support an exemption.

   d.   Administrator Knauss ultimately voted to support granting the exemption for 13 timber sales. Administrator Reilly ultimately voted against the exemption.

   e.   The terms of the ... ESC's final decision were presented to most of the ESC for the first time at the ESC's meeting on May 14. These terms were discussed directly and repeatedly in direct contacts between Administrator Knauss and his staff at NOAA (on the one hand), and Clayton Yeutter and his staff at the White House (on the other); other ESC members and staff may have been involved as well. [A series of written drafts of the final decision passed between the White House and NOAA prior to the ESC's meeting,] and White House staff provided substantive comments and recommendations on draft versions of the Amendment.

Assume that you are an attorney at the United States Department of Justice who is assigned to defend the government against the law suit brought by the environmental group. Your boss would like you to assess candidly the probability that the government will prevail.

   (1) Assuming that the information alleged by the environmentalists is true, what is likely to be the response of the court? Do you need additional facts to reach a judgment, and if so, what are they?

   (2) If the vote had been 6–1 instead of 5–2, would that make a difference in the likely outcome of the case? Why or why not?

   (3) Finally, assuming that the court determines that the APA has been violated, what remedy would you expect?

Problem 3–4: Internal Agency Contacts

The Department of the Army has dismissed Theodore Blake from his position as civilian supervisory inspector, GSC9, at the Military Clothing and Textile Supply Agency, Philadelphia Quartermaster Depot, for filing false and fraudulent travel vouchers. Before the removal, Mr. Blake had been notified of the charges against him and was given the opportunity to seek review under the Army grievance procedures.

The pertinent regulations (Army Civilian Personnel Regulations E 2) provide that:

the resolution of employee grievances is an integral part of the installation commander's responsibility. This function may not be delegated. However, to relieve commanders of the burden of hearing all grievances personally, grievance committees will be established at the installation level to make findings of fact, hear and evaluate evidence, and make recommendations to the commander as to appropriate disposition of individual cases. Grievance committee determinations are advisory, constituting privileged staff guidance to the commander.

Pursuant to those procedures, a hearing was held before the Grievance Committee of the Quartermaster Depot. At the hearing, Mr. Blake was represented by his lawyer and the agency was represented by its lawyer, Ms. Jones. Witnesses were called and testified on direct and cross-examination, exhibits were received in evidence, and counsel for both parties made summary arguments. The Grievance Committee recommended to the commander of the depot, Maj. Gen. Denise Thompson, that the plaintiff not be removed from his position. The Committee was of the view that the Army had not proven the allegations against Mr. Blake.

After the General received the case, but before she took any action, the General Counsel of the Agency, Julius Cohen, prepared and submitted a legal opinion to General Anderson in which he stated, *inter alia:*

> After a complete and diligent analysis of all the facts and applicable laws, it is my considered opinion that the [the plaintiff should be removed], notwithstanding the recommendation of the Agency's Grievance Committee.

Thereafter, General Thompson overruled the Committee, decided that Mr. Blake be removed, and so informed him by letter.

Mr. Blake's lawyer has become aware that Mr. Jones, who represented the agency in the hearing before the Committee, spoke with Mr. Cohen, before he submitted his legal opinion to General Thompson. This was part of a process in which Mr. Cohen questioned approximately half a dozen attorneys in the General Counsel's office, including Ms. Jones, as to their opinion of Mr. Blake's case. After listening to and discussing with each attorney his or her views on the case, Cohen formed his own opinion, which was then embodied in the legal opinion for General Thompson.

Mr. Blake's lawyer has filed a lawsuit contesting his dismissal, which argues that the firing was invalid because of the conversations between Ms. Jones and Mr. Cohen. You are the civilian attorney in the Department of the Army, who is responsible for defending the lawsuit brought by Mr. Blake. What is the likelihood that Mr. Blake will succeed in obtaining a reversal of the decision to fire him? Your research reveals that the Department of the Army is not subject to the APA for purposes of this employment action.

Problem Materials

PROFESSIONAL AIR TRAFFIC CONTROLLERS ORGANIZATION v. FEDERAL LABOR RELATIONS AUTHORITY

685 F.2d 547 (D.C.Cir.1982).

HARRY T. EDWARDS, CIRCUIT JUDGE:

Federal employees have long been forbidden from striking against their employer, the federal government, and thereby denying their services to the public at large.... Congress provided that the Federal Labor Relations Authority ("FLRA" or "Authority") shall "revoke the exclusive recognition status" of a recognized union, or "take any other appropriate disciplinary action" against any labor organization, where it is found that the union has called, participated in or condoned a strike, work stoppage or slowdown against a federal agency in a labor-management dispute.

In this case we review the first application of section 7120(f) by the FLRA. After the Professional Air Traffic Controllers Organization ("PATCO") called a nationwide strike of air traffic controllers against the Federal Aviation Administration ("FAA") in the summer of 1981, the Authority revoked PATCO's status as exclusive bargaining representative for the controllers. For the reasons set forth below, we affirm the decision of the Authority.

I. BACKGROUND

The Professional Air Traffic Controllers Organization has been the recognized exclusive bargaining representative for air traffic controllers employed by the Federal Aviation Administration since the early 1970s. Faced with the expiration of an existing collective bargaining agreement, PATCO and the FAA began negotiations for a new contract in early 1981. A tentative agreement was reached in June, but was overwhelmingly rejected by the PATCO rank and file. Following this rejection, negotiations began again in late July. PATCO announced a strike deadline of Monday, August 3, 1981.

Failing to reach a satisfactory accord, PATCO struck the FAA on the morning of August 3. Over seventy percent of the nation's federally employed air traffic controllers walked off the job, significantly reducing the number of private and commercial flights in the United States.

In prompt response to the PATCO job actions, the Government obtained restraining orders against the strike, and then civil and criminal contempt citations when the restraining orders were not heeded. The Government also fired some 11,000 striking air traffic controllers who did not return to work by 11:00 a. m. on August 5, 1981. In addition, on August 3, 1981, the FAA filed an unfair labor practice charge against PATCO with the Federal Labor Relations Authority. On that same day, an FLRA Regional Director issued a complaint on the unfair labor practice charge, alleging strike activity prohibited by [law] and seeking revocation of PATCO's certification under the Civil Service Reform Act. [After a hearing before an ALJ, who recommended revocation of PATCO's certification, the FLRA heard briefs and arguments on the recommended decision. The FLRA concluded to revoke the certification—which constituted a death penalty for the union. The union appealed to the D.C. Circuit.]

II.   Ex Parte Communications During the FLRA Proceedings

Unfortunately, allegations of improprieties during the FLRA's consideration of this case forced us to delay our review on the merits.... Without assuming that anything improper had in fact occurred or had affected the FLRA Decision in this case, we ordered the FLRA "to hold, with the aid of a specially-appointed administrative law judge, an evidentiary hearing to determine the nature, extent, source and effect of any and all ex parte communications and other approaches that may have been made to any member or members of the FLRA while the PATCO case was pending before it."

Following our remand on the ex parte communications issue, John M. Vittone, an Administrative Law Judge with the Civil Aeronautics Board, was appointed to preside over an evidentiary proceeding....

A.   A.L.J. Vittone's Findings

A.L.J. Vittone's inquiry led to the disclosure of a number of communications with FLRA Members that were at least arguably related to the Authority's consideration of the PATCO case. We find the vast majority of these communications unobjectionable. Three occurrences, however, are somewhat more troubling and require our careful review and discussion.

1.   The Meeting Between Member Applewhaite and FLRA General Counsel Gordon

On August 10, 1981 (one week after the unfair labor practice complaint against PATCO was filed), H. Stephan Gordon, the FLRA General Counsel,* was in Member Applewhaite's office discussing administrative matters unrelated to the PATCO case. During Gordon's discussion with Member Applewhaite, Ms. Ellen Stern, an attorney with the FLRA Solicitor's office,** entered Member Applewhaite's office to deliver a copy of a memorandum entitled "Decertification of Labor Organization Participating in the Conduct of a Strike in Violation of Section 7116(b)(7) of the Statute." ... With General Counsel Gordon present, Ms. Stern proceeded to discuss her memorandum, which dealt with whether the Civil Service Reform Act makes revocation of a striking

---

* [editors' note] The General Counsel is the "prosecutor" for the agency in a decertification proceeding.

** [editors' note] The Solicitor is the general legal advisor of the FLRA, including the Members. The Solicitor also represents the FLRA on appeals from FLRA orders and in other legal proceedings.

union's exclusive recognition status mandatory or discretionary and, assuming it is discretionary, what other disciplinary actions might be taken.

During Ms. Stern's discussion, both Member Applewhaite and General Counsel Gordon asked her general questions (e.g., regarding the availability of other remedies and whether she had researched the relevant legislative history). General Counsel Gordon did not ask Member Applewhaite any questions or express any views on the issues discussed in the memorandum. Nor did Member Applewhaite express any opinion on the correct statutory interpretation. While the conversation at least implicitly focused on the PATCO case, the facts of the case and the appropriate disposition were not discussed. The discussion ended after ten or fifteen minutes.

A.L.J. Vittone concluded that "[t]he conversation had no effect or impact on Member Applewhaite's ultimate decision in the PATCO case."

2. Secretary Lewis' Telephone Calls to Members Frazier and Applewhaite

During the morning of August 13, 1981, Secretary of Transportation Andrew L. Lewis, Jr. telephoned Member Frazier. Secretary Lewis stated that he was not calling about the substance of the PATCO case, but wanted Member Frazier to know that, contrary to some news reports, no meaningful efforts to settle the strike were underway. Secretary Lewis also stated that the Department of Transportation would appreciate expeditious handling of the case. Not wanting to discuss the PATCO case with Secretary Lewis, Member Frazier replied, "I understand your position perfectly, Mr. Secretary." . . .

Member Frazier discussed Secretary Lewis' call with FLRA Solicitor Robert Freehling, describing it as relating to status and settlement. Solicitor Freehling advised Member Frazier that the communication did not fall within the ex parte prohibitions of the FLRA Rules.

Member Frazier also advised Member Applewhaite of Secretary Lewis' telephone call. In anticipation of a call, Member Applewhaite located the FLRA Rules regarding the time limits for processing an appeal from an A.L.J. decision in an unfair labor practice case. When Secretary Lewis telephoned and stated his concern that the case not be delayed, Member Applewhaite interrupted the Secretary to inform him that if he wished to obtain expedited handling of the case, he would have to comply with the FLRA Rules and file a written motion. Secretary Lewis stated that he was unaware that papers had to be filed and that he would contact his General Counsel immediately. The conversation ended without further discussion. . . .

3. Member Applewhaite's Dinner with Albert Shanker

Since 1974 Albert Shanker has been President of the American Federation of Teachers, a large public-sector labor union, and a member of the Executive Council of the AFL–CIO. . . . Through their contacts in New York, Mr. Shanker and Member Applewhaite had become professional and social friends.... On September 21, Mr. Shanker made arrangements to have dinner with Member Applewhaite that evening. Although he did not inform Member Applewhaite of his intentions when he made the arrangements, Mr. Shanker candidly admitted that he wanted to have dinner with Member Applewhaite because he felt strongly about the PATCO case and wanted to communicate directly to Member Applewhaite his sentiments, previously expressed in public statements, that PATCO should not be severely punished for its strike. In particular, Mr. Shanker believed that revocation of PATCO's exclusive recognition status would be an excessive punishment.... Near the end of the dinner, ... the conversation turned to labor law matters relevant to the PATCO case. The two men discussed various approaches to public employee strikes in New York, Pennsylvania and the federal government. Mr. Shanker expressed his view that the punishment of a striking union should fit the crime and that revocation of certification as a punishment for an illegal strike was tantamount to "killing a union." The record is clear that Mr. Shanker made no threats or promises to Member Applewhaite; likewise, the evidence also indicates that Member Applewhaite never revealed his position regarding the PATCO case....

The FLRA Decisional Process. On the afternoon of September 21, before the Applewhaite/Shanker dinner, the FLRA Members had their first formal conference on the PATCO case. Members Frazier and Applewhaite both favored revocation of PATCO's exclusive recognition status. Member Frazier favored an indefinite revocation; Member Applewhaite favored a revocation for a fixed period of one to three years....

After September 21, Member Applewhaite considered other remedies, short of revocation, to deal with the PATCO strike.... [E]fforts to agree on an alternative solution failed and, on October 9, Member Applewhaite finally decided to vote with Member Frazier for revocation....

The A.L.J.'s Conclusions. A.L.J. Vittone concluded: "The Shanker–Applewhaite dinner had no effect on the ultimate decision of Mr. Applewhaite in the PATCO case. Member Applewhaite's final decision in the PATCO case was substantially the same as the position he discussed at the September 21 meeting of the members." ... At the very most, the effect was transitory in nature, and occurred from September 21 to October 9.

B. The Parties' Positions

Each of the FLRA Members argue that their individual contacts with persons outside of the Authority were not improper. In addition, each of the Members supports A.L.J. Vittone's findings that the various contacts, their own and their colleagues', had no effect on the ultimate decision of the PATCO case....

PATCO [is] less sanguine about the implications of Judge Vittone's findings. [It argues] that the disclosed communications were improper and require remedial action.... PATCO contends that the contacts with Authority Members by General Counsel Gordon and Secretary Lewis require a remand with instructions that the FLRA General Counsel and the FAA be required to show cause why the complaint should not be dismissed.

C. Applicable Legal Standards

1. The Statutory Prohibition of Ex Parte Contacts and the FLRA Rules

The Civil Service Reform Act requires that FLRA unfair labor practice hearings, to the extent practicable, be conducted in accordance with the provisions of the Administrative Procedure Act. Since FLRA unfair labor practice hearings are formal adjudications within the meaning of the APA, section 557(d) governs ex parte communications. . . .

Three features of the prohibition on ex parte communications in agency adjudications are particularly relevant to the contacts here at issue. First, by its terms, section 557(d) applies only to ex parte communications to or from an "interested person." Congress did not intend, however, that the prohibition on ex parte communications would therefore have only a limited application. A House Report explained:

The term "interested person" is intended to be a wide, inclusive term covering any individual or other person with an interest in the agency proceeding that is greater than the general interest the public as a whole may have. The interest need not be monetary, nor need a person to (sic) be a party to, or intervenor in, the agency proceeding to come under this section. The term includes, but is not limited to, parties, competitors, public officials, and nonprofit or public interest organizations and associations with a special interest in the matter regulated. The term does not include a member of the public at large who makes a casual or general expression of opinion about a pending proceeding.

Second, the [APA] defines an "ex parte communication" as "an oral or written communication not on the public record to which reasonable prior notice to all parties is not given, but . . . not includ[ing] requests for status reports on any matter or proceeding. . . ." Requests for status reports are thus allowed under the statute, even when directed to an agency decisionmaker rather than to another agency employee. Nevertheless, the legislative history of the Act cautions:

A request for a status report or a background discussion may in effect amount to an indirect or subtle effort to influence the substantive outcome of the proceedings. The judgment will have to be made whether a particular communication could affect the agency's decision on the merits. In doubtful cases the agency official should treat the communication as ex parte so as to protect the integrity of the decision making process.

Third, and in direct contrast to status reports, section 557(d) explicitly prohibits communications "relevant to the merits of the proceeding." The congressional reports state that the phrase should "be construed broadly and . . . include more than the phrase 'fact in issue' currently used in (section 554(d)(1) of) the Administrative Procedure Act." [Nevertheless,] the scope of this provision is not unlimited. Congress explicitly noted that the statute does not prohibit procedural inquiries or other communications "not relevant to the merits."

In sum, Congress sought to establish common-sense guidelines to govern ex parte contacts in administrative hearings, rather than rigidly defined and woodenly applied rules. The disclosure of ex parte communications serves two distinct interests. Disclosure is important in its own right to prevent the appearance of impropriety from secret communications in a proceeding that is required to be decided on the record. Disclosure is also important as an instrument of fair decisionmaking; only if a party knows the arguments presented to a decisionmaker can the party respond effectively and ensure that its position is fairly considered. When these interests of openness and opportunity for response are threatened by an ex parte communication, the communication must be disclosed. It matters not whether the communication comes from someone other than a formal party or if the communication is clothed in the guise of a procedural inquiry. If, however, the communication is truly not relevant to the merits of an adjudication and, therefore, does not threaten the interests of openness and effective response, disclosure is unnecessary. Congress did not intend to erect meaningless procedural barriers to effective agency action. It is thus with these interests in mind that the statutory prohibition on ex parte communications must be applied.

2. Remedies for Ex Parte Communications

Section 557(d) contains two possible administrative remedies for improper ex parte communications. The first is disclosure of the communication and its content. The second requires the violating party to "show cause why his claim or interest in the proceeding should not be dismissed, denied, disregarded, or otherwise adversely affected on account of (the) violation." Congress did not intend, however, that an agency would require a party to "show cause" after every violation or that an agency would dismiss a party's interest more than rarely. Indeed, the statutory language clearly states that a party's interest in the proceeding may be adversely affected only "to the extent consistent with the interests of justice and the policy of the underlying statutes."

The [APA] contains no specific provisions for judicial remedy of improper ex parte communications. However, we may infer from approving citations in the House and Senate Reports that Congress did not intend to alter the existing case law regarding ex parte communications and the legal effect of such contacts on agency decisions.

Under the case law in this Circuit, improper ex parte communications, even when undisclosed during agency proceedings, do not necessarily void an agency decision. Rather, agency proceedings that have been blemished by ex parte communications have been held to be voidable. In enforcing this standard, a court must consider whether, as a result of improper ex parte communications, the agency's decisionmaking process was irrevocably tainted so as to make the ultimate judgment of the agency unfair, either to an innocent party or to the public interest that the agency was obliged to protect. In making this determination, a number of considerations may be relevant: the gravity of the ex parte communications; whether the contacts may have influenced the agency's ultimate decision; whether the party making the improper contacts benefited from the agency's ultimate decision; whether the contents of the communications were unknown to opposing parties, who therefore had no opportunity to respond; and whether vacation of the agency's decision and remand for new proceedings would serve a useful purpose. Since the principal concerns of the court are the integrity of the process and the fairness of the result, mechanical rules have little place in a judicial decision whether to vacate a voidable agency proceeding. Instead, any such decision must of necessity be an exercise of equitable discretion.

D. Analysis of the Alleged Ex Parte Communications with FLRA Members

With the foregoing considerations in mind, we have analyzed A.L.J. Vittone's findings thoroughly and given careful thought to the positions urged by the parties. As we noted earlier, the vast majority of the reported contacts between FLRA Members and persons outside the Authority are not troubling . . . [41]

After extensive review of the three troubling incidents that we describe in Part II.A. supra, we believe that they too provide insufficient reason to vacate the FLRA Decision or to remand this case for further proceedings before the Authority. . . . We conclude that at least one and possibly two of the contacts documented by the A.L.J. probably infringed the statutory prohibitions on ex parte communications. The incidents reported by the A. L. J. also included some evident, albeit unintended, indiscretions in a highly charged and widely publicized case. Nevertheless, we agree with A.L.J. Vittone that the ex parte contacts here at issue had no effect on the ultimate decision of the FLRA. Moreover, we conclude that the statutory infringements and other indiscretions are not so serious as to require us to vacate the FLRA Decision or to remand the case to the Authority. . . .

1. The Meeting Between Member Applewhaite and FLRA General Counsel Gordon

When General Counsel Gordon met with Member Applewhaite on August 10, the General Counsel's office was prosecuting the unfair labor practice complaint against PATCO before Chief A.L.J. Fenton. General Counsel Gordon was therefore a "person outside the agency" within the meaning of section 557(d) and the FLRA rules. Still, the undisputed

41. . . . Over several months Member Applewhaite had contacts with a Senate staff member and with an Administration official about his possible appointment as FLRA Chairman and about his reappoint- ment, respectively. The PATCO case was discussed in none of these instances, and they had no effect on Member Applewhaite's decision.

purpose of the meeting was to discuss budgetary and administrative matters. It was therefore entirely appropriate. The shared concerns of the Authority are not put on hold whenever the General Counsel prosecutes an unfair labor practice complaint.

The discussion relevant to the PATCO case arose only when Ms. Stern delivered a copy of her memorandum regarding decertification of striking unions to Member Applewhaite. Thus, the ex parte contact, such as it was, was entirely inadvertent. More important, the contents of the discussion were entirely innocuous. Neither the General Counsel nor Member Applewhaite expressed any view on the correct statutory interpretation, the General Counsel made no arguments to Member Applewhaite, and the facts of the PATCO case were not mentioned.

Some occasional and inadvertent contacts between the prosecuting and adjudicating arms of a small agency like the FLRA may be inevitable. While we cannot countenance any contacts or overlap in functions that threaten to bias administrative adjudications, accidental or passing references to a pending case do not per se deprive a party of a fair proceeding. . . .

In hindsight, it may have been preferable if Member Applewhaite had postponed even this general conversation with Ms. Stern or if General Counsel Gordon had temporarily excused himself from Member Applewhaite's office. Nonetheless, we do not believe that this contact tainted the proceeding or unfairly advantaged the General Counsel in the prosecution of the case. Thus, we conclude that the conversation at issue here, even though possibly indiscreet and undesirable, does not void the FLRA Decision in this case.

2.   *Secretary Lewis' Telephone Calls to Members Frazier and Applewhaite*

Transportation Secretary Lewis was undoubtedly an "interested person" within the meaning of section 557(d) and the FLRA Rules when he called Members Frazier and Applewhaite on August 13. Secretary Lewis' call clearly would have been an improper ex parte communication if he had sought to discuss the merits of the PATCO case. The Secretary explicitly avoided the merits, however, and mentioned only his view on the possibility of settlement and his desire for a speedy decision. On this basis, Solicitor Freehling and Member Frazier concluded the call was not improper.

We are less certain that Secretary Lewis' call was permissible. Although Secretary Lewis did not in fact discuss the merits of the case, even a procedural inquiry may be a subtle effort to influence an agency decision. We do not doubt that Member Frazier and Solicitor Freehling concluded in good faith that the communications were not improper, but it would have been preferable for them to heed Congress' warning, to assume that close cases like these are improper, and to report them on the public record.

We need not decide, however, whether Secretary Lewis' contacts were in fact improper. Even if they were, the contacts did not taint the proceedings or prejudice PATCO. Secretary Lewis' central concern in his conversations with Member Frazier and Member Applewhaite was that the case be handled expeditiously. Member Applewhaite explicitly told Secretary Lewis that if he wanted the case handled more quickly than the normal course of FLRA business, then the FAA would have to file a written request. If, as A.L.J. Vittone found likely, Member Applewhaite's comments led to the FAA's Motion to Modify Time Limits, that was exactly the desired result. Once the FAA filed a motion, PATCO filed its own responsive motions, and the FLRA was able to decide the timing issue based on the pleadings before it.

We believe that the Authority did exactly that.... In the end, the FLRA denied all of the motions and only reduced the time for filing exceptions from twenty-five days to nineteen days. In these circumstances, and given A.L.J. Vittone's inability to find any effect of the calls on the Members' decision, we cannot find that the disposition of the motions was improperly influenced....

3.   Member Applewhaite's Dinner with Albert Shanker

Of course, the most troublesome ex parte communication in this case occurred during the September 21 dinner meeting between Member Applewhaite and American Federation of Teachers President Albert Shanker....

At the outset, we are faced with the question whether Mr. Shanker was an "interested person" to the proceeding under section 557(d) and the FLRA Rules. Mr. Shanker argues that he was not. He suggests that his only connection with the unfair labor practice case was his membership on the Executive Council of the AFL–CIO which, unbeknownst to him, had participated as amicus curiae in the oral argument of the PATCO case before the FLRA. This relationship to the proceeding, Mr. Shanker contends, is too tenuous to qualify him as an "interested person" forbidden to make ex parte communications to the Authority Members.

As noted above, Congress did not intend such a narrow construction of the term "interested person." The Senate Committee on Government Operations deleted a provision in the original bill that exempted ex parte communications involving persons who were neither parties, intervenors nor government officials. The House and Senate Reports agreed that the term covers "any individual or other person with an interest in the agency proceeding that is greater than the general interest the public as a whole may have. The interest need not be monetary, nor need a person be a party to, or intervenor in, the agency proceeding...."

We believe that Mr. Shanker falls within the intended scope of the term "interested person." Mr. Shanker was (and is) the President of a major public-sector labor union. As such, he has a special and well-known interest in the union movement and the developing law of labor relations in the public sector. The PATCO strike, of course, was the subject of extensive media coverage and public comment. Some union leaders undoubtedly felt that the hard line taken against PATCO by the Administration might have an adverse effect on other unions, both in the federal and in state and local government sectors. Mr. Shanker apparently shared this concern. From August 3, 1981 to September 21, 1981, Mr. Shanker and his union made a series of widely publicized statements in support of PATCO. Mr. Shanker urged repeatedly in public statements that disproportionately severe punishment not be inflicted on PATCO. He spoke frequently on this subject, was interviewed about the PATCO strike on a nationally televised news program, and published a number of columns in the New York Times discussing the PATCO situation. Thus, Mr. Shanker's actions, as well as his union office, belie his implicit claim that he had no greater interest in the case than a member of the general public.

Even if we were to adopt Mr. Shanker's position that he was not an interested person, we are astonished at his claim that he did nothing wrong.... In case any doubt still lingers, we take the opportunity to make one thing clear: It is simply unacceptable behavior for any person directly to attempt to influence the decision of a judicial officer in a pending case outside of the formal, public proceedings. This is true for the general public, for "interested persons," and for the formal parties to the case. This rule applies to administrative adjudications as well as to cases in Article III courts....

We do not hold, however, that Member Applewhaite committed an impropriety when he accepted Mr. Shanker's dinner invitation. Member Applewhaite and Mr. Shanker were professional and social friends. We recognize, of course, that a judge "must have neighbors, friends and acquaintances, business and social relations, and be a part of his day and generation." Similarly, Member Applewhaite was not required to renounce his friendships, either personal or professional, when he was appointed to the FLRA. When Mr. Shanker called Member Applewhaite on September 21, Member Applewhaite was unaware of Mr. Shanker's purpose in arranging the dinner. He therefore had no reason to reject the invitation.

The majority of the dinner conversation was unrelated to the PATCO case. Only in the last fifteen minutes of the dinner did the discussion become relevant to the PATCO dispute.... At this point, and as the conversation turned to the discipline appropriate for a striking union like PATCO, Member Applewhaite should have promptly terminated the discussion. Had Mr. Shanker persisted in discussing his views of the PATCO case, Member Applewhaite should have informed him in no uncertain terms that such behavior was inappropriate. Unfortunately, he did not do so.

This indiscretion, this failure to steer the conversation away from the PATCO case, eventually led to the special evidentiary hearing in this case.... We now know that Mr. Shanker did not in any way threaten Member Applewhaite during their dinner. Mr. Shanker did not tell

Member Applewhaite that if he voted to decertify PATCO he would be unable to get cases as an arbitrator if and when he left the FLRA. Mr. Shanker did not say that he was speaking "for top AFL–CIO officials" or that Member Applewhaite would need labor support to secure reappointment. Moreover, Mr. Shanker did not make any promises of any kind to Member Applewhaite, and Member Applewhaite did not reveal how he intended to vote in the PATCO case.

In these circumstances, we do not believe that it is necessary to vacate the FLRA Decision and remand the case. First, while Mr. Shanker's purpose and conduct were improper, and while Member Applewhaite should not have entertained Mr. Shanker's views on the desirability of decertifying a striking union, no threats or promises were made. Though plainly inappropriate, the ex parte communication was limited to a ten or fifteen minute discussion, often couched in general terms, of the appropriate discipline for a striking public employee union. This behavior falls short of ... "corrupt tampering with the adjudicatory process." ...

Second, A.L.J. Vittone found that the Applewhaite/Shanker dinner had no effect on the ultimate decision of Member Applewhaite or of the FLRA as a whole in the PATCO case. None of the parties have disputed this finding.

Third, no party benefited from the improper contact. The ultimate decision was adverse to PATCO, the party whose interests were most closely aligned with Mr. Shanker's position. The final decision also rejected the position taken by the AFL–CIO as amicus curiae and by Mr. Shanker in his dinner conversation with Member Applewhaite....

F. Conclusion

Our review of the record of the special evidentiary hearing, and of the findings of Judge Vittone, leads us to a simple conclusion: There is no reason to vacate the FLRA decision or to remand the case to the FLRA for any further proceedings. We have not found any ex parte communications that irrevocably tainted the Authority's decision. Nor have the proceedings effected procedural unfairness on any of the parties.

STONE v. FEDERAL DEPOSIT INSURANCE CORPORATION

179 F.3d 1368 (Federal Circuit 1999).

GAJARSA, CIRCUIT JUDGE.

Milton R. Stone seeks review of the final decision of the Merit Systems Protection Board ("Board"), dated September 11, 1997, affirming the April 1, 1997 initial decision of the Administrative Judge ("AJ"). The Board sustained Mr. Stone's removal from his position as a bank examiner at the Federal Deposit Insurance Corporation ("FDIC"). For the reasons set forth below, we vacate the decision of the Board and remand for further proceedings consistent with this opinion.

BACKGROUND

Mr. Stone was employed as a GS–12 bank examiner in the FDIC's Division of Supervision, Englewood, Colorado. Mr. Stone submitted applications for approved leave using Standard Form 71s on four occasions. He admitted that he signed these forms with the names of doctors who were purportedly excusing the absences that he requested.

The FDIC decided to begin removal proceedings against Mr. Stone for the submission of false requests for leave.... [The case was assigned to a "deciding official" in FDIC, who recommended that that Mr. Stone be removed, which led FDIC to terminate his employment. Mr. Stone appealed his dismissal to the Merit Systems Protection Board, which assigned the case to an Administrative Law Judge. In preparation for a hearing before the ALJ, Mr. Stone's lawyer made a request for relevant documents from FDIC.] In response to this request, Mr. Stone discovered that an ex parte memorandum from the official recommending his dismissal (the "proposing official") had been sent to the deciding official. Mr. Stone also discovered that the deciding official received a second ex parte memorandum from another FDIC official urging Mr. Stone's removal. In an affidavit, the deciding official stated that he would have concluded that Mr. Stone should be removed whether or not he had seen the ex parte memo from the proposing official.

Mr. Stone appealed the FDIC's decision to the Board, alleging, among other things, that harmful error occurred in the removal proceeding because the deciding official received ex parte communications. In response to this argument, the AJ explained:

> I find nothing erroneous in that fact [that the proposing official had ex parte communications with the deciding official]; indeed, the purpose of a reply is for the appellant to present his side of the case for the agency's consideration. There is no statutory or regulatory prohibition against ex parte communications between the proposing and deciding officials and other officials or persons during the agency's decision-making process.

The AJ did not apply any type of "harmless error" test with respect to the ex parte communications.

On appeal, Mr. Stone argues that the ex parte memoranda improperly introduced new, highly prejudicial, and unchallenged charges and information against him. Mr. Stone argues that the introduction of these ex parte memoranda was a violation of his right to due process and should automatically void his removal. In the alternative, Mr. Stone urges us to adopt an "objective" harmless error test to determine whether consideration of these ex parte memoranda constituted an error that should void the removal proceeding. The objective test would not focus on whether the deciding official actually would have reached the same result if there had been no procedural defect, but rather would focus on whether the error is so likely to have prejudiced the deciding official that the proceeding should be void.

The government argues that Andersen's subjective test for harmless error applies in this case and that Mr. Stone has failed to submit evidence sufficient to meet this test. This subjective test proposed by the government requires the disciplined federal employee to prove the following:

1. that new allegations or information were introduced which the appellant has not had the benefit of reviewing or responding to;

2. that the deciding official was influenced by the new allegations or information in his or her decision making process; and

3. that the procedural error of considering the new allegations or information likely had a harmful effect upon the outcome before the agency.

The government argues that the information contained in the ex parte memoranda was not "new" and that the deciding official has testified that he would have recommended removal regardless of the ex parte communication. The government, therefore, urges us to use a subjective test to find that any procedural error was harmless. The government does not respond to Mr. Stone's constitutional due process arguments.

DISCUSSION

... Mr. Stone's federal constitutional due process claim depends on his having a property right in continued employment.... [The Court held that because, as a Civil Service employee, Mr. Stone could not be dismissed except for cause or unacceptable performance, he had the requisite property right.]

The next question we face is what process is due Mr. Stone before he can be deprived of his property interest....

The process due a public employee prior to removal from office has been explained in [*Cleveland Bd. Of Educ. v. Loudermill*, 470 U.S. 532, 542–46, 105 S.Ct. 1487, 84 L.Ed.2d 494 (1985)]. The Supreme Court has stated:

> ... The essential requirements of due process ... are notice and an opportunity to respond. The opportunity to present reasons, either in person or in writing, why proposed action should not be taken is a fundamental due process requirement.... The tenured employee is entitled to oral or written notice of the charges against him, an explanation of the employer's evidence, and an opportunity to present his side of the story.... To require more than this prior to termination would intrude to an unwarranted extent on the government's interest in quickly removing an unsatisfactory employee.

The Supreme Court expressly noted that the need for a meaningful opportunity for the public employee to present his or her side of the case is important in enabling the agency to reach an accurate result for two reasons. First, dismissals for cause will often involve factual disputes and consideration of the employee's response may help clarify such disputes.

In addition, even if the facts are clear, "the appropriateness or necessity of the discharge may not be; in such cases, the only meaningful opportunity to invoke the discretion of the decisionmaker is likely to be before the termination takes effect."

Thus, the Supreme Court expressly recognized that the employee's response is essential not only to the issue of whether the allegations are true, but also with regard to whether the level of penalty to be imposed is appropriate. . . .

The introduction of new and material information by means of ex parte communications to the deciding official undermines the public employee's constitutional due process guarantee of notice (both of the charges and of the employer's evidence) and the opportunity to respond. When deciding officials receive such ex parte communications, employees are no longer on notice of the reasons for their dismissal and/or the evidence relied upon by the agency. Procedural due process guarantees are not met if the employee has notice only of certain charges or portions of the evidence and the deciding official considers new and material information. It is constitutionally impermissible to allow a deciding official to receive additional material information that may undermine the objectivity required to protect the fairness of the process. Our system is premised on the procedural fairness at each stage of the removal proceedings. An employee is entitled to a certain amount of due process rights at each stage and, when these rights are undermined, the employee is entitled to relief regardless of the stage of the proceedings.

However, not every ex parte communication is a procedural defect so substantial and so likely to cause prejudice that it undermines the due process guarantee and entitles the claimant to an entirely new administrative proceeding. Only ex parte communications that introduce new and material information to the deciding official will violate the due process guarantee of notice. In deciding whether new and material information has been introduced by means of ex parte contacts, the Board should consider the facts and circumstances of each particular case. Among the factors that will be useful for the Board to weigh are: whether the ex parte communication merely introduces "cumulative" information or new information; whether the employee knew of the error and had a chance to respond to it; and whether the ex parte communications were of the type likely to result in undue pressure upon the deciding official to rule in a particular manner. Ultimately, the inquiry of the Board is whether the ex parte communication is so substantial and so likely to cause prejudice that no employee can fairly be required to be subjected to a deprivation of property under such circumstances.

If the Board finds that an ex parte communication has not introduced new and material information, then there is no due process violation. On the other hand, if the Board finds new and material information has been received by the deciding official by means of ex parte communications, then a due process violation has occurred and the former employee is entitled to a new constitutionally correct removal procedure. As we have explained previously, when a procedural due process violation has occurred because of ex parte communications, such a violation is not subject to the harmless error test.

In this case, because Mr. Stone had a property interest in continued employment with the FDIC, he was entitled by the Due Process Clause to meaningful notice of the reasons for his removal and a meaningful opportunity to respond. Because of the ex parte contacts between FDIC officials and the deciding official, Mr. Stone's procedural due process rights may have been undermined. . . .

We therefore vacate the Board's decision and remand the case for proceedings consistent with this opinion.

E. DUE PROCESS HEARINGS

When the procedures of the APA do not apply, one must look to other statutes that may provide certain procedures for the adjudication. Usually, agencies will have adopted procedural regulations governing the type of procedure applicable to the adjudication. Often the question will arise whether the procedure provided complies with the Due Process Clause. Because the Due Process Clause appears both in the Fifth Amendment (with respect to the federal government) and in the Fourteenth Amendment (with respect to state and local governments), the adequacy of administrative procedure under the Due Process Clause can arise in either federal or state actions.

The Due Process Clause provides that no person shall be deprived of life, liberty, or property without due process of law. There are two strands to the law of Due Process: substantive due process and procedural due process. Substantive due process is traditionally discussed in courses on Constitutional Law, while procedural due process, because it focuses on procedure, is traditionally reserved to courses on Administrative Law. Hereafter, the discussion involves procedural due process, not substantive due process.

In determining the procedural requirements of the Due Process Clause, the first issue is whether the clause applies at all; the second issue, assuming the clause applies, is what procedures are required. The Due Process Clause requires the government to hold some type of hearing before it deprives an individual of "life, liberty, or property" based on the resolution of disputed factual issues pertaining to that person. We first examine the two prerequisites to whether due process applies: individualized decisionmaking and the deprivation of a property or liberty interest. We then turn to the type of hearing that the government is obligated to give if the Due Process Clause applies. In other words, what hearing procedures, such as the right to appear in person, present witnesses, or cross-examine witnesses, are necessary to satisfy the government's obligation of due process?

1. INDIVIDUALIZED DECISIONMAKING

The limitation that the Due Process Clause only applies to ~~alized decisionmaking dates back to the following two cases decide~~ the early 1900s. The Court has continued the distinction betw~~ individualized deprivations of property or liberty, which require due process, and policy-based deprivations affecting a class of individuals, which do not.

LONDONER v. DENVER

210 U.S. 373, 28 S.Ct. 708, 52 L.Ed. 1103 (1908).

MR. JUSTICE MOODY delivered the opinion of the court: . . .

The plaintiffs in error began this proceeding in a state court of Colorado to relieve lands owned by them from an assessment of a tax for the cost of paving a street upon which the lands abutted. The relief sought was granted by the trial court, but its action was reversed by the supreme court of the state, which ordered judgment for the defendants. The case is here on writ of error. The supreme court held that the tax was assessed in conformity with the Constitution and laws of the state, and its decision of that question is conclusive. . . .

The tax complained of was assessed under the provisions of the charter of the city of Denver, which confers upon the city the power to make local improvements and to assess the cost upon property specially benefited. . . .

It appears from the charter that, in the execution of the power to make local improvements and assess the cost upon the property specially benefited, the main steps to be taken by the city authorities are plainly marked and separated: 1. The board of public works must transmit to the city council a resolution ordering the work to be done and the form of an ordinance authorizing it and creating an assessment district. This it can do only upon certain conditions, one of which is that there shall first be filed a petition asking the improvement, signed by the owners of the majority of the frontage to be assessed. 2. The passage of that ordinance by the city council, which is given authority to determine conclusively whether the action of the board was duly taken. 3. The assessment of the cost upon the landowners after due notice and opportunity for hearing. . . .

The [landowner] raises . . . the question whether the assessment was made without notice and opportunity for hearing to those affected by it, thereby denying to them due process of law. The trial court found as a fact that no opportunity for hearing was afforded, and the Supreme Court did not disturb this finding. . . .

In the assessment, apportionment, and collection of taxes upon property within their jurisdiction, the Constitution of the United States imposes few restrictions upon the states. In the enforcement of such restrictions as the Constitution does impose, this court has regarded substance, and not form. But where the legislature of a state, instead of fixing the tax itself, commits to some subordinate body the duty of determining whether, in what amount, and upon whom it shall be levied, and of making its assessment and apportionment, due process of law requires that, at some stage of the proceedings, before the tax becomes irrevocably fixed, the taxpayer shall have an opportunity to be heard, of which he must have notice, either personal, by publication, or by a law fixing the time and place of the hearing.

If it is enough that, under such circumstances, an opportunity is given to submit in writing all objections to and complaints of the tax to the board, then there was a hearing afforded in the case at bar. But we think that something more than that, even in proceedings for taxation, is required by due process of law. Many requirements essential in strictly judicial proceedings may be dispensed with in proceedings of this nature. But even here a hearing, in its very essence, demands that he who is entitled to it shall have the right to support his allegations by argument, however brief, and, if need be, by proof, however informal. It is apparent that such a hearing was denied to the plaintiffs in error. The denial was by the city council, which, while acting as a board of equalization, represents the state. The assessment was therefore void, and the plaintiffs in error were entitled to a decree discharging their lands from a lien on account of it . . . .

BI–METALLIC INVESTMENT COMPANY v. STATE BOARD OF EQUALIZATION

239 U.S. 441, 36 S.Ct. 141, 60 L.Ed. 372 (1915).

MR. JUSTICE HOLMES delivered the opinion of the court:

This is a suit to enjoin the State Board of Equalization and the Colorado Tax Commission from putting in force and the defendant Pitcher, as assessor of Denver, from obeying, an order of the boards, increasing the valuation of all taxable property in Denver 40 per cent. The order was sustained and the suit directed to be dismissed by the Supreme Court of the State. The plaintiff is the owner of real estate in Denver, and brings the case here on the ground that it was given no opportunity to be heard, and that therefore its property will be taken without due process of law, contrary to the 14th Amendment of the Constitution of the United States.

. . . The question, then, is whether all individuals have a constitutional right to be heard before a matter can be decided in which all are equally concerned . . . .

Where a rule of conduct applies to more than a few people, it is impracticable that everyone should have a direct voice in its adoption. The Constitution does not require all public acts to be done in town meeting or an assembly of the whole. General statutes within the state power are passed that affect the person or property of individuals, sometimes to the point of ruin, without giving them a chance to be heard. Their rights are protected in the only way that they can be in a complex society, by their power, immediate or remote, over those who make the rule. If the result in this case had been reached, as it might have been by the state's doubling the rate of taxation, no one would suggest that the 14th Amendment was violated unless every person affected had been allowed an opportunity to raise his voice against it before the body intrusted by the state Constitution with the power.... There must be a limit to individual argument in such matters if government is to go on. In *Londoner v. Denver*, a local board had to determine "whether, in what amount, and upon whom" a tax for paving a street should be levied for special benefits. A relatively small number of persons was concerned, who were exceptionally affected, in each case upon individual grounds, and it was held that they had a right to a hearing. But that decision is far from reaching a general determination dealing only with the principle upon which all the assessments in a county had been laid.

Notes and Questions

1. In *Bi–Metallic*, Justice Holmes explains that the home owners in *Londoner* were entitled to a hearing because "a relatively small number of persons was concerned, who were exceptionally affected, in each case upon individualized grounds." This distinction draws on three factors: number of persons affected, extent of the impact on each person, and the factual basis for determining the impact on each person. Commentators have focussed on two of these factors as justifying limiting due process to individualized decisionmaking. As the following notes elaborate, some analysts focus on the number of persons affected, while other commentators focus on the factual basis of the decision.

2. Justice Holmes emphasizes that individualized hearings are impracticable when more than a "small number of persons" are impacted by a governmental decision, and that when many persons are affected, they can resort to the political system to vindicate their interests. "In such cases, there is much less need for due process protection than when the government singles out an individual for particularly disadvantageous treatment. Moreover, it is far too cumbersome to permit large numbers of potentially affected persons to present testimony and to cross-examine witnesses in agency proceedings that are intended to produce policy decisions that affect large numbers of people." RICHARD J. PIERCE, JR., SIDNEY A. SHAPIRO, & PAUL R. VERKUIL, ADMINISTRATIVE LAW & PROCESS 251–52 (3d ed. 1999).

3. Professor Davis argues that the Due Process Clause applied in *Londoner* because the landowners were each affected on *individualized grounds*. As discussed in Chapter 2, Davis makes a distinction between "adjudicative" and "legislative" facts. He argues that hearing procedures are necessary for the accurate resolution of disputes concerning adjudicative facts, which involve the questions of who did what, where, when, how, why, and with what motive or intent, but that such proce-

dures are normally unnecessary for the resolution of legislative facts, which do not concern the immediate parties but are the general facts which help the tribunal decide questions of law and policy and discretion. *See* 2 KENNETH CULP DAVIS, ADMINISTRATIVE LAW TREATISE § 12.2 (2d ed. 1979). Davis explains, "The crucial difference between the two cases is that in *Londoner* specific facts about the particular property were disputed, but in *Bi–Metallic* no such specific facts were disputed, for the problem was the broad and general problem involving all taxpayers of Denver. The principle emerging from the two cases may be that a dispute about facts that have to be found on 'individual grounds' must be resolved through trial procedure, but a dispute on a question of policy need not be resolved through trial procedure even if the decision is made in part on the basis of broad and general facts of the kind that contribute to the determination of a question of policy." *Id.* at 412.

4. Whether *Bi–Metallic*'s distinction from *Londoner* is based upon the number of people affected, the nature of the facts in issue, or some combination of the two is not just an academic dispute. The Supreme Court has not further specified how to distinguish those types of proceedings that implicate the Due Process Clause from those that do not, so lawyers must assess whether due process is required from the tea leaves of these early cases.

2.   PROTECTED INTERESTS

The following facts, which relate to a student's dismissal from law school, will be used in the next three problems. This problem asks whether the school's actions have deprived the student of a "property" or "liberty" interest. The subsequent problems address what process is due assuming that the Due Process Clause applies. Problem 3–5 considers what procedures the school must use in determining whether the student has committed plagiarism, while problem 3–6 addresses the extent to which due process guarantees a neutral decisionmaker.

Problem 3–5: Definition of Property and Liberty

Jeremy is a second-semester, first-year student at the University of Alaska School of Law (a fictional institution for purposes of this problem). As a result of a legal writing assignment to write an appellate brief, the school charged him with plagiarism, an Honor Code violation. Specifically, he was charged with the failure to indicate by quotation marks six sentences quoted verbatim from judicial decisions and four sentences quoted verbatim from law review articles, although all the documents were cited generically, and with the general appropriation of the three legal arguments in the brief from three actual appellate briefs on file in the library that were merely paraphrased and were not cited.

The legal writing instructor, a former attorney with the U.S. Department of Justice, had originally recognized the appropriation of other work, but as she said one day in the faculty lounge, "In the Justice

Department we learned that, because most of the litigation involved issues that had been considered and briefed before, unless you were plagiarizing someone else's work, you were wasting time." She thought it was interesting that a student had learned this so early in law school. It did not occur to her that this might be an Honor Code violation.

Word of this discussion in the Faculty Lounge got back to the Dean, who called the instructor in to his office and asked her if it was true. The Dean then informed the instructor that "such action was a clear violation" of the school's Honor Code, which defined plagiarism as including: "copying another person's exact language without placing quotation marks around that language and citing to the source (it is not sufficient merely to cite to the source)" and "paraphrasing of another person's work to an extent or degree that you are in effect using the other person's writing." The instructor, who was hired on a year-to-year contract without tenure, then reported the student pursuant to the school's Honor Code procedures.

The Honor Code procedures provide that a teacher who discovers an Honor Code offense shall report it to the Honor Committee, which consists of the Associate Dean for Students (a non-faculty administrator, who is hired by and serves at the pleasure of the Dean) as chair, one tenured faculty member chosen by the Dean, and one student elected annually by the student body. The Committee investigates the alleged violation and determines whether a violation has occurred. It reports its findings and conclusions to the Dean, and if it determines that a violation has occurred, it includes a recommended sanction to the Dean, who imposes the sanction he deems appropriate. The Honor Code does not specify much procedure, stating only that the student shall be given an opportunity to address the Committee and provide his or her side of the story.

Jeremy was in fact given notice of the charge (and was told by the Legal Writing instructor the background to the charge) and was invited to address the Committee, which he did. He requested to be accompanied by counsel, but that request was denied. He pleaded ignorance of the rule, although he admitted that he had been provided a copy of the Honor Code at orientation (along with a lot of other material) and that the initial lecture in Legal Writing had stressed the importance of not plagiarizing, but the lecture had not defined the term. He also told the Committee that his older sister is a lawyer with the Public Defender, and he had often heard her tell how she uses other people's briefs in her own. He asked to call other students to testify as to their understanding and to call practicing lawyers as to what is appropriate behavior in "the real world." These requests were denied.

The Committee unanimously found that Jeremy had committed plagiarism, a violation of the Honor Code, and by a two-to-one vote (the student dissenting) recommended that Jeremy be suspended for one year. The Committee was uncertain whether Jeremy's intent was relevant, but committee members did not believe that Jeremy appropriated the other work in the innocent belief that it was appropriate behavior. Instead, the committee concluded Jeremy had attempted to reduce his own workload, and the lack of citation was an effort to conceal this attempt.

Neither the finding nor recommendation were provided to Jeremy before the Dean imposed his sanction—expulsion. In the letter to Jeremy explaining his decision, the Dean stated: "From Watergate to Whitewater the honesty and integrity of lawyers have been found wanting. A law school must set an example for its students that honesty and integrity in the law are of the utmost importance and cannot be compromised. Any sanction less than the ultimate sanction would suggest that dishonesty and duplicity can be forgiven. This is not a message I wish this school to send."

Jeremy's transcript is closed with the notation: "Expelled for Honor Code violation." Federal law generally protects the privacy of educational records from transmission to third parties without the written permission of the person whose records are involved.

Jeremy challenges his expulsion, arguing that the school violated his due process rights. Did the law school deprive Jeremy of a "property" or "liberty" interest? What arguments might he make? What arguments might the defendants make in response? How would you expect a court to rule?

a. *Property Interest*

To determine whether the due process clause applies, a court must assess whether the government's action constitutes a deprivation of life, liberty, or property, for if it does not, due process is not required at all. Historically, "life, liberty, and property" included the common law or fundamental rights that persons held by reason of membership in the body politic. They did not include the "privileges" that government might grant to persons, such as government employment and welfare payments. Thus, the law distinguished between "rights" and "privileges," with the former protected from deprivation without due process and the latter not. During the early 1970s, the Supreme Court expanded the reach of the Due Process Clause by expanding the definitions of "property" and "liberty."

The Court's abandonment of the "rights/privileges" distinction began in *Goldberg v. Kelly*, 397 U.S. 254, 90 S.Ct. 1011, 25 L.Ed.2d 287 (1970), where a due process challenge to a welfare termination by the state of New York reached the Supreme Court. The state conceded that procedural due process was required; the only argument concerned what procedure due process required. The Court reasoned that in modern society the loss of a government entitlement, such as a welfare benefit, had the same adverse impact on a person as when the government deprived someone of private property. Moreover, the Court believed that citizens had an expectation that entitlements, like private property, were protected by the government's obligation of due process. Finally, the

Court noted that its historical approach to defining property protected the entitlements of the rich, which were in the form of private property, but not of the poor, which were in the form of government benefits. After *Goldberg*, the Court set out to give content to the terms "property" and "liberty" whose deprivation triggers due process concerns.

BOARD OF REGENTS v. ROTH

408 U.S. 564, 92 S.Ct. 2701, 33 L.Ed.2d 548 (1972).

MR. JUSTICE STEWART delivered the opinion of the Court.

In 1968 the respondent, David Roth, was hired for his first teaching job as assistant professor of political science at Wisconsin State University–Oshkosh. He was hired for a fixed term of one academic year. The notice of his faculty appointment specified that his employment would begin on September 1, 1968, and would end on June 30, 1969. The respondent completed that term. But he was informed that he would not be rehired for the next academic year. . . .

The respondent then brought this action in Federal District Court alleging that the decision not to rehire him for the next year infringed his Fourteenth Amendment rights. [H]e . . . alleged that the failure of University officials to give him notice of any reason for nonretention and an opportunity for a hearing violated his right to procedural due process of law. . . .

The requirements of procedural due process apply only to the deprivation of interests encompassed by the Fourteenth Amendment's protection of liberty and property. When protected interests are implicated, the right to some kind of prior hearing is paramount. But the range of interests protected by procedural due process is not infinite. . . .

"While this court has not attempted to define with exactness the liberty . . . guaranteed (by the Fourteenth Amendment), the term has received much consideration and some of the included things have been definitely stated. Without doubt, it denotes not merely freedom from bodily restraint but also the right of the individual to contract, to engage in any of the common occupations of life, to acquire useful knowledge, to marry, establish a home and bring up children, to worship God according to the dictates of his own conscience, and generally to enjoy those privileges long recognized . . . as essential to the orderly pursuit of happiness by free men." *Meyer v. Nebraska*, 262 U.S. 390, 399.

There might be cases in which a State refused to re-employ a person under such circumstances that interests in liberty would be implicated. But this is not such a case.

The State, in declining to rehire the respondent, did not make any charge against him that might seriously damage his standing and associations in his community. It did not base the nonrenewal of his contract on a charge, for example, that he had been guilty of dishonesty, or immorality. Had it done so, this would be a different case. For "[w]here a person's good name, reputation, honor, or integrity is at stake because of what the government is doing to him, notice and an opportunity to be heard are essential." *Wisconsin v. Constantineau*, 400 U.S. 433, 437....

Similarly, there is no suggestion that the State, in declining to re-employ the respondent, imposed on him a stigma or other disability that foreclosed his freedom to take advantage of other employment opportunities....

The Fourteenth Amendment's procedural protection of property is a safeguard of the security of interests that a person has already acquired in specific benefits. These interests—property interests—may take many forms.

... To have a property interest in a benefit, a person clearly must have more than an abstract need or desire for it. He must have more than a unilateral expectation of it. He must, instead, have a legitimate claim of entitlement to it. It is a purpose of the ancient institution of property to protect those claims upon which people rely in their daily lives, reliance that must not be arbitrarily undermined. It is a purpose of the constitutional right to a hearing to provide an opportunity for a person to vindicate those claims.

Property interests, of course, are not created by the Constitution. Rather they are created and their dimensions are defined by existing rules or understandings that stem from an independent source such as state law—rules or understandings that secure certain benefits and that support claims of entitlement to those benefits. Thus, the welfare recipients in *Goldberg v. Kelly* had a claim of entitlement to welfare payments that was grounded in the statute defining eligibility for them. The recipients had not yet shown that they were, in fact, within the statutory terms of eligibility. But we held that they had a right to a hearing at which they might attempt to do so....

Notes and Questions

1. In *Goldberg*, federal law created the entitlement that qualified as property because welfare benefits were a matter of "statutory entitlement for persons qualified to receive them." *Roth* holds that state law—common law or statutory law—can also constitute "property" when there are "rules or understandings that secure benefits and that support claims of entitlement to those benefits."

2. In *Roth*, the Court granted summary judgment for the defendant because the plaintiff could not point to any statute or common law right that established that he could retain his job:

> ... [Roth's] "property" interest in employment at Wisconsin State University–Oshkosh was created and defined by the terms of his appointment. Those terms secured his interest in employment up to June 30, 1969. But the important fact in this case is that they specifically provided that the respondent's employment was to ter-

minate on June 30. They did not provide for contract renewal absent "sufficient cause." Indeed, they made no provision for renewal whatsoever.

Thus, the terms of [Roth's] appointment secured absolutely no interest in re-employment for the next year. They supported absolutely no possible claim of entitlement to re-employment. Nor, significantly, was there any state statute or University rule or policy that secured his interest in re-employment or that created any legitimate claim to it.

408 U.S. at 578, 92 S.Ct. at 2709.

3. The result in *Roth* can be contrasted with the outcome in *Perry v. Sindermann,* 408 U.S. 593, 92 S.Ct. 2694, 33 L.Ed.2d 570 (1972), decided the same day as *Roth.* In *Sindermann,* the plaintiff was a professor who was not rehired and who was not protected by a formal tenure system. Sindermann, however, alleged that, in light of the policies and practices of the institution, he had an implied contract to continue employment. The Court agreed that, if under state law Sindermann had such an implied contract, he would have a "legitimate claim of entitlement" that would trigger due process protections.

b. *Liberty Interest*

Historically, liberty meant freedom from bodily restraint or injury. Ordinarily, the government cannot restrain someone except as incident to the criminal process, which ensures due process of law. In *Meyer v. Nebraska,* 262 U.S. 390, 43 S.Ct. 625, 67 L.Ed. 1042 (1923), the Court said "liberty" also includes all of "those privileges long recognized . . . as essential to the orderly pursuit of happiness by free men." According to *Meyer,* the right to engage in a common calling or profession is one such interest. Thus, the Court has held that the government triggers due process protections when it denies or revokes a person's license to engage in a profession. *See, e.g., Gibson v. Berryhill,* 411 U.S. 564, 93 S.Ct. 1689, 36 L.Ed.2d 488 (1973) (optometrists); *Schware v. Board of Bar Examiners,* 353 U.S. 232, 238–39, 77 S.Ct. 752, 755–56, 1 L.Ed.2d 796 (1957) (lawyers). Similarly, *Roth* said the government would trigger due process protections if "the State, in declining to rehire [the teacher,] has imposed on him a stigma or other disability that foreclosed his freedom to take advantage of other employment opportunities. . . ." Nevertheless, the Court held that Roth was not deprived of a liberty interest because Wisconsin did not make any charge against him when it declined to rehire him. As a result, the state's action did not create a barrier that would prevent Roth from obtaining other employment.

In a pre-*Roth* case, *Wisconsin v. Constantineau,* 400 U.S. 433, 91 S.Ct. 507, 27 L.Ed.2d 515 (1971), the Court suggested that government action that adversely affected a person's reputation might be a denial of liberty without any adverse impact on the individual's job opportunities. In response to a state law that required the posting of the names of "public drunkards" at places where alcoholic beverages were sold, the

Court stated that "[w]here a person's good name, reputation, honor, or integrity is at stake because of what the government is doing to him, [due process is] essential." *Roth*, however, found that Wisconsin's mere failure to rehire the plaintiff, with no reasons being given, did not harm Roth's reputation. The Court returned to the definition of liberty in the following case.

PAUL v. DAVIS

424 U.S. 693, 96 S.Ct. 1155, 47 L.Ed.2d 405 (1976).

MR. JUSTICE REHNQUIST delivered the opinion of the Court.

We granted certiorari in this case to consider whether respondent's charge that petitioners' defamation of him, standing alone and apart from any other governmental action with respect to him, stated a claim for relief under ... the Fourteenth Amendment. For the reasons hereinafter stated, we conclude that it does not.

Petitioner Paul is the Chief of Police of the Louisville, Ky., Division of Police, while petitioner McDaniel occupies the same position in the Jefferson County, Ky., Division of Police. In late 1972 they agreed to combine their efforts for the purpose of alerting local area merchants to possible shoplifters who might be operating during the Christmas season. In early December petitioners distributed to approximately 800 merchants in the Louisville metropolitan area a "flyer," which began as follows:

"TO: BUSINESS MEN IN THE METROPOLITAN AREA

"The Chiefs of The Jefferson County and City of Louisville Police Departments, in an effort to keep their officers advised on shoplifting activity, have approved the attached alphabetically arranged flyer of subjects known to be active in this criminal field.

"This flyer is being distributed to you, the business man, so that you may inform your security personnel to watch for these subjects. These persons have been arrested during 1971 and 1972 or have been active in various criminal fields in high density shopping areas.

"Only the photograph and name of the subject is shown on this flyer, if additional information is desired, please forward a request in writing. . . ."

The flyer consisted of five pages of "mug shot" photos, arranged alphabetically. Each page was headed:

"NOVEMBER 1972
CITY OF LOUISVILLE
JEFFERSON COUNTY
POLICE DEPARTMENTS
ACTIVE SHOPLIFTERS"

In approximately the center of page 2 there appeared photos and the name of the respondent, Edward Charles Davis III. . . .

Respondent's due process claim is grounded upon his assertion that the flyer, and in particular the phrase "Active Shoplifters" appearing at the head of the page upon which his name and photograph appear, impermissibly deprived him of some "liberty" protected by the Fourteenth Amendment. His complaint asserted that the "active shoplifter" designation would inhibit him from entering business establishments for fear of being suspected of shoplifting and possibly apprehended, and would seriously impair his future employment opportunities. Accepting that such consequences may flow from the flyer in question, respondent's complaint would appear to state a classical claim for defamation actionable in the courts of virtually every State. Imputing criminal behavior to an individual is generally considered defamatory *per se*, and actionable without proof of special damages....

... The words "liberty" and "property" as used in the Fourteenth Amendment do not in terms single out reputation as a candidate for special protection over and above other interests that may be protected by state law. While we have in a number of our prior cases pointed out the frequently drastic effect of the "stigma" which may result from defamation by the government in a variety of contexts, this line of cases does not establish the proposition that reputation alone, apart from some more tangible interests such as employment, is either "liberty" or "property" by itself sufficient to invoke the procedural protection of the Due Process Clause.... While not uniform in their treatment of the subject, we think that the weight of our decisions establishes no constitutional doctrine converting every defamation by a public official into a deprivation of liberty within the meaning of the Due Process Clause of the Fifth or Fourteenth Amendment....

MR. JUSTICE BRENNAN, with whom MR. JUSTICE MARSHALL concurs and MR. JUSTICE WHITE concurs in part, dissenting.

I dissent. The Court today holds that police officials, acting in their official capacities as law enforcers, may on their own initiative and without trial constitutionally condemn innocent individuals as criminals and thereby brand them with one of the most stigmatizing and debilitating labels in our society. If there are no constitutional restraints on such oppressive behavior, the safeguards constitutionally accorded an accused in a criminal trial are rendered a sham, and no individual can feel secure that he will not be arbitrarily singled out for similar *ex parte* punishment by those primarily charged with fair enforcement of the law. The Court accomplishes this result by excluding a person's interest in his good name and reputation from all constitutional protection, regardless of the character of or necessity for the government's actions....

Notes and Questions

1. In *Paul*, the Court distinguished *Constantineau* on the grounds that the branding of persons as public drunkards legally disabled them from purchasing alcohol, whereas branding a person an active shoplifter had no legal consequences. The *Paul* analysis has been described as the

"stigma-plus" test; that is, in order to trigger due process protections, the government action not only must harm a person's reputation, but it must also subject the individual to some other disability, such as the loss of a job or the ability to purchase alcohol.

2.   Although the government cannot jail someone accused of a crime without due process, the question arises whether, or to what extent, a person convicted of a crime and receiving a sentence retains any liberty interests. In *Morrissey v. Brewer*, 408 U.S. 471, 92 S.Ct. 2593, 33 L.Ed.2d 484 (1972), the Court "solved" this problem by finding that, just as government could create a property interest by conferring a legal entitlement on someone, government could also create a liberty interest in persons who had been deprived of their natural liberty interest. In *Morrissey*, the Court found that the state had created a parole system that created an entitlement to continued parole so long as a person met the required conditions. A decision to revoke parole, therefore, triggered due process requirements. *Accord Gagnon v. Scarpelli*, 411 U.S. 778, 93 S.Ct. 1756, 36 L.Ed.2d 656 (1973) (probation). Similarly, in *Wolff v. McDonnell*, 418 U.S. 539, 94 S.Ct. 2963, 41 L.Ed.2d 935 (1974), the Court held that a state law that created a "good time" credit system, by which inmates could reduce their sentences, created a liberty interest in those credits, which meant that they could not be taken away without providing due process. Thus, where the government has affirmatively granted a prisoner some right, the deprivation of that liberty or right triggers due process.

3.   By comparison, the Court has held that the test for whether a prisoner has a protectable liberty interest concerning prison discipline does not turn on whether prison regulations grant some benefit or restrict imposition of some penalty. *Sandin v. Conner*, 515 U.S. 472, 115 S.Ct. 2293, 132 L.Ed.2d 418 (1995). Although states may create liberty interests protected by due process, the Court limited due process protection to "freedom from restraint which ... imposes atypical and significant hardship on the inmate in relation to the ordinary incidents of prison life." The Court rejected the plaintiff's claim that disciplinary segregation was such an interest, because "discipline by prison officials in response to a wide range of misconduct falls within the expected parameters of the sentence imposed by a court of law." Thus, where a prisoner suffers deprivation as an incident of his conviction or incarceration, the state's action does not usually implicate the Due Process Clause. *Meachum v. Fano*, 427 U.S. 215, 96 S.Ct. 2532, 49 L.Ed.2d 451 (1976) (transfer from medium-security facility to maximum-security facility); *Bell v. Wolfish*, 441 U.S. 520, 99 S.Ct. 1861, 60 L.Ed.2d 447 (1979) (body cavity searches). It is possible, however, for a deprivation incident to a conviction to be outside the terms of confinement "ordinarily contemplated by a prison sentence." Thus, transfer to a mental hospital for mandatory behavior modification invaded a liberty interest not extinguished by conviction and normal incarceration. *Vitek v. Jones*, 445 U.S. 480, 100 S.Ct. 1254, 63 L.Ed.2d 552 (1980).

Problem Materials

CODD v. VELGER

429 U.S. 624, 97 S.Ct. 882, 51 L.Ed.2d 92 (1977).

PER CURIAM.

[Respondent Velger alleged that he had been wrongly dismissed without a hearing or a statement of reasons from his position as a patrolman with the New York City Police Department, and under 42 U.S.C. § 1983, sought reinstatement and damages for the resulting injury to his reputation and future employment prospects. Because he held only a probationary position, he had no property interest in the position, but he alleged that he was entitled to a hearing due to the stigmatizing effect of certain material placed by the City Police Department in his personnel file. He alleged that the derogatory material had brought about his subsequent dismissal from a position with the Penn–Central Railroad Police Department, and that it had also prevented him from finding other employment of a similar nature for which his scores on numerous examinations otherwise qualified him.]

The case came on for a bench trial before Judge Werker, who ... determined that the only issue [worthy of discussion] was whether petitioners, in discharging respondent had "imposed a stigma on Mr. Velger that foreclosed his freedom to take advantage of other employment opportunities." After discussing the evidence bearing upon this issue, Judge Werker concluded that "[i]t is clear from the foregoing facts that plaintiff has not proved that he has been stigmatized by defendants."

Among the specific findings of fact made by the District Court was that an officer of the Penn–Central Railroad Police Department was shown the City Police Department file relating to respondent's employment, upon presentation of a form signed by respondent authorizing the release of personnel information. From an examination of the file, this officer "gleaned that plaintiff had been dismissed because while still a trainee he had put a revolver to his head in an apparent suicide attempt." The Penn–Central officer tried to verify this story, but the Police Department refused to cooperate with him, advising him to proceed by letter. In rendering judgment against the respondent, the court also found that he had failed to establish "that information about his Police Department service was publicized or circulated by defendants in any way that might reach his prospective employers."

Respondent successfully appealed this decision to the Court of Appeals for the Second Circuit. That court held that the finding of no stigma was clearly erroneous. It reasoned that the information about the apparent suicide attempt was of a kind which would necessarily impair employment prospects for one seeking work as a police officer. It also decided that the mere act of making available personnel files with the employee's consent was enough to place responsibility for the stigma on the employer, since former employees had no practical alternative but to consent to the release of such information if they wished to be seriously considered for other employment.

We granted certiorari, and the parties have urged us to consider whether the report in question was of a stigmatizing nature, and whether the circumstances of its apparent dissemination were such as to fall within the language of *Board of Regents v. Roth* . . . . We find it unnecessary to reach these issues, however, because of respondent's failure to allege or prove one essential element of his case.

Assuming all of the other elements necessary to make out a claim of stigmatization under *Roth* . . . , the remedy mandated by the Due Process Clause of the Fourteenth Amendment is "an opportunity to refute the charge." . . . But if the hearing mandated by the Due Process Clause is to serve any useful purpose, there must be some factual dispute between an employer and a discharged employee which has some significant bearing on the employee's reputation. Nowhere in his pleadings or elsewhere has respondent affirmatively asserted that the report of the apparent suicide attempt was substantially false. . . . When we consider the nature of the interest sought to be protected, we believe the absence of any such allegation or finding is fatal to respondent's claim under the Due Process Clause that he should have been given a hearing. . . .

MR. JUSTICE STEWART, dissenting. . . .

The Court holds that respondent's failure to allege falsity negates his right to damages for the State's failure to give him a hearing. This holding does not appear to rest on the view that a discharged employee has no right to a hearing unless the charge against him is false. If it did, it would represent a radical departure from a principle basic to our legal system the principle that the guilty as well as the innocent are entitled to a fair trial. . . . If the charge, whether true or false, involves a deprivation of liberty, due process must accompany the deprivation. . . .

. . . In short, the purpose of the hearing, as is true of any other hearing which must precede a deprivation of liberty, is two-fold: First, to establish the truth or falsity of the charge, and second, to provide a basis for deciding what action is warranted by the facts. Even when it is perfectly clear that the charge is true, the Constitution requires that procedural safeguards be observed. For these reasons, I disagree with the Court's assertion that the purpose of the hearing is "solely" to provide the person with an opportunity to clear his name.

Even if I agreed with the Court that this was the sole purpose of the hearing, I could not agree with its holding that failure to demonstrate falsity is fatal to the employee's suit. Surely the burden should be on the State to show that failure to provide due process was harmless error because the charges were true.[7] Moreover, failure to provide a hearing

---

7. The Court's contrary approach would produce perverse results when the relief sought by the plaintiff includes an administrative hearing. To establish his right to

might give rise to damages unrelated to the possible outcome of the hearing. . . .

SHANDS v. CITY OF KENNETT

993 F.2d 1337 (8th Cir.1993).

WOLLMAN, CIRCUIT JUDGE.

[The city council dismissed the plaintiffs, who were volunteer firemen, because they attempted to undermine the authority of the Fire Chief. Without the Chief's knowledge, the plaintiffs had asked a member of the council to block the appointment of a new volunteer fireman requested by the Chief and to support instead the appointment of a friend of plaintiffs. The City's dismissal letters stated that the plaintiffs had been discharged for acts of insubordination and misconduct. The four discharged firemen appeared at a city council meeting to say they had done nothing wrong. Thereafter, the Council held a special closed session to consider the discharges. Witnesses testified concerning the reasons for the discharges, and the dismissed firemen, with the aid of counsel, were allowed to question these witnesses and make their own statements. The city council voted not to reinstate the four men. The council found that their attempt to interfere with the hiring process constituted a sufficient basis for their discharges. The council released a statement to dispel rumors and misinformation concerning the discharges. The release stated that the discharged firemen had not been accused of or dismissed for any financial misdealings, illegal activities, or activities involving moral turpitude. Rather, the discharges were the result of fire department personnel matters. Among other things, the plaintiffs alleged that the city had deprived them of a Fourteenth Amendment liberty interest without due process of law.]

. . . Plaintiffs alleged in Count II that Mayor Karsten, Councilman Talley, and Mallott had made false and stigmatizing statements about them to the news media in connection with their discharge and thus implicated their Fourteenth Amendment liberty interests. They further alleged that defendants had deprived them of procedural due process by failing to provide a fair and meaningful hearing for them to publicly clear their names.

In their motion for judgment notwithstanding the verdict, defendants argued that plaintiffs had failed to show that any stigmatizing charges were made against them in connection with their discharges. Defendants also alleged that assuming, arguendo, that such charges had been made and had thereby implicated plaintiffs' liberty interests, defendants had nonetheless afforded plaintiffs procedural due process. The district court agreed with these arguments and granted defendants' motion.

such relief, the plaintiff would have to plead and presumably prove that the charges against him are false. But once it is established that the charges are false, there is no longer any reason to hold an administrative hearing on that subject.

A government employee is entitled to procedural due process in connection with being discharged from employment only when he has been deprived of a constitutionally protected property or liberty interest. Plaintiffs alleged that they were deprived of liberty interests. To establish protected liberty interests, plaintiffs were required to establish that a city official, in connection with discharging plaintiffs, publicly made allegedly untrue charges against them that would stigmatize them so as to seriously damage their standings and associations in their community, or foreclose their freedom to take advantage of other employment opportunities.

... According to the record, Mallott was the only city official to make public statements directly concerning plaintiffs. In an interview with Linda Redeffer on April 11, 1989, Mallott said that the reason for the dismissals "was a personnel matter that was dealt with according to city policy." Also on April 11, Mallott told a television news reporter that plaintiffs had been discharged for acts of insubordination and misconduct. In a subsequent interview with Redeffer, Mallott said that plaintiffs had been dismissed because they "were insubordinate to a standing order to city policy." He explained, however, that they "were not insubordinate to a direct order from me."

We hold that these statements did not create the level of stigma required to implicate a constitutionally protected liberty interest. An employee's liberty interest is implicated where the employer levels accusations at the employee that are so damaging as to make it difficult or impossible for the employee to escape the stigma of those charges. The requisite stigma has generally been found in cases in which the employer has accused the employee of dishonesty, immorality, criminality, racism, or the like. A charge of insubordination alone is normally insufficient to implicate a liberty interest. Although misconduct could conceivably include accusations serious enough to implicate a liberty interest, the general allegation of misconduct in this case does not by itself rise to the level of constitutional stigma....

3. WHAT HEARING PROCEDURES MUST BE USED?

After one has decided that due process is implicated, the next question is what does due process require. The seminal case of *Goldberg v. Kelly*, 397 U.S. 254, 90 S.Ct. 1011, 25 L.Ed.2d 287 (1970), addressed this issue in the context of the termination of welfare benefits. Under the state system in effect, the welfare recipient was given notice of the proposal to terminate and the reasons therefor, as well as an opportunity to respond in writing, before the termination took place. After termination, the recipient was entitled to a full-blown administrative hearing equivalent to what is provided under the APA, and if successful there, was entitled to back payments for the period after termination. The Supreme Court found this inadequate. Because welfare was the last safety net and termination deprives the recipient "of the very means by which to live while he waits," the Court concluded that due process required an evidentiary hearing before termination. The Court recognized the state's interest in expedition and cost-minimization, saying that "[t]hese considerations justify the limitation of the pre-termination hearing to minimum procedural safeguards" and that it was not imposing "any procedural requirements beyond those demanded by rudimentary due process." What it required, however, was significant: timely and adequate notice detailing the reasons for the proposed termination; an effective opportunity to defend by confronting and cross-examining adverse witnesses and by presenting his own arguments and evidence orally, although informal procedures would suffice; the right to be represented by counsel, although not the right to have counsel provided; a decision that rests solely on the evidence adduced at the hearing; an impartial decisionmaker; and a statement by the decisionmaker explaining his decision and the evidence relied upon, although the statement need not be a "full opinion" or contain "formal findings of fact and conclusions of law." Thus, despite its protestations, the Court required not only a pre-termination hearing but also one that included most of the procedures associated with highly formalized adjudication.

Although *Goldberg* has never been overruled, it has for practical purposes been limited to its facts. Thus, within a year, in *Richardson v. Perales*, 402 U.S. 389, 91 S.Ct. 1420, 28 L.Ed.2d 842 (1971), the Court held that there was no right to confront or cross-examine doctors who provided written evidence in Social Security disability decisions. What had seemed so important in *Goldberg* seemed to the Court less important where credibility and veracity were not likely to be at issue. Moreover, the Court seemed impressed with the volume of cases that would be affected. Later, in *Goss v. Lopez*, 419 U.S. 565, 95 S.Ct. 729, 42 L.Ed.2d 725 (1975), where the Court held that a student in a public high school had a legitimate entitlement to continued enrollment, so that a 10–day suspension required due process, the Court found due process satisfied by minimal procedures. The Court held that due process was satisfied if the student received "oral or written notice of the charges against him and, if he denies them, an explanation of the evidence the authorities have and an opportunity to present his side of the story." The Court said there was no right to counsel, to call one's own witnesses, to confront or cross-examine witnesses against him, to an impartial decisionmaker, to a written decision, or a decision based upon evidence in a given proceeding. The Court justification for these truncated procedures was pragmatic: the harm suffered by the student was minimal and the number of such student disciplinary actions potentially large, so that the costs imposed on educational institutions would be disproportionate to the benefit received by students. This balancing approach was made explicit and given a formula a year later in the next case.

MATHEWS v. ELDRIDGE

424 U.S. 319, 96 S.Ct. 893, 47 L.Ed.2d 18 (1976).

MR. JUSTICE POWELL delivered the opinion of the Court.

The issue in this case is whether the Due Process Clause of the Fifth Amendment requires that prior to the termination of Social Security disability benefit payments the recipient be afforded an opportunity for an evidentiary hearing.

Cash benefits are provided to workers during periods in which they are completely disabled under the disability insurance benefits program created by the 1956 amendments to Title II of the Social Security Act. Respondent Eldridge was first awarded benefits in June 1968. In March 1972, he received a questionnaire from the state agency charged with monitoring his medical condition. Eldridge completed the questionnaire, indicating that his condition had not improved and identifying the medical sources, including physicians, from whom he had received treatment recently. The state agency then obtained reports from his physician and a psychiatric consultant. After considering these reports and other information in his file the agency informed Eldridge by letter that it had made a tentative determination that his disability had ceased in May 1972. The letter included a statement of reasons for the proposed termination of benefits, and advised Eldridge that he might request reasonable time in which to obtain and submit additional information pertaining to his condition.

In his written response, Eldridge disputed one characterization of his medical condition and indicated that the agency already had enough evidence to establish his disability. The state agency then made its final determination that he had ceased to be disabled in May 1972. This determination was accepted by the Social Security Administration which notified Eldridge in July that his benefits would terminate after that month. The notification also advised him of his right to seek reconsideration by the state agency of this initial determination within six months.

Instead of requesting reconsideration Eldridge commenced this action challenging the constitutional validity of the administrative procedures established by the Secretary of Health, Education, and Welfare for assessing whether there exists a continuing disability.... In support of his contention that due process requires a pretermination hearing, Eldridge relied exclusively upon this Court's decision in *Goldberg v. Kelly* which established a right to an "evidentiary hearing" prior to termination of welfare benefits....

... "[D]ue process is flexible and calls for such procedural protections as the particular situation demands." Accordingly, resolution of the issue whether the administrative procedures provided here are constitutionally sufficient requires analysis of the governmental and private interests that are affected. More precisely, our prior decisions indicate that identification of the specific dictates of due process generally requires consideration of three distinct factors: First, the private interest that will be affected by the official action; second, the risk of an erroneous deprivation of such interest through the procedures used, and the probable value, if any, of additional or substitute procedural safeguards; and finally, the Government's interest, including the function involved and the fiscal and administrative burdens that the additional or substitute procedural requirement would entail....

Since a recipient whose benefits are terminated is awarded full retroactive relief if he ultimately prevails, his sole interest is in the uninterrupted receipt of this source of income pending final administrative decision on his claim....

Only in *Goldberg* has the Court held that due process requires an evidentiary hearing prior to a temporary deprivation. It was emphasized there that welfare assistance is given to persons on the very margin of subsistence.... Eligibility for disability benefits, in contrast, is not based upon financial need. Indeed, it is wholly unrelated to the worker's income or support from many other sources, such as earnings of other family members, workmen's compensation awards, tort claims awards, savings, private insurance, public or private pensions, veterans' benefits, food stamps, public assistance, or the "many other important programs, both public and private, which contain provisions for disability payments affecting a substantial portion of the work force...."

As *Goldberg* illustrates, the degree of potential deprivation that may be created by a particular decision is a factor to be considered in assessing the validity of any administrative decisionmaking process. The potential deprivation here is generally likely to be less than in *Goldberg*, although the degree of difference can be overstated....

An additional factor to be considered here is the fairness and reliability of the existing pretermination procedures, and the probable value, if any, of additional procedural safeguards. Central to the evaluation of any administrative process is the nature of the relevant inquiry. In order to remain eligible for benefits the disabled worker must demonstrate by means of "medically acceptable clinical and laboratory diagnostic techniques," that he is unable "to engage in any substantial gainful activity by reason of any medically determinable physical or mental impairment...." In short, a medical assessment of the worker's physical or mental condition is required. This is a more sharply focused and easily documented decision than the typical determination of welfare entitlement. In the latter case, a wide variety of information may be deemed relevant, and issues of witness credibility and veracity often are critical to the decisionmaking process....

By contrast, the decision whether to discontinue disability benefits will turn, in most cases, upon "routine, standard, and unbiased medical reports by physician specialists" concerning a subject whom they have personally examined....

In striking the appropriate due process balance the final factor to be assessed is the public interest. This includes the administrative burden and other societal costs that would be associated with requiring, as a matter of constitutional right, an evidentiary hearing upon demand in all cases prior to the termination of disability benefits. The most visible burden would be the incremental cost resulting from the increased number of hearings and the expense of providing benefits to ineligible recipients pending decision. No one can predict the extent of the increase, but the fact that full benefits would continue until after such hearings would assure the exhaustion in most cases of this attractive option. Nor would the theoretical right of the Secretary to recover undeserved benefits result, as a practical matter, in any substantial offset to the added outlay of public funds. The parties submit widely varying estimates of the probable additional financial cost. We only need say that experience with the constitutionalizing of government procedures suggests that the ultimate additional cost in terms of money and administrative burden would not be insubstantial.

Financial cost alone is not a controlling weight in determining whether due process requires a particular procedural safeguard prior to some administrative decision. But the Government's interest, and hence that of the public, in conserving scarce fiscal and administrative resources is a factor that must be weighed. At some point the benefit of an additional safeguard to the individual affected by the administrative action and to society in terms of increased assurance that the action is just, may be outweighed by the cost. Significantly, the cost of protecting those whom the preliminary administrative process has identified as likely to be found undeserving may in the end come out of the pockets of the deserving since resources available for any particular program of social welfare are not unlimited.

But more is implicated in cases of this type than ad hoc weighing of fiscal and administrative burdens against the interests of a particular category of claimants. The ultimate balance involves a determination as to when, under our constitutional system, judicial-type procedures must be imposed upon administrative action to assure fairness. We reiterate the wise admonishment of Mr. Justice Frankfurter that differences in the origin and function of administrative agencies "preclude wholesale transplantation of the rules of procedure, trial and review which have evolved from the history and experience of courts." The judicial model of an evidentiary hearing is neither a required, nor even the most effective, method of decisionmaking in all circumstances. The essence of due process is the requirement that "a person in jeopardy of serious loss [be given] notice of the case against him and opportunity to meet it." All that is necessary is that the procedures be tailored, in light of the decision to be made, to "the capacities and circumstances of those who are to be heard," to insure that they are given a meaningful opportunity to present their case. . . .

We conclude that an evidentiary hearing is not required prior to the termination of disability benefits and that the present administrative procedures fully comport with due process. . . .

Notes and Questions

1. Many of the due process cases, including *Goldberg* and *Mathews*, involve the question of the appropriate procedure *before* the government action takes place, when a full administrative hearing will be available after the action. Obviously, when there are exigent circumstances, the balance in favor of more summary or no prior proceedings is greater. Thus, for example, the Court has upheld seizures of allegedly misbranded drugs or unhealthful food without a prior hearing. *Ewing v. Mytinger & Casselberry, Inc.*, 339 U.S. 594, 70 S.Ct. 870, 94 L.Ed. 1088 (1950); *North American Cold Storage Co. v. Chicago*, 211 U.S. 306, 29 S.Ct. 101, 53 L.Ed. 195 (1908). Similarly, the Court upheld a summary proceeding for the closing of a mine for safety reasons, where a full hearing was available after the fact. *Hodel v. Virginia Surface Mining Ass'n*, 452 U.S. 264, 101 S.Ct. 2352, 69 L.Ed.2d 1 (1981).

In *Cleveland Board of Education v. Loudermill*, 470 U.S. 532, 105 S.Ct. 1487, 84 L.Ed.2d 494 (1985), the Court suggested that, absent exigent circumstances, at least some pre-deprivation hearing would be required, but as in *Mathews*, the pre-deprivation hearing need not provide full protections if there is an opportunity for a full due process hearing subsequent to the deprivation. In *Gilbert v. Homar*, 520 U.S. 924, 17 S.Ct. 1807, 138 L.Ed.2d 120 (1997), however, the Court utilized the *Mathews* three-part test to clarify that, even absent exigent circumstances, a pre-deprivation hearing would not always be required to suspend an employee without pay. In *Gilbert*, a university security guard had been arrested and charged with possession of marijuana with intent to deliver while off-duty and off-campus. The guard was immediately suspended without pay and without any prior notice or hearing at all. Thereafter the charges against him were dismissed. The guard sued, alleging he had been denied due process of law because he had received no hearing before his suspension without pay. The Court held that the university had a substantial interest in immediately removing from its security force any person accused of a felony. The individual's interest was only in his uninterrupted receipt of this paycheck, because if he were ultimately cleared, he would get his pay back to the date of suspension. Moreover, there had been an "adequate assurance" that the suspension was not erroneous, because it was based upon the determination of an independent actor that there was probable cause the guard had committed the offense—the police in arresting the guard—and the mere fact of arrest for a felony (whether or not the underlying facts were true) raise a serious public concern justifying suspension.

2. Because an after-the-fact lawsuit to challenge governmental action is almost always available, the question has arisen whether such an action can satisfy due process. In *Paul v. Davis*, in which the distribution of a flyer naming a person an active shoplifter was held not to implicate due process, the Court also indicated that what the police chief had done was a common law tort of defamation, suggesting that the

plaintiff might appropriately have a tort action, rather than a claim of a constitutional violation. This concept was elaborated in *Parratt v. Taylor*, 451 U.S. 527, 101 S.Ct. 1908, 68 L.Ed.2d 420 (1981), where a prisoner sued for a deprivation of property without due process of law when the prison authorities negligently lost a hobby kit that had been sent to the prisoner in the mail. Because no pre-deprivation hearing could ever be held for a negligent action, only a post-deprivation hearing would be possible, and the Court concluded that the state's tort claims procedure would satisfy any such requirement. In *Daniels v. Williams*, 474 U.S. 327, 106 S.Ct. 662, 88 L.Ed.2d 662 (1986), the Court overruled *Parratt's* determination that the due process clause applied at all, holding that only "deliberate decisions of government officials" trigger procedural due process, eliminating cases involving negligent conduct altogether. Nevertheless, *Parratt's* determination that, at least in some circumstances, subsequent litigation might suffice to satisfy due process requirements remains.

3. At one point the Court seemed to flirt with the idea that when due process applied because of a positive grant of some entitlement from government, and that grant included particular procedures for its termination, then those procedures were all that due process could require. In *Arnett v. Kennedy*, 416 U.S. 134, 94 S.Ct. 1633, 40 L.Ed.2d 15 (1974), the Court upheld the summary pre-termination procedures applicable to firing government employees, when they were followed with a full administrative hearing after termination. Justice Rehnquist wrote the plurality opinion for himself and two others that concluded "that where the grant of a substantive right is inextricably intertwined with the limitations on the procedures which are to be employed in determining that right, a litigant . . . must take the bitter with the sweet." This view, however, never commanded a majority of the Court, and in *Cleveland Board of Education v. Loudermill*, 470 U.S. 532, 105 S.Ct. 1487, 84 L.Ed.2d 494 (1985), the Court explicitly disavowed it over Justice Rehnquist's dissent.

4. In *Walters v. National Association of Radiation Survivors*, 473 U.S. 305, 105 S.Ct. 3180, 87 L.Ed.2d 220 (1985), the Court upheld a statute that limited to $10 the fee that could be paid to an attorney who represented a veteran seeking benefits from the Veterans Administration for service-connected deaths or disabilities. The Court held that the fee limitation did not violate due process merely because it frustrated an applicant's access to legal representation. Applying *Mathews*, the Court gave "great weight" to the Government's interest at stake—Congress had limited the fee to ensure a claimant would receive the entirety of any award and to promote an informal and nonadversarial adjudicatory process. In light of this interest, the Court declared, "It would take an extraordinarily strong showing of probability of error under the present system—and the probability that the presence of attorneys would sharply diminish that possibility—to warrant holding that the fee limitation denies claimants due process of law."

The plaintiffs had presented evidence demonstrating in how many cases the VA overruled an initial decision to deny benefits. In 1978, 66,000 persons appealed an initial adverse decision and about 15 percent of these appeals were successful in the first step of the appeals process. Approximately 36,000 persons used the second (and final) step of the appeals process. About 12 percent of these applicants prevailed and another 13 percent won a remand for additional proceedings. The Court concluded, however, that this evidence failed to produce the "extraordinarily strong showing of probability of error" necessary to overcome the government's interest. The opinion explained, "It is simply not possible to determine on this record whether any of the claims of the named plaintiffs, or of other declarants who are not parties to the action, were wrongfully rejected at the [first or second appeals level], nor is it possible to quantify the 'erroneous deprivations' among the general class of rejected claimants."

The Court also considered the value that the additional procedure—having a lawyer—might have in reducing error. The success rate of an appeal depending on the type of representation of the applicant was: American Legion (16.2%), American Red Cross (16.8%), Disabled American Veterans (16.6%), Veterans of Foreign Wars (16.7%), other nonattorney (15.8%), no representation (15.2%), and attorney/agent (18.3%). The Court concluded that the difference in the success rate for lawyers as compared to other groups was not sufficient to warrant a conclusion that an attorney in VA cases is necessary to satisfy due process.

Do the statistics "prove" that the presence of lawyers would significantly improve the accuracy of the VA determinations? Are you surprised by the Court's apparent hostility to the value of lawyers?

Problem 3–6: Due Process Hearing Procedures

Based on the facts in Problem 3–5, did the law school deny Jeremy due process by refusing his requests to be accompanied by his lawyer when he addressed the Honor Code Committee and to call other students and practicing lawyers to testify? What arguments might Jeremy make? What arguments might the defendants make in response? How would you expect a court to rule?

Problem Materials

BOARD OF CURATORS OF THE UNIVERSITY OF MISSOURI v. HOROWITZ

435 U.S. 78, 98 S.Ct. 948, 55 L.Ed.2d 124 (1978).

MR. JUSTICE REHNQUIST delivered the opinion of the Court.

Respondent, a student at the University of Missouri–Kansas City Medical School, was dismissed by petitioner officials of the school during her final year of study for failure to meet academic standards. Respondent sued petitioners under 42 U.S.C. § 1983 in the United States District Court for the Western District of Missouri alleging, among other constitutional violations, that petitioners had not accorded her procedural due process prior to her dismissal.... We granted certiorari to consider what procedures must be accorded to a student at a state educational institution whose dismissal may constitute a deprivation of "liberty" or "property" within the meaning of the Fourteenth Amendment....

[Student performance in clinical rotations (*e.g.*, supervised student practice in various medical disciplines, such as pediatrics and surgery) was graded by a "Council on Evaluation," consisting of faculty and students. After Horowitz received low ratings for clinical performance during her third year of medical school, she was advanced to her final year on a probationary basis. Faculty expressed dissatisfaction with Horowitz's clinical skills, which were consistently rated below that of her classmates, and often rated as "unsatisfactory," and with her behavior, which consisted of erratic attendance at clinical sessions and a lack of concern for her personal hygiene. After she received additional critical evaluations, the Council recommended that she not be permitted to graduate, and that unless her performance improved, that she be dropped from medical school. Horowitz was then reviewed by seven practicing physicians in the area, for whom she had worked, and by additional faculty in new clinical rotations. Because these recommendations likewise were almost all negative, the Council recommended that she be dismissed from school, and the Dean concurred. Horowitz, appealed in writing to the University's Provost for Health Sciences, who sustained the school's actions after reviewing the record compiled in the earlier proceedings.]

To be entitled to the procedural protections of the Fourteenth Amendment, respondent must in a case such as this demonstrate that her dismissal from the school deprived her of either a "liberty" or a "property" interest. Respondent has never alleged that she was deprived of a property interest. Because property interests are creatures of state law, respondent would have been required to show at trial that her seat at the Medical School was a "property" interest recognized by Missouri state law. Instead, respondent argued that her dismissal deprived her of "liberty" by substantially impairing her opportunities to continue her medical education or to return to employment in a medically related field....

We need not decide, however, whether respondent's dismissal deprived her of a liberty interest in pursuing a medical career. Nor need we decide whether respondent's dismissal infringed any other interest constitutionally protected against deprivation without procedural due process. Assuming the existence of a liberty or property interest, respondent has been awarded at least as much due process as the Fourteenth Amendment requires. The school fully informed respondent of the faculty's dissatisfaction with her clinical progress and the danger that this posed to timely graduation and continued enrollment. The ultimate decision to dismiss respondent was careful and deliberate. These procedures were sufficient under the Due Process Clause of the Fourteenth Amendment....

. . . In *Goss*, this Court felt that suspensions of students for disciplinary reasons have a sufficient resemblance to traditional judicial and administrative factfinding to call for a "hearing" before the relevant school authority.... Even in the context of a school disciplinary proceeding, however, the Court stopped short of requiring a formal hearing since "further formalizing the suspension process and escalating its formality and adversary nature may not only make it too costly as a regular disciplinary tool but also destroy its effectiveness as a part of the teaching process."

Academic evaluations of a student, in contrast to disciplinary determinations, bear little resemblance to the judicial and administrative factfinding proceedings to which we have traditionally attached a full-hearing requirement.... The decision to dismiss respondent, by comparison, rested on the academic judgment of school officials that she did not have the necessary clinical ability to perform adequately as a medical doctor and was making insufficient progress toward that goal. Such a judgment is by its nature more subjective and evaluative than the typical factual questions presented in the average disciplinary decision. Like the decision of an individual professor as to the proper grade for a student in his course, the determination whether to dismiss a student for academic reasons requires an expert evaluation of cumulative information and is not readily adapted to the procedural tools of judicial or administrative decisionmaking.

Under such circumstances, we decline to ignore the historic judgment of educators and thereby formalize the academic dismissal process by requiring a hearing.... We decline to further enlarge the judicial presence in the academic community and thereby risk deterioration of many beneficial aspects of the faculty-student relationship....

OSTEEN v. HENLEY

13 F.3d 221 (7th Cir.1993).

POSNER, CHIEF JUDGE.

Late one night, as Thomas Osteen, an undergraduate at Northern Illinois University, was leaving a bar in the company of two male friends and the girlfriend of one of them, the girlfriend began "mouthing off to a male [another student] who was outside of a bar who decided to mouth off to her and the two of them mouthed out to each other and he didn't realize she was with three football players so when he realized that he was mouthing off to a young lady that was being accompanied by three football players one of which was her boyfriend, it was a little bit too late for him." (We are quoting, not Gertrude Stein, but one of the defendants, university judicial officer Larry Bolles.) "I'm told without one word, Mr. Osteen, not one word out of his mouth he stomps this guy in the head with some cowboy boots. This is what the guy said, he had on some boots and he stomped him.'' Osteen's kick or stomp broke the other student's nose. Another student, apparently a friend of the one whom Osteen had just assaulted, approached Osteen, who again without a word "broke his face with one punch.'' Osteen had broken his second nose for the night. The incident, aggravated in Bolles's mind by the fact that the woman whose honor Osteen was defending in this violent manner was not even Osteen's own girlfriend, led to Osteen's expulsion for two years and to this lawsuit (dismissed by the district court), in which Osteen challenges the expulsion as a deprivation of property without due process of law, in violation of the Fourteenth Amendment. Although it is an open question in this circuit whether a college student as distinct from an elementary school or high school student has a property right in continued attendance, the defendants have not raised it, so we shall not attempt to answer it. . . .

Bolles mailed Osteen a notice of charges and a copy of the university's student judicial code, thus initiating disciplinary proceedings. According to the code, Bolles's function as university judicial officer was to meet with Osteen and attempt to resolve the matter without a hearing, but if this failed he was to present the case against Osteen at a hearing. The two met and in Bolles's presence Osteen signed a form in which he pleaded guilty to the charges but requested a hearing on Bolles's proposed sanction, which was a two-year expulsion. The hearing was held before an appeals board consisting of the university's assistant judicial officer (i.e., assistant to Bolles) presiding and in addition one faculty member and two students. The case against Osteen was presented by Bolles, Osteen being represented by a student advocate. Osteen, his advocate, and Bolles addressed the board (we quoted part of Bolles's statement earlier), which in addition considered character references and other documents and concluded that the two-year expulsion was the proper sanction. Osteen attempted to appeal to the university's vice-president for student affairs but was told that the vice-president's authority under the judicial code had been delegated to an associate vice-president. After considering Osteen's appeal that officer upheld the expulsion but postponed it to the end of the semester. . . .

In his opening brief in this court Osteen raised just three issues. . . . The issues he raised are the defendants' failure to comply with all the requirements of the student judicial code, the interruption of himself and his advocate by the appeals board, and the denial of a right to counsel. The first point has no possible merit. As we tirelessly but unavailingly remind counsel in this court, a violation of state law (for purposes of this case the student judicial code may be treated as a state law) is not a denial of due process, even if the state law confers a procedural right. The standard of due process is federal.

As for the interruption of his student advocate, Osteen had by pleading guilty to the charges against him conceded his guilt, so the presiding officer was entitled to cut off what appeared to be an attempt to reopen the issue. Osteen was allowed to make a statement in mitigation; his advocate was interrupted only when it appeared that she was trying to revisit the issue of guilt. The interruption, designed to confine the proceeding to relevant matters, was well within the outer bounds of the presiding officer's discretionary authority over the scope of the hearing—and it is the outer bounds that the due process clause patrols.

The most interesting question is whether there is a right to counsel, somehow derived from the due process clause of the Fourteenth Amendment, in student disciplinary proceedings. An oldish case (by the standards of constitutional law at any rate) says yes, but the newer cases say no, at most the student has a right to get the advice of a lawyer; the lawyer need not be allowed to participate in the proceeding in the usual way of trial counsel, as by examining and cross-examining witnesses and addressing the tribunal. Especially when the student faces potential criminal charges (Osteen was charged with two counts of aggravated battery; the record is silent on the disposition of the charges), it is at least arguable that the due process clause entitles him to consult a lawyer, who might for example advise him to plead the Fifth Amendment. . . .

Even if a student has a constitutional right to consult counsel . . . we do not think he is entitled to be represented in the sense of having a lawyer who is permitted to examine or cross-examine witnesses, to submit and object to documents, to address the tribunal, and otherwise to perform the traditional function of a trial lawyer. To recognize such a right would force student disciplinary proceedings into the mold of adversary litigation. The university would have to hire its own lawyer to prosecute these cases and no doubt lawyers would also be dragged in—from the law faculty or elsewhere—to serve as judges. The cost and complexity of such proceedings would be increased, to the detriment of discipline as well as of the university's fisc. . . . The danger that without the procedural safeguards deemed appropriate in civil and criminal litigation public universities will engage in an orgy of expulsions is slight. The relation of students to universities is, after all, essentially that of customer to seller. That is true even in the case of public universities, though they are much less dependent upon the academic marketplace than private universities are. Northern Illinois University can't have been happy to lose a student whom it had wanted so much that it had given him a football scholarship, and who had made the team to the greater glory of the institution.

The canonical test for how much process is due, laid down by the Supreme Court in *Mathews v. Eldridge*, and applied to school or college disciplinary proceedings . . ., requires consideration of the cost of the additional procedure sought, the risk of error if it is withheld, and the consequences of error to the person seeking the procedure. The cost of judicializing disciplinary proceedings by recognizing a right to counsel is nontrivial, while the risk of an error—specifically the risk that Osteen was unjustly "sentenced"—is rather trivial. Not only has the university, as we have said, no incentive to jerry-rig its proceedings against the student—and there is no indication of that here, for even permanent expulsion would not have been an excessive sanction for Osteen's brutal and gratuitous misuse of his football player's strength. In addition the issue of the proper sanction generally and here involves no subtleties of law or fact, being judgmental rather than rule-guided, like federal sentencing before the Sentencing Guidelines. Finally, the consequence for Osteen—a nonpermanent expulsion that did not prevent him from enrolling in another college—is not so grave as to entitle him to the procedural protections thought necessary in litigation because large interests of liberty or property may be at stake.

The last point gives us the most pause, as we suspect, though the record is barren on the point, that the expulsion cost Osteen scholarship assistance that he or his family needed. But when we consider all the factors bearing on his claim to a right of counsel, we conclude that the Constitution does not confer such a right on him. We doubt that it does in any student disciplinary proceeding....

4. NEUTRAL DECISIONMAKER

Many formulations of the basic requirements of due process include the need for a neutral decisionmaker, but how neutral has been a recurring question. The following case indicates the Supreme Court's approach to this issue.

WITHROW v. LARKIN

421 U.S. 35, 95 S.Ct. 1456, 43 L.Ed.2d 712 (1975).

MR. JUSTICE WHITE delivered the opinion of the Court.

The statutes of the State of Wisconsin forbid the practice of medicine without a license from an Examining Board composed of practicing physicians. The statutes also define and forbid various acts of professional misconduct.... To enforce these provisions, the Examining Board is empowered ... to warn and reprimand, temporarily to suspend the license, and "to institute criminal action or action to revoke license when it finds probable cause therefor under criminal or revocation statute...." When an investigative proceeding before the Examining Board was commenced against him, appellee brought this suit against appellants, the individual members of the Board, seeking an injunction against the enforcement of the statutes. The District Court issued a preliminary injunction, the appellants appealed, and we noted probable jurisdiction.

... On June 20, 1973, the Board sent to appellee a notice that it would hold an investigative hearing on July 12, 1973 ... to determine whether he had engaged in certain proscribed acts....

The Board proceeded with its investigative hearing on July 12 and 13, 1973; numerous witnesses testified and appellee's counsel was present throughout the proceedings. Appellee's counsel was subsequently informed that appellee could if he wished, appear before the Board to explain any of the evidence which had been presented.

On September 18, 1973, the Board sent to appellee a notice that a "contested hearing" would be held on October 4, 1973, to determine whether appellee had engaged in certain prohibited acts and that based upon the evidence adduced at the hearing the Board would determine whether his license would be suspended temporarily . . . Appellee moved for a restraining order against the contested hearing. The District Court granted the motion on October 1, 1973. Because the Board had moved from purely investigative proceedings to a hearing aimed at deciding whether suspension of appellee's license was appropriate, the District Court concluded that a substantial federal question had arisen, namely, whether the authority given to appellants both "to investigate physicians and present charges [and] to rule on those charges and impose punishment, at least to the extent of reprimanding or temporarily suspending" violated appellee's due process rights. . . .

On November 19, 1973, the three-judge District Court found . . . that [the combination in the Board of the prosecutorial and judicial functions] was unconstitutional as a violation of due process guarantees. . . .

The District Court framed the constitutional issue, which it addressed as being whether "for the board temporarily to suspend Dr. Larkin's license at its own contested hearing on charges evolving from its own investigation would constitute a denial to him of his rights to procedural due process." . . .

Concededly, a "fair trial in a fair tribunal is a basic requirement of due process." This applies to administrative agencies which adjudicate as well as to courts. Not only is a biased decisionmaker constitutionally unacceptable but "our system of law has always endeavored to prevent even the probability of unfairness." In pursuit of this end, various situations have been identified in which experience teaches that the probability of actual bias on the part of the judge or decisionmaker is too high to be constitutionally tolerable. Among these cases are those in which the adjudicator has a pecuniary interest in the outcome and in which he has been the target of personal abuse or criticism from the party before him.

The contention that the combination of investigative and adjudicative functions necessarily creates an unconstitutional risk of bias in administrative adjudication has a much more difficult burden of persuasion to carry. It must overcome a presumption of honesty and integrity in those serving as adjudicators; and it must convince that, under a realistic appraisal of psychological tendencies and human weakness, conferring investigative and adjudicative powers on the same individuals poses such a risk of actual bias or prejudgment that the practice must be forbidden if the guarantee of due process is to be adequately implemented.

Very similar claims have been squarely rejected in prior decisions of this Court. In *FTC v. Cement Institute*, 333 U.S. 683 (1948), the Federal Trade Commission had instituted proceedings concerning the respondents' multiple basing-point delivered-price system. It was demanded that the Commission members disqualify themselves because long before the Commission had filed its complaint it had investigated the parties and reported to Congress and to the President, and its members had testified before congressional committees concerning the legality of such a pricing system. At least some of the members had disclosed their opinion that the system was illegal. The issue of bias was brought here and confronted "on the assumption that such an opinion had been formed by the entire membership of the Commission as a result of its prior official investigations."

The Court rejected the claim saying: "[T]he fact that the Commission had entertained such views as the result of its prior ex parte investigations did not necessarily mean that the minds of its members were irrevocably closed on the subject of the respondents' basing point practices. Here, in contrast to the Commission's investigations, members of the cement industry were legally authorized participants in the hearings. They produced evidence—volumes of it. They were free to point out to the Commission by testimony, by cross-examination of witnesses, and by arguments, conditions of the trade practices under attack which they thought kept these practices within the range of legally permissible business activities." In specific response to a due process argument, the Court asserted: "No decision of this Court would require us to hold that it would be a violation of procedural due process for a judge to sit in a case after he had expressed an opinion as to whether certain types of conduct were prohibited by law. In fact, judges frequently try the same case more than once and decide identical issues each time, although these issues involve questions both of law and fact. Certainly, the Federal Trade Commission cannot possibly be under stronger constitutional compulsions in this respect than a court." ...

That is not to say that there is nothing to the argument that those who have investigated should not then adjudicate. The issue is substantial, it is not new, and legislators and others concerned with the operations of administrative agencies have given much attention to whether and to what extent distinctive administrative functions should be performed by the same persons. No single answer has been reached.... For the generality of agencies, Congress has been content with § 5 of the Administrative Procedure Act, 5 U.S.C. § 554(d), which provides that no employee engaged in investigating or prosecuting may also participate or advise in the adjudicating function, but which also expressly exempts from this prohibition "the agency or a member or members of the body comprising the agency." ...

... Of course, we should be alert to the possibilities of bias that may lurk in the way particular procedures actually work in practice. The processes utilized by the Board, however, do not in themselves contain an unacceptable risk of bias. The investigative proceeding had been closed to the public, but appellee and his counsel were permitted to be present throughout; counsel actually attended the hearings and knew the facts presented to the Board. No specific foundation has been presented for suspecting that the Board had been prejudiced by its investigation or would be disabled from hearing and deciding on the basis of the evidence to be presented at the contested hearing. The mere exposure to evidence presented in nonadversary investigative procedures is insufficient in itself to impugn the fairness of the board members at a later adversary hearing. Without a showing to the contrary, state administrators "are assumed to be men of conscience and intellectual discipline, capable of judging a particular controversy fairly on the basis of its own circumstances." ...

We are of the view, therefore, that the District Court was in error when it entered the restraining order against the Board's contested hearing and when it granted the preliminary injunction based on the untenable view that it would be unconstitutional for the Board to suspend appellee's license "at its own contested hearing on charges evolving from its own investigation...." The contested hearing should have been permitted to proceed....

Notes and Questions

1. The result in *Withrow* raises the question of what sort of evidence would suffice to show prejudice. As the Court indicates, to have a predisposed view of the law involved in a case is not sufficient because judges are not disqualified from sitting in a case even if by prior rulings they have indicated a particular view of the law.

2. Where a decisionmaker has already decided the facts of a case, there can be a problem. In *Texaco v. FTC*, 336 F.2d 754 (D.C.Cir.1964), *vacated and remanded on other grounds*, 381 U.S. 739, 85 S.Ct. 1798, 14 L.Ed.2d 714 (1965), the Chairman of the Federal Trade Commission made a speech during the pendency of an unfair trade practice case against Texaco in which he indicated that the FTC was aware of illegal practices, and he specifically mentioned the type of practice involved in the Texaco case, and of the companies involved in them, and he specifically named several, including Texaco. The court held that a disinterested person "could hardly fail to conclude that he had in some measure decided that Texaco had violated the Act," and, therefore, his participation in the hearing denied due process. This case, however, is extraordinary and may only have the effect of causing more careful editing of decisionmakers' speeches.

Problem 3–7: Neutral Decisionmaker

Based on the facts in Problem 3–5, was Jeremy deprived of his right to a neutral decisionmaker? Recall that the instructor reported the violation only after the Dean's intervention, and that the Dean informed the instructor that "such action [referring to Jeremy's behavior] was a clear violation of the School's Honor Code...." The Dean also selected one member of the Honor Committee, and another member held her job at the pleasure of the Dean. After these actions, the Dean made the final determination concerning whether Jeremy violated the Code and what was an appropriate punishment.

F. JUDICIAL REVIEW

After an agency has rendered a decision in an adjudication, a disappointed party ordinarily may sue for judicial review of that decision. Review would take place in federal district court unless the agency's mandate authorized review in one or more federal courts of appeal. Thus, for example, Congress has generally authorized appellate court review for the independent agencies that conduct formal adjudication, such as the National Labor Relations Board, the Federal Communications Commission, and the Federal Trade Commission. Colloquially, one often refers to appealing an agency's decision. Indeed, there is some similarity between an appeal of a trial court's decision to an appellate court and obtaining judicial review of an agency decision.

Section 706 of the APA specifies the grounds for judicial review of any agency action, and a litigant might be able to challenge the agency's adjudicatory decision on any of the grounds listed in the APA. For example, if an agency which was bound to utilize formal adjudication did not provide an Administrative Law Judge to preside over the hearing, but instead merely provided an agency attorney, the order resulting from that adjudication could be overturned as "without observance of procedure required by law," 5 U.S.C.A. § 706(2)(D). In the context of adjudication, however, 5 U.S.C.A. § 706(2)(E) is probably the most important provision.

1. THE SUBSTANTIAL EVIDENCE STANDARD

Section 706(2)(E) provides that agency action is to be held unlawful if it is "unsupported by substantial evidence in a case subject to sections 556 and 557 of this title or otherwise reviewed on the record of an agency hearing provided by statute." While this provision also applies equally to rulemaking and adjudication, it only applies to *formal* agency action. Given the rarity of formal rulemaking, section 706(2)(E) is used primarily for review of formal adjudications. Prior to the APA, the Supreme Court apparently considered the substantial evidence test as highly deferential. Substantial evidence was "more than a mere scintilla," or "such relevant evidence as a reasonable mind might accept as adequate to support a conclusion." *Consolidated Edison Co. v. National Labor Relations Board*, 305 U.S. 197, 229, 59 S.Ct. 206, 216, 83 L.Ed. 126 (1938). After *Consolidated Edison*, the Court apparently interpreted "substantial evidence" as referring only to the evidence supporting the agency decision; it did not include any contrary evidence. Consequently, if there was "more than a mere scintilla" of evidence supporting the agency's decision, even though there might be a ton of evidence against it, a court was to uphold the agency action as supported by substantial evidence.

After the APA was passed, the Court decided that Congress had changed the prior practice. In *Universal Camera Corp. v. National Labor Relations Board*, 340 U.S. 474, 71 S.Ct. 456, 95 L.Ed. 456 (1951), the Court held that the substantial evidence test applied to the evidence in the whole record on both sides:

> To be sure, the requirement for canvassing the "whole record" in order to ascertain substantiality does not furnish a calculus of value by which a reviewing court can assess the evidence. Nor was it intended to negative the function of the Labor Board as one of those agencies presumably equipped or informed by experience to deal with a specialized field of knowledge, whose findings within that field carry the authority of an expertness which courts do not possess and therefore must respect. Nor does it mean that even as to matter not requiring expertise a court may displace the Board's choice between two fairly conflicting views, even though the court would justifiably have made a different choice had the matter been before it *de novo*. Congress has merely made it clear that a reviewing court is not barred from setting aside a Board decision when it cannot conscientiously find that the evidence supporting that decision is substantial, when viewing in a light that the record in its entirely furnishes, including the body of evidence opposed to the Board's view.

340 U.S. at 488, 71 S.Ct. at 464.

The substantial evidence standard remains, even after *Universal Camera*, a highly deferential standard. Considering the whole record, including both the evidence for and against the agency decision, substantial evidence is the equivalent of the evidence necessary to withstand a motion for a directed verdict. Thus, the court's role is not to weigh or to reweigh the evidence and determine where the preponderance lies. Instead, the court is determining whether the agency decision meets a particular legal standard—the substantial evidence standard.

You might think that a court's function in reviewing an agency's decision is similar to the review an appellate court makes of a trial court's findings of fact. The latter, however, is governed by a "clearly erroneous" standard of review, which is considered to be *less* deferential than the substantial evidence test. In *In re Zurko*, 527 U.S. 150, 119 S.Ct. 1816, 1823, 144 L.Ed.2d 143 (1999), the Court had the following to say about the difference in the two standards of review:

> This Court has described the APA court/agency "substantial evidence" standard as requiring a court to ask whether a "reasonable mind might accept" a particular evidentiary record as "adequate" to support a conclusion. It has described the court/court "clearly erroneous" standard in terms of whether a reviewing judge has a "definite and firm conviction" that an error has been committed. And it has suggested that the former is somewhat less strict than the latter. At the same time, the Court has stressed the importance of not simply rubber-stamping agency fact-finding. The

APA requires meaningful review; and its enactment meant stricter review of agency factfinding than some courts had previously concluded.

The upshot in terms of judicial review is some practical difference in outcome depending upon which standard is used. The court/agency standard, as we have said, is somewhat less strict than the court/court standard. But the difference is a subtle one—so fine that (apart from the present case) we have failed to uncover a single instance in which a reviewing court conceded that use of one standard rather than the other would have in fact produce a different result.

2. SUBSTANTIAL EVIDENCE AND THE ALJ'S CREDIBILITY FINDINGS

What weight to assign to the ALJ's decision is a particular issue involved in applying the "substantial evidence" standard to review of an agency adjudication. In the usual case involving judicial review under the "substantial evidence" test, an ALJ has first reached a decision, making findings of fact and conclusions of law, and the agency on appeal then also made a decision that includes findings of fact and conclusions of law. When both of these decisions are consistent, there is no particular problem, but if the agency makes findings inconsistent with the ALJ's, the question arises how the reviewing court should treat the ALJ's findings. Under § 557 of the APA, the agency in making its decision on review "has all the powers which it would have in making the initial decision. . . ." This authority has been interpreted to mean that the agency makes its decision *de novo* and that the agency is not required to defer to the ALJ's findings and conclusions.

In light of this *de novo* review, courts believed that the ALJ's decision was an irrelevancy in reviewing the agency's decision, but the Supreme Court in *Universal Camera* decided otherwise. The Court clarified that because the ALJ's decision was part of the whole record, a reviewing court must take it into account when assessing whether an agency has substantial evidence for its findings and conclusions. The Court explained:

> We do not require that the examiner's findings be given more weight than in reason and in light of judicial experience they deserve. The "substantial evidence" standard is not modified in any way when the [National Labor Relations] Board and its examiner disagree. We intend only to recognize that evidence supporting a conclusion may be less substantial when an impartial, experienced examiner who has observed the witnesses and lived with the case has drawn conclusions different from the Board's than when he has reached the same decision. The findings of the examiner are to be considered along with the consistency and inherent probability of testimony. The significance of his report, depending largely on the importance of credibility in the particular case. . . .

340 U.S. at 496, 71 S.Ct. at 468.

As the Supreme Court notes, a judge should take particular note of the ALJ's findings when these conclusions are based upon the demeanor of the witness in the hearing. The agency only has the cold record by which to judge the credibility of the witness; it has not seen and heard the witness. As a result, it may be difficult for an agency to avoid judicial reversal when the only evidence in favor of the agency's decision is the testimony of a witness (or witnesses) that have been discredited by the ALJ on the basis of the person's demeanor.

The next problem explores the relationship of the substantial evidence test and findings made by an ALJ. The problem cases focus on the extent to which an ALJ receives deference for findings based on the demeanor of a witness.

Problem 3–8: ALJ Findings of Fact

The General Counsel of the NLRB brought an unfair labor case against Darby, Inc., a trucking company. The General Counsel alleged that Dan Darby, the President, had made statements to Helen Jones, a driver, that violate employees' right to form, join, or assist labor organizations without being interfered with, coerced, or restrained.

Helen Jones testified that, while the Teamsters were attempting to organize Darby, Inc., Dan Darby told her on one occasion, "If the union gets in, life is going to be pretty hard for a doll like you." On another occasion, she testified that he said, "The only reason a skirt like you gets to drive that big truck is I like you. If the union gets in, you can kiss your driving goodbye." Finally, on yet another occasion, she testified that Darby said, "Those union boys won't let girls like you drive." On cross-examination, Ms. Jones could not remember exactly when those conversations took place. Moreover, she denied that she harbored a grudge against Darby because he hadn't taken her out, but he took out the secretaries.

Dan Darby denied absolutely that he said anything like what Helen Jones alleged. He testified that the only possible explanation for her story is that she may have resented him for not paying more attention to her. He admitted that he had dated secretaries of the company. He testified that Helen Jones had once asked him why he didn't like her. He indicated that he interpreted her question as a come on.

The ALJ found that the General Counsel had failed to prove that Helen Jones had been coerced, interfered with, or restrained from joining a union. The ALJ, a man, found Dan Darby's testimony credible and Helen Jones's testimony incredible. His findings were:

> I cannot help but say that Mr. Darby struck me as sincere, forthright, and candid. He admitted dating secretaries, although he is married, but denied ever making the alleged statements to Miss Jones. Moreover, in his testimony he did not use the type of language which Miss Jones attributed to him. On the other hand,

Miss Jones struck me as wholly incredible. Her manner was brusque and opinionated. Moreover, she was unable to verify the times and places where the alleged conversations took place, suggesting that she made them up.

The General Counsel has appealed the ALJ's decision to the Board. You are a staff member to a Board member who would like to reverse the ALJ. He asks you whether the Board can reverse the ALJ? If so, what does the Board need to do to maximize its chances of prevailing in judicial review?

Problem Materials

PENASQUITOS VILLAGE, INC. v. NATIONAL LABOR RELATIONS BOARD
565 F.2d 1074 (9th Cir.1977).

WALLACE, CIRCUIT JUDGE:

The National Labor Relations Board (the Board), reversing the decision of an administrative law judge, held that Penasquitos Village, Inc. and affiliated companies (Penasquitos) had ... wrongfully discharged employees [Tony Rios and Ysidro Martinez] in violation of section 8(a)(3) of the National Labor Relations Act (the Act). Penasquitos petitioned us to review and set aside the Board's order, alleging that it was not supported by substantial evidence. The Board cross-petitioned for enforcement. We refuse enforcement and set aside the order.

I.

... The dispute is basically factual, and the central legal principle requiring clarification concerns the respective and related roles of the administrative law judge, the Board and the Court of Appeals in resolving factual disputes, particularly those turning on the credibility of witnesses. . . .

We treat as conclusive the factual determinations in a Board decision if they are "supported by substantial evidence on the record considered as a whole." This statutorily mandated deference to findings of fact runs in favor of the Board, not in favor of the initial trier-of-facts, the administrative law judge. Nevertheless, the administrative law judge's findings of fact constitute a part of that whole record which we must review. We give those initial findings some weight, whether they support or contradict the Board's factual conclusions.

The most difficult problem facing the reviewing court arises when, as in this case, the Board and the administrative law judge disagree on the facts. . . .

... [W]e have found no decision, nor has one been cited to us, sustaining a finding of fact by the Board which rests solely on testimonial evidence discredited either expressly or by clear implication by the administrative law judge. A typical case demonstrating the need for independent, credited evidence is *Amco Electric v. NLRB*, 358 F.2d 370 (9th Cir.1966). There the legality of a discharge turned on a narrow question of fact: Did the discharged employee use the company's car radio to give orders to another employee or merely to contact the union steward? The trial examiner (now referred to as an administrative law judge) discredited the testimony of both the discharged employee and the employee receiving the call. The Board, however, disagreed and accepted the discharged employee's version. In refusing to enforce the Board's order against the company, we stated:

> Considering the record as a whole *the only evidence* which we believe supports the Board's findings is the [discredited] testimony of the [discharged employee]. While the Board is not bound by the credibility determinations of the trial examiner, nevertheless the probative weight which may be properly given to testimony is severely reduced when an impartial experienced examiner who has observed the witnesses and lived with the case has drawn different conclusions. . . .

We also conclude that basic policy considerations support the course these cases have taken and particularly the distinction often made in the cases between credibility determinations based on demeanor sometimes referred to as testimonial inferences and inferences drawn from the evidence itself sometimes referred to as derivative inferences. These policy considerations can be illuminated by reference to the source of the deference accorded an administrative law judge's findings and the different source of the deference accorded the Board's findings.

Weight is given the administrative law judge's determinations of credibility for the obvious reason that he or she "sees the witnesses and hears them testify, while the Board and the reviewing court look only at cold records." All aspects of the witness's demeanor—including the expression of his countenance, how he sits or stands, whether he is inordinately nervous, his coloration during critical examination, the modulation or pace of his speech and other non-verbal communication— may convince the observing trial judge that the witness is testifying truthfully or falsely. These same very important factors, however, are entirely unavailable to a reader of the transcript, such as the Board or the Court of Appeals. But it should be noted that the administrative law judge's opportunity to observe the witnesses' demeanor does not, by itself, require deference with regard to his or her derivative inferences. Observation of demeanor makes weighty only the observer's testimonial inferences.

Deference is accorded the Board's factual conclusions for a different reason—Board members are presumed to have broad experience and expertise in labor-management relations. Further, it is the Board to which Congress has delegated administration of the Act. The Board, therefore, is viewed as particularly capable of drawing inferences from the facts of a labor dispute. Accordingly, it has been said that a Court of Appeals must abide by the Board's derivative inferences, if drawn from not discredited testimony, unless those inferences are "irrational," "tenuous" or "unwarranted." As already noted, however, the Board, as a reviewing body, has little or no basis for disputing an administrative law judge's testimonial inferences. . . .

We emphasize that we do not hold that the administrative law judge's determinations of credibility based on demeanor are conclusive on the Board. Many circuits, including ours, have held that they are not. We simply observe that the special deference deservedly afforded the administrative law judge's factual determinations based on testimonial inferences will weigh heavily in our review of a contrary finding by the Board. . . .

Recognition of the distinction between testimonial inferences and derivative inferences, and an appreciation of the different sources of deference accorded the Board and the administrative law judge, provide helpful guidance in those cases where the Board and the administrative law judge disagree about the facts. That recognition and appreciation do not, however, eliminate all difficulty for the reviewing court. Cases may still arise where the administrative law judge's position is well supported by testimonial inferences, while the contrary position of the Board is equally well supported by valid derivative inferences.

II.

Applying these principles of judicial review to the present case, we conclude that the record considered as a whole does not contain substantial evidence of unfair labor practices. . . .

B.   *The Discharges*

It is axiomatic that an employer's discharge of an employee because of his union activities or sympathies violates section 8(a)(3) of the Act. . . . The determinative factual issue, therefore, is the employer's motive.

In this case, the administrative law judge and the Board disagreed on Penasquitos' motive. Whether, in light of this disagreement, the Board's conclusion is sustainable because it is based on substantial evidence is an extremely close question. We conclude, however, that the Board's finding of improper motive cannot be sustained, primarily because a significant number of the Board's derivative inferences were drawn from discredited testimony.

The keystone of the administrative law judge's finding of proper motive was his conviction that [the employees' supervisor, Zamora,] told the truth. Zamora testified that he observed Rios and Martinez working slowly and watching several women sunbathe in bikinis some distance from the employees' worksite. Upset with their performance, Zamora approached Rios and Martinez and stated that "if you want to see girls wearing bikinis there were some better ones at the beach." Zamora then left, verified with his superior that he had authority to fire, returned and discharged the two men. At the hearing before the administrative law judge, Martinez admitted that he was working at a slow pace on the day he was fired.

The administrative law judge relied on other evidence also. Several months prior to the discharge, Zamora and another supervisor watched for 5 or 10 minutes while Rios and two other employees stood under a tree, doing no work. When Zamora approached and demanded an explanation, the employees stated that they had no work to do and were waiting for quitting time. Zamora then suspended them, a fact initially denied by the mendacious Rios during cross-examination, but later clearly established.

In reaching a contrary conclusion regarding Zamora's motive, the Board relied on a variety of inferences. First, the Board transferred to Zamora's action in discharging Rios and Martinez the anti-union animus it found in his alleged threats and unlawful interrogations. But, . . . that finding of anti-union animus was [itself] not supported by substantial evidence [because that finding relied on the Board's contrary view, to that of the Examiner, of the credibility of witnesses to the alleged threats and interrogations]. The Board also ascribed an improper motive to Zamora for the discharge because of [other] alleged statements. . . . Again, the witnesses testifying about that incident were not credited by the administrative law judge, thus vitiating the inference the Board attempted to draw from it.

The Board also relied on the fact that Martinez and Rios had signed authorization cards for the union and that Cuevas had informed Zamora that those two, among others, were the leaders of the organizing effort. But against this must be placed the credited testimony of Zamora that he was unconcerned about who was doing the organizing because "I thought they were all in the Union. . . ."

The Board drew two inferences, however, from uncontroverted facts. First, the discharge was abrupt. Rios and Martinez received no warning prior to their discharge that a failure to speed up their work would result in termination. Second, the discharge came only two days after the Board's Regional Director issued a Decision and Direction of Election ordering an election among the Penasquitos employees under Zamora's supervision. These derivative inferences undoubtedly carry weight, which is not diminished by the fact that the administrative law judge drew a contrary inference from the timing of the discharge. As noted before, special deference is accorded the Board when, in the application of its expertise and experience, it derives such inferences from the facts of a labor dispute.

But in this case, credibility played a dominant role. The administrative law judge's testimonial inferences reduce significantly the substantiality of the Board's contrary derivative inferences. Particularly, removing the Board's finding of anti-union animus based upon alleged unlawful threats and interrogations leaves poorly substantiated the Board's other conclusion that the discharges were improperly motivated. Considering the record as a whole, we conclude that the Board's conclusion that Penasquitos committed unlawful labor practices is not supported by substantial evidence and must, therefore, be set aside.

DUNIWAY, CIRCUIT JUDGE (dissenting in part):

[I have] reservations relat[ing] to Judge Wallace's adoption of the dichotomy between "credibility determinations based on demeanor … *testimonial inferences*" and those based on "inferences drawn from the evidence itself … *derivative inferences*. . . ." … Judge Wallace is careful to emphasize that the administrative law judge's determinations of credibility are not conclusive, but I am concerned lest the dichotomy that he adopts may result in future decisions that are merely mechanical applications of labels, which hinder rather than help the intelligent and principled application or growth of the law. I fear that Judge Wallace's opinion may have just such an effect, one which, I am sure, he does not intend, and which he properly disavows. . . .

In his opinion, Judge Wallace fleshes … out [his view of testimonial inferences]:

> All aspects of the witnesses's demeanor including the expression of his countenance, how he sits or stands, whether he is inordinately nervous, his coloration during critical examination, the modulation or pace of his speech and other non-verbal communication may convince the observing trial judge that the witness is testifying truthfully or falsely. . . .

Here is where I begin to have difficulty. I venture to suggest that, as to every one of the factors that Judge Wallace lists, one trier of fact may take it to indicate that the witness is truthful and another may think that it shows that the witness is lying.

I am convinced, both from experience as a trial lawyer and from experience as an appellate judge, that much that is thought and said about the trier of fact as a lie detector is myth or folklore. Every trial lawyer knows, and most trial judges will admit, that it is not unusual for an accomplished liar to fool a jury (or, even, heaven forbid, a trial judge) into believing him because his demeanor is so convincing. The expression of his countenance may be open and frank; he may sit squarely in the chair, with no squirming; he may show no nervousness; his answers to questions may be clear, concise and audible, and given without hesitation; his coloration may be normal neither pale nor flushed. In short, he may appear to be the trial lawyer's ideal witness. He may also be a consummate liar. In such a case, the fact finder may fit Iago's description of Othello:

> The Moor is of a free and open nature, That thinks men honest that but seem to be so;

> And will as tenderly be led by the nose as asses are.

(Othello, Act 1, Sc. 3, 1. 405–8)

On the other hand, another fact finder seeing and hearing the same witness may conclude that he is just too good a testifier, that he is an expert actor, and that he is also a liar.

Conversely, many trial lawyers, and some trial judges, will admit that the demeanor of a perfectly honest but unsophisticated or timid witness may be or can be made by an astute cross-examiner to be such that he will be thought by the jury or the judge to be a liar. He may be unable to face the cross-examiner, the jury, or the judge; he may slouch and squirm in the chair; he may be obviously tense and nervous; his answers to questions may be indirect, rambling, and inaudible; he may hesitate before answering; he may alternately turn pale and blush. In short, he may, to the trier of fact, be a liar, but in fact be entirely truthful. Again, however, another fact finder, seeing and hearing the same witness, may attribute his demeanor to the natural timidity of the average not very well educated and non-public sort of person when dragged to court against his will and forced to testify and face a hostile cross-examiner, and conclude that the witness is telling the truth.

While there are innumerable cases that state and restate the importance of a witness's demeanor to the trier of fact, there are very few that deal with the proper effect of this or that aspect of demeanor. Those that I can find tend to confirm my view that myth and folklore are involved. . . .

I write to suggest that Judge Wallace's dichotomy should not be taken to protect the myth and folklore behind an almost impenetrable wall. I do not want fact finders to believe that to make their findings almost totally unassailable they need only use the right incantation: "I don't (or I do) believe him because of his demeanor," or "on the basis of testimonial inferences."

I doubt if there are many cases in which the fact finder relies on demeanor alone. There may not be any; I hope that there are none. I think that in every case in which he thinks about what he is doing, the fact finder should and does consider both the demeanor of the witness and what he says—the content of his testimony—and weighs those factors in relation to the fact finder's knowledge of life's realities, the internal consistency of what the witness is saying, and its consistency, or lack of it, with the other evidence in the case, testimonial, documentary, and physical. The fact finding as to credibility of the witness should be, and is, based on all of these things. Judge Wallace's dichotomy seems to me to give to demeanor a more important effect than it ought to be given, considering the inherent ambiguities in demeanor itself. Anyone who really believes that he can infallibly determine credibility solely on the basis of observed demeanor is naive. . . .

I do not concur in part II B. As Judge Wallace observes, the question is "extremely close." In such a case, I give more weight to the experience and expertise of the Board than he does. I refer particularly to the two uncontradicted facts, the abruptness and the timing of the discharges. I cannot say that the inferences that the Board drew from these facts are "irrational" or "tenuous" or "unwarranted," or "arbitrary."

I would enforce that part of the Board's order that deals with the discharges of Rios and Martinez.

CHOY, CIRCUIT JUDGE (concurring):

I concur in the results reached by Judge Wallace. . . .

However, I share the concern that Judge Duniway feels about Judge Wallace's treatment of demeanor evidence and testimonial inferences. I, therefore, concur in Judge Duniway's eloquent exposition of his reservations contained in part I of his concurring and dissenting opinion.

JACKSON v. VETERANS ADMINISTRATION

768 F.2d 1325 (Fed.Cir.1985).

NIES, CIRCUIT JUDGE.

Based on five separate incidents of misconduct, Mr. Jackson was removed from his supervisory position with the Veterans Administration for sexual harassment of a subordinate. Following a hearing before the presiding official designated to hear the appeal, the presiding official reversed Mr. Jackson's removal. The presiding official heard testimony from a number of witnesses relevant to each of five alleged incidents of misconduct, and concluded that none of the incidents was established by the requisite preponderance of the evidence. Upon review at the request of the agency, the board reversed the decision of the presiding official. The board concluded that two incidents (A and D) were supported by a preponderance of the evidence, and that the penalty of removal was not unreasonable based only on those occurrences when Mr. Jackson's past disciplinary record was also considered. Mr. Jackson appealed to this court. . . .

Incident A

One incident found by the board to have been proved is that Mr. Jackson kissed a subordinate employee, Ms. LaSalle, while she was talking on the telephone. At the hearing, Ms. LaSalle testified that, while she was sitting on the floor in a basement hallway talking to her roommate on the telephone, Mr. Jackson walked up and kissed her. Mr. Jackson had never done this to her before, and Ms. LaSalle testified that she had done nothing to encourage him. Ms. LaSalle testified that Mr. Jackson entered the basement hallway through some usually closed double doors, but she did not see or hear him until he bent down to kiss her. She testified that the incident occurred shortly after her roommate moved in at the end of August (1981) and thought the date of the incident was the end of September. Although offended, she did not report the incident to appropriate authorities until more than a year later when she was asked about it by an investigator.

The roommate to whom Ms. LaSalle was speaking at the time of the alleged kiss was Mr. Kester. Mr. Kester testified that, during the subject phone conversation, he heard what he thought was a kiss, and Ms. LaSalle told him Mr. Jackson kissed her. He estimated that the subject phone conversation occurred in about the first week of September; that it might have occurred in the second week; but that it was not in the third or fourth weeks of that month. He did not hear any door slam during the subject telephone conversation.

Mr. Jackson testified at the hearing, denying that he kissed Ms. LaSalle. He testified that it would have been impossible for him to surprise Ms. LaSalle, as she claims, because the doors through which he would have entered the area make a lot of noise.

Mr. Knopp, an Acting Supervisor, testified that he works in the basement where the alleged kiss occurred. He was familiar with the doors through which one entered the hallway where the phone was located. Mr. Knopp testified to the effect that if one opened a door and let it go, it could be heard from one end of the hallway to the other.

Having considered the testimony pertaining to the kiss, the presiding official concluded:

In reviewing this entire matter, I find that Ms. LaSalle, was unclear as to when the action took place. I further find that her statement as to the approximate time and the statement by her former roommate were in direct conflict. I find no reason to disbelieve the appellant when he testified that he had not kissed Ms. LaSalle while she was on the phone. Accordingly, I find that the agency has not supported this charge by the preponderance of the evidence.

The board reversed the above finding for the following reason:

Despite appellant's denial, the record contains the subordinate's testimony and the testimony of the other person on the telephone regarding this incident. While neither of these witnesses could recall the exact date of the kiss, their testimony is consistent, and corroborates the agency's charge. Thus, the Board finds that this reason is supported by the requisite preponderant evidence.

Incident D

The second basis for finding sexual harassment by Mr. Jackson involved his repeatedly asking Ms. LaSalle for a kiss in response to her periodic requests to leave a few minutes early on her regular bowling night. In connection with this charge, Ms. LaSalle testified that she went bowling on Tuesday nights during September and October of 1981. On those occasions, a Ms. Herring, another VA Hospital employee, would come to the research building and wait for Ms. LaSalle to get off work. Ms. LaSalle testified that, when she asked for Mr. Jackson's permission to leave early, he would ask for a kiss in return. She testified, however, that she never actually had to give him a kiss in order to leave.

Ms. Herring testified that she did go to the research building on bowling nights to wait for Ms. LaSalle. She testified that they would occasionally ask Mr. Jackson if Ms. LaSalle could leave early. Ms. Herring testified that his response, on a few occasions, was "Sure, if you give me a little kiss." She stated that she and Ms. LaSalle would usually just look at him and laugh. Mr. Jackson denied ever having made such requests.

In regard to this incident, the presiding official made no mention of Ms. Herring's corroborative testimony. Instead, the presiding official analyzed the record as follows:

> In his testimony, appellant was not evasive, nor did he seem insincere. Accordingly, I again find that I have contradictory evidence and I have no reason to disbelieve appellant in his denials. Moreover, Ms. LaSalle testified that it had not been her idea to file charges against the appellant. It had been suggested to her by a third person. In view of the uncertainness of Ms. LaSalle in the exact time of the alleged offenses, Ms. LaSalle's statement that she had not been the person to want to file charges, and appellant's own denials, I find that the agency has not sustained this charge by the preponderance of the evidence. Accordingly, this charge is dismissed.

On review, the board stated that "the testimony of another co-worker [Ms. Herring], who was present, is sufficient to establish" the alleged misconduct by preponderant evidence....

Analysis

[O]n appeal to this court, when a finding by the presiding official of this nature has been reversed by the board, we cannot sustain the board's decision unless the board has articulated a sound reason, based on the record, for its contrary evaluation of the testimonial evidence. The board is not free simply to disagree with the presiding official's assessment of credibility....

Applying these principles to the present case, the issue before this court becomes whether or not the board's evaluation of the weight of the evidence is reasonable (i.e., supported by substantial evidence) taking into consideration that the presiding official, who heard the witnesses, had evaluated the agency's evidence as insufficient to meet the preponderance of evidence standard.

As an initial matter, it must be noted that the presiding official made no determination that Ms. LaSalle's and Mr. Kester's testimony respecting Incident A (the kiss at the basement telephone) was not credible because of their demeanor. Rather, the testimony was rejected expressly on the basis of the content of their testimony. In reviewing that testimony, the board discounted the importance of their recollection as to the precise date and time that the incident occurred. Ordinarily, we would find the reasons articulated by the board entirely reasonable as a basis for reversing a credibility determination. The testimony of Ms.

LaSalle and Mr. Kester was consistent in the important matter—that the incident occurred. Had Mr. Jackson not testified, we would have no difficulty affirming the board. However, the board gave no reason for rejecting Mr. Jackson's testimony while the presiding official favorably commented on his demeanor.

Under these circumstances, we cannot agree that a reasonable fact-finder would accept the agency's proof as sufficient to establish by a preponderance of the evidence, i.e., as more likely than not, that the incident occurred, apart from a credibility determination based on demeanor. Mr. Kester had no knowledge of what actually happened except what Ms. LaSalle told him. In our view, such testimony does not raise the agency's entire evidence to the level of a preponderance considering the entirety of the record. In essence, there is only Ms. LaSalle vis-a-vis Mr. Jackson and no basis for the board to choose between them. Having rejected the presiding official's rationale on credibility, the matter could have been remanded for a redetermination. However that may be, it was not, and we are faced, in effect, with conflicting determinations concerning credibility. On that matter, the presiding official is without question the better judge of who to believe. Thus, with respect to the decision by the board on incident A, we conclude that substantial evidence does not support the board's decision.

With respect to incident D, requests for kisses from Ms. LaSalle, we hold that the board reasonably found that the agency established the facts by a preponderance of the evidence. This incident—in contrast to incident A—was the subject of direct testimony by another witness to the events, Ms. Herring. The analysis by the presiding official failed to take her testimony into account. The presiding official did not discredit it, but ignored it. Contrary to petitioner's argument, the board did not simply overturn the presiding official's credibility determination. Rather, the board's weighing of the evidence of record was more complete. Thus, we hold that the board's holding that the preponderance of the evidence supports this basis for the charge against petitioner is reasonable or, in the terms of the statute, is "supported by substantial evidence."

Notes and Questions

1. As you read, an agency has *de novo* decisionmaking authority under the APA, which means it does not have to defer to the ALJ's findings and conclusions. Why did Congress vest an agency with this authority? How is the situation different than appellate judicial review of a trial court decision in which the appellate court will defer to the trial court's findings and conclusions?

2. Agencies can choose to defer to an ALJ's findings and conclusions, and sometimes they formally decide to do so. In *Brinks, Inc. v. Herman*, 148 F.3d 175 (2d Cir.1998), for example, the court reversed a decision by the Department of Labor because the Department's regulations required the Secretary to affirm an ALJ's finding and conclusions if

they were supported by "substantial evidence." The ALJ had held that Brinks had not fired an employee because he complained about safety violations at the company, which would have been a violation of the Surface Transportation Assistance Act, which protects whistle-blowers who identify safety problems associated with interstate trucking. The ALJ had found that the employee was fired because of insubordination, and the court held that this conclusion was supported by substantial evidence. Why might the Department of Labor adopt a regulation that deprived it of *de novo* review of an ALJ's findings and conclusions?

3. As you read earlier, some states deny agencies the authority to make final decisions in at least some cases. In these states, the ALJ's decision is appealed directly to a state court or to a separate "administrative court" and its decisions can be appealed directly to the state courts. Should agencies have an opportunity to affirm or reverse an ALJ's decisions? Assuming that a state opts for direct judicial review of an ALJ's decisions, what should be the scope of review? *See* Jim Rossi, *ALJ Final Orders on Appeal: Balancing Independence With Accountability*, 19 J. NAT'L ASSOC. OF ADMIN. LAW JUDGES 1, 13–14 (Fall, 1999) (arguing that state courts that directly review ALJ's findings and conclusions should not engage in deferential review). If a state legislative requires state courts to treat ALJ decisions like the courts treat the decisions of a lower court, have such states effectively created a new court system?

3. MIXED QUESTIONS OF LAW AND FACT

The "substantial evidence" standard applies when there is a dispute concerning the facts found by the agency. If, however, there is a legal issue, a different standard applies. Section 706 authorizes a court to hold unlawful and set aside agency action that is unconstitutional, "in excess of statutory jurisdiction, authority, or limitations, or short of statutory right", or "otherwise not in accordance with law." 5 U.S.C. §§ 706(2)(A)–(C).

A question of fact relates to disputed facts and the resolution of this dispute does not require reference to the statute under which the agency is operating. For example, a typical question presented in hearings at the National Labor Relations Board is whether a person was fired because of union activity or because the person was a bad worker. This issue can be resolved without any reference to the National Labor Relations Act. By comparison, a legal issue is an issue that can be resolved without any consideration of the facts in a particular case. For example, if the law makes discharge of an employee for engaging in union activities an unlawful labor practice, it is a question of law whether this prohibition requires that the employer's motivation for the discharge to be solely or only partially based on the employee's union activity to make it illegal.

A large number of issues, however, do not fall conveniently into one or the other of these two camps. In the next case, the Supreme Court considered what scope of review to apply to such mixed questions of law and fact.

NATIONAL LABOR RELATIONS BOARD v. HEARST

322 U.S. 111, 64 S.Ct. 851, 88 L.Ed. 1170 (1944).

MR. JUSTICE RUTLEDGE delivered the opinion of the Court.

[The publishers of four Los Angeles daily newspapers refused to bargain collectively with a union representing "newsboys" who distributed newspapers on the streets of that city. Despite their name, "newsboys" were adults who sold the newspapers, full or part-time, in a variety of locations including street corners. The union filed an unfair labor charge against the publishers with the National Labor Relations Board. The Board rejected the publishers' contention that the newsboys were not "employees" within the meaning of the Act. The Act requires employers to engage in collective bargaining with their "employees" but Congress did not define the scope of the term "employee."]

The principal question is whether the newsboys are "employees." Because Congress did not explicitly define the term, respondents [i.e., the publishers] say its meaning must be determined by reference to common-law standards. In their view "common-law standards" are those the courts have applied in distinguishing between "employees" and "independent contractors" when working out various problems unrelated to the Wagner Act's purposes and provisions. . . .

II.

[The Court rejected the respondent's interpretation. It determined that the terms and purposes of the National Labor Relations Act, as well as its legislative history, indicated that Congress had not meant to define the term "employee" under the Act in the same way that it had been defined by common law. According to the Court, Congress intended to provide the opportunity to join a union to some persons who might be considered "independent contractors" under the common law definition.]

To eliminate the causes of labor disputes and industrial strife, Congress thought it necessary to create a balance of forces in certain types of economic relationships. . . . Congress recognized those economic relationships cannot be fitted neatly into the containers designated "employee" and "employer" which an earlier law had shaped for different purposes. Its Reports on the bill disclose clearly the understanding that "employers and employees not in proximate relationship may be drawn into common controversies by economic forces," and that the very disputes sought to be avoided might involve "employees [who] are at times brought into an economic relationship with employers who are not their employers." In this light, the broad language of the Act's definitions, which in terms reject conventional limitations on such conceptions as "employee," "employer," and "labor dispute," leaves no doubt that its applicability is to be determined broadly, in doubtful situations, by underlying economic facts rather than technically and exclusively by previously established legal classifications. . . .

It is not necessary in this case to make a completely definitive limitation around the term "employee." That task has been assigned primarily to the agency created by Congress to administer the Act. Determination of "where all the conditions of the relation require protection" involves inquiries for the Board charged with this duty. Everyday experience in the administration of the statute gives it familiarity with the circumstances and backgrounds of employment relationships in various industries, with the abilities and needs of the workers for self organization and collective action, and with the adaptability of collective bargaining for the peaceful settlement of their disputes with their employers. The experience thus acquired must be brought frequently to bear on the question who is an employee under the Act. Resolving that question, like determining whether unfair labor practices have been committed, "belongs to the usual administrative routine" of the Board.

In making that body's determinations as to the facts in these matters conclusive, if supported by evidence, Congress entrusted to it primarily the decision whether the evidence establishes the material facts. Hence in reviewing the Board's ultimate conclusions, it is not the court's function to substitute its own inferences of fact for the Board's, when the latter have support in the record. Undoubtedly questions of statutory interpretation, especially when arising in the first instance in judicial proceedings, are for the courts to resolve, giving appropriate weight to the judgment of those whose special duty is to administer the questioned statute. But where the question is one of specific application of a broad statutory term in a proceeding in which the agency administering the statute must determine it initially, the reviewing court's function is limited. . . . [T]he Board's determination that specified persons are "employees" under this Act is to be accepted if it has "warrant in the record" and a reasonable basis in law.

. . . Stating that "the primary consideration in the determination of the applicability of the statutory definition is whether effectuation of the declared policy and purposes of the Act comprehend securing to the individual the rights guaranteed and protection afforded by the Act," the Board concluded that the newsboys are employees. The record sustains the Board's findings and there is ample basis in the law for its conclusion. . . .

Notes and Questions

1. The scope of review chosen by *Hearst* recognizes that a court has two functions when it reviews a mixed question of law and fact. First, the court reviews the facts found by the agency and determines whether these conclusions have a "warrant in the record." In *Hearst*, the Court had to determine whether the record supported the NLRB's conclusions

about the working conditions of the newsboys, such as the terms of their compensation and the number of hours that they worked. Second, the court reviews the agency's explanation for its decision to decide whether it has a "reasonable basis in law." In *Hearst*, the court reviewed the NLRB's justification of why, in light of the facts that the agency found, it would serve the goals and purposes of the National Labor Relations Act to permit employees to join a labor union.

2. Not all courts clearly separate legal and factual issues in mixed questions of law and fact. Moreover, many courts refer to the scope of review of either, or both, issues as "substantial evidence." These courts will ask, for example, whether the agency's explanation for its decision is supported by substantial evidence. The court's function, however, is the same. It determines whether the agency has justified why the outcome is consistent with the agency's mandate.

For example, the general requirement for workers compensation payments is that a worker's injury or death "arose out of or in connection with employment." A celebrated case, *O'Leary v. Brown–Pacific–Maxon, Inc.*, 340 U.S. 504, 71 S.Ct. 470, 95 L.Ed. 483 (1951), applied the substantial evidence standard in resolving this issue. Brown Pacific maintained for its employees on Guam a recreation center near the shoreline, along which ran a channel so dangerous that signs prohibiting swimming were erected. An employee who was spending a weekend afternoon at the center saw two men standing on the reefs beyond the channel signaling for help. He dove in and attempted a rescue but drowned instead. The question was whether this qualified for workers compensation. Under the above taxonomy, this issue is clearly neither a question of fact nor a question of law. The facts concerning how the employee died were not disputed. Thus, there was no purely factual dispute. Likewise, there was no purely legal dispute. The determination of whether the employee's death "arose out of or in connection" with his employment could not be resolved without consideration of the facts concerning how and when he died. Thus, the issue involved applying the legal rules to the facts at hand and exercising judgment to determine whether they fit or not. The Court said that the agency's findings "are to be accepted unless they are unsupported by substantial evidence on the record considered as a whole." *Id.* at 508.

3. Although the courts may not indicate how they determine whether an issue is a mixed question of law and fact, judges employ in effect a two step approach similar to the one that the Supreme Court employs in *Chevron*. A court will first ask whether Congress has defined the term or whether it has delegated that responsibility to the agency. To determine if Congress has defined the term, a court will look at legal sources. It will consider the statutory language and the structure of the statute, and it may consider the goals of the statute and its legislative history. If the court is satisfied that Congress has defined the term from these sources, it will conclude that the issue is "purely" legal and apply the legislative definition. In *Hearst*, you will recall, the Court determined from the language of the Act and its legislative history that Congress had

"not" adopted the common law definition of "employee" or any other definition of that term. If the Court is satisfied that Congress has not defined the term, it will conclude, as did *Hearst*, that the "question is one of specific application of a broad statutory term" and that deferential review is therefore appropriate.

The following problem raises the issue just discussed. You are asked to apply the substantial evidence standard in the context of a mixed question of law and fact.

Problem 3–9: Mixed Question of Law and Fact

The Tennessee Valley Authority employed a ranger named Lund to protect park and forest areas owned by TVA against illegal hunting. He was expected to do much of his patrolling at night, and TVA furnished him with a vehicle the interior of which could be converted into a bed to allow him to rest or sleep while in the woods. Lund one morning was found dead in the automobile. Next to his body was the dead body of a woman, whose car was parked next to his; the two bodies were clad respectively in shorts and panties and were partially covered by a blanket. The deaths were caused by carbon monoxide poisoning and the time of death was between 1 A.M. and 3 A.M. The ranger had no fixed hours of employment, and he had been on patrol the preceding evening. The car was parked in an area which previously had been under surveillance for illegal spotlight killing of deer, and there was no rule against having company while on duty. The ranger's uniform, boots, and gun were out of reach underneath the seat of his car. He had told his wife he was going on patrol and would not be home that night.

The ranger's widow seeks compensation under the Longshore and Harbor Workers' Compensation Act, as amended to apply to TVA employees. That act provides for the employer, here TVA, to pay workers compensation for any injury or death of an employee "arising out of and in the course of employment." In Lund's case, the agency denied compensation, finding that his death had not arisen out of his employment, because he was engaged in immoral activity at the time of death rather than being engaged in patrolling. Lund's widow seeks judicial review. If you represent Lund's widow, what arguments can you effectively make? If you represent TVA, what arguments can you effectively make?

Problem Materials

EVENING STAR NEWSPAPER COMPANY v. KEMP

533 F.2d 1224 (D.C.Cir.1976).

VAN PELT, SENIOR DISTRICT JUDGE.

The petitioner, Evening Star Newspaper Company (Evening Star), seeks reversal of an order awarding to the widow of an employee, compensation under the Longshoremen's and Harbor Workers' Compensation Act, as made applicable to the District of Columbia by Congress.... Following an evidentiary hearing the Administrative Law Judge found for respondent widow. This ruling was affirmed by the Department of Labor's Benefits Review Board. We affirm....

The decedent, Nathan Kemp, was employed by the Evening Star as a truck driver delivering newspapers. He also owned a taxicab which he operated part-time.

On August 10, 1971, while Mr. Kemp was on pay status with the Evening Star, he was killed by a gunshot wound under the following circumstances:

Kemp had returned from his first delivery run at about 3:30 p.m. on that day. He was not due to make another run until 4:25 p.m. Thus he had approximately one hour in which he could do as he pleased. However, he was still on pay status ("on the clock"). From employee Ward he learned that his taxicab, which was parked in a lot one-half block from the Star building, had been hit. Ward suggested to Kemp getting Andrews, who was another "on the clock" driver and who did body work. All three then walked over to the lot to check out the accident.

Andrews looked at the dent in the taxicab and stated that if he had a rubber mallet he could fix it enough for Kemp to get through inspection. Kemp got the gun out of the car and Ward and Kemp began playing with the gun. The three men then left in the taxicab to go to the New Star Garage about three blocks away to get the rubber mallet. It is not clear whether decedent placed the handgun back in the trunk or placed it under the seat of the taxicab.

While at the garage, Andrews began working on the car and the other two men again got the gun out. It is unclear whether Ward or the decedent got the gun out of the car the second time. In the course of handling the gun, it went off while Ward was holding it. Ward's testimony was: "And like I had the gun in my hand, and he said, Oh, man, come on, let's stop this playing. And he made a motion towards me and hit my hand and the gun went off." Mr. Kemp was killed by the shot.

At the hearing before the Administrative Law Judge there was testimony that the decedent carried the gun because he was afraid of being robbed in his taxicab and because he was afraid of things that might happen while he was driving the Evening Star's delivery truck. He had carried the gun on at least one delivery trip and his wife a couple of times noticed that he was carrying the gun when she went to the Evening Star building to pick up his pay check. There was also testimony that other Evening Star drivers had been called names or had been threatened on their delivery runs. However, none carried guns on their trucks, although some carried them in their cars.

The drivers were required to deliver papers into some rural areas and were sometimes required to carry money for the company. The trucks they drove were very similar to the trucks regularly used to carry the Evening Star's money.

Evidence was also presented at the hearing concerning the "free time" the drivers had between their runs. During this time they remained "on the clock" for pay computation but were allowed to leave and do whatever they wanted. Frequently the drivers were required to go to the garage, the scene of the accident, for various employer-related reasons. On occasion the drivers had gone to the garage to work on their private automobiles, to consult with the Evening Star's mechanics about such automobiles, and to borrow tools. The Evening Star's supervisory personnel were aware of these activities and permitted them to occur.

Based on these facts, the Administrative Law Judge awarded compensation and the Benefits Review Board agreed with such order.

We must consider two basic rules in deciding this appeal. The first concerns the scope of judicial review. It is well-settled that if the Administrative Law Judge's decision is supported by the evidence as a whole and is not inconsistent with the law, it should be upheld.

> "The rule of judicial review has therefore emerged that the inferences drawn by the Deputy Commissioner [Administrative Law Judge] are to be accepted unless they are irrational or unsupported by substantial evidence on the record . . . as a whole."

The second rule is the strong legislative and judicial policy favoring awards in workmen's compensation cases. . . .

We conclude that the Administrative Law Judge's finding that the decedent's death resulted from injuries sustained in the course of and arising out of his employment is supported by substantial evidence, and that, under the rules just mentioned and the cited portion of the Act, we should affirm the Benefits Review Board.

The decedent was injured during an enforced lull, which was a condition of his employment. His presence at the Star Garage was not against company policy. On the contrary, it was acquiesced in by the employer.

Viewing the facts in a light most favorable to decedent and his widow, it appears that he was killed by a fellow employee who was handling the decedent's personal handgun. At the time decedent was on pay status with the Evening Star and was on the sidewalk adjacent to the employer's premises. The handgun was carried for the decedent's personal protection as well as for protection of the employer's property. The handling of the gun was instigated by the fellow employee, and the accident occurred when the decedent attempted to stop the activity. The evidence does not show that the two were engaged in reckless, irresponsible "horseplay."

Although it is true that an employer should not be held liable for an accident that results from a "new and added peril to which the employee by his own conduct has needlessly exposed himself," the enforced lull in this case sheds a different light on the facts of the accident. The enforced lull was a part of that employment. If the employees engaged in an activity that hindsight proves was lacking in reasoned thought, so long as it was not illegal, the employer cannot be heard to complain. The employees cannot be expected to remain idle during this time. It is to be expected that they will engage in activities that will relieve their boredom. Unless the activity is so totally unreasonable that it severs the employee's connection with the employer, any accident resulting therefrom should be considered as sustained in the course of and arising out of the employment.

The ultimate question is whether the fact that a gun was involved in the accident in this case works such a severance. Had the injury been sustained in, say, a brawl wherein some ready-to-hand weapon was used, like a pipe, the employer would obviously be liable.... The result is not changed because decedent's death was due to the discharge of his gun, provided there was an employment nexus for the gun, the injury occurred on the employer's premises during work-time, and decedent was not the instigator of the fatal gun handling. As to the employment nexus, the findings of the Administrative Law Judge (ALJ) establish that the availability of a gun was not unrelated to the hazards of the job.... We are aware of the fact stressed by our dissenting colleague, that decedent had already taken one run in a truck without a pistol, but this did not negate the possibility that another assigned run, after a waiting period, might involve a function (being given money to turn in), time, or route that would lead him to carry a gun in the truck. The gun did not provide an automatic severance from employment as may be established by saying we think it plain ... that there would be compensation if the gun had remained in the trunk and had been discharged accidentally upon the trunk being pounded at the garage by means of a mallet. The additional facts that the gun was withdrawn from the taxi cab and the accident arose from ensuing handling of the gun during an "enforced lull" do not defeat compensation....

It is unnecessary for this court to say how it would have decided the case in the first instance. It need only evaluate whether the administrative decision was arbitrary or capricious or unsupported by substantial evidence. A review of the record here supports the conclusion that plaintiff's evidence can be termed substantial.

Resolving doubts in favor of the employee we conclude that the Review Board's determination should stand. Therefore, we affirm.

DANAHER, SENIOR CIRCUIT JUDGE (dissenting):

... Whether the fatal shooting "arose out of" Kemp's employment then became and still remains the issue here presented. Unless Kemp's fatal injury so "arose," the claim for compensation must fall.

Appropriately to be regarded is the test presented by Mr. Justice Frankfurter, speaking for the Court in *O'Leary v. Brown–Pacific–Maxon*:

All that is required is that the "obligations or conditions" of employment create the "zone of special danger" out of which the injury arose....

... Courts have realized fully that compensation is not confined by common-law concepts of the scope of employment; that the test of recovery is not a causal relation between the nature of employment of the injured person and the accident; but it would seem beyond peradventure that Kemp was not engaged at the time of the injury in an activity of benefit to The Star—nor was it necessary that Kemp be so engaged. As matters stood, up to the moment of injury, there was thus not a scintilla of evidence that the death "arose out of" the employment....

... It would seem the ALJ felt bound to develop on the entire record, that there was a zone of danger arising from the conditions and circumstances of the employment. So he found that The Star had provided no areas of relaxation for its truck drivers during the periods between delivery runs. Moreover such employees were not prohibited from going to The Star garage to dump trash, to pick up batteries, to exchange accessory items or to procure gasoline for their trucks. The Star's employees might obtain help and advice from the mechanics at the garage. Kemp, with Ward and Andrews, was not prohibited from borrowing Michael's rubber mallet. After they had approached the garage but before the repair job on Kemp's taxicab was commenced, it seemed important to the ALJ, the cab was parked on a black-top area between the building line and the curb line of the street. Are such "facts" relevant? ...

... The Act does not, and never was intended to, provide automatic insurance for every industrial accident. It was intended to pass along to industry the cost of alleviating injurious results which arise out of the employment of an injured claimant. Broadly and liberally interpreting the purpose and the plan of the Act, as we are bound to do when the facts will so permit, equally we are duty bound to deny relief unless the injury "arose out of" the employment. Whatever might have been the case if while out delivering newspapers Kemp had suffered an injury even by the accidental discharge of his own pistol, such is not this situation. Here, obviously, however "fearful" Kemp might have been, he did not even take the gun on his delivery run on the morning of August 10, 1971.

As the ALJ had interpreted the record, the claimant would have been entitled to recover if his gun had been discharged by a fall down the front steps of his house. Such a misfortune, surely, cannot properly be said to arise out of his employment.

Thus analyzed, if we cannot conscientiously find that the evidence supporting an award is substantial when viewed in the light that the record in its entirety furnishes, a reviewing court should set aside the award.

And that is this case.

DURRAH v. WASHINGTON METROPOLITAN AREA TRANSIT AUTHORITY

760 F.2d 322 (D.C.Cir.1985).

GINSBURG, CIRCUIT JUDGE:

Michael L. Durrah commenced employment with the Washington Metropolitan Area Transit Authority (WMATA) as a special police officer on July 30, 1979. The accident at issue occurred some three weeks later, on August 22, 1979. Durrah, at the time of the accident, was on duty on the midnight to 8:00 a.m. shift at a large Metrobus depot. That night, for the second time since he began working for WMATA, Durrah was assigned to Post No. 1, where he was responsible for monitoring all traffic entering or leaving the depot. At approximately 4:00 a.m., Durrah left the guardhouse and purchased a soda from a vending machine WMATA had installed in the employees' lounge on the premises. In alleged contravention of WMATA's instructions, Durrah did not report that he was leaving the guardhouse and obtain a substitute to cover Post No. 1 in his absence. Upon leaving the lounge to return to Post No. 1, Durrah slipped on a staircase. He immediately complained of a knee injury and in due course sought benefits under the Longshoremen's and Harbor Workers' Compensation Act. An administrative law judge (ALJ) denied Durrah's claim, and the Benefits Review Board (BRB) affirmed. On Durrah's petition for review, we reverse the BRB's decision and remand the case for further proceedings consistent with this opinion.

Durrah alleges an injury occurring on his employer's premises in the course of his workday. There is no dispute that this injury would be one "arising out of and in the course of employment," if Durrah had obtained both permission and a substitute to cover Post No. 1 before going to the employees' lounge. We hold that his fall was securely within the time and space boundaries of his employment.

The lounge and staircase were facilities WMATA expected its employees to use. Moreover, Durrah's conduct—getting a soft drink—is generally incidental to day- (or night-) long employment. The soda machine Durrah visited was maintained by the employer on the employer's premises. Employee use of the machine was an anticipated occurrence in the course of a workday.... It is not "necessary that the employee be engaged at the time of the injury in activity of benefit to his employer. All that is required is that the 'obligations or conditions' of employment create the 'zone of special danger' out of which the injury arose." In short, had Durrah first secured a replacement, his injury would unquestionably have "take[n] place within the period of the employment, at a place where the employee reasonably may be, and while he [was] engaged in doing something incidental [to the employment]."

The ALJ found, however, that Durrah violated a WMATA rule in taking a soda break: he left his duty station to go to and from the lounge area without requesting permission and without obtaining a substitute to cover Post No. 1. That finding alone determined the case for the ALJ and the BRB. The ALJ ruled, and the BRB agreed, that "[Durrah's] actions were removed from the course of employment when [he] knowingly violated the employer's rule that officers stationed at Post No. 1 never leave the post without express permission." . . .

[V]iewing the facts in the light most favorable to WMATA, we do not comprehend how it can be maintained that Durrah's transgression "so thoroughly disconnected [him] from the service of his employer that it would be entirely unreasonable to say that injuries suffered by him arose out of and in the course of his employment." The asserted violation did not place Durrah in the path of new risks not inherent in his employment situation. Had Durrah followed his employer's alleged instructions to the letter in obtaining permission to take a mid-shift break at the employees' lounge soda machine, his injury would have occurred in the very same place on WMATA's premises, at the same time, and in the same manner. Far from severing the link between employment circumstances and injury, Durrah's deviation did not determine the time or place of his injury, and did not render his activity nonincidental to employment.

. . . Fault on Durrah's part there may be, but to deny compensation solely because of misconduct that does nothing to alter the relationship between employment setting and injury would be alien to the workers' compensation scheme. Whatever discipline Durrah's alleged rule violation may have warranted, it distorts workers' compensation precedent, and the basis in law and reason for that precedent, to describe his staircase slip as outside the risk zone that the conditions of his employment created.

4. ARBITRARY AND CAPRICIOUS REVIEW

a. *Informal Adjudication*

If 5 U.S.C. § 706(2)(E) provides the standard of review of questions of fact in formal adjudication, what is the standard in informal adjudication? Section 706(2)(F) provides for the courts to determine the facts independently by authorizing a court to overturn an agency decision if it is "unwarranted by the facts to the extent that the facts are subject to trial *de novo* by the reviewing court." The question is *when* are the facts subject to trial *de novo* by the reviewing court. Prior to the APA, it was common practice for courts to hold trials to take evidence to decide disputed facts where a full administrative hearing had not taken place. The drafters of the APA apparently intended to continue this practice. Whatever the original understanding, however, the next decision changed the legal landscape.

CITIZENS TO PRESERVE OVERTON PARK v. VOLPE

401 U.S. 402, 91 S.Ct. 814, 28 L.Ed.2d 136 (1971).

Opinion of the Court by MR. JUSTICE MARSHALL, announced by MR. JUSTICE STEWART.

The growing public concern about the quality of our natural environment has prompted Congress in recent years to enact legislation designed to curb the accelerating destruction of our country's natural beauty. We are concerned in this case with § 4(f) of the Department of Transportation Act of 1966 and the Federal–Aid Highway Act of 1968. These statutes prohibit the Secretary of Transportation from authorizing the use of federal funds to finance the construction of highways through public parks if a "feasible and prudent" alternative route exists. If no such route is available, the statutes allow him to approve construction through parks only if there has been "all possible planning to minimize harm" to the park.

Petitioners, private citizens as well as local and national conservation organizations, contend that the Secretary has violated these statutes by authorizing the expenditure of federal funds for the construction of a six-lane interstate highway through a public park in Memphis, Tennessee. Their claim was rejected by the District Court, which granted the Secretary's motion for summary judgment, and the Court of Appeals for the Sixth Circuit affirmed. After oral argument, this Court granted a stay that halted construction and, treating the application for the stay as a petition for certiorari, granted review. We now reverse the judgment below and remand for further proceedings in the District Court.

Overton Park is 342-acre city park located near the center of Memphis. The park contains a zoo, a nine-hole municipal golf course, an outdoor theater, nature trails, a bridle path, an art academy, picnic areas, and 170 acres of forest. The proposed highway, which is to be a six lane, high-speed, expressway, will sever the zoo from the rest of the park. . . .

. . . In April 1968, the Secretary announced that he concurred in the judgment of local officials that I–40 should be built through the park. . . . Final approval for the project—the route as well as the design—was not announced until November 1969. . . . Neither announcement approving the route and design of I–40 was accompanied by a statement of the Secretary's factual findings. He did not indicate why he believed there were no feasible and prudent alternative routes or why design changes could not be made to reduce the harm to the park. . . .

. . . For [the standard of review] we must look to § 706 of the Administrative Procedure Act which provides that a "reviewing court shall * * * hold unlawful and set aside agency action, findings, and conclusions found" not to meet six separate standards. In all cases agency action must be set aside if the action was "arbitrary, capricious, an abuse of discretion, or otherwise not in accordance with law" or if the action failed to meet statutory, procedural, or constitutional requirements. In certain narrow, specifically limited situations, the agency action is to be set aside if the action was not supported by "substantial evidence." And in other equally narrow circumstances the reviewing court is to engage in a *de novo* review of the action and set it aside if it was "unwarranted by the facts."

Petitioners argue that the Secretary's approval of the construction of I–40 through Overton Park is subject to one or the other of these latter two standards of limited applicability. First, they contend that the "substantial evidence" standard of § 706(2)(E) must be applied. In the alternative, they claim that § 706(2)(F) applies and that there must be a *de novo* review to determine if the Secretary's action was "unwarranted by the facts" Neither of these standards is, however, applicable.

Review under the substantial-evidence test is authorized only when the agency action is taken pursuant to a rulemaking provision of the Administrative Procedure Act itself,* 5 U.S.C. § 553, or when the agency action is based on a public adjudicatory hearing. See 5 U.S.C. §§ 556, 557. The Secretary's decision to allow the expenditure of federal funds to build I–40 through Overton Park was plainly not an exercise of a rulemaking function. And the only hearing that is required by either the Administrative Procedure Act or the statutes regulating the distribution of federal funds for highway construction is a public hearing conducted by local officials for the purpose of informing the community about the proposed project and eliciting community views on the design and route. The hearing is nonadjudicatory, quasi-legislative in nature. It is not designed to produce a record that is to be the basis of agency action—the basic requirement for substantial-evidence review.

Petitioners' alternative argument also fails. *De novo* review of whether the Secretary's decision was "unwarranted by the facts" is authorized by § 706(2)(F) in only two circumstances. First, such *de novo* review is authorized when the action is adjudicatory in nature and the agency fact finding procedures are inadequate. And, there may be independent judicial fact finding when issues that were not before the agency are raised in a proceeding to enforce nonadjudicatory agency action. Neither situation exists here. . . .

Even though there is no *de novo* review in this case and the Secretary's approval of the route of I–40 does not have ultimately to meet the substantial-evidence test, the generally applicable standards of § 706 require the reviewing court to engage in a substantial inquiry. . . .

The court is first required to decide whether the Secretary acted within the scope of his authority. This determination naturally begins with a delineation of the scope of the Secretary's authority and discretion. . . . Also involved in this initial inquiry is a determination of

* [editors' note] The Court should have   is applicable to "formal" rulemaking.
said that the substantial evidence standard

whether on the facts the Secretary's decision can reasonably be said to be within that range. The reviewing court must consider whether the Secretary properly construed his authority to approve the use of park land as limited to situations where there are no feasible alternative routes or where feasible alternative routes involve uniquely difficult problems. And the reviewing court must be able to find that the Secretary could have reasonably believed that in this case there are no feasible alternatives or that alternatives do involve unique problems.

Scrutiny of the facts does not end, however, with the determination that the Secretary has acted within the scope of his statutory authority. Section 706(2)(A) requires a finding that the actual choice made was not "arbitrary, capricious, an abuse of discretion, or otherwise not in accordance with law." To make this finding the court must consider whether the decision was based on a consideration of the relevant factors and whether there has been a clear error of judgment. Although this inquiry into the facts is to be searching and careful, the ultimate standard of review is a narrow one. The court is not empowered to substitute its judgment for that of the agency.

The final inquiry is whether the Secretary's action followed the necessary procedural requirements. Here the only procedural error alleged is the failure of the Secretary to make formal findings and state his reason for allowing the highway to be built through the park.

Undoubtedly, review of the Secretary's action is hampered by his failure to make such findings, but the absence of formal findings does not necessarily require that the case be remanded to the Secretary. Neither the Department of Transportation Act nor the Federal–Aid Highway Act requires such formal findings. Moreover, the Administrative Procedure Act requirements that there be formal findings in certain rulemaking and adjudicatory proceedings do not apply to the Secretary's action here.

. . . Moreover, there is an administrative record that allows the full, prompt review of the Secretary's action . . . without additional delay which would result from having a remand to the Secretary.

That administrative record is not, however, before us. The lower courts based their review on the litigation affidavits that were presented. These affidavits were merely "post hoc" rationalizations, which have traditionally been found to be an inadequate basis for review. And they clearly do not constitute the "whole record" compiled by the agency: the basis for review required by § 706 of the Administrative Procedure Act.

Thus it is necessary to remand this case to the District Court for plenary review of the Secretary's decision. That review is to be based on the full administrative record that was before the Secretary at the time he made his decision. But since the bare record may not disclose the factors that were considered or the Secretary's construction of the evidence it may be necessary for the District Court to require some explanation in order to determine if the Secretary acted within the scope of his authority and if the Secretary's action was justifiable under the applicable standard.

The court may require the administrative officials who participated in the decision to give testimony explaining their action. Of course, such inquiry into the mental processes of administrative decisionmakers is usually to be avoided. *United States v. Morgan*, 313 U.S. 409, 422 (1941). And where there are administrative findings that were made at the same time as the decision, as was the case in *Morgan*, there must be a strong showing of bad faith or improper behavior before such inquiry may be made. But here there are no such formal findings and it may be that the only way there can be effective judicial review is by examining the decisionmakers themselves.

The District Court is not, however, required to make such an inquiry. It may be that the Secretary can prepare formal findings ... that will provide an adequate explanation for his action. Such an explanation will, to some extent, be a "post hoc rationalization" and thus must be viewed critically. If the District Court decides that additional explanation is necessary, that court should consider which method will prove the most expeditious so that full review may be had as soon as possible.

Reversed and remanded.

Notes and Questions

1. As you have read, the Court said that *de novo* review was not required because Section 706(2)(F) only applies "when the action is adjudicatory in nature and the agency fact finding procedures are inadequate" and "when issues that were not before the agency are raised in a proceeding to enforce non-adjudicatory agency action." The Court said neither situation existed in *Overton Park*, but it did not explain why the first circumstance did not apply. Subsequent lower court cases have interpreted *Overton Park* on this point as indicating that the absence of a hearing or particular adjudicatory proceeding does not render the "fact finding procedures inadequate." As a result, Section 706(2)(F) has lapsed into desuetude.

2. Instead of applying *de novo* review, *Overton Park* applied the "arbitrary and capricious" standard in section 706(2)(A). Application of this standard in the context of rulemaking was covered in the last chapter, and, substantively, the standard is the same in informal adjudication. The problem arises in how to assess the reasonableness of the agency's decision in the absence of the record that normally accompanies formal adjudication (or formal rulemaking). In *Overton Park*, as you read, the Court said that there was "an administrative record" which could be the subject of judicial review. The Court apparently meant that the district court could review whatever documents were before the Secretary of Transportation at the time he approved the grant of highway funds to Memphis. The Court also recognized, however, that

these documents may not explain the basis of the Secretary's approval. If this was the case, the Court said that the lower court could determine the basis for the decision either by testimony before the district court or the Secretary could make a *post hoc* written explanation of his decision. Since *Overton Park,* the Court has expressed a clear preference for courts to remand a decision back to an agency to prepare an explanation, rather than to require testimony in court. *See, e.g., Pension Benefit Guaranty Corp. v. LTV Corp.*, 496 U.S. 633, 654, 110 S.Ct. 2668, 2680, 110 L.Ed.2d 579 (1990).

3.   Although *Overton Park* allowed the lower courts to require the Secretary to testify if necessary, it cited *United States v. Morgan* for the proposition that an "inquiry into the mental processes of administrative decisionmakers is generally to be avoided." *Morgan* was the final appeal in a series of cases heard by the Court concerning rate orders issued by the Secretary of Agriculture. Persons dissatisfied with the order alleged that the Secretary had made his decision "without having heard or read any of the evidence or having read or considered the briefs which the plaintiffs submitted," and that "the only information that the Secretary had as to the proceeding was what he derived from consultation with employees of the Department." The Court permitted the plaintiffs to take the Secretary's deposition to determine what documents he had read before making his decision, but it subsequently decided that the Secretary should not have been subject to this examination: "But the short of the business is that the Secretary should never have been subjected to this examination.... Just as a judge cannot be subjected to such a scrutiny, so the integrity of the administrative process must be equally respected." How did the Court distinguish the situation in *Overton Park* from that in *Morgan*?

4.   Litigation and controversy concerning the proposed highway at issue in *Overton Park* continued until 1977 when the City gave up on the roadway. For a fascinating history of these events and their implication for administrative law, *see* Peter L. Strauss, *Revisiting* Overton Park: *Political and Judicial Controls Over Administrative Action Affecting the Community*, 39 U.C.L.A. L. Rev. 1251 (1992).

b.   *Review for "Adequate Reasons"*

The same requirement of "adequate reasons" that courts apply in the review of agency rules also applies in judicial review of adjudication. As you read in Chapter Two, the *State Farm* case interpreted the "arbitrary and capricious" scope of review under the APA as requiring agencies to "articulate a satisfactory explanation for its action including 'a rational connection between the facts found and the choice made.'" Since § 706(2)(a) also applies to review of adjudication, agencies have the same obligation in defending these decisions. While this requirement is not as often the focus of judicial review, it can provide a basis for a litigant to obtain a court order to remand a decision back to agency for a more elaborate justification. In *Allentown Mack Sales & Service Inc. v. National Labor Relations Board*, 522 U.S. 359, 118 S.Ct. 818, 139

L.Ed.2d 797 (1998), the Court elaborated on an agency's obligation to provide "adequate reasons":

> The Administrative Procedure Act, which governs the proceedings of administrative agencies and related judicial review, establishes a scheme of "reasoned decisionmaking." *Motor Vehicle Mfrs. Ass'n. of United States, Inc. v. State Farm Mut. Automobile Ins. Co.,* 463 U.S. 29, 52 (1983). Not only must an agency's decreed result be within the scope of its lawful authority, but the process by which it reaches that result must be logical and rationale. Courts enforce this principle with regularity when they set aside agency regulations, which well within the agencies' scope of authority, are not supported by the reasons that the agencies adduce. The National Labor Relations Board, uniquely among major federal administrative agencies, has chosen to promulgate virtually all the legal rules in its field through adjudication rather than rulemaking.... But adjudication is subject to the requirement of reasoned decisionmaking as well.

c. *Review for "Consistency"*

After *Overton Park*, the courts apply the "arbitrary and capricious" standard in the same manner in informal rulemaking and informal adjudication. However, there is a line of cases applying the "arbitrary and capricious" standard of review in a manner unique to adjudication, whether formal or informal. Inasmuch as adjudication mirrors the judicial process, courts have been disturbed by agencies reaching different results in cases that appear to be similar or identical. The judicial model would expect agency adjudication to be bound by notions of precedent and stare decisis. In a word, like cases should be decided alike. To the extent that these differing decisions are based upon the exercise of agency discretion within the bounds authorized by statute, however, it would be lawful for agencies to decide like cases differently if they decided to change their policy. At the same time, a different decision might simply be the result of the agency ignoring through oversight an earlier decision, or rejecting it for irrelevant reasons—such as, that was the policy of the former administration. Courts enforcing a norm imported from the judicial context accordingly require agencies to explain inconsistent decisions, otherwise the fact of inconsistency is interpreted as evidence of the agency acting arbitrarily and capriciously.

The following problem involves an informal adjudication that might be subject to a challenge as arbitrary and capricious.

Problem 3–10: Arbitrary and Capricious Standard of Judicial Review

Daniel Jones, after twelve years of excellent service in the military, wrote to the Secretary of the Air Force, through his commanding officers, that he had concluded that his "sexual preferences are homosexual as opposed to heterosexual." He added that in his view his sexual preferences would in no way interfere with his Air Force duties and that he considered himself fully qualified for further military service. He asked that Air Force regulations relating to the discharge of homosexuals be waived in his case. There are two references in the regulation concerning a waiver. The regulation says the Air Force may grant a waiver "where the most unusual circumstances exist and provided that the airman's ability to perform military service has not been compromised." It also says that "an exception is not warranted simply because the airman has extensive service or because of intoxication."

Jones' letter triggered an investigation by the Air Force Office of Special Investigation, and the Air Force began involuntary administrative discharge proceedings against Jones as a result of the investigation. An Administrative Discharge Board held a four-day hearing at which appellant was represented by counsel. In addition to general testimony on homosexuality, appellant presented evidence on his own service in the Air Force and his ability to continue to give effective service. It was stipulated that he had committed homosexual acts during his current enlistment period, but that none of these were with Air Force personnel. The Board so found and recommended that he be given a general discharge for unfitness, based on his homosexual acts.

There was also a stipulation that the Air Force had in the past retained Air Force members on active duty who had engaged in homosexual activity. The Board, however, declined to waive the discharge regulation in this case. It recognized that Jones had an "outstanding" record, but it summarily concluded "that an outstanding military record without other unusual circumstances is not sufficient basis to compel a member's retention." In confirming the Correction Board's determination, the Secretary of the Air Force also found that an outstanding record was not enough to merit a waiver. He said only that he found no "unusual circumstances."

Assume that you have been hired to represent Mr. Jones, who seeks to appeal his dismissal from the Air Force. On what grounds can you seek an appeal? How would you rate the probability of success?

Problem Materials

YEPES–PRADO v. U.S. IMMIGRATION AND NATURALIZATION SERVICE

10 F.3d 1363 (9th Cir.1993).

REINHARDT, CIRCUIT JUDGE:

Rigoberto Yepes–Prado is a thirty-eight-year-old individual who was lawfully admitted to the United States as a permanent resident on November 29, 1974. He has lived here since that date and has maintained steady employment. On April 14, 1984, he was arrested for possession of 14.25 grams of heroin with intent to distribute in violation of California law. He was convicted of that charge on January 15, 1986 and sentenced to one year in the county jail and two years probation.

Nothing in the record suggests that Yepes–Prado has ever been arrested for, let alone convicted of, any other criminal offense since he arrived in the United States almost twenty years ago.

On the basis of the 1986 drug conviction, the Immigration and Naturalization Service ("INS") ordered Yepes–Prado to show cause why he should not be deported under section 241 as an alien who has been convicted of a violation of a law relating to a controlled substance. Yepes–Prado conceded that he was eligible for deportation, but sought a discretionary waiver under section 212(c). Although an immigration judge ("IJ") found that several equities weighed in Yepes–Prado's favor, he denied the waiver. Yepes–Prado then appealed the IJ's decision to the Board of Immigration Appeals ("BIA"). The BIA found that Yepes–Prado had "outstanding equities" and was eligible for relief, but found no error in the IJ's decision. Yepes–Prado's petition for review of the BIA's decision is now before us.... We vacate and remand.

Section 212(c) of the Immigration and Naturalization Act allows the Attorney General to grant discretionary relief from deportation or exclusion to lawful permanent residents who, like Yepes–Prado, meet the provision's seven-year residency requirement....

The BIA has enumerated several factors to be considered in determining whether or not to grant a section 212(c) petition. Favorable considerations include: 1) family ties within the United States; 2) residence of long duration in this country (particularly when residence began at a young age); 3) hardship to the petitioner or petitioner's family if relief is not granted; 4) service in the United States armed forces; 5) a history of employment; 6) the existence of business or property ties; 7) evidence of value and service to the community; 8) proof of rehabilitation if a criminal record exists; 9) other evidence attesting to good character. To be weighed against these factors are 1) the nature and underlying circumstances of the exclusion or deportation ground at issue; 2) additional violations of the immigration laws; 3) the existence, seriousness, and recency of any criminal record; 4) other evidence of bad character or the undesirability of the applicant as a permanent resident. Where a 212(c) petitioner has committed a particularly grave criminal offense, he must make a heightened showing that his case presents unusual or outstanding equities to warrant discretionary relief. However, there are cases in which the adverse considerations are so serious that a favorable exercise is not warranted even in the face of unusual or outstanding equities ...

In making a discretionary immigration decision, the agency must indicate "how it weighed the factors involved" and "how it arrived at its conclusion." Without such an explanation, a reviewing court cannot tell whether the IJ or BIA has departed from established policies in deciding a particular 212(c) application and thereby abused its discretion. While agencies must have significant flexibility to adapt their practices to meet changed circumstances or the facts of a particular case, they cannot reach their decisions capriciously. Agencies abuse their discretion no less by arriving at plausible decisions in an arbitrary fashion than by reaching unreasonable results. In this case, the IJ ... failed to offer a reasoned explanation of why the only adverse factor, the single drug conviction, outweighed all of the equities in Yepes–Prado's favor....

Because the IJ ... failed to offer a reasoned explanation of why that conviction outweighed all the equities in Yepes–Prado's favor, he abused his discretion, and vacation of the BIA's decision upholding his discretionary ruling is required.

DAVILA–BARDALES v. IMMIGRATION AND NATURALIZATION SERVICE

27 F.3d 1 (1st Cir.1994).

SELYA, CIRCUIT JUDGE.

Ricardo Davila–Bardales asks us to review a decision of the Board of Immigration Appeals (BIA) in which the BIA affirmed an Immigration Judge's (IJ's) deportation order. The parties agree that the BIA's decision rests upon the IJ's finding that in late July of 1989 Davila–Bardales, then age 15, entered this country unlawfully, without inspection by an immigration officer. The parties also agree that rules of the Immigration and Naturalization Service (INS) require "clear, unequivocal and convincing" evidentiary support for such a finding. They disagree about whether the INS, under its own rules and practices, could properly consider the evidence that showed unlawful entry in this case—evidence that consists primarily of Davila–Bardales's own statements and admissions.

[INS regulations prohibit the use in an immigration hearing of an admission of deportability from an unrepresented person under 16 not accompanied by a guardian, relative, or friend. Davila–Bardales was under 16 and unaccompanied at his deportation hearing. He admitted there that he illegally entered the country. When shown a form I–213, which is filled out by the Border Patrol officer who apprehends the alien and which also indicated that Davila–Bardales had illegally entered the country, Davila–Bardales admitted it was correct. The INS argued that his admission as to the correctness of the I–213 was not an admission of deportability within the meaning of its regulations, but the court rejected that argument.]

Little daunted, the INS points to [another] kind of evidence admitted at the hearing: the I–213 form itself. That form purports to memorialize an interview between Davila–Bardales and a Border Patrol officer. According to petitioner, this interview took place sometime after midnight at the "frontier" on the day he entered this country, before an official who "spoke little Spanish," and who (petitioner says) "hit" him "in the face."

We agree with the INS that the regulation does not explicitly apply to this evidence. After all, the regulation, in context, seems to refer to the immigration hearing and the IJ's acceptance of an "admission" of deportability at that hearing. It says nothing about admissions made at other times and under other circumstances.

Nonetheless, the BIA, in its case law, has expressed considerable skepticism about the admissibility of similar statements made to Border Patrol officers by persons who are both unrepresented and under the age of sixteen. . . .

What is more, on the very day the BIA decided this case, it stated in the course of deciding a different case that, if the INS seeks to admit an I–213 form against a juvenile, "the circumstances surrounding the Service's preparation of the Form I–213 must be carefully examined to insure that alienage has been properly established." The BIA added that,

> where the Service seeks to establish alienage based on alleged admissions during the interrogation of an unaccompanied minor, the Service should present evidence from the arresting officers in order to demonstrate that the interview was conducted in a non-coercive environment and that the respondent was competent to respond to the questions posed to him.

We do not see how the BIA can reconcile these statements, made in other cases, with its position in this case. The matter at hand seems to present exactly the sort of circumstances that the BIA, in those other cases, addressed. It involves a midnight Border Patrol investigation, an underage suspect, an absence of legal representation, and an allegation of physical abuse. Yet, here, the INS presented no evidence from the arresting officers. Its records do not indicate that it carefully examined the circumstances surrounding the preparation of form I–213. Nor did the IJ . . . treat the admissions made by Davila–Bardales (an unaccompanied minor) as "inherently suspect." And as a crowning blow, the BIA's opinion in this case, albeit stating in a conclusory fashion that petitioner understood the questions and answers at the hearing, does not discuss the integrity or reliability of the Border Patrol's interrogation.

Though the law does not require that all officials of a large agency "react similarly or interpret regulations identically" in every case, it does prohibit an agency from adopting significantly inconsistent policies that result in the creation of "conflicting lines of precedent governing the identical situation." The purpose of this doctrine, as we have explained before, is "to prevent the agency itself from significantly changing [its] policies without conscious awareness of, and consideration of the need for, change." . . .

We need go no further. For the reasons set forth herein, we grant the petition for review, vacate the BIA's decision, and remand the case for further proceedings consistent with this opinion.

Chapter 4

CHOICE OF PROCEDURES AND NONLEGISLATIVE RULES

Up to this point, you have been exposed to an agency adopting new policies either through rulemaking or adjudication. As you saw, an agency can make a decision through adjudication that is binding on the parties to the adjudication and may be precedent with respect to non-parties in future adjudications. Or, it can promulgate a rule that is binding on all those subject to the rule. The agency can then seek to enforce its regulation in agency adjudications, if its mandate so provides, or in judicial action. Adjudication and rulemaking, however, do not exhaust an agency's options. It can also promulgate a nonlegislative rule.

A nonlegislative rule is an agency pronouncement that advises the public of the agency's view on an issue. By itself, a nonlegislative rule does not have binding legal effect on third parties. Nevertheless, such statements are "rules" because they fit the APA's definition of rule, which you studied in Chapter 1. Recall that a rule "means the whole or a part of an agency statement of general or particular applicability and future effect designed to implement, interpret, or prescribe law or policy...." 5 U.S.C.A. § 551(4). Rules adopted by the notice and comment process are called "legislative rules" because they are legally binding. 5 U.S.C.A. § 553. Other rules are called "nonlegislative rules" and need not be adopted by notice and comment rulemaking, because they are *not* legally binding. Section 553 identifies two types of nonlegislative rules—"interpretative rules" and "general statements of policy"—that are exempt from the notice and comment procedures of section 553.* The distinction between legislative and nonlegislative rules will be covered in more detail at a later point in this chapter. For now, you need only understand that such rules are part of a third pathway that an agency can use to adopt new policies.

This chapter considers three major issues. First, why might an agency prefer a particular process option in a given situation? Second,

---

* Recall from Chapter 2 that there are other types of rules exempt from notice-and-comment rulemaking, e.g., procedural rules, emergency rules, military and foreign affairs rules, etc., but these can have binding legal effect on third parties.

what are the advantages and disadvantages of such options from the perspective of the public or a regulated entity? Third, are there legal limitations that constrain the choice of particular options, such as the agency's statutory mandate, the APA, or the due process clause?

A. OPTION ONE: ADJUDICATION

1. ADVANTAGES AND DISADVANTAGES

If an agency has the authority to engage in both adjudication and rulemaking, it must determine which approach to use. Consider the Federal Trade Commission (FTC or Commission). Congress has authorized the FTC "to prevent persons, partnerships, or corporations ... from using unfair methods of competition in or affecting commerce and unfair or deceptive acts of practices in or affecting commerce." 15 U.S.C.A. § 55(a)(6). If the Commission finds in an adjudication that a firm has violated the Act, it orders the firm to "cease and desist" from the activity in the future. *Id.* § 45(b). A firm that violates a cease and desist order is subject to judicially imposed fines of up to $10,000 for each violation. *Id.* § 45(*l*).

The Commission used adjudication for most of its history to determine what acts or practices were "unfair" or "deceptive" in part because it was not clear whether the FTC had rulemaking authority. *See National Petroleum Refiners Assoc. v. Federal Trade Commission*, 482 F.2d 672 (D.C.Cir.1973), *cert. denied* 415 U.S. 951, 94 S.Ct. 1475, 39 L.Ed.2d 567 (1974) (describing this history). In 1974, Congress passed legislation that expressly authorized the FTC to promulgate legislative rules. Federal Trade Commission Improvement Act of 1974, 15 U.S.C.A. § 57a (generally known as the Magnuson–Moss Act). Thus, the FTC now has a choice between using adjudication or rulemaking to determine what constitutes an unfair or deceptive practice. On the one hand, it may bring an administrative action against a person thought to be engaged in such a practice and in that adjudication decide both what constitutes a deceptive or unfair practice and whether the party-defendant engaged in that practice. On the other hand, the FTC may first adopt a rule defining the deceptive or unfair practice and later, if someone violates the rule, use adjudication to impose a cease-and-desist order against the violator.

To illustrate the impact of this choice, consider the issue of whether a grocery store chain commits a deceptive practice if it fails to have an adequate supply of advertised goods in stock. If the Commission uses adjudication to make this decision, the particular defendant chosen by the FTC is in an unenviable position. The defendant may be found to have violated the FTC Act although there was no prior warning that such practices were unlawful. Even if the defendant does not pay a fine for its violation, it is likely to regard this "surprise" as unfair, especially if the FTC gave no prior indication that it might adopt this policy. At a minimum, the defendant is forced to undertake the legal costs of litigating its position, or at least admitting its violation and settling the case.

Rulemaking may be fairer in the previous circumstance for two reasons. Since rulemaking has only a prospective effect, a determination that such practices are unfair or deceptive does not mean that any grocery store chain has violated the Act. Rulemaking also avoids the problem that adjudication focuses only on one defendant. A grocery store chain may be only one of several companies that is engaged in the same practice, but if it is the object of an adjudication, it alone is forced to contest the adoption of the FTC's revised policy. By comparison, "the availability of notice before promulgation and wide public participation in rule-making avoids the problem of singling out a single defendant among a group of competitors for initial imposition of a new and inevitably costly legal obligation." *National Petroleum Refiners Assoc.*, *supra*, at 683. In addition, when an agency uses rulemaking, all competitors are bound to follow the new policy. An adjudicatory order, by comparison, is legally binding only on the entity against which it is issued.

Regulated entities or others may benefit from the use of rulemaking, as may an agency. Judge Skelly Wright has explained, "[T]here is little reason to question that the availability of substantive rulemaking gives the agency an invaluable resource-saving-flexibility in carrying out its tasks of regulating parties subject to its statutory mandate." *Id.* at 681. Also, "utilizing rulemaking procedures opens up the process of agency policy innovation to a broad range of criticism, advice, and data that is ordinarily less likely to be forthcoming in an adjudication." *Id.* at 683. Why is rulemaking more efficient for an agency? Why does it expose the agency to more input from interested parties? Rulemaking can have another advantage for the agency. If the agency uses rulemaking, it can establish a bright-line policy, which is clearer and more precise than a policy developed on case-by-case basis in adjudication. This clarity should increase the level of compliance with the policy and decrease opportunistic behavior by regulated entities that seek to avoid the new policy.

In light of these advantages, agencies might be expected to use rulemaking to adopt new policies, and many do so. But some agencies, such as the National Labor Relations Board (NLRB), continue to use adjudication to adopt new policies. In *Securities and Exchange Commission v. Chenery Corporation*, 332 U.S. 194, 67 S.Ct. 1575, 91 L.Ed. 1995 (1947), the Supreme Court identified some of the reasons why rulemaking might not be suitable for the adoption of new policies in the context of the regulation of labor relations by the NLRB:

> Since the Commission, unlike a court, does have the ability to make new law prospectively through the exercise of its rule-making powers, it has less reason to rely upon ad hoc adjudication to formulate new standards of conduct within the framework of the Holding Company Act. The function of filling in the interstices of the Act should be performed, as much as possible, through this

quasi-legislative promulgation of rules to be applied in the future. But any rigid requirement to that effect would make the administrative process inflexible and incapable of dealing with many of the specialized problems which arise. Not every principle essential to the effective administration of a statute can or should be cast immediately into the mold of a general rule. Some principles must await their own development, while others must be adjusted to meet particular, unforeseeable situations. In performing its important functions in these respects, therefore, an administrative agency must be equipped to act either by general rule or by individual order. To insist upon one form of action to the exclusion of the other is to exalt form over necessity.

In other words, problems may arise in a case which the administrative agency could not reasonably foresee, problems which must be solved despite the absence of a relevant general rule. Or the agency may not have had sufficient experience with a particular problem to warrant rigidifying its tentative judgment into a hard and fast rule. Or the problem may be so specialized and varying in nature as to be impossible of capture within the boundaries of a general rule. In those situations, the agency must retain power to deal with the problems on a case-to-case basis if the administrative process is to be effective. There is thus a very definite place for the case-by-case evolution of statutory standards. And the choice made between proceeding by general rule or by individual, ad hoc litigation is one that lies primarily in the informed discretion of the administrative agency.

332 U.S. at 202–03.

Notes and Questions

1. As discussed in Chapter 3, the APA establishes a right of other persons (as opposed to parties) to appear before an agency in any proceeding "so far as the orderly conduct of public business permits." 5 U.S.C.A. § 555; *see also*, 15 U.S.C.A. § 45(b) (authorizing intervenors in FTC hearings "upon good cause shown"). Will allowing other persons to appear reduce the unfairness of using adjudication? What are the advantages and disadvantages from an agency's point of view of having others participate through adjudication?

2. Critics of adjudication argue that legislative procedures are preferable to adjudicative procedures for rule creation, and that agencies should be forced to use those procedures. *See, e.g.*, Peter L. Strauss, *Rules, Adjudications, and Other Sources of Law in an Executive Department: Reflections on the Interior Department's Administration of the Mining Law*, 74 COLUM. L. REV. 1231, 1233 (1974); J. Skelly Wright, *The Courts and the Rulemaking Process: The Limits of Judicial Review*, 59 CORNELL L. REV. 375, 376 (1974); Glen O. Robinson, *The Making of Administrative Policy: Another Look at Rulemaking and Adjudication and Administrative Procedure Reform*, 118 U. PA. L. REV. 485 (1970).

Although it may be preferable for agencies to articulate policy legislatively, is a degree of nonlegislative policy articulation inevitable? Mr. Justice Frankfurter, writing about legislative drafting, once stated that:

> Anything that is written may present a problem of meaning. . . . The problem derives from the very nature of words. They are symbols of meaning. But unlike mathematical symbols, the phrasing of a document, especially a complicated enactment, seldom attains more than approximate precision. If individual words are inexact symbols, with shifting variables, their configuration can hardly achieve invariant meaning or assured definiteness.

Felix Frankfurter, *Some Reflections on the Reading of Statutes*, 47 COLUM. L. REV. 527, 528 (1947). Professor Karl Llewellyn identified a second problem: policy makers are not prescient and cannot anticipate every situation that will arise. *See* Karl Llewellyn, *Remarks on the Theory of Appellate Decision and the Rules or Canons About How Statutes Are To Be Construed*, 3 VAND. L. REV. 395, 400 (1949). If legislative drafting is imprecise, and regulatory drafters are not prescient, won't agencies be forced to resolve some issues on a case-by-case basis? *See* Russell L. Weaver, *Chenery II: A Forty–Year Retrospective*, 40 AD. L. REV. 161 (1988) (commenting on the necessity of agencies making "adjudicative rules").

3. As noted, the NLRB generally prefers adjudication to rulemaking for the adoption of new policies. In fact, the NLRB did not conduct its first rulemaking until the late 1980s. Why do you suppose the NLRB is so reluctant to use rulemaking? Recall from the prior chapters that ex parte contacts are prohibited in formal adjudication, which the NLRB uses, but not in informal rulemaking. How might this difference explain the Board's reluctance to use rulemaking? Professor Grunewald suggests that the NLRB is attempting to avoid being lobbied by management and unions regarding labor policies. Mark H. Grunewald, *The NLRB's First Rulemaking: An Exercise in Pragmatism*, 41 DUKE L.J. 274 (1991).

4. In addition to insulating itself from political pressure, there are other pragmatic reasons why an agency might prefer adjudication to rulemaking. First, rulemaking is more likely to engage national interests, such as national organizations and large companies, able to mount extensive and expensive campaigns to oppose a rule, often involving political and media forces. On the other hand, proceeding by adjudication is likely to attract less attention, so that the agency can proceed without large-scale organized opposition.

Second, proceeding against one individual or firm is likely to be significantly less expensive and time consuming than a rulemaking applicable to the entire nation. Investigating and obtaining detailed information on one company is a much more manageable operation than obtaining the same information for an entire industry.

Third, if the agency proceeds by adjudication, it gets to pick its defendant. This can mean picking the weakest defendant, perhaps in terms of having the most egregious practices or perhaps in terms of lack of resources.

Fourth, the substantial and increasing procedural requirements for rulemaking, such as cost-benefit analyses and OMB and congressional reviews, can create burdens not applicable to adjudication.

How do you think these concerns weigh against the arguments for fairness and for more informed policymaking touted for rulemaking?

Problem 4–1: FTC Adjudication

Most customers who purchase new automobiles execute an installment sales contract that requires monthly payments and grants a security interest in the automobile as protection against nonpayment. The dealer assigns this contract to the lending institution which lent the consumer the money for the purchase. If the customer defaults on the loan and the creditor repossesses the car, the dealer is obligated to pay the creditor the outstanding balance on the loan and the creditor returns the car to the dealer for resale.

According to the Uniform Commercial Code, a dealer is obligated to refund to the borrower any "surplus" produced by the resale of the car, but the method to calculate whether there is a surplus is not specified. Most dealers calculate the average *wholesale* price of the resold car rather than the actual resale (*retail*) price to determine the surplus. For example, if the outstanding balance had been $6000, and the dealer resold the car for $9000, but the average wholesale price was $7000, the customer whose car had been repossessed would only receive a $1000 payment, rather than $3000.

The FTC has no trade rules concerning this practice, and it has not previously litigated the legality of the practice, but it has received a number of complaints from around the country relating to this practice. One of the dealers identified in some consumer complaints is Country Bob's.

The FTC staff believes that this practice is "unfair" under the FTC Act. The staff argues that the FTC should act because consumers are unlikely to challenge this practice. A consumer law suit is unlikely because a consumer's legal fees would almost certainly be greater than the amount the person could recover in a private action brought in state court under the UCC.

Assume that you work for the Director of the FTC Bureau of Consumer Protection. He asks you to assess whether the FTC should use adjudication or rulemaking to decide whether the previous practice violates the FTC Act. In particular, he would like to know the advantages and disadvantages of using each process.

2. LEGAL CONSTRAINTS

In *Chenery*, the Supreme Court recognized that the NLRB's choice of adjudication over rulemaking might disadvantage some litigants. If the Board had used rulemaking, the promulgation of a rule would have warned companies subject to the Board's jurisdiction that it had adopted a new policy. By using adjudication, the Board not only adopted a new policy, it gave the change retroactive effect. Thus, the employer in *Chenery* had no prior warning that the Board was going to change its policy. Nevertheless, *Chenery* held that the NLRB was not precluded from using adjudication merely because it had a retroactive effect. Instead, the Court compared the impact of the retroactive effect on the defendant to the benefit to the public of using adjudication to adopt a new policy:

> [W]e refuse to say that the Commission, which had not previously been confronted with the problem of management trading during reorganization, was forbidden from utilizing this particular proceeding for announcing and applying a new standard of conduct. That such action might have a retroactive effect was not necessarily fatal to its validity. Every case of first impression has a retroactive effect, whether the new principle is announced by a court or by an administrative agency. But such retroactivity must be balanced against the mischief of producing a result which is contrary to a statutory design or to legal and equitable principles. If that mischief is greater than the ill effect of the retroactive application of a new standard, it is not the type of retroactivity which is condemned by law. . . .

332 U.S. at 203.

This section explores the legal constraints that apply to an agency's choice of rulemaking or adjudication as the method to adopt a new policy. The following problem presents this problem in the context of the FTC enforcement action described in Problem 4–1. The problem materials provide more recent case law that addresses this issue.

Problem 4–2: FTC Adjudication

In Problem 4–1, you were asked to assess the advantages and disadvantages of using adjudication or rulemaking to decide whether Country Bob's credit practices violate the FTC Act.

(1) Assume that the FTC proceeded against Country Bob's in an adjudication and found that the dealer had violated the FTC Act. As Country Bob's attorney, what arguments can you make on appeal that the court should require the FTC to use rulemaking to prohibit the dealers' practice. As the FTC's attorney, what counter-arguments can you make?

(2) On appeal, how would you expect a court to rule? How might the court be influenced if the FTC was in the process of receiving comments on a proposed trade rule on this subject at the time of the adjudication involving Country Bob's? How might the court be influenced by the fact that the FTC must use hybrid procedures for rulemaking? A study of these procedures has found that they can be substantially burdensome.

Barry Boyer, Report on the Trade Regulation Rulemaking Procedures of the Federal Trade Commission (Phase II), 1979 ACUS ANN. REP. 41 (1979), 316. Finally, how might the court be influenced by the fact that as a remedy the FTC will issue a cease and desist order?

(3) Assume that the FTC, using adjudication, concluded that Country Bob's engaged in a deceptive practice and that it is now considering the remedy. You work for a FTC Commissioner who thinks it is unfair to order Country Bob to refund the difference between the wholesale and retail prices to past customers whose cars were repossessed and sold. Congress has authorized the FTC to order such consumer refunds. What additional arguments can you make against the FTC ordering a refund? How do you think a court will rule if Country Bob's seeks judicial review of the Commission's refund order?

Problem Materials

NATIONAL LABOR RELATIONS BOARD v. BELL AEROSPACE COMPANY DIVISION OF TEXTRON INC.

416 U.S. 267, 94 S.Ct. 1757, 40 L.Ed.2d 134 (1974).

MR. JUSTICE POWELL delivered the opinion of the Court.

This case presents two questions: first, whether the National Labor Relations Board properly determined that all "managerial employees," except those whose participation in a labor organization would create a conflict of interest with their job responsibilities, are covered by the National Labor Relations Act; and second, whether the Board must proceed by rulemaking rather than by adjudication in determining whether certain buyers are "managerial employees." We answer both questions in the negative.

[A union sought to unionize "buyers" in Bell's plant, but Bell argued that the "buyers" were "managerial employees" and thus not subject to the National Labor Relations Act (NLRA). When this issue was litigated in an adjudication before the NLRB, the Board reversed its prior policy that all managerial employees were exempt from the Act, finding that only those managerial employees with labor-management responsibilities were exempt. The Board concluded the buyers, who did not have such responsibilities, were subject to the NLRA. The Supreme Court, however, decided that the NLRB's original policy was the correct interpretation of the NLRA—all managerial employees are exempt—and it reversed the Board. As a result, there was still an issue whether "buyers" were managerial employees. Because the NLRB had not decided that issue, the Court remanded it back to the agency. It then addressed whether the NLRB could resolve this issue in an adjudication.]

The Court of Appeals also held that, although the Board was not precluded from determining that buyers or some types of buyers were not "managerial employees," it could do so only by invoking its rulemaking procedures under § 6 of the Act. We disagree.

At the outset, the precise nature of the present issue must be noted. The question is not whether the Board should have resorted to rulemaking, or in fact improperly promulgated a "rule," when in the context of the prior representation proceeding it held that the Act covers all "managerial employees" except those meeting the new "conflict of interest in labor relations" touchstone. Our conclusion that the Board applied the wrong legal standard makes consideration of that issue unnecessary. Rather, the present question is whether on remand the Board must invoke its rulemaking procedures if it determines, in light of our opinion, that these buyers are not "managerial employees" under the Act. The Court of Appeals thought that rulemaking was required because any Board finding that the company's buyers are not "managerial" would be contrary to its prior decisions and would presumably be in the nature of a general rule designed "to fit all cases at all times."

A similar issue was presented to this Court in its second decision in *SEC v. Chenery Corp.*, 332 U.S. 194 (1947). There, the respondent corporation argued that in an adjudicative proceeding the Commission could not apply a general standard that it had formulated for the first time in that proceeding. Rather, the Commission was required to resort instead to its rulemaking procedures if it desired to promulgate a new standard that would govern future conduct. In rejecting this contention, the Court ... concluded that "the choice made between proceeding by general rule or by individual, ad hoc litigation is one that lies primarily in the informed discretion of the administrative agency."

And in *NLRB v. Wyman–Gordon Co.*, 394 U.S. 759 (1969), the Court upheld a Board order enforcing [a requirement] first promulgated in an earlier adjudicative proceeding.... The plurality opinion ... recognized that "[a]djudicated cases may and do ... serve as vehicles for the formulation of agency policies, which are applied and announced therein," and that such cases "generally provide a guide to action that the agency may be expected to take in future cases." ...

The views expressed in [*Chenery*] and *Wyman-Gordon* make plain that the Board is not precluded from announcing new principles in an adjudicative proceeding and that the choice between rulemaking and adjudication lies in the first instance within the Board's discretion. Although there may be situations where the Board's reliance on adjudication would amount to an abuse of discretion or a violation of the Act, nothing in the present case would justify such a conclusion. Indeed, there is ample indication that adjudication is especially appropriate in the instant context. As the Court of Appeals noted, "[t]here must be tens of thousands of manufacturing, wholesale and retail units which employ buyers, and hundreds of thousands of the latter." Moreover, duties of buyers vary widely depending on the company or industry. It is doubtful whether any generalized standard could be framed which would have more than marginal utility. The Board thus has reason to proceed with caution, developing its standards in a case-by-case manner with attention to the specific character of the buyers' authority and duties in each company. The Board's judgment that adjudication best serves this purpose is entitled to great weight.

The possible reliance of industry on the Board's past decisions with respect to buyers does not require a different result. It has not been shown that the adverse consequences ensuing from such reliance are so substantial that the Board should be precluded from reconsidering the issue in an adjudicative proceeding. Furthermore, this is not a case in which some new liability is sought to be imposed on individuals for past actions which were taken in good-faith reliance on Board pronouncements. Nor are fines or damages involved here. In any event, concern about such consequences is largely speculative, for the Board has not yet finally determined whether these buyers are "managerial."

It is true, of course, that rulemaking would provide the Board with a forum for soliciting the informed views of those affected in industry and labor before embarking on a new course. But surely the Board has discretion to decide that the adjudicative procedures in this case may also produce the relevant information necessary to mature and fair consideration of the issues. Those most immediately affected, the buyers and the company in the particular case, are accorded a full opportunity to be heard before the Board makes its determination. . . .

RETAIL, WHOLESALE AND DEPARTMENT STORE UNION v. NATIONAL LABOR RELATIONS BOARD

466 F.2d 380 (D.C.Cir.1972).

McGOWAN, CIRCUIT JUDGE:

The decision of the National Labor Relations Board now before us arises out of a strike by the Retail, Wholesale and Department Store Union against Coca Cola Bottling Works, Inc. . . . The most significant issue relates to the propriety of the Board's retroactive application of a change in policy effectuated by it through adjudication rather than rule making. For the reasons set forth hereinafter, the order of the Board is enforced only in part.

[The Board held that the employer had committed an unfair labor practice because it failed to hire workers who were permanently replaced during a strike to fill new job openings. This decision reflected a new policy. Prior to 1968,] it was a well settled rule, enunciated and applied by the Board, that when an employer permanently replaced an economic striker, he was under no obligation thereafter to treat that striker other than as a new applicant for employment. Although he was not permitted to discriminate against a former striker on the basis of his prior protected activity, he was not obliged actively to seek out and to offer former strikers reinstatement in preference to other applicants, or to accord rehired strikers their full former accrued rights and pay. . . . [In

June 1968, however, the Board reassessed this rule in light of a recent Supreme Court decision, *NLRB v. Fleetwood Trailer Co.*, 389 U.S. 375, 88 S.Ct. 543, 19 L.Ed.2d 614 (1967), and in a case entitled *The Laidlaw Corporation*] overturned this rule, and held that former strikers, although not entitled to reinstatement in preference to replacements permanently hired during the strike, are entitled to offers of reinstatement to vacancies resulting from the subsequent departure of permanent replacements; and they remain so entitled until they have obtained "other regular and substantially equivalent employment."

Applying the *Laidlaw* rule, the Board in this case determined that the Company committed unfair labor practices in failing to seek out and to offer to former strikers reinstatement to vacancies occasioned by the departure of replacements hired during the strike, and has imposed backpay liability against the Company on the basis of these unfair labor practices. Since all of the events relevant to this determination occurred before the Board's decision in *Laidlaw*, the Company protests the seeming inequity of branding as unfair, and imposing a back-pay remedy for, actions which, when undertaken, were squarely within explicitly articulated Board policy as sustained by the courts.

The Company does not assail the validity of the *Laidlaw* rule itself; and, were the validity of that rule directly before us, we would have no difficulty in joining the growing number of circuits that have upheld it. The issue presently before us involves only the question of its retroactive reach in the circumstances of this case.

Whether to give retroactive effect to new rules adopted in the course of agency adjudication is a difficult and recurring problem in the field of administrative law. It has arisen with notable frequency in the review of decisions by the Board. In order to establish an alternative procedure where inequity may be avoided, the Administrative Procedure Act has authorized agencies to conduct formal rule making proceedings, in which all interested parties are notified, hearings conducted, and new rules thereby adopted. Rules so adopted are prospective in application only. 5 U.S.C. § 551(4) (1970). Despite substantial and repeated scholarly and judicial criticism, the Board has largely ignored the rule making process, and has chosen rather to fashion new standards and to abrogate old ones in the context of case-by-case adjudication. . . .

In deciding whether to grant or deny retroactive force to newly adopted administrative rules, reviewing courts must look to the standard established by the Supreme Court in *SEC v. Chenery*:

> . . . [R]etroactivity must be balanced against the mischief of producing a result which is contrary to a statutory design or to legal and equitable principles. If that mischief is greater than the ill effect of the retroactive application of a new standard, it is not the type of retroactivity which is condemned by law.

Which side of this balance preponderates is in each case a question of law, resolvable by reviewing courts with no overriding obligation of deference to the agency decision, and courts have not infrequently declined to enforce administrative orders when in their view the inequity of retroactive application has not been counterbalanced by sufficiently significant statutory interests.

Among the considerations that enter into a resolution of the problem are (1) whether the particular case is one of first impression, (2) whether the new rule represents an abrupt departure from well established practice or merely attempts to fill a void in an unsettled area of law, (3) the extent to which the party against whom the new rule is applied relied on the former rule, (4) the degree of the burden which a retroactive order imposes on a party, and (5) the statutory interest in applying a new rule despite the reliance of a party on the old standard. Taking all of these considerations into account, we find that the inequity of applying the *Laidlaw* rule to the facts of this case far outweighs the interests that might be furthered if it were applied.

First, while the Supreme Court has observed in *Chenery* that "[E]very case of first impression has a retroactive effect . . .," this is not a case of first, but of second impression. The case in which the rule in question was adopted by the Board was *Laidlaw* itself, and, although the Seventh Circuit upheld its application to the employer there, it must be recognized that "[t]he problem of retroactive application has a somewhat different aspect in cases not of first but of second impression." The Supreme Court has identified a number of reasons calling for the application of a new rule to the parties to the adjudicatory proceeding in which it is first announced—reasons that do not apply with the same force to subsequent proceedings Thus the Court has suggested that to deny the benefits of a change in the law to the very parties whose efforts were largely responsible for bringing it about might have adverse effects on the incentive of litigants to advance new theories or to challenge outworn doctrines The Court has also made reference to "[s]ound policies of decisionmaking, rooted in the command of Article III of the Constitution that we resolve issues solely in concrete cases or controversies. . . ."

This approach may have a special legitimacy in the agency field. In *NLRB v. Wyman-Gordon Co.*, 394 U.S. 759 (1969), a plurality of the members of the Supreme Court differentiated sharply between the Board's quasi-legislative (rule making) and quasi-judicial (adjudicatory) powers, suggesting that both the Board's own statute and the Administrative Procedure Act limit the Board's use of the latter to promulgate rules of wholly prospective application. In the various expressions to this effect, there was emphasis upon the circumstance that the Board, in its earlier purported adjudication relied upon by it in that case, had concluded to make its decision announcing a new principle of labor relations prospective only; and this circumstance was strongly intimated to be a potent indicator of rule making.

Whatever may be the precise reach of *Wyman-Gordon* in terms of agency power to engage in wholly prospective adjudication, it does not prevent an agency in adjudication from declining in subsequent cases to apply a new rule retroactively if equitable or statutory considerations militate against it, any more than Article III prevents a federal court from limiting the retroactive scope of new legal principles articulated in judicial decision. Nor does *Wyman-Gordon* prevent reviewing courts from refusing to enforce such retroactive orders when the circumstances so dictate. In short, some of the considerations which support retroactivity in cases of first impression are, in subsequent cases, absent from the scale on which a court must weigh its decision.

The standard to which the Company attempted to conform its conduct in this case was well established and long accepted by the Board. Unlike *Chenery*, this is not the kind of case where the Board "had not previously been confronted by the problem" and was required by the very absence of a previous standard and the nature of its duties to exercise the "function of filling in the interstices of the Act." Rather it is a case where the Board had confronted the problem before, had established an explicit standard of conduct, and now attempts to punish conformity to that standard under a new standard subsequently adopted.

The record shows that in this case the Company at all times sought and closely followed the advice of counsel.... Unless the burden of imposing the new standard is de minimis, or the newly discovered statutory design compels its retroactive application, the principles which underlie the very notion of an ordered society, in which authoritatively established rules of conduct may fairly be relied upon, must preclude its retroactive effect....

Therefore, enforcement of the Board's order, insofar as it relates to reinstatement and back-pay liability for any period before the Supreme Court's decision in *Fleetwood*, is denied. As we have said hereinabove, the advent of *Fleetwood* marks the earliest point at which the Company could be said to have been put on notice that it must deal differently with former striking employees in respect of reemployment....

Notes and Questions

1. How does a "cease and desist" remedy take some of the sting out of the application of a policy that is new and unanticipated by the defendant? Should Congress give the FTC legal authority to fine firms for violations found as the result of an adjudication? EPA, for example, can assess civil penalties against firms that violate the Clean Water Act.

2. Once an adjudication is finished, other regulated entities are warned by the decision that the agency has adopted a new policy. If such an entity continues to engage in behavior that violates the agency's new policy, it can hardly claim that it is surprised by an agency action to enforce the new policy against it. There is a category of potential defendants, however, that can claim surprise despite the results of the adjudication. These are firms that engaged in the behavior now prohibited by the agency before it announced this result in an adjudication. This was the status of the firm in *Retail, Wholesale, and Department Store Union.*

3.   The FTC has the option of more than one remedy. Besides a cease and desist order, it can order a seller to make refunds to consumers in certain cases. Thus, even if the Commission issues a cease and desist order, it still has the option whether it will also order refunds. Thus, a court can review the legality of the Commission's decision to order refunds independently of the FTC's decision to use adjudication to declare Country Bob's credit practices to be a violation of the FTC act.

4.   Unlike the FTC, some agencies lack the authority to impose more than one remedy. The remedy available to the NLRB, for example, is to order a new election if it finds that a prior election was illegal. Can the NLRB declare a prior election to be invalid and refuse to order a new election? In *National Labor Relations Board v. Wyman–Gordon Co.*, 394 U.S. 759, 89 S.Ct. 1426, 22 L.Ed.2d 709 (1969), a majority of the Supreme Court suggested, but did not decide, that the answer was "no." Its analysis was that, if the agency's decision did not include an order to the party, but only had future effect as a general rule of precedence, the agency's decision looked more like a rule, which the APA defines as an "agency statement of general . . . applicability and future effect designed to . . . prescribe law or policy. . . ." 5 U.S.C. § 551(4). However, the agency had gone through the procedures applicable to adjudication, not rulemaking, so the final decision, if characterized as a rule, would be invalid. In *Wyman–Gordon,* though, the Court was still willing to allow the NLRB to use the decision as precedent in a subsequent adjudication, so whether the agency's original decision was valid or not, it had precisely the effect the NLRB desired it to have.

5.   Consider the following:

[A]n absolute prohibition against retroactivity would be extreme. In many instances new or altered interpretations are not novel or unanticipated, and thus implicate only minimally the concerns associated with retroactivity. Moreover, an absolute rule against retroactivity would produce undesirable side effects. The regulated person would be discouraged from seeking interpretive guidance from the responsible agency. Until the agency or a court announced an interpretation and gave fair notice of its existence, the interpretation could not be applied to anyone. By seeking interpretive guidance, the regulated individual might alert the agency to an interpretive problem and prompt it to render an undesired interpretation.

[Moreover, the adjudicative] process of rule creation and retroactive application is not always unfair. Unfairness depends on the extent to which the interpretation is novel and unanticipated, as well as on the severity of its impact. Retroactive application might be particularly necessary or appropriate when an initial interpretation proves to be totally unworkable or permits wholesale evasion of regulatory requirements. In such a situation, it may be desirable to replace that interpretation with a new one. It may also be appropriate to purge the initial interpretation immediately, especially if it produces particularly anomalous or undesirable results.

Russell L. Weaver, *Retroactive Regulatory Interpretations: An Analysis of Judicial Responses*, 61 NOTRE DAME L. REV. 167 (1986).

6. Generally, the practice in the states has mirrored the federal courts' tendency to state its preference for policy making by rulemaking but to show reluctance in overturning policy making by adjudication. *See* ARTHUR BONFIELD, STATE ADMINISTRATIVE RULE MAKING § 4.1.1 (1993 supplement). However, Bonfield notes that a few state courts have required agencies to adopt new policies through rulemaking, at least in certain circumstances. *Id.*, at § 4.3.1A (discussing cases in Oregon, New Jersey, Colorado, and Hawaii). *See also Project: State Judicial Review of Administrative Action*, 43 ADMIN. L. REV. 571, 738–739 (1991) (identifying New Jersey as "especially active" and citing a case from Colorado). Bonfield has been a tireless advocate of legislative requirements to require rulemaking for adopting new policies. *See* Arthur Bonfield, *State Administrative Policy Formulation and the Choice of Lawmaking Methodology*, 42 ADMIN. L. REV. 121 (1990). As Reporter for the 1981 version of the Model State Administrative Procedure Act of the National Conference of Commissioners on Uniform State Laws, Bonfield managed the inclusion of a requirement that agencies, "as soon as feasible and to the extent practicable, adopt rules ... embodying appropriate standards, principles, and procedural safeguards that the agency will apply to the law it administers." Section 2–104(3), 1981 MSAPA. According to Bonfield, this language requires agencies, when feasible and practicable, to adopt policy by rulemaking rather than adjudication. No state, however, has adopted this language from the 1981 MSAPA. BONFIELD, STATE ADMINISTRATIVE RULE MAKING, *supra*, at § 4.4.1. (noting somewhat similar language in the APAs of Wisconsin, Utah, Florida, and Washington).

In 1996 Florida distinguished itself among the states by adopting a new APA that takes a hard line against rulemaking. Nevertheless, it retained the provision noted by Bonfield requiring agencies to use rulemaking for any statement of generally applicability and future effect if to do so is feasible and practicable. *See generally* Jim Rossi, *Florida's 1996 Revised APA*, ADMIN. & REG. L. NEWS (Fall 1996, Vol. 22, No. 1).

B.   OPTION TWO: RULEMAKING

If an agency can engage in rulemaking and adjudication, it can adopt a new policy and make it legally binding through rulemaking and then, if necessary, enforce it through adjudication or judicial action. This section considers four legal issues that arise when an agency pursues this option. First, does the agency have the authority to promulgate substantive rules? Second, can an agency restrict the scope of adjudicatory hearing rights by promulgating a rule that eliminates the materiality of facts that otherwise would be subject to resolution in a hearing? Third, can an agency give retroactive effect to a rule? Finally, to what extent does due process limit an agency's authority to use adjudication to clarify an ambiguity in a rule?

1. RULEMAKING AUTHORITY

An agency has the authority to promulgate legislative rules if Congress (or a state legislature) has given it this power. Usually, an agency's mandate is clear concerning whether it has this authority, but there can be an issue regarding the existence of such authority, as demonstrated by *National Petroleum Refiners Association v. Federal Trade Commission*, 482 F.2d 672 (D.C.Cir.1973).

In *Petroleum Refiners*, the National Petroleum Refiners Association (NPRA), a trade group, challenged a rule on the ground that Congress had not given the FTC the authority to promulgate legislative rules. The regulation prohibited retail sales of gasoline without the posting of the octane rating of the gasoline on the pump. The FTC indicated that the rule would end a deceptive practice because consumers were purchasing gasoline with a higher octane rating than necessary to run their cars. According to the FTC Act in effect at that time, the Commission could "[f]rom time to time ... classify corporations and ... make such rules and regulations for the purpose of carrying out [its mandate]." NPRA argued that this grant only authorized the FTC to promulgate procedural rules.

The legislative history did not support the FTC's position that it had the power to promulgate substantive rules. For one thing, the FTC Act was passed at a time (1914) when it was unusual for Congress to grant an agency rulemaking power. Moreover, the placement and wording of the previous section of the Act supported the NPRA's position that the FTC was limited to issuing procedural rules. Nevertheless, the court held for the FTC. The court first characterized the legislative history somewhat disingenuously as ambiguous evidence of Congress' intent. It then pointed out all of the policy advantages of permitting an agency to promulgate legislative rules. The advantages identified by the court are described in the first section of this chapter. Finally, the court reasoned that Congress must have intended to delegate the power to issue legislative rules to the FTC because of all of the advantages of using rulemaking. *See* RICHARD A. PIERCE, SIDNEY A. SHAPIRO, & PAUL R. VERKUIL, ADMINISTRATIVE LAW & PROCESS 283–85 (3d ed. 1999) (analyzing *Petroleum Refiners*).

2. IMPACT ON ADJUDICATION RIGHTS

Statutes or regulations may give individuals a right to formal adjudication of a dispute before an agency. By adopting a legislative rule, however, an agency may be able to restrict the scope of such rights. For example, assume that the FTC promulgated a rule that prohibited Country Bob and other automobile dealers from using the "average" price in the calculation of any surplus from the resale of repossessed cars. If the FTC then seeks enforcement of its rule, the only relevant issue for an adjudication is whether a dealer is in compliance with the rule. Thus, the defendant could not call expert witnesses to testify concerning whether such a prohibition is good or bad for consumers. By comparison, if the FTC attempts to adopt the same policy in an adjudication, the defendant could call such witnesses to testify concerning the potential benefits and costs of such a policy.

In *United States v. Storer Broadcasting Company*, 351 U.S. 192, 76 S.Ct. 763, 100 L.Ed. 1081 (1956), the Supreme Court held that the use of rulemaking in this context is permissible despite this impact. Under the Communications Act of 1934, applicants for broadcast radio and television licenses were entitled to a "full hearing" before the Federal Communications Commission (FCC) could deny their application. Everyone was agreed that "full hearing" meant a formal adjudication under the APA. The FCC had adopted a regulation intended to limit concentration in the broadcast industry, thereby furthering the Act's requirement that the FCC regulate the airwaves for the public interest. The regulation limited the total number of broadcast licenses that the FCC would issue to any one broadcaster. Because Storer already owned the maximum number of stations, the FCC determined that no hearing was necessary to reject Storer's application for another license. Although Storer did not contest the fact that it already owned the maximum number of stations, it argued that the Commission was required by its statute to conduct a formal adjudication before it could reject an application, presumably to allow Storer to argue (and present evidence) against the policy embodied in the regulation. The Court rejected Storer's argument. It held that the FCC had no duty to hold a formal adjudicatory hearing if there were no material facts to be resolved in such a hearing, even though the rulemaking did not provide Storer with all the procedural rights to question the FCC's evidence or to present its own that it would have in a formal adjudication.

Although *Storer* permitted the FCC to use rulemaking to eliminate the need to hold an adjudicatory hearing on some factual issues, the Court suggested that a such a rule might have to provide an opportunity for an applicant to seek an adjudicatory hearing in an effort to justify an exception to, or waiver of, the rule. In *FCC v. WNCN Listeners Guild*, 450 U.S. 582, 101 S.Ct. 1266, 67 L.Ed.2d 521 (1981), however, the Court backed away from this earlier dicta. The Commission had promulgated a rule that eliminated entertainment format as a factor in licensing hearings. Prior to the rule, the Commission based its licensing decision, in part, on the nature of the programming that an applicant planned to offer. Further, the rule completely foreclosed any possibility that the Commission would reexamine its new policy in the context of a particular licensing decision. The dissenting justices would have required the FCC to have a "safety valve"—a procedure to consider applications for exceptions based on special circumstances. The majority, however, concluded the FCC was not required to offer such a procedure. According to the majority, *Storer Broadcasting* "did not hold that the Commission may never adopt a rule that lacks a waiver provision." 450 U.S. at 601 n. 44, 101 S.Ct. at 1278 n. 44.

This concept of determining certain facts incident to a policy adopted in a regulatory proceeding has been used by agencies in a variety of contexts, not just in broadcast licensing. *See, e.g., Heckler v. Campbell*, 461 U.S. 458, 103 S.Ct. 1952, 76 L.Ed.2d 66 (1983) (HHS regulation creates medical-vocational guidelines defining the relationship between physical ability, age, education, and work experience necessary to qualify for Social Security disability benefits, although statute provides for determining an applicant's eligibility in an adjudicatory hearing); *Vermont Yankee Nuclear Power Corp. v. NRDC*, 435 U.S. 519, 98 S.Ct. 1197, 55 L.Ed.2d 460 (1978) (Atomic Energy Commission regulation determining for purposes of future nuclear power plant licensing proceedings what the environmental impact would be of the nuclear waste generated by the plant).

An agency is not required to provide a safety valve for rules by permitting regulated entities to apply for a waiver or exception, but agencies often find it advisable to do so. For example, an exception process permits the agency to adjust a regulation in light of unanticipated consequences. If any agency permits too many exceptions, however, it can reintroduce the disadvantages of reaching policy decisions through adjudication rather than rulemaking. For a discussion of this and related problems, *see* Alfred Aman, *Administrative Equity: An Analysis of Exceptions To Administrative Rules*, 1982 DUKE L.J. 277.

3. RETROACTIVE RULEMAKING

Normally we think of rulemaking as prospective. Nevertheless, for many years agencies sometimes adopted regulations that had retroactive effect. Usually this was the result of judicial invalidation of one regulation and the agency's belief that it was necessary to substitute a valid regulation for the invalidated one, not only prospectively but also retroactively. In a pre-APA case, *Addison v. Holly Hill Fruit Products, Inc.*, 322 U.S. 607, 64 S.Ct. 1215, 88 L.Ed. 1488 (1944), the Supreme Court seemed to endorse this notion. There the Supreme Court held that the particular regulatory definition of "area of production," for the purpose of exempting certain food processors from the wage and hours law of the Fair Labor Standards Act, was beyond the Administrator's statutory authority. In an opinion by Justice Frankfurter, an acknowledged expert in administrative law, the Court remanded the case to the district court to hold it until the Administrator adopted a valid regulation (that would operate both retroactively and prospectively) governing which processors were exempt. In 1988, however, the Supreme Court reached a different conclusion in a case involving the Medicare program.

In *Bowen v. Georgetown University Hospital*, 488 U.S. 204, 109 S.Ct. 468, 102 L.Ed.2d 493 (1988), the Court reviewed an attempt by the Department of Health and Human Services (HHS) to give retroactive effect to a 1984 rule setting limits on the levels of Medicaid costs for which hospitals could obtain reimbursement. The rule was retroactive to July 1, 1981, which was the date that a district court had invalidated an essentially identical rule on the ground that HHS had violated the APA.

As the Court recognized, "In effect, the Secretary had promulgated a rule retroactively, and the net result was as if the original rule had never been set aside. . . ." A group of hospitals which were required by the new rule to reimburse the government over $2 million sought judicial review. Applying *Retail, Wholesale, and Department Store Union*, which you read earlier, the D.C. Circuit held that retroactive application was not justified under the circumstances of the case. The Supreme Court affirmed, but on a different ground.

The Court declared that an agency's power to issue rules is limited to the authority delegated by Congress, and that agencies do not have the power to give rules retroactive effect without an express grant of such authority by Congress:

> Retroactivity is not favored in the law. Thus, congressional enactments and administrative rules will not be construed to have retroactive effect unless their language requires this result. By the same principle, a statutory grant of legislative rulemaking authority will not, as a general matter, be understood to encompass the power to promulgate retroactive rules unless that power is conveyed by Congress in express terms. Even where some substantial justification for retroactive rulemaking is presented, courts should be reluctant to find such authority absent an express statutory grant. . . .

The Court found that the "statutory provisions establishing the Secretary's general rulemaking power contain no express authorization of retroactive rulemaking . . . ," and that the legislative history indicated that "no such authority was contemplated. . . ."

Problem 4–3: Copyright Fees

The Copyright Act establishes a compulsory license system that permits cable television operators to retransmit copyrighted broadcast programming without having to secure permission from each individual copyright owner. The cable operators pay royalties twice a year to the Copyright Office, according to a statutory formula based on the operator's "gross receipts." Congress has delegated to the Copyright Office the responsibility to implement the Act including the collection and distribution of royalties. The Register of Copyrights, who is appointed by the Librarian of Congress, is the administrator of the Office.

To permit the Office to implement its functions, Congress established the following rulemaking authority in the Copyright Office:

> The Register of Copyrights is authorized to establish regulations not inconsistent with law for the administration of the functions and duties made the responsibility of the Register under this title. All regulations established by the Register under this title are subject to the approval of the Librarian of Congress.

The Office promulgated a rule that established the method by which "gross receipts" were to be calculated when the fee that an operator charged a homeowner covered both broadcast and nonbroadcast programming. When cable operators sought judicial review of the rule, the district court held it was inconsistent with the Act. After the Office appealed the decision, the appellate court upheld the rule. After the appellate court decision, the operators paid the royalties for the seventeen-month period that elapsed between the district court and appellate decisions.

A group of broadcasters petitioned the Copyright Office to promulgate a rule that requires the operators to pay interest on the delayed payments.

The Register of Copyrights asks you, as a lawyer for the Office, whether the Register could adopt such a regulation.

Notes and Questions

1. By requiring a clear statement by Congress that an agency has the authority to promulgate retroactive rules, *Bowen* drastically limits the authority of most agencies to issue such rules. Congress has expressly authorized some agencies, however, to issue such rules. The Internal Revenue Service, for example, "may prescribe the extent, if any, to which any ruling or regulation, relating to the internal revenue laws, shall be applied without retroactive effect." 26 U.S.C.A. § 7805(b).

2. Are regulated entities better off if most agencies do not have the power to promulgate retroactive rules? *Bowen* certainly makes it easier for lawyers to advise their clients concerning the state of the law. Before *Bowen*, courts policed the use of retroactive rules by applying the test announced in *Retail, Wholesale and Department Store Union v. NLRB*. As noted, this was the approach of the D.C. Circuit in *Bowen*. As you may recall, *Retail, Wholesale and Department Store Union* used a balancing test to determine the retroactive reach of an adjudicatory decision. The courts considered the same factors in addressing the retroactive reach of a rule. Is this approach sufficient to protect the interests of regulated entities where they had justifiably relied on a different rule? Consider the following conclusion of Professor Luneburg:

> There is a constant tension in the law between the need for clear guidance in the private and public sectors in order to determine what is permissible and the desire to maintain flexibility to deal appropriately with individual situations. *Bowen* promises clear guidance: Formal retroactivity is only permissible if Congress has clearly provided for it by statute. A case-by-case balancing analysis inevitably creates uncertainty and accompanying costs for both the regulators and the regulated. Yet the legal system tolerates retroactivity to such a degree, whether in the adjudicative or legislative contexts, that the risk of adverse effects on reliance interests is always present and substantial. Accordingly, it is difficult to believe that the aggregate costs of uncertainty are increased significantly by permitting agencies to adopt retroactive rules when the benefits of retroactivity outweigh the costs even in the absence of clear delegations of

authority. This is particularly true because formally retroactive rules are only infrequently adopted, and their numbers are not likely to increase substantially even with the adoption of a balancing test.

William V. Luneburg, *Retroactivity And Administrative Rulemaking*, 1991 DUKE L.J. 106, 140–41.

3. In *Bowen*, the hospitals sued because they were disadvantaged by the HHS's decision to give the cost-limit rule retroactive effect. Regulated entities can also benefit from the retroactive application of a rule. Imagine, for example, that HHS's original rule had been upheld, but that HHS was convinced in the course of the litigation that the rule was too stingy. Could HHS have retroactively changed the rule back to its pre–1981 status? In *General Motors Corp. v. National Highway Traffic Safety Administration*, 898 F.2d 165 (D.C.Cir.1990), the agency denied a petition from automobile manufacturers to amend retroactively fuel economy standards for passenger cars. The companies sought relief because their failure to meet the existing regulation subjected them to possible fines. The court upheld the agency's determination that its statutory mandate did not permit it to issue such a retroactive rule.

4. AMBIGUOUS RULES

When an agency adopts a rule and then enforces it as necessary, this approach reduces the problem of surprise, but it does not eliminate it. The problem is reduced because by first adopting a rule, the agency notifies regulated entities that a new policy will be in effect. The problem of surprise is not eliminated, however, because the rule may be ambiguous or unclear. A regulated entity may therefore be subject to an enforcement action under circumstances it did not anticipate. If the enforcement occurs in a judicial forum, the court will interpret the meaning of the regulation, with possible issues of deference to the agency if the agency has expressed an interpretation of the regulation. If, however, the enforcement occurs in an agency adjudication, the agency interprets the regulation. In this case, normally the ALJ (or other administrative judge, if the adjudication is not formal) makes the first interpretation, with possible review by the head of the agency or an appellate administrative entity. The following case is an example of an agency interpreting its regulation.

GENERAL ELECTRIC COMPANY v. U.S. ENVIRONMENTAL PROTECTION AGENCY

53 F.3d 1324 (D.C.Cir.1995).

TATEL, CIRCUIT JUDGE:

The Environmental Protection Agency fined the General Electric Company $25,000 after concluding that it had processed polychlorinated biphenyls in a manner not authorized under EPA's interpretation of its regulations. We conclude that EPA's interpretation of those regulations is permissible, but because the regulations did not provide GE with fair warning of the agency's interpretation, we vacate the finding of liability and set aside the fine.

I.

GE's Apparatus Service Shop in Chamblee, Georgia decommissioned large electric transformers. Inside these transformers was a "dielectric fluid" that contained high concentrations of polychlorinated biphenyls ("PCBs"), which are good conductors of electricity. PCBs are also dangerous pollutants. "[A]mong the most stable chemicals known," they are extremely persistent in the environment and have both acute and chronic affects on human health. Recognizing the dangers of PCBs, Congress has required their regulation under the Toxic Substances Control Act. 15 U.S.C. §§ 2601–29 (1988 & Supp. V 1993) ("TSCA"). Pursuant to TSCA, the EPA promulgated detailed regulations governing the manufacture, use, and disposal of PCBs. See 40 C.F.R. pt. 761 (1994).

Because GE's transformers were contaminated with PCBs, the company had to comply with the disposal requirements of 40 C.F.R. § 761.60. Section 761.60(b)(1) requires the disposal of transformers by either incinerating the transformer, or by placing it into a chemical waste landfill after the PCB-laced dielectric fluid has been drained and the transformer rinsed with a PCB solvent. GE chose the "drain-and-landfill" option of section 761.60(b)(1)(i)(B).

The drain-and-landfill alternative required GE to dispose of the liquid drained from the transformer "in accordance with" the terms of section 761.60(a). Since the dielectric fluid contained extremely high concentrations of PCBs, the relevant provision of section 761.60(a) was section (1), a catch-all section applicable to liquids contaminated with more than 500 parts per million ("ppm") of PCBs. This section required those disposing of these particularly dangerous materials to do so solely by incineration in an approved facility. In accord with that requirement, GE incinerated the dielectric fluid after draining it from the transformers. It then soaked the transformers in a PCB solvent—in this case, freon—for 18 hours, drained the contaminated solvent, and immediately incinerated it as well.

In March, 1987, GE changed these procedures, beginning a process that ultimately led to the EPA complaint in this case. While GE continued to incinerate the dielectric fluid, it began a recycling process that recovered a portion of the dirty solvent through distillation. . . .

GE and EPA agree that the regulations require the incineration of the solvent. They disagree about whether the intervening distillation and recycling process violated the regulations.

. . . EPA charged the company with violating the PCB disposal regulations. After a hearing, an ALJ agreed and assessed a $25,000 fine. On appeal, the Environmental Appeals Board modified the ALJ's reasoning, but agreed with the disposition of the complaint and upheld the

$25,000 penalty. In other proceedings, the agency found the company liable for distillation it performed in six other locations, but suspended the fines for those violations pending the outcome of this appeal.

II.

GE argues that EPA's complaint is based on an arbitrary, capricious, and otherwise impermissible interpretation of its regulations. See 5 U.S.C. § 706(2)(A) (1988). To prevail on this claim, GE faces an uphill battle. We accord an agency's interpretation of its own regulations a "high level of deference," accepting it "unless it is plainly wrong." . . .

Particularly in the context of this comprehensive and technically complex regulatory scheme, EPA's interpretation of the regulations is permissible. Although GE's interpretation may also be reasonable, at stake here is the proper disposal of a highly toxic substance. We defer to the reasonable judgment of the agency to which Congress has entrusted the development of rules and regulations to ensure its safe disposal.

Had EPA merely required GE to comply with its interpretation, this case would be over. But EPA also found a violation and imposed a fine. Even if EPA's regulatory interpretation is permissible, the company argues, the violation and fine cannot be sustained consistent with fundamental principles of due process because GE was never on notice of the agency interpretation it was fined for violating. It is to this issue that we now turn.

III.

Due process requires that parties receive fair notice before being deprived of property. The due process clause thus "prevents . . . deference from validating the application of a regulation that fails to give fair warning of the conduct it prohibits or requires." In the absence of notice—for example, where the regulation is not sufficiently clear to warn a party about what is expected of it—an agency may not deprive a party of property by imposing civil or criminal liability. Of course, it is in the context of criminal liability that this "no punishment without notice" rule is most commonly applied. But as long ago as 1968, we recognized this "fair notice" requirement in the civil administrative context. In *Radio Athens, Inc. v. FCC*, we held that when sanctions are drastic—in that case, the FCC dismissed the petitioner's application for a radio station license—"elementary fairness compels clarity" in the statements and regulations setting forth the actions with which the agency expects the public to comply. This requirement has now been thoroughly "incorporated into administrative law."

Although the agency must always provide "fair notice" of its regulatory interpretations to the regulated public, in many cases the agency's pre-enforcement efforts to bring about compliance will provide adequate notice. If, for example, an agency informs a regulated party that it must seek a permit for a particular process, but the party begins processing without seeking a permit, the agency's pre-violation contact with the regulated party has provided notice, and we will enforce a finding of liability as long as the agency's interpretation was permissible. In some cases, however, the agency will provide no pre-enforcement warning, effectively deciding "to use a citation [or other punishment] as the initial means for announcing a particular interpretation"—or for making its interpretation clear. This, GE claims, is what happened here. In such cases, we must ask whether the regulated party received, or should have received, notice of the agency's interpretation in the most obvious way of all: by reading the regulations. If, by reviewing the regulations and other public statements issued by the agency, a regulated party acting in good faith would be able to identify, with "ascertainable certainty," the standards with which the agency expects parties to conform, then the agency has fairly notified a petitioner of the agency's interpretation.

. . . Although we defer to EPA's interpretation regarding distillation because it is "logically consistent with the language of the regulation[s]," we must, because the agency imposed a fine, nonetheless determine whether that interpretation is "ascertainably certain" from the regulations. . . . [W]e conclude that the interpretation is so far from a reasonable person's understanding of the regulations that they could not have fairly informed GE of the agency's perspective. We therefore reverse the agency's finding of liability and the related fine.

On their face, the regulations reveal no rule or combination of rules providing fair notice that they prohibit pre-disposal processes such as distillation. To begin with, such notice would be provided only if it was "reasonably comprehensible to people of good faith" that distillation is indeed a means of "disposal." While EPA can permissibly conclude, given the sweeping regulatory definition of "disposal," that distillation is a means of disposal, such a characterization nonetheless strays far from the common understanding of the word's meaning. A person "of good faith," would not reasonably expect distillation—a process which did not and was not intended to prevent the ultimate destruction of PCBs—to be barred as an unapproved means of "disposal."

Not only do the regulations fail clearly to bar distillation, they apparently permit it. Section 761.20(c)(2) permits processing and distribution of PCBs "for purposes of disposal." This language would seem to allow parties to conduct certain pre-disposal processes without authorization as long as they facilitate the ultimate disposal of PCBs and are done "in compliance with the requirements of this Part"—i.e., in accordance with other relevant regulations governing the handling, labeling, and transportation of PCBs. EPA argues—permissibly, as we concluded above—that the section allows parties to "use" PCBs in the described manner, but that those uses must still comply with the disposal requirements of section 761.60, including the requirement that unauthorized methods of disposal receive a disposal permit from the agency. This permissible interpretation, however, is by no means the most obvious interpretation of the regulation, particularly since, under EPA's view, section 761.20(c)(2) would not need to exist at all. If every process "for purposes of disposal" also requires a disposal permit, section 761.20(c)(2) does nothing but lull regulated parties into a false sense of security by hinting that their processing "for purposes of disposal" is authorized. While the mere presence of such a regulatory trap does not reflect an irrational agency interpretation, it obscures the agency's interpretation of the regulations sufficiently to convince us that GE did not have fair notice that distillation was prohibited. . . .

We thus conclude that EPA did not provide GE with fair warning of its interpretation of the regulations. Where, as here, the regulations and other policy statements are unclear, where the petitioner's interpretation is reasonable, and where the agency itself struggles to provide a definitive reading of the regulatory requirements, a regulated party is not "on notice" of the agency's ultimate interpretation of the regulations, and may not be punished. EPA thus may not hold GE responsible in any way—either financially or in future enforcement proceedings—for the actions charged in this case. Although we conclude that EPA's interpretation of the regulations is permissible, we grant the petition for review, vacate the agency's finding of liability, and remand for further proceedings consistent with this opinion.

Problem 4–4: OSHA Penalties

The Occupational Safety and Health Administration (OSHA) issued a citation against the Johnson Construction Company for violation of a regulation applicable to tunnels and shafts. Johnson is one of a number of contractors engaged in the construction of a subway tunnel extension project. The OSHA regulation provides:

> Bureau of Mines approved self-rescuers shall be available near the advancing face to equip each face employee. Such equipment shall be on the haulage equipment and in other areas where employees might be trapped by smoke or gas, and shall be maintained in good condition.

A "self-rescuer" is a canister-like device which tunnel employees can use to breathe in the event of a loss of oxygen caused by a cave-in or other similar emergency. An "advancing face" is the wall of earth at the end of a tunnel upon which excavation work is being done.

At the time that the company was cited, none of its employees were working near the "advancing face." Nevertheless, the Occupational Health and Safety Review Commission (OSHRC) upheld the citation on a 2 to 1 vote. The majority gave deference to OSHA's interpretation. OSHA had taken the position that the second sentence imposed a requirement that the safety equipment was required in areas other than the advancing edge where employees might be trapped by smoke or gas. Because Johnson's employees were in such an other area, the majority upheld OSHA's citation. The dissent held that the regulation was clear on its face that it applied only to workers in the area of an "advancing edge." The Commission ordered the company to pay a $20,000 fine.

Should the company seek judicial review of the Commission's decision? What arguments can you make on behalf of the company that imposition of a fine violates the due process clause? What counter arguments can OSHA make?

Notes and Questions

1. In *GE v. EPA*, the court found it a violation of due process to let EPA enforce a reasonable interpretation of its regulations because the defendants did not have fair warning of what was substantively required by the regulation. In Chapter 3, you studied another (and different) "due process" issue concerning fair notice. The earlier issue was whether an agency had given adequate notice of the charges to a defendant in an adjudication (whether administrative or judicial).

2. If enforcing a reasonable interpretation of EPA's regulation was a violation of due process in *GE v. EPA*, why was it not also a violation of due process to enforce a new interpretation of law in *Bell Aerospace*, or *Retail, Wholesale, and Department Union*? Does it turn on the nature of the enforcement action? In *GE v. EPA*, the court refers to EPA "punishing" GE and to EPA depriving GE of property.

3. After *GE v. EPA*, can EPA bring enforcement actions against other companies that use recycling programs like GE with respect to activities occurring before *GE v. EPA*? Can EPA bring charges with respect to activities occurring after *GE v. EPA*?

C. OPTION THREE: NONLEGISLATIVE RULES

Another option for an agency is to issue a nonlegislative rule. As discussed at the beginning of the chapter, Section 553 recognizes two types of nonlegislative rules: interpretive rules and statements of policy. An *interpretive rule* is a statement "issued by an agency to advise the public of the agency's construction of the statutes and rules which it administers." ATTORNEY GENERAL'S MANUAL ON THE ADMINISTRATIVE PROCEDURE ACT 30 n. 3 (1947), *reprinted in* ADMINISTRATIVE CONFERENCE OF THE UNITED STATES, FEDERAL ADMINISTRATIVE PROCEDURE SOURCEBOOK 96 (2d ed. 1992). A *policy statement* is a statement "issued by an agency to advise the public prospectively of the manner in which the agency proposes to exercise a discretionary power." *Id.* The distinction between these two types of nonlegislative rules will be considered in greater detail below. For now, it is sufficient to know that these rules warn the public of an agency interpretation or policy.

After a discussion of the advantages and disadvantages of nonlegislative rules, this section considers three legal issues that arise from agency's use of this option. First, although an agency can promulgate nonlegislative rules without use of notice and comment rulemaking, the APA does impose some requirements concerning the publication of such rules. Failure to follow these requirements may limit an agency's use of a nonlegislative rule. Second, a party might challenge a nonlegislative rule on the ground that the pronouncement is really a legislative rule. The entity would argue that the rule is invalid because the agency failed to use notice and comment procedures as required by the APA. In such cases, a court must determine whether the rule is "nonlegislative" or "legislative." Third, when an agency issues a nonlegislative rule, the issue arises concerning what are the consequences when a member of the public relies on this statement and then the government later refuses to follow it. When this situation arises, a court must determine whether a member of the public has any remedy because of the person's reliance on the agency's prior policy.

1. ADVANTAGES AND DISADVANTAGES OF OPTION THREE

Agencies generally find nonlegislative rules to be an efficient and beneficial way to implement regulatory policy. These rules are efficient because they are not subject to the procedural requirements of the APA, and they generally are also exempt from the various other statutory and administrative procedures applicable to rulemaking. They are beneficial for two primary reasons. First, a nonlegislative rule is a means of informing the public as to the agency's views and intentions. Second, a nonlegislative rule can be used as a management tool to issue guidance to agency employees, thereby ensuring centralized policy control and administrative uniformity.

Informing the public of the agency's interpretations and policies can have two separate salutary effects from the agency's perspective. First, most members of the regulated community will change their behavior in accordance with the expressed views of the agency. Whether because they wish to do the "right" thing, curry the agency's favor, or merely avoid the expense and problems of being the object of an enforcement action, regulated entities typically comply with nonlegislative rules, even though they are not legally binding. The second benefit from the agency's perspective is that, if the agency does need to take enforcement action to implement the expressed policy, the regulated community will not be able to claim surprise. As demonstrated in earlier sections, when an agency uses adjudication to adopt a new interpretation or policy, the defendant may lack prior warning of its intentions. In the *GE v. EPA* case, for example, if EPA had issued an interpretive rule interpreting its regulation governing disposal of PCBs, GE would not be able to complain that it did not have fair warning for any activities taken after the interpretive rule was issued.

As indicated in Chapter 1, in order to implement wide ranging regulatory statutes throughout the nation, most agencies act by means of numerous and widely dispersed regional offices. Absent centralized instruction, these different offices could develop different responses to similar problems and politically responsive officials in Washington, D.C., would not be able to take care that the laws would be faithfully executed. Accordingly, agencies develop staff manuals as one means of regularizing employee action that directly affects the public. OSHA, for example, has established guidelines for agency inspectors concerning which employers to target for inspections, how to conduct the inspections, and how to determine whether to cite employers for violations. Agencies could, of course, use legislative rules for this purpose, but as noted nonlegislative rules are more easily issued.

In light of these various considerations, it is no surprise that nonlegislative rules have become the "bread and butter" of the administrative process. Peter L. Strauss, *The Rulemaking Continuum*, 1992 DUKE L.J. 1463, 1468. Not everyone, however, views this development as entirely positive.

First, nonlegislative rules may be adopted without public input. A person who believes the rule to be unwise or illegal must either comply, or challenge the policy in an enforcement proceeding or, if possible, in pre-enforcement judicial review. Because of the time and expense of challenging a nonlegislative rule, however, members of the public may simply comply. Moreover, as Chapter 5 will make clear, problems of ripeness and finality may prevent pre-enforcement review. In cases where review is not sought or is unavailable, members of the public will have no opportunity to contest the rule, unless they were in a position to oppose it by lobbying the agency before the rule was adopted, and the agency is denied the educative value of their facts and arguments. Robert A. Anthony, *Interpretative Rules, Policy Statements, Guidance, Manuals, and the Like—Should Federal Agencies Use Them To Bind The Public?*, 1992 DUKE L.J. 1311, 1317.

Second, an agency may treat a nonlegislative rule as binding on members of the public. This can occur because of inadvertence—agency personnel erroneously assume the policy is legally binding—or strategic behavior—agency personnel treat the policy as legally binding in the hope that members of the public will acquiesce in its enforcement, thereby enabling the agency to avoid notice and comment rulemaking. Persons who challenge this behavior are protected as long as a court detects that the agency has imposed a binding obligation. But those who acquiesce are denied the opportunity to comment on legislative rules which is afforded them under the APA. PIERCE, SHAPIRO, & VERKUIL, *supra*, at §§ 6.4.4a-b.

Finally, because members of the public rely on nonlegislative rules as authoritative guidance of an agency's intentions, these persons may be adversely affected by their reliance. This can occur, for example, when an agency asserts in an enforcement proceeding a position different than that adopted in an existing nonlegislative rule on which the defendant relied. Agencies sometimes warn individuals not to rely on nonlegislative rules, but such warnings are often disregarded for good reasons. For example, the agency may adopt a policy statement for the express purpose of guiding the public. Moreover, there is a reasonable expectation that agency employees will follow staff instructions and manuals. Nevertheless, an agency can ordinarily disown a nonlegislative rule without prior notice because it has not been adopted by notice-and-comment rulemaking. The courts, however, have devised some protections for parties who justifiably rely on a nonlegislative rule, and you will study the extent to which these apply later in the chapter.

Problem 4–5: OSHA Policy Statement

The Occupational Safety and Health Administration Act ("the Act") requires employers to permit an employee representative to accompany an Occupational Safety and Health Administration (OSHA) inspector as that person inspects a workplace. An inspector's physical inspection of a workplace is called a "walk around." The Act states in relevant part:

> Subject to regulations issued by the Secretary [of Labor], a representative of the employer and a representative authorized by his employees shall be given an opportunity to accompany the Secretary or his authorized representative during the physical inspection of any workplace . . . for the purpose of aiding such inspection.

The Act also prohibits any employer from discriminating against an employee because the person exercises his or her rights under the Act:

> No person shall discharge or in any manner discriminate against any employee because such employee has filed any complaint or instituted or caused to be instituted any proceeding under or related to this chapter or has testified or is about to testify in any such proceeding or because of the exercise by such employee on behalf of himself or others of any right afforded by this chapter.

OSHA has discovered that many employers refuse to pay the employee representative for the time that person spends accompanying the OSHA inspector, which OSHA calls "walk around pay." The Assistant Secretary of Labor for OSHA believes that these companies are in violation of the Act's anti-discrimination requirement. She asks the Solicitor of Labor to advise her how OSHA should establish that such a refusal is a violation of the Act.

Assess from OSHA's perspective the three options described at the beginning of this chapter. Recall from Chapter 3 that the Occupational Safety and Health Act uses a split-enforcement model, not typical of most agencies, where OSHA acts as prosecutor only, with the ALJ and administrative appellate review provided by the Occupational Safety and Health Review Commission (OSHRC).

Notes and Questions

1. The Administrative Conference of the United States (ACUS) recommended that agencies voluntarily comply with the requirements of section 553 of the APA when issuing policy statements and interpretive rules, except in cases where it would be impracticable, unnecessary, or contrary to the public interest. ACUS also recommended that when there has been no prepromulgation notice and opportunity to comment, the public be notified of an opportunity to submit post-adoption com-

ments. Recommendation 76–5, 1 C.F.R. § 305.76–5 (1992); *see* Michael Asimow, *Public Participation in the Adoption of Interpretive Rules and Policy Statements*, 75 MICH. L. REV. 520 (1977) (report for ACUS concerning public participation). The American Bar Association has endorsed the ACUS recommendation, and it has recommended that Congress should consider amending the APA to require the use of notice and comment rulemaking for policy statements and interpretative rules if agencies fail to utilize these procedures voluntarily. American Bar Association, Recommendation on Nonlegislative Rulemaking, August, 1989.

Would you advise OSHA to use notice and comment rulemaking in the previous problem if it decides to issue a nonlegislative rule? If OSHA were required to use notice and comment before adopting an interpretive rule, is there any reason why it would not go ahead and promulgate a legislative rule instead? What does your answer suggest concerning the likely response of agencies to a law requiring nonlegislative rules to be preceded by notice and comment?

2. The Administrative Conference also recommended that agencies establish internal agency procedures that would permit persons to challenge the legality of nonlegislative rules or to seek a waiver from their application. Concerning policy statements, ACUS recommended:

> Agencies that issue policy statements should examine and, where necessary, change their formal and informal procedures, where they already exist, to allow as an additional subject requests for modification or reconsideration of such statements. Agencies should also consider new procedures separate from the context in which the policy statement is actually applied. The procedures should not merely consist of an opportunity to challenge the applicability of the document or request waivers or exemption from it; rather, affected persons should be afforded a fair opportunity to challenge the legality or wisdom of the document or to suggests alternative choices in an agency forum that assures adequate consideration by responsible agency officials. The opportunity should take place at or before the time the policy statement is applied to affected persons unless it is inappropriate or impracticable to do so.

Concerning instructions to agency staff, ACUS stated: "Agencies are encouraged to obtain public comment on such guidance." Agency Policy Statements, Recommendation 92B2, 57 Fed. Reg. 30103 (1992).

Why might such procedures be necessary in addition to the opportunity to comment on nonlegislative rules before they are issued or shortly thereafter? Are persons more likely to use such procedures to challenge a nonlegislative rule than to seek judicial review?

3. The 1961 Model State Administrative Procedure Act, which most states have adopted at least in part, does not exempt interpretive rules from notice and comment procedures. Thus, most states' APAs require state agencies to use notice and comment procedures for interpretive rules. When the 1981 MSAPA was written, however, the drafters reversed the earlier position, and the 1981 Act does exempt interpretive

rules from notice and public participation requirements. Most states, however, have not adopted the 1981 MSAPA provisions. Nevertheless, an increasing number of states have provided exemptions from notice and comment for interpretive rules. *See* BONFIELD, STATE ADMINISTRATIVE RULE MAKING, *supra*, § 6.9.2(a). (identifying statutes in Michigan, North Carolina, Virginia, Idaho, New York, Wyoming, Utah, and Washington). Moreover, Bonfield alleges that "agencies in virtually all states requiring notice and comment rulemaking for interpretive rules have completely ignored that requirement in practice, and have done so with impunity." *Id.*, § 6.9.2(b). Primarily, this is due to the fact that, if the rule properly interprets the statute, then even if the rule itself is not given effect, the effect of the statute is the same.

4.   When state agencies do use notice and comment for interpretive rules, states avoid the problem that plagues federal case law of determining which rules are interpretive and which are legislative. Similarly, when state agencies use notice and comment for interpretive rules, courts give them the same deference that they give to legislative rules.

5.   The 1961 MSAPA invented a new form of agency action called declaratory rulings (which should not be confused with declaratory judgements that one learns about in civil procedure). The same concept, renamed declaratory orders, was continued in the 1981 MSAPA. There is no equivalent recognized in the federal APA. Both involve a right of a person to seek a determination from an agency as to the applicability of a statute, rule, or order. *See* Section 8, 1961 MSAPA; Section 2–103, 1981 MSAPA. Many states have included in their APAs such a provision, although the so-called "right" is invariably qualified in some ways. Generally, the proceeding by which the determination is made involves a contested case proceeding (formal adjudication procedure), and the agency's final determination is subject to judicial review in the same manner as an order in a contested case proceeding. The determination by the agency is binding between the agency and the requesting party.

Because these actions require a relatively formal procedure for their issuance and because they are instituted at the initiative of the public, rather than the agency, state agencies are generally reluctant to issue declaratory rulings and orders.

2. APA PROCEDURES

Although section 553 exempts interpretive rules and policy statements from the notice and comment rulemaking, the APA does mandate procedures for nonlegislative rules concerning their publication. Section 552 of the APA, also known as the Freedom of Information Act (FOIA), requires each agency to publish in the Federal Register "statements of general policy or interpretations of general applicability formulated and adopted by the agency." *Id.* § 552(a)(1)(D). The APA also states: "[A] person may not in any manner be required to resort to, or be adversely affected by, a matter required to be published in the Federal Register and not so published," except if the person "has actual and timely notice of the terms" of the matter. *Id.* § 552. When a person proves that an agency failed in this legal duty to make information available, a court can provide appropriate relief.

In *Anderson v. Butz*, 550 F.2d 459 (9th Cir.1977), for example, the Secretary of Agriculture issued a revised instruction concerning the calculation of income to determine eligibility to receive food stamps. The instruction indicated that housing subsidies paid by the Department of Housing and Urban Development were to be treated as income for food stamp purposes. Although the instruction was placed in an administrative staff manual containing instructions to state agencies administering the Food Stamp Act, it was not published in the *Federal Register*. The Secretary was sued by recipients of food stamps who were declared ineligible for food stamps because they received housing subsidies. The Ninth Circuit, which treated the instruction as an "interpretive rule," held that the Secretary's failure to publish the rule violated the § 552(a)(1)(D) publication requirement. It also held that the Secretary could not circumvent this requirement by claiming that the plaintiffs had "actual and timely notice" of the unpublished instruction. The court observed, "Such notification occurred when the instruction took effect. This is not the timely notice contemplated by Congress when it enacted that exemption to the standard FOIA procedures." *Id.* at 463. The court therefore affirmed the district court's order requiring the Secretary to refund any sums that the plaintiffs were overcharged because the instruction was applied to them.

Notes and Questions

1. One commentator notes that judicial authority to give relief when an agency fails to publish a nonlegislative rule "is rarely exercised, perhaps because agencies make so much available and perhaps because few citizens have ever demanded their full statutory rights." JAMES T. O'REILLY, FEDERAL INFORMATION DISCLOSURE, § 6.05 at 6–19 (2d ed. 1995).

2. Because nonlegislative rules must be made available to the public by publishing them in the *Federal Register*, or making them available for copying, Professor Strauss describes these rules as "publication rules." PETER L. STRAUSS, AN INTRODUCTION TO ADMINISTRATIVE JUSTICE IN THE UNITED STATES 157–58 (1989). Although the more familiar term of "nonlegislative rules" is used in the text, that term is intended to be coextensive with Strauss' concept.

3. DISTINGUISHING NONLEGISLATIVE FROM LEGISLATIVE RULES

It is important to distinguish between nonlegislative and legislative rules because nonlegislative rules are exempt from notice and comment rulemaking procedures. Yet, it is not always easy to tell the difference between legislative and nonlegislative rules, just as earlier it was not always easy to tell the difference between procedural and substantive rules. This issue arises when someone challenges an agency pronouncement on the ground it constitutes an invalid legislative rule because the agency failed to use notice and comment rulemaking procedures to issue the rule. The agency will defend its action by arguing that its announcement fits within the exemption in section 553 for interpretive rules or statements of policy.

a. Policy Statements

Policy statements are issued by an agency to advise the public prospectively of the manner in which the agency proposes to exercise a discretionary power in subsequent adjudication or a rulemaking. A policy statement does not purport to interpret an existing duty in a regulation or statute. Instead, it announces that the agency intends to adopt a new duty in some future adjudication or rulemaking. Of course, the policy announced is not binding on the public until it is adopted by one of those means. Courts therefore use a "binding effect" test to distinguish policy statements from legislative rules. A court will ask whether the statement of the agency imposes a new duty or merely announces the intention to impose a new duty at some future time.

Determining whether an agency has or has not imposed a "duty" can be difficult. The difficulty usually arises because an agency has been ambiguous about its intentions. In one passage, an agency will characterize the intended effect of its statement in the language of commitment such as "regulatees must" take some action. In another passage, the agency characterizes its intended effect in the language of preference, such as "regulatees should" take some action. This ambiguity might be the result of agency oversight or sloppiness, but an agency might also be attempting to give a statement binding effect without using notice and comment rulemaking procedures. Professor Pierce notes that the "beauty of the 'binding effect' test lies in its ability to frustrate this illegitimate goal." DAVIS & PIERCE, *supra*, § 6.2, at 229. If a court finds that the agency has adopted a new duty, its statement is a rule that can be promulgated only through the use of rulemaking procedures. A court will therefore refuse to give the statement any legal effect. By comparison, if a court finds that the statement is actually a "policy statement," the agency still does not obtain any benefit from its attempt to bypass notice and comment rulemaking procedures. Because the rule is a "policy statement," a court will not permit the agency to give it binding effect.

Problem 4–6: OSHA Policy Statement

In problem 4–5, OSHA was trying to determine how it should proceed concerning the issue of walk around pay. Recall that OSHA was considering promulgating a legislative rule or announcing a nonlegislative rule.

Assume that the Assistant Secretary resolved this issue by giving a speech on the subject before a national convention of workplace safety professionals. She announced that "any employer who fails to compensate employees for walkabout times will be charged with discriminating against their workers under the OSHA Act." OSHA then issued an amendment of its Employee Manual to instruct inspectors to cite employers who failed to compensate employees for walk around time. The change was made without use of the notice and comment procedures of Section 553.

The National Association of Businesses (NAB) has sought judicial review of OSHA's rule. NAB seeks a declaratory judgment that the OSHA rule is invalid. OSHA responds that the rule is exempt from the APA's notice and comment procedures because it is a nonlegislative rule.

(1) What arguments would you make if you represented OSHA? What arguments would you make on NAB's behalf? How would you expect a court to resolve this issue?

(2) How would a court's decision likely be impacted if the court had held previously that the Act neither compels nor prohibits walk around pay? In other words, what is the impact of an earlier judicial ruling that Congress had not specifically considered this issue?

Problem Materials

AMERICAN HOSPITAL ASSOCIATION v. BOWEN

834 F.2d 1037 (D.C.Cir.1987)

WALD, CHIEF JUDGE:

We face here the issue of whether the Department of Health and Human Services ("HHS"), in implementing the system of "peer review" of Medicare outlays called for by Congress in its 1982 amendments to the Medicare Act, erred in not first undertaking the notice and comment rulemaking generally prescribed by the Administrative Procedure Act ("APA"), 5 U.S.C. § 553....

I. THE FACTUAL SETTING OF THIS CASE

Since 1965, the Medicare program has provided for the reimbursement by the federal government of those medical expenses incurred by persons over 65 and of persons suffering from certain disabilities. Typically, this reimbursement has been paid directly to the hospitals and doctors who provide health care to Medicare recipients.

In 1982, Congress amended the Medicare Act to provide for a new method of reviewing the quality and appropriateness of the health care provided by these medical providers to Medicare beneficiaries. It did so by passing the Peer Review Improvement Act of 1982, 42 U.S.C. §§ 1320c *et seq.*, which called for HHS to contract with "peer review organizations," or PROs, private organizations of doctors that would monitor "some or all of the professional activities" of the provider of Medicare services in their areas. A primary goal of Congress was to put into place a review system that would crack down on excessive reimbursements to hospitals for treatments of Medicare patients.

In passing the 1982 amendments, Congress painted with a broad brush, leaving HHS to fill in many important details of the workings of peer review. The amendments require HHS to designate geographic areas generally corresponding to each state, to be served by individual peer review organizations. HHS must then enter into an agreement, initially for a two-year term, with a PRO in each area. . . .

Under the 1982 amendments, hospitals, in turn, must enter into contracts with the HHS-designated PRO in their area in order to participate in the Medicare program and thus be eligible for reimbursements. The hospital must agree, as part of its contract with the PRO, to allow the PRO to review the validity of diagnostic information provided by the hospital, to review the completeness, adequacy and quality of care provided, to review the appropriateness of hospital admissions, and to review the appropriateness of care provided for which the hospital or health care provider seeks extra Medicare payments. . . .

The principal function of a PRO, once having been designated by HHS and having entered into agreements with hospitals in its jurisdiction, is to review for conformance with the substantive standards of the Medicare Act the professional activities of physicians, hospitals, and other providers of health care. . . .

Beyond those relatively skeletal requirements, Congress left much of the specifics of the hospital-PRO relationship to the inventiveness of HHS, empowering it to promulgate regulations governing PROs in order to implement the peer review program. . . .

The initial flurry of regulations promulgated by HHS filled in a variety of these details regarding PRO procedures. . . .

The parties to this case agree that these regulations were promulgated in conformance with the Administrative Procedure Act, 5 U.S.C. § 553, and thus they are not under challenge here.

In addition to these regulations, HHS issued a series of directives and transmittals governing the PRO program that are the subject of this lawsuit. These communications include [a] Request for Proposals ("RFP"), a document soliciting proposed contracts from entities seeking to become PROs. The RFP, among other things, told would-be PROs what review procedures their proposals must address, and what provisions their bids must contain. The contracts entered into between HHS and the PROs contain the provisions required by the RFP.

HHS concedes that neither the transmittals, the RFP, nor the contracts ultimately entered into were issued pursuant to the notice and comment procedures generally required by § 553 of the APA.

The plaintiff in this action is the American Hospital Association ("AHA"), an Illinois nonstock corporation that represents 6,000 member hospitals, serving approximately 30 million patients per year, more than 9 million of them Medicaid beneficiaries. . . .

II. DISCUSSION

... The function of the second § 553 exemption, for "general policy statements," is to allow agencies to announce their "tentative intentions for the future," without binding themselves. We have previously contrasted "a properly adopted substantive rule" with a "general statement of policy," observing that while a substantive rule "establishes a standard of conduct which has the force of law" in subsequent proceedings,

> [a] general statement of policy, on the other hand, does not establish a "binding norm." It is not finally determinative of the issues or rights to which it is addressed. The agency cannot apply or rely upon a general statement of policy as law because a general statement of policy only announces what the agency seeks to establish as policy.

The perimeters of the exemption for general statements of policy, like those for interpretive pronouncements, are fuzzy. See *Community Nutrition Institute v. Young*, 818 F.2d 943, 946 (D.C.Cir.1987) (quoting authorities describing the distinction between legislative rules and general policy statements as "tenuous," "blurred," "baffling," and even "enshrouded in considerable smog"). Nevertheless, our prior cases, in seeking to discern the line between these two types of agency pronouncements, have provided considerable guidance. One useful formulation is the two-criteria test set forth by Judge McGowan in *American Bus Association v. United States*:

> First, courts have said that, unless a pronouncement acts prospectively, it is a binding norm. Thus ... a statement of policy may not have a present effect: "a 'general statement of policy' is one that does not impose any rights and obligations"....

> The second criterion is whether a purported policy statement genuinely leaves the agency and its decisionmakers free to exercise discretion.

In applying these two criteria, we have observed that an agency's characterization of its own action, while not decisive, is a factor that we do consider....

Before examining the specific contractual provisions at issue, we turn first to analyze the role of the RFP in the process of contract formation between HHS and the PROs. The request for proposals is a document issued by HHS soliciting proposed contracts from entities seeking to become PROs. It is a mammoth sheaf full of detailed specifications, charts, and forms: the RFP included in the joint appendix in this case runs 335 pages and spells out in some detail the arrangements HHS expected to see in PRO contracts. Broadly stated, the RFP describes the technical procedures HHS expects PROs to follow, sets forth guidelines ... on the sampling strategies it wishes its enforcement agents to deploy, including special focus on particular areas of medicine and on ["diagnosis related groups"] whose average admission rates in the area exceeds the national average. Many of the terms set forth in the RFP are duplicative of the transmittals to PROs already discussed. Because it concluded that several of these terms contained legislative rules, not interpretive ones, the district court invalidated the RFP as containing "legislative rules," and the appellees seek affirmance under a similar theory.

We disagree. We instead regard the RFP as a nonbinding "general statement of policy," exempt from notice and comment requirements under § 553. The RFP binds neither the agency nor the PROs to whom it is sent. Rather, like the initial communication between parties negotiating to hammer out a contract, it establishes "talking points" and provides a foundation from which the agency and the would-be PRO can negotiate. In § 553 jargon, it allows the agency to announce its "tentative intentions for the future," while leaving the agency open to modifications based on the demands or requests of local PRO aspirants.

It is surely true that in negotiations over PRO contracts, HHS is a monopolist and thus has the upper hand in bargaining. However, final PRO contracts have been known to differ from the RFP, and in any event our cases construing this exemption make plain that even the possibility of the nonapplication of a given statement can entitle the agency to claim shelter under the "general statement of policy" exemption. See, e.g., *Pacific Gas & Electric Co.* (agency free to abandon tentative plans for gas rationing in event of shortage); *Brock v. Cathedral Bluffs* (agency free not to apply guidelines on mine operator violations because such guidelines were only a "general rule"). Under the *American Bus Association* formulation described earlier, the RFP neither has "a present effect" nor does it prevent future exercises of discretion on the part of agency decisionmakers. Accordingly, we conclude that the district court wrongly invalidated those parts of the RFP it deemed legislative in character ...

Notes and Questions

1. Normally, when courts look to see if a policy statement has legally binding effect, they look to see the impact on the regulated community. What should be the outcome if the agency binds itself and not the regulated community?

In *Community Nutrition Institute (CNI) v. Young*, 818 F.2d 943 (D.C.Cir.1987), the Food and Drug Administration had issued a notice to the food industry identifying "action levels," levels of contamination in food, below which FDA would not institute enforcement proceedings. In other words, the notice identified "acceptable" contamination for food producers. A consumer group challenged this approach on the ground FDA had promulgated a legislative rule. FDA defended on the ground that it was merely a statement of agency enforcement policy. The court noted that the statement was binding on the agency—it promised not to proceed against a food producer if the contamination remained below the action level—and accordingly concluded that the action levels were legislative rules. According to the court, a rule is legislative if it is binding on an agency, regardless of whether it is also binding on regulated entities.

2.   Cases like *CNI, see, e.g., W.C. v. Bowen*, 807 F.2d 1502, 1505 (9th Cir.1987) (invalidating Bellmon Review Program used by HHS Secretary because it limited agency discretion), have made agencies reluctant to commit themselves to abide by nonlegislative regulations. FDA, for example, has proposed a procedural rule that warns:

> an advisory opinion does not bind the agency, and it does not create or confer any rights, privileges, or benefits for or on any person. FDA may, in its discretion, recommend or initiate legal or administrative action against a person or product with respect to an action taken in conformity with an advisory opinion, provided that the legal or administrative action is consistent with applicable statutes and regulations.

57 Fed. Reg. 47314 (1992).

Professor Thomas argues that this understandable reluctance by agencies to commit to abiding by nonlegislative rules harms the public:

> In short, under those cases following the reasoning of *CNI*, the more unstructured, variable, and undisciplined the agency's prosecutorial approach, the more shielded an agency's prosecutorial discretion will be from public participation and, ultimately, from judicial review. But, if regularity of agency enforcement action, centralized control of agency personnel, and imposition of public, agency-wide policy are desired—and they are desired by most citizens—then a rule that essentially penalizes an agency for restricting the discretion of its own personnel would appear to be counter-productive.

Richard M. Thomas, *Prosecutorial Discretion and Agency Self–Regulation*: CNI v. Young *and the Aflatoxin Dance*, 44 ADMIN. L. REV. 131, 155 (1992).

Should the courts distinguish between nonlegislative rules that bind regulated entities and those that bind only agencies?

b.   Interpretive Rules

An "interpretive rule" interprets or clarifies the nature of the duties previously established by an agency's statutory mandate or by a regulation promulgated by the agency. In an interpretive rule, an agency announces how an existing law or statute is binding on those who are subject to it. The interpretive rule, however, is not itself binding. Until the interpretation is adopted in a legislative rule or an adjudication, persons are free to ignore the interpretation. For example, a regulation of the FTC might be susceptible to two interpretations; *i.e.*, a regulated entity is required to take action "A" or action "B." If the FTC issues an interpretive rule that says that the regulation requires persons to take action "A", regulated entities would not be legally bound to take action "A." The FTC's interpretation would become legally binding only if it took one of two actions. It could enforce its regulation and interpret the regulation to require action "A" in an adjudication, or it could use rulemaking and promulgate a rule that requires action "A." Thus, an interpretive rule differs from a legislative rule because, by itself, it does not establish any new duties. The duty to take action "A", if the FTC's interpretation is correct, was established by the regulation that the FTC adopted. However, to say that the interpretive rule is not binding and does not establish new duties is not to say it has no legal significance. As will be discussed later, courts may defer to the agency's interpretation, so regulated entities would ignore such interpretations at their peril.

When Congress has not granted an agency the authority to make legally binding rules, any rule that the agency issues is necessarily interpretive. If an agency has the authority to promulgate legislative rules, the courts look generally at two factors to determine whether to accept the rule as interpretive. *See* DAVIS & PIERCE, *supra*, § 6.3 (describing factors).

One factor is the agency's characterization of its actions. Courts are not bound by this declaration, but they usually give it some (difficult to define) minimal level of deference. *See e.g. Brock v. Cathedral Bluffs Shale Oil Co.*, 796 F.2d 533, 537 (D.C.Cir.1986) ("there is deference and there is deference—and the degree accorded to the agency on a point such as this is not overwhelming"); *General Motors Corp. v. Ruckelshaus*, 742 F.2d 1561, 1565 (D.C.Cir.1984) ("the agency's own label, while relevant, is not dispositive"); *Chamber of Commerce v. Occupational Safety and Health Administration*, 636 F.2d 464, 468 (D.C.Cir.1980) ("agency's own label is indicative, but not dispositive").

The other, and usually more important factor, is the source of the duty a party is obligated to obey. *See, e.g., Community Nutrition Institute v. Young*, 818 F.2d 943, 947 (D.C.Cir.1987) ("courts are to give far greater weight to the language actually used by the agency" than its characterization). If an agency is describing with greater clarity or precision a duty that a statute or regulation has already established, a court will conclude that the agency has issued a "nonlegislative rule." If a court determines that the agency is creating a entirely new duty, it will hold that the agency has violated section 553 by its failure to use rulemaking procedures.

The determination of the source of a duty may be easy or difficult. If, for example, a regulation contains a phrase that is clearly susceptible of two interpretations, the court is likely to accept as an interpretive rule an announcement that resolves this ambiguity. At other times, this analysis is more difficult. Consider, for example, the situation where a phrase in a regulation has an obvious definition, but an argument can be made that the phrase means something other than its obvious meaning. If the agency interprets the rule in a way that contradicts the obvious meaning of the phrase, has it imposed a "new duty" on regulated entities, or has it "merely" clarified the meaning of an existing duty?

Problem 4–7: USDA Interpretive Rule

The Animal Welfare Act, 7 U.S.C. §§ 2131 *et seq*, enacted in 1966, requires the Secretary of Agriculture to formulate standards "to govern the humane handling, care, treatment, and transportation of animals by dealers," and these standards must include minimum requirements "for handling, housing, feeding, watering, sanitation," etc. The Act authorizes the Secretary "to promulgate such rules, regulations, and orders as [the Secretary] may deem necessary in order to effectuate the purposes of [the Act]." Utilizing this authority, USDA promulgated a regulation, according to the APA's notice and comment procedures, entitled "structural strength," which provides that "the facility [housing animals] must be constructed of material and of such strength as appropriate for the animals involved." The regulation further provides that "the indoor and outdoor housing facilities shall be structurally sound and shall be maintained in good repair to protect the animals from injury and to contain the animals."

Patricia Jones has been a dealer in exotic animals on her farm outside of Wichita, Kansas since 1992. In a 25–acre compound, she regularly raises a variety of animals including "Big Cats"—such as lions, tigers, cougars and snow leopards. The animals are in pens, and there is a containment fence around the pens. In addition, there is a perimeter fence around the entire compound. When Jones started her animal dealership in 1992, she made the perimeter fence six feet high.

In 1998, USDA issued an internal memorandum that "dangerous animals," defined as including, among members of the cat family, lions, tigers, and leopards, "must be inside a perimeter fence at least eight feet high." The memorandum was addressed to the USDA inspectors responsible for assuring compliance with the Animal Welfare Act and regulations promulgated to implement it.

When an USDA inspector informs Ms. Jones that she must build a higher fence or she will be fined for non-compliance, she contacts you, her lawyer. She informs you that would cost her thousands of dollars to build a higher perimeter fence and that she likely would be forced out of business if she has to do so. On her behalf, you file a lawsuit claiming that the memorandum is really a legislative rule that is subject to the rulemaking requirements of section 553, which USDA did not observe.

What arguments can you make on your client's behalf? What arguments would you expect from USDA? How would you expect a court to rule?

Problem Materials

AMERICAN MINING CONGRESS v. MINE SAFETY & HEALTH ADMINISTRATION

995 F.2d 1106 (D.C.Cir.1993).

STEPHEN F. WILLIAMS, CIRCUIT JUDGE:

This case presents a single issue: whether Program Policy Letters of the Mine Safety and Health Administration, stating the agency's position that certain x-ray readings qualify as "diagnose[s]" of lung disease within the meaning of agency reporting regulations, are interpretive rules under the Administrative Procedure Act. We hold that they are.

* * *

The Federal Mine Safety and Health Act, 30 U.S.C. § 801 et seq., extensively regulates health and safety conditions in the nation's mines and empowers the Secretary of Labor to enforce the statute and relevant regulations. In addition, the Act requires "every operator of a ... mine ... [to] establish and maintain such records, make such reports, and provide such information, as the Secretary ... may reasonably require from time to time to enable him to perform his functions." The Act makes a general grant of authority to the Secretary to issue "such regulations as ... [he] deems appropriate to carry out" any of its provisions.

Pursuant to its statutory authority, the Mine Safety and Health Administration (acting on behalf of the Secretary of Labor) maintains regulations known as "Part 50" regulations, which cover the "Notification, Investigation, Reports and Records of Accidents, Injuries, Illnesses, Employment, and Coal Production in Mines." See 30 CFR Part 50. These were adopted via notice-and-comment rulemaking. Subpart C deals with the "Reporting of Accidents, Injuries, and Illnesses" and requires mine operators to report to the MSHA within ten days "each accident, occupational injury, or occupational illness" that occurs at a mine. Of central importance here, the regulation also says that whenever any of certain occupational illnesses are *"diagnosed,"* the operator must similarly report the diagnosis within ten days. Among the occupational illnesses covered are "[s]ilicosis, asbestosis, coal worker's pneumoconiosis, and other pneumoconioses." An operator's failure to report may lead to citation and penalty.

As the statute and formal regulations contain ambiguities, the MSHA from time to time issues Program Policy Letters ("PPLs") intended to coordinate and convey agency policies, guidelines, and interpretations to agency employees and interested members of the public. One subject on which it has done so—apparently in response to inquiries from mine operators about whether certain x-ray results needed to be reported as "diagnos[es]"—has been the meaning of the term diagnosis for purposes of Part 50.

[The agency had issued three PPL's that purported to interpret when x-ray results constituted a "diagnosis" of silicosis or one of the other pneumonoconioses covered by the Part 50 regulation. Although the three PPLs varied to some extent, all three agreed that such a diagnosis occurred when there was a chest x-ray of a miner who had a history of exposure to pneumonoconiosis-causing dust that rated 1/0 or higher on the International Labor Office (ILO) classification system. The ILO classification system uses a 12–step scale to measure the concentration of opacities (i.e., areas of darkness or shading) on chest x-rays. A 1/0 rating is the fourth most severe of the ratings. MSHA issued the last of the PPL's in August, 1992.]

The MSHA did not follow the notice and comment requirements of 5 U.S.C. § 553 in issuing any of the three PPLs. In defending its omission of notice and comment, the agency relies solely on the interpretive rule exemption of § 553(b)(3)(A).

We note parenthetically that the agency also neglected to publish any of the PPLs in the Federal Register, but distributed them to all mine operators and independent contractors with MSHA identification numbers, as well as to interested operator associations and trade unions. Compare 5 U.S.C. § 552(a)(1)(D) (requiring publication in the Federal Register of all "interpretations of general applicability") with id. at § 552(a)(2)(B) (requiring agencies to make available for public inspection and copying "those statements of policy and interpretations which have been adopted by the agency and are not published in the Federal Register"). Petitioners here make no issue of the failure to publish in the Federal Register.

* * *

The distinction between those agency pronouncements subject to APA notice-and-comment requirements and those that are exempt has been aptly described as "enshrouded in considerable smog," *General Motors Corporation v. Ruckelshaus*, 742 F.2d 1561, 1565 (D.C.Cir.1984) (en banc) (quoting *Noel v. Chapman*, 508 F.2d 1023, 1030 (2d Cir.1975)); see also *American Hospital Association v. Bowen*, 834 F.2d 1037, 1046 (D.C.Cir.1987) (calling the line between interpretive and legislative rules "fuzzy"); *Community Nutrition Institute v. Young*, 818 F.2d 943, 946 (D.C.Cir.1987) (quoting authorities describing the present distinction between legislative rules and policy statements as "tenuous," "blurred" and "baffling").

Given the confusion, it makes some sense to go back to the origins of the distinction in the legislative history of the Administrative Procedure Act. Here the key document is the Attorney General's Manual on the Administrative Procedure Act (1947), which offers "the following working definitions":

> *Substantive rules*—rules, other than organizational or procedural under section 3(a)(1) and (2), issued by an agency pursuant to statutory authority and which implement the statute, as, for exam-

ple, the proxy rules issued by the Securities and Exchange Commission pursuant to section 14 of the Securities Exchange Act of 1934 (15 U.S.C. 78n). Such rules have the force and effect of law.

Interpretative rules—rules or statements issued by an agency to advise the public of the agency's construction of the statutes and rules which it administers. . . .

General statements of policy—statements issued by an agency to advise the public prospectively of the manner in which the agency proposes to exercise a discretionary power.

Our own decisions have often used similar language, inquiring whether the disputed rule has "the force of law". We have said that a rule has such force only if Congress has delegated legislative power to the agency and if the agency intended to exercise that power in promulgating the rule.

On its face, the "intent to exercise" language may seem to lead only to more smog, but in fact there are a substantial number of instances where such "intent" can be found with some confidence. The first and clearest case is where, in the absence of a legislative rule by the agency, the legislative basis for agency enforcement would be inadequate. The example used by the Attorney General's Manual fits exactly—the SEC's proxy authority under § 14 of the Securities Exchange Act of 1934, 15 U.S.C. § 78n. Section 14(b), for example, forbids certain persons, "to give, or to refrain from giving a proxy" "in contravention of such rules and regulations as the Commission may prescribe". The statute itself forbids *nothing* except acts or omissions to be spelled out by the Commission in "rules or regulations". The present case is similar, as to Part 50 itself, in that § 813(h) merely requires an operator to maintain "such records . . . as the Secretary . . . may reasonably require from time to time". 30 U.S.C. § 813(h). Although the Secretary might conceivably create some "require[ments]" ad hoc, clearly some agency creation of a duty is a necessary predicate to any enforcement against an operator for failure to keep records. Analogous cases may exist in which an agency may offer a government benefit only after it formalizes the prerequisites.

Second, an agency seems likely to have intended a rule to be legislative if it has the rule published in the Code of Federal Regulations; 44 U.S.C. § 1510 limits publication in that code to rules "having general applicability and legal effect".

Third, " '[i]f a second rule repudiates or is irreconcilable with [a prior legislative rule], the second rule must be an amendment of the first; and, of course, an amendment to a legislative rule must itself be legislative.' " . . .

Accordingly, insofar as our cases can be reconciled at all, we think it almost exclusively on the basis of whether the purported interpretive rule has "legal effect", which in turn is best ascertained by asking (1) whether in the absence of the rule there would not be an adequate legislative basis for enforcement action or other agency action to confer benefits or ensure the performance of duties, (2) whether the agency has published the rule in the Code of Federal Regulations, (3) whether the agency has explicitly invoked its general legislative authority, or (4) whether the rule effectively amends a prior legislative rule. If the answer to any of these questions is affirmative, we have a legislative, not an interpretive rule.

Here we conclude that the August 1992 PPL is an interpretive rule. The Part 50 regulations themselves require the reporting of diagnoses of the specified diseases, so there is no legislative gap that required the PPL as a predicate to enforcement action. Nor did the agency purport to act legislatively, either by including the letter in the Code of Federal Regulations, or by invoking its general legislative authority under 30 U.S.C. § 811(a). See *MSHA Program Information Bulletin No. 88–03* (August 19, 1988) (characterizing PPLs generally as "[i]nterpretation"). The remaining possibility therefore is that the August 1992 PPL is a de facto amendment of prior legislative rules, namely the Part 50 regulations.

A rule does not, in this inquiry, become an amendment merely because it supplies crisper and more detailed lines than the authority being interpreted. If that were so, no rule could pass as an interpretation of a legislative rule unless it were confined to parroting the rule or replacing the original vagueness with another.

Although petitioners cite some definitions of "diagnosis" suggesting that with pneumoconiosis and silicosis, a diagnosis requires more than a chest x-ray—specifically, additional diagnostic tools as tissue examinations or at least an occupational history—MSHA points to some administrative rules that make x-rays at the level specified here the basis for a finding of pneumoconiosis. A finding of a disease is surely equivalent, in normal terminology, to a diagnosis, and thus the PPLs certainly offer no interpretation that repudiates or is irreconcilable with an existing legislative rule.

We stress that deciding whether an interpretation is an amendment of a legislative rule is different from deciding the substantive validity of that interpretation. An interpretive rule may be sufficiently within the language of a legislative rule to be a genuine interpretation and not an amendment, while at the same time being an incorrect interpretation of the agency's statutory authority. Here, petitioners have made no attack on the PPLs' substantive validity. Nothing that we say upholding the agency's decision to act without notice and comment bars any such substantive claims.

Accordingly, the petitions for review are

Dismissed.

METROPOLITAN SCHOOL DISTRICT v. DAVILA

969 F.2d 485 (7th Cir.1992).

BAUER, CHIEF JUDGE.

In this appeal, Robert Davila on behalf of the United States Department of Education challenges the district court's grant of summary judgment in favor of the Metropolitan School District of Wayne Township and the plaintiff class. The district court held that a letter purporting to interpret part B of the Individuals with Disabilities Education Act, 20 U.S.C. §§1411–20 ("the IDEA–B" or "the Act"), was a legislative ruling subject to the notice and comment procedures of the Administrative Procedure Act, 5 U.S.C. § 553 ("APA"). We reverse, and remand for entry of summary judgment in favor of Davila and the Department of Education.

The IDEA–B provides federal funding to states to support the education of disabled children. In order to qualify for funds, a state must establish a policy assuring a free appropriate education ("FAPE") to all disabled children. Most states distribute the federal monies to local educational agencies that provide services to eligible children. The Office of Special Education and Rehabilitative Services of the United States Department of Education ("OSERS") administers the Act. The rule at issue here was announced by OSERS in a letter written by Davila, the Assistant Secretary for Special Education and Rehabilitative Services, in response to an inquiry from Frank E. New, the Director of Special Education for the Ohio Department of Education.

New asked whether the IDEA requires states to provide educational services to disabled children who are expelled or suspended for an extended period for reasons unrelated to their disability. In his letter, Davila stated that OSERS interpreted the IDEA to require states to continue services in these circumstances. The relevant facts are undisputed: this position was not published in the Federal Register or the Code of Federal Regulations, and public comments were not solicited before it was issued.

The School District for Wayne Township sued the Secretary on behalf of itself and all similarly situated providers of educational services. The School District asserts that OSERS' position places a large financial burden on school districts, and that the districts are entitled to notice of the proposed rule and the opportunity to comment. Both parties filed motions for summary judgment. The district court agreed with the School District that OSERS' position is a legislative rule subject to the notice and comment requirements of the APA. The district court acknowledged that "the issue is whether ... the New Letter is a 'legislative rule' requiring notice and comment under the APA, or ... merely an 'interpretive rule' exempt from the APA's requirements." ...

... In this case, we believe Davila and the Department of Education are entitled to judgment as a matter of law. The APA does not require administrative agencies to follow notice and comment procedures in all situations. Section 553(b)(3)(A) specifically excludes "interpretive rules, general statements of policy, or rules of agency organization, procedure, or practice," from the notice and comment procedures. Based upon our review of Davila's letter and controlling authority, we conclude that the letter announced OSERS' construction of the IDEA, and hence is an interpretive rule that does not trigger the APA's notice and comment requirements....

... The District of Columbia Circuit, sitting *en banc*, has set forth the general principles to be used to determine whether a rule is interpretive, and, therefore, exempt from APA's notice and comment requirements. The "starting point" of the analysis is the agency's characterization of the rule. The agency's characterization is not dispositive, but is a relevant factor.

After considering the agency's characterization, the ... court outlined the more general distinction between interpretive and legislative rules:

> An interpretive rule simply states what the administrative agency thinks the [underlying] statute means, and only reminds affected parties of existing duties. On the other hand, if by its action the agency intends to create new law, rights, or duties, the rule is properly considered to be a legislative rule.

[For example, in one case the court determined a rule was interpretive, because] "the 'entire justification for the rule was comprised of reasoned statutory interpretation, with reference to the language, purpose, and legislative history' of the statute." In other words, " 'interpretive rules are statements as to what the administrative officer thinks the statute or regulation means,' whereas legislative rules have 'effects completely independent of the statute.' "

This court has noted with approval Professor Davis' test for distinguishing interpretive from legislative rules. Davis' formulation provides:

> [R]ules are legislative when the agency is exercising delegated power to make law through rules, and rules are interpretative when the agency is not exercising such delegated power in issuing them. When an agency has no granted power to make law through rules, the rules it issues are necessarily interpretative; when an agency has such granted power, the rules are interpretative unless it intends to exercise the granted power....

... Professor Davis' formulation focuses upon the kind of power the agency is using, and hence the force and effect of the rule. Legislative rules have the force and effect of law—they are as binding upon courts as congressional enactments. Interpretive rules, although they are entitled to deference, do not bind reviewing courts. But this formulation is of limited value when an agency, like the Department of Education, has both delegated rulemaking authority and the power to issue interpretive rules. All agencies charged with enforcing and administering a statute have "inherent authority to issue interpretive rules informing the public of the procedures and standards it intends to apply in exercising its discretion." Basically, then, this test returns us to the starting point set forth by the District of Columbia Circuit—what kind of rule does the agency think it has promulgated?

Here, Secretary Davila's letter purports to be an interpretation of the IDEA. Davila based the OSERS' interpretation upon the Supreme Court's decision in *Honig v. Doe*, 484 U.S. 305 (1988), and other cases interpreting IDEA, the language of both the statute and an implementing regulation (34 C.F.R. § 300.121(a)), and the legislative history of the Act. These are the classic tools a reviewing body, be it court or agency, relies upon to determine the meaning of a statute. Thus, the first factor in our analysis, and an "important" one according to the governing authority, weighs in favor of a determination that the rule is interpretive.

Under the more general inquiry, we must determine whether the rule merely states what OSERS thinks the statute means, or creates new law, rights, or duties. . . .

[A]n agency's change in its reading of a statute does not necessarily make the rule announcing the change legislative. That rules "may have altered administrative duties or other hardships does not make them substantive [legislative]." Further, as we have pointed out, the issue here is a new one, and the agency's ruling does not constitute a change in policy.

The rule announced in Davila's letter satisfies the general test of an interpretive rule. It relies upon the language of the statute and its legislative history to determine "that Congress did not intend for educational services to cease for children with handicaps who were removed from schools as a result of behavioral problems." This represents the paradigmatic case of an interpretive rule. The rule is based on specific statutory provisions ("all handicapped children"), and its validity stands or falls on the correctness of the agency's interpretation of the statute. In these circumstances, it is clear that the rule is an interpretive one. . . .

Notes and Questions

1.   Prevailing authority rejects the use of the "substantial impact" test as an independent means to distinguish nonlegislative and legislative rules. *E.g.*, *Mada-Luna v. Fitzpatrick*, 813 F.2d 1006, 1016 (9th Cir.1987); *Cabais v. Egger*, 690 F.2d 234 (D.C.Cir.1982). The substantial impact test asks whether or not an agency pronouncement has a "substantial impact" on the rights or duties of the public. This test was introduced in the 1970s by judges who reasoned that if a rule has such an impact, an agency should use notice and comment procedures. *E.g.*, *Independent Broker–Dealers' Trade Ass'n. v. SEC*, 442 F.2d 132, 144 (D.C.Cir.1971); *Pickus v. U.S. Bd. of Parole*, 507 F.2d 1107, 1113B14 (D.C.Cir.1974).

Judges generally have rejected the test because it is inconsistent with section 553, which exempts nonlegislative rules regardless of their impact. In addition, after *Vermont Yankee Nuclear Power Corp. v. Natural Resources Defense Council, Inc.*, 435 U.S. 519, 98 S.Ct. 1197, 55 L.Ed.2d 460 (1978), the courts have noted that they cannot require agencies to use procedures more demanding than those required by statute or the Constitution. *See* Michael Asimow, *Nonlegislative Rulemaking and Regulatory Reform*, 1985 DUKE L.J. 381, 401 (discussing the demise of the substantial impact test).

2. Professor Asimow would have reviewing courts give more deference to the agency's characterization of its action as an interpretive rule or policy statement. The agency's description of the purpose and intended effect of its action "should be of central importance in characterizing its product" because such deference would promote certainty and predictability. Asimow, *supra*, at 389–90. Would the public be better off if the courts adopted Professor Asimow's recommendation? Why or why not?

3. Is there any way to give some legal effect to nonlegislative rules that stops short of the rule having a "binding effect"? Consider Professor Strauss' proposal for nonlegislative rules which, as mentioned earlier, he describes as publication rules:

> Would it not be preferable, as strongly suggested by the equation between publication rules and adjudicatory results in the diction of Section 552(a), to treat publication rules as ordinarily having the force of precedent for the agency and its personnel. Significant differences from legislative rules would remain. One may assert in the course of agency adjudication that a publication rule is inappropriate on the facts, whereas a legislative rule binds the agency adjudicator as well as a court; and an agency is not permitted to treat departure from the advice of a publication rule as an infraction—it must make its case in terms of the statute or rule underlying the publication rule. But it does not follow that the agency or its staff are free to disregard validly adopted publication rules on which a private party may have relied *absent* the demonstration of its inappropriateness. The whole point of the exercise is to structure discretion, to provide warning and context for efficient interaction between the agency and the affected public.

Peter L. Strauss, *The Rulemaking Continuum*, 41 DUKE L.J. 1463, 1486 (1992).

4. In *American Mining Congress,* the D.C. Circuit said one of the factors to consider in determining an agency's intent whether a rule is interpretative or legislative is whether the agency published the rule in the Code of Federal Regulations, because the CFR is supposed to contain rules "having general applicability and legal effect." However, shortly thereafter, the same judge elaborated on this factor, saying that in "none of the cases citing the distinction [based on publication in the Code of Federal Regulations], however, has the court taken publication in the

Code of Federal Regulations, or its absence, as anything more than a snippet of evidence of agency intent." *Health Ins. Ass'n. of America, Inc. v. Shalala,* 23 F.3d 412 (D.C.Cir.1994). Why might an agency publish an interpretative rule in the CFR even if it did not want it to be of "legal effect"? Wouldn't it be convenient to the public to have one source in which to find an agency's official interpretations, rather than have to search through old Federal Registers?

4. LEGAL PROTECTION OF RELIANCE ON NONLEGISLATIVE RULES

As discussed earlier, when an agency issues a nonlegislative rule, it may hope (or even intend) that regulated entities will follow the policy announced in the rule, because such compliance may eliminate the need for the agency to adopt the policy as legally binding. The government issues interpretations and policy statements in other circumstances as well. For example, a member of the public calls the Internal Revenue Service when filling out his income tax return to get advice as to how to fill it out.

When the government offers its view as to what the law requires, the question arises as to what are the consequences when a member of the public relies on this statement and the government later refuses to follow it. For example, an agency might decide that there is a better policy than the one that the government originally announced it intended to follow. Since nonlegislative rules are not legally binding, it is easy enough for an agency to change its mind and change is policy. In the case of advice given by an agency employee, the advice might simply be wrong, and the government seeks to implement the correct policy. Whatever the government's reason for abandoning its earlier position, a regulated entity or a member of the public might be left in the lurch. By relying on a nonlegislative rule, which the government has abandoned, a regulated entity might find itself not be in compliance with a regulatory requirement. Can the government nevertheless fine the entity for noncompliance? By erroneously relying on the advice of a government employee, a member of the public might end up owing more taxes or the person may fail to qualify for a government benefit. Does the person have any recourse if he or she reasonably relied on the advice given by a government agent? This section considers when, and under what legal theories, a court might protect persons who reasonably rely on nonlegislative rules

Problem 4–8: USDA Interpretive Rule

In Problem 4–7, Patricia Jones sought to challenge an USDA memorandum that a perimeter fence around an animal compound must be eight feet tall. At the time she constructed the compound, a veterinarian employed by the Agriculture Department, who was assigned to inspect the facility when Jones started her animal dealership, told her that she should make the fence six feet high, which she did. USDA has threatened to bring an enforcement action against Ms. Jones, but it has not yet done so. In the prior problem, Jones challenged the interpretation on the ground that it was really a legislative rule, which USDA had issued without notice and comment procedures.

As Ms. Jones' lawyer, what grounds do you have based on the following case law for arguing that USDA's interpretive rule—requiring an eight-foot fence—is invalid? How likely is it that you will succeed?

Problem Materials

ALASKA PROFESSIONAL HUNTERS ASSOCIATION, INC. v. FEDERAL AVIATION ADMINISTRATION
177 F.3d 1030 (D.C.Cir.1999).

RANDOLPH, CIRCUIT JUDGE:

In January 1998 the Federal Aviation Administration published a "Notice to Operators" aimed at Alaskan hunting and fishing guides who pilot light aircraft as part of their guiding service. The Notice required these guide pilots to abide by FAA regulations applicable to commercial air operations. The question in this petition for judicial review, brought by a guide organization and individual guides, is whether § 553 of the Administrative Procedure Act required the FAA to proceed by way of notice and comment rule making rather than by announcement in the Federal Register.

Fishing and hunting are big business in the State of Alaska. A large proportion of the State's population depends on the income these activities generate. Small lodges in remote regions of the State cater to hunters and fisherman, providing food and shelter, guide services, and air transportation to and from the lodge and on side trips, all for a flat fee. It is common for a fishing or hunting guide to serve as the pilot of the light aircraft typically used in these operations. Beginning in 1963, the FAA, through its Alaskan Region, consistently advised guide pilots that they were not governed by regulations dealing with commercial pilots.

The advice stemmed from *Administrator v. Marshall*, 39 C.A.B. 948 (1963), a decision rejecting the FAA's attempt to sanction Ralph E. Marshall, a registered Alaskan hunting and fishing guide and the holder of an FAA-issued private pilot's license. [At the time of the case, the Civil Aeronautics Board (CAB) was responsible for the safety of air transportation, a function that was subsequently transferred to the FAA. The case held that the pilot did not require a commercial aviation license because Marshall's flight with the hunter in search of polar bear was "merely incidental" to his guiding business, in part because he had not billed for it separately. The applicable regulation, at the time of the case and to the present, required a commercial license for persons who operate aircraft "for compensation or hire."]

... In view of *Marshall*, the FAA's Alaskan Region concluded that these regulations did not govern guide pilots whose flights were incidental to their guiding business and were not billed separately.... Although the Alaskan Region never set forth its interpretation of [the applicable regulation] in a written statement, all agree that FAA personnel in Alaska consistently followed the interpretation in official advice to guides and guide services....

Whether FAA officials in Washington, D.C. were aware of the advice being given by their counterparts in Alaska is uncertain. No correspondence or other writing bearing on the question has surfaced....

[In the 1990's, the FAA began studying guiding operations in Alaska, and a 1992 report expressed concern about the safety record of guide pilots who did not have commercial aviation licenses. Aware of this concern, the Alaska Professional Hunters Association submitted a petition for rulemaking, which proposed that the FAA require that guides be subject to additional licensing requirements, but that they not be required to obtain commercial aviation licenses.] In January 1998, without having responded to the Association's petition, the FAA published its "Notice to Operators" in the Federal Register.

The Notice, which is the subject of the Association's petition for judicial review, announced that ... the FAA would [in the future] treat these guides as commercial operators or air carriers, transporting passengers for compensation or hire. The FAA acknowledged that the Alaskan Region had not enforced [the regulation requiring a commercial aviation license] against guide pilots in the past. But it attributed this to a misreading of the *Marshall* case....

The Association, joined by two Alaskan guide pilots, contends that the Notice to Operators altered the FAA's well-established interpretation of its regulations and should have been promulgated pursuant to notice and comment rule making....

Our analysis of these arguments draws on *Paralyzed Veterans of America v. D.C. Arena*, 117 F.3d 579, 586 (D.C.Cir.1997), in which we said: "Once an agency gives its regulation an interpretation, it can only change that interpretation as it would formally modify the regulation itself: through the process of notice and comment rulemaking." We there explained why an agency has less leeway in its choice of the method of changing its interpretation of its regulations than in altering its construction of a statute. "Rule making," as defined in the APA, includes not only the agency's process of formulating a rule, but also the agency's process of modifying a rule. 5 U.S.C. § 551(5). When an agency has given its regulation a definitive interpretation, and later significantly revises that interpretation, the agency has in effect amended its rule, something it may not accomplish without notice and comment....

The FAA thinks *Paralyzed Veterans* is inapposite because its January 1998 Notice to Operators did not fundamentally change any "authoritative interpretation" of its regulations. The FAA is confident that the Alaskan Region's advice to guide pilots for more than 30 years stemmed from a misreading of the *Marshall* decision and so could not have represented the view of the agency. . . .

Even if the FAA as a whole somehow had in mind an interpretation different from that of its Alaskan Region, guides and lodge operators in Alaska had no reason to know this. Those regulated by an administrative agency are entitled to "know the rules by which the game will be played." See Holmes, *Holdsworth's English Law*, 25 LAW QUARTERLY REV. 414 (1909). Alaskan guide pilots and lodge operators relied on the advice FAA officials imparted to them—they opened lodges and built up businesses dependent on aircraft, believing their flights were subject to part 91's requirements only. That advice became an authoritative departmental interpretation, an administrative common law applicable to Alaskan guide pilots. The FAA's current doubts about the wisdom of the regulatory system followed in Alaska for more than thirty years does not justify disregarding the requisite procedures for changing that system. Throughout this period, guide pilots and lodge operators had no opportunity to participate in the development of the part 135 regulations and to argue in favor of special rules for their operations. Air transportation regulations have evolved considerably since 1963 and part 135 has been the subject of numerous rule making proceedings. Had guides and lodge operators been able to comment on the resulting amendments and modifications to part 135, they could have suggested changes or exceptions that would have accommodated the unique circumstances of Alaskan air carriage. As the FAA pointed out in its brief, the agency's regulations have, in several respects, treated Alaska differently from the continental United States. There is no reason to suppose that with the participation of Alaskan guide pilots and lodge operators, the regulations [regarding commercial aviation licenses] would not have been affected. If the FAA now wishes to apply those regulations to these individuals, it must give them an opportunity to comment before doing so. The Notice to Operators was published without notice and comment and it is therefore invalid. . . .

So ordered.

ASSOCIATION OF AMERICAN RAILROADS v. DEPARTMENT OF TRANSPORTATION
198 F.3d 944 (D.C.Cir.1999).

TATEL, CIRCUIT JUDGE: . . .

I

Congress directed the Secretary of Transportation to "prescribe regulations and issue orders for every area of railroad safety. . . ." To "carry out all railroad safety laws of the United States," Congress created the Federal Railroad Administration, also a respondent in this case.

The Rail Safety Enforcement and Review Act of 1992 directs the Secretary to review and revise federal rules relating to railroad track safety. Responding to that directive, the FRA conducted a study and found that from 1989 to 1993 twenty-two roadway workers were struck and killed by trains or on-track equipment. Based on these findings and the results of a similar study by a joint labor-management task force, the FRA established a federal advisory committee comprised of representatives from management, labor, and the agency to engage in a negotiated rulemaking on the subject of roadway worker safety. The advisory committee eventually produced the Roadway Worker Protection Rule, which, following notice and comment, became effective in January 1997.

The Roadway Worker Protection Rule establishes procedures to protect roadway workers from accidents involving trains or other on-track equipment. At issue in this case is the Rule's procedure for demarcating portions of track where railroad employees are working and on-track accidents generally occur. The Rule refers to these areas as "working limits."

[The rule gives railroads a number of options concerning how to notify on-coming trains that they are about to encounter employees working on or near the tracks. A railroad is required to] mark the boundaries of working limits with a flagman, a fixed signal displaying "Stop," a station identified in the railroad's timetable, a clearly identifiable milepost, or, in language central to this case, any other "clearly identifiable physical location prescribed by the operating rules of the railroad that trains may not pass without proper authority." We will refer to this last option as "paragraph (c)(5)."

Railroads taking advantage of the paragraph (c)(5) option often use unattended red flags to mark the boundaries of working limits. When a train enters a segment of controlled track containing working limits, a dispatcher directs the train engineer to travel at restricted speed until the train arrives at the unattended red flag, at which point it stops and awaits instructions from the roadway worker in charge of the working limits. The Rule provides that the roadway worker in charge may not allow trains to pass the red flag and enter the working limits until certain specified steps are taken to protect the safety of roadway workers.

The dispute in this case centers on the precise amount of information about the red flag that paragraph (c)(5) requires the dispatcher to give the train engineer. Petitioner, the Association of American Railroads (AAR), argues that paragraph (c)(5) requires the dispatcher to tell approaching trains nothing more than that they will encounter a red flag somewhere within the segment of controlled track. The FRA, supported by intervenor, the Brotherhood of Maintenance of Way Employees, reads the regulation to mean that the train engineer must be told not just that a red flag exists somewhere within the segment of controlled track, but of the flag's precise location. . . .

Two years after issuing the Roadway Worker Protection Rule, the FRA incorporated its view of paragraph (c)(5) in Workplace Safety Technical Bulletin WPS–99–01 (January 1999). Issued without notice and comment, the technical bulletin directs that when unattended red flags or other passive devices are used to demarcate working limits, trains "must be provided with advance notification of the type and exact location of these devices."

In this petition for review, the AAR does not challenge the advance notice requirement as an unreasonable interpretation of the Roadway Worker Protection Rule. Rather, claiming that the FRA had previously interpreted paragraph (c)(5) as not requiring advance notice of precise flag location and that the bulletin amounts to an "abrupt departure" from that interpretation, the AAR argues that the Administrative Procedure Act required the agency to issue the bulletin through notice and comment rulemaking. . . .

II

. . . In support, the AAR relies on our recent decision *in Alaska Professional Hunters Ass'n, Inc. v. FAA*, 177 F.3d 1030 (D.C.Cir. 1999). . . .

The AAR claims that this case is like *Alaska Professional Hunters*. Just as the FAA had definitively ruled that Alaskan guides were not subject to commercial air regulations, the AAR argues, the FRA had determined that prior notice of a red flag's precise location was unnecessary. The AAR detects this definitive interpretation in the Roadway Worker Protection Rule's Preamble, in an email and two letters from agency personnel, and in the agency's own safety manual. . . .

Even interpreting the evidence in the light most favorable to the AAR, however, we think it is quite clear that the FRA never adopted a definitive interpretation of paragraph (c)(5) that it could change only through notice and comment rulemaking. Although the AAR has unearthed some documents that seem, albeit sometimes vaguely, to support its argument that the agency—or at least some of its employees—may have interpreted paragraph (c)(5) as not requiring notice of precise flag location, none of those documents even comes close to the express, direct, and uniform interpretation present in *Alaska Professional Hunters*. Also, unlike *Alaska Professional Hunters*, where the regional office's position was reflected in official agency adjudications holding that Alaskan guides need not comply with commercial pilot standards, nothing in this record indicates that the FRA ever held that the Roadway Worker Protection Rule did not require advance notice of red flag location. Indeed, as far as we can tell, prior to the technical bulletin, the issue regarding notice of flag location had been the subject of no official agency proceeding. In other words, this record reveals no "administrative common law" (this court's words in *Alaska Professional Hunters*) that paragraph (c)(5) does not require notice of precise flag location.

This case differs from *Alaska Professional Hunters* in another important respect. Believing that they were exempt from commercial pilot regulations, "Alaskan guide pilots and lodge operators relied on the advice FAA officials imparted to them—they opened lodges and built up businesses dependent on aircraft." Nothing in this record suggests that railroads relied on the Gavalla letter or other documents in any comparable way. The AAR does not claim that its members made large capital expenditures based on their interpretation of paragraph (c)(5) or altered their business practices in any significant manner. Instead, the AAR claims that the railroads' agreement with the outcome of the negotiated rulemaking was "critically dependent on their ability (consistent with the regulations) to use red flags [alone] to demarcate working limits." Yet the AAR points to no evidence to support this assertion; all evidence in the record is post-negotiated rulemaking. Even if true, moreover, agreement to a negotiated rulemaking based on a presumptive interpretation of ambiguous language hardly compares to the three decades of business development that had occurred in *Alaska Professional Hunters*.

To sum up, we see the record in this case quite differently than does the AAR. We read the various letters and other documents relied on by the AAR not as evidence of a firm agency policy, but rather as the agency's initial efforts to respond to the dispute over the meaning of paragraph (c)(5) that flared up shortly after the Roadway Worker Protection Rule was issued. As one would expect when agency personnel face controversies of this kind, their responses were often ambiguous and incomplete. Not until the agency issued the technical bulletin was the controversy officially and definitively resolved. If, as the AAR urges, the record in this case reflects a definitive interpretation of paragraph (c)(5), it would mean that an agency's initial, often chaotic process of considering an unresolved issue could prematurely freeze its thinking into a position that it would then be unable to change without formal rulemaking. Not only would this blur the distinction between definitive agency action and informal, uncoordinated communications, it would seriously hamstring agency efforts to interpret and apply their own policies. The Administrative Procedure Act requires no such result....

Notes and Questions

1. Until *Alaska Professional Hunters*, it was assumed that an agency did not have to use notice and comment procedures to change an existing interpretive rule. Since a nonlegislative rule can be issued or amended simply by publishing it (or by making it available to a person affected by it), the APA appears to permit an agency immediately to make a change.

2. In *Alaska Professional Hunters*, the court justifies its holding in part on the fact that the bush pilots relied to their detriment on the first interpretation that they were not required to obtain commercial pilots licenses. The court in *Association of American Railroads* distinguished *Alaska Professional Hunters* on the ground that the railroads did not have the same type of reliance as the bush pilots. What is the relevance of "reliance" to the issue of whether the APA requires notice and comment rulemaking?

3. What other justification does the court in *Alaska Professional Hunters* give for holding the FAA had to use notice and comment rulemaking to issue the second interpretive rule? Is this justification valid in light of *Vermont Yankee*? Recall from Chapter Two that the Supreme Court in *Vermont Yankee* prohibited the lower courts from imposing procedural obligations on agencies that were not required by the APA. Do you anticipate that the Supreme Court will overrule the doctrine adopted in *Alaska Professional Hunters*?

4. Besides the degree of reliance, is there any other factor that determines when an agency must use notice and comment rulemaking to replace a prior interpretive rule? Consider the following distinction of the Third Circuit Court of Appeals:

> Taken together, the cases indicate that agencies can alter the interpretation of their regulations in modest ways without requiring notice and comment. However, if an agency's new interpretation will result in significantly different rights and duties than existed under a prior interpretation, notice and comment is required. This distinction, which is not precise, is akin to the distinction that is generally made between substantive and interpretive rules. *See Dia Navigation Co. v. Pomeroy*, 34 F.3d 1255, 1264 (3d Cir.1994) (although the line between substantive and interpretive rules is "incapable of being drawn with much analytical precision," and the tests formulated to draw the line "are often circular," the "basic determination . . . involves whether . . . the agency intends to create new law, rights or duties") (quotations omitted). In that context, we have indicated that it is "helpful to analyze a rule with an eye to the policies animating the APA's notice and comment requirement." "The essential purpose of according § 553 notice and comment opportunities is to reintroduce public participation and fairness to affected parties after governmental authority has been delegated to unrepresentative agencies."

Caruso v. Blockbuster–Sony Music Entertainment Centre, 174 F.3d 166, 177 (3d Cir. 1999).

In an earlier note, we observed that prevailing authority rejects use of the "substantial impact" test as an independent means to distinguish nonlegislative and legislative rules. Has the Third Circuit reintroduced this concept?

Problem 4–9: Animal Welfare Act Advice

The Animal Welfare Act (AWA or "the Act") authorizes the Secretary of Agriculture to promulgate regulations governing the transportation and handling of various animals in interstate commerce. One of the goals of the Act is the "humane treatment of animals during transportation in commerce." The Act requires the Secretary to "promulgate standards to govern the humane handling, treatment, and transportation of animals by dealers, research facilities, and exhibitors."

The Secretary promulgated extensive regulations including provisions relating to the transportation of dogs in interstate commerce. One such regulation limits the temperatures that dogs can be subjected to during transportation: "When dogs are transported in interstate commerce, they shall not be subjected to excessive heat or cold." The regulations apply to dealers and intermediate handlers. Dealers or intermediate handlers violate the regulations, if they "knew, or should have known," that animals are being shipped in violation of the regulations.

Appellant Happy Puppy Farms, Inc. (HPF), which breeds and sells puppies in Port Royal, Kentucky, has been cited for violation of the excessive heat regulation concerning a shipment of Collie puppies to the "Puppies and More" store in Kansas City, Missouri. At the time of the citation, the dogs were located in a cage in a hanger at the Louisville Airport. The Department of Agriculture inspector, who issued the citation, seized the puppies and delivered them to the Louisville Humane Society. At the time, Kentucky was suffering from a heat wave that began at the end of June and continued through the end of August. During this period, temperatures frequently exceeded 95 degrees. The hanger was not air-conditioned.

HPF would have preferred to ship the Collie puppies, which were born on April 15, 1993, before June 15, 1993, but it did not have a customer for them until the Puppies and More order of July 3, 1993. HPF's manager, hoping to ship on July 23, but fearing that AWA regulations might still prohibit the shipment, telephoned the United States Department of Agriculture's (USDA) Louisville regional office for advice. The manager was concerned because if the puppies could not be shipped by that date, HPF would have to euthanize them. After being informed of HPF's situation, a USDA field inspector gave his opinion that it was permissible to ship the puppies on the 23rd if the temperature dropped into the low 90s. When the temperature did dip until the low 90s, HPF sent the puppies to the airport for shipment to Kansas City.

After reviewing Inspector Collins' citation, USDA's Office of Compliance (OC) decided to seek civil penalties against HPF. The judicial officer (JO) at USDA concluded that the regulation prohibited carriers from subjecting 13 week-old puppies to 93–degree heat. The JO also held that HPF had improperly relied on the advice of Inspector Johnson, noting that the USDA has detailed procedures governing the issuance of interpretive rulings under the AWA. HPF had attempted to obtain such a ruling, but USDA had informed it that it would take 8 to 10 weeks. The JO's decision imposing a penalty of $2,000 constituted final agency action and became the USDA's final decision.

If you represent HPF, what arguments should you make on its behalf when you appeal the USDA decision. If you represented USDA, what arguments would you make in response? How would you expect an appellate court to decide this case?

Problem Materials

HECKLER v. COMMUNITY HEALTH SERVICES

467 U.S. 51, 104 S.Ct. 2218, 81 L.Ed.2d 42 (1984).

JUSTICE STEVENS delivered the opinion of the Court.

Under what is recognized for present purposes as an incorrect interpretation of rather complex federal regulations, during 1975, 1976, and 1977 respondent received and expended $71,480 in federal funds to provide health care services to Medicare beneficiaries to which it was not entitled. The question presented is whether the Government is estopped from recovering those funds because respondent relied on the express authorization of a responsible Government agent in making the expenditures.

I

Under the Medicare program, providers of health care services are reimbursed for the reasonable cost of services rendered to Medicare beneficiaries as determined by the Secretary of Health and Human Services (Secretary). Providers receive interim payments at least monthly covering the cost of services they have rendered. Congress recognized, however, that these interim payments would not always correctly reflect the amount of reimbursable costs, and accordingly instructed the Secretary to develop mechanisms for making appropriate retroactive adjustments when reimbursement is found to be inadequate or excessive. Pursuant to this statutory mandate, the Secretary requires providers to submit annual cost reports which are then audited to determine actual costs. The Secretary may reopen any reimbursement determination within a 3–year period and make appropriate adjustments.

The Act also permits a provider to elect to receive reimbursement through a "fiscal intermediary." If the intermediary the provider has nominated meets the Secretary's requirements, the Secretary then enters into an agreement with the intermediary to have it perform those administrative responsibilities she assigns it. These duties include receipt, disbursement, and accounting for funds used in making Medicare payments, auditing the records of providers in order to ensure payments have been proper, resolving disputes over cost reimbursement, reviewing and reconsidering payments to providers, and recovering overpayments to providers. The fiscal intermediary must also "serve as a center for, and communicate to providers, any information or instructions furnished to it by the Secretary, and serve as a channel of communication from providers to the Secretary."

Respondent Community Health Services of Crawford County, Inc. (hereafter respondent), is a nonprofit corporation. In 1966 it entered into a contract with [the government] to provide home health care services to individuals eligible for benefits under Part A of the Medicare program.

Under the contract, respondent received reimbursement through a fiscal intermediary, the Travelers Insurance Cos. (Travelers).

[Uncertain about its eligibility to receive government reimbursement for certain expenses, Community Health Services contacted Travelers to ask whether it was eligible to recover the expenses in question. Traveler's Medicare manager orally informed the company that the expenses were reimbursable under the Medicate program. Relying on Travelers' advice, Community Health Services asked for and obtained reimbursement.]

It is undisputed that correct administrative practice required Travelers to refer respondent's inquiry to the Department of Health and Human Services for a definitive answer. However, Travelers did not do this until August 7, 1977, when a written request for instructions was finally submitted to the Philadelphia office of the Department's Bureau of Health Insurance. Travelers was then formally advised that [the expenses in question were not reimbursable] and therefore had to be subtracted from respondent's Medicare reimbursement. On October 7, 1977, Travelers formally notified respondent of this determination. Travelers then reopened respondent's cost reports for the preceding three years and recomputed respondent's reimbursable costs, determining that respondent had been overpaid a total of $71,480.

In May 1978 Travelers made a formal demand for repayment of the disputed amount. Respondent filed suit and obtained temporary injunctive relief against the Secretary and Travelers; in November 1979, the parties entered into a stipulation providing that the Secretary would postpone any attempts at recoupment and that the civil action would be stayed pending the outcome of administrative review. [The administrative review confirmed that the government should not have repaid Community Health Services for the expenses and, after the health provider sued HHS, the district court affirmed the administrative determination.]

The Court of Appeals reversed, reaching only the estoppel question. It held that the Government may be estopped by the "affirmative misconduct" of its agents and that Travelers' erroneous advice coupled with its failure to refer the question to the Secretary constituted such misconduct. It rejected as "clearly erroneous" the District Court's finding that it was unreasonable for respondent to rely on Travelers' advice, concluding instead that respondent acted reasonably because the relevant regulation had no clear meaning and respondent had no source other than Travelers to which it could turn for advice.

II

Estoppel is an equitable doctrine invoked to avoid injustice in particular cases. While a hallmark of the doctrine is its flexible application, certain principles are tolerably clear:

> "If one person makes a definite misrepresentation of fact to another person having reason to believe that the other will rely

upon it and the other in reasonable reliance upon it does an act . . .
the first person is not entitled

* * *

"(b) to regain property or its value that the other acquired by
the act, if the other in reliance upon the misrepresentation and
before discovery of the truth has so changed his position that it
would be unjust to deprive him of that which he thus acquired."
Restatement (Second) of Torts § 894(1) (1979).

Thus, the party claiming the estoppel must have relied on its adversary's
conduct "in such a manner as to change his position for the worse," and
that reliance must have been reasonable in that the party claiming the
estoppel did not know nor should it have known that its adversary's
conduct was misleading.

When the Government is unable to enforce the law because the
conduct of its agents has given rise to an estoppel, the interest of the
citizenry as a whole in obedience to the rule of law is undermined. It is
for this reason that it is well settled that the Government may not be
estopped on the same terms as any other litigant. Petitioner urges us to
expand this principle into a flat rule that estoppel may not in any
circumstances run against the Government. We have left the issue open
in the past,[12] and do so again today. Though the arguments the Government advances for the rule are substantial, we are hesitant, when it is
unnecessary to decide this case, to say that there are no cases in which
the public interest in ensuring that the Government can enforce the law
free from estoppel might be outweighed by the countervailing interest of
citizens in some minimum standard of decency, honor, and reliability in
their dealings with their Government. But however heavy the burden
might be when an estoppel is asserted against the Government, the
private party surely cannot prevail without at least demonstrating that
the traditional elements of an estoppel are present. We are unpersuaded
that that has been done in this case with respect to either respondent's
change in position or its reliance on Travelers' advice.

III

To analyze the nature of a private party's detrimental change in
position, we must identify the manner in which reliance on the Govern-

---

12. . . . In fact, at least two of our cases
seem to rest on the premise that when the
Government acts in misleading ways, it
may not enforce the law if to do so would
harm a private party as a result of governmental deception. See *United States v.
Pennsylvania Industrial Chemical Corp.*,
411 U.S. 655, 670–675, 93 S.Ct. 1804, 1814–
1817, 36 L.Ed.2d 567 (1973) (criminal defendant may assert as a defense that the
Government led him to believe that its conduct was legal); *Moser v. United States*, 341
U.S. 41, 71 S.Ct. 553, 95 L.Ed. 729 (1951)
(applicant cannot be deemed to waive right
to citizenship on the basis of a form he
signed when he was misled as to the effect
signing would have on his rights). This
principle also underlies the doctrine that an
administrative agency may not apply a new
rule retroactively when to do so would unduly intrude upon reasonable reliance interests. See *NLRB v. Bell Aerospace Co.*, 416
U.S. 267, 295, 94 S.Ct. 1757, 1772, 40
L.Ed.2d 134 (1974); . . . *SEC v. Chenery
Corp.*, 332 U.S. 194, 203, 67 S.Ct. 1575,
1580, 91 L.Ed. 1995 (1947).

ment's misconduct has caused the private citizen to change his position for the worse. In this case the consequences of the Government's misconduct were not entirely adverse. Respondent did receive an immediate benefit as a result of the double reimbursement. Its detriment is the inability to retain money that it should never have received in the first place. Thus, this is not a case in which the respondent has lost any legal right, either vested or contingent, or suffered any adverse change in its status. When a private party is deprived of something to which it was entitled of right, it has surely suffered a detrimental change in its position. Here respondent lost no rights but merely was induced to do something which could be corrected at a later time.

There is no doubt that respondent will be adversely affected by the Government's recoupment of the funds that it has already spent. It will surely have to curtail its operations and may even be forced to seek relief from its debts through bankruptcy. However, there is no finding as to the extent of the likely curtailment in the volume of services provided by respondent, much less that respondent will reduce its activities below the level that obtained when it was first advised that the double reimbursement was proper. . . .

A for-profit corporation could hardly base an estoppel on the fact that the Government wrongfully allowed it the interest-free use of taxpayers' money for a period of two or three years, enabling it to expand its operation. . . .

IV

Justice Holmes wrote: "Men must turn square corners when they deal with the Government." *Rock Island, A. & L.R. Co. v. United States*, 254 U.S. 141, 143, 41 S.Ct. 55, 56, 65 L.Ed. 188 (1920). This observation has its greatest force when a private party seeks to spend the Government's money. Protection of the public fisc requires that those who seek public funds act with scrupulous regard for the requirements of law; respondent could expect no less than to be held to the most demanding standards in its quest for public funds. This is consistent with the general rule that those who deal with the Government are expected to know the law and may not rely on the conduct of Government agents contrary to law.

As a participant in the Medicare program, respondent had a duty to familiarize itself with the legal requirements for cost reimbursement. Since it also had elected to receive reimbursement through Travelers, it also was acquainted with the nature of and limitations on the role of a fiscal intermediary. When the question arose concerning respondent's [Comprehensive Employment and Training Act] funds, respondent's own action in consulting Travelers demonstrates the necessity for it to have obtained an interpretation of the applicable regulations; respondent indisputably knew that this was a doubtful question not clearly covered by existing policy statements. The fact that Travelers' advice was erroneous is, in itself, insufficient to raise an estoppel, as is the fact that petitioner had not anticipated this problem and made a clear resolution available to respondent. There is simply no requirement that the Government anticipate every problem that may arise in the administration of a complex program such as Medicare; neither can it be expected to ensure that every bit of informal advice given by its agents in the course of such a program will be sufficiently reliable to justify expenditure of sums of money as substantial as those spent by respondent. Nor was the advice given under circumstances that should have induced respondent's reliance. As a recipient of public funds well acquainted with the role of a fiscal intermediary, respondent knew Travelers only acted as a conduit; it could not resolve policy questions. The relevant statute, regulations, and Reimbursement Manual, with which respondent should have been and was acquainted, made that perfectly clear. Yet respondent made no attempt to have the question resolved by the Secretary; it was satisfied with the policy judgment of a mere conduit.

The appropriateness of respondent's reliance is further undermined because the advice it received from Travelers was oral. It is not merely the possibility of fraud that undermines our confidence in the reliability of official action that is not confirmed or evidenced by a written instrument. Written advice, like a written judicial opinion, requires its author to reflect about the nature of the advice that is given to the citizen, and subjects that advice to the possibility of review, criticism, and reexamination. The necessity for ensuring that governmental agents stay within the lawful scope of their authority, and that those who seek public funds act with scrupulous exactitude, argues strongly for the conclusion that an estoppel cannot be erected on the basis of the oral advice that underlay respondent's cost reports. That is especially true when a complex program such as Medicare is involved, in which the need for written records is manifest.

In sum, the regulations governing the cost reimbursement provisions of Medicare should and did put respondent on ample notice of the care with which its cost reports must be prepared, and the care which would be taken to review them within the relevant 3–year period. Yet respondent prepared those reports on the basis of an oral policy judgment by an official who, it should have known, was not in the business of making policy. That is not the kind of reasonable reliance that would even give rise to an estoppel against a private party. It therefore cannot estop the Government.

Thus, assuming estoppel can ever be appropriately applied against the Government, it cannot be said that the detriment respondent faces is so severe or has been imposed in such an unfair way that petitioner ought to be estopped from enforcing the law in this case. Accordingly, the judgment of the Court of Appeals is reversed, and the case is remanded to that court for further proceedings consistent with this opinion.

It is so ordered.

OFFICE OF PERSONNEL MANAGEMENT
v. RICHMOND

496 U.S. 414, 110 S.Ct. 2465, 110 L.Ed.2d 387 (1990).

MR. JUSTICE KENNEDY delivered the opinion of the Court.

This case presents the question whether erroneous oral and written advice given by a Government employee to a benefits claimant may give rise to estoppel against the Government and so entitle the claimant to a monetary payment not otherwise permitted by law. We hold that payments of money from the Federal Treasury are limited to those authorized by statute, and we reverse the contrary holding of the Court of Appeals.

I

Not wishing to exceed a statutory limit on earnings that would disqualify him from a disability annuity, respondent Charles Richmond sought advice from a federal employee and received erroneous information. As a result he earned more than permitted by the eligibility requirements of the relevant statute and lost six months of benefits. Respondent now claims that the erroneous and unauthorized advice should give rise to equitable estoppel against the Government, and that we should order payment of the benefits contrary to the statutory terms. Even on the assumption that much equity subsists in respondent's claim, we cannot agree with him or the Court of Appeals that we have authority to order the payment he seeks. . . .

A divided panel of the Court of Appeals . . . accept[ed the Richmond's] contention that the misinformation from Navy personnel estopped the Government, and that the estoppel required payment of disability benefits despite the statutory provision to the contrary. The Court of Appeals acknowledged the longstanding rule that "ordinarily the government may not be estopped because of erroneous or unauthorized statements of government employees when the asserted estoppel would nullify a requirement prescribed by Congress." Nonetheless, the Court of Appeals focused on this Court's statement in an earlier case that "we are hesitant . . . to say that there are no cases" where the Government might be estopped. . . .

II

From our earliest cases, we have recognized that equitable estoppel will not lie against the Government as it lies against private litigants. . . .

The principles of these and many other cases were reiterated in *Federal Crop Ins. Corporation v. Merrill*, 332 U.S. 380 (1947), the leading case in our modern line of estoppel decisions. . . .

Despite the clarity of these earlier decisions, dicta in our more recent cases have suggested the possibility that there might be some situation in which estoppel against the Government could be appropriate. . . .

The language in our decisions has spawned numerous claims for equitable estoppel in the lower courts. . . . In sum, Courts of Appeals have taken our statements as an invitation to search for an appropriate case in which to apply estoppel against the Government, yet we have reversed every finding of estoppel that we have reviewed. Indeed, no less than three of our most recent decisions in this area have been summary reversals of decisions upholding estoppel claims. Summary reversals of courts of appeals are unusual under any circumstances. The extraordinary number of such dispositions in this single area of the law provides a good indication that our approach to these cases has provided inadequate guidance for the federal courts and served only to invite and prolong needless litigation.

The Solicitor General proposes to remedy the present confusion in this area of the law with a sweeping rule. As it has in the past, the Government asks us to adopt "a flat rule that estoppel may not in any circumstances run against the Government." The Government bases its broad rule first upon the doctrine of sovereign immunity. Noting that the " 'United States, as sovereign, is immune from suit save as it consents to be sued,' "petitioner asserts that the courts are without jurisdiction to entertain a suit to compel the Government to act contrary to a statute, no matter what the context or circumstances. Petitioner advances as a second basis for this rule the doctrine of separation of powers. Petitioner contends that to recognize estoppel based on the misrepresentations of Executive Branch officials would give those misrepresentations the force of law, and thereby invade the legislative province reserved to Congress. This rationale, too, supports the petitioner's contention that estoppel may never justify an order requiring executive action contrary to a relevant statute, no matter what statute or what facts are involved.

We have recognized before that the "arguments the Government advances for the rule are substantial." And we agree that this case should be decided under a clearer form of analysis than "we will know an estoppel when we see one." But it remains true that we need not embrace a rule that no estoppel will lie against the Government in any case in order to decide this case. We leave for another day whether an estoppel claim could ever succeed against the Government. A narrower ground of decision is sufficient to address the type of suit presented here, a claim for payment of money from the Public Treasury contrary to a statutory appropriation.

III

The Appropriations Clause of the Constitution, Art. I, § 9, cl. 7, provides that: "No Money shall be drawn from the Treasury, but in Consequence of Appropriations made by Law." For the particular type of claim at issue here, a claim for money from the Federal Treasury, the

Clause provides an explicit rule of decision. Money may be paid out only through an appropriation made by law; in other words, the payment of money from the Treasury must be authorized by a statute. All parties here agree that the award respondent seeks would be in direct contravention of the federal statute upon which his ultimate claim to the funds must rest. . . .

Our cases underscore the straightforward and explicit command of the Appropriations Clause. "It means simply that no money can be paid out of the Treasury unless it has been appropriated by an act of Congress." . . .

Extended to its logical conclusion, operation of estoppel against the Government in the context of payment of money from the Treasury could in fact render the Appropriations Clause a nullity. If agents of the Executive were able, by their unauthorized oral or written statements to citizens, to obligate the Treasury for the payment of funds, the control over public funds that the Clause reposes in Congress in effect could be transferred to the Executive. . . .

It may be argued that a rule against estoppel could have the opposite result, that the Executive might frustrate congressional intent to appropriate benefits by instructing its agents to give claimants erroneous advice that would deprive them of the benefits. But Congress may always exercise its power to expand recoveries for those who rely on mistaken advice should it choose to do so. In numerous other contexts where Congress has been concerned at the possibility of significant detrimental reliance on the erroneous advice of Government agents, it has provided appropriate legislative relief. . . .

APPEAL OF ENO
(NEW HAMPSHIRE DEPARTMENT OF EMPLOYMENT SECURITY)

126 N.H. 650, 495 A.2d 1277 (N.H.1985).

SOUTER, JUSTICE.

The plaintiff appeals from an order of the Appeal Tribunal of the New Hampshire Department of Employment Security. The department's denial of unemployment benefits was sustained by the tribunal on the ground that the plaintiff had failed to "expose herself to the labor market to the extent commensurate with the economic conditions and the efforts of a reasonably prudent person seeking work." We reverse.

. . . On February 19, she was laid off [from her job with the New England Telephone and Telegraph Company], and on March 3 she applied for unemployment compensation benefits . . . to begin with the week ending on March 6.

An employee of the department took the plaintiff's application, although she was not authorized to approve it. She advised the plaintiff to reapply for benefits each week pending a determination of her eligibility. On plaintiff's second visit she received a pamphlet entitled "Your Rights and Obligations." So far as it is relevant here, the pamphlet stated the conditions of eligibility in these paragraphs: "5. You must be ready, willing, and able to accept and perform suitable work on all the shifts and during all the hours for which there is a market for the services you offer. 6. You must be available for and seeking permanent full-time work for which you are qualified."

There was no further explanation of the requirement that an applicant be seeking work as a condition of eligibility. On this occasion, and on all of the plaintiff's subsequent visits to file weekly applications, an employee of the department simply asked the plaintiff if she was seeking work. Each time the plaintiff answered yes. There was never any further questioning or advice on the subject. Over the course of the ensuing eleven weeks the plaintiff answered some want ads by telephone calls and by sending out her resume, and the department gave her one lead. The plaintiff did not make personal visits to possible employers, however, and none of her efforts led to a job within the time in question here.

[Ultimately, she was determined ineligible for unemployment compensation] on the ground that the plaintiff had made insufficient efforts to obtain work during that time.

[W]e believe that the record before us raises a narrow[ ]issue: whether the department may deny benefits to the plaintiff on the ground that she made insufficient efforts to find work, over a period of time in which the department led her to believe that her efforts were sufficient. This issue is at the nub of her claim that the denial of benefits offends standards of due process, to which we turn.

The plaintiff's claim of entitlement to unemployment compensation benefits is a claim to a property interest that is itself subject to protection under the due process guarantees. . . . At its most basic level, the requirement to afford due process forbids the government from denying or thwarting claims of statutory entitlement by a procedure that is fundamentally unfair. We agree with the plaintiff that the department's action suffers from such a degree of unfairness.

At the outset we should say that if we were to consider the plaintiff's efforts to find work simply in the light of the statutory standard of eligibility, we would find no error in the denial of benefits. . . .

But to do this is to view the case with blinders, and on the issue of due process we must look further at the department's contacts with the plaintiff.

As instructed, the plaintiff made weekly visits to the department's local office. Each time she was asked the general question whether she was seeking work, and each time she answered yes. Her answers were not false, for the questions were not such as to elicit any detail about the extent of an applicant's search.

Since the statute calls for eligibility determinations on a week-to-week basis, the reason for asking questions is to determine whether the applicant has satisfied the conditions of eligibility for that week. When an applicant's answers are accepted without further question or inquiry, the natural impression is that the answers satisfy the eligibility conditions to which they relate. Such an impression has particular force when the condition in question, the need to be seeking work, is stated to the applicant in only the most general of terms.

The impression thus created does more, however, than merely comfort an applicant in the hope that the condition has been satisfied thus far. For the condition that an applicant be seeking work does not refer only to some past event that is over and done with when the applicant files an application; it is a condition that the applicant must continue to meet. The department's response to the applicant's answer relating to this condition is therefore a signal about what the applicant is expected to do in a continuing effort to satisfy the condition. If an applicant is told that his efforts to find work have been insufficient, he can make greater effort in the following week. If he is given the impression that he has satisfied the condition thus far, he can reasonably infer that the same level of effort will do for the future.

We believe that the record in this case can reasonably be read only as supporting just such an inference. In effect, the department led the plaintiff to believe that she need not do more to establish her eligibility than she had done. She acted accordingly, only to have the appeal tribunal deny her benefits for failing to do more. This was fundamentally unfair and thus amounted to a denial of due process. . . .

Before concluding this opinion it is only fair to note that the record indicates that during the time in question the department was both understaffed and confronted with a large number of applications. These conditions may well explain why the plaintiff did not receive more specific attention when she made her weekly appearances to apply for benefits. We also note that since the time in question the department has revised the pamphlet of instructions for applicants, which now indicates that personal visits to possible employers are normally appropriate. The facts before us are therefore unlikely to recur.

Having found that the department's denial of benefits for the weeks in question worked a denial of due process, we reverse the decision of the appeal tribunal and remand the case for entry of an order finding the plaintiff eligible for benefits during the disputed period.

Notes and Questions

1. Should the Supreme Court bar the use of estoppel in cases that do not implicate the Appropriations Clause on one of the grounds cited by the Solicitor General in *Office of Personnel Management v. Rich-*

mond? Or should the Court retain the doctrine as a means of protecting individuals (or companies) that have reasonably relied on what they were told by the government?

2.   Some lower federal courts have recognized the doctrine of estoppel in non-appropriations cases, but most decisions refuse to apply the doctrine because the plaintiff failed to prove that there was "reasonable" reliance on the government's pronouncement, *see, e.g., Emery Mining Corp. v. Secretary of Labor*, 744 F.2d 1411 (10th Cir.1984), or because the court will not use equitable estoppel to contradict a clear Congressional mandate, *see, e.g., Worley v. Harris*, 666 F.2d 417, 422 (9th Cir.1982). Some courts require a showing of affirmative misconduct to estop the government. *See Lurch v. United States*, 719 F.2d 333, 341 & n. 12 (10th Cir.1983); *cert. denied* 466 U.S. 927, 104 S.Ct. 1710, 80 L.Ed.2d 182 (1984). For a description of the disarray in the case law, see Peter Raven-Hansen, *Regulatory Estoppel: When Agencies Break Their Own Laws*, 64 Tex. L. Rev. 1, 27–54 (1985); Joshua I. Schwartz, *The Irresistible Force Meets The Immovable Object: Estoppel Remedies For An Agency's Violation of Its Own Regulations Or For Other Misconduct*, 44 Admin. L. Rev. 653, 660–93 (1992).

3.   As might be reflected in *Eno*, the states seem more willing than federal courts (and especially the United States Supreme Court) to apply estoppel. *See generally Project: State Judicial Review of Administrative Action*, 43 Admin. L. Rev. 571, 813 (1991). First, when the government acts in a proprietary, rather than governmental, capacity, several states have found equitable estoppel applicable. *See Project, supra*, at 813 (citing cases in Texas, Virginia, and Wyoming). Second, equitable estoppel may be applied when state or local agencies have engaged in "affirmative misconduct." *See id.* (citing cases in Minnesota and Missouri). Third, some states are willing to find equitable estoppel simply when there is some stronger basis than would justify equitable estoppel against a private party. *See id.* (citing cases in South Carolina, Alaska, Connecticut, and Hawaii). Typically, this may be phrased as "to the extent justice requires" or "to prevent manifest injustice." For example, in *Kellams v. Public School Employees' Retirement Board*, 486 Pa. 95, 403 A.2d 1315 (1979), the state retirement system tried to recover overpayments made to retirees over a number of years, but the state courts would not allow it, citing the "manifest hardship" of forcing repayment from retirees.

4.   By comparison to the law on equitable estoppel, it is relatively well established that one cannot be held criminally responsible for acting in reasonable reliance upon the advice of a government agent. In *United States v. Pennsylvania Industrial Chemical Corporation*, 411 U.S. 655, 93 S.Ct. 1804, 36 L.Ed.2d 567 (1973), for example, the government filed a criminal indictment against a company that had discharged industrial refuse into the Monongahela River. The Court held that the district court had erred in disallowing the company's offer of proof that it had been affirmatively misled by the Army Corps of Engineers into believing that it did not have to obtain a permit for the discharges. The Court

explained that "to the extent that [the Corp's] regulations deprived PICCO of fair warning as to what conduct the Government intended to make criminal, we think that there can be no doubt that traditional notions of fairness inherent in our system of criminal justice prevent the Government from proceeding with the prosecution." 411 U.S. at 674. For other similar cases, see *Raley v. State of Ohio*, 360 U.S. 423, 79 S.Ct. 1257, 3 L.Ed.2d 1344 (1959) (person could not be held in contempt of state legislature after being told by the legislative committee prior to refusing to answer questions that he had a right not to answer); *Cox v. Louisiana*, 379 U.S. 559, 85 S.Ct. 476, 13 L.Ed.2d 487 (1965) (protesters could not be prosecuted for interfering with law enforcement when sheriff told them they could protest across the street and they did). This concept is not rooted in common law equitable estoppel, but in due process.

5. If the government cannot be "estopped" and if due process does not apply, the courts sometimes use some other tactic to give relief to a deserving plaintiff. When the State Department failed to warn a foreign national that failure to register for the draft would bar him from applying for citizenship, for example, the Supreme Court refused to bar his application even though he did not make himself available for the draft. *Moser v. United States*, 341 U.S. 41, 71 S.Ct. 553, 95 L.Ed. 729 (1951). The Court said there was "no need" to evaluate his claim of estoppel because the plaintiff "did not knowingly and intelligently waive his rights to citizenship" and that "nothing less than an intelligent waiver is required by elementary fairness." *Id*. at 47.

6. Another way that courts might give relief, depending on the facts, is to apply the prohibition against inconsistent application. Recall that one basis for finding agency action arbitrary and capricious is if the agency acts inconsistently with past decisions without explaining the basis for the change. Also, to the extent that the agency is asking a court to defer to its new interpretation, courts may refuse that deference because the agency has not been consistent. In *North Haven Board of Education v. Bell*, 456 U.S. 512, 102 S.Ct. 1912, 72 L.Ed.2d 299 (1982), for example, the Supreme Court rejected an administrative interpretation because the agency had changed its interpretation of a regulation several times, once during the course of the judicial proceedings. The Court concluded that there was no interpretation to which to defer.

This approach might seem inconsistent with *Chevron v. NRDC*, which explicitly stated that the agency's change of position was not a relevant consideration to deference in that case. One of the first cases after *Chevron*, however, was *Immigration and Naturalization Service v. Cardoza-Fonseca*, 480 U.S. 421, 107 S.Ct. 1207, 94 L.Ed.2d 434 (1987), where the Court refused to defer to the INS' interpretation of a statutory provision. The Court held that the case involved "a pure matter of statutory construction" as to which no deference was necessary. In dicta, the Court (per Justice Stevens, the author of *Chevron*) stated that the agency's interpretation would not in any event have been entitled to deference:

An additional reason for rejecting the INS's request for heightened deference to its position is the inconsistency of the positions the BIA has taken through the years. An agency interpretation of a relevant provision which conflicts with the agency's earlier interpretation is "entitled to considerably less deference" than a consistently held agency view. [The BIA's prior decisions] and the long pattern of erratic treatment of this issue make it apparent that the BIA has not consistently agreed, and even today does not completely agree, with the INS's litigation position that the two standards are equivalent.

Still later, in *Rust v. Sullivan*, 500 U.S. 173, 111 S.Ct. 1759, 114 L.Ed.2d 233 (1991), the Court returned to *Chevron's* statement that consistency is not necessary to obtain deference, at least where the agency justifies the change with a reasoned analysis. In other words, the Supreme Court has not been totally consistent. Or viewed another way, there may be *Chevron* deference and there may be other deference. As discussed in more detail in the next section, there is more than one form of deference.

D. JUDICIAL DEFERENCE

The previous discussion considered some of the advantages and disadvantages of the different procedures by which an agency can adopt new policies or revise old ones, and it identified the legal constraints that apply to an agency's choice of procedures. This section considers one last issue that impacts on an agency's choice of procedures: How does the level of deference that a court will give to a decision vary according to the procedure that the agency used to adopt that decision?

In Chapter 2, you read *Chevron v. NRDC*, which considered judicial review of interpretations of law contained in legislative rules. According to *Chevron*, a court will defer to an agency's statutory interpretation if it concludes that a statutory term is ambiguous and that the agency's interpretation of the term is "reasonable" or "permissible." After *Chevron*, the courts confronted a related issue: what level of deference should be given to interpretations of law that are contained in an interpretive rule.

This issue arose because of an older case that involved judicial review of an interpretive rule, *Skidmore v. Swift & Co.*, 323 U.S. 134, 65 S.Ct. 161, 89 L.Ed. 124 (1944), which you will read below. *Skidmore* was less deferential to agency interpretations of law than the scope of review adopted in *Chevron*. This lesser level of deference is commonly described as *"Skidmore"* deference to distinguish it from so-called *Chevron* deference. In 2000, the Supreme Court decided *Christensen v. Harris County*, 529 U.S. 576, 120 S.Ct. 1655, 146 L.Ed.2d 621 (2000), which resolved this issue. *Christensen* ruled that the courts owed *Skidmore* deference, not *Chevron* deference, to interpretive rules.

While the Supreme Court has determined the level of deference courts are to give interpretive rules, the issue of the appropriate level of deference comes up in other contexts where as yet there is no definitive Supreme Court decision. Consider, for example, informal adjudication. In Chapter Three, you read *NLRB v. Hearst*, which adopted a deferential scope of review of formal adjudication. According to *Hearst*, a court is to accept the result of an adjudication if the decision has "warrant in the record" and a "reasonable basis in law." The Court has not definitively indicated whether a similar (or the same) level of deference applies to informal adjudication.

This section considers the level of deference that courts will give to agency decisions adopted in formats other than informal rulemaking or formal adjudication. You will first consider the deference that applies to interpretive rules. You will then consider the level of deference that applies when an agency uses informal adjudication or other formats concerning which the scope of review remains uncertain.

1. INTERPRETIVE RULES

SKIDMORE v. SWIFT & CO.

323 U.S. 134, 65 S.Ct. 161, 89 L.Ed. 124 (1944).

MR. JUSTICE JACKSON delivered the opinion of the Court.

Seven employees of the Swift and Company packing plant at Fort Worth, Texas, brought an action under the Fair Labor Standards Act, 29 U.S.C.A. § 201 *et seq.*, to recover overtime, liquidated damages, and attorneys' fees, totaling approximately $77,000. The District Court rendered judgment denying this claim wholly, and the Circuit Court of Appeals for the Fifth Circuit affirmed.

It is not denied that the daytime employment of these persons was working time within the Act. Two were engaged in general fire hall duties and maintenance of fire-fighting equipment of the Swift plant. The others operated elevators or acted as relief men in fire duties. They worked from 7:00 a.m. to 3:30 p.m., with a half-hour lunch period, five days a week. They were paid weekly salaries.

Under their oral agreement of employment, however, petitioners undertook to stay in the fire hall on the Company premises, or within hailing distance, three and a half to four nights a week.... The Company provided a brick fire hall equipped with steam heat and air-conditioned rooms. It provided sleeping quarters, a pool table, a domino table, and a radio. The men used their time in sleep or amusement as they saw fit, except that they were required to stay in or close by the fire hall and be ready to respond to alarms.... The trial court found ... as a "conclusion of law" that "the time plaintiffs spent in the fire hall subject to call to answer fire alarms does not constitute hours worked, for which overtime compensation is due them under the Fair Labor Standards Act...." The Circuit Court of Appeals affirmed....

Congress did not utilize the services of an administrative agency to find facts and to determine in the first instance whether particular cases fall within or without the Act. Instead, it put this responsibility on the courts. But it did create the office of Administrator [of the Wage and Hour Division of the Department of Labor], impose upon him a variety of duties, endow him with powers to inform himself of conditions in industries and employments subject to the Act, and put on him the duties of bringing injunction actions to restrain violations. Pursuit of his duties has accumulated a considerable experience in the problems of ascertaining working time in employments involving periods of inactivity and a knowledge of the customs prevailing in reference to their solution. From these he is obliged to reach conclusions as to conduct without the law, so that he should seek injunctions to stop it, and that within the law, so that he has no call to interfere. He has set forth his views of the application of the Act under different circumstances in an interpretative bulletin and in informal rulings. They provide a practical guide to employers and employees as to how the office representing the public interest in its enforcement will seek to apply it.

The Administrator thinks the problems presented by inactive duty require a flexible solution, rather than the all-in or all-out rules respectively urged by the parties in this case, and his Bulletin endeavors to suggest standards and examples to guide in particular situations....

There is no statutory provision as to what, if any, deference courts should pay to the Administrator's conclusions. And, while we have given them notice, we have had no occasion to try to prescribe their influence. The rulings of this Administrator are not reached as a result of hearing adversary proceedings in which he finds facts from evidence and reaches conclusions of law from findings of fact. They are not, of course, conclusive, even in the cases with which they directly deal, much less in those to which they apply only by analogy. They do not constitute an interpretation of the Act or a standard for judging factual situations which binds a district court's processes, as an authoritative pronouncement of a higher court might do. But the Administrator's policies are made in pursuance of official duty, based upon more specialized experience and broader investigations and information than is likely to come to a judge in a particular case. They do determine the policy which will guide applications for enforcement by injunction on behalf of the Government. Good administration of the Act and good judicial administration alike require that the standards of public enforcement and those for determining private rights shall be at variance only where justified by very good reasons. The fact that the Administrator's policies and standards are not reached by trial in adversary form does not mean that they are not entitled to respect. This Court has long given considerable and in some cases decisive weight to Treasury Decisions and to interpretative regulations of the Treasury and of other bodies that were not of adversary origin.

We consider that the rulings, interpretations and opinions of the Administrator under this Act, while not controlling upon the courts by reason of their authority, do constitute a body of experience and informed judgment to which courts and litigants may properly resort for guidance. The weight of such a judgment in a particular case will depend upon the thoroughness evident in its consideration, the validity of its reasoning, its consistency with earlier and later pronouncements, and all those factors which give it power to persuade, if lacking power to control.

... [I]n this case, although the District Court referred to the Administrator's Bulletin, its evaluation and inquiry were apparently restricted by its notion that waiting time may not be work, an understanding of the law which we hold to be erroneous. Accordingly, the judgment is reversed and the cause remanded for further proceedings consistent herewith.

Reversed.

CHRISTENSEN v. HARRIS COUNTY

529 U.S. 576, 120 S.Ct. 1655, 146 L.Ed.2d 621 (2000).

JUSTICE THOMAS delivered the opinion of the Court.

Under the Fair Labor Standards Act of 1938 (FLSA), States and their political subdivisions may compensate their employees for overtime by granting them compensatory time or "comp time," which entitles them to take time off work with full pay. If the employees do not use their accumulated compensatory time, the employer is obligated to pay cash compensation under certain circumstances. Fearing the fiscal consequences of having to pay for accrued compensatory time, Harris County adopted a policy requiring its employees to schedule time off in order to reduce the amount of accrued compensatory time. Employees of the Harris County Sheriff's Department sued, claiming that the FLSA prohibits such a policy. The Court of Appeals rejected their claim. Finding that nothing in the FLSA or its implementing regulations prohibits an employer from compelling the use of compensatory time, we affirm.

I

The FLSA generally provides that hourly employees who work in excess of 40 hours per week must be compensated for the excess hours at a rate not less than 1 1/2 times their regular hourly wage. [In recognition that this requirement might present a budgetary hardship for states and their political subdivisions and local governments, Congress amended the FLSA to permit these governmental units] to compensate employees for overtime by granting them compensatory time at a rate of 1 1/2 hours for every hour worked. To provide this form of compensation, the employer must arrive at an agreement or understanding with employees that compensatory time will be granted instead of cash compensation. . . .

Petitioners are 127 deputy sheriffs employed by respondents Harris County, Texas, and its sheriff, Tommy B. Thomas (collectively, Harris County). It is undisputed that each of the petitioners individually agreed to accept compensatory time, in lieu of cash, as compensation for overtime.

As petitioners accumulated compensatory time, Harris County became concerned that it lacked the resources to pay monetary compensation to employees who worked overtime after reaching the statutory cap on compensatory time accrual and to employees who left their jobs with sizable reserves of accrued time. As a result, the county began looking for a way to reduce accumulated compensatory time. It wrote to the United States Department of Labor's Wage and Hour Division, asking "whether the Sheriff may schedule non-exempt employees to use or take compensatory time." The Acting Administrator of the Division replied:

> "[I]t is our position that a public employer may schedule its nonexempt employees to use their accrued FLSA compensatory time as directed if the prior agreement specifically provides such a provision. . . .

> "Absent such an agreement, it is our position that neither the statute nor the regulations permit an employer to require an employee to use accrued compensatory time." Opinion Letter from Dept. of Labor, Wage and Hour Div. (Sept. 14, 1992) (Opinion Letter).

After receiving the letter, Harris County implemented a policy under which the employees' supervisor sets a maximum number of compensatory hours that may be accumulated. When an employee's stock of hours approaches that maximum, the employee is advised of the maximum and is asked to take steps to reduce accumulated compensatory time. If the employee does not do so voluntarily, a supervisor may order the employee to use his compensatory time at specified times. . . .

II

Both parties, and the United States as amicus curiae, concede that nothing in the FLSA expressly prohibits a State or subdivision thereof from compelling employees to utilize accrued compensatory time. Petitioners and the United States, however, contend that the FLSA implicitly prohibits such a practice in the absence of an agreement or understanding authorizing compelled use. Title 29 U.S.C. § 207(*o*)(5) provides:

> "An employee . . .

> "(A) who has accrued compensatory time off . . . , and

> "(B) who has requested the use of such compensatory time,

> "shall be permitted by the employee's employer to use such time within a reasonable period after making the request if the use of the compensatory time does not unduly disrupt the operations of the public agency."

Petitioners and the United States rely upon the canon *expressio unius est exclusio alterius*, contending that the express grant of control to employees to use compensatory time, subject to the limitation regarding undue disruptions of workplace operations, implies that all other methods of spending compensatory time are precluded. . . .

At bottom, we think the better reading of § 207(*o*)(5) is that it imposes a restriction upon an employer's efforts to prohibit the use of compensatory time when employees request to do so; that provision says nothing about restricting an employer's efforts to require employees to use compensatory time. Because the statute is silent on this issue and because Harris County's policy is entirely compatible with § 207(*o*)(5), petitioners cannot . . . prove that Harris County has violated § 207. . . .

III

In an attempt to avoid the conclusion that the FLSA does not prohibit compelled use of compensatory time, petitioners and the United States contend that we should defer to the Department of Labor's opinion letter, which takes the position that an employer may compel the use of compensatory time only if the employee has agreed in advance to such a practice. Specifically, they argue that the agency opinion letter is entitled to deference under our decision in *Chevron U.S.A. Inc. v. Natural Resources Defense Council, Inc.*, 467 U.S. 837, 104 S.Ct. 2778, 81 L.Ed.2d 694 (1984). In *Chevron*, we held that a court must give effect to an agency's regulation containing a reasonable interpretation of an ambiguous statute.

Here, however, we confront an interpretation contained in an opinion letter, not one arrived at after, for example, a formal adjudication or notice-and-comment rulemaking. Interpretations such as those in opinion letters—like interpretations contained in policy statements, agency manuals, and enforcement guidelines, all of which lack the force of law— do not warrant *Chevron*-style deference. Instead, interpretations contained in formats such as opinion letters are "entitled to respect" under our decision in *Skidmore v. Swift & Co.*, 323 U.S. 134, 140, 65 S.Ct. 161, 89 L.Ed. 124 (1944), but only to the extent that those interpretations have the "power to persuade," *ibid*. As explained above, we find unpersuasive the agency's interpretation of the statute at issue in this case. . . .

JUSTICE SCALIA, concurring in part and concurring in the judgment.

I join the judgment of the Court and all of its opinion except Part III, which declines to give effect to the position of the Department of Labor in this case because its opinion letter is entitled only to so-called "*Skidmore* deference." *Skidmore* deference to authoritative agency views is an anachronism, dating from an era in which we declined to give agency interpretations (including interpretive regulations, as opposed to "legislative rules") authoritative effect. This former judicial attitude accounts for that provision of the 1946 Administrative Procedure Act which exempted "interpretative rules" (since they would not be authoritative) from the notice-and-comment requirements applicable to rulemaking, see 5 U.S.C. § 553(b)(A).

That era came to an end with our watershed decision in *Chevron*, which established the principle that "a court may not substitute its own construction of a statutory provision for a reasonable interpretation made by the administrator of an agency."* While *Chevron* in fact involved an interpretive regulation, the rationale of the case was not limited to that context: " 'The power of an administrative agency to administer a congressionally created ... program necessarily requires the formulation of policy and the making of rules to fill any gap left, implicitly or explicitly, by Congress.' "

In my view, therefore, the position that the county's action in this case was unlawful unless permitted by the terms of an agreement with the sheriff's department employees warrants *Chevron* deference if it represents the authoritative view of the Department of Labor....

I nonetheless join the judgment of the Court because, for the reasons set forth in Part II of its opinion, the Secretary's position does not seem to me a reasonable interpretation of the statute.

JUSTICE STEVENS, with whom JUSTICE GINSBURG and JUSTICE BREYER join, dissenting.

... As I read the statute, the employer has no right to impose compensatory overtime payment upon its employees except in accordance with the terms of the agreement authorizing its use....

Finally, it is not without significance in the present case that the Government department responsible for the statute's enforcement shares my understanding of its meaning. Indeed, the Department of Labor made its position clear to the county itself in response to a direct question posed by the county before it decided—agency advice notwithstanding—to implement its forced-use policy nonetheless.... Because there is no reason to believe that the Department's opinion was anything but thoroughly considered and consistently observed, it unquestionably merits our respect. *See Skidmore v. Swift & Co.*, 323 U.S. 134, 140, 65 S.Ct. 161, 89 L.Ed. 124 (1944).[2] ...

I respectfully dissent.

---

* I do not comprehend Justice BREYER's contention that *Skidmore* deference—that special respect one gives to the interpretive views of the expert agency responsible for administering the statute—is not an anachronism because it may apply in "circumstances in which *Chevron*-type deference is inapplicable." *Chevron*-type deference can be inapplicable for only three reasons: (1) the statute is unambiguous, so there is no room for administrative interpretation; (2) no interpretation has been made by personnel of the agency responsible for administering the statute; or (3) the interpretation made by such personnel was not authoritative, in the sense that it does not represent the official position of the expert agency. All of these reasons preclude *Skidmore* deference as well. The specific example of the inapplicability of *Chevron* that Justice BREYER posits, viz., "where one has doubt

that Congress actually intended to delegate interpretive authority to the agency," appears to assume that, after finding a statute to be ambiguous, we must ask in addition, before we can invoke *Chevron* deference, whether Congress intended the ambiguity to be resolved by the administering agency. That is not so. *Chevron* establishes a presumption that ambiguities are to be resolved (within the bounds of reasonable interpretation) by the administering agency. The implausibility of Congress's leaving a highly significant issue unaddressed (and thus "delegating" its resolution to the administering agency) is assuredly one of the factors to be considered in determining whether there is ambiguity, but once ambiguity is established the consequences of *Chevron* attach.

2. I should add that I fully agree with Justice BREYER's comments on *Chevron*.

JUSTICE BREYER, with whom JUSTICE GINSBURG joins, dissenting.

Justice SCALIA may well be right that the position of the Department of Labor, set forth in both brief and letter, is an "authoritative" agency view that warrants deference under *Chevron*. But I do not object to the majority's citing *Skidmore* instead. And I do disagree with Justice SCALIA's statement that what he calls "*Skidmore* deference" is "an anachronism."

Skidmore made clear that courts may pay particular attention to the views of an expert agency where they represent "specialized experience," even if they do not constitute an exercise of delegated lawmaking authority. The Court held that the "rulings, interpretations and opinions of" an agency, "while not controlling upon the courts by reason of their authority, do constitute a body of experience and informed judgment to which courts and litigants may properly resort for guidance." As Justice Jackson wrote for the Court, those views may possess the "power to persuade," even where they lack the "power to control."

Chevron made no relevant change. It simply focused upon an additional, separate legal reason for deferring to certain agency determinations, namely, that Congress had delegated to the agency the legal authority to make those determinations. And, to the extent there may be circumstances in which *Chevron*-type deference is inapplicable—e.g., where one has doubt that Congress actually intended to delegate interpretive authority to the agency (an "ambiguity" that *Chevron* does not presumptively leave to agency resolution)—I believe that *Skidmore* nonetheless retains legal vitality. If statutes are to serve the human purposes that called them into being, courts will have to continue to pay particular attention in appropriate cases to the experienced-based views of expert agencies.

I agree with Justice STEVENS that, when "thoroughly considered and consistently observed," an agency's views, particularly in a rather technical case such as this one, "meri[t] our respect." And, of course, I also agree with Justice STEVENS that, for the reasons he sets forth, the Labor Department's position in this matter is eminently reasonable, hence persuasive, whether one views that decision through *Chevron*'s lens, through *Skidmore*'s, or through both.

Problem 4–10: Agricultural Worker Protection Act

The Agricultural Workers Protection Act (Act) is intended to "assure necessary protection" for migrant and seasonal farm workers. The Act requires farm labor contractors, or anyone who solicits, recruits, hires, and transports farm workers, to obtain a certificate of registration from the Department of Labor. Furthermore, the Department may suspend or revoke the certificate of any contractor that violates the Act or any regulations promulgated under it. The Act requires that contractors keep certain information and records, make prompt payment of wages, and comply with federal and state health and safety standards applicable to housing. The Act authorizes the Department to promulgate regulations necessary to ensure the safe transportation of workers. Finally, the Act establishes a private right of action:

29 U.S.C.A. § 1854. Private Right of Action

(a) Maintenance of civil action in district court by aggrieved person

Any person aggrieved by a violation of this chapter or any regulation under this chapter by a farm labor contractor ... may file suit in any district court of the United States having jurisdiction of the parties, without respect to the amount in controversy and without regard to the citizenship of the parties ...

(c) Award of damages or other equitable relief; amount; criteria; appeal

(1) If the court finds that the respondent has intentionally violated any provision of this chapter or any regulation under this chapter, it may award damages up to and including an amount equal to the amount of actual damages, or statutory damages of $500 per plaintiff per violation, or other equitable relief....

Ramsford Barret and several other farm workers were injured in an accident while being transported in the back of a pickup truck owned by their employer, Farm Contractors, Inc. Mr. Barret contacts Florida Legal Services, for whom you work, to determine whether he can sue Farm Contractors for damages under 29 U.S.C.A. § 1854. Your investigation of the claim reveals that, after the truck hit a hole in the road, Mr. Barret and several other workers fell from the truck bed and were injured when they hit the ground.

Florida law does not prohibit persons from riding in the back of a pickup truck, and Farm Contractors argues that this suggests that it has not violated the requirement of the Agricultural Protection Act that it "assure adequate protection" for migrant and seasonal farm workers. The Department of Labor has not promulgated a regulation that prohibits the transportation of workers in the back of a pickup truck. The Department, however, has issued a "Labor Bulletin" that states: "The Department understands an employer's obligation to assure necessary protection of workers to include protection of workers during their transportation, including the provision of seat belts for each worker."

You are to assess for Mr. Barret the likelihood that he will prevail in his lawsuit. In order to make this judgment, you must assess what level of deference a court will give to the Department's "Labor Bulletin," and the likelihood that a court will defer to the Department's understanding of what actions the Act requires concerning the transportation of workers.

Notes and Questions

1. Why is an agency not entitled to *Chevron* deference if it has not used its lawmaking powers (or if it does not have such powers)? If an agency has not used its law-making powers (or it does not have such powers), why is it entitled to any deference when it interprets statutory language. That is, what is the rationale of a court giving so-called "*Skidmore*" deference in this circumstance?

2. Does it matter to the outcome of a case whether a court applies *Chevron* or *Skidmore* deference? What is the difference in the two standards? *Skidmore* deference, as Justice Thomas' opinion suggests, is considered to be less deferential than *Chevron* deference. In *Christensen*, however, Justice Scalia applies *Chevron* deference, but does not uphold the agency's interpretation, while Justices Stevens, Breyer and Ginsburg would uphold the agency interpretation under *Skidmore* deference. How can this be?

3. Justice Breyer notes that there may be cases where, although statutory language is ambiguous, a court would not defer to a reasonable interpretation of that language by an agency under step two of *Chevron*. As you read in Chapter Two, the Court in *Brown & Williamson* found *Chevron* inapplicable because it had doubts that Congress actually intended to delegate interpretive authority to FDA, notwithstanding the presence of a statutory ambiguity. In the footnote to his concurrence in *Christensen*, Justice Scalia rejects this interpretation of when *Chevron* deference applies.

2. INFORMAL ADJUDICATION

In *Christensen*, the Court indicated that an interpretive rule was not entitled to *Chevron* deference because such rules were not an exercise of an agency's law-making powers. The opinion stated that interpretations, which "lack the force of law," "do not warrant *Chevron*-style deference." If an agency's uses "formal adjudication" or "rulemaking" to adopt an interpretation of a statute, it obviously is engaged in lawmaking. In *Christensen*, however, Justice Thomas seemed to say that these formats may not be the only form of lawmaking that the Court would recognize as entitling an interpretation to greater deference than *Skidmore*-type deference:

> Here, however, we confront an interpretation contained in an opinion letter, not one arrived at after, for example, a formal adjudication or notice-and-comment rulemaking. Interpretations such as those in opinion letters—like interpretations contained in policy statements, agency manuals, and enforcement guidelines, all of which lack the force of law—do not warrant *Chevron*-style deference.

529 U.S. at 587, 120 S.Ct. at 1662. This section considers whether another format–informal adjudication–is also entitled to *Chevron*-type deference

Problem 4–11: Regulation of Proxy Solicitation

A "proxy" is an agreement by which a shareholder authorizes another person to represent him or her and vote the person's shares at the shareholders' meeting in according with the shareholder's instructions. In the Securities Act of 1934, Congress has assigned the Securities and Exchange Commission (SEC) the responsibility of regulating proxy solicitation in order to protect the interests of shareholders who do not attend an annual meeting. The SEC has promulgated a series of rules that govern proxy solicitation. 17 C.F.R. § 240.14a–1 *et seq.*

The Amalgamated Clothing and Textile Workers Union (Union) has requested the management of the Bishop Corporation, a company that operates hundreds of retail stores, to notify other shareholders about a resolution that the Union intends to offer at the annual shareholders' meeting of the Bishop Corporation. The Union owns stock in Bishop.

After receiving this request, Bishop asked the SEC to issue a "no-action" letter. In a no-action letter, the SEC indicates to a corporation whether it will start an enforcement action against the corporation under specified circumstances. The SEC authorizes certain members of its staff to issue no-action letters and the full Commission retains the authority to overrule no-action decisions by those staff members. In its "no-action" letter, the SEC said Bishop was not required to notify shareholders of the Union's proposal according to the statutory language of the 1934 Act.

Since the 1934 Act authorizes individual stockholders, as well as the SEC, to sue to enforce statutory requirements, the Union has sued Bishop over its failure to engage in the notification that the Union requested. Bishop argues that it is not required by the 1934 Act to engage in such notification, and it cites the SEC's decision not to seek an enforcement action against it. The Judge is trying to determine what deference she should give to the SEC's judgment that the 1934 Act does not require Bishop to honor the Union's request.

(1) As the judge's law clerk, please advise her whether the SEC's interpretation of the 1934 Act is entitled to *Chevron* deference or *Skidmore* deference.

(2) Would your answer change if the SEC based its decision not to start an enforcement action on an interpretation of one of its own regulations, rather than an interpretation of the 1934 Securities Act?

Problem Materials

GONZALEZ v. RENO
212 F.3d 1338 (11th Cir.2000).

Edmondson, Circuit Judge:

This case, at first sight, seems to be about little more than a child and his father. But, for this Court, the case is mainly about the separation of powers under our constitutional system of government: a statute enacted by Congress, the permissible scope of executive discretion under that statute, and the limits on judicial review of the exercise of that executive discretion.

Elian Gonzalez ("Plaintiff"), a six-year-old Cuban child, arrived in the United States alone. His father in Cuba demanded that Plaintiff be returned to Cuba. Plaintiff, however, asked to stay in the United States; and asylum applications were submitted on his behalf. The Immigration and Naturalization Service ("INS")—after, among other things, consulting with Plaintiff's father and considering Plaintiff's age—decided that Plaintiff's asylum applications were legally void and refused to consider their merit.

Plaintiff then filed this suit in federal district court, seeking on several grounds to compel the INS to consider and to determine the merit of his asylum applications. The district court dismissed Plaintiff's suit.

[After Elian Gozalez's mother died at sea during an effort to escape Cuba and immigrate to the United States, officials of the Immigration and Naturalization Service (INS) decided not to remove the boy immediately to Cuba. Instead, the INS deferred Plaintiff's immigration inspection and paroled Plaintiff into the custody and care of the boy's great uncle, Lazaro Gonzalez. Mr. Gonzalez thereafter filed an application for asylum on Elian's behalf with the INS. This application was followed by a second application signed by Elian. A third asylum application was filed by Mr. Gonzalez on Elian's behalf after a state court awarded temporary custody of Elian to Lazaro.

After an investigation, the INS Commissioner] rejected [the] asylum applications as legally void. The Commissioner—concluding that six-year-old children lack the capacity to file personally for asylum against the wishes of their parents—determined that [Elian] could not file his own asylum applications. Instead, according to the Commissioner, [he] needed an adult representative to file for asylum on his behalf. The Commissioner—citing the custom that parents generally speak for their children and finding that no circumstance in this case warranted a departure from that custom—concluded that the asylum applications submitted by [Elian and his great-uncle] were legally void and required no further consideration. Plaintiff asked the Attorney General to overrule the Commissioner's decision; the Attorney General declined to do so. . . .

Plaintiff [i.e., Elian Gonzalez] contends that the district court erred in rejecting his statutory claim based on 8 U.S.C. § 1158. Section 1158 provides that "[a]ny alien . . . may apply for asylum." Plaintiff says that, because he is "[a]ny alien," he may apply for asylum. Plaintiff insists that, by the applications signed and submitted by himself and Lazaro, he, in fact, did apply for asylum within the meaning of section 1158. In addition, Plaintiff argues that the summary rejection by the INS of his applications as invalid violated the intent of Congress as set out in the statute.

The INS responds that section 1158 is silent about the validity of asylum applications filed on behalf of a six-year-old child, by the child himself and a non-parental relative, against the wishes of the child's parent. The INS argues that, because the statute does not spell out how a young child files for asylum, the INS was free to adopt a policy requiring, in these circumstances, that any asylum claim on Plaintiff's behalf be filed by Plaintiff's father. As such, the INS urges that the rejection of Plaintiff's purported asylum applications as legally void was lawful. According to the INS, because the applications had no legal effect, Plaintiff never applied at all within the meaning of the statute.

Guided by well-established principles of statutory construction, judicial restraint, and deference to executive agencies, we accept that the rejection by the INS of Plaintiff's applications as invalid did not violate section 1158.

Our consideration of Plaintiff's statutory claim must begin with an examination of the scope of the statute itself. In *Chevron*, the Supreme Court explained: "First, always, is the question whether Congress has directly spoken to the precise question at issue. If the intent of Congress is clear, that is the end of the matter; for the court, as well as the agency, must give effect to the unambiguously expressed intent of Congress." We turn, therefore, to the plain language of the statute.

Because the statute is silent on the issue, Congress has left a gap in the statutory scheme. From that gap springs executive discretion. As a matter of law, it is not for the courts, but for the executive agency charged with enforcing the statute (here, the INS), to choose how to fill such gaps. Moreover, the authority of the executive branch to fill gaps is especially great in the context of immigration policy. Our proper review of the exercise by the executive branch of its discretion to fill gaps, therefore, must be very limited. . . .

In this case, because the law—particularly section 1158—is silent about the validity of Plaintiff's purported asylum applications, it fell to the INS to make a discretionary policy choice. The INS, exercising its gap-filling discretion, determined these things: (1) six-year-old children lack the capacity to sign and to submit personally an application for asylum; (2) instead, six-year-old children must be represented by an adult in immigration matters; (3) absent special circumstances, the only proper adult to represent a six-year-old child is the child's parent, even when the parent is not in this country; and, (4) that the parent lives in a communist-totalitarian state (such as Cuba), in and of itself, does not constitute a special circumstance requiring the selection of a non-parental representative. Our duty is to decide whether this policy might be a reasonable one in the light of the statutory scheme.

But we first address Plaintiff's contention that the "policy" relied on by the INS in this case is really no policy at all but is, in reality, just a litigating position. An after-the-fact rationalization of agency action—an explanation developed for the sole purpose of defending in court the agency's acts—is usually entitled to no deference from the courts. But we are unable to say that the position of the INS here is just an after-the-fact rationalization.

The INS policy toward Plaintiff's application was not created by INS lawyers during litigation, but instead was developed in the course of administrative proceedings before litigation commenced. While the policy announced by the INS may not harmonize perfectly with earlier INS interpretative guidelines (which are not law), the parties have cited, and we have found, no statutory provision, no regulatory authority, and no prior agency adjudication that "flatly contradicts" the policy. That the INS policy was developed in the course of an informal adjudication, rather than during formal rulemaking, may affect the degree of deference appropriate but does not render the policy altogether unworthy of deference. And that the INS policy may not be a longstanding one likewise affects only the degree of deference required. The INS policy, therefore, is entitled to, at least, some deference under *Chevron*; and that deference, when we take account of the implications of the policy for foreign affairs, becomes considerable.

We accept that the INS policy at issue here comes within the range of reasonable choices.

. . . We now examine the INS's application of its facially reasonable policy to Plaintiff in this case. Although based on a policy permissible under *Chevron*, if the ultimate decision of the INS—to treat Plaintiff's asylum applications as invalid—was "arbitrary, capricious, [or] an abuse of discretion," the decision is unlawful. But whatever we personally might think about the decisions made by the Government, we cannot properly conclude that the INS acted arbitrarily or abused its discretion here. . . .

. . . Because the preexisting law compelled no particular policy, the INS was entitled to make a policy decision. The policy decision that the INS made was within the outside border of reasonable choices. And the INS did not abuse its discretion or act arbitrarily in applying the policy and rejecting Plaintiff's purported asylum applications. The Court neither approves nor disapproves the INS's decision to reject the asylum applications filed on Plaintiff's behalf, but the INS decision did not contradict 8 U.S.C. § 1158.

GONZALEZ v. RENO

215 F.3d 1243 (11th Cir. 2000).

On Petition for Rehearing and Petition for Rehearing En Banc

Per Curiam:

Our decision of 1 June hung largely on two ideas: (1) that the policy adopted by the INS in this case—a policy developed in what we called "informal adjudication"—was due "some deference" because 8 U.S.C.

1158(a) was silent on the precise question at issue and because the INS had the duty to set how the statute was to be applied when the statute was silent, and (2) that the level of deference due the INS policy was strengthened—becoming "considerable"—when we also took into account the foreign policy implications of the administrative decisions dealing with immigration. Among other things, our opinion spoke of *Chevron, U.S.A., Inc. v. Natural Resources Defense Council, Inc.*, 467 U.S. 837, 104 S.Ct. 2778, 81 L.Ed.2d 694 (1984)

When our opinion was written, we knew of *Christensen v. Harris County*, 529 U.S. 576, 120 S.Ct. 1655, 146 L.Ed.2d 621 (2000), a Fair Labor Standards Act (FLSA) decision. But no lawyer in this case had cited or argued *Christensen* to us. More important, we thought that *Christensen*—which involved no immigration law, no foreign policy consideration, and no kind of agency adjudication—was noncrucial to this case. So, we never mentioned *Christensen*.

Now in the petition for rehearing, Plaintiff stresses *Christensen*. Therefore, we will write briefly about it.

First, Christensen involved an opinion letter from the Department of Labor giving advice to Harris County, Texas. The letter, in itself, did not decide Harris County's rights; it did not stop and did not purport to be able to stop Harris County from acting against the advice given. The letter was in no way binding on Harris County. And later when *Christensen* arose as active litigation, Harris County was not sued by the Department of Labor, but by private citizens: county employees who contended that Harris County was misconstruing the FLSA. The Supreme Court said that the administrative position taken in the opinion letter was not due *Chevron* deference. As we read it, the Supreme Court's opinion also indicated that the view of the pertinent statute taken in the opinion letter was wrong and unreasonable: "[T]his view is exactly backwards."

In our case, the INS did directly decide Plaintiff's specific right to file certain asylum applications under the pertinent statute and did so after receiving and weighing some evidence. The INS acted in the context of an actual and concrete dispute with and before that agency. The INS decision was final and binding on Plaintiff unless he, in effect, appealed it to a court. The sovereign power of the United States—per the INS and the Attorney General—had determined that neither Plaintiff himself nor Lazaro Gonzalez could file for asylum on Plaintiff's behalf over the objections of Plaintiff's father. This kind of administrative decisionmaking—which we think no one can seriously question was the deliberate and official position of the pertinent agencies of the executive branch of our government—is substantially different from and more than the opinion letter in *Christensen*. We considered the administrative decisionmaking in this case to be adjudication and to be outside *Christensen*'s scope.[3] In our view, to apply *Christensen* to this case would not be following *Christensen*, but would be an extension of *Christensen*.

---

3. The Supreme Court opinion gives some examples of the kinds of agency acts that are due *Chevron* deference. In setting out some examples, "formal adjudication"

Second, we thought, even when *Christensen* does apply, administrative decisions of agencies are still due some deference. And we believed that under *Chevron* or *Christensen*, when the foreign-policy impact of immigration law was added as a separate source of judicial deference, we were justified in exercising the judicial restraint that marked our opinion. In addition, we did conclude that the executive branch decisions under section 1158 were reasoned and reasonable.

The petition for rehearing is DENIED . . .

Notes and Questions

1. What type of deference should be given to an agency interpretation of its statutory mandate when that interpretation is adopted in informal adjudication? Is an informal adjudication of the type that occurred in *Gonzalez* an "exercise" of law-making power? Since persons subject to the jurisdiction of the INS are legally liable to comply with its decisions regarding their immigration status, it would appear that the INS decision was an exercise of law-making power. Regarding the level of deference, should it matter that informal adjudication provides affected persons with fewer procedural rights than formal adjudication.

2. The Court may provide some clarification regarding what constitutes "law-making" power in *The Mead Corporation v. United States*, 185 F.3d 1304 (Fed.Cir.1999), *cert. granted* 120 S.Ct. 2193, 147 L.Ed.2d 231 (2000). In *Mead*, the company challenged a "classification ruling" by the U.S. Custom's service. In an informal adjudication, the Service determined that "day planners" imported by the Mead Corporation were "bound diaries" for purposes of paying custom's duties. A day planner is a notebook that contains a calendar, a section for notes, etc. The adjudication was an interpretation of a regulation that was ambiguous concerning whether "day planners" were included in the definition of "bound diaries." The Federal Circuit held that the Service's interpretation was entitled to no deference because the interpretation was not adopted by notice and comment rulemaking. Having concluded that the interpretation was not entitled to *Chevron*-type deference, the Federal Circuit did not apply *Skidmore*-type deference, and the opinion did not explain the court's failure to do so.

3. In *Gonzalez*, the court determined the level of deference it owed to an agency's statutory interpretation arrived at in informal adjudication. A related issue is the level of deference that a court will give to an agency's interpretation of its own regulations when the agency does not exercise its law-making powers. The Supreme Court has generally deferred to an agency's interpretation of its own regulations without regard to the format used to adopt that interpretation.

is mentioned. We have described what happened before the INS in our case as informal adjudication. We understand the listing in *Christensen* to be illustrative and not to be an exhaustive or complete list of agency acts due deference.

The principle that agencies are entitled to deference for an interpretation of their own regulations dates back to *Bowles v. Seminole Rock & Sand Co.*, 325 U.S. 410, 65 S.Ct. 1215, 89 L.Ed. 1700 (1945), where the Court observed, "The intention of Congress or the principles of the Constitution in some situations may be relevant in the first instance in choosing between various constructions. But the ultimate criterion is the administrative interpretation, which becomes of controlling weight unless it is plainly erroneous or inconsistent with the regulation." 325 U.S. at 410, 65 S.Ct. at 1217. In more recent cases, the Court has deferred to an agency's interpretation of its regulations contained in an amicus brief filed by the Department of Labor at the request of the Supreme Court, *Auer v. Robbins*, 519 U.S. 452, 117 S.Ct. 905, 137 L.Ed.2d 79 (1997), in an interpretive rule issued by the United States Sentencing Commission, *Stinson v. United States*, 508 U.S. 36, 113 S.Ct. 1913, 123 L.Ed.2d 598 (1993), and in an OSHA citation alleging that a regulation had been violated, *Martin v. Occupational Safety and Health Review Commission*, 499 U.S. 144, 111 S.Ct. 1171, 113 L.Ed.2d 117 (1991).

4. In *Christensen*, after concluding that the Department of Labor's opinion letter interpreting the FLSA was entitled to *Skidmore*-deference, because it was not an exercise of the Department's law-making powers, Justice Thomas acknowledged the Court's treatment an agency's non-binding interpretation of its own regulations was different. 120 S.Ct. at 1663. Thus, despite the result in *Christensen*, the majority apparently anticipates continuation of the prior law regarding judicial deference to agency interpretations of an agency's own legislative rules. Why are interpretive rules that interpret legislative rules entitled to stronger deference than interpretive rules that interpret an agency's statutory mandate?

5. As noted in paragraph 3, *Auer v. Robbins* involved the interpretation of a legislative rule in an amicus brief. In *Christensen*, Justice Scalia's concurring opinion rejected the argument that the Department's interpretation was unreliable because it was formulated in a legal brief. This rejection was based on the fact that the agency was not a party in the litigation. Likewise, the lawsuit in *Auer* was between the St. Louis police department and some of its employees, and it concerned whether the police department owed the employees overtime pay. Supreme Court decisions do indicate that an agency's interpretation of one of its own regulations is not entitled to deference when it is a "litigating position" offered for the first time in a reviewing court. *See, e.g., Bowen v. Georgetown Univ. Hospital*, 488 U.S. 204, 212, 109 S.Ct. 468, 474, 102 L.Ed.2d 493 (1988); *Burlington Truck Lines, Inc. v. United States*, 371 U.S. 156, 168, 83 S.Ct. 239, 245, 9 L.Ed.2d 207 (1962). Why did the difference circumstance in *Auer* justify the Court in deferring to the Department's interpretation?

Chapter 5

REVIEWABILITY

A. INTRODUCTION

Each of the last three chapters has culminated in judicial review of agency action. In those chapters we assumed that a person could obtain judicial review of the agency action in question, but that is not always a good assumption. In this chapter the focus is on what is necessary for one to obtain judicial review, or viewed from the government's perspective, the focus is on the various legal arguments that may be raised in order to have a plaintiff's case dismissed without reaching the merits.

Some of these prerequisites arise from the Constitution, others from statute, and still others from common law. Some prerequisites delay when plaintiffs are able to obtain review, while others effectively preclude any review. The effect of precluding review altogether is obvious; the effect of delaying it or conditioning it is not always so obvious. As you consider the problems, ask yourself how delaying or conditioning review will affect the conduct of the private party and the government, as well as how it will affect their litigation.

The first question in federal courts is whether the court has jurisdiction. *See Steel Co. v. Citizens for a Better Environment*, 523 U.S. 83, 118 S.Ct. 1003, 140 L.Ed.2d 210 (1998). This is an issue that never goes away, can be raised by the court on its own motion, and is not waived even if not raised by the government. One element of jurisdiction is that the plaintiff must have **standing** to bring the case. The doctrine of standing comes from the Constitution and focuses on whether the person bringing the lawsuit is an appropriate person to bring the suit.

If a plaintiff has standing, a court must still have a **statutory grant of jurisdiction** over the particular type of case. This is usually not a problem in administrative law for two reasons. First, many statutory regimes contain specific jurisdictional provisions. For example, the Clean Air Act specifically provides for judicial review of various actions by the Environmental Protection Agency (EPA), indicating that some are to be reviewed in the U.S. Court of Appeals for the District of Columbia and others are to be reviewed in the "appropriate" U.S. Circuit Court of Appeals. *See* 42 U.S.C.A. § 7607(b). Similarly, the Communications Act of 1934, which created the Federal Communications Commission (FCC), specifically provides for judicial review in the U.S. Court of Appeals for the District of Columbia of a variety of different orders issued by the FCC. *See* 47 U.S.C.A. § 402(b). Second, if a plaintiff does not have jurisdiction under a particular statutory regime, the general federal question jurisdictional statute is normally available. According to 28 U.S.C.A. § 1331: "The district courts shall have original jurisdiction of all civil actions arising under the Constitution, laws, or treaties of the United States." The Administrative Procedure Act (APA) itself does not grant jurisdiction.

The next requirement is that the plaintiff state a **cause of action**. In essence, this means there is a statute granting the plaintiff some judicially enforceable right. Where there are specific judicial review provisions, they can provide both jurisdiction and a "cause of action." For example, the same section of the Occupational Safety and Health Act establishes jurisdiction to review regulations promulgated by OSHA and indicates who may sue: "Any person who may be adversely affected by a standard ... may at any time prior to the sixtieth day after such standard is promulgated file a petition challenging the validity of such standard" in an appropriate Court of Appeals. 29 U.S.C.A. § 655(f). For matters not covered by the specific review provisions, the APA's section 702 is the fall-back provision. It establishes a "cause of action" for "[a] person suffering legal wrong because of agency action, or adversely affected by agency action within the meaning of a relevant statute." 5 U.S.C.A. § 702. This cause of action is sometimes referred to as "non-statutory review" to distinguish it from review under a specific statutory provision.

To successfully assert a cause of action under the APA, a plaintiff must meet four requirements established by the APA. The Government must raise any objections to the adequacy of the plaintiff's satisfaction of the APA's cause of action requirements or waive them. *See Air Courier Conference v. American Postal Workers Union*, 498 U.S. 517, 523 n. 3, 111 S.Ct. 913, 917 n. 3, 112 L.Ed.2d 1125 (1991) (Postal Service's failure to raise inapplicability of the APA to the Postal Service in a lower court can waive the issue).

First, the appeal must be one that is not **excluded from review**. Section 701(a) states that the APA's judicial review provisions do not apply "to the extent that (1) statutes preclude judicial review; or (2) agency action is committed to agency discretion by law." While there are relatively few statutes that expressly preclude judicial review, and these are usually narrowly construed by the courts, it is possible for statutes to preclude review by implication. As you might guess, the case law concerning when a statute "impliedly" precludes judicial review is difficult. Similarly, it is often difficult to assess whether action has been "committed to agency discretion by law." The mere fact that the agency can exercise discretion is clearly not enough to escape judicial review under the APA; after all, one of the grounds for invalidating agency action is that the action is an abuse of discretion.

Second, section 702's cause of action is limited to persons suffering "legal wrong" or those "adversely affected or aggrieved ... within the meaning of a relevant statute." A "legal wrong" in the context of the APA means an action by the government that interferes with a person's constitutional, statutory, or common law rights. Such "legal wrongs" occur, for example, when the government takes your property (perhaps by fining you), interferes with your liberty (perhaps by limiting the manner in which you conduct your business), or denies you a statutory right (perhaps by not granting you a benefit to which a statute entitles you). The government, by comparison, does not commit a "legal wrong" when it decides to build a ski resort in a wilderness area in which you hike. You, however, might have a cause of action under the second part of section 702, which authorizes lawsuits by persons who assert "interests" that are "arguably within the zone of interests to be protected or regulated by the statute ... in question." *Association of Data Processing Service Organizations, Inc. v. Camp*, 397 U.S. 150, 153, 90 S.Ct. 827, 829, 25 L.Ed.2d 184 (1970). If a federal statute limits the type of development that can occur in a wilderness area, hikers are probably within the **zone of interests** that Congress intended to protect because unlimited development would adversely affect hikers' enjoyment of the wilderness. Although the "adversely affected or aggrieved" language of section 702 concerns whether a plaintiff has a "cause of action," courts often refer to the zone of interests requirement as an aspect of standing.

Third, section 704 of the APA provides that only agency action specifically reviewable by statute or "final agency action for which there is no adequate remedy in a court" is reviewable under the APA. The requirement for final agency action is known as the **finality** doctrine. As a general matter, this requirement is intended to protect against piece-meal litigation by requiring persons to wait until an agency has reached its final conclusion in the matter.

Fourth, section 704 also states that an agency action is final for purposes of judicial review even if a person has not appealed within the agency, unless the agency by rule requires such an appeal and stays its action pending that appeal, in which case the action would be final only after the conclusion of that appeal. The Supreme Court has declared this language a statutory **exhaustion of remedies** provision, replacing the common law exhaustion of remedies requirement that courts had previously applied. *Darby v. Cisneros*, 509 U.S. 137, 113 S.Ct. 2539, 125 L.Ed.2d 113 (1993).

There still remains a common law requirement that plaintiffs must meet known as the **ripeness** doctrine. The purpose of this doctrine is to assure that the case is in a posture appropriate for judicial determination and that the courts will not unnecessarily interfere in the administrative process. Much of the litigation in this area relates to "pre-enforcement review"—for example, review of a regulation before the agency tries to enforce that regulation. If review is not "ripe," persons subject to the regulation would have to wait until the agency enforces the regulation against them, and then they could obtain judicial review of the regulation as a defense to the enforcement action. Some regulatory statutes require persons to bring pre-enforcement challenges to rules within a set period of time or forever lose their ability to challenge the rule. *See, e.g.,* 42 U.S.C.A. § 7607(b)(1) (certain Clean Air Act regulations must be challenged within 60 days of promulgation). In these circumstances, because of the statutory requirement, ripeness is not an issue. Such statutes are, however, unusual.

Notes and Questions

1.   When a statutory mandate contains a jurisdictional provision, it also includes a direction concerning **venue.** Venue refers to the power of an individual court to function. A typical venue provision for the circuit courts, for example, permits a plaintiff to bring suit in the circuit in which that person resides, in which the person's principal place of business is located, or in which the particular activity under review took place. *See, e.g.,* 29 U.S.C.A. §§ 655(f), 660 (providing review of occupational safety and health standards in the U.S. Court of Appeals where the plaintiff resides and review of orders from the Occupational Safety and Health Review Commission in the U.S. Court of Appeals where the violation occurred, where the employer has its principal office, or of the District of Columbia). A lawsuit filed under general federal question jurisdiction, 28 U.S.C.A. § 1331, may be brought "in any judicial district in which (1) a defendant in the action resides, (2) a substantial part of the events or omissions giving rise to the claim occurred, or a substantial part of property that is the subject of the action is situated, or (3) the plaintiff resides if no real property is involved in the action."

2.   Distinct from the previous doctrines is another common law doctrine, known as **Primary Jurisdiction.** When a court is faced with an issue over which an agency also has jurisdiction, the court may stay the court case pending a determination of the issue by the agency with "primary jurisdiction." This doctrine is different from the others because it is not a way for an agency to avoid or delay judicial review of its actions. Instead, it arises in litigation between private parties, rather than in litigation to review agency action. For example, some regulatory systems in effect authorize agencies to exempt firms or activities from the antitrust laws. A firm sued for antitrust violations by a competitor might invoke the doctrine of primary jurisdiction to afford the agency an opportunity to determine whether the complained of conduct is exempted from the antitrust laws. If the agency determines that the exemption applies, the court case would be dismissed, but if the agency does not, the court case could go forward. *See, e.g., Ricci v. Chicago Mercantile Exchange,* 409 U.S. 289, 93 S.Ct. 573, 34 L.Ed.2d 525 (1973). Another common situation involves disputes over rates that are subject to federal regulation. For example, a gas pipeline might sue a customer for sums arguably due it under a tariff filed with the Federal Energy Regulatory Commission. Because of FERC's expertise with these tariffs, a court is likely to find primary jurisdiction in the agency, deferring the court case

until the agency has heard and decided the issue. *See, e.g., Williams Pipe Line Co. v. Empire Gas Corp.*, 76 F.3d 1491 (10th Cir.1996).

B. STANDING

Standing relates to the connection between the plaintiff and the lawsuit. Stemming from the constitutional limitation of federal judicial power to "Cases" and "Controversies," U.S. CONST. art. III, § 2, standing to bring a case in a federal court requires a sufficient connection between the plaintiff and the lawsuit. If the connection is not sufficient, the court has no jurisdiction, because the lawsuit is not a "case" or "controversy."

The basic constitutional test for standing is easily stated: has the plaintiff suffered an injury (or is the plaintiff about to suffer an injury) caused (or about to be caused) by the alleged illegal action, and would a favorable court decision remedy (or avoid) that injury? Application of this test is not always simple, and courses in Constitutional Law typically spend some time on this issue. For purposes of Administrative Law, there are a number of recurring issues.

When government takes action against a person, either generally by rulemaking or particularly by adjudication, so as to interfere with that person's liberty or property, the standing test is easily met. When government takes action (or does not take action) with respect to a third person, however, such as when an environmental group wishes to challenge agency action as inadequate regulation of polluters, two questions arise concerning whether the plaintiff has a cause of action. First, what type of injury must the plaintiff prove? Second, what chain of causation (and redressability) between the injury suffered and the government action must the plaintiff prove?

1. INJURY IN FACT

In the past half-century, the Court has expanded the types of injuries that will qualify for standing. In the 1960s, if not before, the courts made it clear that "injury in fact" would satisfy the standing requirement. If government action or inaction injures a third person in some real fashion, then the person has suffered a sufficient injury for standing purposes. *Association of Data Processing Service Organizations v. Camp*, 397 U.S. 150, 90 S.Ct. 827, 25 L.Ed.2d 184 (1970); *Federal Communications Commission v. Sanders Bros. Radio Station*, 309 U.S. 470, 60 S.Ct. 693, 84 L.Ed. 869 (1940). The "injury in fact" test replaced an earlier, more restrictive "legal injury" test. Under that more restrictive approach, a person did not have standing to challenge an action of the government unless the person had a right not to be injured conferred by common or statutory law. *See Alexander Sprunt & Son v. United States*, 281 U.S. 249, 50 S.Ct. 315, 74 L.Ed. 832 (1930); *Chicago Junction Case*, 264 U.S. 258, 44 S.Ct. 317, 68 L.Ed. 667 (1924).

The requirement of "injury in fact" raises its own questions. As a general matter, the Court has resisted including purely ideological or theoretical injury within the concept of injury in fact. Thus, a citizen is not deemed injured simply because the government acts unlawfully and the person is upset with that. Similarly, a federal taxpayer is generally not deemed to be injured by an agency's actions simply because they involve the illegal expenditure of federal funds. *United States v. Richardson*, 418 U.S. 166, 94 S.Ct. 2940, 41 L.Ed.2d 678 (1974). In *Sierra Club v. Morton*, 405 U.S. 727, 92 S.Ct. 1361, 31 L.Ed.2d 636 (1972), however, the Supreme Court allowed that injury to environmental, aesthetic, or recreational interests actually suffered by persons could qualify as injury in fact. In that case, the Court held that the Sierra Club did not suffer injury in fact solely by reason of being an organization interested in the environment. Rather, when government action harms some area of the environment, individuals would actually have to use that area in order to be "injured in fact" in their environmental, aesthetic, or recreational interests.

Despite *Sierra Club*, public interest and environmental groups can have standing under the doctrine of "associational" or "representational" standing. Under this doctrine, an association can sue in its own name on behalf of its members if: (1) one of its members would have standing to bring the action, (2) the lawsuit relates to the purposes of the organization, and (3) neither the claim asserted nor the relief requested requires the participation of individual members (which in practical terms means the action is not for damages, but is for declaratory or injunctive relief). *See Hunt v. Washington State Apple Advertising Commn.*, 432 U.S. 333, 97 S.Ct. 2434, 53 L.Ed.2d 383 (1977). Thus, much public interest and environmental litigation requires these groups to find members who actually would suffer an injury.

2. CAUSATION AND REDRESSABILITY

Even when a person can demonstrate "injury in fact," a court must still determine whether the injury is the result of the government action and that a favorable court decision would remedy the injury. *Simon v. Eastern Ky. Welfare Rights Organization (EKWRO)*, 426 U.S. 26, 96 S.Ct. 1917, 48 L.Ed.2d 450 (1976), illustrates the difficulty that a plaintiff can have in satisfying the causation and redressability requirements. EKWRO, a welfare rights organization, challenged an Internal Revenue Service (IRS) regulation that reduced the amount of free medical care that hospitals had to provide in order to qualify as tax exempt charitable institutions. The Internal Revenue Code exempts nonprofit organizations, including hospitals, from paying taxes if they operate "exclusively for ... charitable ... purposes." For thirteen years prior to the new regulation, the IRS had interpreted the Code to require hospitals, as a condition of being granted tax exempt status, to accept patients in need of care who could not pay for such services. The new regulation permitted hospitals to be tax exempt as long as they provided emergency services to persons who could not pay, even if they turned such persons away for non-emergency treatment. EKWRO alleged that the IRS had " 'encouraged' " hospitals to deny services to indigents, but the Court held that the plaintiffs lacked standing.

The Court found the complaint deficient concerning both causation and redressability. Concerning causation, it was "purely speculative whether the denials in service specified in the complaint can be traced to the [IRS's] 'encouragement' or instead result from decisions made by the hospitals without regard to tax implications." Concerning redressability, it was "equally speculative" whether a judgment in favor of EKWRO "would result in the availability of [medical] services." According to the Court, it was "just as plausible that the hospitals to which [EKWRO's members] may apply for service would elect to forgo favorable tax treatment to avoid the undetermined financial drain of an increase in the level of uncompensated services."

The Court has expressed a similarly skeptical attitude concerning causation and redressability in other cases where the government is regulating a third party. *See, e.g., Warth v. Seldin*, 422 U.S. 490, 95 S.Ct. 2197, 45 L.Ed.2d 343 (1975) (poor persons did not have standing to challenge a city's zoning requirements which prevented the construction of low cost housing because the lack of low cost housing could be attributable to other factors).

The Court has not always been so demanding. In *United States v. Students Challenging Regulatory Agency Procedures*, 412 U.S. 669, 93 S.Ct. 2405, 37 L.Ed.2d 254 (1973), a group of law students challenged railroad tariffs approved by the Interstate Commerce Commission (ICC) on the ground that the ICC was required to prepare an Environment Impact Statement before approving the new prices. The complaint alleged that the students used the forests, streams, and mountains in the Washington, D.C. area for camping, hiking, and fishing, and that this use would be "disturbed" by the adverse environmental impact caused by a reduction in recyclable goods attributable to the higher railroad rates. That is, because the higher railroad rates would cause manufacturers to recycle fewer goods, there would be more trash in the woods. Despite the attenuated nature of this claim, which relied on a long chain of causation, the Court decided that the complaint was sufficient to withstand the government's motion to dismiss. It held that a plaintiff is entitled to prove that the government's actions caused an injury if its pleadings more than "sham" allegations.

3. PRUDENTIAL REQUIREMENTS

Beyond the constitutional requirements for standing, the Supreme Court has established "prudential" standing requirements intended to assure that courts do not exercise judicial power unnecessarily. These requirements are "prudential" because they are not based on the constitutional requirement of "case and controversy." For this reason, they are subject to amendment by statute. As prudential requirements, the Court requires that the injury suffered is not a generalized grievance suffered equally by large numbers of people and that the plaintiff is not asserting the rights of a third person.

The requirement that the injury not be one suffered equally by large numbers of persons is intended to limit judicial power in an area where more representative forms of government might be more appropriate. Section 702 of the APA, however, limits judicial reliance on this requirement by providing a cause of action to any person "suffering legal wrong because of agency action, or adversely affected or aggrieved by agency action within the meaning of a relevant statute," whether or not large numbers of other persons are equally affected. Consequently, any person meeting the APA's requirement will not be denied standing on the basis that it is only a generalized grievance.

The requirement that a person cannot assert the rights of others reflects the Court's judgment that it is generally unsuitable to have someone litigate the rights of another person even if the potential plaintiff can claim an actual injury. For example, the Court held that a physician did not have standing to assert that a state law that prohibited the prescription of contraceptives violated the constitutional rights of his patients. *Tileston v. Ullman*, 318 U.S. 44, 63 S.Ct. 493, 87 L.Ed. 603 (1943). The physician, however, had an actual (financial) injury because the statute prohibited him from seeing patients for the purpose of prescribing contraceptives. For administrative law purposes, section 702 again delimits this prudential requirement. For example, if the Occupational Safety and Health Administration (OSHA) adopted a regulation prohibiting employers from employing women in certain kinds of jobs, an employer could challenge that regulation as denying equal protection of the laws to women employees. The employer would be asserting the rights of third persons—the right of women to equal protection. But the employer has a cause of action under section 702 to make this argument because the employer is suffering a "legal wrong" because of agency action. OSHA's action interferes with the employer's freedom to contract.

There is another important exception to the limitation that a person cannot assert the rights of others. As explained previously, the Court will permit associations to represent their members under the doctrine of "associational standing."

4. STANDING IN THE STATES

The above discussion of standing all relates to federal court cases and hence federal administrative law. Because the constitutional limitation of federal judicial power to "cases and controversies" does not apply to state judicial power, federal standing law does not apply in state courts and hence in state administrative law. Most states have developed their own rules of standing through either their own constitutions or common law, and those rules may have something in common with federal law but need not. *See generally Project: State Judicial Review of Administrative Action*, 43 ADMIN. L. REV. 571, 603–660 (1991).

5. LITIGATION OF STANDING

The next two cases provide additional information concerning how the Supreme Court approaches the requirement of standing and provide a context for the problems that follow.

LUJAN v. DEFENDERS OF WILDLIFE

504 U.S. 555, 112 S.Ct. 2130, 119 L.Ed.2d 351 (1992).

JUSTICE SCALIA delivered the opinion of the Court with respect to Parts I, II, III–A, and IV, and an opinion with respect to Part III–B in which the CHIEF JUSTICE, JUSTICE WHITE, and JUSTICE THOMAS join.

This case involves a challenge to a rule promulgated by the Secretary of the Interior interpreting § 7 of the Endangered Species Act of 1973 (ESA), in such fashion as to render it applicable only to actions within the United States or on the high seas. The preliminary issue, and the only one we reach, is whether the respondents here, plaintiffs below, have standing to seek judicial review of the rule.

I

[The ESA, which is administered jointly by the Secretaries of Interior and Commerce, provides in § 7(a) that Federal agencies must consult with either the Secretary of Interior or Commerce before undertaking actions that might jeopardize the continued existence of any endangered species or threatened species. In 1978, the Fish and Wildlife Service (FWS) and the National Marine Fisheries Service (NMFS), on behalf of the Secretary of the Interior and the Secretary of Commerce respectively, promulgated a joint regulation stating that this obligation extends to Federal actions taken in foreign nations. In 1986, however, these agencies issued a revised regulation, reinterpreting the ESA, to limit the consultation obligation to Federal actions taken in the United States or on the high seas. Shortly thereafter, respondents, organizations dedicated to wildlife conservation causes, filed this action against the Secretary of the Interior, seeking a declaratory judgment that the new regulation is in error as to the geographic scope of this requirement of the ESA and an injunction requiring the Secretary to promulgate a new regulation restoring the initial interpretation. The District Court granted the Secretary's motion to dismiss for lack of standing, and the Eighth Circuit reversed.]

II

While the Constitution of the United States divides all power conferred upon the Federal Government into "legislative Powers," Art. I, § 1, "[t]he executive Power," Art. II, § 1, and "[t]he judicial Power," Art. III, § 1, it does not attempt to define those terms. To be sure, it limits the jurisdiction of federal courts to "Cases" and "Controversies," but an executive inquiry can bear the name "case" (the Hoffa case) and a legislative dispute can bear the name "controversy" (the Smoot-

Hawley controversy). Obviously, then, the Constitution's central mechanism of separation of powers depends largely upon common understanding of what activities are appropriate to legislatures, to executives, and to courts.... One of those landmarks, setting apart the "Cases" and "Controversies" that are of the justiciable sort referred to in Article III ... is the doctrine of standing. Though some of its elements express merely prudential considerations that are part of judicial self-government, the core component of standing is an essential and unchanging part of the case-or-controversy requirement of Article III.

Over the years, our cases have established that the irreducible constitutional minimum of standing contains three elements: First, the plaintiff must have suffered an "injury in fact"—an invasion of a legally-protected interest which is (a) concrete and particularized[1] and (b) "actual or imminent, not 'conjectural' or 'hypothetical.'" Second, there must be a causal connection between the injury and the conduct complained of—the injury has to be "fairly ... trace[able] to the challenged action of the defendant, and not ... th[e] result [of] the independent action of some third party not before the court." Third, it must be "likely," as opposed to merely "speculative," that the injury will be "redressed by a favorable decision."

The party invoking federal jurisdiction bears the burden of establishing these elements. Since they are not mere pleading requirements but rather an indispensable part of the plaintiff's case, each element must be supported in the same way as any other matter on which the plaintiff bears the burden of proof, *i.e.*, with the manner and degree of evidence required at the successive stages of the litigation....

When the suit is one challenging the legality of government action or inaction, the nature and extent of facts that must be averred (at the summary judgment stage) or proved (at the trial stage) in order to establish standing depends considerably upon whether the plaintiff is himself an object of the action (or forgone action) at issue. If he is, there is ordinarily little question that the action or inaction has caused him injury, and that a judgment preventing or requiring the action will redress it. When, however, as in this case, a plaintiff's asserted injury arises from the government's allegedly unlawful regulation (or lack of regulation) of someone else, much more is needed. In that circumstance, causation and redressability ordinarily hinge on the response of the regulated (or regulable) third party to the government action or inaction—and perhaps on the response of others as well. The existence of one or more of the essential elements of standing "depends on the unfettered choices made by independent actors not before the courts and whose exercise of broad and legitimate discretion the courts cannot presume either to control or to predict," and it becomes the burden of the plaintiff to adduce facts showing that those choices have been or will be

---

1. By particularized, we mean that the injury must affect the plaintiff in a personal and individual way.

made in such manner as to produce causation and permit redressability of injury. . . .

III

We think the Court of Appeals failed to apply the foregoing principles in denying the Secretary's motion for summary judgment. Respondents had not made the requisite demonstration of (at least) injury and redressability.

A.

Respondents' claim to injury is that the lack of consultation with respect to certain funded activities abroad "increas[es] the rate of extinction of endangered and threatened species." Of course, the desire to use or observe an animal species, even for purely aesthetic purposes, is undeniably a cognizable interest for purpose of standing. "But the 'injury in fact' test requires more than an injury to a cognizable interest. It requires that the party seeking review be himself among the injured." To survive the Secretary's summary judgment motion, respondents had to submit affidavits or other evidence showing, through specific facts, not only that listed species were in fact being threatened by funded activities abroad, but also that one or more of respondents' members would thereby be "directly" affected apart from their " 'special interest' in th[e] subject."

With respect to this aspect of the case, the Court of Appeals focused on the affidavits of two Defenders' members—Joyce Kelly and Amy Skilbred. Ms. Kelly stated that she traveled to Egypt in 1986 and "observed the traditional habitat of the endangered Nile crocodile there and intend[s] to do so again, and hope[s] to observe the crocodile directly," and that she "will suffer harm in fact as a result of [the] American . . . role . . . in overseeing the rehabilitation of the Aswan High Dam on the Nile . . . and [in] develop[ing] . . . Egypt's . . . Master Water Plan." Ms. Skilbred averred that she traveled to Sri Lanka in 1981 and "observed th[e] habitat" of "endangered species such as the Asian elephant and the leopard" at what is now the site of the Mahaweli Project funded by the Agency for International Development (AID), although she "was unable to see any of the endangered species;" "this development project," she continued, "will seriously reduce endangered, threatened, and endemic species habitat including areas that I visited . . . [, which] may severely shorten the future of these species;" that threat, she concluded, harmed her because she "intend[s] to return to Sri Lanka in the future and hope[s] to be more fortunate in spotting at least the endangered elephant and leopard." When Ms. Skilbred was asked at a subsequent deposition if and when she had any plans to return to Sri Lanka, she reiterated that "I intend to go back to Sri Lanka," but confessed that she had no current plans. . . .

We shall assume for the sake of argument that these affidavits contain facts showing that certain agency-funded projects threaten listed species—though that is questionable. They plainly contain no facts, however, showing how damage to the species will produce "imminent" injury to Mss. Kelly and Skilbred. That the women "had visited" the areas of the projects before the projects commenced proves nothing. As we have said in a related context, " '[p]ast exposure to illegal conduct does not in itself show a present case or controversy regarding injunctive relief ... if unaccompanied by any continuing, present adverse effects.' "And the affiants' profession of an "inten[t]" to return to the places they had visited before—where they will presumably, this time, be deprived of the opportunity to observe animals of the endangered species—is simply not enough. Such "some day" intentions—without any description of concrete plans, or indeed even any specification of when the some day will be—do not support a finding of the "actual or imminent" injury that our cases require.

Besides relying upon the Kelly and Skilbred affidavits, respondents propose a series of novel standing theories. The first, inelegantly styled "ecosystem nexus," proposes that any person who uses any part of a "contiguous ecosystem" adversely affected by a funded activity has standing even if the activity is located a great distance away. This approach, as the Court of Appeals correctly observed, is inconsistent with our opinion in *National Wildlife Federation*, which held that a plaintiff claiming injury from environmental damage must use the area affected by the challenged activity and not an area roughly "in the vicinity" of it....

Respondents' other theories are called, alas, the "animal nexus" approach, whereby anyone who has an interest in studying or seeing the endangered animals anywhere on the globe has standing; and the "vocational nexus" approach, under which anyone with a professional interest in such animals can sue. Under these theories, anyone who goes to see Asian elephants in the Bronx Zoo, and anyone who is a keeper of Asian elephants in the Bronx Zoo, has standing to sue because the Director of AID did not consult with the Secretary regarding the AID-funded project in Sri Lanka. This is beyond all reason.... It is clear that the person who observes or works with a particular animal threatened by a federal decision is facing perceptible harm, since the very subject of his interest will no longer exist. It is even plausible—though it goes to the outermost limit of plausibility—to think that a person who observes or works with animals of a particular species in the very area of the world where that species is threatened by a federal decision is facing such harm, since some animals that might have been the subject of his interest will no longer exist. It goes beyond the limit, however, and into pure speculation and fantasy, to say that anyone who observes or works with an endangered species, anywhere in the world, is appreciably harmed by a single project affecting some portion of that species with which he has no more specific connection.

B.

Besides failing to show injury, respondents failed to demonstrate redressability.... Since the agencies funding the projects were not parties to the case, the District Court could accord relief only against the Secretary: He could be ordered to revise his regulation to require consultation for foreign projects. But this would not remedy respondents' alleged injury unless the funding agencies were bound by the Secretary's regulation, which is very much an open question. . . .

A further impediment to redressability is the fact that the agencies generally supply only a fraction of the funding for a foreign project. AID, for example, has provided less than 10% of the funding for the Mahaweli Project. Respondents have produced nothing to indicate that the projects they have named will either be suspended, or do less harm to listed species, if that fraction is eliminated. . . . [I]t is entirely conjectural whether the nonagency activity that affects respondents will be altered or affected by the agency activity they seek to achieve. There is no standing.

IV

The Court of Appeals found that respondents had standing for an additional reason: because they had suffered a "procedural injury." The so-called "citizen-suit" provision of the ESA provides, in pertinent part, that "any person may commence a civil suit on his own behalf (A) to enjoin any person, including the United States and any other governmental instrumentality or agency . . . who is alleged to be in violation of any provision of this chapter." The court held that, because § 7(a) requires interagency consultation, the citizen-suit provision creates a "procedural righ[t]" to consultation in all "persons"—so that *anyone* can file suit in federal court to challenge the Secretary's (or presumably any other official's) failure to follow the assertedly correct consultative procedure, notwithstanding their inability to allege any discrete injury flowing from that failure. To understand the remarkable nature of this holding one must be clear about what it does not rest upon: This is not a case where plaintiffs are seeking to enforce a procedural requirement the disregard of which could impair a separate concrete interest of theirs (*e.g.*, the procedural requirement for a hearing prior to denial of their license application, or the procedural requirement for an environmental impact statement before a federal facility is constructed next door to them)[7] . . . Rather, the court held that the injury-in-fact requirement had been satisfied by congressional conferral upon all persons of an abstract,

---

7.   There is this much truth to the assertion that "procedural rights" are special: The person who has been accorded a procedural right to protect his concrete interests can assert that right without meeting all the normal standards for redressability and immediacy. Thus, under our case-law, one living adjacent to the site for proposed construction of a federally licensed dam has standing to challenge the licensing agency's failure to prepare an Environmental Impact Statement, even though he cannot establish with any certainty that the Statement will cause the license to be withheld or altered, and even though the dam will not be completed for many years. (That is why we do not rely, in the present case, upon the Government's argument that, *even if* the other agencies were obliged to consult with the Secretary, they might not have followed his advice.) What respondents' "procedural rights" argument seeks, however, is quite different from this: standing for persons who have no concrete interests affected— persons who live (and propose to live) at the other end of the country from the dam.

self-contained, noninstrumental "right" to have the Executive observe the procedures required by law. We reject this view[8]

We have consistently held that a plaintiff raising only a generally available grievance about government—claiming only harm to his and every citizen's interest in proper application of the Constitution and laws, and seeking relief that no more directly and tangibly benefits him than it does the public at large—does not state an Article III case or controversy. . . .

To be sure, our generalized-grievance cases have typically involved Government violation of procedures assertedly ordained by the Constitution rather than the Congress. But there is absolutely no basis for making the Article III inquiry turn on the source of the asserted right. Whether the courts were to act on their own, or at the invitation of Congress, in ignoring the concrete injury requirement described in our cases, they would be discarding a principle fundamental to the separate and distinct constitutional role of the Third Branch—one of the essential elements that identifies those "Cases" and "Controversies" that are the business of the courts rather than of the political branches. "The province of the court," as Chief Justice Marshall said in *Marbury v. Madison,* "is, solely, to decide on the rights of individuals." Vindicating the *public* interest (including the public interest in government observance of the Constitution and laws) is the function of Congress and the Chief Executive. The question presented here is whether the public interest in proper administration of the laws (specifically, in agencies' observance of a particular, statutorily prescribed procedure) can be converted into an individual right by a statute that denominates it as such, and that permits all citizens (or, for that matter, a subclass of citizens who suffer no distinctive concrete harm) to sue. If the concrete injury requirement has the separation-of-powers significance we have always said, the answer must be obvious: To permit Congress to convert the undifferentiated public interest in executive officers' compliance with the law into an "individual right" vindicable in the courts is to permit Congress to transfer from the President to the courts the Chief Executive's most important constitutional duty, to "take Care that the Laws be faithfully executed," Art. II, § 3. . . .

Nothing in this contradicts the principle that "[t]he . . . injury required by Art. III may exist solely by virtue of 'statutes creating legal

---

8. . . . We do *not* hold that an individual cannot enforce procedural rights; he assuredly can, so long as the procedures in question are designed to protect some threatened concrete interest of his that is the ultimate basis of his standing. The dissent, however, asserts that there exist "classes of procedural duties . . . so enmeshed with the prevention of a substantive, concrete harm that an individual plaintiff may be able to demonstrate a sufficient likelihood of injury just through the breach of that procedural duty." If we understand this correctly, it means that the government's violation of a certain (undescribed) class of procedural duty satisfies the concrete-injury requirement by itself, without any showing that the procedural violation endangers a concrete interest of the plaintiff (apart from his interest in having the procedure observed). We cannot agree. The dissent is unable to cite a single case in which we actually found standing solely on the basis of a "procedural right" unconnected to the plaintiff's own concrete harm. . . .

rights, the invasion of which creates standing.' "[But the cases in which this was said] involved Congress's elevating to the status of legally cognizable injuries concrete, *de facto* injuries that were previously inadequate in law (namely, injury to an individual's personal interest in living in a racially integrated community and injury to a company's interest in marketing its product free from competition.) As we said in *Sierra Club v. Morton*, "[Statutory] broadening [of] the categories of injury that may be alleged in support of standing is a different matter from abandoning the requirement that the party seeking review must himself have suffered an injury." [I]t is clear that in suits against the government, at least, the concrete injury requirement must remain.

JUSTICE KENNEDY, with whom JUSTICE SOUTER joins, concurring in part and concurring in the judgment.

. . . While it may seem trivial to require that Mss. Kelly and Skilbred acquire airline tickets to the project sites or announce a date certain upon which they will return, this is not a case where it is reasonable to assume that the affiants will be using the sites on a regular basis, nor do the affiants claim to have visited the sites since the projects commenced. With respect to the Court's discussion of respondents' "ecosystem nexus," "animal nexus," and "vocational nexus" theories, I agree that on this record respondents' showing is insufficient to establish standing on any of these bases. I am not willing to foreclose the possibility, however, that in different circumstances a nexus theory similar to those proffered here might support a claim to standing. . . .

I also join Part IV of the Court's opinion with the following observations. As government programs and policies become more complex and far-reaching, we must be sensitive to the articulation of new rights of action that do not have clear analogs in our common-law tradition. Modern litigation has progressed far from the paradigm of Marbury suing Madison to get his commission, or Ogden seeking an injunction to halt Gibbons' steamboat operations. In my view, Congress has the power to define injuries and articulate chains of causation that will give rise to a case or controversy where none existed before, and I do not read the Court's opinion to suggest a contrary view. In exercising this power, however, Congress must at the very least identify the injury it seeks to vindicate and relate the injury to the class of persons entitled to bring suit. The citizen-suit provision of the Endangered Species Act does not meet these minimal requirements, because while the statute purports to confer a right on "any person . . . to enjoin . . . the United States and any other governmental instrumentality or agency . . . who is alleged to be in violation of any provision of this chapter," it does not of its own force establish that there is an injury in "any person" by virtue of any "violation."

The Court's holding that there is an outer limit to the power of Congress to confer rights of action is a direct and necessary consequence of the case and controversy limitations found in Article III. I agree that it would exceed those limitations if, at the behest of Congress and in the absence of any showing of concrete injury, we were to entertain citizen-suits to vindicate the public's nonconcrete interest in the proper administration of the laws. While it does not matter how many persons have been injured by the challenged action, the party bringing suit must show that the action injures him in a concrete and personal way. This requirement is not just an empty formality. It preserves the vitality of the adversarial process by assuring both that the parties before the court have an actual, as opposed to professed, stake in the outcome, and that "the legal questions presented ... will be resolved, not in the rarefied atmosphere of a debating society, but in a concrete factual context conducive to a realistic appreciation of the consequences of judicial action." In addition, the requirement of concrete injury confines the Judicial Branch to its proper, limited role in the constitutional framework of government....

JUSTICE STEVENS, concurring in the judgment.

Because I am not persuaded that Congress intended the consultation requirement in § 7(a)(2) of the ESA, to apply to activities in foreign countries, I concur in the judgment of reversal. I do not, however, agree with the Court's conclusion that respondents lack standing because the threatened injury to their interest in protecting the environment and studying endangered species is not "imminent." Nor do I agree with the plurality's additional conclusion that respondents' injury is not "redressable" in this litigation.

In my opinion a person who has visited the critical habitat of an endangered species, has a professional interest in preserving the species and its habitat, and intends to revisit them in the future has standing to challenge agency action that threatens their destruction. Congress has found that a wide variety of endangered species of fish, wildlife, and plants are of "aesthetic, ecological, educational, historical, recreational, and scientific value to the Nation and its people." Given that finding, we have no license to demean the importance of the interest that particular individuals may have in observing any species or its habitat, whether those individuals are motivated by aesthetic enjoyment, an interest in professional research, or an economic interest in preservation of the species....

The Court nevertheless concludes that respondents have not suffered "injury in fact" because they have not shown that the harm to the endangered species will produce "imminent" injury to them. I disagree. An injury to an individual's interest in studying or enjoying a species and its natural habitat occurs when someone (whether it be the government or a private party) takes action that harms that species and habitat. In my judgment, therefore, the "imminence" of such an injury should be measured by the timing and likelihood of the threatened environmental harm, rather than by the time that might elapse between the present and the time when the individuals would visit the area if no such injury should occur....

Although I believe that respondents have standing, I nevertheless concur in the judgment of reversal because I am persuaded that the Government is correct in its submission that § 7(a)(2) does not apply to activities in foreign countries. . . .

JUSTICE BLACKMUN, with whom JUSTICE O'CONNOR joins, dissenting.

I part company with the Court in this case in two respects. First, I believe that respondents have raised genuine issues of fact—sufficient to survive summary judgment—both as to injury and as to redressability. Second, I question the Court's breadth of language in rejecting standing for "procedural" injuries. I fear the Court seeks to impose fresh limitations on the constitutional authority of Congress to allow citizen-suits in the federal courts for injuries deemed "procedural" in nature. I dissent.

. . . Were the Court to apply the proper standard for summary judgment, I believe it would conclude that the sworn affidavits and deposition testimony of Joyce Kelly and Amy Skilbred advance sufficient facts to create a genuine issue for trial concerning whether one or both would be imminently harmed by the Aswan and Mahaweli projects. In the first instance, as the Court itself concedes, the affidavits contained facts making it at least "questionable" (and therefore within the province of the factfinder) that certain agency-funded projects threaten listed species. The only remaining issue, then, is whether Kelly and Skilbred have shown that they personally would suffer imminent harm. . . .

By requiring a "description of concrete plans" or "specification of when the some day [for a return visit] will be," the Court, in my view, demands what is likely an empty formality. No substantial barriers prevent Kelly or Skilbred from simply purchasing plane tickets to return to the Aswan and Mahaweli projects. This case differs from other cases in which the imminence of harm turned largely on the affirmative actions of third parties beyond a plaintiff's control. . . .

The Court also concludes that injury is lacking, because respondents' allegations of "ecosystem nexus" failed to demonstrate sufficient proximity to the site of the environmental harm. To support that conclusion, the Court mischaracterizes our decision in *Lujan v. National Wildlife Federation*, as establishing a general rule that "a plaintiff claiming injury from environmental damage must use the area affected by the challenged activity." In *National Wildlife Federation*, the Court required specific geographical proximity because of the particular type of harm alleged in that case: harm to the plaintiff's visual enjoyment of nature from mining activities. One cannot suffer from the sight of a ruined landscape without being close enough to see the sites actually being mined. Many environmental injuries, however, cause harm distant from the area immediately affected by the challenged action. Environmental destruction may affect animals traveling over vast geographical ranges, see, *e.g., Japan Whaling Assn. v. American Cetacean Soc.*, 478 U.S. 221 (1986) (harm to American whale watchers from Japanese whaling activities), or rivers running long geographical courses, see, *e.g., Arkansas v. Oklahoma*, 503 U.S. 91 (1992) (harm to Oklahoma residents from wastewater treatment plant 39 miles from border). It cannot seriously be contended that a litigant's failure to use the precise or exact site where animals are slaughtered or where toxic waste is dumped into a river means he or she cannot show injury.

The Court also rejects respondents' claim of vocational or professional injury. The Court says that it is "beyond all reason" that a zoo "keeper" of Asian elephants would have standing to contest his government's participation in the eradication of all the Asian elephants in another part of the world. I am unable to see how the distant location of the destruction necessarily (for purposes of ruling at summary judgment) mitigates the harm to the elephant keeper. If there is no more access to a future supply of the animal that sustains a keeper's livelihood, surely there is harm . . . .

The Court concludes that any "procedural injury" suffered by respondents is insufficient to confer standing. It rejects the view that the "injury-in-fact requirement . . . [is] satisfied by congressional conferral upon *all* person of an abstract, self-contained, noninstrumental 'right' to have the Executive observe the procedures required by law." Whatever the Court might mean with that very broad language, it cannot be saying that "procedural injuries" *as a class* are necessarily insufficient for purposes of Article III standing.

Most governmental conduct can be classified as "procedural." Many injuries caused by governmental conduct, therefore, are categorizable at some level of generality as "procedural" injuries. Yet, these injuries are not categorically beyond the pale of redress by the federal courts. When the Government, for example, "procedurally" issues a pollution permit, those affected by the permittee's pollutants are not without standing to sue. Only later cases will tell just what the Court means by its intimation that "procedural" injuries are not constitutionally cognizable injuries. In the meantime, I have the greatest of sympathy for the courts across the country that will struggle to understand the Court's standardless exposition of this concept today.

The Court expresses concern that allowing judicial enforcement of "agencies' observance of a particular, statutorily prescribed procedure" would "transfer from the President to the courts the Chief Executive's most important constitutional duty, to 'take Care that the Laws be faithfully executed,' Art. II, sec. 3." In fact, the principal effect of foreclosing judicial enforcement of such procedures is to transfer power into the hands of the Executive at the expense—not of the courts—but of Congress, from which that power originates and emanates . . . .

It is to be hoped that over time the Court will acknowledge that some classes of procedural duties are so enmeshed with the prevention of a substantive, concrete harm that an individual plaintiff may be able to demonstrate a sufficient likelihood of injury just through the breach of that procedural duty. For example, in the context of the NEPA requirement of environmental impact statements, this Court has acknowledged "it is now well settled that NEPA itself does not mandate particular results [and] simply prescribes the necessary process," but "these procedures are almost certain to affect the agency's substantive decision." This acknowledgment of an inextricable link between procedural and substantive harm does not reflect improper appellate factfinding. It reflects nothing more than the proper deference owed to the judgment of a coordinate branch—Congress—that certain procedures are directly tied to protection against a substantive harm. . . .

FEDERAL ELECTION COMMISSION v. AKINS

524 U.S. 11, 118 S.Ct. 1777, 141 L.Ed.2d 10 (1998).

JUSTICE BREYER delivered the opinion of the Court.

The Federal Election Commission (FEC) has determined that the American Israel Public Affairs Committee (AIPAC) is not a "political committee" as defined by the Federal Election Campaign Act of 1971 (FECA) and, for that reason, the Commission has refused to require AIPAC to make disclosures regarding its membership, contributions, and expenditures that FECA would otherwise require. We hold that respondents, a group of voters, have standing to challenge the Commission's determination in court, and we remand this case for further proceedings.

[The Federal Election Committee Act, among other obligations, requires groups that fall within the Act's definition of a "political committee" to undertake extensive record keeping and disclosure requirements. Such groups must register with the FEC, appoint a treasurer, keep names and addresses of contributors, track the amount and purpose of disbursements, and file complex FEC reports. Akins and five other voters, who held views contrary to those supported by AIPAC, filed a complaint with the FEC alleging that AIPAC had failed to comply with the previous requirements. AIPAC asked the FEC to dismiss the claim on the ground it was not a "political committee" within the meaning of FECA. The FEC held that AIPAC was not subject to the previous requirements and it dismissed the complaint of Akins and the other voters. After a Court of Appeals decision reversing the FEC decision, the Supreme Court granted the Government's request that it hear the case.]

The Solicitor General argues that respondents lack standing to challenge the FEC's decision not to proceed against AIPAC. He claims that they have failed to satisfy the "prudential" standing requirements upon which this Court has insisted. He adds that respondents have not shown that they "suffe[r] injury in fact," that their injury is "fairly traceable" to the FEC's decision, or that a judicial decision in their favor would "redres[s]" the injury. In his view, respondents' District Court petition consequently failed to meet Article III's demand for a "case" or "controversy."

We do not agree with the FEC's "prudential standing" claim. Congress has specifically provided in FECA that "[a]ny person who believes a violation of this Act . . . has occurred, may file a complaint with the Commission." It has added that "[a]ny party aggrieved by an order of the Commission dismissing a complaint filed by such party ... may file a petition" in district court seeking review of that dismissal. History associates the word "aggrieved" with a congressional intent to cast the standing net broadly—beyond the common-law interests and substantive statutory rights upon which "prudential" standing traditionally rested.

Moreover, prudential standing is satisfied when the injury asserted by a plaintiff " 'arguably [falls] within the zone of interests to be protected or regulated by the statute ... in question.' " The injury of which respondents complain—their failure to obtain relevant information—is injury of a kind that FECA seeks to address. We have found nothing in the Act that suggests Congress intended to exclude voters from the benefits of these provisions, or otherwise to restrict standing, say, to political parties, candidates, or their committees.

Given the language of the statute and the nature of the injury, we conclude that Congress, intending to protect voters such as respondents from suffering the kind of injury here at issue, intended to authorize this kind of suit. Consequently, respondents satisfy "prudential" standing requirements.

Nor do we agree with the FEC or the dissent that Congress lacks the constitutional power to authorize federal courts to adjudicate this lawsuit. Article III, of course, limits Congress' grant of judicial power to "cases" or "controversies." That limitation means that respondents must show, among other things, an "injury in fact"—a requirement that helps assure that courts will not "pass upon ... abstract, intellectual problems," but adjudicate "concrete, living contest[s] between adversaries." In our view, respondents here have suffered a genuine "injury in fact."

The "injury in fact" that respondents have suffered consists of their inability to obtain information—lists of AIPAC donors ... and campaign-related contributions and expenditures—that, on respondents' view of the law, the statute requires that AIPAC make public. There is no reason to doubt their claim that the information would help them (and others to whom they would communicate it) to evaluate candidates for public office, especially candidates who received assistance from AIPAC, and to evaluate the role that AIPAC's financial assistance might play in a specific election. Respondents' injury consequently seems concrete and particular. Indeed, this Court has previously held that a plaintiff suffers an "injury in fact" when the plaintiff fails to obtain information which must be publicly disclosed pursuant to a statute. *Public Citizen v. Department of Justice*, 491 U.S. 440, 449 (1989) (failure to obtain information subject to disclosure under Federal Advisory Committee Act "constitutes a sufficiently distinct injury to provide standing to sue"). *See also Havens Realty Corp. v. Coleman*, 455 U.S. 363, 373–374 (1982) (deprivation of information about housing availability constitutes "specific injury" permitting standing).

The dissent refers to *United States v. Richardson*, 418 U.S. 166 (1974), a case in which a plaintiff sought information (details of Central Intelligence Agency expenditures) to which, he said, the Constitution's Accounts Clause, Art. I, § 9, cl. 7, entitled him. The Court held that the plaintiff there lacked Article III standing. The dissent says that *Richardson* and this case are "indistinguishable." But as the parties' briefs suggest—for they do not mention *Richardson*—that case does not control the outcome here.

Richardsons's plaintiff claimed that a statute permitting the CIA to keep its expenditures nonpublic violated the Accounts Clause, which requires that "a regular Statement and Account of the Receipts and Expenditures of all public Money shall be published from time to time." The Court held that the plaintiff lacked standing because there was "no 'logical nexus' between the [plaintiff's] asserted status of taxpayer and the claimed failure of the Congress to require the Executive to supply a more detailed report of the [CIA's] expenditures."

In this case, however, the "logical nexus" inquiry is not relevant. Here, there is no constitutional provision requiring the demonstration of the "nexus".... Rather, there is a statute which, as we previously pointed out, does seek to protect individuals such as respondents from the kind of harm they say they have suffered, i.e., failing to receive particular information about campaign-related activities.

The fact that the Court in *Richardson* focused upon taxpayer standing, not voter standing, places that case at still a greater distance from the case before us. We are not suggesting, as the dissent implies, that *Richardson* would have come out differently if only the plaintiff had asserted his standing to sue as a voter, rather than as a taxpayer. Faced with such an assertion, the *Richardson* court would simply have had to consider whether "the Framers ... ever imagined that general directives [of the Constitution] ... would be subject to enforcement by an individual citizen." But since that answer (like the answer to whether there was taxpayer standing in *Richardson*) would have rested in significant part upon the Court's view of the Accounts Clause, it still would not control our answer in this case. All this is to say that the legal logic which critically determined *Richardson*'s outcome is beside the point here.

The FEC's strongest argument is its contention that this lawsuit involves only a "generalized grievance." (Indeed, if *Richardson* is relevant at all, it is because of its broad discussion of this matter, not its basic rationale.) The Solicitor General points out that respondents' asserted harm (their failure to obtain information) is one which is " 'shared in substantially equal measure by all or a large class of citizens.' "Whether styled as a constitutional or prudential limit on standing, the Court has sometimes determined that where large numbers of Americans suffer alike, the political process, rather than the judicial process, may provide the more appropriate remedy for a widely shared grievance.

The kind of judicial language to which the FEC points, however, invariably appears in cases where the harm at issue is not only widely shared, but is also of an abstract and indefinite nature—for example, harm to the "common concern for obedience to law." The abstract nature of the harm—for example, injury to the interest in seeing that the law is obeyed—deprives the case of the concrete specificity that characterized those controversies which were "the traditional concern of the courts at Westminster," and which today prevents a plaintiff from obtaining what would, in effect, amount to an advisory opinion.

Often the fact that an interest is abstract and the fact that it is widely shared go hand in hand. But their association is not invariable, and where a harm is concrete, though widely shared, the Court has found "injury in fact." Thus the fact that a political forum may be more readily available where an injury is widely shared (while counseling against, say, interpreting a statute as conferring standing) does not, by itself, automatically disqualify an interest for Article III purposes. Such an interest, where sufficiently concrete, may count as an "injury in fact." This conclusion seems particularly obvious where (to use a hypothetical example) large numbers of individuals suffer the same common-law injury (say, a widespread mass tort), or where large numbers of voters suffer interference with voting rights conferred by law. We conclude that similarly, the informational injury at issue here, directly related to voting, the most basic of political rights, is sufficiently concrete and specific such that the fact that it is widely shared does not deprive Congress of constitutional power to authorize its vindication in the federal courts.

Respondents have also satisfied the remaining two constitutional standing requirements. The harm asserted is "fairly traceable" to the FEC's decision about which respondents complain. Of course, as the FEC points out, it is possible that even had the FEC agreed with respondents' view of the law, it would still have decided in the exercise of its discretion not to require AIPAC to produce the information. But that fact does not destroy Article III "causation," for we cannot know that the FEC would have exercised its prosecutorial discretion in this way. Agencies often have discretion about whether or not to take a particular action. Yet those adversely affected by a discretionary agency decision generally have standing to complain that the agency based its decision upon an improper legal ground. If a reviewing court agrees that the agency misinterpreted the law, it will set aside the agency's action and remand the case—even though the agency (like a new jury after a mistrial) might later, in the exercise of its lawful discretion, reach the same result for a different reason. Thus respondents' "injury in fact" is "fairly traceable" to the FEC's decision not to issue its complaint, even though the FEC might reach the same result exercising its discretionary powers lawfully. For similar reasons, the courts in this case can "redress" respondents' "injury in fact." . . .

[The majority declined to reach the issue of whether AIPAC was a "political committee" with the meaning of the FACA and remanded the issue to the FEC for further consideration in light of legal developments which occurred after the FEC's decision.]

JUSTICE SCALIA, with whom JUSTICE O'CONNOR AND Justice Thomas JOIN, DISSENTING. . . .

It is clear that the Federal Election Campaign Act does not intend that all persons filing complaints with the Commission have the right to seek judicial review of the rejection of their complaints. This is evident from the fact that the Act permits a complaint to be filed by "[a]ny person who believes a violation of this Act . . . has occurred," but accords a right to judicial relief only to "[a]ny party aggrieved by an order of the Commission dismissing a complaint filed by such party." The interpretation that the Court gives the latter provision deprives it of almost all its limiting force. Any voter can sue to compel the agency to require registration of an entity as a political committee, even though the "aggrievement" consists of nothing more than the deprivation of access to information whose public availability would have been one of the consequences of registration.

. . . A person demanding provision of information that the law requires the agency to furnish—one demanding compliance with the Freedom of Information Act or the Advisory Committee Act, for example—can reasonably be described as being "aggrieved" by the agency's refusal to provide it. What the respondents complain of in this suit, however, is not the refusal to provide information, but the refusal (for an allegedly improper reason) to commence an agency enforcement action against a third person. That refusal itself plainly does not render respondents "aggrieved" within the meaning of the Act, for in that case there would have been no reason for the Act to differentiate between "person" . . . and "party aggrieved" in [the Act]. Respondents that each of them is elevated to the special status of a "party aggrieved" by the fact that the requested enforcement action (if it was successful) would have had the effect, among others, of placing certain information in the agency's possession, where respondents, along with everyone else in the world, would have had access to it. It seems to me most unlikely that the failure to produce that effect—both a secondary consequence of what respondents immediately seek, and a consequence that affects respondents no more and with no greater particularity than it affects virtually the entire population—would have been meant to set apart each respondent as a "party aggrieved" (as opposed to just a rejected complainant) within the meaning of the statute. . . .

In *Richardson*, we dismissed for lack of standing a suit whose "aggrievement" was precisely the "aggrievement" respondents assert here: the Government's unlawful refusal to place information within the public domain. The only difference, in fact, is that the aggrievement there was more direct, since the Government already had the information within its possession, whereas here the respondents seek enforcement action that will bring information within the Government's possession and then require the information to be made public. The plaintiff in

Richardson challenged the Government's failure to disclose the expenditures of the Central Intelligence Agency (CIA), in alleged violation of the constitutional requirement, Art. I, § 9, cl. 7, that "a regular Statement and Account of the Receipts and Expenditures of all public Money shall be published from time to time." We held that such a claim was a nonjusticiable "generalized grievance" because "the impact on [plaintiff] is plainly undifferentiated and common to all members of the public."

. . . According to the Court, "*Richardson* focused upon taxpayer standing, ... not voter standing." In addition to being a silly distinction, given the weighty governmental purpose underlying the "generalized grievance" prohibition—viz., to avoid "something in the nature of an Athenian democracy or a New England town meeting to oversee the conduct of the National Government by means of lawsuits in federal courts"—this is also a distinction that the Court in *Richardson* went out of its way explicitly to eliminate. It is true enough that the narrow question presented in *Richardson* was " '[w]hether a federal taxpayer has standing.' " But the *Richardson* Court did not hold only, as the Court today suggests, that the plaintiff failed to qualify for the exception to the rule of no taxpayer standing established by the "logical nexus" test of *Flast v. Cohen*, 392 U.S. 83 (1968). The plaintiff's complaint in *Richardson* had also alleged that he was " 'a member of the electorate,' " and he asserted injury in that capacity as well. The *Richardson* opinion treated that as fairly included within the taxpayer-standing question, or at least as plainly indistinguishable from it:

> "The respondent's claim is that without detailed information on CIA expenditures—and hence its activities—he cannot intelligently follow the actions of Congress or the Executive, nor can he properly fulfill his obligations as a member of the electorate in voting for candidates seeking national office. . . ."

If *Richardson* left voter-standing unaffected, one must marvel at the unaccustomed ineptitude of the American Civil Liberties Union Foundation, which litigated *Richardson*, in not immediately refiling with an explicit voter-standing allegation. Fairly read, and applying a fair understanding of its important purposes, *Richardson* is indistinguishable from the present case.

The Court's opinion asserts that our language disapproving generalized grievances "invariably appears in cases where the harm at issue is not only widely shared, but is also of an abstract and indefinite nature." "Often," the Court says, "the fact that an interest is abstract and the fact that it is widely shared go hand in hand. But their association is not invariable, and where a harm is concrete, though widely shared, the Court has found 'injury in fact.' " If that is so—if concrete generalized grievances (like concrete particularized grievances) are OK, and abstract generalized grievances (like abstract particularized grievances) are bad— one must wonder why we ever developed the superfluous distinction between generalized and particularized grievances at all. But of course the Court is wrong to think that generalized grievances have only concerned us when they are abstract. One need go no further than *Richardson* to prove that—unless the Court believes that deprivation of information is an abstract injury, in which event this case could be disposed of on that much broader ground.

What is noticeably lacking in the Court's discussion of our generalized-grievance jurisprudence is all reference to two words that have figured in it prominently: "particularized" and "undifferentiated." "Particularized" means that "the injury must affect the plaintiff in a personal and individual way." If the effect is "undifferentiated and common to all members of the public," the plaintiff has a "generalized grievance" that must be pursued by political rather than judicial means. These terms explain why it is a gross oversimplification to reduce the concept of a generalized grievance to nothing more than "the fact that [the grievance] is widely shared," thereby enabling the concept to be dismissed as a standing principle by such examples as "large numbers of individuals suffer[ing] the same common-law injury (say, a widespread mass tort), or . . . large numbers of voters suffer[ing] interference with voting rights conferred by law." The exemplified injuries are widely shared, to be sure, but each individual suffers a particularized and differentiated harm. One tort victim suffers a burnt leg, another a burnt arm—or even if both suffer burnt arms they are different arms. One voter suffers the deprivation of his franchise, another the deprivation of hers. With the generalized grievance, on the other hand, the injury or deprivation is not only widely shared but it is undifferentiated. The harm caused to Mr. *Richardson* by the alleged disregard of the Statement-of-Accounts Clause was precisely the same as the harm caused to everyone else: unavailability of a description of CIA expenditures. Just as the (more indirect) harm caused to Mr. Akins by the allegedly unlawful failure to enforce FECA is precisely the same as the harm caused to everyone else: unavailability of a description of AIPAC's activities.

The Constitution's line of demarcation between the Executive power and the judicial power presupposes a common understanding of the type of interest needed to sustain a "case or controversy" against the Executive in the courts. A system in which the citizenry at large could sue to compel Executive compliance with the law would be a system in which the courts, rather than of the President, are given the primary responsibility to "take Care that the Laws be faithfully executed," Art. II, § 3. We do not have such a system because the common understanding of the interest necessary to sustain suit has included the requirement, affirmed in *Richardson*, that the complained-of injury be particularized and differentiated, rather than common to all the electorate. When the Executive can be directed by the courts, at the instance of any voter, to remedy a deprivation which affects the entire electorate in precisely the same way—and particularly when that deprivation (here, the unavailability of information) is one inseverable part of a larger enforcement scheme—there has occurred a shift of political responsibility to a branch designed not to protect the public at large but to protect individual rights . . . .

Problem 5–1: Standing and Animal Rights

Under the Animal Welfare Act, the Department of Agriculture is required to adopt regulations establishing "standards to govern the humane handling, care, treatment, and transportation of animals by dealers, research facilities, and exhibitors," which includes zoos. Such standards "shall include minimum requirements" for, among other things, "a physical environment adequate to promote the psychological well-being of primates." While the Department has adopted regulations, the Animal Legal Defense Fund believes they are totally inadequate. For example, nothing in the regulations prohibits zoos from housing primates in individual cages, although all primates are communal animals. What facts would the group have to allege (and be prepared to offer evidence on) in order to establish standing to challenge these regulations?

Problem 5–2: Standing and Procedural Injury

Problem 3–3 concerned ex parte communications between a presidential aide and members of the Endangered Species Committee during the consideration of a petition for an exemption from the Endangered Species Act for a number of Bureau of Land Management timber sales. These timber sales would result in cutting timber in the habitat of the threatened Northern Spotted Owl. An environmental group wishes to challenge the grant of the exemption on the basis that the APA forbids ex parte communications in formal adjudications. What facts would the group need to allege (and be prepared to offer evidence on) in order to establish standing to challenge the decision on this basis?

Notes and Questions

1. In *Defenders* Justice Scalia writes for six members of the Court, including Chief Justice Rehnquist and Justices Kennedy and Souter, while Justices Stevens, O'Connor, and Blackmun dissented on the standing issue. In *Akins*, only six years later, Justice Scalia writes the dissent joined by only two others—one being Justice Thomas, who had joined him in *Defenders* and the other being Justice O'Connor, who had not. What happened? Justices Kennedy and Souter perhaps signaled their leanings in their concurrence in *Defenders*. The cause of action created in the Federal Election Campaign Act may well have been precisely the "articulation of new rights of action," to which they said the Court must be sensitive. Justice White, who joined the majority in *Defenders*, was replaced by Justice Ginsburg, who voted with the majority in *Akins*. That accounts for the three-vote swing. Justice Breyer, the author of *Akins*, had replaced Justice Blackmun. Nevertheless, why do you suppose the Chief Justice and Justice O'Connor switched sides?* In any case, *Defenders* continues to be cited by the Court as the basic restatement of standing law.

* If the Chief Justice is in the majority, he chooses the persons to be the author of the majority opinion; otherwise, the senior justice in the majority chooses, who would

2.   The Court in recent years seemingly had been hostile to environmentalists, denying standing in other environmental cases besides *Defenders. See Lujan v. National Wildlife Federation*, 497 U.S. 871, 110 S.Ct. 3177, 111 L.Ed.2d 695 (1990) (lack of injury); *Steel Co. v. Citizens for a Better Environment*, 523 U.S. 83, 118 S.Ct. 1003, 140 L.Ed.2d 210 (1998) (lack of redressability). *Cf., Bennett v. Spear*, 520 U.S. 154, 117 S.Ct. 1154, 137 L.Ed.2d 281 (1997) (finding standing for "anti-environmentalists"). Subsequent to *Akins*, however, the Court decided *Friends of the Earth v. Laidlaw*, 528 U.S. 167, 120 S.Ct. 693, 145 L.Ed.2d 610 (2000), which found standing for environmental plaintiffs. The lower court had found that the defendant polluter's discharge to a river had caused "no demonstrated proof of harm to the environment." The Supreme Court, now with only Justices Scalia and Thomas dissenting, responded: "[t]he relevant showing for purposes of Article III standing, however, is not injury to the environment but injury to the plaintiff." Here the injury to the plaintiffs consisted of their not being able to swim and fish in the river because of their "reasonable fear" caused by defendant's pollution. Thus, their injury fell within the rubric of recreational injury, approved by *Sierra Club v. Morton*. Prior to *Laidlaw* some lower courts had denied standing to environmental plaintiffs who were able to show that defendants illegally polluted some waters, but were unable to show that the pollution actually injured them, either because the pollutant, while illegal, was not dangerous or because the discharge took place far removed from where plaintiffs used the waters. After *Laidlaw*, it would appear that a plaintiff need only show that the defendant's acts cause the plaintiff a "reasonable fear." Is a fear reasonable if the pollutant is not dangerous, does not result in a violation of water quality standards, or is discharged so far from plaintiff's use that it is effectively diluted by the time it reaches plaintiff? Some have suggested that *Laidlaw*'s real effect is to shift the burden from the plaintiff of showing actual injury to the defendant polluter to show absence of injury and therefore no reasonable basis for fear.

3.   Supreme Court decisions in the 1960s and 1970s opened the court house doors to statutory beneficiaries to challenge agency actions. Statutory beneficiaries were aided by the Court's adoption of the "injury in fact" test, by the inclusion of environmental, aesthetic, and recreational interests as such injuries, and by the creation of "associational standing." In addition, the Court did not strictly enforce the causation and redressability requirements. Finally, statutory beneficiaries were aided by the Court's interpretation of Section 702 of the APA to give a cause of action to persons that Congress intended to protect by adoption of a statute.

have been Justice Stevens. Some Court watchers have suggested that the Chief Justice sometimes votes in the majority, when his vote is not the deciding vote, solely for the purpose of depriving the senior justice from the ability to determine the author of the majority opinion.

Prior to these decisions, regulated entities were often the only parties that had standing and a cause of action to challenge agency decisions. Thus, the Court "reformed" administrative law by adopting similar treatment of statutory beneficiaries and regulated entities. Richard Stewart, *The Reformation of American Administrative Law*, 88 HARV. L. REV. 1669 (1975). The Court's actions can be justified under a "private attorney general" theory. When an agency decides in favor of regulated entities, they have no incentive to challenge the legality of agency action. Unless statutory beneficiaries can sue, the courts will not have the opportunity to determine the legality of the agency's decision. When they sue, statutory beneficiaries serve as "private attorneys generals" who can vindicate the interests of the public by obtaining judicial review. Moreover, such lawsuits can signal to Congress when agencies may have gone astray. *See* Peter L. Strauss, *Revisiting* Overton Park: *Political and Judicial Controls Over Administrative Action Affecting the Community*, 39 U.C.L.A. L. REV. 1251, 1324–25 (1992).

What motivated the Court to adopt stricter standing requirements? If expanded standing requirements serve the private attorney general theory, what goals or values are served by a restrictive standing theory? Justice Scalia in his majority opinion in *Defenders* and his dissent in *Akins* argues that the whole notion of "private attorneys general" is contrary to the Constitution's vesting of executive powers in the President–not the courts. Professor Pierce, however, suggests that the Court's approach to standing is part of a broader agenda to reduce the judicial role in government policy making, but he criticizes using standing as an element of judicial restraint. He is concerned that an agency will be able to ignore legislative commands because no one will be eligible to sue to hold the agency accountable. Richard J. Pierce, Lujan v. Defenders of Wildlife: *Standing As A Judicially Imposed Limit on Legislative Power*, 42 DUKE L.J. 1170 (1993). Others respond that "the outer limits set by *Defenders* will not, in practice, affect most lawsuits" and that the Court must respect the constitutional requirement of "case and controversy" even if it means rejecting some causes of action created by Congress. Marshall Breger, *Defending* Defenders: *Remarks on Nichol and Pierce*, 42 DUKE L.J. 1202, 1218 (1993).

4. In *Defenders of Wildlife*, Justice Scalia indicates that the injury suffered by the plaintiff must be "fairly traceable" to the government's action and that it must be " 'likely' as opposed to merely 'speculative' "that the injury will be redressed by a favorable decision. Professor Pierce argues that the manner in which the Court has sometimes applied the causation and redressability tests, such as in the *EKWRO* case described earlier under causation and redressability, was so demanding as to constitute an "insurmountable hurdle" to standing, while in other cases the Court has "applied a pragmatic test of causation based on probabilities." KENNETH CULP DAVIS & RICHARD J. PIERCE, III, ADMINISTRATIVE LAW TREATISE 38 (1994); *see also* Cass R. Sunstein, *What's Standing After* Lujan?: *Of Citizen Suits, "Injuries," and Article III*, 91 MICH.L.REV. 163, 203–04 (1992) (comparing inconsistent application of standing tests in

EKWRO and *Regents of the University of California v. Bakke*, 438 U.S. 912, 98 S.Ct. 3140, 57 L.Ed.2d 1158 (1978)).

Duke Power Co. v. Carolina Environmental Study Group, 438 U.S. 59, 98 S.Ct. 2620, 57 L.Ed.2d 595 (1978), is an example of the more lenient approach. The environmental group challenged the constitutionality of the Price–Anderson Act, which establishes a cap on the tort liability of the operators of nuclear power plants in the case of a catastrophic accident. The group claimed that its members were injured by the operation of a nuclear plant by the Duke Power Company because of the plant's adverse impact on the nearby environment. They also contended that the Price–Anderson Act "caused" this injury because Duke Power would not have built the plant if Congress has not passed the Act, and that the injury would be "redressed" if the Act were void, because the company would not continue to operate the plant without the protection of the Act. The Court acknowledged that these last two claims might not be true. The company might have built the plant if the Act had not passed, and if it were void, they might continue to operate the plant. Nevertheless, the Court held that the plaintiffs had standing because there was a "substantial likelihood" that the plaintiff's claims were true.

The Supreme Court's inconsistency has generated considerable conflict in the circuit courts. In *Center for Auto Safety v. Thomas*, 847 F.2d 843 (D.C.Cir.1988), for example, the court sitting en banc split 5–5 over standing. The plaintiffs sought to challenge a rule promulgated by EPA that reduced the penalties that automobile manufacturers would pay for failing to build a sufficient number of high mileage automobiles. Five judges held that consumers had standing because the reduced penalties made it less likely that the companies would build as many high mileage cars in the future. The other five judges objected that it was speculative how the companies would react because there are many factors that impact the production decisions of car companies.

5. One explanation of inconsistent standing decisions is that the Court engages in a result-oriented manipulation of the standing doctrine. *See* Richard E. Levy & Robert L. Glicksman, *Judicial Activism and Restraint in the Supreme Court's Environmental Law Decisions*, 42 VAND. L. REV. 343 (1989). Assuming that this observation is at least sometimes true, what does it mean for the litigants? What strategy would you adopt to have the Court apply the standing tests more or less strictly depending on which application benefits your client?

C. CAUSE OF ACTION

In addition to meeting the requirements of standing, a person must have a cause of action to sue. As noted earlier, Congress sometimes establishes a cause of action in the agency's statutory mandate. Other times, a plaintiff will seek to rely on section 702 of the APA. The next two cases interpret the "zone of interest" test established in section 702.

The problem which follows requires you to apply these cases to resolve a "cause of action" issue.

AIR COURIER CONFERENCE OF AMERICA v. AMERICAN POSTAL WORKERS UNION, AFL–CIO

498 U.S. 517, 111 S.Ct. 913, 112 L.Ed.2d 1125 (1991).

CHIEF JUSTICE REHNQUIST delivered the opinion of the Court.

This case requires us to decide whether postal employees are within the "zone of interests" of the Private Express Statutes (PES), so that they may challenge the action of the United States Postal Service in suspending the operation of the PES with respect to a practice of private courier services called "international remailing." We hold that they are not.

Since its establishment, the United States Postal Service has exercised a monopoly over the carriage of letters in and from the United States. The postal monopoly is codified in a group of statutes known as the Private Express Statutes. The monopoly was created by Congress as a revenue protection measure for the Postal Service to enable it to fulfill its mission. It prevents private competitors from offering service on low-cost routes at prices below those of the Postal Service, while leaving the Service with high-cost routes and insufficient means to fulfill its mandate of providing uniform rates and service to patrons in all areas, including those that are remote or less populated.

A provision of the PES allows the Postal Service to "suspend [the PES restrictions] upon any mail route where the public interest requires the suspension." [The Postal Service adopted a rule suspending the PES restrictions for "international remailing," whereby private courier systems, like Federal Express, take mail from the United States to foreign countries and deposit it in foreign postal systems, bypassing the U.S. Postal Service.]

Respondents, the American Postal Workers Union, AFL–CIO, and the National Association of Letter Carriers, AFL–CIO (Unions), sued in the United States District Court for the District of Columbia, challenging the international remailing regulation pursuant to the judicial review provisions of the Administrative Procedure Act, 5 U.S.C. § 702 (APA). They claimed that the rulemaking record was inadequate to support a finding that the suspension of the PES for international remailing was in the public interest ...

The United States Postal Service, nominally a respondent, argues along with Air Courier Conference of America that the Unions do not have standing to challenge the Postal Service's suspension of the PES for international remailing. . . .

To establish standing to sue under § 702 of the APA, respondents must establish that they have suffered a legal wrong because of the challenged agency action, or are adversely affected or "aggrieved by agency action within the meaning of a relevant statute." Once they have shown that they are adversely affected, i.e., have suffered an "injury in fact," the Unions must show that they are within the zone of interests sought to be protected through the PES. Specifically, "the plaintiff must establish that the injury he complains of (his aggrievement, or the adverse effect upon him) falls within the 'zone of interests' sought to be protected by the statutory provision whose violation forms the legal basis of his complaint." The District Court found that the Unions had satisfied the injury-in-fact test because increased competition through international remailing services might have an adverse effect on employment opportunities of postal workers. This finding of injury in fact was not appealed. The question before us, then, is whether the adverse effects on the employment opportunities of postal workers resulting from the suspension is within the zone of interests encompassed by the PES—the statutes which the Unions assert the Postal Service has violated in promulgating the international remailing rule.

The Court of Appeals found that the Unions had standing because "the revenue protective purposes of the PES, standing alone, plausibly relate to the Unions' interest in preventing the reduction of employment opportunities." This view is mistaken, for it conflates the zone-of-interests test with injury in fact. In *Lujan* [*v. National Wildlife Federation*, 497 U.S. 871 (1990)], this Court gave the following example illustrating how injury in fact does not necessarily mean one is within the zone of interests to be protected by a given statute:

> "[T]he failure of an agency to comply with a statutory provision requiring 'on the record' hearings would assuredly have an adverse effect upon the company that has the contract to record and transcribe the agency's proceedings; but since the provision was obviously enacted to protect the interests of the parties to the proceedings and not those of the reporters, that company would not be 'adversely affected within the meaning' of the statute."

We must inquire then, as to Congress' intent in enacting the PES in order to determine whether postal workers were meant to be within the zone of interests protected by those statutes. The particular language of the statutes provides no support for respondents' assertion that Congress intended to protect jobs with the Postal Service....

Nor does the history of this legislation—such as it is—indicate that the PES were intended for the benefit of postal workers....

The legislative history of the sections of the Act limiting private carriage of letters shows a two-fold purpose. First, the Postmaster General and the States most distant from the commercial centers of the Northeast believed that the postal monopoly was necessary to prevent users of faster private expresses from taking advantage of early market intelligence and news of international affairs that had not yet reached the general populace through the slower mails. Second, it was thought to be the duty of the Government to serve outlying, frontier areas, even if it meant doing so below cost. Thus, the revenue protection provisions were not seen as an end in themselves, nor in any sense as a means of insuring certain levels of public employment, but rather were seen as the means to achieve national integration and to ensure that all areas of the Nation were equally served by the Postal Service.

The postal monopoly, therefore, exists to ensure that postal services will be provided to the citizenry at-large, and not to secure employment for postal workers.

. . . The foregoing discussion has demonstrated that the PES were not designed to protect postal employment or further postal job opportunities, but the Unions argue that the courts should look beyond the PES to the entire 1970 Postal Reorganization Act in applying the zone-of-interests test. The Unions argue that because one of the purposes of the labor-management provisions of the PRA was to stabilize labor-management relations within the Postal Service, and because the PES is the "linchpin" of the Postal Service, employment opportunities of postal workers are arguably within the zone of interests covered by the PES. The Unions rely upon our opinion in *Clarke v. Securities Industry Assn.*, 479 U.S. 388, 107 S.Ct. 750 (1987), to support this contention.

. . . In *Clarke,* we said that "we are not limited to considering the statute under which respondents sued, but may consider any provision that helps us to understand Congress' overall purposes in the National Bank Act." This statement, like all others in our opinions, must be taken in the context in which it was made. In the next paragraph of the opinion, the Court pointed out that 12 U.S.C. § 36, which the plaintiffs in that case claimed had been misinterpreted by the Comptroller, was itself "a limited exception to the otherwise applicable requirement of [12 U.S.C.] § 81," limiting the places at which a national bank could transact business to its headquarters and any "branches" permitted by § 36. Thus the zone-of-interests test was to be applied not merely in the light of § 36, which was the basis of the plaintiffs' claim on the merits, but also in the light of § 81, to which § 36 was an exception.

The situation in the present case is quite different. The only relationship between the PES, upon which the Unions rely for their claim on the merits, and the labor-management provisions of the PRA, upon which the Unions rely for their standing, is that both were included in the general codification of postal statutes embraced in the PRA. The statutory provisions enacted and re-enacted in the PRA are spread over some 65 pages in the United States Code, and take up an entire title of that volume. We said in *Lujan,* that "the relevant statute [under the APA] of course, is the statute whose violation is the gravamen of the complaint." To adopt petitioners' contention would require us to hold that the "relevant statute" in this case is the PRA, with all of its various provisions united only by the fact that they deal with the Postal Service. But to accept this level of generality in defining the "relevant statute" could deprive the zone-of-interests test of virtually all meaning. . . .

None of the documents constituting the PRA legislative history suggests that those concerned with postal reforms saw any connection between the PES and the provisions of the PRA dealing with labor-management relations. The Senate and House Reports simply note that the proposed bills continue existing law without change and require the Postal Service to conduct a study of the PES.

It would be a substantial extension of our holdings ... to allow the Unions in this case to leapfrog from their asserted protection under the labor-management provisions of the PRA to their claim on the merits under the PES. We decline to make that extension, and hold that the Unions do not have standing to challenge the Postal Service's suspension of the PES to permit private couriers to engage in international remailing. We therefore do not reach the merits of the Unions' claim that the suspension was not in the public interest.

NATIONAL CREDIT UNION ADMIN. v. FIRST NATIONAL BANK & TRUST CO.

522 U.S. 479, 118 S.Ct. 927, 140 L.Ed.2d 1 (1998).

Justice Thomas delivered the opinion of the Court.

[In] 1934, during the Great Depression, Congress enacted the [Federal Credit Union Act (FCUA)], which authorizes the chartering of credit unions at the national level and provides that federal credit unions may, as a general matter, offer banking services only to their members. Section 109 of the FCUA, which has remained virtually unaltered since the FCUA's enactment, expressly restricts membership in federal credit unions. In relevant part, it provides:

[Federal] credit union membership shall be limited to groups having a common bond of occupation or association, or to groups within a well-defined neighborhood, community, or rural district.

Until 1982, the National Credit Union Administration and its predecessors consistently interpreted § 109 to require that the same common bond of occupation unite every member of an occupationally defined federal credit union. In 1982, however, the NCUA reversed its longstanding policy in order to permit credit unions to be composed of multiple unrelated employer groups. It thus interpreted § 109's common bond requirement to apply only to each employer group in a multiple-group credit union, rather than to every member of that credit union. . . . Since 1982, therefore, the NCUA has permitted federal credit unions to be composed of wholly unrelated employer groups, each having its own distinct common bond.

After the NCUA revised its interpretation of § 109, petitioner AT&T Family Federal Credit Union (ATTF) expanded its operations considerably by adding unrelated employer groups to its membership. As a result, ATTF now has approximately 110,000 members nationwide, only 35% of whom are employees of AT&T and its affiliates. The remaining members are employees of such diverse companies as the Lee Apparel

Company, the Coca–Cola Bottling Company, the Ciba–Geigy Corporation, the Duke Power Company, and the American Tobacco Company.

In 1990, after the NCUA approved a series of amendments to ATTF's charter that added several such unrelated employer groups to ATTF's membership, respondents brought this action. Invoking the judicial review provisions of the Administrative Procedure Act (APA), respondents claimed that the NCUA's approval of the charter amendments was contrary to law because the members of the new groups did not share a common bond of occupation with ATTF's existing members, as respondents alleged § 109 required. . . .

Respondents claim a right to judicial review of the NCUA's chartering decision under § 10(a) of the APA. . . . Based on [our] prior cases finding that competitors of financial institutions have standing to challenge agency action relaxing statutory restrictions on the activities of those institutions, we hold that respondents' interest in limiting the markets that federal credit unions can serve is arguably within the zone of interests to be protected by § 109. Therefore, respondents have prudential standing under the APA to challenge the NCUA's interpretation.

Our prior cases [have] consistently held that for a plaintiff's interests to be arguably within the "zone of interests" to be protected by a statute, there does not have to be an "indication of congressional purpose to benefit the would-be plaintiff." The proper inquiry is simply "whether the interest sought to be protected by the complainant is *arguably* within the zone of interests to be protected . . . by the statute." Hence in applying the "zone of interests" test, we do not ask whether, in enacting the statutory provision at issue, Congress specifically intended to benefit the plaintiff. Instead, we first discern the interests "arguably [to] be protected" by the statutory provision at issue; we then inquire whether the plaintiff's interests affected by the agency action in question are among them.

Section 109 provides that "[f]ederal credit union membership shall be limited to groups having a common bond of occupation or association, or to groups within a well-defined neighborhood, community, or rural district." By its express terms, § 109 limits membership in every federal credit union to members of definable "groups." Because federal credit unions may, as a general matter, offer banking services only to members, § 109 also restricts the markets that every federal credit union can serve. Although these markets need not be small, they unquestionably are limited. The link between § 109's regulation of federal credit union membership and its limitation on the markets that federal credit unions can serve is unmistakable. Thus, even if it cannot be said that Congress had the specific purpose of benefiting commercial banks, one of the interests "arguably . . . to be protected" by § 109 is an interest in limiting the markets that federal credit unions can serve.[6] This interest

6. . . . During the Great Depression, in contrast to widespread bank failures at both the state and national level, there were no involuntary liquidations of state-is precisely the interest of respondents affected by the NCUA's interpretation of § 109. As competitors of federal credit unions, respondents certainly have an interest in limiting the markets that federal credit unions can serve, and the NCUA's interpretation has affected that interest by allowing federal credit unions to increase their customer base. . . .

Petitioners attempt to distinguish this case principally on the ground that there is no evidence that Congress, when it enacted the FCUA was at all concerned with the competitive interests of commercial banks, or indeed at all concerned with competition. . . .

The difficulty with this argument is that similar arguments were made unsuccessfully in each of [our prior banking cases]. [I]n *Clarke* [*v. Securities Industry Ass'n*, 479 U.S. 388 (1987), involving a challenge by securities dealers to a ruling by the Comptroller of the Currency that banks could offer discount brokerages], we did not debate whether the Congress that enacted the McFadden Act was concerned about the competitive position of securities dealers. The provisions at issue in [that case], moreover, could be said merely to be safety-and-soundness provisions, enacted only to protect national banks and their depositors and without a concern for competitive effects. We nonetheless did not hesitate to find standing. . . .

Petitioners also mistakenly rely on our decision in *Air Courier Conference v. Postal Workers*. In *Air Courier*, . . . we noted that although the statute in question regulated competition, the interests of the plaintiff employees had nothing to do with competition. In this case, not only do respondents have "competitive and direct injury," but, as the foregoing discussion makes clear, they possess an interest that is "arguably . . . to be protected" by § 109. . . .

[Having decided that ATTF was within the zone of interests of the FCUA's common bond requirement, the Court went on to the merits, holding that the NCUA's interpretation of the common bond requirement violated the plain language of the provision and hence was unlawful.]

Justice O'Connor, WITH WHOM Justice Stevens, Justice Souter, AND Justice Breyer JOIN, DISSENTING.

[U]nder a proper conception of the inquiry, "the interest sought to be protected by" respondents in this case is not "arguably within the zone of interests to be protected" by the common bond provision.

[In] each of the competitor standing cases, [we] found that Congress had enacted an "anti-competition limitation," or, alternatively, that Congress had "legislated [against] competition," and accordingly,

chartered credit unions. The cooperative nature of the institutions, which state-law common bond provisions reinforced, was believed to have contributed to this result. . . . The legislative history thus confirms that § 109 was thought to reinforce the cooperative nature of credit unions, which in turn was believed to promote their safety and soundness and allow access to credit to persons otherwise unable to borrow. . . .

that the plaintiff-competitor's "commercial interest was sought to be protected by the anti-competition limitation" at issue. We determined, in other words, that "the injury [the plaintiff] complain[ed] of [fell] within the zone of interests sought to be protected by the [relevant] statutory provision." The Court fails to undertake that analysis here.

Applying the proper zone-of-interests inquiry to this case, I would find that competitive injury to respondents' commercial interests does not arguably fall within the zone of interests sought to be protected by the common bond provision. The terms of the statute do not suggest a concern with protecting the business interests of competitors. The common bond provision limits "[f]ederal credit union membership [to] groups having a common bond of occupation or association, or to groups within a well-defined neighborhood, community, or rural district." * * * The language suggests that the common bond requirement is an internal organizational principle concerned primarily with defining membership in a way that secures a financially sound organization. There is no indication in the text of the provision or in the surrounding language that the membership limitation was even arguably designed to protect the commercial interests of competitors.

Nor is there any nontextual indication to that effect. [The] common bond requirement does not purport to restrict credit unions from becoming large, nationwide organizations, as might be expected if the provision embodied a congressional concern with the competitive consequences of credit union growth.

[T]he common bond requirement speaks only to whether a *particular* credit union's membership can include a given group of customers, not to whether credit unions *in general* can serve that group. Even if a group of would-be customers does not share the requisite bond with a particular credit union, nothing in the common bond provision prevents that same group from joining a different credit union that is within the same "neighborhood, community, or rural district" or with whose members the group shares an adequate "occupation[al] or association[al]" connection. Also, the group could conceivably form its own credit union. In this sense, the common bond requirement does not limit credit unions collectively from serving any customers, nor does it bar any customers from being served by credit unions.

[The] circumstances surrounding the enactment of the FCUA also indicate that Congress did not intend to legislate against competition through the common bond provision. As the Court explains, the FCUA was enacted in the shadow of the Great Depression; Congress thought that the ability of credit unions to "come through the depression without failures, when banks have failed so notably, is a tribute to the worth of cooperative credit and indicates clearly the great potential value of rapid national credit union extension." Credit unions were believed to enable the general public, which had been largely ignored by banks, to obtain credit at reasonable rates. The common bond requirement "was seen as the cement that united credit union members in a cooperative venture, and was, therefore, thought important to credit unions' continued success." "Congress assumed implicitly that a common bond amongst members would ensure both that those making lending decisions would know more about applicants and that borrowers would be more reluctant to default."

The requirement of a common bond was thus meant to ensure that each credit union remains a cooperative institution that is economically stable and responsive to its members' needs. As a principle of internal governance designed to secure the viability of individual credit unions in the interests of the membership, the common bond provision was in no way designed to impose a restriction on all credit unions in the interests of institutions that might one day become competitors. . . .

[N]either the terms of the common bond provision, nor the way in which the provision operates, nor the circumstances surrounding its enactment, evince a congressional desire to legislate against competition. This, then, is a case where "the plaintiff's interests are so marginally related to or inconsistent with the purposes implicit in the statute that it cannot reasonably be assumed that Congress intended to permit the suit." . . .

Problem 5–3: NEPA's Zone of Interests

The National Environmental Policy Act of 1969 states that "[t]he purposes of this chapter are: To declare a national policy which will encourage productive and enjoyable harmony between man and his environment; to promote efforts which will prevent or eliminate damage to the environment and biosphere and stimulate the health and welfare of man; [and] to enrich the understanding of the ecological systems and natural resources important to the Nation. . . ." 42 U.S.C. § 4321. The Act further states that "Congress . . . declares that it is the continuing policy of the Federal Government . . . to use all practicable means and measures . . . in a manner calculated to foster and promote the general welfare, to create and maintain productive harmony, and fulfill the social, economic, and other requirements of present and future generations of Americans." 42 U.S.C. § 4331(a). In order to achieve these purposes and policies, NEPA states: "The Congress authorizes and directs that, to the fullest extent possible: . . . all agencies of the Federal Government shall . . . include in every recommendation or report on . . . major Federal actions significantly affecting the quality of the human environment, [an Environmental Impact Statement (EIS)] by the responsible official on the environmental impact of the proposed action, any adverse environmental effects which cannot be avoided if the proposal is implemented, alternatives to the proposed action, the relationship between local short-term uses of man's environment and the maintenance and enhancement of long-term productivity, and any irreversible and irretrievable commitments of resources which would be involved in the proposed action should it be implemented." 42 U.S.C. § 4332(2)(c).

The National Forest Service is responsible for vast areas of land owned by the federal government. Historically, the Service has allowed ranchers to graze cattle and sheep on some of this land pursuant to a permit system. Under the National Forest Management Act (NFMA), the Forest Service is required to make, and from time-to-time revise, Land Resource Management Plans (LRMP) governing how its lands are to be used. LRMPs govern use of the individual forests, and they must fulfill the Forest Service's mandate to "provide for multiple use and sustained yield ... includ[ing] coordination of outdoor recreation, range, timber, watershed, wildlife and fish, and wilderness." 16 U.S.C. § 1604(e)(1). In addition, LRMPs are to set the standards for managing the use of the resource use in order maintain multiple use and sustained yield from the resource. 16 U.S.C. § 1604(e)(2). The congressional findings in NFMA explain the purposes of this planning process. Congress determined that planning function is necessary because: the management of the Nation's renewable resources is highly complex; the public interest is served by creating a renewable resource program and periodically reviewing it; planning is best accomplished by a comprehensive assessment of present and anticipated uses, which includes an analysis of environmental and economic impacts, and by public participation in developing the program; the public is served by multiple use and sustained yield of products and services from renewable resources, including coordination of outdoor recreation, range, timber, watershed, wildlife and fish, and wilderness; and the Forest Service should be a leader in assuring that resources will be used in a manner that will meet the requirements of our people in perpetuity.

The Service issued a revised LRMP for the Muir National Forest which, among other things, changed the extent to which, and the conditions under which, new permits for cattle and sheep grazing should be granted. As part of review, the Service prepared an EIS.

An association of ranchers, whose members currently possess permits for grazing in the forest, is concerned that the new LRMP will drastically reduce the areas available for grazing permits and substantially reduce the number of cattle or sheep that will be allowed to graze in approved areas. While the LRMP does not affect existing permits, it will govern the issuance of new permits when current permits expire. In the association's view, the EIS erroneously describes the environmental effects of grazing and does not consider alternatives that would maintain grazing at close to existing levels but would mitigate adverse effects on the environment. The association sues to enjoin implementation of the LRMP on the ground that the EIS was inadequate and that the decision reducing the acreage and stock numbers was arbitrary and capricious.

(1) As a Justice Department attorney defending the Forest Service, what arguments might you make that the association is not within the zone of interests of NEPA? Of NFMA? Also, assess the likelihood of success of those arguments.

(2) As a Justice Department attorney defending the Forest Service, what arguments might you make that the association does not have standing? What is the likely success of those arguments?

Notes and Questions

1. In 1997 the Supreme Court decided *Bennett v. Spear*, 520 U.S. 154, 117 S.Ct. 1154, 137 L.Ed.2d 281 (1997), in which ranchers challenged actions of the U.S. Fish and Wildlife Service under both the citizens suit provision of the Endangered Species Act and under the APA, alleging violations of the ESA by the Service. The lower court had held that the ranchers' commercial interests were not within the zone of interests of the ESA, and therefore they could not sue under either its citizen suit provision or the APA. The Supreme Court reversed. First, as noted in *Defenders of Wildlife*, the ESA allows "any person" to sue under its citizen suit provision. While this language must be limited by constitutional standing requirements, the Court held that it either eliminated any zone of interests requirement, or alternatively extended the zone of interests to all persons with constitutional standing, for suits brought under the citizen suit provision. As to the APA claim, however, the Court held that the zone of interests is determined not by the citizen suit provision in the ESA but by reference to the particular provision of the ESA allegedly violated. In *Bennett*, the ranchers alleged that the Service had made its jeopardy determination without using "the best scientific and commercial data available," as required by the ESA. The Court held that this requirement evidenced a congressional intent to assure that

> the ESA not be implemented haphazardly, on the basis of speculation or surmise. While this no doubt serves to advance the ESA's overall goal of species preservation, we think it readily apparent that another objective (if not indeed the primary one) is to avoid needless economic dislocation produced by agency officials zealously but unintelligently pursuing their environmental objectives.... Petitioners' claim that they are victims of such a mistake is plainly within the zone of interests that the provision protects.

2. When an agency regulates a person, that person always has a cause of action under Section 702 to challenge the lawfulness of that regulation. There is no requirement for the person to show he is within any particular zone of interests of the statute. Thus, if the National Credit Union Administration had taken away a credit union's charter because the Administration did not believe the credit union's membership was appropriately limited, the credit union could challenge that action, and no one would ask whether the credit union was within the zone of interests of the Act. The credit union would be a "person suffering legal wrong because of agency action." The zone of interests test only comes up when the person who challenges the agency action is otherwise injured by the agency action, for example, when the agency action benefits a competitor (as in *NCUA v. First National Bank & Trust*

Co.) or the agency action may result in the loss of a government benefit (as in the problem case) or protection (arguably the case in *Air Courier Conference*). If the zone of interests test is very strictly applied, so that it is difficult for these types of persons to obtain judicial review of agency action injuring them, there is an asymmetry in the judicial review of agency action—regulated entities can obtain review but others cannot. This might result in agencies, because they are litigation-averse, tending to err to the benefit of regulated entities, knowing that the non-regulated but disadvantaged entities could not sue. A liberal interpretation of the zone of interests test, however, enables symmetry in judicial review. Thus, as was discussed in the section on Standing, the courts can be used to assure not only that agencies do not exceed their statutory authority in regulating persons but also to assure that they are faithful to their statutory duties to serve the public interest.

D. EXCLUSIONS FROM JUDICIAL REVIEW UNDER THE APA

1. STATUTORY PRECLUSION

Section 701(a) of the APA provides that the judicial review chapter applies "except to the extent that—(1) statutes preclude judicial review; or (2) agency action is committed to agency discretion by law." Statutes that expressly preclude judicial review are relatively rare. Moreover, statutes that do preclude review usually do not preclude it altogether, but rather limit it to particular circumstances. For example, the Immigration Reform and Control Act of 1986 (IRCA), Pub. L. 99–603, 100 Stat. 3359, made a number of changes to our immigration law, including the establishment of programs to allow certain types of previously illegal aliens to become legal aliens. This was to be accomplished by means of an adjustment of status proceeding. The Act explicitly provided that "[t]here shall be no administrative or judicial review of a determination respecting an application for adjustment of status ... except in accordance with this subsection." 8 U.S.C.A. § 1160(e)(1). The Act then established an administrative appellate review system for reviews of denials of an adjustment of status. As for judicial review, it stated, "There shall be judicial review of such a denial only in the judicial review of an order of exclusion or deportation...." *Id.* § 1160(e)(3)(A). In other words, there was to be no direct judicial review of the denial of the adjustment of status, but if and when the Immigration and Naturalization Service (INS) tried to deport the person, and the person appealed the deportation order to the courts, then the person could defend against the deportation on the grounds that the adjustment of status denial was wrong. The Act also specified that judicial review: "shall be based solely upon the administrative record established at the time of the review by the appellate authority, and the findings of fact and determinations contained in the record shall be conclusive unless the applicant can establish abuse of discretion or that the findings are contrary to clear and convincing facts contained in the record considered as a whole." *Id.* § 1160(e)(3)(B).

The Supreme Court's response to a claim brought outside of the specified review provision in IRCA is also typical. In *McNary v. Haitian Refugee Center, Inc.*, 498 U.S. 479, 111 S.Ct. 888, 112 L.Ed.2d 1005 (1991), the question was whether the language of the Act precluded a class action lawsuit alleging that INS's implementation of the Special Agricultural Workers adjustment program violated due process. The Court found that the choice of language used in the preclusion provision—review of "a determination respecting an application"—was inapt to a suit challenging as a general matter the basic procedures used by the agency. Moreover, were reviews of this issue limited by the specified administrative and judicial review procedure in the Act, the affected aliens would be denied any meaningful review of their claims. Review would be hindered because an appellate court would not have the benefit of evidence concerning a pattern of INS practices, and it would lack the fact finding and record-developing capabilities of a district court.

This type of restrictive interpretation of preclusion statutes, especially when the effect would be to foreclose *any* review, and particularly when it would preclude constitutional claims, is the norm. This stems from two considerations. First, preclusion of judicial review of constitutional claims is probably unconstitutional. The Supreme Court has never directly answered this question, preferring to interpret statutes to avoid it. Accordingly, courts tend to interpret statutes not to preclude constitutional claims. Second, the Administrative Procedure Act is perceived as codifying a presumption of affording judicial review to those adversely affected or aggrieved by agency action. This presumption was articulated in the case of *Abbott Laboratories v. Gardner*, a seminal case on reviewability, which you will read next. This is not to say, however, that statutes cannot be held to preclude review, especially review under the APA. They can and are. In essence, it is an issue of statutory construction: in light of the considerations discussed above, does the statute preclude review?

Just as statutes may explicitly preclude judicial review, statutes may also be construed to preclude review implicitly. *Abbott Laboratories* itself involved such a claim. The following Supreme Court cases are the leading cases on preclusion of review and provide the background for the problem that follows them.

ABBOTT LABORATORIES v. GARDNER

387 U.S. 136, 87 S.Ct. 1507, 18 L.Ed.2d 681 (1967).

Mr. Justice Harlan delivered the opinion of the Court.

In 1962 Congress amended the Federal Food, Drug, and Cosmetic Act to require manufacturers of prescription drugs to print the "established name" of the drug "prominently and in type at least half as large as that used thereon for any proprietary name or designation for such drug," on labels and other printed material.... The underlying purpose of the 1962 amendment was to bring to the attention of doctors and patients the fact that many of the drugs sold under familiar trade names are actually identical to drugs sold under their "established" or less familiar trade names at significantly lower prices. The Commissioner of Food and Drugs ... promulgated the following regulation for the "efficient enforcement" of the Act:

> "If the label or labeling of a prescription drug bears a proprietary name or designation for the drug or any ingredient thereof, the established name, if such there be, corresponding to such proprietary name or designation, shall accompany each appearance of such proprietary name or designation."

A similar rule was made applicable to advertisements for prescription drugs.

The present action was brought by a group of 37 individual drug manufacturers and by the Pharmaceutical Manufacturers Association, of which all the petitioner companies are members, and which includes manufacturers of more than 90% of the Nation's supply of prescription drugs. They challenged the regulations on the ground that the Commissioner exceeded his authority under the statute by promulgating an order requiring labels, advertisements, and other printed matter relating to prescription drugs to designate the established name of the particular drug involved every time its trade name is used anywhere in such material.

The first question we consider is whether Congress by the Federal Food, Drug, and Cosmetic Act intended to forbid pre-enforcement review of this sort of regulation promulgated by the Commissioner. The question is phrased in terms of "prohibition" rather than "authorization" because a survey of our cases shows that judicial review of a final agency action by an aggrieved person will not be cut off unless there is persuasive reason to believe that such was the purpose of Congress. Early cases in which this type of judicial review was entertained, have been reinforced by the enactment of the Administrative Procedure Act, which embodies the basic presumption of judicial review to one "suffering legal wrong because of agency action, or adversely affected or aggrieved by agency action within the meaning of a relevant statute," so long as no statute precludes such relief or the action is not one committed by law to agency discretion. The Administrative Procedure Act provides specifically not only for review of "[a]gency action made reviewable by statute" but also for review of "final agency action for which there is no other adequate remedy in a court." The legislative material elucidating that seminal act manifests a congressional intention that it cover a broad spectrum of administrative actions, and this Court has echoed that theme by noting that the Administrative Procedure Act's "generous review provisions" must be given a "hospitable" interpretation. [And this] Court [has] held that only upon a showing of "clear and convincing evidence" of a contrary legislative intent should the courts restrict access to judicial review.

Given this standard, we are wholly unpersuaded that the statutory scheme in the food and drug area excludes this type of action. The Government relies on no explicit statutory authority for its argument that pre-enforcement review is unavailable, but insists instead that because the statute includes a specific procedure for such review of certain enumerated kinds of regulations, not encompassing those of the kind involved here, other types were necessarily meant to be excluded from any pre-enforcement review. The issue, however, is not so readily resolved; we must go further and inquire whether in the context of the entire legislative scheme the existence of that circumscribed remedy evinces a congressional purpose to bar agency action not within its purview from judicial review. As a leading authority in this field has noted, "The mere fact that some acts are made reviewable should not suffice to support an implication of exclusion as to others. The right to review is too important to be excluded on such slender and indeterminate evidence of legislative intent."

In this case the Government has not demonstrated such a purpose; indeed, a study of the legislative history shows rather conclusively that the specific review provisions were designed to give an additional remedy and not to cut down more traditional channels of review.... At the time the Food, Drug, and Cosmetic Act was under consideration, in the late 1930's, the Administrative Procedure Act had not yet been enacted, the Declaratory Judgment Act was in its infancy, and the scope of judicial review of administrative decisions under the equity power was unclear. It was these factors that led to the form the statute ultimately took. There is no evidence at all that members of Congress meant to preclude traditional avenues of judicial relief....

The main issue in contention was whether these methods of review were satisfactory....

Against this background we think it quite apparent that the special-review procedures provided in [the FDCA], applying to regulations embodying technical factual determinations, were simply intended to assure adequate judicial review of such agency decisions, and that their enactment does not manifest a congressional purpose to eliminate judicial review of other kinds of agency action.

This conclusion is strongly buttressed by the fact that the Act itself states, "The remedies provided for in this subsection shall be in addition to and not in substitution for any other remedies provided by law." ...

We conclude that nothing in the Food, Drug, and Cosmetic Act itself precludes this action. [The Court's decision on ripeness is provided later.]

BLOCK v. COMMUNITY NUTRITION INSTITUTE

467 U.S. 340, 104 S.Ct. 2450, 81 L.Ed.2d 270 (1984).

JUSTICE O'CONNOR delivered the opinion of the Court.

This case presents the question whether ultimate consumers of dairy products may obtain judicial review of milk market orders issued by the Secretary of Agriculture (Secretary) under the authority of the Agricultural Marketing Agreement Act of 1937 (Act). We conclude that consumers may not obtain judicial review of such orders.

In the early 1900's, dairy farmers engaged in intense competition in the production of fluid milk products. To bring this destabilizing competition under control, the 1937 Act authorizes the Secretary to issue milk market orders setting the minimum prices that handlers (those who process dairy products) must pay to producers (dairy farmers) for their milk products. The "essential purpose [of this milk market order scheme is] to raise producer prices," and thereby to ensure that the benefits and burdens of the milk market are fairly and proportionately shared by all dairy farmers. . . .

The Secretary currently has some 45 milk market orders in effect. Each order covers a different region of the country, and collectively they cover most, though not all, of the United States. The orders divide dairy products into separately priced classes based on the uses to which raw milk is put. Raw milk that is processed and bottled for fluid consumption is termed "Class I" milk. Raw milk that is used to produce milk products such as butter, cheese, or dry milk powder is termed "Class II" milk.

For a variety of economic reasons, fluid milk products would command a higher price than surplus milk products in a perfectly functioning market. Accordingly, the Secretary's milk market orders require handlers to pay a higher order price for Class I products than for Class II products. . . .

In particular, the Secretary has regulated the price of "reconstituted milk"—that is, milk manufactured by mixing milk powder with water—since 1964. The Secretary's orders assume that handlers will use reconstituted milk to manufacture surplus milk products. Handlers are therefore required to pay only the lower Class II minimum price. However, handlers are required to make a "compensatory payment" on any portion of the reconstituted milk that their records show has not been used to manufacture surplus milk products. The compensatory payment is equal to the difference between the Class I and Class II milk product prices. . . . [The consumers group is upset because if reconstituted milk can be sold as fluid milk (i.e., in jugs and cartons like regular milk), but for a much lower price as a Class II milk product, poor people will be able to buy it more readily than they can buy regular fluid milk. On the other hand, milk producers would not like this arrangement because it would cut demand for Class I milk, for which they receive the highest payments.]

Respondents filed this suit under the Administrative Procedure Act (APA). The APA confers a general cause of action upon persons "adversely affected or aggrieved by agency action within the meaning of a relevant statute," but withdraws that cause of action to the extent the relevant statute "preclude[s] judicial review." Whether and to what extent a particular statute precludes judicial review is determined not only from its express language, but also from the structure of the statutory scheme, its objectives, its legislative history, and the nature of the administrative action involved. Therefore, we must examine this statutory scheme "to determine whether Congress precluded all judicial review, and, if not, whether Congress nevertheless foreclosed review to the class to which the [respondents] belon[g]."

It is clear that Congress did not intend to strip the judiciary of all authority to review the Secretary's milk market orders.... Congress [included] a mechanism by which dairy handlers could obtain review of the Secretary's market orders. That mechanism ... requires handlers first to exhaust the administrative remedies made available by the Secretary. After these formal administrative remedies have been exhausted, handlers may obtain judicial review of the Secretary's ruling in [a] federal district court.... These provisions for handler-initiated review make evident Congress' desire that some persons be able to obtain judicial review of the Secretary's market orders.

The remainder of the statutory scheme, however, makes equally clear Congress' intention to limit the classes entitled to participate in the development of market orders.... Handlers and producers—but not consumers—are entitled to participate in the adoption and retention of market orders. The Act provides for agreements among the Secretary, producers, and handlers, for hearings among them, and for votes by producers and handlers. Nowhere in the Act, however, is there an express provision for participation by consumers in any proceeding. In a complex scheme of this type, the omission of such a provision is sufficient reason to believe that Congress intended to foreclose consumer participation in the regulatory process.

To be sure, the general purpose sections of the Act allude to general consumer interests. But the preclusion issue does not only turn on whether the interests of a particular class like consumers are implicated. Rather, the preclusion issue turns ultimately on whether Congress intended for that class to be relied upon to challenge agency disregard of the law. The structure of this Act indicates that Congress intended only producers and handlers, and not consumers, to ensure that the statutory objectives would be realized.

Respondents would have us believe that, while Congress unequivocally directed handlers first to complain to the Secretary that the prices set by milk market orders are too high, it was nevertheless the legislative judgment that the same challenge, if advanced by consumers, does not require initial administrative scrutiny.... Congress channeled disputes concerning marketing orders to the Secretary in the first instance because it believed that only he has the expertise necessary to illuminate and resolve questions about them. Had Congress intended to allow consumers to attack provisions of marketing orders, it surely would have required them to pursue the administrative remedies . . . as well. The restriction of the administrative remedy to handlers strongly suggests that Congress intended a similar restriction of judicial review of market orders.

Allowing consumers to sue the Secretary would severely disrupt this complex and delicate administrative scheme. It would provide handlers with a convenient device for evading the statutory requirement that they first exhaust their administrative remedies. . . . Suits of this type would effectively nullify Congress' intent to establish an "equitable and expeditious procedure for testing the validity of orders, without hampering the Government's power to enforce compliance with their terms." For these reasons, we think it clear that Congress intended that judicial review of market orders issued under the Act ordinarily be confined to suits brought by handlers. . . .

The Court of Appeals viewed the preclusion issue from a somewhat different perspective. First, it recited the presumption in favor of judicial review of administrative action that this Court usually employs. It then noted that the Act has been interpreted to authorize producer challenges to the administration of market order settlement funds, and that no legislative history or statutory language directly and specifically supported the preclusion of consumer suits. In these circumstances, the Court of Appeals reasoned that the Act could not fairly be interpreted to overcome the presumption favoring judicial review and to leave consumers without a judicial remedy. We disagree with the Court of Appeals' analysis.

The presumption favoring judicial review of administrative action is just that—a presumption. This presumption, like all presumptions used in interpreting statutes, may be overcome by specific language or specific legislative history that is a reliable indicator of congressional intent. The congressional intent necessary to overcome the presumption may also be inferred from contemporaneous judicial construction barring review and the congressional acquiescence in it, or from the collective import of legislative and judicial history behind a particular statute. More important for purposes of this case, the presumption favoring judicial review of administrative action may be overcome by inferences of intent drawn from the statutory scheme as a whole. In particular, at least when a statute provides a detailed mechanism for judicial consideration of particular issues at the behest of particular persons, judicial review of those issues at the behest of other persons may be found to be impliedly precluded. . . .

In this case, the Court of Appeals did not take the balanced approach to statutory construction. . . . Rather, it recited this Court's oft-quoted statement that "only upon a showing of 'clear and convincing evidence' of a contrary legislative intent should the courts restrict access to judicial review." *Abbott Laboratories v. Gardner.* According to the Court of Appeals, the "clear and convincing evidence" standard required it to find unambiguous proof, in the traditional evidentiary sense, of a congressional intent to preclude judicial review at the consumers' behest. Since direct statutory language or legislative history on this issue could not be found, the Court of Appeals found the presumption favoring judicial review to be controlling.

This Court has, however, never applied the "clear and convincing evidence" standard in the strict evidentiary sense the Court of Appeals thought necessary in this case. Rather, the Court has found the standard met, and the presumption favoring judicial review overcome, whenever the congressional intent to preclude judicial review is "fairly discernible in the statutory scheme." In the context of preclusion analysis, the "clear and convincing evidence" standard is not a rigid evidentiary test but a useful reminder to courts that, where substantial doubt about the congressional intent exists, the general presumption favoring judicial review of administrative action is controlling. That presumption does not control in cases such as this one, however, since the congressional intent to preclude judicial review is "fairly discernible" in the detail of the legislative scheme. Congress simply did not intend for consumers to be relied upon to challenge agency disregard of the law. . . .

The structure of this Act implies that Congress intended to preclude consumer challenges to the Secretary's market orders. Preclusion of such suits does not pose any threat to realization of the statutory objectives; it means only that those objectives must be realized through the specific remedies provided by Congress and at the behest of the parties directly affected by the statutory scheme. . . .

Problem 5–4: Environmentalists and Land Exchanges

The Federal Land Policy and Management Act (FLPMA) authorizes the Bureau of Land Management (BLM) to exchange federal lands for non-federal lands if the public interest will be served by the trade, 43 U.S.C. § 1716(a), and the value of the public lands conveyed away is equal to the value of the non-federal lands to be acquired, taking into account any cash included as part of the exchange, 43 U.S.C. § 1716(b). Pursuant to these provisions, the BLM transferred approximately 1,745 acres of federal land at $610,914 to the Mesquite Regional Landfill. In return, BLM acquired from the Landfill 2,642 acres with an appraised value of $609,995 and $919 in cash. Members of the Sierra Club object to this exchange because it will result in land they currently use for recreation being used for a regional landfill. They have filed a complaint alleging that the exchange is illegal because it relies on an outdated appraisal that undervalued the federal lands, thereby violating 43 U.S.C. § 1716(b). In response, the Department of Justice has filed a motion to dismiss on the grounds that plaintiffs are not within the zone of interests protected by 1716(b) and that their suit is impliedly precluded by FLPMA Section 206(d) which provides for arbitration by the parties to a land exchange when there is a dispute over the proper valuation of properties involved in an exchange.

What arguments should be made on behalf of the Sierra Club members?

Notes and Questions

1. In *Abbott Laboratories*, the Court required "clear and convincing evidence" that Congress intended to preclude judicial review, but in *Block* the Court indicated that this standard is satisfied if congressional intent to preclude review is "fairly discernible in the statutory standard." Did the Court change its test for statutory preclusion? Did it lack "clear and convincing" evidence of statutory preclusion in *Block*?

2. In *Leedom v. Kyne*, 358 U.S. 184, 79 S.Ct. 180, 3 L.Ed.2d 210 (1958), the Supreme Court held that a person who alleged the National Labor Relations Board had acted "in excess of its delegated authority and contrary to a specific prohibition" could obtain district court review despite a general preclusion of district court review of Board certifications of bargaining units. "To litigants seeking review under a variety of circumstances where review was precluded either explicitly or impliedly, the rule of *Leedom v. Kyne* was attractive; it suggested an exception to preclusion whenever the agency allegedly had acted *ultra vires*. Courts over the years, however, have interpreted the exception narrowly, finding the exception to exist only where the agency action was *plainly* beyond its authority, or, as one court put it, when the agency action is 'infused with an error which is of a summa or magna quality as contraposed to decisions which are simply cum error.' " William Funk, *Supreme Court News*, 17 ADMIN. L. NEWS 5 (Spring, 1992).

2. COMMITTED TO AGENCY DISCRETION

Section 701 also excludes agency action from judicial review under the APA if the action is "committed to agency discretion by law." This exclusion is particularly confusing in light of Section 706's provision for judicial review for "abuse of discretion." In *Citizens to Preserve Overton Park v. Volpe*, 401 U.S. 402, 91 S.Ct. 814, 28 L.Ed.2d 136 (1971), the Supreme Court addressed this part of Section 701, stating that it was a "very narrow exception" that applied only where a statute was phrased in such broad terms that "there was no law to apply." In other words, if a statute grants discretion to an agency, and the law does not establish a standard against which to assess the exercise of that discretion (so that a court can determine if there was an abuse of discretion), then Congress has committed that action to agency discretion by law.

In subsequent cases, one issue has been the application of the "no law to apply" test from *Overton Park*. Another issue has been whether this test is the exclusive test of whether judicial review is impliedly precluded. This section addresses these issues.

HECKLER v. CHANEY

470 U.S. 821, 105 S.Ct. 1649, 84 L.Ed.2d 714 (1985).

JUSTICE REHNQUIST delivered the opinion of the Court.

Respondents have been sentenced to death by lethal injection of drugs under the laws of the States of Oklahoma and Texas.... Respondents first petitioned the Food and Drug Administration (FDA), claiming that the drugs used by the States for this purpose, although approved by the FDA for the medical purposes stated on their labels, were not approved for use in human executions. They alleged that the drugs had not been tested for the purpose for which they were to be used, and that, given that the drugs would likely be administered by untrained personnel, it was also likely that the drugs would not induce the quick and painless death intended. They urged that use of these drugs for human execution was the "unapproved use of an approved drug" and constituted a violation of the Act's prohibitions against "misbranding." They also suggested that the Federal Food, Drug, and Cosmetics Act's (FDCA) requirements for approval of "new drugs" applied, since these drugs were now being used for a new purpose. Accordingly, respondents claimed that the FDA was required to approve the drugs as "safe and effective" for human execution before they could be distributed in interstate commerce. They therefore requested the FDA to take various investigatory and enforcement actions to prevent these perceived violations....

The FDA Commissioner responded, refusing to take the requested actions. The Commissioner first detailed his disagreement with respondents' understanding of the scope of FDA jurisdiction over the unapproved use of approved drugs for human execution, concluding that FDA jurisdiction in the area was generally unclear but in any event should not be exercised to interfere with this particular aspect of state criminal justice systems. He went on to state:

> "Were FDA clearly to have jurisdiction in the area, moreover, we believe we would be authorized to decline to exercise it under our inherent discretion to decline to pursue certain enforcement matters. The unapproved use of approved drugs is an area in which the case law is far from uniform. Generally, enforcement proceedings in this area are initiated only when there is a serious danger to the public health or a blatant scheme to defraud. We cannot conclude that those dangers are present under State lethal injection laws, which are duly authorized statutory enactments in furtherance of proper State functions...." ...

... Petitioner urges that the decision of the FDA to refuse enforcement is an action "committed to agency discretion by law" under § 701(a)(2).

This Court has not had occasion to interpret this second exception in § 701(a) in any great detail. On its face, the section does not obviously lend itself to any particular construction; indeed, one might wonder what difference exists between § (a)(1) and § (a)(2). The former section seems easy in application; it requires construction of the substantive statute involved to determine whether Congress intended to preclude judicial review of certain decisions.... But one could read the language "committed to agency discretion by law" in § (a)(2) to require a similar inquiry. In addition, commentators have pointed out that construction of § (a)(2) is further complicated by the tension between a literal reading of § (a)(2), which exempts from judicial review those decisions committed to agency "discretion," and the primary scope of review prescribed by § 706(2)(A)—whether the agency's action was "arbitrary, capricious, or an abuse of discretion." ...

This Court first discussed § (a)(2) in *Citizens to Preserve Overton Park v. Volpe.* That case dealt with the Secretary of Transportation's approval of the building of an interstate highway through a park in Memphis, Tennessee.... Interested citizens challenged the Secretary's approval under the APA, arguing that he had not satisfied the substantive statute's requirements. This Court first addressed the "threshold question" of whether the agency's action was at all reviewable. After setting out the language of § 701(a), the Court stated:

> "In this case, there is no indication that Congress sought to prohibit judicial review and there is most certainly no 'showing of "clear and convincing evidence" of a ... legislative intent' to restrict access to judicial review. *Abbott Laboratories v. Gardner.*

> "Similarly, the Secretary's decision here does not fall within the exception for action 'committed to agency discretion.' This is a very narrow exception.... The legislative history of the Administrative Procedure Act indicates that it is applicable in those rare instances where 'statutes are drawn in such broad terms that in a given case there is no law to apply.' "

The above quote answers several of the questions raised by the language of § 701(a), although it raises others. First, it clearly separates the exception provided by § (a)(1) from the § (a)(2) exception. The former applies when Congress has expressed an intent to preclude judicial review. The latter applies in different circumstances; even where Congress has not affirmatively precluded review, review is not to be had if the statute is drawn so that a court would have no meaningful standard against which to judge the agency's exercise of discretion. In such a case, the statute ("law") can be taken to have "committed" the decisionmaking to the agency's judgment absolutely. This construction avoids conflict with the "abuse of discretion" standard of review in § 706—if no judicially manageable standards are available for judging how and when an agency should exercise its discretion, then it is impossible to evaluate agency action for "abuse of discretion." ...

To this point our analysis does not differ significantly from that of the Court of Appeals. That court purported to apply the "no law to apply" standard of *Overton Park.* We disagree, however, with that court's insistence that the "narrow construction" of § (a)(2) required application of a presumption of reviewability even to an agency's decision not to undertake certain enforcement actions. Here we think the Court of Appeals broke with tradition, case law, and sound reasoning.

Overton Park did not involve an agency's refusal to take requested enforcement action. It involved an affirmative act of approval under a statute that set clear guidelines for determining when such approval should be given. Refusals to take enforcement steps generally involve precisely the opposite situation, and in that situation we think the presumption is that judicial review is not available. This Court has recognized on several occasions over many years that an agency's decision not to prosecute or enforce, whether through civil or criminal process, is a decision generally committed to an agency's absolute discretion. This recognition of the existence of discretion is attributable in no small part to the general unsuitability for judicial review of agency decisions to refuse enforcement.

The reasons for this general unsuitability are many. First, an agency decision not to enforce often involves a complicated balancing of a number of factors which are peculiarly within its expertise. Thus, the agency must not only assess whether a violation has occurred, but whether agency resources are best spent on this violation or another, whether the agency is likely to succeed if it acts, whether the particular enforcement action requested best fits the agency's overall policies, and, indeed, whether the agency has enough resources to undertake the action at all. An agency generally cannot act against each technical violation of the statute it is charged with enforcing. The agency is far better equipped than the courts to deal with the many variables involved in the proper ordering of its priorities. . . .

In addition to these administrative concerns, we note that when an agency refuses to act it generally does not exercise its coercive power over an individual's liberty or property rights, and thus does not infringe upon areas that courts often are called upon to protect. Similarly, when an agency does act to enforce, that action itself provides a focus for judicial review, inasmuch as the agency must have exercised its power in some manner. . . . Finally, we recognize that an agency's refusal to institute proceedings shares to some extent the characteristics of the decision of a prosecutor in the Executive Branch not to indict—a decision which has long been regarded as the special province of the Executive Branch, inasmuch as it is the Executive who is charged by the Constitution to "take Care that the Laws be faithfully executed." U.S. Const., Art. II, § 3.

We of course only list the above concerns to facilitate understanding of our conclusion that an agency's decision not to take enforcement action should be presumed immune from judicial review under § 701(a)(2). For good reasons, such a decision has traditionally been "committed to agency discretion," and we believe that the Congress enacting the APA did not intend to alter that tradition. In so stating, we emphasize that the decision is only presumptively unreviewable; the presumption may be rebutted where the substantive statute has provided guidelines for the agency to follow in exercising its enforcement powers.[4] Thus, in establishing this presumption in the APA, Congress did not set agencies free to disregard legislative direction in the statutory scheme that the agency administers. Congress may limit an agency's exercise of enforcement power if it wishes, either by setting substantive priorities, or by otherwise circumscribing an agency's power to discriminate among issues or cases it will pursue. How to determine when Congress has done so is the question left open by *Overton Park*.

Dunlop v. Bachowski, 421 U.S. 560 (1975), relied upon heavily by respondents and the majority in the Court of Appeals, presents an example of statutory language which supplied sufficient standards to rebut the presumption of unreviewability. [The law there] provided that, upon filing of a complaint by a union member, "[t]he Secretary shall investigate such complaint and, if he finds probable cause to believe that a violation ... has occurred ... he shall ... bring a civil action...." ... This Court held that review was available. It rejected the Secretary's argument that the statute precluded judicial review, and in a footnote it stated its agreement with the conclusion of the Court of Appeals that the decision was not "an unreviewable exercise of prosecutorial discretion." ... The Court of Appeals, in turn, had found the "principle of absolute prosecutorial discretion" inapplicable, because the language of the [Act] indicated that the Secretary was required to file suit if certain "clearly defined" factors were present. The decision therefore was not " 'beyond the judicial capacity to supervise.' "

Dunlop is thus consistent with a general presumption of unreviewability of decisions not to enforce. The statute being administered quite clearly withdrew discretion from the agency and provided guidelines for exercise of its enforcement power.... The danger that agencies may not carry out their delegated powers with sufficient vigor does not necessarily lead to the conclusion that courts are the most appropriate body to police this aspect of their performance. That decision is in the first instance for Congress, and we therefore turn to the FDCA to determine whether in this case Congress has provided us with "law to apply." If it has indicated an intent to circumscribe agency enforcement discretion, and has provided meaningful standards for defining the limits of that discretion, there is "law to apply" under § 701(a)(2), and courts may require that the agency follow that law; if it has not, then an agency refusal to institute proceedings is a decision "committed to agency discretion by law" within the meaning of that section.

---

4. We do not have in this case a refusal by the agency to institute proceedings based solely on the belief that it lacks jurisdiction. Nor do we have a situation where it could justifiably be found that the agency has "consciously and expressly adopted a general policy" that is so extreme as to amount to an abdication of its statutory responsibilities. Although we express no opinion on whether such decisions would be unreviewable under § 701(a)(2), we note that in those situations the statute conferring authority on the agency might indicate that such decisions were not "committed to agency discretion."

... The Act's general provision for enforcement provides only that "[t]he Secretary is authorized to conduct examinations and investigations...." Unlike the statute at issue in *Dunlop*, [the FDCA] gives no indication of when an injunction should be sought, and [the section] providing for seizures, is framed in the permissive—the offending food, drug, or cosmetic "shall be liable to be proceeded against." The section on criminal sanctions states baldly that any person who violates the Act's substantive prohibitions "shall be imprisoned ... or fined." Respondents argue that this statement mandates criminal prosecution of every violator of the Act but they adduce no indication in case law or legislative history that such was Congress' intention in using this language, which is commonly found in the criminal provisions of Title 18 of the United States Code. We are unwilling to attribute such a sweeping meaning to this language, particularly since the Act charges the Secretary only with recommending prosecution; any criminal prosecutions must be instituted by the Attorney General. The Act's enforcement provisions thus commit complete discretion to the Secretary to decide how and when they should be exercised....

We therefore conclude that the presumption that agency decisions not to institute proceedings are unreviewable under 5 U.S.C. § 701(a)(2) is not overcome by the enforcement provisions of the FDCA. The FDA's decision not to take the enforcement actions requested by respondents is therefore not subject to judicial review under the APA. The general exception to reviewability provided by § 701(a)(2) for action "committed to agency discretion" remains a narrow one, but within that exception are included agency refusals to institute investigative or enforcement proceedings, unless Congress has indicated otherwise. In so holding, we essentially leave to Congress, and not to the courts, the decision as to whether an agency's refusal to institute proceedings should be judicially reviewable. No colorable claim is made in this case that the agency's refusal to institute proceedings violated any constitutional rights of respondents, and we do not address the issue that would be raised in such a case.

JUSTICE BRENNAN, concurring.

Today the Court holds that individual decisions of the Food and Drug Administration not to take enforcement action in response to citizen requests are presumptively not reviewable under the Administrative Procedure Act. I concur in this decision. This general presumption is based on the view that, in the normal course of events, Congress intends to allow broad discretion for its administrative agencies to make particular enforcement decisions, and there often may not exist readily discernible "law to apply" for courts to conduct judicial review of nonenforcement decisions.

I also agree that, despite this general presumption, "Congress did not set agencies free to disregard legislative direction in the statutory scheme that the agency administers." Thus the Court properly does not decide today that nonenforcement decisions are unreviewable in cases where (1) an agency flatly claims that it has no statutory jurisdiction to reach certain conduct; (2) an agency engages in a pattern of nonenforcement of clear statutory language, as in *Adams v. Richardson*, 480 F.2d 1159 (1973) (en banc); (3) an agency has refused to enforce a regulation lawfully promulgated and still in effect; or (4) a nonenforcement decision violates constitutional rights. It is possible to imagine other nonenforcement decisions made for entirely illegitimate reasons, for example, nonenforcement in return for a bribe, judicial review of which would not be foreclosed by the nonreviewability presumption. It may be presumed that Congress does not intend administrative agencies, agents of Congress' own creation, to ignore clear jurisdictional, regulatory, statutory, or constitutional commands, and in some circumstances including those listed above the statutes or regulations at issue may well provide "law to apply" under 5 U.S.C. § 701(a)(2). Individual, isolated nonenforcement decisions, however, must be made by hundreds of agencies each day. It is entirely permissible to presume that Congress has not intended courts to review such mundane matters, absent either some indication of congressional intent to the contrary or proof of circumstances such as those set out above.

JUSTICE MARSHALL, concurring in the judgment.

Easy cases at times produce bad law, for in the rush to reach a clearly ordained result, courts may offer up principles, doctrines, and statements that calmer reflection, and a fuller understanding of their implications in concrete settings, would eschew. In my view, the "presumption of unreviewability" announced today is a product of that lack of discipline that easy cases make all too easy....

I write separately to argue for a different basis of decision: that refusals to enforce, like other agency actions, are reviewable in the absence of a "clear and convincing" congressional intent to the contrary, but that such refusals warrant deference when, as in this case, there is nothing to suggest that an agency with enforcement discretion has abused that discretion....

When a statute does not mandate full enforcement, I agree with the Court that an agency is generally "far better equipped than the courts to deal with the many variables involved in the proper ordering of its priorities." As long as the agency is choosing how to allocate finite enforcement resources, the agency's choice will be entitled to substantial deference, for the choice among valid alternative enforcement policies is precisely the sort of choice over which agencies generally have been left substantial discretion by their enabling statutes. On the merits, then, a decision not to enforce that is based on valid resource-allocation decisions will generally not be "arbitrary, capricious, an abuse of discretion, or otherwise not in accordance with law." The decision in this case is no exception to this principle.

The Court, however, is not content to rest on this ground. Instead, the Court transforms the arguments for deferential review on the merits into the wholly different notion that "enforcement" decisions are presumptively unreviewable altogether—unreviewable whether the resource-allocation rationale is a sham, unreviewable whether enforcement is declined out of vindictive or personal motives, and unreviewable whether the agency has simply ignored the request for enforcement. . . .

Moreover, for at least two reasons it is inappropriate to rely on notions of prosecutorial discretion to hold agency inaction unreviewable. First, . . . even in the area of criminal prosecutions, prosecutorial discretion is not subject to a "presumption of unreviewability." If a plaintiff makes a sufficient threshold showing that a prosecutor's discretion has been exercised for impermissible reasons, judicial review is available.

Second, arguments about prosecutorial discretion do not necessarily translate into the context of agency refusals to act. . . . Criminal prosecutorial decisions vindicate only intangible interests, common to society as a whole, in the enforcement of the criminal law. The conduct at issue has already occurred; all that remains is society's general interest in assuring that the guilty are punished. . . . In contrast, requests for administrative enforcement typically seek to prevent concrete and future injuries that Congress has made cognizable—injuries that result, for example, from misbranded drugs, such as alleged in this case, or unsafe nuclear power plants—or to obtain palpable benefits that Congress has intended to bestow—such as labor union elections free of corruption. Entitlements to receive these benefits or to be free of these injuries often run to specific classes of individuals whom Congress has singled out as statutory beneficiaries. The interests at stake in review of administrative enforcement decisions are thus more focused and in many circumstances more pressing than those at stake in criminal prosecutorial decisions. A request that a nuclear plant be operated safely or that protection be provided against unsafe drugs is quite different from a request that an individual be put in jail or his property confiscated as punishment for past violations of the criminal law.

Perhaps most important, the *sine qua non* of the APA was to alter inherited judicial reluctance to constrain the exercise of discretionary administrative power—to rationalize and make fairer the exercise of such discretion. Since passage of the APA, the sustained effort of administrative law has been to "continuously narro[w] the category of actions considered to be so discretionary as to be exempted from review." . . . Judicial review is available under the APA in the absence of a clear and convincing demonstration that Congress intended to preclude it precisely so that agencies, whether in rulemaking, adjudicating, acting or failing to act, do not become stagnant backwaters of caprice and lawlessness. . . .

WEBSTER v. DOE
486 U.S. 592, 108 S.Ct. 2047, 100 L.Ed.2d 632 (1988).

CHIEF JUSTICE REHNQUIST delivered the opinion of the Court.

Section 102(c) of the National Security Act of 1947 provides that: "[T]he Director of Central Intelligence may, in his discretion, terminate the employment of any officer or employee of the Agency whenever he shall deem such termination necessary or advisable in the interests of the United States...." In this case we decide whether, and to what extent, the termination decisions of the Director under § 102(c) are judicially reviewable.

Respondent John Doe was first employed by the Central Intelligence Agency (CIA or Agency) in 1973 as a clerk-typist. He received periodic fitness reports that consistently rated him as an excellent or outstanding employee. By 1977, respondent had been promoted to a position as a covert electronics technician. In January 1982, respondent voluntarily informed a CIA security officer that he was a homosexual.... On April 14, 1982, a CIA security agent informed respondent that the Agency's Office of Security had determined that respondent's homosexuality posed a threat to security, but declined to explain the nature of the danger. After reviewing respondent's records and the evaluations of his subordinates, the Director "deemed it necessary and advisable in the interests of the United States to terminate [respondent's] employment with this Agency pursuant to section 102(c) of the National Security Act...." ...

Respondent then filed an action against petitioner in the United States District Court for the District of Columbia. Respondent alleged that the Director's decision to terminate his employment violated the Administrative Procedure Act (APA), because it was arbitrary and capricious, represented an abuse of discretion, and was reached without observing the procedures required by law and CIA regulations.... He also complained that the Director's termination of his employment deprived him of constitutionally protected rights to property, liberty, and privacy in violation of the First, Fourth, Fifth, and Ninth Amendments. Finally, he asserted that his dismissal transgressed the procedural due process and equal protection of the laws guaranteed by the Fifth Amendment.

Petitioner moved to dismiss respondent's amended complaint on the ground that '102(c) of the National Security Act (NSA) precludes judicial review of the Director's termination decisions under the provisions of the APA.... The ... availability [of review] at all is predicated on satisfying the requirements of § 701, which provides: "(a) This chapter applies, according to the provisions thereof, except to the extent that—"(1) statutes preclude judicial review; or "(2) agency action is committed to agency discretion by law." ...

II

... In *Citizens to Preserve Overton Park, Inc. v. Volpe*, 401 U.S. 402 (1971), this Court explained the distinction between §§ 701(a)(1) and (a)(2). Subsection (a)(1) is concerned with whether Congress expressed an intent to prohibit judicial review; subsection (a)(2) applies "in those rare instances where 'statutes are drawn in such broad terms that in a given case there is no law to apply.'"

We further explained what it means for an action to be "committed to agency discretion by law" in *Heckler v. Chaney*.... We noted that, under § 701(a)(2), even when Congress has not affirmatively precluded judicial oversight, "review is not to be had if the statute is drawn so that a court would have no meaningful standard against which to judge the agency's exercise of discretion." Since the statute conferring power on the Food and Drug Administration to prohibit the unlawful misbranding or misuse of drugs provided no substantive standards on which a court could base its review, we found that enforcement actions were committed to the complete discretion of the FDA to decide when and how they should be pursued.

Both *Overton Park* and *Heckler* emphasized that § 701(a)(2) requires careful examination of the statute on which the claim of agency illegality is based. In the present case, respondent's claims against the CIA arise from the Director's asserted violation of § 102(c) of the NSA. As an initial matter, it should be noted that § 102(c) allows termination of an Agency employee whenever the Director "shall *deem* such termination necessary or advisable in the interests of the United States" (emphasis added), not simply when the dismissal is necessary or advisable to those interests. This standard fairly exudes deference to the Director, and appears to us to foreclose the application of any meaningful judicial standard of review. Short of permitting cross-examination of the Director concerning his views of the Nation's security and whether the discharged employee was inimical to those interests, we see no basis on which a reviewing court could properly assess an Agency termination decision. The language of § 102(c) thus strongly suggests that its implementation was "committed to agency discretion by law."

So too does the overall structure of the NSA. Passed shortly after the close of the Second World War, the NSA created the CIA and gave its Director the responsibility "for protecting intelligence sources and methods from unauthorized disclosure." Section 102(c) is an integral part of that statute, because the Agency's efficacy, and the Nation's security, depend in large measure on the reliability and trustworthiness of the Agency's employees....

We thus find that the language and structure of § 102(c) indicate that Congress meant to commit individual employee discharges to the Director's discretion, and that § 701(a)(2) accordingly precludes judicial review of these decisions under the APA. We reverse the Court of Appeals to the extent that it found such terminations reviewable by the courts.

III

In addition to his claim that the Director failed to abide by the statutory dictates of § 102(c), respondent also alleged a number of constitutional violations in his amended complaint.... Respondent asserts that he is entitled, under the APA, to judicial consideration of these claimed violations.[7]

Petitioner maintains that, no matter what the nature of respondent's constitutional claims, judicial review is precluded by the language and intent of § 102(c). In petitioner's view, all Agency employment termination decisions, even those based on policies normally repugnant to the Constitution, are given over to the absolute discretion of the Director, and are hence unreviewable under the APA. We do not think § 102(c) may be read to exclude review of constitutional claims. We emphasized in *Johnson v. Robison,* 415 U.S. 361 (1974), that where Congress intends to preclude judicial review of constitutional claims its intent to do so must be clear. We require this heightened showing in part to avoid the "serious constitutional question" that would arise if a federal statute were construed to deny any judicial forum for a colorable constitutional claim.

Our review of § 102(c) convinces us that it cannot bear the preclusive weight petitioner would have it support. As detailed above, the section does commit employment termination decisions to the Director's discretion, and precludes challenges to these decisions based upon the statutory language of § 102(c). A discharged employee thus cannot complain that his termination was not "necessary or advisable in the interests of the United States," since that assessment is the Director's alone. Subsections (a)(1) and (a)(2) of § 701, however, remove from judicial review only those determinations specifically identified by Congress or "committed to agency discretion by law." Nothing in § 102(c) persuades us that Congress meant to preclude consideration of colorable constitutional claims arising out of the actions of the Director pursuant to that section; we believe that a constitutional claim based on an individual discharge may be reviewed by the District Court. . . .

JUSTICE SCALIA, dissenting.

I agree with the Court's apparent holding . . . that the Director's decision to terminate a CIA employee is "committed to agency discretion by law" within the meaning of 5 U.S.C. § 701(a)(2). But because I do not see how a decision can, either practically or legally, be both unreviewable and yet reviewable for constitutional defect, I regard Part III of the opinion as essentially undoing Part II. I therefore respectfully dissent from the judgment of the Court.

Before proceeding to address Part III of the Court's opinion, which I think to be in error, I must discuss one significant element of the analysis in Part II. Though I subscribe to most of that analysis, I disagree with the Court's description of what is required to come within

---

7. We understand that petitioner concedes that the Agency's failure to follow its *own regulations* can be challenged under the APA as a violation of § 102(c). The Court of Appeals, however, found that the CIA's own regulations plainly protect the discretion granted the Director by § 102(c), and that the regulations "provid[e] no independent source of procedural or substantive protections." Thus, since petitioner prevailed on this ground below and does not seek further review of the question here, we do not reach that issue.

subsection (a)(2) of § 701, which provides that judicial review is unavailable "to the extent that ... agency action is committed to agency discretion by law." The Court's discussion suggests that the Court of Appeals below was correct in holding that this provision is triggered only when there is "no law to apply." Our precedents amply show that "commit[ment] to agency discretion by law" includes, but is not limited to, situations in which there is "no law to apply."

The Court relies for its "no law to apply" formulation upon our discussion in *Heckler v. Chaney*—which, however, did not apply that as the sole criterion of § 701(a)(2)'s applicability, but to the contrary discussed the subject action's "general unsuitability" for review, and adverted to "tradition, case law, and sound reasoning." Moreover, the only supporting authority for the "no law to apply" test cited in *Chaney* was our observation in *Citizens to Preserve Overton Park, Inc. v. Volpe*, that "[t]he legislative history of the Administrative Procedure Act indicates that [§ 701(a)(2)] is applicable in those rare instances where 'statutes are drawn in such broad terms that in a given case there is no law to apply.' "Perhaps *Overton Park* discussed only the "no law to apply" factor because that was the only basis for nonreviewability that was even arguably applicable. It surely could not have believed that factor to be exclusive, for that would contradict the very legislative history, both cited and quoted in the opinion, from which it had been derived, which read in full: "The basic exception of matters committed to agency discretion would apply even if not stated at the outset [of the judicial review Chapter]. If, *for example,* statutes are drawn in such broad terms that in a given case there is no law to apply, courts of course have no statutory question to review."

The "no law to apply" test can account for the nonreviewability of certain issues, but falls far short of explaining the full scope of the areas from which the courts are excluded. For the fact is that there is no governmental decision that is not subject to a fair number of legal constraints precise enough to be susceptible of judicial application—beginning with the fundamental constraint that the decision must be taken in order to further a public purpose rather than a purely private interest; yet there are many governmental decisions that are not at all subject to judicial review. A United States Attorney's decision to prosecute, for example, will not be reviewed on the claim that it was prompted by personal animosity. Thus, "no law to apply" provides much less than the full answer to whether § 701(a)(2) applies.

The key to understanding the "committed to agency discretion *by law*" provision of § 701(a)(2) lies in contrasting it with the "*statutes* preclude judicial review" provision of § 701(a)(1). Why "statutes" for preclusion, but the much more general term "law" for commission to agency discretion? The answer is, as we implied in *Chaney*, that the latter was intended to refer to "the 'common law' of judicial review of agency action,"—a body of jurisprudence that had marked out, with more or less precision, certain issues and certain areas that were beyond the range of judicial review. That jurisprudence included principles ranging from the "political question" doctrine, to sovereign immunity (including doctrines determining when a suit against an officer would be deemed to be a suit against the sovereign), to official immunity, to prudential limitations upon the courts' equitable powers, to what can be described no more precisely than a traditional respect for the functions of the other branches. . . . Only if all that "common law" were embraced within § 701(a)(2) could it have been true that, as was generally understood, "[t]he intended result of [§ 701(a)] is to restate the existing law as to the area of reviewable agency action." Because that is the meaning of the provision, we have continued to take into account for purposes of determining reviewability, post-APA as before, not only the text and structure of the statute under which the agency acts, but such factors as whether the decision involves "a sensitive and inherently discretionary judgment call"; whether it is the sort of decision that has traditionally been nonreviewable; and whether review would have "disruptive practical consequences." . . .

If and when this Court does come to consider the reviewability of a dismissal such as the present one on the ground that it violated the agency's regulations—a question the Court avoids today—the difference between the "no law to apply" test and what I consider the correct test will be crucial. Perhaps a dismissal in violation of the regulations can be reviewed, but not simply because the regulations provide a standard that makes review possible. Thus, I agree with the Court's holding in Part II of its opinion (though, as will soon appear, that holding seems to be undone by its holding in Part III), but on different reasoning. . . .

[Justice Scalia argued that the statute clearly commits the Director's decision to his discretion. Accordingly, the APA excepts it from judicial review. According to Justice Scalia, this commitment does not authorize the Director to act unconstitutionally, or even illegally, but it does insulate his decision from judicial review.]

Perhaps, then, a constitutional right is by its nature so much more important to the claimant than a statutory right that a statute which plainly excludes the latter should not be read to exclude the former unless it says so. That principle has never been announced—and with good reason, because its premise is not true. An individual's contention that the Government has reneged upon a $100,000 debt owing under a contract is much more important to him—both financially and, I suspect, in the sense of injustice that he feels—than the same individual's claim that a particular federal licensing provision requiring a $100 license denies him equal protection of the laws, or that a particular state tax violates the Commerce Clause. A citizen would much rather have his statutory entitlement correctly acknowledged after a constitutionally inadequate hearing, than have it incorrectly denied after a proceeding that fulfills all the requirements of the Due Process Clause. . . .

The harm done by today's decision is that, contrary to what Congress knows is preferable, it brings a significant decision-making process of our intelligence services into a forum where it does not belong.

Neither the Constitution, nor our laws, nor common sense gives an individual a right to come into court to litigate the reasons for his dismissal as an intelligence agent. It is of course not just valid constitutional claims that today's decision makes the basis for judicial review of the Director's action, but all colorable constitutional claims, whether meritorious or not. And in determining whether what is colorable is in fact meritorious, a court will necessarily have to review the entire decision....

Problem 5–5: Refusal To Waive Regulation

Congress has authorized the Department of Transportation (DOT) to issue and enforce regulations concerning commercial motor vehicle safety. Pursuant to this authority, DOT has promulgated a rule that a person is physically qualified to drive a commercial motor vehicle if that "person ... [h]as no established medical history or clinical diagnosis of epilepsy...."

Your client has epilepsy, but anticonvulsant medicine has kept the seizures under control. He has had no seizures at all since 1990, but his employer suspended him from his job as an interstate commercial truck driver after discovering his medical history, as DOT regulations require. He then sought to have DOT waive application of the regulation in his case. Congress has authorized the Secretary of Transportation "in his discretion to waive ... application of any regulation." The Secretary refused to grant the waiver.

Your law firm was brought into the case to appeal DOT's decision at the behest of the National Epilepsy Foundation. The Foundation asserts that the DOT's decision violates the federal Rehabilitation Act which stipulates: "No otherwise qualified individual with handicaps, ... shall by reason of her or his handicap, be ... subjected to discrimination ... under any program or activity conducted by any Executive agency...." The Foundation argues this Act makes it unlawful for DOT to prohibit your client from driving a truck "by reason of ... his handicap" if he can prove that his medical condition does not prevent him from being a safe driver.

After you file a lawsuit challenging DOT's decision, the government moves to dismiss the case on the ground that the Secretary's decision is "committed to agency discretion by law" under § 701(a)(2). The government's brief argues the Secretary's discretion to waive DOT regulations "is so broad" that a reviewing court has "no law to apply," and that the Secretary's decision is of the type traditionally that has been regarded as "committed to agency discretion by law."

What counter arguments can you make on your client's behalf? Would you expect that the reviewing court will refuse to dismiss the case?

Notes and Questions

1. In *Lincoln v. Vigil*, 508 U.S. 182, 113 S.Ct. 2024, 124 L.Ed.2d 101 (1993), the Court held that review of a spending decision by the Indian Health Service (IHS) was precluded under section 701(a)(2). The IHS, which is an agency within the Public Health Service of the Department of Health and Human Services, established and ran diagnostic and treatment centers for disabled Indian children for several years. After the IHS shut down the centers, children who had been receiving services sued and claimed that the closures were contrary to law and a violation of the APA. Congress had never expressly appropriated money for the centers; instead the IHS had allocated money for their support from a lump sum appropriation.

The Court justified its decision on the ground that certain types of administrative decisions, including this one, were of the type that courts have traditionally regarded as committed to agency discretion:

> Over the years, we have read § 701(a)(2) to preclude judicial review of certain categories of administrative decisions that courts traditionally have regarded as "committed to agency discretion." . . . [For example], in *ICC v. Locomotive Engineers*, 482 U.S. 270, 107 S.Ct. 2360, 96 L.Ed.2d 222 (1987), we held that § 701(a)(2) precludes judicial review of another type of administrative decision traditionally left to agency discretion, an agency's refusal to grant reconsideration of an action because of material error. In so holding, we emphasized "the impossibility of devising an adequate standard of review for such agency action." Finally, in *Webster*, we held that § 701(a)(2) precludes judicial review of a decision by the Director of Central Intelligence to terminate an employee in the interests of national security, an area of executive action "in which courts have long been hesitant to intrude."
>
> The allocation of funds from a lump-sum appropriation is another administrative decision traditionally regarded as committed to agency discretion. After all, the very point of a lump-sum appropriation is to give an agency the capacity to adapt to changing circumstances and meet its statutory responsibilities in what it sees as the most effective or desirable way. . . .
>
> Like the decision against instituting enforcement proceedings, then, an agency's allocation of funds from a lump-sum appropriation requires "a complicated balancing of a number of factors which are peculiarly within its expertise": whether its "resources are best spent" on one program or another; whether it "is likely to succeed" in fulfilling its statutory mandate; whether a particular program "best fits the agency's overall policies"; and, "indeed, whether the agency has enough resources" to fund a program "at all." . . .

508 U.S. at 191–93, 113 S.Ct. at 2030–32.

2. Professor Levin observes:

The Court's defense of the "law to apply" test rests primarily on what I call the "futility" theory. This theory maintains that an administrative action is unreviewable if and only if judicial review of the decision would be infeasible. . . .

[T]he major premise of the futility theory—that extremely broad statutory language makes judicial review infeasible—is . . . mistaken. Even a broad statutory mandate, which gives an agency wide latitude to strike a balance among varied public policy factors, can have teeth when a litigant alleges that the agency failed to take the prescribed factors into account. Furthermore, the courts have derived a number of doctrines with which they can test an action for arbitrariness without relying on the statutory language under which the agency acted. . . .

Of course, lower courts would have to follow the "law to apply" approach to section 701(a)(2) if Supreme Court precedent clearly mandated the test. Despite lip service to the futility theory, however, the court has never relied solely on that rationale to hold agency action unreviewable. . . .

Ronald M. Levin, *Understanding Unreviewability in Administrative Law*, 74 MINN. L. REV. 689, 734–35, 738 (1990). In addition to the "presence or absence of law to apply," what other factors did the Court use in the previous cases to determine if judicial review was precluded?

3.   When you studied rulemaking petitions in Chapter 2, you read about the highly deferential scope of review employed in *American Horse Protection Association (AHPA) v. Lyng*, 812 F.2d 1 (D.C.Cir.1987), to review an agency's decision not to grant a rulemaking petition. In a portion of *Heckler* not reproduced, the Court expressed no opinion whether there was a presumption of unreviewability concerning an agency decision not to issue a rule. In *AHPA*, the D. C. Circuit held it could review such decisions, and other circuits have followed this decision. *AHPA* distinguished *Heckler v. Chaney* in the following manner:

The *Chaney* Court relied on three features of nonenforcement decisions in arriving at its negative presumption. First, such decisions require a high level of agency expertise and coordination in setting priorities. Second, the agency in such situations will not ordinarily be exercising "its coercive power over an individual's liberty or property rights." Third, such nonenforcement decisions are akin to prosecutorial decisions not to indict, which traditionally involve executive control and judicial restraint. The first and second of these features are likely to be involved in an agency's refusal to institute a rulemaking, but the third is another matter.

Chaney says little about this third feature. To a degree, of course, it recapitulates and underscores the prior points about resource allocation and non-coercion. The analogy between prosecutorial discretion and agency nonenforcement is strengthened, however, by two other shared characteristics. First, both prosecutors and agencies constantly make decisions not to take enforcement steps;

such decisions thus are numerous. Second, both types of nonenforcement are typically based mainly on close consideration of the facts of the case at hand, rather than on legal analysis. Refusals to institute rulemakings, by contrast, are likely to be relatively infrequent and more likely to turn upon issues of law. . . .

Furthermore, the [APA] serves to distinguish between *Chaney* nonenforcement decisions and refusals to institute rulemakings. The *Chaney* Court noted that "when an agency does act to enforce, that action itself provides a focus for judicial review" since a court can "at least . . . determine whether the agency exceeded its statutory powers." APA provisions governing agency refusals to initiate rulemakings give a similar focal point. The APA requires agencies to allow interested persons to "petition for the issuance, amendment, or repeal of a rule," 5 U.S.C.A. § 553(e)(1982), and, when such petitions are denied, to give "a brief statement of the grounds for denial," id. § 555(e). These two provisions suggest that Congress expected that agencies denying rulemaking petitions must explain their actions.

Thus, refusals to institute rulemaking proceedings are distinguishable from other sorts of nonenforcement decisions insofar as they are less frequent, more apt to involve legal as opposed to factual analysis, and subject to special formalities, including a public explanation. *Chaney* therefore does not appear to overrule our prior decisions allowing review of agency refusals to institute rulemakings.

812 F.2d at 4.

E.   TIMING

Three principles impact on the timing of judicial review. First, a party can obtain judicial review only of **final** agency actions unless Congress has authorized review at an earlier stage. Second, a party may have to **exhaust** any administrative remedies as a prerequisite to judicial review. Finally, a party can obtain judicial review of any agency action only if that action is **ripe** for review. This section defines these concepts and indicates how they are applied. Although each concept is discussed separately, these principles do overlap, as you will see.

1. FINALITY

Section 704 states that "agency action made reviewable by statute and final agency action for which there is no adequate remedy in a court" are judicially reviewable. When a particular statute specifically provides for judicial review of agency action, then the review proceeds pursuant to that statute, not the APA. If there is no specific statutory provision for judicial review, section 704 restricts review to "final agency action for which there is no other adequate remedy."

In *Franklin v. Massachusetts*, 505 U.S. 788, 112 S.Ct. 2767, 120 L.Ed.2d 636 (1992), the Court rejected an attack on the validity of the 1990 census because there was no "final agency action" to review. The plaintiffs challenged certain adjustments made by the Department of Commerce (and its Census Bureau) in its count of the persons who lived in Massachusetts. As required by the census statute, the Secretary of Commerce submitted the Massachusetts census (and the census of the other states) to the President, who in turn reported the census to Congress to permit a reapportionment of the House of Representatives. Because the Department submitted its results to the President, the Court analyzed whether its action was "final":

> To determine when an agency action is final, we have looked to, among other things, whether its impact "is sufficiently direct and immediate" and has a "direct effect on . . . day-to-day business." An agency action is not final if it is only "the ruling of a subordinate official," or "tentative." The core question is whether the agency has completed its decisionmaking process, and whether the result of that process is one that will directly affect the parties. In this case, the action that creates an entitlement to a particular number of Representatives and has a direct effect on the reapportionment is the President's statement to Congress, not the Secretary's report to the President.

> . . . Section 2a does not expressly require the President to use the data in the Secretary's report. . . . There is no statute forbidding amendment of the "decennial census" itself after the Secretary submits the report to the President. For potential litigants, therefore, the "decennial census" still presents a moving target, even after the Secretary reports to the President. . . .

505 U.S. at 796–97, 112 S.Ct. at 2773–74. As discussed in Chapter 1, the Court then denied review of the President's action, because he was not an "agency" within the meaning of the APA. Out of respect for separation of powers, it refused to subject actions of the President to review under the APA without an express declaration to that effect by Congress.

While in *Franklin* the Court referred to a "direct effect" or an immediate and direct impact, sometimes the Court has stated that for an agency action to be "final" it must be one "by which 'rights or obligations have been determined,' or from which "legal consequences will flow." *Bennett v. Spear*, 520 U.S. 154, 178, 117 S.Ct. 1154, 1168, 137 L.Ed.2d 281 (1997). Often there is no conflict between these two descriptions, but if the agency action is, for example, a non-legislative rule, then the rule does not have binding legal consequences, even though it may have real, practical consequences. The following problem raises this question.

Problem 5-6: Finality of Agency Statements

You represent an old friend who owns and runs two small health care companies. One, Home Health Care, Inc., is a Medicare and Medicaid certified home health agency; the other, Managed Health Services, Inc., provides home health services to non-Medicare patients who have private insurance or some other source of funds available to them. The two entities have separate offices, home health licenses, federal tax identification numbers, insurance coverage, and bank accounts. Home Health Care does not maintain a large full-time staff of health care personnel, because its needs vary from month to month depending on the number of patients it is serving at any given time. In fact, Home Health Care warns its employees that it cannot guarantee them a full-time (i.e. 40 hours per week) job. They may, however, apply to work with Managed Health Services if they want more hours of work. Some employees took Home Health Care up on the invitation.

The Fair Labor Standards Act, which sets federal standards for overtime pay, requires that persons working a combined number of hours for "joint employers" in excess of 40 hours receive overtime pay for those excess hours. The purpose of this provision is to protect against firms creating bogus companies and manipulating employment under two employers so that an employee who works more than 40 hours a week for the two employers, but less than 40 hours a week for either one, would not be paid overtime pay.

A former employee of Home Health Care and Managed Health Services filed a complaint with the Wage and Hour Division of the Department of Labor. At the conclusion of its investigation you receive the following letter:

> This is in reference to our investigation of your client, Home Health Care, Inc. and Managed Health Service, Inc., under the Fair Labor Standards Act.

> You are advised that after reviewing the circumstances involved in this case I will be closing our investigation with no further action. I want to stress, however, that it is the Department of Labor's position that employees concurrently working for the two corporate entities must have their hours of work combined and be paid overtime when the total is over 40 hours in a week. At a minimum, a joint employment relationship exists in this situation. If your client fails to pay overtime in accordance with this enforcement position it does so at its own peril.

> The Department of Labor has authority to conduct investigations as provided under section 11(a). It is not necessary for a complaint to be filed in order for such an investigation to be scheduled. It is my intention to consider a follow-up investigation at some later date to determine whether your client is complying with the Act.

I would like to direct your attention to section 16(e) of the FLSA and Regulations, Part 578. As you will note, section 16(e) provides for the assessment of a civil money penalty for any repeated or willful violations of section 6 or 7, in an amount not to exceed $1,000 for each such violation. No penalty is being assessed as a result of this investigation. If at any time in the future your client is found to have violated the monetary provisions of the FLSA, it will be subject to such penalties.

> Sincerely,
> Dean A. Campbell
> Assistant District Director

You do not think that Home Health Care and Managed Health Services meet the definition of "joint employers" in the Department of Labor regulations. Can you challenge the determination reflected in the letter in court?

TAYLOR–CALLAHAN–COLEMAN COUNTIES DISTRICT ADULT PROBATION DEPARTMENT v. DOLE

948 F.2d 953 (5th Cir.1991).

CLARK, CHIEF JUDGE:

[Under the Fair Labor Standards Act of 1938, as amended (FLSA), overtime requirements do not apply to "any employee employed in a bona fide executive, administrative or professional capacity ... as such terms are defined and delimited from time to time by regulations of the Secretary." Since 1940 DOL has had regulations interpreting these terms. In 1974 the Wage and Hour Administrator issued an opinion letter advising the requesting party that the probation officers described in the request were exempt as administrative employees. However, in 1988, the DOL issued two opinion letters in response to new requests in which the Administrator stated that under the fact circumstances provided by the requesting parties, those probation officers were not exempt as administrative, executive or professional employees. The Taylor–Callahan–Coleman Counties District Adult Probation Department (the District) challenged these two opinion letters on the grounds that they were legislative rules that had not gone through notice and comment and that they were inconsistent with the prior regulations and the statute.] Since the DOL action complained of is not final agency action, we affirm the district court's order dismissing for lack of subject matter jurisdiction.

... The District must also establish a waiver of sovereign immunity before relief can be granted. In this case, a waiver must be found in the APA. That Act does not make every agency action subject to judicial review. Section 704 of that Act limits judicial review to "[a]gency action made reviewable by statute and [to] final agency action for which there is no adequate remedy in a court...." [T]he District asserts the DOL treats its 1988 opinion letters as binding precedent for all parties and that this treatment makes those particular letters final agency action.

... Precedent requires that we gauge the finality of agency action in a pragmatic way.

We begin by noting the DOL has authoritatively addressed the function and finality which it will place on opinion letters.

Advisory interpretations announced by the Administrator [of the Wage and Hour Division] serve only to indicate the construction of the law which will guide the Administrator in the performance of his administrative duties unless he is directed otherwise by the authoritative ruling of the courts, or unless he shall subsequently decide that his prior interpretation is incorrect.

... Advisory opinions issued by the Wage and Hour Administrator are to guide the DOL in its operations. They are neither final nor binding on employers or employees. Rather they are expressly issued subject to change by the Administrator. The 1974 opinion letter was not final agency action which fixed the rights of probation officers. The 1988 opinion letters are not final agency action which fixed the rights of the District. After substantial legal changes had occurred in the area of public employment, the Administrator changed the opinions he had held previously. The 1974 letter was not issued after public notice and comment. The 1988 letters required no such procedure....

All of the letters involved here are expressly limited to the factual situation presented by the requesting party. "[Y]ou are advised that based on the job descriptions submitted, [the probation officers] would meet the conditions for exemption...." "Therefore, it is our opinion on the basis of the information you provide that the employees ... cannot qualify...."

The District has not requested an opinion as to any part of its own situation. Instead, it claims that such a request would be futile because the policy of the Administrator is well defined in the two most recent opinion letters. This claim ignores their own contention that the Administrator decided to change his prior interpretation. If the 1974 and 1988 positions and conditions were identical and the legal situation was the same so that the Administrator did make a change, he is logically free to change again. Rather than constituting agency action which is definitive, broadly applicable and demanding of compliance by all employers of probation officers, the letters involved here state only that they respond to particularized inquiries. Since the opinions are intended to guide DOL officials in similar situations, they surely are carefully reasoned. Nevertheless it is the regulations, not the opinion letters, which fix rights.

In *Abbott Laboratories v. Gardner* the Supreme Court reviewed several factors it found to be significant in determining the finality of agency action. First, whether the challenged action is a definitive statement of the agency's position; second, whether the actions have the status of laws with penalties for noncompliance; third, whether the impact on the plaintiff is direct and immediate; and fourth, whether immediate compliance was expected. When the Supreme Court applied these four factors to a Federal Trade Commission (FTC) complaint based on its alleged "reason to believe" that a violation had occurred, it held the action unreviewable because it was not final agency action....

The District relies principally on two cases to support its contention that opinion letters are final agency action. Since both are distinguishable on their facts we need not determine here whether our construction of the effect of DOL opinion letters would conflict with these rulings. In the first, *National Automatic Laundry and Cleaning Council v. Shultz*, 443 F.2d 689 (D.C.Cir.1971), the District of Columbia Circuit held that an opinion letter issued by the Administrator to an association stating that coin-operated launderettes and dry-cleaning services were "engaged in laundering or cleaning clothing or fabrics within the meaning of the act" was agency action subject to judicial review. The court found that the opinion letter constituted final agency action because it was in response to an actual situation and the Wage and Hour Division intended the letter to be a "deliberative determination of the agency's position at the highest available level on a question of importance ..." that affected an entire industry group. The court also decided that the ruling of the head of an agency is presumptively final, absent evidence on the face of the ruling that it is tentative. The court also held that opinion letter rose to the level of "expected conformity" which applied to the businessman and agency personnel.

National Laundry is distinguishable on several grounds. First, the opinion letter in that case was issued to the plaintiff whereas the opinion letters in this case were not issued to the District. Second, the addressee was a national trade association and its request was made and responded to on behalf of a significant portion of an industry, not simply some employees of one employer. Third, the opinion letter determined that all standardized coin-operated launderettes or dry-cleaning services were enterprises within the meaning of FLSA. The letter requesting the opinion set forth three typical fact situations prevailing in the coin-operated laundry business. The Administrator's opinion was that in all these situations the launderettes would be covered by FLSA. A wholly different situation confronts this court in today's case.

The opinion letters cited by the District did not have general applicability to machinery used by an industry, nor did they create an expected conformity to be followed by other probation departments or by the DOL. Each of the letters was issued in response to a discreet inquiry by one employer or probation department with respect to its own described personnel operations.

The D.C. Circuit recognized that:

[t]o permit suits for declaratory judgment upon mere informal, advisory, administrative opinions might well discourage the practice

of giving such opinions, with a net loss of far greater proportions to the average citizen than any possible gain which would accrue.

That court also acknowledged the need for informal advisory letters in the administration of FLSA.

The letters involved here were not a "deliberative determination of the agency's position at the highest available level on a question of importance." They were no more than individualized advisory, administrative opinions, subject to modification or change.

The second case the District cites is *International Longshoremen's and Warehousemen's Union v. Meese*, 891 F.2d 1374 (9th Cir.1989). There the Ninth Circuit determined that an Immigration and Naturalization Service (INS) advisory opinion was final because the union had "no administrative remedy to overturn the advisory opinion or policy statement." The court also found, however, that by acting through an advisory opinion, the INS deprived the union members of the protections afforded by the National Labor Relations Board certification procedure.

In *ILWU*, the court held the INS opinion letter stating that King-come's crane operators were "alien crewmen" was final because it resulted in the loss by union members of their opportunity to compete for jobs long considered traditional longshoremen positions but did not provide the union with any remedy. Such is not the situation with the opinion letters and the District. The DOL's opinion letters responding to the specific inquiries of other probation departments do not have such an effect on the District. It is still free to seek its own opinion letter and is free to challenge any opinion letter issued to it by continuing with treatment of its employees which it believes is correct.

The opinion letters involved in today's case are akin to threshold determinations. They give specific entities the Administrator's opinion as to how governing regulations affect the probation officers described in the request. They set out no definitive statement of DOL policy. They do not have the status of law with penalties for noncompliance. They do not have a direct or immediate impact on the District. They do not require immediate compliance by the District. They are not final agency action subject to judicial review.

C. DECLARATORY RELIEF

The District asserts it had no adequate remedy other than this declaratory judgment action. This is incorrect. In a FLSA enforcement action, whether brought by probation officers or the DOL, the District may defend on the basis that the officers are exempt from coverage. The District contends that this option is not viable because as a law enforcement agency it should not engage in civil disobedience. The District also asserts that if it ceases to pay overtime to its probation officers and an enforcement action ensues which it defends without success, the violation would be construed as willful because it is aware of the DOL's position regarding the District's probation officers. Our holding that the opinion letters are not final agency action which binds the District provides a substantial answer to these concerns. While we issue no advisory opinion on any question of willfulness which may later arise, we do hold that the answer to that question cannot turn on ascribing any binding force to the opinion letters. . . .

APPALACHIAN POWER COMPANY v. ENVIRONMENTAL PROTECTION AGENCY

208 F.3d 1015 (D.C.Cir.2000).

RANDOLPH, CIRCUIT JUDGE:

These consolidated petitions for judicial review, brought by electric power companies, and trade associations representing the nation's chemical and petroleum industry, challenge the validity of portions of an EPA document entitled "Periodic Monitoring Guidance," released in 1998. . . .

[Under Title V of the 1990 amendments to the Clean Air Act, stationary sources of air pollution must obtain operating permits from State or local authorities administering their EPA-approved implementation plans. The States must submit to EPA for its review all operating permits and proposed and final permits. EPA has 45 days to object; if it does so, "the permitting authority may not issue the permit." Congress instructed EPA to pass regulations establishing the "minimum elements of a permit program to be administered by any air pollution control agency," including "monitoring and reporting requirements." EPA promulgated rules implementing the Title V permit program in 1992. The rules require that permits contain a requirement for "periodic monitoring sufficient to yield reliable data from the relevant time period that are representative of the source's compliance with the permit." What is not clear is whether this requirement only applies when the regulations governing particular kinds of polluters do not already contain a monitoring requirement, or whether this requirement trumps already existing monitoring requirements that are not "periodic monitoring." In September 1988, EPA issued a document entitled "Periodic Monitoring Guidance for Title V Operating Permits Programs." The "Guidance" was issued over the signature of two EPA officials—the Director of the Office of Regulatory Enforcement, and the Director of the Office of Air Quality Planning and Standards. It is narrative in form, consists of 19 single-spaced, typewritten pages, and is available on EPA's internet web site (www.epa.gov). The Guidance makes clear that permits are to require "periodic monitoring" even in situations in which the source is already subject to another, non-periodic monitoring requirement. Because such periodic monitoring would raise the cost of compliance to many industries, they challenge the Guidance as unlawful.]

The phenomenon we see in this case is familiar. Congress passes a broadly worded statute. The agency follows with regulations containing broad language, open-ended phrases, ambiguous standards and the like. Then as years pass, the agency issues circulars or guidance or memoranda, explaining, interpreting, defining and often expanding the commands in the regulations. One guidance document may yield another and then another and so on. Several words in a regulation may spawn hundreds of pages of text as the agency offers more and more detail regarding what its regulations demand of regulated entities. Law is made, without notice and comment, without public participation, and without publication in the Federal Register or the Code of Federal Regulations. With the advent of the Internet, the agency does not need these official publications to ensure widespread circulation; it can inform those affected simply by posting its new guidance or memoranda or policy statement on its web site. An agency operating in this way gains a large advantage. "It can issue or amend its real rules, i.e., its interpretative rules and policy statements, quickly and inexpensively without following any statutorily prescribed procedures." Richard J. Pierce, Jr., Seven Ways to Deossify Agency Rulemaking, 47 ADMIN.L.REV. 59, 85 (1995).[9] The agency may also think there is another advantage—immunizing its lawmaking from judicial review.

EPA tells us that its Periodic Monitoring Guidance is not subject to judicial review because it is not final, and it is not final because it is not "binding." It is worth pausing a minute to consider what is meant by "binding" in this context. Only "legislative rules" have the force and effect of law. . . . If this were all that "binding" meant, EPA's Periodic Monitoring Guidance could not possibly qualify: it was not the product of notice and comment rulemaking in accordance with the Clean Air Act, and it has not been published in the Federal Register. But we have also recognized that an agency's other pronouncements can, as a practical matter, have a binding effect. See, e.g., *McLouth Steel Prods. Corp. v. Thomas*, 838 F.2d 1317, 1321 (D.C.Cir.1988). If an agency acts as if a document issued at headquarters is controlling in the field, if it treats the document in the same manner as it treats a legislative rule, if it bases enforcement actions on the policies or interpretations formulated in the document, if it leads private parties or State permitting authorities to believe that it will declare permits invalid unless they comply with the terms of the document, then the agency's document is for all practical purposes "binding."[10]

For these reasons, EPA's contention must be that the Periodic Monitoring Guidance is not binding in a practical sense. . . . EPA claims, on the one hand, that the Guidance is a policy statement, rather than an interpretative rule, and is not binding. On the other hand, EPA agrees with petitioners that "the Agency's position on the central legal issue here—the appropriateness of a sufficiency review of all Title V monitor-

9. How much more efficient than, for instance, the sixty rounds of notice and comment rulemaking preceding the final rule in *Motor Vehicle Mfrs. Ass'n v. State Farm Mut. Auto. Ins. Co.*

10. . . . The Guidance issued over the signatures of two high level EPA officials rather than the Administrator. EPA does not, however, contest petitioners' assertion that because "the document was drafted, and reviewed by, high ranking officials in several EPA offices, including EPA's lawyers, there is no reason to doubt the authors' authority to speak for the Agency."

ing requirements—indeed is settled. . . ." In other words, whatever EPA may think of its Guidance generally, the elements of the Guidance petitioners challenge consist of the agency's settled position, a position it plans to follow in reviewing State-issued permits, a position it will insist State and local authorities comply with in setting the terms and conditions of permits issued to petitioners, a position EPA officials in the field are bound to apply.

We should note that the Guidance itself states that it "interprets" § 70.6(a)(3) of the regulations.

Of course, an agency's action is not necessarily final merely because it is binding. Judicial orders can be binding; a temporary restraining order, for instance, compels compliance but it does not finally decide the case. In the administrative setting, "two conditions must be satisfied for agency action to be 'final': First, the action must mark the 'consummation' of the agency's decisionmaking process—it must not be of a merely tentative or interlocutory nature. And second, the action must be one by which 'rights or obligations have been determined,' or from which 'legal consequences will flow.'" The first condition is satisfied here. The "Guidance," as issued in September 1998, followed a draft circulated four years earlier and another, more extensive draft circulated in May 1998. This latter document bore the title "EPA Draft Final Periodic Monitoring Guidance."[16] On the question whether States must review their emission standards and the emission standards EPA has promulgated to determine if the standards provide enough monitoring, the Guidance is unequivocal—the State agencies must do so. On the question whether the States may supersede federal and State standards and insert additional monitoring requirements as terms or conditions of a permit, the Guidance is certain—the State agencies must do so if they believe existing requirements are inadequate, as measured by EPA's multi-factor, case-by-case analysis set forth in the Guidance.

EPA may think that because the Guidance, in all its particulars, is subject to change, it is not binding and therefore not final action. There are suggestions in its brief to this effect. But all laws are subject to change. Even that most enduring of documents, the Constitution of the United States, may be amended from time to time. The fact that a law may be altered in the future has nothing to do with whether it is subject to judicial review at the moment.

On the issue whether the challenged portion of the Guidance has legal consequences, EPA points to the concluding paragraph of the document, which contains a disclaimer: "The policies set forth in this paper are intended solely as guidance, do not represent final Agency action, and cannot be relied upon to create any rights enforceable by any party." This language is boilerplate; since 1991 EPA has been placing it at the end of all its guidance documents. Insofar as the "policies" mentioned in the disclaimer consist of requiring State permitting authorities to search for deficiencies in existing monitoring regulations and

16. In the title to the Guidance we have before us, EPA dropped the word "final."

replace them through terms and conditions of a permit, "rights" may not be created but "obligations" certainly are—obligations on the part of the State regulators and those they regulate. At any rate, the entire Guidance, from beginning to end—except the last paragraph—reads like a ukase. It commands, it requires, it orders, it dictates. Through the Guidance, EPA has given the States their "marching orders" and EPA expects the States to fall in line, as all have done, save perhaps Florida and Texas....

The short of the matter is that the Guidance, insofar as relevant here, is final agency action, reflecting a settled agency position which has legal consequences both for State agencies administering their permit programs and for companies like those represented by petitioners who must obtain Title V permits in order to continue operating....

[The court went on to set aside the Guidance on the basis that it impermissibly went beyond the regulation.]

Notes and Questions

1.   One purpose of restricting review to "final agency action" is to avoid judicial review of preliminary and subsidiary agency actions separate from the final action. For example, an agency in an adjudication might deny a party the ability to subpoena a particular witness. While that action (denying the subpoena) might be final as to that issue, it would not be a final agency action within the meaning of Section 704. Rather, the party would have to wait until the agency had finally ruled against it on the merits. Then the party could obtain judicial review of the "final" action, arguing that it was unlawful because the party was denied the ability to subpoena a particular witness. This is explicit in the second sentence of Section 704: "A preliminary, procedural, or intermediate agency action or ruling not directly reviewable is subject to review on the review of the final agency action."

2.   The finality doctrine also recognizes that it is often more difficult for a court to review agency action before it has resulted in some final decision. Without a final decision, a court often lacks a record of the matter and a complete justification for the agency's action. In addition, a court may not even be able to discern the precise nature of the dispute between the agency and the person seeking an appeal until after the agency has taken a final action.

3.   Section 704 provides that final agency action "for which there is no adequate remedy in a court" is subject to judicial review. This phrase refers to the general notion that equitable remedies, which the APA provides, are only available where there is no adequate remedy "at law." Thus, at least in theory, if a person could obtain full relief through an action at law, review under the APA would not lie. As a practical matter, this provision means that cases that can be brought against the government in the United States Court of Federal Claims are to be brought there, rather than in a district court under the APA.

4. In order for there to be a "final" agency action, there must first be an agency "action." In *Lujan v. National Wildlife Federation*, 497 U.S. 871, 110 S.Ct. 3177, 111 L.Ed.2d 695 (1990), the Court held that environmentalists challenging the Bureau of Land Management's land withdrawal review activities lacked standing. The environmentalists had tried to cure their lack of evidence of injury by submitting additional affidavits. The Court said that even if those affidavits were considered, the environmentalists could not bring the challenge because the BLM's land withdrawal program was not agency action:

> It is impossible that the affidavits would suffice, as the Court of Appeals held, to enable respondent to challenge the entirety of petitioners' so-called "land withdrawal review program." That is not an "agency action" within the meaning of § 702, much less a "final agency action" within the meaning of '704. The term "land withdrawal review program" (which as far as we know is not derived from any authoritative text) does not refer to a single BLM order or regulation, or even to a completed universe of particular BLM orders and regulations. It is simply the name by which petitioners have occasionally referred to the continuing (and thus constantly changing) operations of the BLM in reviewing withdrawal revocation applications and the classifications of public lands and developing land use plans as required by the FLPMA.... As the District Court explained, the "land withdrawal review program" extends to, currently at least, "1250 or so individual classification terminations and withdrawal revocations."

The Court explained further, "If there is in fact some specific order or regulation, applying some particular measure across-the-board to all individual classification terminations and withdrawal revocations, and if that order or regulation is final . . . it can of course be challenged under the APA by a person adversely affected—and the entire 'land withdrawal review program,' insofar as the content of that particular action is concerned, would thereby be affected. But that is quite different from permitting a generic challenge to all aspects of the 'land withdrawal review program,' as though that itself constituted a final agency action."

5. In Chapter 2, you studied agency inaction concerning petitions for rulemaking. The issue was what standard of review a court would use if an agency simply fails to respond to a rulemaking petition and the petitioner asks the court to "compel agency action unlawfully withheld or unreasonably delayed." 5 U.S.C.A. § 706(1). If an agency has failed to rule on a petition, there appears to be no "final" agency action to be reviewed. If the agency rejected the petition, the action would be final because the are no further agency proceedings concerning the petition. If the agency grants the petition, it would not be a "final" action until the agency either completed the rulemaking proceeding or announced that it was ending the proceeding without issuing a rule. Nevertheless, a court may treat administrative inaction as the equivalent of an order denying relief. Otherwise, an agency could immunize itself from relief by simply failing to respond to a petition. *See, e.g., Environmental Defense Fund v.*

Hardin, 428 F.2d 1093 (D.C.Cir.1970) ("[W]hen administrative inaction has precisely the same impact on the rights of the parties as denial of relief, an agency cannot preclude judicial review by casting its decision in the form of inaction rather than in the form of an order denying relief. . . . At some point administrative delay amounts to a refusal to act, with sufficient finality and ripeness to permit judicial review.")

2. EXHAUSTION

Related to the requirement for final agency action is the doctrine of exhaustion of administrative remedies. Before the APA, courts had developed a general requirement that if an agency provided an internal means of review of its decisions, persons should be required to use those means before coming to court. This was similar to the finality requirement in that it husbanded judicial resources by delaying judicial review pending agency proceedings that might eliminate the need for any judicial review. It was different from finality, however, in that the delay pending exhaustion did not have the further purpose of not interfering with on-going agency proceedings.

While application of the exhaustion requirement usually sends a plaintiff back to an agency to use available remedies, thereby delaying judicial review, application of the doctrine can also result in precluding review. For example, if, by the time a court finds that a person has not exhausted available remedies, the deadline for invoking those remedies has passed, the person will be precluded from either further administrative review or judicial review.

Much of the case law relating to the exhaustion doctrine consists of various exceptions carved out by courts to avoid the hardship caused by delaying or precluding judicial review. The next case, *McCarthy v. Madigan*, illustrates this type of case. Because courts had by common law created the exhaustion doctrine, they could equally create exceptions to it. By comparison, courts lack discretion to create exceptions to the requirement of finality, because it is created by statute.

Darby v. Cisneros, which also follows, dramatically changed the exhaustion doctrine. The Court held that although the third sentence in section 704 is phrased in terms of finality, it constitutes a statutory exhaustion provision that substitutes for the common law doctrine. The third sentence reads: "Except as otherwise expressly required by statute, agency action otherwise final is final for the purposes of this section whether or not there has been presented or determined an application for a declaratory order, for any form of reconsideration, or, unless the agency otherwise requires by rule and provides that the action meanwhile is inoperative, for an appeal to superior agency authority."

MCCARTHY v. MADIGAN

503 U.S. 140, 112 S.Ct. 1081, 117 L.Ed.2d 291 (1992).

JUSTICE BLACKMUN delivered the opinion of the Court.

The issue in this case is whether a federal prisoner must resort to the internal grievance procedure promulgated by the Federal Bureau of Prisons before he may initiate a suit, pursuant to the authority of *Bivens v. Six Unknown Named Agents of Federal Bureau of Narcotics*, 403 U.S. 388 (1971), solely for money damages....*

While he was a prisoner in the federal penitentiary at Leavenworth, petitioner John J. McCarthy filed a *pro se* complaint in the United States District Court for the District of Kansas against four prison employees: the hospital administrator, the chief psychologist, another psychologist, and a physician. McCarthy alleged that respondents had violated his constitutional rights under the Eighth Amendment by their deliberate indifference to his needs and medical condition resulting from a back operation and a history of psychiatric problems. On the first page of his complaint, he wrote: "This Complaint seeks Money Damages Only."

The District Court dismissed the complaint on the ground that petitioner had failed to exhaust prison administrative remedies. [Under] the general "Administrative Remedy Procedure for Inmates" at federal correctional institutions, a prisoner may "seek formal review of a complaint which relates to any aspect of his imprisonment." ...

To promote efficient dispute resolution, the procedure includes rapid filing and response timetables. An inmate first seeks informal resolution of his claim by consulting prison personnel. If this informal effort fails, the prisoner "may file a formal written complaint on the appropriate form, within 15 calendar days of the date on which the basis of the complaint occurred." Should the warden fail to respond to the inmate's satisfaction within 15 days, the inmate has 20 days to appeal to the Bureau's Regional Director, who has 30 days to respond. If the inmate still remains unsatisfied, he has 30 days to make a final appeal to the Bureau's General Counsel, who has another 30 days to respond. If the inmate can demonstrate a "valid reason for delay," he "shall be allowed" an extension of any of these time periods for filing....

The doctrine of exhaustion of administrative remedies is one among related doctrines—including abstention, finality, and ripeness—that govern the timing of federal court decisionmaking. Of "paramount importance" to any exhaustion inquiry is congressional intent. Where Congress specifically mandates, exhaustion is required. But where Congress has not clearly required exhaustion, sound judicial discretion governs. Nevertheless, even in this field of judicial discretion, appropriate deference to Congress' power to prescribe the basic procedural scheme under

---

* [editors' note] *Bivens* held that a person is entitled to receive money damages for injuries suffered as the result of unconstitutional actions taken by governmental officials under color of their legal authority.

which a claim may be heard in a federal court requires fashioning of exhaustion principles in a manner consistent with congressional intent and any applicable statutory scheme.

This Court long has acknowledged the general rule that parties exhaust prescribed administrative remedies before seeking relief from the federal courts. Exhaustion is required because it serves the twin purposes of protecting administrative agency authority and promoting judicial efficiency.

As to the first of these purposes, the exhaustion doctrine recognizes the notion, grounded in deference to Congress' delegation of authority to coordinate branches of government, that agencies, not the courts, ought to have primary responsibility for the programs that Congress has charged them to administer. Exhaustion concerns apply with particular force when the action under review involves exercise of the agency's discretionary power or when the agency proceedings in question allow the agency to apply its special expertise. The exhaustion doctrine also acknowledges the common sense notion of dispute resolution that an agency ought to have an opportunity to correct its own mistakes with respect to the programs it administers before it is haled into federal court. Correlatively, exhaustion principles apply with special force when "frequent and deliberate flouting of administrative processes" could weaken an agency's effectiveness by encouraging disregard of its procedures.

As to the second of the purposes, exhaustion promotes judicial efficiency in at least two ways. When an agency has the opportunity to correct its own errors, a judicial controversy may well be mooted, or at least piecemeal appeals may be avoided. And even where a controversy survives administrative review, exhaustion of the administrative procedure may produce a useful record for subsequent judicial consideration, especially in a complex or technical factual context.

Notwithstanding these substantial institutional interests, federal courts are vested with a "virtually unflagging obligation" to exercise the jurisdiction given them.... Accordingly, this Court has declined to require exhaustion in some circumstances even where administrative and judicial interests would counsel otherwise. In determining whether exhaustion is required, federal courts must balance the interest of the individual in retaining prompt access to a federal judicial forum against countervailing institutional interests favoring exhaustion. "[A]dministrative remedies need not be pursued if the litigant's interests in immediate judicial review outweigh the government's interests in the efficiency or administrative autonomy that the exhaustion doctrine is designed to further." Application of this balancing principle is "intensely practical," because attention is directed to both the nature of the claim presented and the characteristics of the particular administrative procedure provided.

This Court's precedents have recognized at least three broad sets of circumstances in which the interests of the individual weigh heavily against requiring administrative exhaustion. First, requiring resort to the administrative remedy may occasion undue prejudice to subsequent assertion of a court action. Such prejudice may result, for example, from an unreasonable or indefinite timeframe for administrative action. Even where the administrative decisionmaking schedule is otherwise reasonable and definite, a particular plaintiff may suffer irreparable harm if unable to secure immediate judicial consideration of his claim. By the same token, exhaustion principles apply with less force when an individual's failure to exhaust may preclude a defense to criminal liability.

Second, an administrative remedy may be inadequate "because of some doubt as to whether the agency was empowered to grant effective relief." For example, an agency, as a preliminary matter, may be unable to consider whether to grant relief because it lacks institutional competence to resolve the particular type of issue presented, such as the constitutionality of a statute. In a similar vein, exhaustion has not been required where the challenge is to the adequacy of the agency procedure itself, such that " 'the question of the adequacy of the administrative remedy . . . [is] for all practical purposes identical with the merits of [the plaintiff's] law suit.' "Alternatively, an agency may be competent to adjudicate the issue presented, but still lack authority to grant the type of relief requested.

Third, an administrative remedy may be inadequate where the administrative body is shown to be biased or has otherwise predetermined the issue before it.

In light of these general principles, we conclude that petitioner McCarthy need not have exhausted his constitutional claim for money damages. As a preliminary matter, we find that Congress has not meaningfully addressed the appropriateness of requiring exhaustion in this context. Although respondents' interests are significant, we are left with a firm conviction that, given the type of claim McCarthy raises and the particular characteristics of the Bureau's general grievance procedure, McCarthy's individual interests outweigh countervailing institutional interests favoring exhaustion. . . .

Because Congress has not required exhaustion of a federal prisoner's Bivens claim, we turn to an evaluation of the individual and institutional interests at stake in this case. The general grievance procedure heavily burdens the individual interests of the petitioning inmate in two ways. First, the procedure imposes short, successive filing deadlines that create a high risk of forfeiture of a claim for failure to comply. Second, the administrative "remedy" does not authorize an award of monetary damages—the only relief requested by McCarthy in this action. The combination of these features means that the prisoner seeking only money damages has everything to lose and nothing to gain from being required to exhaust his claim under the internal grievance procedure. . . .

We do not find the interests of the Bureau of Prisons to weigh heavily in favor of exhaustion in view of the remedial scheme and particular claim presented here. To be sure, the Bureau has a substantial interest in encouraging internal resolution of grievances and in preventing the undermining of its authority by unnecessary resort by prisoners to the federal courts. But other institutional concerns relevant to exhaustion analysis appear to weigh in hardly at all. The Bureau's alleged failure to render medical care implicates only tangentially its authority to carry out the control and management of the federal prisons. Furthermore, the Bureau does not bring to bear any special expertise on the type of issue presented for resolution here.

The interests of judicial economy do not stand to be advanced substantially by the general grievance procedure. No formal factfindings are made. The paperwork generated by the grievance process might assist a court somewhat in ascertaining the facts underlying a prisoner's claim more quickly than if it has only a prisoner's complaint to review. But the grievance procedure does not create a formal factual record of the type that can be relied on conclusively by a court for disposition of a prisoner's claim on the pleadings or at summary judgment without the aid of affidavits. . . .

THE CHIEF JUSTICE, with whom JUSTICE SCALIA and JUSTICE THOMAS join, concurring in the judgment.

I agree with the Court's holding that a federal prisoner need not exhaust the procedures promulgated by the Federal Bureau of Prisons. My view, however, is based entirely on the fact that the grievance procedure at issue does not provide for any award of monetary damages. As a result, in cases such as this one where prisoners seek monetary relief, the Bureau's administrative remedy furnishes no effective remedy at all, and it is therefore improper to impose an exhaustion requirement. . . .

DARBY v. CISNEROS

509 U.S. 137, 113 S.Ct. 2539, 125 L.Ed.2d 113 (1993).

JUSTICE BLACKMUN delivered the opinion of the Court.

This case presents the question whether federal courts have the authority to require that a plaintiff exhaust available administrative remedies before seeking judicial review under the Administrative Procedure Act (APA), where neither the statute nor agency rules specifically mandate exhaustion as a prerequisite to judicial review. At issue is the relationship between the judicially created doctrine of exhaustion of administrative remedies and the statutory requirements of [5 U.S.C. § 704].

[The Department of Housing and Urban Development (HUD) is authorized to provide mortgage insurance as a means of facilitating the construction of housing in poor areas. After Darby, who was a real estate developer, obtained such insurance on several occasions, HUD officials decided that he had violated the eligibility regulations for this financing. HUD notified Darby that it proposed to debar him from further participation in all HUD procurement contracts. After Darby sought a hearing, the ALJ imposed an 18 month debarment. Neither Darby nor any HUD official sought further administrative review of the ALJ's "Initial Decision and Order." According to HUD regulations:

> The hearing officer's determination shall be final unless the Secretary or the Secretary's designee, within 30 days of receipt of a request, decides as a matter of discretion to review the finding of the hearing officer. The 30 day period for deciding whether to review a determination may be extended upon written notice of such extension by the Secretary or his designee. Any party may request such a review in writing within 15 days of receipt of the hearing officer's determination.

Darby then filed suit in District Court and sought a declaration that imposition of the penalty was "not in accordance with law" within the meaning of section 706(2)(A) of the APA. The government moved to dismiss the complaint on the ground that Darby had failed to exhaust his administrative remedies. The District Court denied HUD's motion to dismiss but the Court of Appeals reversed.]

Section 704 of the APA bears the caption "Actions reviewable." It provides in its first two sentences that judicial review is available for "final agency action for which there is no other adequate remedy in a court," and that "preliminary, procedural, or intermediate agency action . . . is subject to review on the review of the final agency action." The last sentence of § 704 reads:

> "Except as otherwise expressly required by statute, agency action otherwise final is final for the purposes of this section whether or not there has been presented or determined an application for a declaratory order, for any form of reconsideration, or, unless the agency otherwise requires by rule and provides that the action meanwhile is inoperative, for an appeal to superior agency authority."

[Darby] argue[s] that this provision means that a litigant seeking judicial review of a final agency action under the APA need not exhaust available administrative remedies unless such exhaustion is expressly required by statute or agency rule. According to [Darby], since § 704 contains an explicit exhaustion provision, federal courts are not free to require further exhaustion as a matter of judicial discretion.

[HUD]contend[s] that § 704 is concerned solely with timing, that is, when agency actions become "final," and that Congress had no intention to interfere with the courts' ability to impose conditions on the timing of their exercise of jurisdiction to review final agency actions. . . .

We have recognized that the judicial doctrine of exhaustion of administrative remedies is conceptually distinct from the doctrine of finality:

> "[T]he finality requirement is concerned with whether the initial decisionmaker has arrived at a definitive position on the issue that

inflicts an actual, concrete injury; the exhaustion requirement generally refers to administrative and judicial procedures by which an injured party may seek review of an adverse decision and obtain a remedy if the decision is found to be unlawful or otherwise inappropriate."

Whether courts are free to impose an exhaustion requirement as a matter of judicial discretion depends, at least in part, on whether Congress has provided otherwise, for "of 'paramount importance' to any exhaustion inquiry is congressional intent," *McCarthy v. Madigan*. We therefore must consider whether § 704, by providing the conditions under which agency action becomes "final for the purposes of" judicial review, limits the authority of courts to impose additional exhaustion requirements as a prerequisite to judicial review.

It perhaps is surprising that it has taken over 45 years since the passage of the APA for this Court definitively to address this question. . . .

This Court has had occasion, however, to consider § 704 in other contexts. For example, we [have] recognized . . . that § 704 "has long been construed by this and other courts merely to relieve parties from the *requirement* of petitioning for rehearing before seeking judicial review (unless, of course, specifically required to do so by statute), but not to prevent petitions for reconsideration that are actually filed from rendering the orders under reconsideration nonfinal." . . .

While some dicta in these cases might be claimed to lend support to [Darby's] interpretation of § 704, the text of the APA leaves little doubt that [Darby is] correct. Under § 702 of the APA, "[a] person suffering legal wrong because of agency action, or adversely affected or aggrieved by agency action within the meaning of a relevant statute, is entitled to judicial review thereof." Although § 702 provides the general right to judicial review of agency actions under the APA, § 704 establishes when such review is available. When an aggrieved party has exhausted all administrative remedies expressly prescribed by statute or agency rule, the agency action is "final for the purposes of this section" and therefore "subject to judicial review" under the first sentence. While federal courts may be free to apply, where appropriate, other prudential doctrines of judicial administration to limit the scope and timing of judicial review, § 704, by its very terms, has limited the availability of the doctrine of exhaustion of administrative remedies to that which the statute or rule clearly mandates.

The last sentence of § 704 refers explicitly to "any form of reconsideration" and "an appeal to superior agency authority." Congress clearly was concerned with making the exhaustion requirement unambiguous so that aggrieved parties would know precisely what administrative steps were required before judicial review would be available. If courts were able to impose additional exhaustion requirements beyond those provided by Congress or the agency, the last sentence of § 704 would make no sense. . . . Section 704 explicitly requires exhaustion of all intra-agency appeals mandated either by statute or by agency rule; it would be inconsistent with the plain language of § 704 for courts to require litigants to exhaust optional appeals as well....

We noted just last Term in a non-APA case that

"appropriate deference to Congress' power to prescribe the basic procedural scheme under which a claim may be heard in a federal court requires fashioning of exhaustion principles in a manner consistent with congressional intent and any applicable statutory scheme."

Appropriate deference in this case requires the recognition that, with respect to actions brought under the APA, Congress effectively codified the doctrine of exhaustion of administrative remedies in § 704. Of course, the exhaustion doctrine continues to apply as a matter of judicial discretion in cases not governed by the APA. But where the APA applies, an appeal to "superior agency authority" is a prerequisite to judicial review only when expressly required by statute or when an agency rule requires appeal before review and the administrative action is made inoperative pending that review. Courts are not free to impose an exhaustion requirement as a rule of judicial administration where the agency action has already become "final" under § 704.

Problem 5–7: Exhaustion of Administrative Remedies

Under the Higher Education Act of 1965, a proprietary institution of higher education is eligible to participate in the federal student loan program if the Department of Education finds that the school meets certain conditions specified in the Act. The Department is also authorized to terminate the eligibility of any such school if and when it no longer meets these conditions. For this purpose, the Department's regulations provide:

§ 668.83 Emergency action.

(a) Under an emergency action, the Secretary may—

(1) Withhold ... program funds from a participating institution ... as applicable; ...

(c)(1) An initiating official takes emergency action against an institution ... only if that official—

(i) Receives information, determined by the official to be reliable, that the institution ... is violating any statutory provision [the Act];....

(f)(1) An emergency action does not extend more than 30 days after initiated unless the Secretary initiates a ... termination proceeding ... against the institution ... within that 30–day period, in which case the emergency action continues until a final decision is issued in that proceeding....

§ 668.86   [T]ermination proceedings.

(b) *Procedures.* (1) A designated department official begins a ... termination proceeding by sending an institution ... a notice by certified mail, return receipt requested ...

(2) If the institution ... does not request a hearing but submits written material, the designated department official, after considering that material, notifies the institution ... that—(i) The proposed action is dismissed; ... or

(iii) The termination is effective as of a specified date.

(3) If the institution ... requests a hearing by the time specified in paragraph (b)(1)(iii) of this section, the designated department official sets the date and place.... The termination ... does not take place until after the requested hearing is held.

§ 668.90   Initial and final decisions—Appeals ...

(c)(1) In a ... termination proceeding, the hearing official's initial decision automatically becomes the Secretary's final decision 30 days after the initial decision is issued and received by both parties unless, within that 30–day period, the institution ..., as applicable, or the designated department official appeals the initial decision to the Secretary....

(vi) The initial decision of the hearing official imposing a fine ... or terminating the institution's participation ... does not take effect pending the appeal.

The Department of Education sent a notice to Richard Crane, owner of the Texas City Driving School, that the Department was withholding loan funds from the school under its emergency powers. The Department gave as its reason that a departmental audit found that two other driving schools owned by Crane had engaged in serious financial improprieties. The Department notified Crane fifteen days later that it intended to terminate the school's eligibility to participate in the federal student loan program for the same reason. Crane requested an administrative hearing concerning the termination.

While the termination proceeding is pending, Crane files a law suit in federal district court alleging that the Department lacks legal authority for its emergency action. Crane argues that the Department does not have legal authority to withhold funds from the Texas City school on the basis of activities at the other schools because the other schools are separate legal entities. Crane claimed an APA cause of action on the ground the Department's emergency action forced him to close the Texas City school resulting in the loss of a significant amount of money.

You are the Justice Department lawyer assigned to defend the Department. Do you have an exhaustion defense? Are you likely to prevail on it?

After the hearing officer makes a decision to terminate the Texas City school's eligibility, Crane files another lawsuit challenging that decision. Does the government have an exhaustion defense?

Notes and Questions

1. In *Ticor Title Insurance Co. v. Federal Trade Commission*, 814 F.2d 731 (D.C.Cir.1987), Judge Williams offered the following comparison of the doctrines of finality and exhaustion:

> First, there is a difference in focus. While exhaustion is directed to the steps a litigant must take, finality looks to the conclusion of activity by the agency. And while ripeness depends on the fitness of issues for judicial review, finality in administrative law plays a role closely akin to the doctrine of the same name restricting interlocutory review of trial courts in the federal system. For our immediate purposes, the more critical distinction is that while exhaustion and ripeness are judge-made prudential doctrines, finality is, where applicable, a jurisdictional requirement.
>
> Thus, a finding of finality (or of an applicable exception) is essential when the court's reviewing authority depends on one of the many statutes permitting appeal only of "final" agency action.

814 F.2d at 745–46.

2. In *McCarthy v. Madigan*, the Court balanced "the interest of the individual in retaining prompt access to a federal judicial forum against countervailing institutional interests favoring exhaustion." The Court was influenced to hear McCarthy's claim because the Bureau of Prisons did not have the legal authority to grant McCarthy's remedy—a constitutional claim for monetary damages. *Darby*, however, may be read to require a plaintiff to exhaust any administrative remedy required by statute or regulation even when traditional common-law exceptions might apply, such as the action would be futile because the agency could not grant the remedy that the plaintiff seeks. Of course, *Darby* did not present this issue and the Court has not yet ruled on it. Some lower courts have read *Darby* in this way; others have not, usually without discussing the issue. *Compare Marine Mammal Conservancy, Inc. v. Dept. of Agriculture*, 134 F.3d 409, 411 (D.C.Cir.1998) (suggesting equitable exceptions are not applicable in an APA case) *with Clouser v. Espy*, 42 F.3d 1522 (9th Cir.1994) (*Darby* cited but exceptions considered, with citations to pre-*Darby* cases).

3. Closely related to the doctrine of exhaustion of administrative remedies is the doctrine of "issue exhaustion." This judge-made doctrine requires that, in the absence of exceptional circumstances, courts will not consider arguments not first presented in an administrative proceeding. This doctrine, like the requirement of exhaustion of remedies, ensures that an agency has an opportunity to consider an issue, including all relevant arguments before it acts. A recent Supreme Court decision addressed "issue exhaustion" in Social Security Disability cases.

There, because such administrative procedures, while formal adjudications, are not adversary in nature, often the person challenging the denial of benefits is unrepresented by counsel, and because the agency's regulations suggested that issue exhaustion was not required, a split Court held that no issue exhaustion was required. *See Sims v. Apfel*, 530 U.S. 103, 120 S.Ct. 2080, 147 L.Ed.2d 80 (2000). Nevertheless, a majority of the justices made clear that "issue exhaustion" was normally required and that a simple change in the agency regulations would enable Social Security to require it as well. In addition to the prudential, judge-made doctrine, there are statutes that prohibit courts from considering arguments not raised before an agency. *E.g.*, 29 U.S.C.A. § 160(e) ("No objection that has not been urged before the [National Labor Relations] Board, its member, agent, or agency, shall be considered by the court unless the failure or neglect to urge such objections shall be excused because of extraordinary circumstances.").

4. Whether "issue exhaustion" or even exhaustion of administrative remedies applies to informal rulemaking is an unsettled question, although probably the right answer is that it should not. As the Court suggested in *Sims v. Apfel*, one of the underlying reasons for the judge-made exhaustion rules is the similarity between administrative adjudication and judicial litigation. Where they are similar, exhaustion should apply. Informal rulemaking, however, is *not* like adjudication or litigation. Most notably informal rulemaking does not have "parties." Some statutes specifically require some form of issue exhaustion with respect to particular types of rulemakings. *See, e.g.*, 47 U.S.C. § 405 (requiring a petition for reconsideration of a communications rule as a prerequisite for judicial review, unless the issue was already considered by the Commission). Some courts have cited to cases arising under this provision in circumstances in which there is no statutory requirement for exhaustion. *See, e.g., National Ass'n of Manufacturers v. Department of the Interior*, 134 F.3d 1095 (D.C.Cir.1998). Other courts, however, have totally rejected the notion of an exhaustion requirement with respect to informal rulemaking. *See, e.g., American Forest and Paper Ass'n v. U.S. E.P.A.*, 137 F.3d 291 (5th Cir.1998). It is also unclear whether there is an exhaustion requirement with respect to informal adjudications that look more like rulemaking than an adjudication, such as environmental impact statements incident to informal adjudications. Because these proceedings have many of the characteristics of rulemakings and involve commenters who are not "parties" to the adjudication, it can be argued that they should be treated like rulemakings, so that a commenter might not be foreclosed from arguing a point in judicial review of the agency action that it had not raised in its comments on the EIS. Of course, without regard to exhaustion issues, a commenter would be well advised to provide all the information and arguments it would like to raise later, because any judicial review will likely be limited to the record compiled in the proceeding, and the agency's failure to consider an argument or information not in the record is less likely to be adjudged arbitrary and capricious.

5.   In the states, exhaustion requirements may stem from statute or from judge-made law. The 1961 Model State APA, which many states have followed, contains an explicit statement that "a person who has exhausted all administrative remedies available within the agency ... is entitled to judicial review." Section 15(a). Generally, state law reflects the principles behind the exhaustion requirement and its common law exceptions described in *Madigan. See generally Project: State Judicial Review of Administrative Action*, 43 ADMIN. L. REV. 571, 661–679 (1991). One notable difference in some states is the allowance that agencies may consider arguments in adjudications that their statutory mandates are unconstitutional and that their regulations are unlawful. If so convinced, the agency refuses to enforce the provisions. The effect of this on exhaustion claims is to eliminate the exception for constitutional issues or futility. *See, e.g., Llewellyn v. Board of Chiropractic Examiners*, 318 Or. 120, 127, 863 P.2d 469 (1993).

6.   In *Darby*, Darby ignored the administrative review procedure available, and because that review procedure did not meet the requirements of Section 704, it did not require Darby to exhaust that procedure before going to court. What if Darby had utilized HUD's review procedure, but after the Secretary decided to review the hearing officer's decision and before the Secretary's decision, Darby had second thoughts and sued in federal court under the APA? Would he still be excused from exhausting the review procedure? In both *Darby* and in a later case, *Stone v. INS*, 514 U.S. 386, 392, 115 S.Ct. 1537, 131 L.Ed.2d 465 (1995), the Court in dicta answered in the negative—once a person has invoked existing administrative procedures, the agency decision becomes unfinal, even if it would have been final if the person had not invoked the procedures. The lower court cases uniformly follow the Court's dicta.

3.   RIPENESS

The ripeness doctrine, like finality and exhaustion, relates to the proper time for a court to review agency action. The original and still the leading case on ripeness is *Abbott Labs*, reproduced below, the portion of which dealing with reviewability generally we read earlier. It deals with an attempt to obtain "pre-enforcement" judicial review; that is, review of an agency action before the agency tries to enforce that action against the person in court.

After the *Abbott Labs* selection is the Court's most recent case dealing with ripeness, *Ohio Forestry*. Here the doctrine is used to deny an environmental group the ability to obtain judicial review of a forest plan before it is put into effect.

ABBOTT LABORATORIES v. GARDNER
387 U.S. 136, 87 S.Ct. 1507, 18 L.Ed.2d 681 (1967).

MR. JUSTICE HARLAN delivered the opinion of the Court.

[The facts and the decision as to whether the statute precluded review are printed earlier.]

A further inquiry must, however, be made. The injunctive and declaratory judgment remedies are discretionary, and courts traditionally have been reluctant to apply them to administrative determinations unless these arise in the context of a controversy 'ripe' for judicial resolution. Without undertaking to survey the intricacies of the ripeness doctrine it is fair to say that its basic rationale is to prevent the courts, through avoidance of premature adjudication, from entangling themselves in abstract disagreements over administrative policies, and also to protect the agencies from judicial interference until an administrative decision has been formalized and its effects felt in a concrete way by the challenging parties. The problem is best seen in a twofold aspect, requiring us to evaluate both the fitness of the issues for judicial decision and the hardship to the parties of withholding court consideration.

As to the former factor, we believe the issues presented are appropriate for judicial resolution at this time. First, all parties agree that the issue tendered is a purely legal one: whether the statute was properly construed by the Commissioner to require the established name of the drug to be used every time the proprietary name is employed. Both sides moved for summary judgment in the District Court, and no claim is made here that further administrative proceedings are contemplated. It is suggested that the justification for this rule might vary with different circumstances, and that the expertise of the Commissioner is relevant to passing upon the validity of the regulation. This of course is true, but the suggestion overlooks the fact that both sides have approached this case as one purely of congressional intent, and that the Government made no effort to justify the regulation in factual terms.

Second, the regulations in issue we find to be "final agency action" within the meaning of 5 U.S.C.A. § 704, as construed in judicial decisions.... The cases dealing with judicial review of administrative actions have interpreted the "finality" element in a pragmatic way. Thus in *Columbia Broadcasting System v. United States*, 316 U.S. 407, ... this Court held reviewable a regulation of the Federal Communications Commission setting forth certain proscribed contractual arrangements between chain broadcasters and local stations. The FCC did not have direct authority to regulate these contracts, and its rule asserted only that it would not license stations which maintained such contracts with the networks. Although no license had in fact been denied or revoked, and the FCC regulation could properly be characterized as a statement only of its intentions, the Court held that "such regulations have the force of law before their sanctions are invoked as well as after. When as here they are promulgated by order of the Commission and the expected conformity to them causes injury cognizable by a court of equity, they are appropriately the subject of attack." ...

We find decision in the present case following *a fortiori* from these precedents. The regulation challenged here, promulgated in a formal manner after announcement in the Federal Register and consideration of comments by interested parties is quite clearly definitive. There is no hint that this regulation is informal, or only the ruling of a subordinate official, or tentative. It was made effective upon publication, and the Assistant General Counsel for Food and Drugs stated in the District Court that compliance was expected.

The Government argues, however, that the present case can be distinguished from [other] cases ... on the ground that in those instances the agency involved could implement its policy directly, while here the Attorney General must authorize criminal and seizure actions for violations of the statute. In the context of this case, we do not find this argument persuasive. These regulations are not meant to advise the Attorney General, but purport to be directly authorized by the statute. Thus, if within the Commissioner's authority, they have the status of law and violations of them carry heavy criminal and civil sanctions. . . .

This is also a case in which the impact of the regulations upon the petitioners is sufficiently direct and immediate as to render the issue appropriate for judicial review at this stage. These regulations purport to give an authoritative interpretation of a statutory provision that has a direct effect on the day-to-day business of all prescription drug companies; its promulgation puts petitioners in a dilemma that it was the very purpose of the Declaratory Judgment Act to ameliorate. As the District Court found on the basis of uncontested allegations, "Either they must comply with the every time requirement and incur the costs of changing over their promotional material and labeling or they must follow their present course and risk prosecution." ... If petitioners wish to comply they must change all their labels, advertisements, and promotional materials; they must destroy stocks of printed matter; and they must invest heavily in new printing type and new supplies. The alternative to compliance—continued use of material which they believe in good faith meets the statutory requirements, but which clearly does not meet the regulation of the Commissioner—may be even more costly. That course would risk serious criminal and civil penalties for the unlawful distribution of "misbranded" drugs.

It is relevant at this juncture to recognize that petitioners deal in a sensitive industry, in which public confidence in their drug products is especially important. To require them to challenge these regulations only as a defense to an action brought by the Government might harm them severely and unnecessarily. Where the legal issue presented is fit for judicial resolution, and where a regulation requires an immediate and significant change in the plaintiffs' conduct of their affairs with serious penalties attached to noncompliance, access to the courts under the Administrative Procedure Act and the Declaratory Judgment Act must be permitted, absent a statutory bar or some other unusual circumstance, neither of which appears here. . . .

The Government further contends that the threat of criminal sanctions for noncompliance with a judicially untested regulation is unrealistic; the Solicitor General has represented that if court enforcement becomes necessary, "the Department of Justice will proceed only civilly for an injunction ... or by condemnation." We cannot accept this argument as a sufficient answer to petitioners' petition. This action at its inception was properly brought and this subsequent representation of the Department of Justice should not suffice to defeat it.

Finally, the Government urges that to permit resort to the courts in this type of case may delay or impede effective enforcement of the Act. We fully recognize the important public interest served by assuring prompt and unimpeded administration of the Pure Food, Drug, and Cosmetic Act, but we do not find the Government's argument convincing. First, in this particular case, a pre-enforcement challenge by nearly all prescription drug manufacturers is calculated to speed enforcement. If the Government prevails, a large part of the industry is bound by the decree; if the Government loses, it can more quickly revise its regulation. . . .

In addition to all these safeguards against what the Government fears, it is important to note that the institution of this type of action does not by itself stay the effectiveness of the challenged regulation. There is nothing in the record to indicate that petitioners have sought to stay enforcement of the "every time" regulation pending judicial review. See 5 U.S.C. § 705. If the agency believes that a suit of this type will significantly impede enforcement or will harm the public interest, it need not postpone enforcement of the regulation and may oppose any motion for a judicial stay on the part of those challenging the regulation. It is scarcely to be doubted that a court would refuse to postpone the effective date of an agency action if the Government could show, as it made no effort to do here, that delay would be detrimental to the public health or safety. . . .

MR. JUSTICE FORTAS, with whom THE CHIEF JUSTICE and MR. JUSTICE CLARK join . . . dissenting. . . .

The Court, by today's decisions, has opened Pandora's box. Federal injunctions will now threaten programs of vast importance to the public welfare. The Court's holding here strikes at programs for the public health. The dangerous precedent goes even further. It is cold comfort—it is little more than delusion—to read in the Court's opinion that "It is scarcely to be doubted that a court would refuse to postpone the effective date of an agency action if the Government could show . . . that delay would be detrimental to the public health or safety." Experience dictates, on the contrary, that it can hardly be hoped that some federal judge somewhere will not be moved as the Court is here, by the cries of anguish and distress of those regulated, to grant a disruptive injunction.

The difference between the majority and me . . . is not with respect to the existence of jurisdiction to enjoin, but to the definition of occasions on which such jurisdiction may be invoked. . . .

. . . . Where Congress has provided a method of review, the requisite showing to induce the courts otherwise to bring a governmental program to a halt may not be made by a mere showing of the impact of the regulation and the customary hardships of interim compliance. At least in cases where the claim is of erroneous action rather than the lack of jurisdiction or denial of procedural due process, a suit for injunctive or declaratory relief will not lie absent a clear demonstration that the type of review available under the statute would not be "adequate," that the controversies are otherwise "ripe" for judicial decision, and that no public interest exists which offsets the private values which the litigation seeks to vindicate . . . .

In evaluating the destructive force and effect of the Court's action in these cases, it is necessary to realize that it is arming each of the federal district judges in this Nation with power to enjoin enforcement of regulations and actions under the federal law designed to protect the people of this Nation against dangerous drugs and cosmetics. Restraining orders and temporary injunctions will suspend application of these public safety laws pending years of litigation—a time schedule which these cases illustrate.[10]

The Court, however, moved by petitioners' claims as to the expense and inconvenience of compliance and the risks of deferring challenge by noncompliance, decrees that the manufacturers may have their suit for injunction at this time. The Court says that this confronts the manufacturer with a "real dilemma." But the fact of the matter is that the dilemma is no more than citizens face in connection with countless statutes and with the rules of the SEC, FTC, FCC, ICC, and other regulatory agencies. This has not heretofore been regarded as a basis for injunctive relief unless Congress has so provided. The overriding fact here is—or should be—that the public interest in avoiding the delay in implementing Congress' program far outweighs the private interest; and that the private interest which has so impressed the Court is no more than that which exists in respect of most regulatory statutes or agency rules. Somehow, the Court has concluded that the damage to petitioners if they have to engage in the required redesign and reprint of their labels and printed materials without threshold review outweighs the damage to the public of deferring during the tedious months and years of litigation a cure for the possible danger and asserted deceit of peddling plain medicine under fancy trademarks and for fancy prices which, rightly or wrongly, impelled the Congress to enact this legislation. I submit that a much stronger showing is necessary than the expense and trouble of compliance and the risk of defiance. Actually, if the Court refused to permit this shotgun assault, experience and reasonably sophisticated common sense show that there would be orderly compliance without the disaster so dramatically predicted by the industry, reasonable adjustments by the agency in real hardship cases, and where extreme intransigence involving substantial violations occurred, enforcement actions in which legality of the regulation would be tested in specific, concrete situations. I respectfully submit that this would be the correct and appropriate result . . . .

10. The 'every time' regulation was published about four years ago, on June 20, 1963, 28 Fed. Reg. 6375. As a result of litigation begun in September of 1963, it has not yet been put into force.

OHIO FORESTRY ASSOCIATION, INC. v. SIERRA CLUB

523 U.S. 726, 118 S.Ct. 1665, 140 L.Ed.2d 921 (1998).

JUSTICE BREYER delivered the opinion of the Court.

The Sierra Club challenges the lawfulness of a federal land and resource management plan adopted by the United States Forest Service for Ohio's Wayne National Forest on the ground that the plan permits too much logging and too much clearcutting. We conclude that the controversy is not yet ripe for judicial review.

The National Forest Management Act of 1976 (NFMA) requires the Secretary of Agriculture to "develop, maintain, and, as appropriate, revise land and resource management plans for units of the National Forest System." . . . . The National Forest Service, which manages the System, develops land and resource management plans pursuant to NFMA, and uses these forest plans to "guide all natural resource management activities," including use of the land for "outdoor recreation, range, timber, watershed, wildlife and fish, and wilderness." In developing the plans, the Service must take both environmental and commercial goals into account.

This case focuses upon a plan that the Forest Service has developed for the Wayne National Forest located in southern Ohio. When the Service wrote the plan, the forest consisted of 178,000 federally owned acres (278 sq. mi.) in three forest units that are interspersed among privately owned lands, some of which the Forest Service plans to acquire over time. The Plan permits logging to take place on 126,000 (197 sq. mi.) of the federally owned acres. At the same time, it sets a ceiling on the total amount of wood that can be cut—a ceiling that amounts to about 75 million board feet over 10 years, and which, the Plan projects, would lead to logging on about 8,000 acres (12.5 sq. mi.) during that decade. According to the Plan, logging on about 5,000 (7.8 sq. mi.) of those 8,000 acres would involve clearcutting, or other forms of what the Forest Service calls "even-aged" tree harvesting.

Although the Plan sets logging goals, selects the areas of the forest that are suited to timber production, and determines which "probable methods of timber harvest," are appropriate, it does not itself authorize the cutting of any trees. Before the Forest Service can permit the logging, it must: (a) propose a specific area in which logging will take place and the harvesting methods to be used; (b) ensure that the project is consistent with the Plan; (c) provide those affected by proposed logging notice and an opportunity to be heard; (d) conduct an environmental analysis pursuant to the National Environmental Policy Act of 1969 (NEPA) to evaluate the effects of the specific project and to contemplate alternatives; and (e) subsequently take a final decision to permit logging, which decision affected persons may challenge in an administrative appeals process and in court. Furthermore, the statute requires the Forest Service to "revise" the Plan "as appropriate". Despite the considerable legal distance between the adoption of the Plan and the moment when a tree is cut, the Plan's promulgation nonetheless makes logging more likely in that it is a logging precondition; in its absence logging could not take place.

When the Forest Service first proposed its Plan, the Sierra Club and the Citizens Council on Conservation and Environmental Control each objected. In an effort to bring about the Plan's modification, they (collectively Sierra Club), pursued various administrative remedies. The Sierra Club then brought this lawsuit in federal court, initially against the Chief of the Forest Service, the Secretary of Agriculture, the Regional Forester, and the Forest Supervisor. The Ohio Forestry Association, some of whose members harvest timber from the Wayne National Forest or process wood products obtained from the forest, later intervened as a defendant.

The Sierra Club's Second Amended Complaint sets forth its legal claims. That Complaint initially states facts that describe the Plan in detail and allege that erroneous analysis leads the Plan wrongly to favor logging and clearcutting. The Complaint then sets forth three claims for relief:

The first claim for relief says that the "defendants in approving the plan for the Wayne [National Forest] and in directing or permitting below-cost timber sales accomplished by means of clearcutting" violated various laws including the National Forestry Management Act, the National Environmental Policy Act, and the Administrative Procedure Act.

The second claim says that the "defendants' actions in directing or permitting below-cost timber sales in the Wayne [National Forest] under the plan violate [their] duties as public trustees."

The third claim says that, in selecting the amount of the forest suitable for timber production, the defendants followed regulations that failed properly to identify "economically unsuitable lands." It adds that, because the Forest Service's regulations thereby permitted the Service to place "economically unsuitable lands" in the category of land where logging could take place, the regulations violated their authorizing statute and were "arbitrary, capricious, an abuse of discretion, and not in accordance with law," pursuant to the Administrative Procedure Act.

The Complaint finally requests as relief: (a) a declaration that the plan "is unlawful as are the below-cost timber sales and timbering, including clearcutting, authorized by the plan," (b) an "injunction prohibiting the defendants from permitting or directing further timber harvest and/or below-cost timber sales" pending plan revision, (c) costs and attorneys fees, and (d) "such other further relief as may be appropriate." . . .

Petitioner alleges that this suit is nonjusticiable both because the Sierra Club lacks standing to bring this case and because the issues

before us—over the Plan's specifications for logging and clearcutting—
are not yet ripe for adjudication. We find that the dispute is not
justiciable, because it is not ripe for court review.

As this Court has previously pointed out, the ripeness requirement
is designed "to prevent the courts, through avoidance of premature
adjudication, from entangling themselves in abstract disagreements over
administrative policies, and also to protect the agencies from judicial
interference until an administrative decision has been formalized and its
effects felt in a concrete way by the challenging parties." *Abbott Laboratories v. Gardner.*

In deciding whether an agency's decision is, or is not, ripe for
judicial review, the Court has examined both the "fitness of the issues
for judicial decision" and the "hardship to the parties of withholding
court consideration." To do so in this case, we must consider: (1)
whether delayed review would cause hardship to the plaintiffs; (2)
whether judicial intervention would inappropriately interfere with further administrative action; and (3) whether the courts would benefit
from further factual development of the issues presented. These considerations, taken together, foreclose review in the present case.

First, to "withhol[d] court consideration" at present will not cause
the parties significant "hardship" as this Court has come to use that
term. For one thing, the provisions of the Plan that the Sierra Club
challenges do not create adverse effects of a strictly legal kind, that is,
effects of a sort that traditionally would have qualified as harm. [T]hey
do not command anyone to do anything or to refrain from doing
anything; they do not grant, withhold, or modify any formal legal license,
power or authority; they do not subject anyone to any civil or criminal
liability; they create no legal rights or obligations. Thus, for example, the
Plan does not give anyone a legal right to cut trees, nor does it abolish
anyone's legal authority to object to trees' being cut.

Nor have we found that the Plan now inflicts significant practical
harm upon the interests that the Sierra Club advances—an important
consideration in light of this Court's modern ripeness cases. As we have
pointed out, before the Forest Service can permit logging, it must focus
upon a particular site, propose a specific harvesting method, prepare an
environmental review, permit the public an opportunity to be heard, and
(if challenged) justify the proposal in court. The Sierra Club thus will
have ample opportunity later to bring its legal challenge at a time when
harm is more imminent and more certain. Any such later challenge
might also include a challenge to the lawfulness of the present Plan if
(but only if) the present Plan then matters, i.e., if the Plan plays a causal
role with respect to the future, then-imminent, harm from logging.
Hence we do not find a strong reason why the Sierra Club must bring its
challenge now in order to get relief.

Nor has the Sierra Club pointed to any other way in which the Plan
could now force it to modify its behavior in order to avoid future adverse
consequences, as, for example, agency regulations can sometimes force

immediate compliance through fear of future sanctions. Cf. *Abbott Laboratories*.

The Sierra Club does say that it will be easier, and certainly cheaper, to mount one legal challenge against the Plan now, than to pursue many challenges to each site-specific logging decision to which the Plan might eventually lead. It does not explain, however, why one initial site-specific victory (if based on the Plan's unlawfulness) could not, through preclusion principles, effectively carry the day. And, in any event, the Court has not considered this kind of litigation cost-saving sufficient by itself to justify review in a case that would otherwise be unripe. The ripeness doctrine reflects a judgment that the disadvantages of a premature review that may prove too abstract or unnecessary ordinarily outweigh the additional costs of—even repetitive—post-implementation litigation.

Second, from the agency's perspective, immediate judicial review directed at the lawfulness of logging and clearcutting could hinder agency efforts to refine its policies: (a) through revision of the Plan, e.g., in response to an appropriate proposed site-specific action that is inconsistent with the Plan or (b) through application of the Plan in practice, e.g., in the form of site-specific proposals, which proposals are subject to review by a court applying purely legal criteria. Hearing the Sierra Club's challenge now could thus interfere with the system that Congress specified for the agency to reach forest logging decisions.

Third, from the courts' perspective, review of the Sierra Club's claims regarding logging and clearcutting now would require time-consuming judicial consideration of the details of an elaborate, technically based plan, which predicts consequences that may affect many different parcels of land in a variety of ways, and which effects themselves may change over time. That review would have to take place without benefit of the focus that a particular logging proposal could provide. Thus, for example, the court below in evaluating the Sierra Club's claims had to focus upon whether the Plan as a whole was "improperly skewed," rather than focus upon whether the decision to allow clearcutting on a particular site was improper, say, because the site was better suited to another use or logging there would cumulatively result in too many trees' being cut. And, of course, depending upon the agency's future actions to revise the Plan or modify the expected methods of implementation, review now may turn out to have been unnecessary.

This type of review threatens the kind of "abstract disagreements over administrative policies," *Abbott Laboratories*, that the ripeness doctrine seeks to avoid. In this case, for example, the Court of Appeals panel disagreed about whether or not the Forest Service suffered from a kind of general "bias" in favor of timber production and clear-cutting. Review where the consequences had been "reduced to more manageable proportions," and where the "factual components [were] fleshed out, by some concrete action" might have led the panel majority either to demonstrate that bias and its consequences through record citation (which it did not do) or to abandon the claim. All this is to say that further factual development would "significantly advance our ability to deal with the legal issues presented" and would "aid us in their resolution."

Finally, Congress has not provided for pre-implementation judicial review of forest plans. Those plans are tools for agency planning and management. The Plan is consequently unlike agency rules that Congress has specifically instructed the courts to review "pre-enforcement." Cf. 15 U.S.C. § 2618 (Toxic Substances Control Act) (providing pre-enforcement review of agency action); 30 U.S.C. § 1276(a) (Surface Mining Control and Reclamation Act of 1977) (same); 42 U.S.C. § 6976 (Resource Conservation and Recovery Act of 1976) (same); § 7607(b) (Clean Air Act) (same); 43 U.S.C. § 1349(c)(3) (Outer Continental Shelf Lands Act). Nor does the Plan, which through standards guides future use of forests, resemble an environmental impact statement prepared pursuant to NEPA. That is because in this respect NEPA, unlike the NFMA, simply guarantees a particular procedure, not a particular result. Compare, 16 U.S.C. § 1604(e) (requiring that forest plans provide for multiple coordinated use of forests, including timber and wilderness) with 42 U.S.C. § 4332 (requiring that agencies prepare environmental impact statements where major agency action would significantly affect the environment). Hence a person with standing who is injured by a failure to comply with the NEPA procedure may complain of that failure at the time the failure takes place, for the claim can never get riper.

The Sierra Club makes one further important contrary argument. It says that the Plan will hurt it in many ways that we have not yet mentioned. Specifically, the Sierra Club says that the Plan will permit "many intrusive activities, such as opening trails to motorcycles or using heavy machinery," which activities "will go forward without any additional consideration of their impact on wilderness recreation." At the same time, in areas designated for logging, "affirmative measures to promote undisturbed backcountry recreation, such as closing roads and building additional hiking trails" will not take place. These are harms, says the Sierra Club, that will not take place at a distant future time. Rather, they will take place now.

This argument suffers from the legally fatal problem that it makes its first appearance here in this Court in the briefs on the merits. The Complaint, fairly read, does not include such claims. Instead, it focuses on the amount and method of timber harvesting. The Sierra Club has not referred us to any other court documents in which it protests the Plan's approval of motorcycles or machinery, the Plan's failure to close roads or to provide for the building of trails, or other disruptions that the Plan might cause those who use the forest for hiking. As far as we can tell, prior to the argument on the merits here, the harm to which the Sierra Club objected consisted of too much, and the wrong kind of, logging.

The matter is significant because the Government concedes that if the Sierra Club had previously raised these other kinds of harm, the ripeness analysis in this case with respect to those provisions of the Plan that produce the harm would be significantly different. . . .

And, at oral argument, the Solicitor General agreed that if the Sierra Club's claim was "that [the] plan was allowing motorcycles into a bird-watching area or something that like, that would be immediately justiciable." Thus, we believe these other claims that the Sierra Club now raises are not fairly presented here, and we cannot consider them. . . .

Problem 5–8: Ripeness and Regulatory Beneficiaries

Imagine that the FDA had not adopted the "every time" rule in *Abbott Labs*, but rather had adopted a rule requiring that the generic name merely appear somewhere on the label or advertising. If a consumers' organization then brought suit to challenge the FDA's rule on the grounds that it was contrary to the statute, and the government asked the Court to dismiss the case as not ripe, how should the Court rule? What would Justice Fortas say?

Problem 5–9: Ripeness and Regulated Entities

The Clean Water Act authorizes EPA to proceed against persons who fail to seek a permit before filling in wetlands in several ways. One option is for EPA to seek an injunction in federal district court to prohibit the filling of such wetlands until a permit is obtained. Another option is for EPA to issue an "administrative compliance order" which orders the person to comply with the permit requirement. Any person who violates a compliance order is subject to fines of up to $25,000 per day for each violation assessed by a court.

After a developer begins a construction project, the company is informed by the Corps of Engineers that the land under development is "wetland" and that the company cannot fill it without a permit. After the developer disputes that the land is a "wetland," EPA issues a compliance order—ordering the company not to fill the wetland without a permit. The developer then sues under the APA to obtain review of the compliance order. It asks the court to declare that the land is not a wetland.

What arguments can EPA make that the court should dismiss the case?

Problem 5–10: Ripeness and the FOIA

The Freedom of Information Act provides generally that persons who request documents from the government for "commercial use" must pay the costs of searching for the documents, reviewing the documents to determine if they are exempt from disclosure, and copying the documents. If the request is not for "commercial use," and the requester is an educational or noncommercial scientific institution, whose purpose is scholarly or scientific research, or a representative of the news media, only duplication costs may be charged. In addition, no fee is to be charged if the disclosure is in the public interest because it is likely to contribute significantly to public understanding of the operations of government and is not primarily in the commercial interest of the requester.

The Department of Transportation, after notice and comment, adopts a regulation interpreting the terms "commercial use" and "commercial interest" in the Act to include the use of information by nonprofit organizations to further those organizations' purposes. The theory is that such organizations, in order to survive economically, must provide certain services attractive to customers, donors, or grantors. When they provide those services, the theory goes on, they are acting like any other commercial organization attempting to provide a product that will attract money in the marketplace. The cost of doing business by such groups is increased significantly by the change in the regulations because the groups have to reimburse the agency for the cost of finding, reviewing, and copying the documents, rather than just copying costs. A suit is brought jointly by the Motor Vehicle Manufacturers Association and the Public Interest Research Group challenging the validity of this regulation under the FOIA.

As a Justice Department attorney, what arguments do you make to attempt to get the court to dismiss the suit? How do you assess your chances of winning?

Notes and Questions

1. The same day that *Abbott Laboratories* was decided, *Toilet Goods Association v. Gardner*, 387 U.S. 158, 87 S.Ct. 1520, 18 L.Ed.2d 697 (1967), refused to review another FDA regulation because it was not ripe for review. The regulation provided that the Commissioner "may immediately suspend" FDA's approval to market a product containing a color additive if the manufacturer refused to admit FDA inspectors "free access to all manufacturing facilities, processes, and formulae" involved in the process of producing the product. The Toilet Goods Association, which represented cosmetic manufacturers, sought pre-enforcement review of the regulation on the ground that FDA lacked the legal authority to promulgate the rule.

The Court applied the two part test announced in *Abbott Laboratories*. Although the issue raised by the Association was a "purely legal question," the Court decided that it was not "appropriate for judicial resolution." The problem, according to the Court, was the permissive nature of the regulation:

> The regulation serves notice only that the Commissioner may under certain circumstances order inspection of certain facilities and data,

and that further certification of additives may be refused to those who decline to permit a duly authorized inspection until they have complied in that regard. At this juncture we have no idea whether or when such an inspection will be ordered and what reasons the Commissioner will give to justify his order. The statutory authority asserted for the regulation is the power to promulgate regulations "for the efficient enforcement" of the Act. Whether the regulation is justified thus depends not only, as petitioners appear to suggest, on whether Congress refused to include a specific section of the Act authorizing such inspections, although this factor is to be sure a highly relevant one, but also on whether the statutory scheme as a whole justified promulgation of the regulation. This will depend not merely on an inquiry into statutory purpose, but concurrently on an understanding of what types of enforcement problems are encountered by the FDA, the need for various sorts of supervision in order to effectuate the goals of the Act, and the safeguards devised to protect legitimate trade secrets. We believe that judicial appraisal of these factors is likely to stand on a much surer footing in the context of a specific application of this regulation than could be the case in the framework of the generalized challenge made here.

Further, the case was not analogous to *Abbott Laboratories*, "where the impact of the administrative action could be said to be felt immediately by those subject to it in conducting their day-to-day affairs." As the Court explained, "This is not a situation in which primary conduct is affected—when contracts must be negotiated, ingredients tested or substituted, or special records compiled...." Moreover, unlike the rule in *Abbott Laboratories*, "in which seizure of goods, heavy fines, adverse publicity for distributing 'adulterated' goods, and possible criminal liability might penalize failure to comply," the plaintiffs were not subject to significant penalties if they did not obey the regulation. Instead, a company's refusal to admit an inspector "would at most lead only to a suspension of [approval to manufacture a product], a determination that can then be promptly challenged through an administrative procedure, which in turn is reviewable by a court." The Court elaborated, "We recognize that a denial of certification might under certain circumstances cause inconvenience and possibly hardship.... In the context of the present case we need only say that such inconvenience is speculative and we have been provided with no information that would support an assumption that much weight should be attached to this possibility."

2. In *Ticor Title*, which was discussed in prior notes, Judge Edwards offered the following comparison of the ripeness and exhaustion doctrine:

> If the agency proceeding is still at an early stage and the party seeking review has the right to an administrative hearing or review, the court will decline to hear his appeal on the ground that he has failed to exhaust his administrative remedies. Judicial intervention may not be necessary because the agency can correct any initial errors at subsequent stages of the process; moreover, the agency's

position on important issues of fact and law may not be fully crystallized or adopted in final form....

The ripeness doctrine looks to similar factors in determining the availability of review—that is, the fitness of the issues for judicial determination and the hardship to the parties that would result from granting or denying review—but it has a different focus and a different basis from exhaustion. The exhaustion doctrine emphasizes the position of the party seeking review; in essence, it asks whether he may be attempting to short circuit the administrative process or whether he has been reasonably diligent in protecting his own interests. Ripeness, by contrast, is concerned primarily with the institutional relationships between courts and agencies, and the competence of the courts to resolve disputes without further administrative refinement of the issues. In extreme cases, the ripeness doctrine serves to implement the policy behind Article III of the Constitution. Since the judicial power is limited to cases and controversies, federal courts cannot decide purely abstract or theoretical claims, or render advisory opinions....

814 F.2d at 735 *quoting from* ERNEST GELLHORN & BARRY BOYER, ADMINISTRATIVE LAW & PROCESS 316–19 (1981).

3. In *Thunder Basin Coal Co. v. Reich*, 510 U.S. 200, 114 S.Ct. 771, 127 L.Ed.2d 29 (1994), the Court dealt with a suit for pre-enforcement injunctive relief. Rather than decide the case on ripeness grounds, the Court held the statute governing mine inspections precluded *pre-enforcement* review. That is, the Court used statutory preclusion, not of all review, but of pre-enforcement review to deny the request for pre-enforcement injunctive relief. In deciding that the statute precluded pre-enforcement review, the Court considered the hardship to the petitioner in denying pre-enforcement review and found it not "serious." In short, the analysis focused on the terms of the statute to deny pre-enforcement review, rather than judge-made ripeness doctrine, but it weighed the hardship to the petitioner to help it decide the meaning of the statute. Is this ripeness doctrine in a different suit of clothes?

4. In *Abbott Labs* the Court was unclear whether the "presumption of review" it announced included a presumption of pre-enforcement review. *Toilet Goods* did not directly answer that question, but its denial of pre-enforcement review suggested no presumption of pre-enforcement review. Later cases have reinforced that suggestion. For example, in *Shalala v. Illinois Council on Long Term Care*, 529 U.S. 1, 120 S.Ct. 1084, 146 L.Ed.2d 1 (2000), the Court in dictum referred to pre-enforcement review being an exception that only applies when there is a legal question fit for resolution and there is hardship in denying review. Three justices, led by Justice Thomas, however, stated their view that there is a presumption of judicial review of final agency action, even if it is pre-enforcement review. Justice Scalia was not willing to call it a presumption, but rather a background principle. On the other hand, in *Thunder Basin Coal Co. v. Reich*, in which the Court denied pre-

enforcement review on statutory preclusion grounds, Justice Scalia wrote a concurrence, which Justice Thomas joined, where he referred to pre-enforcement challenges being "the exception," not the rule. Are they confused too?

5.   The issue of ripeness (or finality) often arises in the context of nonlegislative rules. A famous old case, *National Automatic Laundry and Cleaning Council v. Shultz*, 443 F.2d 689 (D.C.Cir.1971), undertook review of a letter from the Administrator of the Wage and Hour Division, an agency in the Department of Labor, to the National Automatic Laundry and Cleaning Council, a national trade association for the coin-operated laundry and dry-cleaning industry. The trade association had requested the Administrator's opinion whether recent legislation had made such laundries subject to the minimum wage and overtime laws. The Administrator replied that the new law did indeed subject the laundries to those laws.

The court proceeded in three steps. It found first that the issue was fit for judicial resolution because it was a purely legal one—whether the new law applied to the industry. It then concluded that the laundries faced the same type of hardship if the court deferred review as did the plaintiffs in *Abbott Laboratories*: "If the Administrator is correct in his interpretation of the 1966 law, the owners of coin-operated laundries who are paying their employees at rates which are in violation of the Act are subject not only to injunctive enforcement proceedings under the Act; and in extreme cases to criminal liability; but also to actions for double damages, [t]he dilemma was that of businessmen required either to change business practices or else stand 'exposed to the imposition of strong sanctions.' " Finally, the court decided that the agency's action was "final" because the letter was signed by the Administrator who was the head of the agency, saying:

> We think the sound course is to accept the ruling of a board or commission, or the head of an agency, as presumptively final. If it does not indicate on its face that it is only tentative, it would be likely to be accepted as authoritative. This presumption could be negatived, of course, if the agency adopted a rule prescribing its procedure in such a way as to identify certain actions as tentative and subject to reconsideration, prescribing the means of obtaining such reconsideration. Indeed, even in the absence of such structuring in regulations prescribing agency procedures, a court might decline to entertain a litigation if it was presented not with legal defenses interposed by counsel, but with an affidavit of the agency head advising the court that the ruling in question was tentative, and outlining the method of seeking reconsideration....

National Automatic Laundry is a relatively old ripeness case. Recall from the section on Finality that some courts today are questioning whether interpretative rulings are final agency action.

6.   Justice Fortas dissented in *Abbott Laboratories* because he feared that rules would be stayed while courts engaged in pre-enforce-

ment review, and this would result, he observed, in ignoring "the damage to the public of deferring during the tedious months and years of litigation" the implementation of a regulation. Contemporary critics of pre-enforcement review, like Professor Mashaw, point to additional problems:

> If the availability of immediate review eliminates the incentives of all parties to begin compliance efforts, then it also eliminates the incentives that otherwise exist to solve some of the feasibility and practicability issues that may loom large in the litigation....
>
> Moreover, the timing of review also radically reshapes the focus of the litigation. Review in an enforcement context often concentrates on one or a few issues of particular moment to a particular firm. Pre-enforcement review invites, and usually produces, the invocation of a laundry list of potential frailties in a rule's substantive content or procedural regularity. The multiplicity of issues available, combined with the unavailability of evidence concerning genuine attempts to comply with the rule, dramatically increase the uncertainties of judicial review.

He concludes, "Moving back toward the older regime of rulemaking review at the time of enforcement thus has much to recommend it, for unnecessary judicial review simultaneously stultifies the policy process, while imperilling judicial *and* administrative legitimacy." Jerry L. Mashaw, *Improving The Environment of Agency Rulemaking: An Essay On Management, Games, and Accountability*, 57 L. & CONTEMP. PROBS. 185, 233–34, 236 (1994).

Others counter that elimination of preenforcement review would deter parties from seeking review of many rules in any context. The problem is that a regulated entity that attempts to defend the legality of a rule in an enforcement proceeding runs a significant risk. "Violation of a rule that is held to be valid often exposes the regulatee to the risk of large civil and criminal penalties, as well as other adverse regulatory and public relations consequences. Those risks are likely to induce regulatees to comply with a rule, even if they believe the rule to be invalid, rather than to take the risks attendant to noncompliance and a subsequent challenge to the validity of the rule in an enforcement case." Richard J. Pierce, *Seven Ways To Deossify Agency Rulemaking*, 47 ADMIN. L. REV. 59, 90 (1995).

7. Why did Justice Fortas assume that the FDA rule would be stayed pending the courts' determination as to the validity of the rule? In Chapter 2 you dealt with a problem where a person considered appealing to delay the effect of the rule. There you learned that Section 705 of the APA authorizes an agency or a court to stay an agency action pending judicial review, but nothing compels the agency to grant a stay, and courts are only to grant stays "to the extent necessary to prevent irreparable injury." Some statutes even prohibit stays pending judicial review of a rule. *See, e.g.,* 42 U.S.C.A. § 7607(g) (Clean Air Act noncom-

pliance penalty regulations). In light of these limits and safeguards, what accounts for the perception that judicial review necessarily delays agency regulations? To what extent do Professor Mashaw's objections really apply to the grant of stays, as opposed to pre-enforcement judicial review *per se*? Would private parties seek pre-enforcement review if they could *not* obtain stays?

Chapter 6

AGENCY STRUCTURE

A. INTRODUCTION

The framers of the United States Constitution envisioned three branches of government each with a distinct task. Yet, as we have seen, administrative agencies confound this vision. Although the Constitution provides that "[a]ll legislative Powers ... shall be vested in a Congress of the United States ...," U.S. Const. art. I, § 1, agencies promulgate regulations that have the force and effect of legislative enactments. Although the Constitution provides that "[t]he judicial Power of the United States, shall be vested in one Supreme Court, and in such inferior Courts as the Congress may from time to time ordain and establish," U.S. Const. art. III, § 1, agencies routinely engage in adjudication. Agency government has another constitutional anomaly. The Constitution provides that "[t]he executive Power shall be vested in a President of the United States of America." U.S. Const. art. II, § 1. The President's responsibility to implement the laws would seem to be hindered if the President can not fire an administrator who fails to adopt policies favored by the President. Nevertheless, Congress has forbidden the President from firing some administrators because of a policy disagreement. As noted earlier, an agency subject to this arrangement is known as an "independent" agency to denote that its administrator(s) have "independence" from the President in terms of establishing agency policies.

Although the Supreme Court has accepted the previous structural features of agencies by refusing to enforce rigidly separation of powers principles, the Court has not always been so accommodating. It has forbidden Congress from appointing or removing administrators, and it has declared unconstitutional the legislative veto. Under a legislative veto, Congress reserves for itself the right to void agency orders or rules by the passage of a resolution by one or both houses of Congress. This chapter addresses the Court's sometimes accommodating and sometimes strict approach to separation of powers.

Agency structure is relevant to administrative law practice in several ways. A lawyer representing a regulated entity might seek to block agency action by arguing the action is invalid because the agency is structured in an unconstitutional manner. The lawyer can also use constitutional arguments for purposes of statutory interpretation. When the meaning of a statutory term is unclear, a litigant may be able to argue that an interpretation proposed by an agency would make the statute unconstitutional. Also, a lawyer might be asked to advise Congress or a state legislature whether a pending bill to create or redesign an agency might violate a constitutional prohibition. The problems that follow illustrate these roles.

Agency structure is relevant to law practice in one more way. As a lawyer, you may be involved in the selection process for federal or state judges, or you may be a candidate for a judgeship. Those who nominate and choose judges are interested in a candidate's approach to constitutional interpretation including the extent to which the person might defer to legislative preferences concerning agency structure. Since the framers of the Constitution did not envision anything like the modern administrative state, a judge's constitutional philosophy will have a significant impact on how the person views issues of agency structure.

Notes and Questions

1. The concept of separation of powers has an impressive heritage in political philosophy. *See, e.g.*, XI BARON MONTESQUIEU, THE SPIRIT OF THE LAWS 202 (1977) ("When the legislative and executive powers are united in the same person, or in the same body of magistracy, there can then be no liberty. . . ."); JOHN LOCKE, THE SECOND TREATISE OF GOVERNMENT 81 (1952) ("the legislative cannot transfer the power of making laws to any other hands; for it being but a delegated power from the people, they who have it cannot pass it over to others."). Yet, its historical roots are obscure. In England, for example, the executive branch, as a reflection of the party in power, dominates the legislative branch. Professor William Gwyn has found that the doctrine is related to the basic proposition of natural justice that no man can be a judge in his own cause. In early England, for example, the King was deprived of the opportunity to review judicial decisions concerning the Crown even though judges were appointed under the King's authority. WILLIAM GWYN, THE MEANING OF SEPARATION OF POWERS 6–7 (1965). "Thus, separation of powers is a necessary condition to avoid the conflicts of interest between law makers, enforcers, and deciders that would arise if each could invade the other's functions. In this manner, the doctrine serves as a fundamental underpinning of limited government." RICHARD J. PIERCE, SIDNEY A. SHAPIRO, PAUL R. VERKUIL, ADMINISTRATIVE LAW & PROCESS 25 (2d ed. 1992).

2. When the Supreme Court concludes that some governmental structure is unconstitutional, it usually takes a formalistic approach to constitutional interpretation. This technique, which interprets constitutional requirements as literally as possible, has the impact of minimizing the extent to which the powers of the three branches overlap. Under this approach, the Court identifies the power being exercised as legislative,

judicial, or executive, and then it determines whether the power is being exercised by an inappropriate branch. In *Youngstown Sheet & Tube Co. v. Sawyer (The Steel Seizure Case)*, 343 U.S. 579, 72 S.Ct. 863, 96 L.Ed. 1153 (1952), for example, the Court struck down President Truman's order directing the Secretary of Commerce to seize and operate the nation's steel mills. It held that Congress did not authorize the seizure, and the President's own power did not justify it. Accordingly, in seizing the mills, the President had improperly aggregated to himself the power to make law: "In the framework of our Constitution, the President's power to see that the laws are faithfully executed refutes the idea that he is to be a lawmaker." 343 U.S. at 587, 72 S.Ct. at 866.

3. When the Court is less strict about separation of powers, it usually uses a functional approach which interprets constitutional powers in a nonliteral manner. It defends this technique, which has the impact of extending the extent to which the powers of the three branches overlap, on the ground that the Constitution itself commingles powers among the three branches. Because the framers contemplated some commingling of functions, the Court has said that separation of powers questions should be determined "according to common sense and the inherent necessities of the governmental coordination." *Buckley v. Valeo*, 424 U.S. 1, 121, 96 S.Ct. 612, 683, 46 L.Ed.2d 659 (1976). Under a functional approach, the Court determines whether Congress has gone too far in commingling of powers by using a "core function" test. *See* Peter L. Strauss, *The Place of Agencies in Government: Separation of Powers and the Fourth Branch*, 84 COLUM. L. REV. 573, 625–26 (1984). This test approves the commingling of powers as long as one branch's exercise of a power does not jeopardize the "core function" of another branch. In other words, "[i]nstead of trumpeting independence as a value in itself, the inquiry becomes whether, in a particular setting, it is a concept necessary to protect fundamental branch interests." PIERCE, SHAPIRO, & VERKUIL, *supra*, at 98.

4. According to Professor Lawson, "The post-New Deal administrative state is unconstitutional, and its validation by the legal system amounts to nothing less than a bloodless constitutional revolution.... In short, the modern administrative state flouts almost every important structural precept of the American constitutional order." Gary Lawson, *The Rise and Rise of the Administrative State*, 107 HARV. L. REV. 1231, 1233 (1994). As you may have guessed, Professor Lawson's conclusions are based on a literal reading of separation of powers. As you read the following materials, you can consider whether such a formalistic approach is necessary or appropriate to enforce separation of powers principles. Or, as discussed in the last note, is a "core function" approach sufficient to promote separation of powers principles?

B. DELEGATION OF LEGISLATIVE POWER

In Chapter 2, you studied the rulemaking process at agencies. The Constitution authorizes the delegation of rulemaking to agencies because

Congress is "[t]o make all Laws which shall be necessary and proper" to carry out its functions under Article I. U.S. Const. art. I, § 8. If Congress enacts legislation to promote airline safety under the Commerce Clause, for example, it may rely on the necessary and proper clause to create the Federal Aviation Agency (FAA) and give it rulemaking powers to accomplish that goal. The question arises, however, what the limits are to Congress's power to delegate such rulemaking authority. After all, the Constitution provides that "[a]ll legislative Powers ... shall be vested in a Congress of the United States...." U.S. Const. art. I, § 1. The Supreme Court has gone through three phases in answering this question. The Court rejected all nondelegation challenges until the 1930s, when it struck down two statutes on this ground. The Court has rejected all additional nondelegation challenges since that time, but it has occasionally used the nondelegation clause to justify narrowly interpreting an agency's statutory authority. This section describes the Court's application of the nondelegation doctrine, compares the approach used in state courts, and considers how the doctrine is used in statutory interpretation.

1. FIRST PHASE

In *Brig Aurora*, 11 U.S. (7 Cranch) 382, 3 L.Ed. 378 (1813), which was the Court's first nondelegation case, it considered a delegation that authorized the President to lift a trade embargo against France and England when these counties no longer violated the "neutral commerce" of United States. The Court held the statute did not violate the nondelegation doctrine because the President's discretion was limited to taking a specific action mandated by Congress if the "named contingency" occurred. In other words, Congress had complied with the nondelegation doctrine because it established a policy and then directed the executive to implement the policy only if certain facts were true. *See also Field v. Clark*, 143 U.S. 649, 12 S.Ct. 495, 36 L.Ed. 294 (1892).

In *J.W. Hampton, Jr. & Co. v. United States*, 276 U.S. 394, 48 S.Ct. 348, 72 L.Ed. 624 (1928), the Court replaced this "named contingency" test. Congress had authorized the President to revise certain tariffs whenever he determined revision to be necessary to "equalize the costs of production in the U.S. and the principal competing country." The Court approved the delegation because Congress had established an "intelligible principle" by which the justices could determine whether the President had acted within his delegated authority. The "named contingency" test was apparently rejected because it did not take into account that presidential fact finding might involve some measure of discretion. By comparison, the intelligible principle permits the delegation of discretion, but it also requires an agency to make decisions which are consistent with the general policies defined by Congress. *See also United States v. Grimaud*, 220 U.S. 506, 31 S.Ct. 480, 55 L.Ed. 563 (1911); *Buttfield v. Stranahan*, 192 U.S. 470, 24 S.Ct. 349, 48 L.Ed. 525 (1904).

The Court has used the "intelligible principle" test since *Hampton* to apply the nondelegation doctrine. Under this approach, Congress does not violate the prohibition against delegating its legislative powers as long as it sets the boundaries of the agency's authority. If, however, a delegation is broad and ambiguous, it may not offer sufficient guidance to the courts concerning the extent of the agency's authority to promulgate rules. In the 1930s, the Court struck down two statutes on this ground.

2. SECOND PHASE

In *Panama Refining Co. v. Ryan*, 293 U.S. 388, 55 S.Ct. 241, 79 L.Ed. 446 (1935), the Court declared unconstitutional a provision of the National Industrial Recovery Act (NIRA) which authorized the President "to prohibit ... the transportation in interstate ... commerce of petroleum ... produced or withdrawn from storage in excess of the amount ... permitted ... by state law ..." Congress was seeking to prevent oil producers from evading state restrictions limiting the amount of oil the producers could sell. The Court concluded that Congress failed to provide an intelligible principle: "As to the transportation of oil production in excess of state permission, the Congress has declared no policy, has established no standard, has laid down no rule. There is no requirement, no definition of circumstances and conditions in which the transportation is to be allowed or prohibited." Justice Cardozo dissented on the ground that an intelligible principle could be found in the first section of the NIRA which indicated the goals and purposes of the legislation. Cardozo reasoned that the President was to stop the interstate sale of oil when it served these legislative purposes.

A unanimous Supreme Court declared another and more important section of the NIRA to be invalid in *A.L.A. Schechter Poultry Corp. v. United States*, 295 U.S. 495, 55 S.Ct. 837, 79 L.Ed. 1570 (1935). Congress had authorized the President to approve codes of "fair competition" jointly established by firms in an industry if three conditions were met. The President could approve a code if it was written by a representative group of businesses, if it did not promote monopolies, and if it served the goals indicated in the first section of the NIRA. The Court held that these restrictions did not establish an intelligible principle that limited the President's authority.

The government argued the NIRA language was similar to limitations that Congress had established for the Federal Trade Commission (FTC), which was authorized to prevent "unfair methods of competition." The Court distinguished this legislation on two grounds. First, it said that the phrase "fair competition" was less limiting than the FTC's mandate. Justice Hughes explained that the act

> supplies no standards for any trade, industry or activity. It does not undertake to prescribe rules of conduct to be applied to particular states of fact determined by appropriate administrative procedure. Instead of prescribing rules of conduct, it authorizes the making of

codes to prescribe them. For that legislative undertaking, section 3 sets up no standards, aside from the statement of the general aims of rehabilitation, correction, and expansion described in section 1. In view of the scope of that broad declaration, and of the nature of the few restrictions that are imposed, the discretion of the President in approving or prescribing codes, and thus enacting laws for the government of trade and industry throughout the country, is virtually unfettered.

295 U.S. at 541–42, 55 S.Ct. at 898.

Second, the Court noted that the FTC Act was implemented through the use of adversarial procedures, but Congress has provided for no such procedure under the NIRA. At the FTC, "Provision was made for a formal complaint, for notice and hearing, and for appropriate findings of fact supported by adequate evidence, and for judicial review to give assurance that the action of the Commission is taken within its statutory authority." *Id.* at 533, 55 S.Ct. at 844. By comparison, the NIRA "dispense[d] with this administrative procedure and with administrative procedure of any character." *Id.*

This time Justice Cardozo agreed that Congress had failed to establish an intelligible principle. He objected that "anything that Congress may do within the limits of the commerce clause for the betterment of business may be done by the President." Accordingly, he concluded, "This is delegation running riot." 295 U.S. at 533, 55 S.Ct. at 844.

The Court declared a third New Deal statute unconstitutional because it delegated legislative power to private persons. In *Carter v. Carter Coal Company*, 298 U.S. 238, 56 S.Ct. 855, 80 L.Ed. 1160 (1936), the Court reviewed legislation which delegated to some mine owners and miners the authority to fix maximum hours of labor which were binding on all mine owners. The Court observed, "The power conferred upon the majority is, in effect, the power to regulate the affairs of an unwilling minority. This is legislative delegation in its most obnoxious form; for it is not even delegation to an official or an official body, presumptively disinterested, but to private persons whose interests may be and often are adverse to the interests of others in the same business." 298 U.S. at 311, 56 S.Ct. at 872.

3. THIRD PHASE

Since the 1930s, the Court has approved all of the legislation it has reviewed for compliance with the nondelegation doctrine, as the next case illustrates.

MISTRETTA v. UNITED STATES
488 U.S. 361, 109 S.Ct. 647, 102 L.Ed.2d 714 (1989).

JUSTICE BLACKMUN delivered the opinion of the Court.

In this litigation, we granted certiorari before judgment in the United States Court of Appeals for the Eighth Circuit in order to consider the constitutionality of the Sentencing Guidelines promulgated by the United States Sentencing Commission. The Commission is a body created under the Sentencing Reform Act of 1984 (Act). The United States District Court for the Western District of Missouri ruled that the Guidelines were constitutional.

I

For almost a century, the Federal Government employed in criminal cases a system of indeterminate sentencing. Statutes specified the penalties for crimes but nearly always gave the sentencing judge wide discretion to decide whether the offender should be incarcerated and for how long, whether he should be fined and how much, and whether some lesser restraint, such as probation, should be imposed instead of imprisonment or fine. This indeterminate-sentencing system was supplemented by the utilization of parole, by which an offender was returned to society under the "guidance and control" of a parole officer....

Serious disparities in sentences, however, were common. Rehabilitation as a sound penological theory came to be questioned and, in any event, was regarded by some as an unattainable goal for most cases....

The Act, as adopted, ... consolidates the power that had been exercised by the sentencing judge and the Parole Commission to decide what punishment an offender should suffer. This is done by creating the United States Sentencing Commission, directing that Commission to devise guidelines to be used for sentencing, and prospectively abolishing the Parole Commission.... It makes the Sentencing Commission's guidelines binding on the courts, although it preserves for the judge the discretion to depart from the guideline applicable to a particular case if the judge finds an aggravating or mitigating factor present that the Commission did not adequately consider when formulating guidelines.

The Commission is established "as an independent commission in the judicial branch of the United States." It has seven voting members (one of whom is the Chairman) appointed by the President "by and with the advice and consent of the Senate." ...

II

On December 10, 1987, John M. Mistretta (petitioner) and another were indicted in the United States District Court for the Western District of Missouri on three counts centering in a cocaine sale. Mistretta moved to have the promulgated Guidelines ruled unconstitutional on the grounds that the Sentencing Commission was constituted in violation of the established doctrine of separation of powers, and that Congress delegated excessive authority to the Commission to structure the Guidelines....

III

Petitioner argues that in delegating the power to promulgate sentencing guidelines for every federal criminal offense to an independent

Sentencing Commission, Congress has granted the Commission excessive legislative discretion in violation of the constitutionally based nondelegation doctrine. We do not agree.

The nondelegation doctrine is rooted in the principle of separation of powers that underlies our tripartite system of Government. The Constitution provides that "[a]ll legislative Powers herein granted shall be vested in a Congress of the United States," U.S. Const., Art. I, § 1, and we long have insisted that "the integrity and maintenance of the system of government ordained by the Constitution" mandate that Congress generally cannot delegate its legislative power to another Branch. We also have recognized, however, that the separation-of-powers principle, and the nondelegation doctrine in particular, do not prevent Congress from obtaining the assistance of its coordinate Branches. In a passage now enshrined in our jurisprudence, Chief Justice Taft, writing for the Court, explained our approach to such cooperative ventures: "In determining what [Congress] may do in seeking assistance from another branch, the extent and character of that assistance must be fixed according to common sense and the inherent necessities of the government co-ordination." So long as Congress "shall lay down by legislative act an intelligible principle to which the person or body authorized to [exercise the delegated authority] is directed to conform, such legislative action is not a forbidden delegation of legislative power."

Applying this "intelligible principle" test to congressional delegations, our jurisprudence has been driven by a practical understanding that in our increasingly complex society, replete with ever changing and more technical problems, Congress simply cannot do its job absent an ability to delegate power under broad general directives. "The Constitution has never been regarded as denying to the Congress the necessary resources of flexibility and practicality, which will enable it to perform its function." Accordingly, this Court has deemed it "constitutionally sufficient if Congress clearly delineates the general policy, the public agency which is to apply it, and the boundaries of this delegated authority."

Until 1935, this Court never struck down a challenged statute on delegation grounds. After invalidating in 1935 two statutes as excessive delegations, we have upheld, again without deviation, Congress' ability to delegate power under broad standards.[7]

In light of our approval of these broad delegations, we harbor no doubt that Congress' delegation of authority to the Sentencing Commission is sufficiently specific and detailed to meet constitutional require-

---

7. In *Schechter* and *Panama Refining* the Court concluded that Congress had failed to articulate any policy or standard that would serve to confine the discretion of the authorities to whom Congress had delegated power. No delegation of the kind at issue in those cases is present here. The Act does not make crimes of acts never before criminalized or delegate regulatory power to private individuals. In recent years, our application of the nondelegation doctrine principally has been limited to the interpretation of statutory texts, and, more particularly, to giving narrow constructions to statutory delegations that might otherwise be thought to be unconstitutional. *See, e.g., Industrial Union Dept. v. American Petroleum Institute*, 448 U.S. 607, 646 (1980).

ments. Congress charged the Commission with three goals: to "assure the meeting of the purposes of sentencing as set forth" in the Act; to "provide certainty and fairness in meeting the purposes of sentencing, avoiding unwarranted sentencing disparities among defendants with similar records ... while maintaining sufficient flexibility to permit individualized sentences," where appropriate; and to "reflect, to the extent practicable, advancement in knowledge of human behavior as it relates to the criminal justice process." Congress further specified four "purposes" of sentencing that the Commission must pursue in carrying out its mandate: "to reflect the seriousness of the offense, to promote respect for the law, and to provide just punishment for the offense"; "to afford adequate deterrence to criminal conduct"; "to protect the public from further crimes of the defendant"; and "to provide the defendant with needed ... correctional treatment."

In addition, Congress prescribed the specific tool—the guidelines system—for the Commission to use in regulating sentencing. More particularly, Congress directed the Commission to develop a system of "sentencing ranges" applicable "for each category of offense involving each category of defendant." Congress instructed the Commission that these sentencing ranges must be consistent with pertinent provisions of Title 18 of the United States Code and could not include sentences in excess of the statutory maxima. . . .

In addition to these overarching constraints, Congress provided even more detailed guidance to the Commission about categories of offenses and offender characteristics. . . .

We cannot dispute petitioner's contention that the Commission enjoys significant discretion in formulating guidelines. The Commission does have discretionary authority to determine the relative severity of federal crimes and to assess the relative weight of the offender characteristics that Congress listed for the Commission to consider. The Commission also has significant discretion to determine which crimes have been punished too leniently, and which too severely. Congress has called upon the Commission to exercise its judgment about which types of crimes and which types of criminals are to be considered similar for the purposes of sentencing.

But our cases do not at all suggest that delegations of this type may not carry with them the need to exercise judgment on matters of policy. In *Yakus v. United States,* 321 U.S. 414 (1944), the Court upheld a delegation to the Price Administrator to fix commodity prices that "in his judgment will be generally fair and equitable and will effectuate the purposes of this Act" to stabilize prices and avert speculation. In *National Broadcasting Co. v.United States*, 319 U.S. 190 (1943), we upheld a delegation to the Federal Communications Commission granting it the authority to promulgate regulations in accordance with its view of the "public interest." In *Yakus*, the Court laid down the applicable principle:

"It is no objection that the determination of facts and the inferences to be drawn from them in the light of the statutory standards and declaration of policy call for the exercise of judgment, and for the formulation of subsidiary administrative policy within the prescribed statutory framework. . . .

". . . Only if we could say that there is an absence of standards for the guidance of the Administrator's action, so that it would be impossible in a proper proceeding to ascertain whether the will of Congress has been obeyed, would we be justified in overriding its choice of means for effecting its declared purpose. . . ."

Congress has met that standard here. The Act sets forth more than merely an "intelligible principle" or minimal standards. One court has aptly put it: "The statute outlines the policies which prompted establishment of the Commission, explains what the Commission should do and how it should do it, and sets out specific directives to govern particular situations."

Developing proportionate penalties for hundreds of different crimes by a virtually limitless array of offenders is precisely the sort of intricate, labor-intensive task for which delegation to an expert body is especially appropriate. Although Congress has delegated significant discretion to the Commission to draw judgments from its analysis of existing sentencing practice and alternative sentencing models, "Congress is not confined to that method of executing its policy which involves the least possible delegation of discretion to administrative officers." We have no doubt that in the hands of the Commission "the criteria which Congress has supplied are wholly adequate for carrying out the general policy and purpose" of the Act. . . .

[The Court considered and rejected other constitutional objections to the Commission.]

Notes and Questions

1. Justice Scalia dissented in *Mistretta* because the legislative delegation was to an agency located in the judicial branch. Although he did not dispute the Court's application of the intelligible principle test, he argued that "because the scope of delegation is largely uncontrollable by the courts, we must be particularly rigorous in preserving the Constitution's structural restrictions that deter excessive delegation." He therefore objected to the delegation because it was to the judicial branch: "The lawmaking function of the Sentencing Commission is completely divorced from any responsibility for execution of the law or adjudication of private rights under the law. It is divorced from responsibility for execution of the law not only because the Commission is not said to be 'located in the Executive Branch' . . .; but, more importantly, because the Commission neither exercises any executive power on its own, nor is subject to the control of the President who does. . . ." 488 U.S. at 416–17, 420, 109 S.Ct. at 677–78, 679.

2. In addition to *Mistretta*, the Court has rejected Justice Scalia's call to "preserve the Constitution's structural restrictions that deter excessive delegation" in yet another context. In *Skinner v. Mid–America Pipeline Co.*, 490 U.S. 212, 109 S.Ct. 1726, 104 L.Ed.2d 250 (1989), for example, the Court rejected the plaintiff's argument that the Court should employ a stricter test under the nondelegation clause when Congress delegates its taxing authority to an agency. The case involved the Consolidated Omnibus Budget Reconciliation Act of 1985, which directed the Secretary of Transportation to establish a system of user fees to cover the costs of administering certain federal pipeline safety programs. Citing and quoting from *Mistretta*, the Court rejected a claim that the Act unconstitutionally delegated the taxing power to the Executive Branch: "We find no support, then, for Mid–America's contention that the text of the Constitution or the practices of Congress require the application of a different and stricter nondelegation doctrine in cases where Congress delegates discretionary authority to the Executive under its taxing power." 490 U.S. at 222–23, 109 S.Ct. at 1732–33.

4. STATE PRACTICE

Unlike the Supreme Court, some state courts have sought to rein in legislative delegation. In *Lincoln Dairy Company v. Finigan*, 170 Neb. 777, 104 N.W.2d 227 (1960), for example, the Nebraska Supreme Court considered a delegation to the Director of the Department of Agriculture "to adopt, by regulation, minimum standards for the sanitary quality, production, processing, distribution, and sale of Grade A milk and Grade A milk products, and for labeling of the same." The legislation also provided for criminal penalties for violation of the act and any regulations issued under it. The Court found the delegation was unconstitutional because the "director and not the Legislature defines what shall be criminal offenses." The justices explained, "It is axiomatic that the power to define crimes and criminal offenses is in the Legislature and it may not delegate such power to an administrative agency." Other state courts, however, have declined to follow Nebraska's approach. *See, e.g. Ohio v. Acme Scrap Iron & Metal*, 49 Ohio App.2d 371, 361 N.E.2d 250 (Ohio.Ct.App.1974) (rejecting challenge to state air pollution regulations on ground that violations were a criminal offense).

Some state courts have also been more precise about what constitutes an "intelligible principle" for purposes of the nondelegation doctrine. For example, the Illinois Supreme Court uses the following test:

> Accordingly, we find that the view which has developed through the decisions of this court in recent years requires that the legislature, in delegating its authority provide sufficient identification of the following:
>
> (1) The persons and activities potentially subject to regulation;
>
> (2) the harm sought to be prevented; and
>
> (3) the general means intended to be available to the administrator to prevent the identified harm.

We recognize that the term "sufficient identification" itself is not free from ambiguity and will have to receive additional content from its application to particular facts and circumstances. The following principles should guide such applications: (1) The legislature must do all that is practical to define the scope of the legislation, i. e., the persons and activities which may be subject to the administrator's authority. This effort is necessary to put interested persons on notice of the possibility of administrative actions affecting them. Of course, the complexity of the subject sought to be regulated may put practical limitations upon the legislature's ability to identify all of the forms the activity may take. (2) With regard to identifying the harm sought to be prevented, the legislature may use somewhat broader, more generic language than in the first element. It is sufficient if, from the language of the statute, it is apparent what types of evil the statute is intended to prevent. Finally, with regard to the means intended to be available, the legislature must specifically enumerate the administrative tools (e.g., regulations, licenses, enforcement proceedings) and the particular sanctions, if any, intended to be available. If sanctions are provided, the legislature also must provide adequate standards and safeguards such as judicial review of the imposition of those sanctions.

Stofer v. Motor Vehicle Casualty Co., 68 Ill.2d 361, 12 Ill.Dec. 168, 172, 369 N.E.2d 875, 879 (Ill.1977).

The Oregon Supreme Court has adopted a different approach to enforcement of the nondelegation doctrine. It has held that there "is no constitutional requirement that all delegation of legislative power must be accompanied by a statement of standard circumscribing its exercise." *Warren v. Marion County*, 222 Or. 307, 353 P.2d 257 (Or.1960). In Oregon, "the important consideration is not whether the statute delegating the power expresses *standards*, but whether the procedure established for the exercise of the power furnishes adequate *safeguards* to those who are affected by administrative action." In *Warren*, for example, the Court upheld a delegation to counties to adopt building codes because the statute required an appeals procedure that "provided a sufficient safeguard to persons wishing to contest administrative action in the enforcement of the code." A statute delegating authority to be exercised in accordance with the state's APA also provides a sufficient safeguard. The Court dismissed the requirement of standards as a meaningless safeguard: "It is now apparent that the requirement of expressed standards has, in most instances, been little more than a judicial fetish for legislative language, the recitation of which provides no additional safeguards to persons affected by the exercise of the delegated authority. Thus, we have learned that it is of little or no significance in the administration of a delegated power that the statute which generated it stated the permissible limits of its exercise in terms of such abstractions as 'public convenience, interest, or necessity' or 'unjust or unreasonable,' or for the 'public health, safety, and morals' and similar phases accepted as satisfying the standards requirement."

5. STATUTORY INTERPRETATION

Although the Supreme Court has not struck down any statutes under the nondelegation doctrine since the 1930's, it has used the doctrine to give narrow constructions to statutes that might otherwise have violated the doctrine. For example, in *Industrial Union Department v. American Petroleum Institute*, 448 U.S. 607, 100 S.Ct. 2844, 65 L.Ed.2d 1010 (1980), popularly known as the *Benzene* case, the Court overturned the Occupational Safety and Health Administration's standard for workplace exposure to benzene. OSHA had interpreted the Occupational Safety and Health Act generally to authorize strict standards governing workers' exposure to toxic materials in any workplace. While four justices found nothing problematic about such an interpretation, four other justices indicated that such an interpretation "would make such a 'sweeping delegation of legislative power' that it might be unconstitutional under the Court's reasoning in *A.L.A. Schechter Poultry Corp. v. United States* and *Panama Refining Co. v. Ryan*. A construction of the statute that avoids that kind of open-ended grant should certainly be favored...." Accordingly, they interpreted the statute to limit OSHA's authority to establish standards for toxic materials to those workplaces where OSHA could demonstrate there was a significant safety risk from exposure to such materials. Then Justice Rehnquist cast the deciding vote against the standard, saying that the statute *was* an unconstitutional delegation of legislative authority because it gave no guidance to OSHA "where on the continuum of relative safety [it] should draw the line."

The following case demonstrates another way the nondelegation doctrine can influence construction of statutes.

INTERNATIONAL UNION, UNITED AUTOMOBILE, AEROSPACE & AGRICULTURAL IMPLEMENT WORKERS OF AMERICA, UAW v. OCCUPATIONAL SAFETY & HEALTH ADMINISTRATION

938 F.2d 1310 (D.C.Cir.1991).

STEPHEN F. WILLIAMS, CIRCUIT JUDGE:

Representatives of labor and industry challenge a regulation of the Occupational Safety and Health Administration, "Control of Hazardous Energy Sources (Lockout/Tagout)". The regulation deals not with the effects of such subtle phenomena as electrical energy fields but with those of ordinary industrial equipment that may suddenly move and cut or crush or otherwise injure a worker. "Lockout" and "tagout" are two procedures designed to reduce these injuries. Lockout is the placement of a lock on an "energy isolating device", such as a circuit breaker, so that equipment cannot start up until the lock is removed. Tagout is the similar placement of a plastic tag to alert employees that the tagged equipment "may not be operated" until the tag is removed. Although OSHA had previously issued specific standards governing especially dangerous equipment, the present rule extends lockout/tagout to virtually all equipment in almost all industries. It generally requires employers to use lockout procedures during servicing and maintenance, unless the employer can show that tagout will provide the same level of safety.

[T]he National Association of Manufacturers [claims] that Congress has given so little guidance for rules issued under § 6(b) but not covered by § 6(b)(5) that as to such rules the Act invalidly delegates legislative authority. Although we reject that claim, we find that the interpretation offered by [OSHA] is, in light of nondelegation principles, so broad as to be unreasonable. We note, however, the existence of at least one interpretation that is reasonable and consistent with the nondelegation doctrine....

I

Section 6(b)(5) of the Act limits [OSHA]'s discretion when [it] is promulgating standards that deal with "toxic materials or harmful physical agents". [OSHA, however, interprets § 6(b)(5) only to apply to health standards, not safety standards.] We uphold [OSHA]'s conclusion that § 6(b)(5) does not govern occupational safety standards that regulate hazards causing immediately noticeable physical harm.

II

The removal of § 6(b)(5) as a direct constraint on OSHA regulations outside the area of toxics (the term we use hereafter as shorthand for "toxic materials or harmful physical agents") gives point to the NAM's claim of an excessive delegation of legislative power. The only evident source of constraints remaining is § 3(8). It defines an "occupational safety and health standard" as

> a standard which requires conditions, or the adoption or use of one or more practices, means, methods, operations, or processes, reasonably necessary or appropriate to provide safe or healthful employment and places of employment.

Though the language is exceedingly vague, the *Benzene* plurality found it the source of a threshold requirement of "significant risk", without which OSHA was not to act under § 6(b) at all. It justified this narrowing construction with the argument (among others) that otherwise "the statute would make such a 'sweeping delegation of legislative power' that it might be unconstitutional under the Court's reasoning in *A.L.A. Schechter Poultry Corp. v. United States* and *Panama Refining Co. v. Ryan.*"

The *Benzene* construction was, of course, a manifestation of the Court's current general practice of applying the nondelegation doctrine mainly in the form of "giving narrow constructions to statutory delegations that might otherwise be thought to be unconstitutional." In effect we require a clear statement by Congress that it intended to test the constitutional waters.

We thus turn to possible constructions.

A

One can imagine broader constructions than the one proposed by OSHA, but not easily. It essentially identifies two boundaries[: that a risk be significant and that avoiding it be feasible.] The upshot is an asserted power, once significant risk is found, to require precautions that take the industry to the verge of economic ruin (so long as the increment reduces a significant risk), or to do nothing at all. All positions in between are evidently equally valid.

The claimed power to roam between the rigor of § 6(b)(5) standards and the laxity of unidentified alternatives would, we believe, raise a serious nondelegation issue. As was true of the standard upset in *Schechter*, the scope of the regulatory program is immense, encompassing all American enterprise. "When the scope increases to immense proportions (as in *Schechter*) the standards must be correspondingly more precise."

[I]t is true that price and wage controls blanketing the entire economy have been sustained under quite vague legislative directions. But in view of the inevitable tensions in such controls between such purposes as price stabilization on the one hand and the need for adjustments on ground of changes in cost and other market conditions on the other, an insistence on greater clarity from Congress would deny it any power to impose price controls at all. Not so here. Congress can readily articulate some principle by which the beneficent health and safety effects of workplace regulation are to be traded off against the adverse welfare effects. "Policy direction is all that was ever required, and policy direction is what is lacking in much contemporary legislation." OSHA's reading of the Act finds no such direction.

[O]SHA's proposed analysis would give the executive branch untrammelled power to dictate the vitality and even survival of whatever segments of American business it might choose. Although in *Benzene* the Court focused perhaps more on the severity of the power claimed by OSHA than on its variability, the plurality's point is apt here: "In the absence of a clear mandate in the Act, it is unreasonable to assume that Congress intended to give [OSHA] the unprecedented power over American industry that would result from the Government's view...." At least if reasonable alternative readings can be found, OSHA's must be rejected as unreasonable.

B

The NAM argues (as a fallback to its nondelegation claim) that Congress's use of "reasonably necessary or appropriate" in § 3(8) contemplates "cost-benefit" analysis. Under this interpretation, in imposing standards under § 6(b) but outside the realm of toxics, OSHA may adopt a safety standard if its benefits outweigh its costs, and not otherwise.

Cost-benefit analysis is certainly consistent with the language of § 3(8). "Reasonableness" has long been associated with the balancing of costs and benefits. The "reasonable" person of tort fame is one who takes a precaution if the gravity of the injuries averted, adjusted for their probability, exceeds the precaution's burden.

[A]s there appear to be many confusions about cost-benefit analysis, it may be important to make clear what we are not saying when we identify it as a reasonable interpretation of § 3(8) as applied outside the § 6(b)(5) realm. Cost-benefit analysis requires identifying values for lost years of human life and for suffering and other losses from non-fatal injuries. Nothing we say here should be taken as confining the discretion of OSHA to choose among reasonable evaluation methods. While critics of cost-benefit analysis argue that any such valuation is impossible, that is so only in the sense that pin-point figures are necessarily arbitrary, so that the decisionmaker is effectively limited to considering some range of values. In fact, we make implicit life and safety valuations each day when we decide, for example, whether to travel by train or car, the former being more costly (at least if several family members are traveling together) but safer per passenger-mile. Where government makes decisions for others, it may reasonably be expected to make the trade-offs somewhat more explicitly than individuals choosing for themselves. The difficulty of securing agreement even on a range of values hardly justifies making decisions on the basis of a pretense that resources are not scarce. . . .

As we accept the NAM's contention that § 3(8)'s "reasonably necessary or appropriate" criterion can reasonably be read as requiring cost-benefit analysis, we must reject its nondelegation claim.

Accordingly, in light of the NAM's nondelegation claim we reject OSHA's view that under § 3(8) it may impose any restriction it chooses so long as it is "feasible", but we also reject the NAM's nondelegation claim in light of our view that § 3(8) may reasonably be read as providing for cost-benefit analysis.

Accordingly, we remand the case to OSHA for further consideration in light of this opinion.

HENDERSON, CIRCUIT JUDGE, concurring:

I concur in Parts I, IIA (with the exception of the last sentence), IIIA, IV and V of the majority's opinion.

Notes and Questions

1. *Schechter* pointed to the lack of procedural protections in the NIRA as one reason why the legislation violated the nondelegation doctrine. How does the presence or absence of such procedures relate to whether Congress has violated the nondelegation doctrine? Do you agree with the Oregon Supreme Court that the presence or absence of such protections is the only relevant test concerning whether a delegation should be approved?

2. Why has the Court permitted Congress to delegate power under such broad and ambiguous terms? In his concurrence in the *Benzene*

case, Justice Rehnquist noted that "a number of observers have suggested that this Court should once more take up its burden of ensuring that Congress does not unnecessarily delegate important choices of social policy to politically unresponsible administrators." He also noted, "Other observers, as might be imagined have disagreed." What is the likely result if the Court did adopt a stricter test for the nondelegation clause? Would Congress comply? Or would a stricter test lead to less legislation because Congress could not comply? *See Symposium: Delegation of Powers To Administrative Agencies*, 36 AM. U. L. REV. 295 (1987).

3. In the *Lockout/Tagout* case, Judge Williams does not interpret the OSH Act to require cost-benefit analysis, but he says that such an interpretation would eliminate delegation problems and absent *some* limiting interpretation the Act would violate the nondelegation doctrine. The court remanded the case to OSHA to provide it an opportunity to adopt an interpretation that would satisfy the nondelegation doctrine. On remand, OSHA did not change its rule but it further explained how it believed the OSH Act constrained its discretion. The court rejected most of the further explanations, but it found one newly explained limitation sufficient: a requirement that a safety standard provide "a high degree of worker protection." *See International Union, United Auto., Aerospace & Agr. Implement Workers of America, UAW v. Occupational Safety & Health Admin.*, 37 F.3d 665 (D.C.Cir.1994). Do you think such a requirement limits OSHA's discretion significantly?

4. Subsequently, in 1999, the D.C. Circuit, again with Judge Williams writing the opinion, found that EPA's interpretation of the Clean Air Act's requirements for National Ambient Air Quality Standards (NAAQS) suffered the same flaw as OSHA's original interpretation of the OSH Act. *See American Trucking Associations, Inc. v. U.S. Environmental Protection Agency*, 175 F.3d 1027 (D.C.Cir.1999). This time, however, the government obtained Supreme Court review. *Whitman v. American Trucking Associations, Inc.*, ___ U.S. ___, 121 S.Ct. 903, ___ L.Ed.2d ___ (2001). The Court interpreted the CAA to reject a cost-benefit standard to govern the stringency of the NAAQS. Nevertheless, the scope of discretion permitted by the CAA was constitutional because it was "in fact well within the outer limits of [the Court's] nondelegation precedents." The Court also observed it had "never suggested that an agency can cure an unlawful delegation of legislative power by adopting in its discretion a limiting construction of the statute."

5. Some legislators would like to make significant new rules subject to approval by a joint resolution of Congress. *See* H.R. 2990, 104th Cong. 2d Sess. § 4 (1996). In other words, these rules would not become effective until Congress enacted them as laws and the President signed the legislation. This would be a different way in which to assure that Congress was making the important policy choices. This approach has not been enthusiastically adopted by either Democrats or Republicans. Why do you suppose that is? Would you favor this approach?

Problem 6–1: Indian Trust Lands

The Lower Brule Tribe of Sioux Indians applied to the Department of the Interior to acquire ninety-one acres of land located seven miles from the tribe's reservation. The purpose of the acquisition would be to create an industrial park in order to stimulate economic development beneficial to the tribe. The Department had the following authorization to acquire such lands:

> The Secretary of the Interior is hereby authorized, in his discretion, to acquire through purchase ... any lands ... within or without existing reservations ... for the purpose of providing land for Indians.

> For the acquisition of such lands ..., there is hereby authorized to be appropriated ... a sum not to exceed $2,000,000 in any one fiscal year: *Provided*, That no part of such funds shall be used to acquire additional land outside of the exterior boundaries of the Navajo Indian Reservation for the Navajo Indians in Arizona and New Mexico....

> Title to any lands or rights acquired pursuant to this Act ... shall be taken in the name of the United States in trust for the Indian tribe ... for which the land is acquired, and such lands shall be exempt from State and local taxation.

25 U.S.C.A. § 465. Congress defined the term "Indian" to include "all persons of Indian descent who are members of any recognized tribe now under Federal jurisdiction, and all persons who are descendants of such members who were, on June 1, 1934, residing within the present boundaries of any reservation, and shall further include all other persons of one-half or more Indian blood." *Id.* § 479.

Section 465 is part of legislation passed by Congress in 1934 in response to the loss of lands originally owned by Indians. Prior to 1934, existing Indian tribal land was allotted to individual Indians, and surplus lands were sold to whites. Under this "allotment policy," Indian land holdings were reduced from 138 million acres to 48 million, a loss of 90 million acres. The loss occurred because individual allotments were sold to non-Indians, lost through tax forfeiture, or otherwise alienated. The purpose of the legislation was "to rehabilitate the Indian's economic life and to give him a chance to develop the initiative destroyed by a century of oppression and paternalism." H.R. Rep. No. 1804, 73rd Cong. 2d Sess. 1 (1934). The legislation also prohibited allotment of reservation land to individual Indians, extended existing periods of trust and restrictions on alienation on any Indian lands, and prohibited the transfer of restricted Indian lands except to Indian tribes.

The legislative history is not explicit but it includes the following statement from the House Report: "Section 5 authorizes the Secretary to purchase or otherwise acquire land for the landless Indians.... He may loan them money for improvements and cultivation, but the continued occupancy of this land will depend on its beneficial use by the Indian occupant and his heirs." A chief sponsor of the legislation said on the House floor: "Section 5 sets up a land acquisition program to provide land for Indians who have no land or insufficient land, and who can use land beneficially.... The program would permit ... progress toward the consolidation of badly checkerboarded Indian reservations, as well as provide additional agricultural land to supplement stock grazing or forestry operations." He went on to say that the acquisition of land for farming is "the keystone of the new Indian policy." Another representative said that the lands would b acquired as "Indian subsistence homesteads."

You represent the City of Oacoma, in which the land at question is located and which will lose tax revenue as a result of the purchase of the land for the tribe. What legal arguments could you make against the purchase? What do you suppose are your chances of obtaining a favorable judgement for your client?

Would the outcome of the case be different if the issue was a matter of state constitutional law in Illinois or Oregon?

C. DELEGATION OF JUDICIAL POWER

Chapter Three revealed that many agencies perform the same adjudicative functions as the federal courts. The following material asks you to consider when such delegations violate Article III, which vests judicial power in the courts, or the Seventh Amendment, which preserves the right to a jury trial for common law disputes.

1. ARTICLE III, § 1

Article III, § 1 provides that the "judicial power of the United States shall be vested in one Supreme Court and such inferior courts as the Congress may from time to time ordain and establish." U.S. Const. art. III, § 1. Since Article III gives judges certain protections, such as lifetime tenure, the Supreme Court must be wary that adjudication by a non-Article III tribunal denies litigants the protections associated with having an Article III adjudicator. For example, because an Article III judge has lifetime tenure, the judge may be less susceptible to political pressure than someone who does not have this protection.

Despite this constitutional imperative, Congress routinely assigns the power to adjudicate to persons other than Article III judges. Administrative adjudication is a common example of such adjudication, but agencies are not the only non-Article III adjudicators. Congress also establishes "legislative" or "Article I" courts. A good example is the Court of Veterans Appeals, which has exclusive initial review jurisdiction over issues of law, fact, and constitutionality, arising under laws administered by the Department of Veterans Affairs (VA), 38 U.S.C.A. § 4061 (1988). The President appoints the Court's seven judges for fifteen year terms, with the concurrence of the Senate, and judges may be removed only for cause. A party may obtain judicial review of the validity of a statute or regulation relied on by the Court of Veterans Appeals, but there is no judicial review of factual determinations or the application of a law or regulation to the facts of a particular case, except for constitutional issues.

Murray's Lessee v. Hoboken Land and Improvement Co., 59 U.S. (18 How.) 272, 15 L.Ed. 372 (1855), supports Congress's decision to limit review in this manner. The case involved the seizure by federal marshals of the property that belonged to a customs collection agent who owed the government money. The Court upheld a summary procedure that permitted the government to recoup money owed it by customs collectors without judicial review of its actions. The Court determined that Article III did not apply because under the doctrine of sovereign immunity the government may be sued only with its consent. Because the government can be sued only with its permission, the Court reasoned that it can establish the terms and conditions of such litigation, including that the matter be resolved by a non-Article III adjudicator. Justice Curtis noted that "there are matters involving public rights, which may be presented in such form that the judicial power is capable of acting on them, and which are susceptible of judicial determination, but which congress may or may not bring within the cognizance of the courts of the United States, as it may deem proper."

The Court used this public versus private rights distinction in *Crowell v. Benson*, 285 U.S. 22, 52 S.Ct. 285, 76 L.Ed. 598 (1932), when it reviewed a decision by the United States Employees' Compensation Commission. Under the Federal Longshoreman and Harbor Workers' Compensation Act (Act), the Commission was authorized to determine whether an employer was liable to pay compensation to an injured worker. Although the Commission's decision was subject to judicial review, its findings, if "supported by evidence and within the scope of the [Commission's] authority," were final and conclusive. *Id.* at 46. In rejecting an argument that Commission fact-finding violated Article III, the Court focussed on the distinction between cases of private right and those which arise between the government and persons subject to its authority in connection with the performance of the constitutional functions of the executive or legislative departments. *Id.* at 50. The Court determined that the Commission was adjudicating a "private right" because it involved the liability of one individual to another. Nevertheless, it held that the Commission could adjudicate the dispute in the first instance because there was review by an Article III court. The Court explained that there had been a long history of juries, masters, and commissioners serving as fact finders subject to appellate review by Article III judges.

Crowell and *Murray's Lessee* provided the framework on which Congress has built administrative adjudication. The cases sanctioned the adjudication of "public rights" by administrative agencies because the government, according to the doctrine of sovereign immunity, determines the terms and conditions on which it can be sued. Moreover, according to this logic, Congress can assign the final adjudication of both facts and law in public rights cases to non-Article III judges. "The whole point of the public rights analysis," as Professor Strauss has pointed out, has been that *"no judicial involvement at all* was required—executive determination alone would suffice." Peter L. Strauss, *The Place of Agencies in Government: Separation of Powers and The Fourth Branch,* 84 COLUM. L. REV. 573, 632 (1984) (emphasis in original).

Congress has been reluctant to take full advantage of this power. Administrative agencies are usually subject to judicial review under Section 706 of the APA. Nevertheless, Section 701(a) of the APA recognizes that Congress can preclude judicial review, and Congress sometimes does so. Factual and legal decisions by the Veterans Department concerning veterans benefits were not reviewable, for example, until Congress established the Court of Veterans Appeals in 1988. *See Gott v. Walters,* 756 F.2d 902 (D.C.Cir.) *vacated* 791 F.2d 172 (D.C.Cir.1985) (en banc) (construing the scope of Congress' preclusion of judicial review).

Whereas *Murray's Lessee* permits Congress to eliminate judicial review completely concerning public rights, *Crowell* requires such review concerning "private" rights, although Congress can require a deferential scope of review. For this reason, courts were forced to distinguish "public" from "private" rights. In *Crowell*, the Court defined a "public right" as one arising in a case "between the government and persons subject to its authority in connection with the performance of the constitutional functions of the executive or legislative departments." 285 U.S. at 50, 52 S.Ct. at 292. A private right was one involving the "liability of one individual to another under the law as defined." *Id.* at 51, 52 S.Ct. at 292.

In 1982, the Court begin to alter its approach to Article III. At first, the Court changed the definition of a private right. In *Northern Pipeline Construction Co. v. Marathon Pipe Line Co.,* 458 U.S. 50, 102 S.Ct. 2858, 73 L.Ed.2d 598 (1982), it held that bankruptcy judges could not adjudicate a contract dispute between the person in bankruptcy and another party because the judges were not Article III judges. The Court distinguished *Crowell* on the ground that Congress created the cause of action that created the dispute between the two private parties in that case. Recall that *Crowell* involved a federal workers compensation law. By comparison, state common law was the source of the cause of action in *Northern Pipeline.* In 1986, the Court made a fundamental change. In *Commodity Futures Trading Commission v. Schor,* it rejected the public/private rights distinction as the appropriate test for determining the scope of Congress' power to rely on non-Article III adjudicators.

COMMODITY FUTURES TRADING COMMISSION v. SCHOR
478 U.S. 833, 106 S.Ct. 3245, 92 L.Ed.2d 675 (1986).

JUSTICE O'CONNOR delivered the opinion of the Court.

The question presented is whether the Commodity Exchange Act (CEA or Act) empowers the Commodity Futures Trading Commission

(CFTC or Commission) to entertain state law counterclaims in reparation proceedings and, if so, whether that grant of authority violates Article III of the Constitution.

[The CFTC regulates the trading of commodity futures including the sales practices of commodity brokers. Among the Commission's duties, it administers a reparations process through which disgruntled customers of professional commodity brokers can seek redress for a broker's violations of the Act or Commission regulations. This case arose when Schor filed a complaint against a broker, Conti Commodity Services, Inc. (Conti). Schor had an account with Conti which contained a negative balance because Schor's net futures trading losses and expenses, such as commissions, exceeded the funds deposited in the account. Schor alleged that this negative balance was the result of Conti's numerous violations of the CEA.

The Commission had promulgated a regulation that allowed it to adjudicate any counterclaims that a broker might assert against a customer if they arose "out of the transaction or occurrence or series of transactions or occurrences set forth in [a] complaint." The broker was not required to assert such counterclaims; it could instead sue the customer in state court by filing a contract action. The CFTC adopted its regulation to permit the efficient resolution of all claims (of customers and brokers) arising out of the same transaction. In response to Schor's action, Conti voluntarily presented its claim against Schor in the CFTC reparations proceeding. It denied violating the CEA and instead insisted that the negative balance resulted from Schor's trading, and was therefore a simple debt owed by Schor.

After the CFTC ruled in Conti's favor on both Schor's claims and Conti's counterclaims, Schor sought judicial review. The Court of Appeals ordered the dismissal of Conti's counterclaims on the ground that Congress did not authorize the Commission to adjudicate Conti's common law allegations. The appeals court interpreted the Commission's authority in this manner to avoid the constitutional question of whether such adjudication violated Article III. The Supreme Court reversed and held that Congress clearly authorized the Commission to adjudicate such counterclaims. The Court therefore considered the issue of whether the CFTC's assumption of jurisdiction over common law counterclaims violated Article III of the Constitution. Schor argued that Article III prohibited Congress from authorizing the initial adjudication of common law counterclaims by the CFTC, because its officers did not enjoy the tenure and salary protections embodied in Article III.]

... Our precedents ... demonstrate ... that Article III does not confer on litigants an absolute right to the plenary consideration of every nature of claim by an Article III court. Moreover, as a personal right, Article III's guarantee of an impartial and independent federal adjudication is subject to waiver, just as are other personal constitutional rights that dictate the procedures by which civil and criminal matters must be tried. . . .

In the instant cases, Schor indisputably waived any right he may have possessed to the full trial of Conti's counterclaim before an Article III court. Schor expressly demanded that Conti proceed on its counterclaim in the reparations proceeding rather than before the District Court, and was content to have the entire dispute settled in the forum he had selected until the ALJ ruled against him on all counts; it was only after the ALJ rendered a decision to which he objected that Schor raised any challenge to the CFTC's consideration of Conti's counterclaim.

Even were there no evidence of an express waiver here, Schor's election to forgo his right to proceed in state or federal court on his claim and his decision to seek relief instead in a CFTC reparations proceeding constituted an effective waiver. . . .

. . . [O]ur precedents establish that Article III, § 1, not only preserves to litigants their interest in an impartial and independent federal adjudication of claims within the judicial power of the United States, but also serves as "an inseparable element of the constitutional system of checks and balances." Article III, § 1 safeguards the role of the Judicial Branch in our tripartite system by barring congressional attempts "to transfer jurisdiction [to non–Article III tribunals] for the purpose of emasculating" constitutional courts, and thereby preventing "the encroachment or aggrandizement of one branch at the expense of the other." To the extent that this structural principle is implicated in a given case, the parties cannot by consent cure the constitutional difficulty for the same reason that the parties by consent cannot confer on federal courts subject-matter jurisdiction beyond the limitations imposed by Article III, § 2. When these Article III limitations are at issue, notions of consent and waiver cannot be dispositive because the limitations serve institutional interests that the parties cannot be expected to protect.

In determining the extent to which a given congressional decision to authorize the adjudication of Article III business in a non-Article III tribunal impermissibly threatens the institutional integrity of the Judicial Branch, the Court has declined to adopt formalistic and unbending rules. Although such rules might lend a greater degree of coherence to this area of the law, they might also unduly constrict Congress' ability to take needed and innovative action pursuant to its Article I powers. Thus, in reviewing Article III challenges, we have weighed a number of factors, none of which has been deemed determinative, with an eye to the practical effect that the congressional action will have on the constitutionally assigned role of the federal judiciary. Among the factors upon which we have focused are the extent to which the "essential attributes of judicial power" are reserved to Article III courts, and, conversely, the extent to which the non-Article III forum exercises the range of jurisdiction and powers normally vested only in Article III courts, the origins and importance of the right to be adjudicated, and the concerns that drove Congress to depart from the requirements of Article III.

An examination of the relative allocation of powers between the CFTC and Article III courts in light of the considerations given prominence in our precedents demonstrates that the congressional scheme does not impermissibly intrude on the province of the judiciary. The CFTC's adjudicatory powers depart from the traditional agency model in just one respect: the CFTC's jurisdiction over common law counterclaims. While wholesale importation of concepts of pendent or ancillary jurisdiction into the agency context may create greater constitutional difficulties, we decline to endorse an absolute prohibition on such jurisdiction out of fear of where some hypothetical "slippery slope" may deposit us . . . .

Of course, the nature of the claim has significance in our Article III analysis quite apart from the method prescribed for its adjudication. The counterclaim asserted in this litigation is a "private" right for which state law provides the rule of decision. It is therefore a claim of the kind assumed to be at the "core" of matters normally reserved to Article III courts. Yet this conclusion does not end our inquiry; just as this Court has rejected any attempt to make determinative for Article III purposes the distinction between public rights and private rights, there is no reason inherent in separation of powers principles to accord the state law character of a claim talismanic power in Article III inquiries.

We have explained that "the public rights doctrine reflects simply a pragmatic understanding that when Congress selects a quasi-judicial method of resolving matters that 'could be conclusively determined by the Executive and Legislative Branches,' the danger of encroaching on the judicial powers" is less than when private rights, which are normally within the purview of the judiciary, are relegated as an initial matter to administrative adjudication. Similarly, the state law character of a claim is significant for purposes of determining the effect that an initial adjudication of those claims by a non-Article III tribunal will have on the separation of powers for the simple reason that private, common law rights were historically the types of matters subject to resolution by Article III courts. The risk that Congress may improperly have encroached on the federal judiciary is obviously magnified when Congress "withdraw[s] from judicial cognizance any matter which, from its nature, is the subject of a suit at the common law, or in equity, or admiralty" and which therefore has traditionally been tried in Article III courts, and allocates the decision of those matters to a non-Article III forum of its own creation. Accordingly, where private, common law rights are at stake, our examination of the congressional attempt to control the manner in which those rights are adjudicated has been searching. In this litigation, however, "[l]ooking beyond form to the substance of what" Congress has done, we are persuaded that the congressional authorization of limited CFTC jurisdiction over a narrow class of common law claims as an incident to the CFTC's primary, and unchallenged, adjudicative function does not create a substantial threat to the separation of powers.

It is clear that Congress has not attempted to "withdraw from judicial cognizance" the determination of Conti's right to the sum represented by the debit balance in Schor's account. Congress gave the CFTC the authority to adjudicate such matters, but the decision to invoke this forum is left entirely to the parties and the power of the federal judiciary to take jurisdiction of these matters is unaffected. In such circumstances, separation of powers concerns are diminished, for it seems self-evident that just as Congress may encourage parties to settle a dispute out of court or resort to arbitration without impermissible incursions on the separation of powers, Congress may make available a quasi-judicial mechanism through which willing parties may, at their option, elect to resolve their differences. This is not to say, of course, that if Congress created a phalanx of non-Article III tribunals equipped to handle the entire business of the Article III courts without any Article III supervision or control and without evidence of valid and specific legislative necessities, the fact that the parties had the election to proceed in their forum of choice would necessarily save the scheme from constitutional attack. But this case obviously bears no resemblance to such a scenario, given the degree of judicial control saved to the federal courts, as well as the congressional purpose behind the jurisdictional delegation, the demonstrated need for the delegation, and the limited nature of the delegation.

When Congress authorized the CFTC to adjudicate counterclaims, its primary focus was on making effective a specific and limited federal regulatory scheme, not on allocating jurisdiction among federal tribunals. Congress intended to create an inexpensive and expeditious alternative forum through which customers could enforce the provisions of the CEA against professional brokers. Its decision to endow the CFTC with jurisdiction over such reparations claims is readily understandable given the perception that the CFTC was relatively immune from political pressures, and the obvious expertise that the Commission possesses in applying the CEA and its own regulations. This reparations scheme itself is of unquestioned constitutional validity. It was only to ensure the effectiveness of this scheme that Congress authorized the CFTC to assert jurisdiction over common law counterclaims. Indeed, as was explained above, absent the CFTC's exercise of that authority, the purposes of the reparations procedure would have been confounded....

... [If we were] to hold that the Legislative Branch may not permit such limited cognizance of common law counterclaims at the election of the parties, it is clear that we would "defeat the obvious purpose of the legislation to furnish a prompt, continuous, expert and inexpensive method for dealing with a class of questions of fact which are peculiarly suited to examination and determination by an administrative agency specially assigned to that task." We do not think Article III compels this degree of prophylaxis....

. . . We conclude that the limited jurisdiction that the CFTC asserts over state law claims as a necessary incident to the adjudication of federal claims willingly submitted by the parties for initial agency adjudication does not contravene separation of powers principles or Article III.

Notes and Questions

1. The Supreme Court in *Crowell* identified an exception to its holding that an agency could adjudicate private rights that may still have some importance. There the Court said that an agency could not finally adjudicate "constitutional facts," the facts that underlie a constitutional claim. The indication was that an Article III court must make a *de novo* determination of such facts. 253 U.S. at 46, 40 S.Ct. at 428; *see also Crowell v. Benson*, 285 U.S. 22, 52 S.Ct. 285, 76 L.Ed. 598 (1932). In a case involving a takings claim under the Fifth Amendment, for example, an Article III court would have to determine the factual issues of whether there had been a taking and whether there had been just compensation. The vitality of this doctrine is uncertain. In *Northern Pipeline*, the plurality said that *Crowell*'s "precise holding" with respect to constitutional facts had "been undermined by later cases. But the general principle of Crowell—distinguishing between congressionally created rights and constitutionally recognized rights—remains valid."

2. Does *Schor* narrow the scope of the public rights approach? In *Schor*, the Court recognizes that Article III's guarantee of an impartial and independent judiciary is a "personal right," but it determined that the right was waived. Is such a right now a constraint on Congress's authority to rely exclusively on non-Article III adjudicators? If so, *Schor*

> tells us nothing about how the Court would have weighed arguments appealing to Article III's fairness value in the absence of consent by the litigants to CFTC's jurisdiction. Moreover, there is still no answer to such basic questions as whether there are necessary threshold justifications for use of a non-Article III tribunal, whether appellate review by an article III court is always necessary, or whether the necessity for or the scope of appellate review varies in a systematic way with the kinds of questions that are at issue. The doctrine, in sum, lacks definition. The Court recognizes that article III literalism is not a feasible alternative, and its aspiration to accommodate competing concerns merits approval. Yet, the Court's methodology is underdeveloped, its standards obscure.

Richard H. Fallon, Jr., *Of Legislative Courts, Administrative Agencies, and Article III*, 101 HARV. L. REV. 915, 932–33 (1988).

3. For Professor Verkuil, the crucial inquiry concerning a person's individual right to Article III protection is "whether anything short of life tenure can adequately protect decisionmakers against conflicts of interest." Paul Verkuil, *Separation of Powers, The Rule of Law, and the Idea of Independence*, 30 WM. & MARY L. REV. 301, 316 (1988). "While

concerns about unbiased decision making implicate separation of powers concerns," Professor Verkuil believes that "the issue can be better resolved as a due process inquiry." After all, "[w]hen due process and separation of powers serve congruent interests, why should the latter be offended if the former is satisfied." Since the APA requires the use of Administrative Law Judges and the separation of functions, Professor Verkuil notes that the litigants in *Schor* were adequately protected against the danger of a biased decisionmaker. Moreover, the litigants in *Schor* also had the protection of judicial review under section 706(2) of the APA.

It is possible, however, that these protections would not apply. First, there is no requirement of due process unless the government has deprived someone of a liberty or property interest. Second, *Murray Lessee* apparently permits Congress to deny such review in cases involving public rights. The Supreme Court, however, has never held that Congress may cut off all judicial review of the administration of an entitlement program. The Court has implied on a number of occasions that there must be review of at least constitutional issues. *E.g.*, *Bowen v. Michigan Academy of Family Physicians*, 476 U.S. 667, 681 n. 12, 106 S.Ct. 2133, 2141 n. 12, 90 L.Ed.2d 623 (1986) (limitation on judicial review in Medicare Act does not apply to constitutional challenges to the Act).

4. Under the public rights approach announced in *Murray Lessee*, Congress is free to delegate the exclusive adjudication of legal and factual issues to non-Article III adjudicators. Professor Fallon is concerned that such an expansive view of public rights "threatens the rule of law" because it "displaces checks against arbitrary and self-interested government action." He would have the Court interpret Article III to preclude Congress from cutting off review of nonconstitutional legal issues concerning public rights: "No less in public than in private disputes, a requirement of judicial review of questions of law emerges from the basic concern that led the framers to fear location of judicial power in executive or legislative hands: that adjudication could become the tool for the selective or arbitrary pursuit of a political program, not authorized by law, that would deprive people of the security that a regime of law should provide." Fallon, *supra*, at 978. He admits that "[r]equiring judicial review of all questions of law would undoubtedly call for substantial revisions of existing practice," but he believes that separation of powers values "call for this conclusion." *Id.* at 983.

Fallon finds that judicial review of agency fact-finding is less necessary for the reasons indicated by Professor Verkuil, but he would retain the possibility that such review is compelled by Article III:

> A presumption against the necessary reviewability of issues of fact does not foreclose the possibility that fairness and integrity values could, in some cases, make review mandatory.... [I]n assessing the extent to which Article III fairness value is threatened, a crucially relevant factor involves the administrative safeguards available to

ensure the fairness of an agency's adjudication. The more generous the administrative procedures, the weaker is that argument that article III requires review of decisions of fact.

Id. at 987–88.

How would Professor Fallon's approach impact the Court of Veterans Appeals? Do you agree with Professor Fallon that rule of law objectives require the Court to interpret Article III to require judicial review of legal issues and of factual issues if administrative procedures do not guarantee fairness?

5. Professor Bruff proposes that Congress expand the Veterans Court. He recommends a new Article I Administrative Court "to have initial review jurisdiction" over high volume, fact-intensive programs, such as veterans and social security benefits, and other federal subjects. Harold H. Bruff, *Specialized Courts in Administrative Law*, 43 ADMIN. L. REV. 329, 364 (1991). Other subjects could include appeals from the International Trade Commission, the National Labor Relations Board, the Merit Systems Protection Board (which adjudicates employee dismissals from the federal civil service), and enforcement cases now decided by split-enforcement tribunals, such as the Occupational Safety and Health Review Commission (OSHRC). Do you approve of this suggestion?

Problem 6–2: Pesticide Royalties and Limited Judicial Review

The Federal Insecticide, Fungicide, and Rodenticide Act (FIFRA) requires any manufacturer of a chemical that may be used to control any pest to obtain a registration for that product from the Environmental Protection Agency (EPA). 7 U.S.C.A. § 136. Applicants for a new registration must provide, among other information, comprehensive animal studies from which the probable effects of a pesticide on humans can be evaluated. If EPA has reason to believe that the studies available to it do not adequately support a prior approval, it may require a registrant to produce additional data at any time.

Most chemicals are patented at the time that EPA issues a registration. When a patent expires, new companies can apply to EPA for a registration to sell the same chemical as the original applicant. Congress determined that it was wasteful for such "follow-on" companies to conduct their own animal testing to obtain regulatory approval. Because follow-on companies sell the same chemical as the original applicant, the animal studies submitted by the original registrant establish the safety of the chemical for additional registrants. Congress recognized, however, that it would be unfair for subsequent registrants to piggy back their applications on data paid for by the original registrant. It therefore established a process to ensure that the original registrant was paid for the use of its data by follow-on applicants. This process became embroiled in litigation, however, and as a result, follow-on pesticide registration ground to a halt.

Congress therefore adopted a new process for determining compensation. As amended, FIFRA authorizes EPA to consider previously submitted data only if a follow-on applicant has offered to compensate the original registrant for use of the data, and it requires binding arbitration if the two parties cannot agree on the amount of compensation. 7 U.S.C.A. § 136a(c)(1)(D). The decision of the arbitrator, who is appointed by the Federal Mediation and Conciliation Service, is subject to judicial review only for "fraud, misrepresentation, or other misconduct." In other words, there is no judicial review of the amount of compensation ordered by the arbitrator unless the dissatisfied party can prove the decision was the result of fraud, misrepresentation, or other misconduct.

The Large Chemical Company has appealed the results of an arbitration decision. It alleges that the compensation process violates Article III because it allocates to arbitrators a judicial function and because it severely restricts judicial review of an arbitrator's decision.

If you represented the chemical company, what arguments would you make that this arrangement violates Article III? If you represented the Justice Department, would arguments would you make that this arrangement does not violate Article III? How would you expect a court to rule?

2. SEVENTH AMENDMENT

When Congress creates a statutory cause of action, it may also state that a jury trial may be provided, thereby establishing a statutory right to a jury trial. When Congress establishes a preference for no jury trial, a party can contest the decision as a violation of the Seventh Amendment. The Seventh Amendment provides that "In suits at common law, where the value in controversy shall exceed $20, the right to trial by jury shall be preserved." U.S. Const., amend. VII. Most administrative adjudications, however, are safe from such a challenge because they involve public rights.

The Court has long sanctioned administrative adjudication of "public rights." In *Atlas Roofing Co. v. Occupational Safety and Health Review Commission*, 430 U.S. 442, 97 S.Ct. 1261, 51 L.Ed.2d 464 (1977), for example, the Court rejected the defendant's claim that the Seventh Amendment required a jury trial concerning the imposition of a financial penalty for violation of the Occupational Safety and Health Act. As you read earlier, the Occupational Safety and Health Review Commission (OSHRC), an independent agency, is responsible for the adjudication of OSHA citations. The Court held that

> when Congress creates new statutory "public rights," it may assign their adjudication to an administrative agency with which a jury trial would be incompatible, without violating the Seventh Amendment's injunction that jury trial is to be "preserved" in "suits at

common law." Congress is not required by the Seventh Amendment to choke the already crowded federal courts with new types of litigation nor prevented from committing some new types of litigation to administrative agencies with special competence in the relevant field. This is the case even if the Seventh Amendment would have required a jury where the adjudication of those rights is assigned instead to a federal court instead of an administrative agency. . . .

The reason is that administrative adjudication of public rights does "not constitute a suit at common law or in the nature of such a suit."

When Congress requires judicial adjudication of statutory public rights, the Seventh Amendment may require a jury trial. A jury trial is required if the plaintiff's cause of action historically is one that was a "legal" claim at common law, or if the cause of action was unknown at common law, if the action is analogous to a "legal" action at common law. The practice of the courts in 1791, when the Seventh Amendment was adopted, is the standard. In *Tull v. United States*, 481 U.S. 412, 107 S.Ct. 1831, 95 L.Ed.2d 365 (1987), for example, the Court held that a jury trial was necessary to determine whether a real estate developer was liable for civil penalties for violations of the Clean Water Act. The government sued the developer for filling in wetlands without the proper permits. A trial was required for the liability issue because the statutory action was analogous to the 18th century common law action of "debt" in the English courts. Conversely, the Court generally permits Congress to exclude jury trials for claims that historically were "equitable." If a claim is the same or similar to an "equitable" action before 1791, there is no right to a jury trial because proceedings in equity were tried before a chancellor in equity, who sat without a jury. For example, there is no right to a jury trial for claims that seek injunctive relief or specific performance.

Notes and Questions

1. Because administrative adjudication of "public rights" does not violate the Seventh Amendment, litigants will want to know the definition of a "public right." The Court uses the same definition that it uses concerning Article III: " 'The distinction is between cases of private right and those which arise *between the Government and persons subject to its authority in connection with the performance of the constitutional functions of the executive or legislative departments . . . .* ' " *Atlas Roofing*, 430 U.S. at 452 *quoting Crowell v. Benson*, 285 U.S. 22, 50–51, 52 S.Ct. 285, 292, 76 L.Ed. 598 (emphasis in original).

2. The definition of "public rights," however, can also include cases in which the government is not a party. In *Granfinanciera v. Nordberg*, 492 U.S. 33, 109 S.Ct. 2782, 106 L.Ed.2d 26 (1989), the issue was whether the Seventh Amendment applied to a dispute between two private parties that arose in the context of bankruptcy litigation. Accord-

ing to the Court, the mere fact that the dispute was between two private parties did not mean that a jury trial was required:

> In our most recent discussion of the "public rights" doctrine as it bears on Congress' power to commit adjudication of a statutory cause of action to a non-Article III tribunal, we rejected the view that "a matter of public rights must at a minimum arise 'between the government and others.'" We held, instead, that the Federal Government need not be a party for a case to revolve around "public rights." The crucial question, in cases not involving the Federal Government, is whether "Congress, acting for a valid legislative purpose pursuant to its constitutional powers under Article I, [has] create[d] a seemingly 'private' right that is so closely integrated into a public regulatory scheme as to be a matter appropriate for agency resolution with limited involvement by the Article III judiciary." If a statutory right is not closely intertwined with a federal regulatory program Congress has power to enact, and if that right neither belongs to nor exists against the Federal Government, then it must be adjudicated by an Article III court. If the right is legal in nature, then it carries with it the Seventh Amendment's guarantee of a jury trial. . . .

492 U.S. at 54–55, 109 S.Ct. at 2796–97.

3. Although *Granfinanciera* did not involve an agency, the Court's definition of "public rights" is important because administrative agencies sometimes adjudicate disputes between private parties. If the Court regards such statutory rights as "closely intertwined with a federal regulatory program that Congress had the power to enact," the rights are "public rights" and the Seventh Amendment does not apply. As *Granfinanciera* stated, "Congress may fashion causes of action that are closely analogous to common-law claims and place them beyond the ambit of the Seventh Amendment by assigning their resolution to a forum in which jury trials are unavailable." Congress, however, cannot simply reclassify a preexisting common law cause of action in order to eliminate a party's Seventh Amendment right to a jury trial. If all that Congress has done is to relabel a cause of action, the Court is unlikely to regard it as one that is "closely intertwined with a federal regulatory program." *See* JACK H. FRIEDENTHAL, MARY KAY KANE, & ARTHUR R. MILLER, CIVIL PROCEDURE 503 (2d ed. 1993).

In *Crowell v. Benson*, the Court approved agency adjudication of a federal worker's compensation claim as consistent with Article III despite the fact that the dispute involved a private right. After *Granfinanciera*, is a defendant in such an adjudication entitled to a jury trial because the right being resolved is a private right? Why or why not?

4. The issue of whether a jury trial is required often arises in a context that does not involve an administrative agency or a legislative court. When Congress creates a new statutory cause of action to be litigated by a private party in a federal district court, it may or may not provide for a jury trial. If it does not, a litigant may claim that one is

required by the Seventh Amendment. For example, this issue has been litigated frequently in enforcement actions brought under the Employee Retirement Income Security Act (ERISA), 29 U.S.C.A. § 1001–1461, which establishes comprehensive federal minimum standards governing private welfare and pension plans. Congress authorized the beneficiaries of such plans to sue plan administrators to enforce statutory requirements intended for their protection. *E.g.,* 29 U.S.C.A. § 1132(a)(1)(B). Most courts have held that Congress did not require a jury trial, and that the Seventh Amendment does not require one either. *See* Note, *The Right To A Jury Trial In Enforcement Actions Under Section 502(a)(1)(B) of ERISA,* 96 HARV. L. REV. 737 (1983).

Problem 6–3: Pesticide Royalties and the Right to a Jury

In Problem 6–2, you were asked to consider whether the method chosen by Congress to determine how much money a follow-on company owes the original company to license its pesticide data violated Article III. The issue arose because Congress significantly limited judicial review of the amount of royalties that an arbitrator might award.

Assume that the chemical company that opposes this arrangement also contends that the method violates the Seventh Amendment. The company contends that FIFRA requires it to sign a licensing agreement with the follow-on applicant, which permits the follow-on company to use its animal testing data, and that any dispute over compensation is therefore a matter of contract law. The Company therefore concludes that the Seventh Amendment entitles it to a jury trial because contract claims are "suits at common law."

If you are a Justice Department attorney, what argument(s) can you make that the compensation scheme does not violate the Seventh Amendment? How would you expect a court to rule?

D. THE LEGISLATIVE VETO

Until the legislative veto was declared to be unconstitutional, Congress reserved for itself the right to veto rules or orders in almost 200 statutes. The veto was popular because Congress could delegate substantial discretion to an agency and still retain the authority to disapprove of specific agency decisions. This section explains why the veto violates the requirements of presentment and bicameralism and discusses the legislative mechanisms that have been used to replace the veto.

1. PRESENTMENT AND BICAMERALISM

IMMIGRATION AND NATURALIZATION SERVICE v. CHADHA

462 U.S. 919, 103 S.Ct. 2764, 77 L.Ed.2d 317 (1983).

CHIEF JUSTICE BURGER delivered the opinion of the Court. . . .

[Chadha, who was born in Kenya, was lawfully admitted into the United States on a nonimmigrant student visa. More than a year after the visa expired, the Immigration and Naturalization Service (INS) began deportation proceedings. Chadha filed an application with the INS to suspend his deportation pursuant to section 244(a)(1) of the Immigration Act. This section permits a person to stay in this country if, among other conditions, deportation would result in an "extreme hardship." After a hearing, the Immigration Judge found that Chadha met the requirements of section 244(a)(1), and the Attorney General, who reviewed the decision, accepted it. The Attorney General, as required by statute, then conveyed its decision to suspend Chadha's deportation to Congress for a possible veto. The Immigration Act provided that the decision of the Attorney General would stand unless "either the Senate or the House of Representatives passes a resolution stating in substance that it does not favor the suspension of such deportation" within two sessions of Congress from the date of the Attorney General's report to Congress. The House of Representatives, without debate or recorded vote, passed a resolution of disapproval, and this lawsuit was brought.]

Explicit and unambiguous provisions of the Constitution prescribe and define the respective functions of the Congress and of the Executive in the legislative process. . . . Art. I provides:

"All legislative Powers herein granted shall be vested in a Congress of the United States, which shall consist of a Senate *and* a House of Representatives." Art. I, § 1. (Emphasis added).

"Every Bill which shall have passed the House of Representatives *and* the Senate, *shall*, before it becomes a Law, be presented to the President of the United States; . . ." Art. I, § 7, cl. 2. (Emphasis added).

"*Every* Order, Resolution, or Vote to which the Concurrence of the Senate and House of Representatives may be necessary (except on a question of Adjournment) *shall be* presented to the President of the United States; and before the Same shall take Effect, *shall be* approved by him, or being disapproved by him, *shall be* repassed by two thirds of the Senate and House of Representatives, according to the Rules and Limitations prescribed in the Case of a Bill." Art. I, § 7, cl. 3. (Emphasis added). . . .

The records of the Constitutional Convention reveal that the requirement that all legislation be presented to the President before becoming law was uniformly accepted by the Framers. . . .

The decision to provide the President with a limited and qualified power to nullify proposed legislation by veto was based on the profound conviction of the Framers that the powers conferred on Congress were the powers to be most carefully circumscribed. It is beyond doubt that lawmaking was a power to be shared by both Houses and the President. . . .

The President's role in the lawmaking process also reflects the Framers' careful efforts to check whatever propensity a particular Congress might have to enact oppressive, improvident, or ill-considered measures. . . .

The bicameral requirement of Art. I, §§ 1, 7 was of scarcely less concern to the Framers than was the Presidential veto and indeed the two concepts are interdependent. By providing that no law could take effect without the concurrence of the prescribed majority of the Members of both Houses, the Framers reemphasized their belief, already remarked upon in connection with the Presentment Clauses, that legislation should not be enacted unless it has been carefully and fully considered by the Nation's elected officials. . . .

. . . It emerges clearly that the prescription for legislative action in Art. I, §§ 1, 7 represents the Framers' decision that the legislative power of the Federal government be exercised in accord with a single, finely wrought and exhaustively considered, procedure.

[We turn then to the question whether the action exercised by the House of Representatives in this case involves legislative action subject to Article I, § 7.] When any Branch acts, it is presumptively exercising the power the Constitution has delegated to it. . . .

Examination of the action taken here by one House pursuant to § 244(c)(2) reveals that it was essentially legislative in purpose and effect. In purporting to exercise power defined in Art. I, § 8, cl. 4 to "establish an uniform Rule of Naturalization," the House took action that had the purpose and effect of altering the legal rights, duties and relations of persons, including the Attorney General, Executive Branch officials and Chadha, all outside the legislative branch. Section 244(c)(2) purports to authorize one House of Congress to require the Attorney General to deport an individual alien whose deportation otherwise would be canceled under § 244. The one-House veto operated in this case to overrule the Attorney General and mandate Chadha's deportation; absent the House action, Chadha would remain in the United States. Congress has acted and its action has altered Chadha's status. . . .

The nature of the decision implemented by the one-House veto in this case further manifests its legislative character. After long experience with the clumsy, time consuming private bill procedure, Congress made a deliberate choice to delegate to the Executive Branch, and specifically to the Attorney General, the authority to allow deportable aliens to remain in this country in certain specified circumstances. . . . Disagreement with the Attorney General's decision on Chadha's deportation—that is, Congress' decision to deport—no less than Congress' original choice to delegate to the Attorney General the authority to make that decision, involves determinations of policy that Congress can implement in only one way; bicameral passage followed by presentment to the President. Congress must abide by its delegation of authority until that delegation is legislatively altered or revoked. . . .

Since it is clear that the action by the House under § 244(c)(2) was not within any of the express constitutional exceptions authorizing one House to act alone, and equally clear that it was an exercise of legislative power, that action was subject to the standards prescribed in Article I. . . .

JUSTICE WHITE, dissenting. . . .

The prominence of the legislative veto mechanism in our contemporary political system and its importance to Congress can hardly be overstated. It has become a central means by which Congress secures the accountability of executive and independent agencies. Without the legislative veto, Congress is faced with a Hobson's choice: either to refrain from delegating the necessary authority, leaving itself with a hopeless task of writing laws with the requisite specificity to cover endless special circumstances across the entire policy landscape, or in the alternative, to abdicate its law-making function to the executive branch and independent agencies. To choose the former leaves major national problems unresolved; to opt for the latter risks unaccountable policymaking by those not elected to fill that role. Accordingly, over the past five decades, the legislative veto has been placed in nearly 200 statutes. . . .

. . . The Constitution does not directly authorize or prohibit the legislative veto. Thus, our task should be to determine whether the legislative veto is consistent with the purposes of Art. I and the principles of Separation of Powers which are reflected in that Article and throughout the Constitution. . . .

. . . If the effective functioning of a complex modern government requires the delegation of vast authority which, by virtue of its breadth, is legislative or "quasi-legislative" in character, I cannot accept that Article I—which is, after all, the source of the non-delegation doctrine— should forbid Congress from qualifying that grant with a legislative veto. . . .

The central concern of the presentation and bicameralism requirements of Article I is . . . fully satisfied by the operation of § 244(c)(2). The President's approval is found in the Attorney General's action in recommending to Congress that the deportation order for a given alien be suspended. The House and the Senate indicate their approval of the Executive's action by not passing a resolution of disapproval within the statutory period. . . .

Thus understood, § 244(c)(2) fully effectuates the purposes of the bicameralism and presentation requirements. . . .

Notes and Questions

1. Mr. Chadha was in desperate trouble at the time his visa to stay in the United States had expired. Although Mr Chadha was born in Kenya, Kenya did not recognize him as a citizen, and although he had come to the United States from the United Kingdom, the United Kingdom did not recognize him as eligible for residence. The Attorney General's decision that Mr. Chadha qualified for a hardship exception was based on the fact that he was literally "stateless." For a fascinating account of Mr. Chadha's plight and the constitutional litigation, SEE BARBARA H. CRAIG, CHADHA: THE STORY OF AN EPIC CONSTITUTIONAL STRUGGLE (1988).

After Chadha's long search for a lawyer, Ms. Craig's book recounts that John Pohlmann, an immigration attorney, agreed to represent him:

> Providence at last rewarded Chadha's perseverance, for in Pohlmann he found a kindred spirit—one who was equally outraged by what Chadha had experienced. Beneath the three-piece, pin-striped lawyer's uniform lurked a sensitive and caring soul. During Pohlmann's long-haired, hippie days as a mid-sixties undergraduate at San Jose State University and at law school in San Francisco, he had developed a sense of fairness and a passion for causes. Although there was little prospect of being paid, he took on the case without hesitation. Of Pohlmann, Chadha says admiringly, "He is a pearl of a human being. He stood behind me and my fight all the way and never would let me pay him a dime, even when I could have afforded to. As long as I live, he will always be someone I remember as having a great effect on my life."

Id. at 25.

Although Pohlmann immediately believed that the veto by Congress was not only unjust, but unconstitutional, his familiarity with constitutional law was "more than a bit rusty." Pohlmann persevered despite this limitation and limited resources. Fortunately for Mr. Chadha, Alan Morrison, a nationally renowned Supreme Court litigator for Public Citizen, a not-for-profit public interest law firm, learned of the case from a contact at the Department of Justice, which was opposed to the veto. After Morrison telephoned Pohlmann to learn about the case, the attorney, with Mr. Chadha's blessing, asked Morrison for assistance. Morrison argued the case in the Supreme Court.

2. Although *Chadha* involved an adjudicatory decision, the Court quickly indicated that rulemaking vetoes were likewise unconstitutional. It affirmed per curiam and without opinion (except to cite to *Chadha*) two decisions by the Court of Appeals for the District of Columbia that had invalidated legislative vetoes of agency rules. *Consumer Energy Council v. FERC,* 673 F.2d 425 (D.C.Cir.1982), *affirmed sub nom. Process Gas Consumers Group v. Consumer Energy Council,* 463 U.S. 1216, 103 S.Ct. 3556, 77 L.Ed.2d 1402 (1983) (one-house veto); *Consum-*

ers Union v. FTC, 691 F.2d 575 (D.C.Cir.1982), *affirmed sub nom. United States Senate v. FTC*, 463 U.S. 1216, 103 S.Ct. 3556, 77 L.Ed.2d 1402 (1983) (veto by concurrent resolution). Because *Chadha* was based on both presentment and bicameralism, even when a statute requires a concurrent resolution of disapproval, the law is invalid for failing to provide for presentment. Joint resolutions, however, are the same as legislation; they require action by both houses and approval by the President (or legislative override of his veto). The only distinction between a joint resolution and a bill is a parliamentary one; resolutions are not subject to amendment, whereas bills are.

3. In *Chadha* the Court determined that the legislative veto in section 244 of the Immigration Act was unconstitutional. But how much of section 244 was unconstitutional—the whole section or just the legislative veto portion? If the whole section was unconstitutional, Chadha would have to be deported, because that section was the source of his right as an illegal alien to stay in the United States, as well as the source of the legislative veto. Indeed, this was Justice Rehnquist's interpretation. He dissented in *Chadha* on the grounds that Chadha did not have standing, because under Justice Rehnquist's interpretation of the effect of a ruling in Chadha's favor, he would still be deported. Hence, Chadha's injury would not be redressed by a favorable court ruling. The issue of how much of a provision is unconstitutional is called "severability" or "separability."

4. The Immigration Act contained a severability clause typical of federal statutes, stating, in effect, that if any portion of the law is found unconstitutional, the rest shall remain. Severing the one-house veto in the Immigration Act from the rest of the section leaves the Attorney General with the requirement to report to Congress his decision to suspend an illegal alien's deportation, and then to wait the two sessions of Congress. At the end of that period of time, the alien's deportation is finally waived. Similarly, with respect to other legislative veto provisions, the agency treats the provision as a "report-and-wait" provision. The agency sends notice of the action to Congress, as required by the statutory provision, waits the requisite period of time provided in the statute for the exercise of the legislative veto, and at the end of the period (whether or not Congress has tried to veto the action) declares the action final.

5. Peter McCutchen has proposed that the Supreme Court engage in a "form of constitutional damage control." Peter B. McCutchen, *Mistakes, Precedent, and the Rise of the Administrative State: Toward A Constitutional Theory of the Second Best*, 80 CORN. L. REV. 1, 2 (1994). McCutchen, like Professor Lawson (discussed earlier), believes that the administrative state is clearly unconstitutional, but he recognizes that the Supreme Court is unlikely to overrule "an immense and deeply rooted body of precedent." *Id.* He therefore proposes that "[w]here unconstitutional institutions are allowed to stand based on a theory of precedent, the Court should allow (or even require) the creation of compensating institutions that seek to move governmental structures

closer to constitutional equilibrium." *Id.* at 3. For example, he would have the Supreme Court overrule *Chadha*. The legislative veto, which would be unconstitutional if considered as an original matter, should be approved because it compensates for the open ended delegations of legislative authority to administrative agencies, which are also unconstitutional. *Id.*

Was Justice White following something like McCutchen's theory in his dissent in *Chadha*? Would you support the Court overruling *Chadha* on the basis proposed by Justice White?

6.   In his dissent, Justice White indicated his belief that the legislative veto was indispensable to modern American government. Do you sense that in the ten-plus years since *Chadha* that the absence of a legislative veto by Congress has seriously affected the government? Is the Hobson's choice real?

2.   POST–VETO DEVELOPMENTS

Congress has recently taken two steps to reassert its authority over agency decisionmaking in the wake of *Chadha*. In 1995, the House of Representatives established "Corrections Day" as a method to expedite review of agency orders and rules. Further, a 1996 law requires agencies to submit all rules to Congress for its review and stays the effective date of major rules to permit legislative review.

a.   *Corrections Day*

Corrections Day involves a process established by the House of Representatives for correction of agency "mistakes." After a House committee approves a bill, it can apply to have it placed on the Corrections Calendar which specifies one or two days a month when the House will consider adoption of the bill under fast-track procedures. The decision to place a bill on the calendar is made by the Speaker after consultation with the Minority Leader and an advisory committee. The rules for Corrections Day expedite consideration of the bill in three ways: there is a limited time for debate; only the chair of the committee with jurisdiction over the bill can move to amend it; and opponents are limited to one motion to recommit the bill. However, a bill must pass by a sixty percent majority on Corrections Day. Any bill that fails to pass can be considered at a later date under normal House rules. The House rules do not limit what type of agency action is eligible for this expedited treatment. 141 Cong. Rec. H6104 (daily ed. June 20, 1995). Of course, even if the bill passes the House, it still must be considered and passed by the Senate (and signed by the President), which has no comparable fast-track procedure.

b.   *Congressional Review of Agency Rulemaking*

The entire Congress will implement fast-track procedures for the review of agency rulemaking. *See* 5 U.S.C.A. §§ 801–808. Agencies must submit all new rules to Congress and the Comptroller General, along with copies of any cost-benefit analysis, regulatory flexibility analysis, and analysis undertaken pursuant to the Unfunded Mandates Reform Act of 1995. The Comptroller General will certify to Congress that an agency has complied with its submission requirements.

A major rule cannot take effect until 60 days after the previous information is submitted to Congress, or after the rule is published in the Federal Register, which ever date is later. A major rule is one with an annual economic impact of $100 million or more or with other significant regulatory impacts identified in the legislation. This stay does not apply if a rule is not a major rule, if the President certifies by Executive Order that immediate implementation is necessary for, among other reasons, an imminent threat to health or safety or other emergency, or if an agency determines that it has good cause for promulgating the rule without prior notice and comment.

If a joint resolution of disapproval is introduced within 60 calendar days after Congress receives a rule, the Senate has 60 *session* days and the House has 60 *legislative* days in which to employ the fast-track procedures to pass the resolution. Since *session* and *legislative* days measure the time in which each House is actually in session, the period for fast-track procedures can last several months. The fast-track procedures are designed primarily to permit consideration of the resolution in the Senate free of procedural roadblocks. A resolution may not amend the agency rule; it can only disapprove it. Further, debate in the Senate over the resolution will be limited to 10 hours (thereby eliminating filibusters); the resolution may not be amended or postponed; and it is not subject to other procedural motions that otherwise would be in order. If one House has passed a resolution, the resolution may not be referred to committee in the other House. Once a vote has taken place in each House, there is no House–Senate conference committee.

If the joint resolution is passed by Congress and signed by the President, a rule will not take effect, or if it has already gone into effect because the 60–day stay expired, the rule will cease to be in effect. In addition, a rule that has been disapproved "may not be reissued in substantially the same form, and a new rule that is substantially the same as such a rule may not be issued, unless the reissued or new rule is specifically authorized by a law enacted after the date of the joint resolution disapproving the original rule."

Notes and Questions

1. Supporters believe Corrections Day will permit the House to act quickly to remedy statutory mistakes and thereby to increase agency accountability to Congress and the public. Critics worry that the expedited process will permit special interest groups to use Corrections Day to undo legislative compromises and gain benefits that they were unable to secure in court, before an agency, or in Congress when the legislation was originally enacted. *See* John C. Nagle, *Corrections Day*, 43 U.C.L.A.

L. Rev. 1267 (1996) (describing the debate over Corrections Day). According to Professor Nagle, legislative debates and House actions on Corrections Day indicate that the House intends to address mistakes that are obvious, dumb or expensive, that were caused by a drafting error, an unintentional ambiguity, or a provision that has become outdated because of changed circumstances, and that have solutions that are noncontroversial, narrowly focussed, and able to receive bipartisan support. *Id.* at 1310–12. Is Corrections Day a good idea? Does your answer depend on whether the House applies the criteria identified by Professor Nagle? If so, why are such limitations necessary?

2. The following assessment of the congressional review procedures predicts that they are unlikely to have a dramatic impact, but it concludes that the procedures are nevertheless a positive development:

> There may be less to these procedures than meets the eye, given the President's ability to veto any resolution of disapproval passed by Congress. Moreover, increasing to sixty calendar days the period before which a major rule goes into effect does not substantially extend the current period [of 30 days in the APA]. Also, while these procedures certainly create and even increase the possibility that a rule would go into effect and then be repealed, this potentiality exists today. Congress can always override or change an existing agency rule if it can secure the President's agreement or override his veto.

> These procedures are likely to be of some effect, however. First, the Comptroller General, who only has fifteen calendar days during which to summarize the rule and report on it to Congress, takes on increased responsibility and power. Second, agencies may well be more likely to informally clear rules with Congress and the relevant congressional committees. Third, the uncertainty concerning whether rules will remain in effect will increase, but probably not dramatically. (There are an estimated 75–100 new major rules each year; Congress will be hard-pressed to act on more than a few of the most controversial ones.) Finally, these procedures will give Congress some accountability for the consequences of their broad delegations to independent agencies. That alone may justify the increased administrative burden that these new procedures will undoubtedly place on agencies.

Daniel E. Troy, *New Congressional Review Procedures of Agency Rules*, 21 ADMIN. & REG. LAW NEWS 4, 19 (Summer, 1996). Do you agree with this assessment? Do you think the legislative review requirement will add to the ossification of rulemaking some have perceived? In fact, as of 2000, Congress has not overturned any rule submitted to it since the law was enacted, and the only resolution of disapproval ever introduced was introduced solely for the purpose of having the resolution voted down so that the rule could go into effect before the full waiting period had expired. Does this say anything about the effectiveness of legislative rule review?

3. In 2000, Congress enacted the Truth in Regulating Act, Pub. L. No. 106–312, which requires the General Accounting Office to evaluate those agencies' cost-benefit analyses referred to it by the chair of a congressional committee. This is a 3–year pilot program. Do you think this will result in more activity by Congress in its rule review?

4. Most states have preceded Congress in establishing legislative mechanisms to review regulations issued by agencies. *See* ARTHUR E. BONFIELD, STATE ADMINISTRATIVE RULEMAKING § 8.3.1(b) (1986). The typical approach is to establish a single, standing committee, composed of members of both Houses. The Model State Administrative Procedure Act recommends that such a committee should "selectively review possible, proposed, or adopted rules and prescribe appropriate committee procedures for that purpose," and that the committee "may receive and investigate complaints from the public with respect to possible, proposed, or adopted rules and hold public proceedings on those complaints." 1981 MSAPA § 3–204. The model code also recommends that when a committee "objects to all or some portion of a rule because the committee considers it to be beyond the procedural or substantive authority delegated to the adopting agency," it can file an objection with the Secretary of State to be published and transmitted to the relevant agency. *Id.* § 3–204(d). Finally, the code indicates that the committee may "recommend that a particular rule be superseded in whole or in part by a statute." *Id.* § 3–204(c). This last provision is consistent with *Chadha* because it requires that a legislature pass a law signed by the governor to overrule an agency rule. State supreme courts have followed *Chadha* in interpreting their state constitutions except in cases where there is an express constitutional provision authorizing some type of legislative veto. BON-FIELD, *supra*, § 8.3.2(c).

Problem 6–4: Legislative Review

There are those in Congress who believe the legislative review law did not go far enough. They are aware that most major rules will slide by without serious congressional review. The Chair of the House Oversight Committee asks you, as an attorney for the committee, to assess the constitutionality of laws that would enact the following additional possible measures:

(a) Any congressional committee may by majority vote further stay the effective date of a major rule for 90 additional days beyond the statutorily required 60.

(b) The Director of the Office of Management and Budget may suspend indefinitely the effect of any rule adopted by any federal agency, if the Director finds that it does not maximize the net benefits to society.

(c) No major rule adopted by any federal agency shall be effective unless approved by a joint resolution of Congress.

E. APPOINTMENT POWER

Congress has also sought to increase its influence over agency administrators by participating in their appointment or removal. It has directly appointed administrators and reserved the right to remove them, limited the President's power to remove administrators, and given itself the authority to veto administrative orders and rules. The Supreme Court has declared all of these efforts to be unconstitutional except the limitations on the President's removal powers.

1. APPOINTMENT OF "OFFICERS OF THE UNITED STATES"

Article II requires that the President "shall nominate, and by and with the Advice and Consent of the Senate, shall appoint Ambassadors, other public Ministers and Consuls, Judges of the Supreme Court, and all other Officers of the United States, whose appointments are not herein otherwise provided for, and which shall be established by law; but the Congress may by Law vest the appointment of such inferior Officers, as they think proper, in the President alone, in the Courts of Law, or in the Heads of Departments." U.S. Const. art. II, § 2. The following case discusses two issues raised by this clause. First, does Article II vest the power to appoint "Officers of the United States" exclusively in the President? Although the clause seems clear on this point, the Supreme Court was required to clarify that Congress does not share this power under the "necessary and proper" clause in Article I. Article I authorizes Congress "To make all Laws which shall be necessary and proper for carrying into Execution the foregoing Powers, and all Powers vested by this Constitution in the Government of the United States, or in any Department or Officer thereof." U.S. Const. art. I, § 8. Second, if "Officers of the United States" must be appointed by the President, are there employees who are not "Officers of the United States" and may therefore be chosen by Congress?

BUCKLEY v. VALEO

424 U.S. 1, 96 S.Ct. 612, 46 L.Ed.2d 659 (1976).

PER CURIAM.

[In the wake of Watergate, Congress passed the Federal Election Campaign Act of 1971 (Act), which required candidates to report campaign donations and expenditures and which limited different types of campaign spending. Congress created the Federal Election Commission (FEC) to administer and implement the Act. The FEC was authorized to promulgate regulations, investigate possible violations of the Act or its rules, and to adjudicate whether violations had actually occurred. The Commission had six voting members. Two were appointed by the President pro tempore of the Senate, after receiving the recommendations of the majority and minority leaders of the Senate, and two more were appointed by the Speaker of the House of Representatives, after receiving the recommendations of its respective majority and minority leaders.

The President appointed the remaining two members. The Secretary of the Senate and the Clerk of the House of Representatives were *ex officio* members without the right to vote.]

Appellants urge that since Congress has given the Commission wide-ranging rulemaking and enforcement powers with respect to the substantive provisions of the Act, Congress is precluded under the principle of separation of powers from vesting in itself the authority to appoint those who will exercise such authority. . . .

Appellee Commission and amici in support of the Commission urge that the Framers of the Constitution, while mindful of the need for checks and balances among the three branches of the National Government, had no intention of denying to the Legislative Branch authority to appoint its own officers. Congress, either under the Appointments Clause or under its grants of substantive legislative authority and the Necessary and Proper Clause in Art. I, is in their view empowered to provide for the appointment to the Commission in the manner which it did because the Commission is performing "appropriate legislative functions."

2.   THE APPOINTMENTS CLAUSE . . .

We think that the term "Officers of the United States" as used in Art. II, defined to include "all persons who can be said to hold an office under the government" . . . is a term intended to have substantive meaning. We think its fair import is that any appointee exercising significant authority pursuant to the laws of the United States is an "Officer of the United States," and must, therefore, be appointed in the manner prescribed by § 2, cl. 2, of that Article . . . .[162]

. . . Unless their selection is elsewhere provided for, all Officers of the United States are to be appointed in accordance with the Clause. Principal officers are selected by the President with the advice and consent of the Senate. Inferior officers Congress may allow to be appointed by the President alone, by the heads of departments, or by the Judiciary. No class or type of officer is excluded because of its special functions. The President appoints judicial as well as executive officers. Neither has it been disputed and apparently it is not now disputed that the Clause controls the appointment of the members of a typical administrative agency even though its functions, as this Court recognized in *Humphrey's Executor v. United States*, 295 U.S. 602 (1935), may be "predominantly quasijudicial and quasilegislative" rather than executive. . . .

Appellee Commission and amici . . . contend, and the majority of the Court of Appeals agreed with them, that whatever shortcomings the provisions for the appointment of members of the Commission might

---

162. "Officers of the United States" does not include all employees of the United States, but there is no claim made that the Commissioners are employees of the United States rather than officers. Employees are lesser functionaries subordinate to officers of the United States, whereas the Commissioners, appointed for a statutory term, are not subject to the control or direction of any other executive, judicial, or legislative authority.

have under Art. II, Congress had ample authority under the Necessary and Proper Clause of Art. I to effectuate this result. We do not agree. The proper inquiry when considering the Necessary and Proper Clause is not the authority of Congress to create an office or a commission, which is broad indeed, but rather its authority to provide that its own officers may make appointments to such office or commission.

So framed, the claim that Congress may provide for this manner of appointment under the Necessary and Proper Clause of Art. I stands on no better footing than the claim that it may provide for such manner of appointment because of its substantive authority to regulate federal elections. Congress could not, merely because it concluded that such a measure was "necessary and proper" to the discharge of its substantive legislative authority, pass a bill of attainder or ex post facto law contrary to the prohibitions contained in § 9 of Art. I. No more may it vest in itself, or in its officers, the authority to appoint officers of the United States when the Appointments Clause by clear implication prohibits it from doing so.

3. THE COMMISSION'S POWERS

Thus, on the assumption that all of the powers granted in the statute may be exercised by an agency whose members have been appointed in accordance with the Appointments Clause, the ultimate question is which, if any, of those powers may be exercised by the present voting Commissioners, none of whom was appointed as provided by that Clause. Our previous description of the statutory provisions disclosed that the Commission's powers fall generally into three categories: functions relating to the flow of necessary information-receipt, dissemination, and investigation; functions with respect to the Commission's task of fleshing out the statute—rulemaking and advisory opinions; and functions necessary to ensure compliance with the statute and rules—informal procedures, administrative determinations and hearings, and civil suits.

Insofar as the powers confided in the Commission are essentially of an investigative and informative nature, falling in the same general category as those powers which Congress might delegate to one of its own committees, there can be no question that the Commission as presently constituted may exercise them. . . .

But when we go beyond this type of authority to the more substantial powers exercised by the Commission, we reach a different result. The Commission's enforcement power, exemplified by its discretionary power to seek judicial relief, is authority that cannot possibly be regarded as merely in aid of the legislative function of Congress. A lawsuit is the ultimate remedy for a breach of the law, and it is to the President, and not to the Congress, that the Constitution entrusts the responsibility to "take Care that the Laws be faithfully executed." Art. II, § 3.

Congress may undoubtedly under the Necessary and Proper Clause create "offices" in the generic sense and provide such method of appointment to those "offices" as it chooses. But Congress' power under that Clause is inevitably bounded by the express language of Art. II, § 2, cl. 2, and unless the method it provides comports with the latter, the holders of those offices will not be "Officers of the United States." They may, therefore, properly perform duties only in aid of those functions that Congress may carry out by itself, or in an area sufficiently removed from the administration and enforcement of the public law as to permit their being performed by persons not "Officers of the United States."

We hold that these provisions of the Act, vesting in the Commission primary responsibility for conducting civil litigation in the courts of the United States for vindicating public rights, violate Art. II, § 2, cl. 2, of the Constitution. Such functions may be discharged only by persons who are "Officers of the United States" within the language of that section.

All aspects of the Act are brought within the Commission's broad administrative powers: rulemaking, advisory opinions, and determinations of eligibility for funds and even for federal elective office itself. These functions, exercised free from day-to-day supervision of either Congress or the Executive Branch, are more legislative and judicial in nature than are the Commission's enforcement powers, and are of kinds usually performed by independent regulatory agencies or by some department in the Executive Branch under the direction of an Act of Congress. Congress viewed these broad powers as essential to effective and impartial administration of the entire substantive framework of the Act. Yet each of these functions also represents the performance of a significant governmental duty exercised pursuant to a public law. While the President may not insist that such functions be delegated to an appointee of his removable at will, *Humphrey's Executor v. United States*, none of them operates merely in aid of congressional authority to legislate or is sufficiently removed from the administration and enforcement of public law to allow it to be performed by the present Commission. These administrative functions may therefore be exercised only by persons who are "Officers of the United States." . . .

Conclusion

In summary, . . . we hold that most of the powers conferred by the Act upon the Federal Election Commission can be exercised only by "Officers of the United States," appointed in conformity with Art. II, § 2, cl. 2, of the Constitution, and therefore cannot be exercised by the Commission as presently constituted. . . .

Notes and Questions

1. Why does the Constitution permit Congress to appoint officers whose function is limited to an investigative or informative nature, but it does not allow the legislative appointment of officers who engage in adjudicative, legislative, or enforcement functions? Why are the FEC Commissioners "officers" of the United States? What definition of "officer" does the Court adopt?

2. After *Buckley*, Congress reconstituted the Commission to permit the President to appoint its six members with the advice and consent of the Senate, but the Secretary of the Senate and the Clerk of the House of Representatives remained as ex officio members. After the Commission brought an enforcement action against the National Rifle Association (NRA) for violation of a campaign finance law, the association moved to dismiss the action on the ground that the composition of the Commission violated separation of powers. The Commission argued that ex officio members were constitutionally harmless because they could not vote in Commission meetings, but the D.C. Circuit rejected this argument because "we cannot conceive why Congress would wish or expect its officials to serve as ex officio members if not to exercise some influence.... Advice ... surely implies influence, and Congress must limit the exercise of its influence, whether in the form of advice or not, to its legislative role." *FEC v. NRA Political Victory Fund*, 6 F.3d 821, 826–27 (D.C.Cir.1993). The FEC petitioned for certiorari, but after the Supreme Court granted certiorari, it subsequently dismissed the petition on the ground that the FEC could not independently petition for certiorari. Pursuant to the statute vesting litigating authority for the United States in the Attorney General; only the Solicitor General could petition for certiorari on behalf of agencies, absent specific statutory authority to the contrary.

Problem 6–5: Legislative Appointments

You are hired by the Citizens for the Abatement of Aircraft Noise (CAAN) which is upset with plans for the operation of Ronald Reagan (formerly known as Washington National) Airport, which is operated by the Metropolitan Washington Airport Authority (MWAA), an interstate compact agency.

The federal government owned National Airport prior to the creation of the MWAA. When Congress transferred ownership, it made most of the important decisions by the MWAA subject to approval by a federal "Board of Review" composed of nine members of Congress, who are appointed by the MWAA from nominations submitted by the leadership of the House and Senate. The leadership submitted only nine names to the MWAA for selection to the Board of Review as the law allowed. The legislation also provided that the members of Congress were to serve in their "individual capacities" as representatives of users of the airport. Congress created the Board of Review in response to objections by some members that surrender of federal control might result in the transfer of flights from National to Dulles Airport, which also serves Washington. National is about a twelve minute ride from the Capital, whereas Dulles requires a drive of about one hour.

The MWAA decided to limit the hours of operation of Ronald Reagan Airport, prohibiting operation after 11 p.m., so as to reduce noise impacts on the surrounding area. In its decision it said that later flights could instead depart from and arrive at Dulles Airport because of its rural location. The Board of Review, however, vetoed the MWAA's decision, so that flights could continue leaving and arriving at Ronald Reagan Airport after 11 p.m.

As CAAN's attorney, what argument can you make that the appointment process for members of the Board of Review is unconstitutional. How likely is it that you will succeed?

2. APPOINTMENT OF "INFERIOR OFFICERS"

Article II vests in the President the power to appoint "Officers of the United States," but it makes alternative arrangements for the appointment of inferior officers: Congress "may by Law vest the appointment of such inferior Officers, as they think proper, in the President alone, in the Courts of Law, or in the Heads of Departments." U.S. Const. art. II, § 2. The next case indicates how the Court distinguishes between "Officers of the United States," who must be appointed by the President with the concurrence of the Senate, and "inferior officers," who may be appointed by any of the three methods indicated in the appointments clause.

MORRISON v. OLSON
487 U.S. 654, 108 S.Ct. 2597, 101 L.Ed.2d 569 (1988).

CHIEF JUSTICE REHNQUIST delivered the opinion of the Court....

I

[The Ethics in Government Act, 28 U.S.C. §§ 591–599, requires the Attorney General, upon receipt of information that is "sufficient to constitute grounds to investigate whether any person [covered by the Act] may have violated any Federal criminal law," to conduct a preliminary investigation of the matter. When this investigation is completed, or 90 days has elapsed, the Attorney General is required to report to the Special Division, which is a special court Congress created to appoint independent counsels. The court is located in the District of Columbia Court of Appeals and consists of three circuit court judges or justices appointed by the Chief Justice of the United States. 28 U.S. § 49. If the Attorney General determines that "there are no reasonable grounds to believe that further investigation is warranted," then the Special Division has no power to appoint an independent counsel. If the Attorney General has determined that there are "reasonable grounds to believe that further investigation or prosecution is warranted," then the court appoints an independent counsel and defines the counsel's prosecutorial jurisdiction. The independent counsel has "full power and independent authority to exercise all investigative and prosecutorial functions and powers of the Department of Justice, the Attorney General, and any other officer or employee of the Department of Justice."]

... In 1982, two Subcommittees of the House of Representatives issued subpoenas directing the Environmental Protection Agency (EPA) to produce certain documents relating to the efforts of the EPA and the Land and Natural Resources Division of the Justice Department to enforce the "Superfund Law." At that time, appellee Olson was the Assistant Attorney General for the Office of Legal Counsel (OLC).... Acting on the advice of the Justice Department, the President ordered the Administrator of EPA to invoke executive privilege to withhold certain of the documents on the ground that they contained "enforcement sensitive information." The Administrator obeyed this order and withheld the documents. In response, the House voted to hold the Administrator in contempt, after which the Administrator and the United States together filed a lawsuit against the House. The conflict abated in March 1983, when the administration agreed to give the House Subcommittees limited access to the documents.

The following year, the House Judiciary Committee began an investigation into the Justice Department's role in the controversy over the EPA documents. During this investigation, appellee Olson testified before a House Subcommittee on March 10, 1983. Both before and after that testimony, the Department complied with several Committee requests to produce certain documents. Other documents were at first withheld, although these documents were eventually disclosed by the Department after the Committee learned of their existence. In 1985, the majority members of the Judiciary Committee published a lengthy report on the Committee's investigation. The report not only criticized various officials in the Department of Justice for their role in the EPA executive privilege dispute, but it also suggested that appellee Olson had given false and misleading testimony to the Subcommittee on March 10, 1983 ... The Chairman of the Judiciary Committee forwarded a copy of the report to the Attorney General with a request ... that he seek the appointment of an independent counsel to investigate the allegations against Olson....

The Attorney General ... requested appointment of an independent counsel to investigate whether Olson's March 10, 1983, testimony "regarding the completeness of [OLC's] response to the Judiciary Committee's request for OLC documents, and regarding his knowledge of EPA's willingness to turn over certain disputed documents to Congress, violated ... any ... provision of federal criminal law." ...

On April 23, 1986, the Special Division appointed James C. McKay as independent counsel.... McKay later resigned as independent counsel, and on May 29, 1986, the Division appointed Morrison as his replacement, with the same jurisdiction....

... [Morrison] caused a grand jury to issue and serve subpoenas ad testificandum and duces tecum on [Olson]. [Olson] moved to quash the subpoenas, claiming, among other things, that the independent counsel provisions of the Act were unconstitutional and that appellant accordingly had no authority to proceed....

III

The parties do not dispute that "[t]he Constitution for purposes of appointment . . . divides all its officers into two classes." As we stated in *Buckley v. Valeo:* "[P]rincipal officers are selected by the President with the advice and consent of the Senate. Inferior officers Congress may allow to be appointed by the President alone, by the heads of departments, or by the Judiciary." The initial question is, accordingly, whether appellant is an "inferior" or a "principal" officer. If she is the latter, as the Court of Appeals concluded, then the Act is in violation of the Appointments Clause.

The line between "inferior" and "principal" officers is one that is far from clear, and the Framers provided little guidance into where it should be drawn. We need not attempt here to decide exactly where the line falls between the two types of officers, because in our view appellant clearly falls on the "inferior officer" side of that line. Several factors lead to this conclusion.

First, appellant is subject to removal by a higher Executive Branch official. Although appellant may not be "subordinate" to the Attorney General (and the President) insofar as she possesses a degree of independent discretion to exercise the powers delegated to her under the Act, the fact that she can be removed by the Attorney General indicates that she is to some degree "inferior" in rank and authority. Second, appellant is empowered by the Act to perform only certain, limited duties. An independent counsel's role is restricted primarily to investigation and, if appropriate, prosecution for certain federal crimes. . . .

Third, appellant's office is limited in jurisdiction. Not only is the Act itself restricted in applicability to certain federal officials suspected of certain serious federal crimes, but an independent counsel can only act within the scope of the jurisdiction that has been granted by the Special Division pursuant to a request by the Attorney General. Finally, appellant's office is limited in tenure. There is concededly no time limit on the appointment of a particular counsel. Nonetheless, the office of independent counsel is "temporary" in the sense that an independent counsel is appointed essentially to accomplish a single task, and when that task is over the office is terminated, either by the counsel herself or by action of the Special Division. . . .

This does not, however, end our inquiry under the Appointments Clause. Appellees argue that even if appellant is an "inferior" officer, the Clause does not empower Congress to place the power to appoint such an officer outside the Executive Branch. They contend that the Clause does not contemplate congressional authorization of "interbranch appointments," in which an officer of one branch is appointed by officers of another branch. The relevant language of the Appointments Clause is worth repeating. It reads: " . . . but the Congress may by Law vest the Appointment of such inferior Officers, as they think proper, in the President alone, in the courts of Law, or in the Heads of Departments." On its face, the language of this "excepting clause" admits of no limitation on interbranch appointments. Indeed, the inclusion of "as they think proper" seems clearly to give Congress significant discretion to determine whether it is "proper" to vest the appointment of, for example, executive officials in the "courts of Law." . . .

We also note that the history of the Clause provides no support for appellees' position. . . . [T]here was little or no debate on the question whether the Clause empowers Congress to provide for interbranch appointments, and there is nothing to suggest that the Framers intended to prevent Congress from having that power.

We do not mean to say that Congress' power to provide for inter-branch appointments of "inferior officers" is unlimited. In addition to separation-of-powers concerns, which would arise if such provisions for appointment had the potential to impair the constitutional functions assigned to one of the branches, . . . Congress' decision to vest the appointment power in the courts would be improper if there was some "incongruity" between the functions normally performed by the courts and the performance of their duty to appoint. . . . We have recognized that courts may appoint private attorneys to act as prosecutor for judicial contempt judgments. Congress, of course, was concerned when it created the office of independent counsel with the conflicts of interest that could arise in situations when the Executive Branch is called upon to investigate its own high-ranking officers. If it were to remove the appointing authority from the Executive Branch, the most logical place to put it was in the Judicial Branch. In the light of the Act's provision making the judges of the Special Division ineligible to participate in any matters relating to an independent counsel they have appointed, we do not think that appointment of the independent counsel by the court runs afoul of the constitutional limitation on "incongruous" interbranch appointments.

Notes and Questions

1. The independent counsel statute was enacted after President Nixon resigned as a result of the Watergate affair. The President had ordered Attorney General Elliot Richardson to fire Archibald Cox, a special prosecutor hired by Richardson under promises of independence to investigate the Watergate burglary. Richardson resigned rather than carry out the order. Deputy Attorney General Ruckelshaus likewise resigned rather than carry out the President's order. The firing of Cox, which was finally ordered by Solicitor General Robert Bork, came to be known as the "Saturday Night Massacre." Do these events establish the need for the appointment process that Congress created? After all, President Nixon was forced to resign in part because of the adverse public reaction to the Saturday Night Massacre.

2. What facts convinced the Court that the independent counsel was an "inferior" officer of the United States? Consider Justice Scalia's objection to this conclusion:

The second reason offered by the Court—that appellant performs only certain, limited duties—may be relevant to whether she is an inferior officer, but it mischaracterizes the extent of her powers. As the Court states: "Admittedly, the Act delegates to appellant [the] *'full power and independent authority to exercise all investigative and prosecutorial functions and powers of the Department of Justice.'* " Moreover, in addition to this general grant of power she is given a broad range of specifically enumerated powers, including a power not even the Attorney General possesses: to "contes[t] in court . . . any claim of privilege or attempt to withhold evidence on grounds of national security." Once all of this is "admitted," it seems to me impossible to maintain that appellant's authority is so "limited" as to render her an inferior officer. The Court seeks to brush this away by asserting that the independent counsel's power does not include any authority to "formulate policy for the Government or the Executive Branch." But the same could be said for all officers of the Government, with the single exception of the President. All of them only formulate policy within their respective spheres of responsibility—as does the independent counsel, who must comply with the policies of the Department of Justice only to the extent possible.

The final set of reasons given by the Court for why the independent counsel clearly is an inferior officer emphasizes the limited nature of her jurisdiction and tenure. Taking the latter first, I find nothing unusually limited about the independent counsel's tenure. To the contrary, unlike most high-ranking Executive Branch officials, she continues to serve until she (or the Special Division) decides that her work is substantially completed. This particular independent prosecutor has already served more than two years, which is at least as long as many Cabinet officials. As to the scope of her jurisdiction, there can be no doubt that is small (though far from unimportant). But within it she exercises more than the full power of the Attorney General. The Ambassador to Luxembourg is not anything less than a principal officer, simply because Luxembourg is small. And the federal judge who sits in a small district is not for that reason "inferior in rank and authority." If the mere fragmentation of executive responsibilities into small compartments suffices to render the heads of each of those compartments inferior officers, then Congress could deprive the President of the right to appoint his chief law enforcement officer by dividing up the Attorney General's responsibilities among a number of "lesser" functionaries. . . .

487 U.S. at 716–18, 108 S.Ct. at 2632–33. Do you agree that the independent counsel should be considered an "inferior officer"?

3. In the aftermath of Kenneth Starr's investigation of President Clinton, Congress refused to extend the Independent Counsel Act. The Starr investigation lasted for more than five years and cost more than $40 million. Although the law expired on June 30th, the five pending independent counsel investigations did not terminate. During the Act's

20 year existence, more than 2 dozen independent counsels were appointed.

Before allowing the law to die, Congress entertained vigorous debate about the wisdom of the Act. Ex-independent counsel Whitney North Seymour, Jr., stated that "I believe strongly in the concept of an independent counsel to guarantee public confidence in the impartiality of any criminal investigation into conduct of top officials in the executive branch of our government." Others disagreed arguing that independent counsel investigations have taken too long, spent too much money, or sought to criminalize conduct that is rarely prosecuted. Attorney General Janet Reno, who recommended the appointment of seven independent counsels during her tenure and who was under fire for her failure to appoint more, specifically urged Congress not to renew the Act. She stated that too many independent counsels investigations get "plunged into the political process", and contended that Congress could do a better job of investigating high-level officials. She argued that, in those instances when the Justice Department faces a conflict of interest, outside counsel could be appointed.

Problem 6–6: Appointment of Trial Judges of the Tax Court

The "Tax Court of the United States" is an independent agency within the Executive Branch. Its nineteen judges, who adjudicate disputes concerning federal tax liability, are appointed by the President for 15 year terms with the Senate's advice and concurrence. Judges may be removed by the President only for inefficiency, neglect of duty, or malfeasance in office. Congress described the Tax Court for most of its history as an independent agency in the Executive Branch, but it designated it an "Article I Court" in 1969.

After the Internal Revenue Service (IRS) rejected deductions worth about $1.5 billion taken by several taxpayers, because the deductions were procured in a sham tax shelter scheme, the taxpayers appealed the IRS's decision to the Tax Court. The Chief Judge appointed a special judge to hear the taxpayers' appeal. The Chief Judge is authorized to appoint "special trial judges" who may hear cases, take evidence, rule on admissibility, enforce compliance orders, prepare proposed findings and write an opinion, but the actual decision is made by a Tax Court judge. In other words, the "special judges" function like Administrative Law Judges. The special judge found for the IRS and his opinion was adopted by the Chief Judge.

The taxpayers, who wish to pursue all potential arguments to upset the Tax Court's decision, have hired you to argue that the appointment of "special trial judges" is unconstitutional. What argument(s) can you make on behalf of your clients? If you represent the government, how would you respond? How would you expect that the Supreme Court would rule on this issue?

3. REMOVAL

While the Constitution speaks directly to the President's authority to appoint "Officers of the United States," it is silent concerning the President's authority to remove them. The authority of the President to fire such officers can be implied from two constitutional provisions. The Constitution vests in the President an "executive power," and it requires that the President "take care that the Laws be faithfully executed." U.S. Const. art. II, §§ 1, 3. The Supreme Court has addressed the issue of Congress's authority to limit the President's authority to remove executive officials in a series of cases which follow. The Court has also considered whether Congress can directly remove executive officials.

a. *Limitations on Presidential Removal*

Myers v. United States, 272 U.S. 52, 47 S.Ct. 21, 71 L.Ed. 160 (1926), is the first case to address the issue of the President's removal powers. Congress had forbidden the President to dismiss a postmaster before the expiration of the official's four year term without the concurrence of the Senate. After President Harding dismissed Myers without the Senate's concurrence, he sued for back pay in the Court of Claims. The Court upheld Myers' dismissal on the ground that the Constitution did not assign to Congress a role in the removal of administrators. The Court distinguished the Senate's role in appointments:

> The power to prevent the removal of an officer who has served under the President is different from the authority to consent to or reject his appointment. When a nomination is made, it may be presumed that the Senate is, or may become, as well advised as to the fitness of the nominee as the President, but in the nature of things the defects in ability or intelligence or loyalty in the administration of the laws of one who has served as an officer under the President are facts as to which the President, or his trusted subordinates, must be better informed than the Senate, and the power to remove him may therefor be regarded as confined for very sound and practical reasons, to the governmental authority which has administrative control. The power of removal is incident to the power of appointment, not to the power of advising and consenting to appointment, and when the grant of the executive power is enforced by the express mandate to take care that the laws be faithfully executed, it emphasizes the necessity for including within the executive power as conferred the exclusive power of removal.

272 U.S. at 121–22, 47 S.Ct. at 26–27.

Myers went on to conclude, "The imperative reasons requiring an unrestricted power to remove the most important of his subordinates in their most important duties must therefore control the interpretation of the Constitution as to all appointed by him." *Id.* at 134, 47 S.Ct. at 31. Nevertheless, the Court soon limited the board scope of *Myers*.

HUMPHREY'S EXECUTOR v. UNITED STATES

295 U.S. 602, 55 S.Ct. 869, 79 L.Ed. 1611 (1935).

MR. JUSTICE SUTHERLAND delivered the opinion of the Court. . . .

[President Roosevelt had fired Humphrey, a Federal Trade Commissioner, in contravention of a statute that said a Commissioner could be removed only for "inefficiency, neglect of duty or malfeasance in office." *See* 15 U.S.C. § 41. When the executor of Humphrey's estate sued for backpay, the government defended on the ground that the restriction was unconstitutional under *Myers*.]

. . . To support its contention that the removal provision of section 1, as we have just construed it, is an unconstitutional interference with the executive power of the President, the government's chief reliance is *Myers v. United States* . . . .

The office of a postmaster is so essentially unlike the office now involved that the decision in the *Myers* case cannot be accepted as controlling our decision here. A postmaster is an executive officer restricted to the performance of executive functions. He is charged with no duty at all related to either the legislative or judicial power. . . .

The Federal Trade Commission is an administrative body created by Congress to carry into effect legislative policies embodied in the statute in accordance with the legislative standard therein prescribed, and to perform other specified duties as a legislative or as a judicial aid. Such a body cannot in any proper sense be characterized as an arm or an eye of the executive. Its duties are performed without executive leave and, in the contemplation of the statute, must be free from executive control. In administering the provisions of the statute in respect of "unfair methods of competition," that is to say, in filling in and administering the details embodied by that general standard, the commission acts in part quasi legislatively and in part quasi judicially. . . .

We think it plain under the Constitution that illimitable power of removal is not possessed by the President in respect of officers of the character of those just named. The authority of Congress, in creating quasi legislative or quasi judicial agencies, to require them to act in discharge of their duties independently of executive control cannot well be doubted; and that authority includes, as an appropriate incident, power to fix the period during which they shall continue, and to forbid their removal except for cause in the meantime. For it is quite evident that one who holds his office only during the pleasure of another cannot be depended upon to maintain an attitude of independence against the latter's will.

The fundamental necessity of maintaining each of the three general departments of government entirely free from the control or coercive influence, direct or indirect, of either of the others, has often been stressed and is hardly open to serious question. So much is implied in the very fact of the separation of the powers of these departments by the Constitution; and in the rule which recognizes their essential coequality. The sound application of a principle that makes one master in his own house precludes him from imposing his control in the house of another who is master there. . . .

The power of removal here claimed for the President falls within this principle, since its coercive influence threatens the independence of a commission, which is not only wholly disconnected from the executive department, but which, as already fully appears, was created by Congress as a means of carrying into operation legislative and judicial powers, and as an agency of the legislative and judicial departments. . . .

In 1988, the court revisited the issue of Congress's authority to limit the President's removal powers. As you will see, the Court changed the basis on which it approved such limitations.

MORRISON v. OLSON

487 U.S. 654, 108 S.Ct. 2597, 101 L.Ed.2d 569 (1988).

CHIEF JUSTICE REHNQUIST delivered the opinion of the Court. . . . [Earlier you read selections from this case regarding inferior officers.]

Two statutory provisions govern the length of an independent counsel's tenure in office. The first defines the procedure for removing an independent counsel. Section 596(a)(1) provides: "An independent counsel appointed under this chapter may be removed from office, other than by impeachment and conviction, only by the personal action of the Attorney General and only for good cause, physical disability, mental incapacity, or any other condition that substantially impairs the performance of such independent counsel's duties." . . .

The other provision governing the tenure of the independent counsel defines the procedures for "terminating" the counsel's office. Under § 596(b)(1), the office of an independent counsel terminates when he or she notifies the Attorney General that he or she has completed or substantially completed any investigations or prosecutions undertaken pursuant to the Act. . . .

We now turn to consider whether . . . the provision of the Act restricting the Attorney General's power to remove the independent counsel to only those instances in which he can show "good cause," taken by itself, impermissibly interferes with the President's exercise of his constitutionally appointed functions. . . .

In *Humphrey's Executor*, the issue was whether a statute restricting the President's power to remove the Commissioners of the Federal Trade Commission (FTC) only for "inefficiency, neglect of duty, or malfeasance in office" was consistent with the Constitution. . . .

[Olson] contend[s] that *Humphrey's Executor* . . . [is] distinguishable from this case because [it] did not involve officials who performed a "core executive function." [He] argue[s] that our decision in *Humphrey's*

Executor rests on a distinction between "purely executive" officials and officials who exercise "quasi-legislative" and "quasi-judicial" powers. In [his] view, when a "purely executive" official is involved, the governing precedent is *Myers*, not *Humphrey's Executor*. And, under *Myers*, the President must have absolute discretion to discharge "purely" executive officials at will.

We undoubtedly did rely on the terms "quasi-legislative" and "quasi-judicial" to distinguish the officials involved in *Humphrey's Executor* ... from those in *Myers*, but our present considered view is that the determination of whether the Constitution allows Congress to impose a "good cause"-type restriction on the President's power to remove an official cannot be made to turn on whether or not that official is classified as "purely executive." The analysis contained in our removal cases is designed not to define rigid categories of those officials who may or may not be removed at will by the President, but to ensure that Congress does not interfere with the President's exercise of the "executive power" and his constitutionally appointed duty to "take care that the laws be faithfully executed" under Article II. *Myers* was undoubtedly correct in its holding, and in its broader suggestion that there are some "purely executive" officials who must be removable by the President at will if he is to be able to accomplish his constitutional role....

Considering for the moment the "good cause" removal provision in isolation from the other parts of the Act at issue in this case, we cannot say that the imposition of a "good cause" standard for removal by itself unduly trammels on executive authority. There is no real dispute that the functions performed by the independent counsel are "executive" in the sense that they are law enforcement functions that typically have been undertaken by officials within the Executive Branch. As we noted above, however, the independent counsel is an inferior officer under the Appointments Clause, with limited jurisdiction and tenure and lacking policymaking or significant administrative authority. Although the counsel exercises no small amount of discretion and judgment in deciding how to carry out his or her duties under the Act, we simply do not see how the President's need to control the exercise of that discretion is so central to the functioning of the Executive Branch as to require as a matter of constitutional law that the counsel be terminable at will by the President.

Nor do we think that the "good cause" removal provision at issue here impermissibly burdens the President's power to control or supervise the independent counsel, as an executive official, in the execution of his or her duties under the Act. This is not a case in which the power to remove an executive official has been completely stripped from the President, thus providing no means for the President to ensure the "faithful execution" of the laws. Rather, because the independent counsel may be terminated for "good cause," the Executive, through the Attorney General, retains ample authority to assure that the counsel is competently performing his or her statutory responsibilities in a manner that comports with the provisions of the Act....

JUSTICE SCALIA, dissenting. . . .

The Court concedes that "[t]here is no real dispute that the functions performed by the independent counsel are 'executive' " . . . Governmental investigation and prosecution of crimes is a quintessentially executive function. . . .

The utter incompatibility of the Court's approach with our constitutional traditions can be made more clear, perhaps, by applying it to the powers of the other two branches. Is it conceivable that if Congress passed a statute depriving itself of less than full and entire control over some insignificant area of legislation, we would inquire whether the matter was "so central to the functioning of the Legislative Branch" as really to require complete control, or whether the statute gives Congress "sufficient control over the surrogate legislator to ensure that Congress is able to perform its constitutionally assigned duties"? Of course we would have none of that. Once we determined that a purely legislative power was at issue we would require it to be exercised, wholly and entirely, by Congress. . . .

The Court has, nonetheless, replaced the clear constitutional prescription that the executive power belongs to the President with a "balancing test." What are the standards to determine how the balance is to be struck, that is, how much removal of Presidential power is too much? . . . Once we depart from the text of the Constitution, just where short of that do we stop? The most amazing feature of the Court's opinion is that it does not even purport to give an answer. It simply announces, with no analysis, that the ability to control the decision whether to investigate and prosecute the President's closest advisers, and indeed the President himself, is not "so central to the functioning of the Executive Branch" as to be constitutionally required to be within the President's control. Apparently that is so because we say it is so. Having abandoned as the basis for our decision-making the text of Article II that "the executive Power" must be vested in the President, the Court does not even attempt to craft a substitute criterion—a "justiciable standard," however remote from the Constitution—that today governs, and in the future will govern, the decision of such questions. Evidently, the governing standard is to be what might be called the unfettered wisdom of a majority of this Court, revealed to an obedient people on a case-by-case basis. This is not only not the government of laws that the Constitution established; it is not a government of laws at all. . . .

Notes and Questions

1. How did *Morrison* redefine the test for when Congress can limit the President's removal power? If the *Morrison* test is applied in *Humphrey's Executor* and *Myers*, does the result of those cases change? Why did the Court redefine the test in *Morrison*?

2. The vast majority of federal government employees are in the civil service system, which means that they cannot be dismissed by the

President except on limited grounds. Why is this limitation constitutional under *Morrison*?

3. Justice Scalia objects that the Court "has ... replaced clear constitutional prescription that the executive power belongs to the President with a 'balancing test.' " Should the Constitution be interpreted to permit the President to remove executive branch officials without restriction? How can the President "run" the government if he cannot dismiss some officials if they implement policies with which the President disagrees? *See* Richard J. Pierce, Morrison v. Olson, *Separation of Powers, and the Structure of Government*, 1988 SUP. CT. REV. 1.

b. *Legislative Removal*

BOWSHER v. SYNAR
478 U.S. 714, 106 S.Ct. 3181, 92 L.Ed.2d 583 (1986).

CHIEF JUSTICE BURGER delivered the opinion of the Court.

The question presented by these appeals is whether the assignment by Congress to the Comptroller General of the United States of certain functions under the Balanced Budget and Emergency Deficit Control Act of 1985 violates the doctrine of separation of powers.

I

On December 12, 1985, the President signed into law the Balanced Budget and Emergency Deficit Control Act of 1985, popularly known as the "Gramm–Rudman–Hollings Act." The purpose of the Act is to eliminate the federal budget deficit. To that end, the Act sets a "maximum deficit amount" for federal spending for each of fiscal years 1986 through 1991. The size of that maximum deficit amount progressively reduces to zero in fiscal year 1991. If in any fiscal year the federal budget deficit exceeds the maximum deficit amount by more than a specified sum, the Act requires across-the-board cuts in federal spending to reach the targeted deficit level, with half of the cuts made to defense programs and the other half made to nondefense programs. The Act exempts certain priority programs from these cuts.

These "automatic" reductions are accomplished through a rather complicated procedure, spelled out in § 251, the so-called "reporting provisions" of the Act. Each year, the Directors of the Office of Management and Budget (OMB) and the Congressional Budget Office (CBO) independently estimate the amount of the federal budget deficit for the upcoming fiscal year. If that deficit exceeds the maximum targeted deficit amount for that fiscal year by more than a specified amount, the Directors of OMB and CBO independently calculate, on a program-by-program basis, the budget reductions necessary to ensure that the deficit does not exceed the maximum deficit amount. The Act then requires the Directors to report jointly their deficit estimates and budget reduction calculations to the Comptroller General.

The Comptroller General, after reviewing the Directors' reports, then reports his conclusions to the President. The President in turn must issue a "sequestration" order mandating the spending reductions specified by the Comptroller General....

Within hours of the President's signing of the Act, Congressman Synar, who had voted against the Act, filed a complaint seeking declaratory relief that the Act was unconstitutional. Eleven other Members later joined Congressman Synar's suit. A virtually identical lawsuit was also filed by the National Treasury Employees Union. The Union alleged that its members had been injured as a result of the Act's automatic spending reduction provisions, which have suspended certain cost-of-living benefit increases to the Union's members....

III ...

The Constitution does not contemplate an active role for Congress in the supervision of officers charged with the execution of the laws it enacts. The President appoints "Officers of the United States" with the "Advice and Consent of the Senate...." Art. II, § 2. Once the appointment has been made and confirmed, however, the Constitution explicitly provides for removal of Officers of the United States by Congress only upon impeachment by the House of Representatives and conviction by the Senate. An impeachment by the House and trial by the Senate can rest only on "Treason, Bribery or other high Crimes and Misdemeanors." Article II, § 4. A direct congressional role in the removal of officers charged with the execution of the laws beyond this limited one is inconsistent with separation of powers....

... Congress cannot reserve for itself the power of removal of an officer charged with the execution of the laws except by impeachment. To permit the execution of the laws to be vested in an officer answerable only to Congress would, in practical terms, reserve in Congress control over the execution of the laws. As the District Court observed: "Once an officer is appointed, it is only the authority that can remove him, and not the authority that appointed him, that he must fear and, in the performance of his functions, obey." The structure of the Constitution does not permit Congress to execute the laws; it follows that Congress cannot grant to an officer under its control what it does not possess....

IV

Appellants urge that the Comptroller General performs his duties independently and is not subservient to Congress. We agree with the District Court that this contention does not bear close scrutiny.

The critical factor lies in the provisions of the statute defining the Comptroller General's office relating to removability. Although the Comptroller General is nominated by the President from a list of three individuals recommended by the Speaker of the House of Representatives and the President pro tempore of the Senate, and confirmed by the Senate, he is removable only at the initiative of Congress. He may be removed not only by impeachment but also by joint resolution of Congress "at any time" resting on any one of the following bases:

"(i) permanent disability";

"(ii) inefficiency";

"(iii) neglect of duty;"

"(iv) malfeasance"; or

"(v) a felony or conduct involving moral turpitude."

... These terms are very broad and, as interpreted by Congress, could sustain removal of a Comptroller General for any number of actual or perceived transgressions of the legislative will....

It is clear that Congress has consistently viewed the Comptroller General as an officer of the Legislative Branch....

Over the years, the Comptrollers General have also viewed themselves as part of the Legislative Branch....

Against this background, we see no escape from the conclusion that, because Congress has retained removal authority over the Comptroller General, he may not be entrusted with executive powers. The remaining question is whether the Comptroller General has been assigned such powers in the Balanced Budget and Emergency Deficit Control Act of 1985.

V

The primary responsibility of the Comptroller General under the instant Act is the preparation of a "report." This report must contain detailed estimates of projected federal revenues and expenditures. The report must also specify the reductions, if any, necessary to reduce the deficit to the target for the appropriate fiscal year. The reductions must be set forth on a program-by-program basis.

In preparing the report, the Comptroller General is to have "due regard" for the estimates and reductions set forth in a joint report submitted to him by the Director of CBO and the Director of OMB, the President's fiscal and budgetary adviser. However, the Act plainly contemplates that the Comptroller General will exercise his independent judgment and evaluation with respect to those estimates. The Act also provides that the Comptroller General's report "shall explain fully any differences between the contents of such report and the report of the Directors."

Appellants suggest that the duties assigned to the Comptroller General in the Act are essentially ministerial and mechanical so that their performance does not constitute "execution of the law" in a meaningful sense. On the contrary, we view these functions as plainly entailing execution of the law in constitutional terms. Interpreting a law enacted by Congress to implement the legislative mandate is the very essence of "execution" of the law. Under § 251, the Comptroller General must exercise judgment concerning facts that affect the application of the Act. He must also interpret the provisions of the Act to determine precisely what budgetary calculations are required. Decisions of that kind are typically made by officers charged with executing a statute.

The executive nature of the Comptroller General's functions under the Act is revealed in § 252(a)(3) which gives the Comptroller General the ultimate authority to determine the budget cuts to be made. Indeed, the Comptroller General commands the President himself to carry out, without the slightest variation (with exceptions not relevant to the constitutional issues presented), the directive of the Comptroller General as to the budget reductions:

> "The [Presidential] order *must provide* for reductions in the manner specified in section 251(a)(3), *must incorporate* the provisions of the [Comptroller General's] report submitted under section 251(b), and *must be consistent with such report in all respects.* The President *may not modify or recalculate any of the estimates, determinations, specifications, bases, amounts, or percentages* set forth in the report submitted under section 251(b) in determining the reductions to be specified in the order with respect to programs, projects, and activities, or with respect to budget activities, within an account...." (emphasis added) . . .

VII . . .

We conclude that the District Court correctly held that the powers vested in the Comptroller General under § 251 violate the command of the Constitution that the Congress play no direct role in the execution of the laws. Accordingly, the judgment and order of the District Court are affirmed. . . .

Problem 6–7: Independent Agencies

The President is a member of one political party, and the Congress is under the control of the country's other political party. This split has led to policy gridlock and left both the President and Congress unhappy with the other. In particular, Congress is upset that the Office of Management and Budget (OMB) is preventing agencies from implementing legislation as Congress intended.

The member of Congress for whom you work is interested in whether Congress can loosen the President's grip over key officials in the government by limiting the President's authority to remove these officials. The legislator anticipates that there will be enough votes to override any presidential veto of legislation. Your employer has several questions for you concerning the constitutionality of actions that Congress might take.

(a) Can Congress make the Secretary of Labor removable by itself instead of the President? As an alternative, can it restrict the authority of the President to remove the Secretary of Labor to situations involving "inefficiency, neglect of duty, or malfeasance"? The Secretary of Labor is charged with the final authority to adjudicate disputes and to promulgate rules under several statutes administered by the Department.

(b) Can Congress restrict the authority of the President to remove the Administrator of the Environmental Protection Agency to situations involving "inefficiency, neglect of duty, or malfeasance"? Recall that EPA is an "independent agency" within the Executive Branch but not a cabinet department.

Chapter 7

INSPECTIONS, REPORTS & SUBPOENAS

A. INTRODUCTION

Administrative agencies need information to perform their many functions. They use this information to set policy through the promulgation of rules and regulations, to keep Congress advised regarding various matters, and to enforce regulatory requirements and prosecute companies for civil and criminal violations. Agencies obtain this information in different ways: they conduct inspections or search an area; they require persons to submit information or produce documents to the agency; and they require persons to keep records, which the government may then wish to inspect or have delivered to it. This chapter considers the legal and constitutional authority of agencies to acquire information, the role of agency lawyers in authorizing such action, and what steps lawyers who represent individuals or companies can take to limit such efforts.

B. INSPECTIONS

A number of agencies regularly inspect buildings and work sites. Health inspectors enter restaurants to determine whether food preparation and service areas are clean, as well as to see whether food is being kept under healthy conditions. Inspectors from the Occupational Safety and Health Administration (OSHA) examine construction and factory sites to make sure that workers are employed in safe and healthy conditions. In some instances, administrative officials even seek to enter people's homes or yards. Child welfare officials, for example, will enter a house looking for abused or neglected children.

1. LEGAL AUTHORITY TO INSPECT

Are such inspections legal? First, an agency's authority to inspect is defined in its enabling act. If Congress (or a state legislature) has not authorized an agency to conduct administrative inspections, it has no legal authority to do so. Moreover, an agency's authority to inspect is only as great as its statutory authorization. For example, the Occupational Safety and Health Act provides:

§ 657.   Inspections, investigations, and recordkeeping

(a) Authority of Secretary to enter, inspect, and investigate places of employment; time and manner

In order to carry out the purposes of this chapter, the Secretary, upon presenting appropriate credentials to the owner, operator, or agent in charge, is authorized—

(1) to enter without delay and at reasonable times any factory, plant, establishment, construction site, or other area, workplace or environment where work is performed by an employee of an employer; and

(2) to inspect and investigate during regular working hours and at other reasonable times, and within reasonable limits and in a reasonable manner, any such place of employment and all pertinent conditions, structures, machines, apparatus, devices, equipment, and materials therein, and to question privately any such employer, owner, operator, agent or employee.

29 U.S.C.A. § 657(a). Thus, OSHA can only inspect workplaces during regular working hours or at other reasonable times and only for the purposes of performing its mandate of protecting workers. Agencies like OSHA are well aware of such statutory limitations and usually obey them.

Second, the Fourth Amendment provides:

The right of the people to be secure in their persons, houses, papers, and effects, against unreasonable searches and seizures, shall not be violated, and no Warrants shall issue, but upon probable cause, supported by Oath or affirmation, and particularly describing the place to be searched, and the persons or things to be seized.

U.S. CONST. Amend IV. Through the Fourteenth Amendment state agencies are also subject to the Fourth Amendment.

Until the 1960s, there was doubt that the Fourth Amendment required a warrant for administrative inspections. For example, in *Frank v. Maryland*, 359 U.S. 360, 79 S.Ct. 804, 3 L.Ed.2d 877 (1959), the Supreme Court held that there was no warrant requirement applicable to administrative inspections because they "touch at most upon the periphery of the important interests safeguarded by the Fourteenth Amendment's protection against official intrusion." In the following case, however, the Court overruled *Frank* and held that administrative searches, like searches in criminal cases, require a prior judicial warrant.

CAMARA v. MUNICIPAL COURT
387 U.S. 523, 87 S.Ct. 1727, 18 L.Ed.2d 930 (1967).

MR. JUSTICE WHITE delivered the opinion of the Court.

[City building inspectors sought to inspect Camara's apartment under a San Francisco ordinance that authorized them to enter buildings "to perform any duty imposed upon them by the Municipal Code." When Camara refused to allow the inspectors to enter his apartment without a warrant, he was charged with violating the municipal code which made it illegal to refuse to permit a lawful inspection.]

[The Fourth Amendment was designed] to safeguard the privacy and security of individuals against arbitrary invasions by governmental officials. The Fourth Amendment thus gives concrete expression to a right of the people which "is basic to a free society." As such, the Fourth Amendment is enforceable against the States through the Fourteenth Amendment.

. . . [E]xcept in certain carefully defined classes of cases, a search of private property without proper consent is "unreasonable" unless it has been authorized by a valid search warrant. . . .

. . . [W]e hold that administrative searches of the kind at issue here are significant intrusions upon the interests protected by the Fourth Amendment, that such searches when authorized and conducted without a warrant procedure lack the traditional safeguards which the Fourth Amendment guarantees to the individual. [Because] of the nature of the municipal programs under consideration, however, these conclusions must be the beginning, not the end, of our inquiry . . .

[In] cases in which the Fourth Amendment requires that a warrant to search be obtained, "probable cause" is the standard by which a particular decision to search is tested against the constitutional mandate of reasonableness . . .

[T]he only effective way to seek universal compliance with the minimum standards required by municipal codes is through routine periodic inspections of all structures. It is here that the probable cause debate is focused, for the agency's decision to conduct an area inspection is unavoidably based on its appraisal of conditions in the area as a whole, not on its knowledge of conditions in each particular building . . .

[Unfortunately,] there can be no ready test for determining reasonableness other than by balancing the need to search against the invasion which the search entails. But we think that a number of persuasive factors combine to support the reasonableness of area code-enforcement inspections. First, such programs have a long history of judicial and public acceptance. Second, the public interest demands that all dangerous conditions be prevented or abated, yet it is doubtful that any other canvassing technique would achieve acceptable results. Many such conditions—faulty wiring is an obvious example—are not observable from outside the building and indeed may not be apparent to the inexpert occupant himself. Finally, because the inspections are neither personal in nature nor aimed at the discovery of evidence of crime, they involve a relatively limited invasion of the urban citizen's privacy. . . .

Having concluded that the area inspection is a "reasonable" search of private property within the meaning of the Fourth Amendment, it is obvious that "probable cause" to issue a warrant to inspect must exist if reasonable legislative or administrative standards for conducting an area inspection are satisfied with respect to a particular dwelling. Such standards, which will vary with the municipal program being enforced, may be based upon the passage of time, the nature of the building (*e.g.*, a multifamily apartment house), or the condition of the entire area, but they will not necessarily depend upon specific knowledge of the condition of the particular dwelling....

Since our holding emphasizes the controlling standard of reasonableness, nothing we say today is intended to foreclose prompt inspections, even without a warrant, that the law has traditionally upheld in emergency situations. *See North American Cold Storage Co. v. City of Chicago*, 211 U.S. 306 (seizure of unwholesome food); *Jacobson v. Commonwealth of Massachusetts*, 197 U.S. 11 (compulsory smallpox vaccination); *Compagnie Francaise De Navigation a Vapeur v. Louisiana State Board of Health*, 186 U.S. 380 (health quarantine); *Kroplin v. Truax*, 119 Ohio St. 610, 165 N.E. 498 (summary destruction of tubercular cattle). On the other hand, in the case of most routine area inspections, there is no compelling urgency to inspect at a particular time or on a particular day. Moreover, most citizens allow inspections of their property without a warrant. Thus, as a practical matter and in light of the Fourth Amendment's requirement that a warrant specify the property to be searched, it seems likely that warrants should normally be sought only after entry is refused unless there has been a citizen complaint or there is other satisfactory reason for securing immediate entry. Similarly, the requirement of a warrant procedure does not suggest any change in what seems to be the prevailing local policy, in most situations, of authorizing entry, but not entry by force, to inspect.

In this case, appellant has been charged with a crime for his refusal to permit housing inspectors to enter his leasehold without a warrant. There was no emergency demanding immediate access; in fact, the inspectors made three trips to the building in an attempt to obtain appellant's consent to search. Yet no warrant was obtained and thus appellant was unable to verify either the need for or the appropriate limits of the inspection. [W]e therefore conclude that appellant had a constitutional right to insist that the inspectors obtain a warrant to search and that appellant may not constitutionally be convicted for refusing to consent to the inspection....

Subsequent History

The decision in *Camara* was extended to administrative inspections of commercial buildings in *See v. City of Seattle*, 387 U.S. 541, 87 S.Ct. 1737, 18 L.Ed.2d 943 (1967), because a "businessman, like the occupant of a residence, has a constitutional right to go about his business free from unreasonable official entries upon his private property."

Having created a new warrant requirement where it had not previously existed, the Court was faced in the following years with a number of cases seeking exceptions from this new administrative search warrant requirement. The Court generally agreed that exceptions were in order where an administrative search was of an industry that had long been subject to close government regulation. The theory was that a person entering such a business had a reduced expectation of privacy. *See Colonnade Catering Corp. v. United States*, 397 U.S. 72, 90 S.Ct. 774, 25 L.Ed.2d 60 (1970) (liquor dealers); *United States v. Biswell*, 406 U.S. 311, 92 S.Ct. 1593, 32 L.Ed.2d 87 (1972) (firearms dealers); *Donovan v. Dewey*, 452 U.S. 594, 101 S.Ct. 2534, 69 L.Ed.2d 262 (1981) (underground mines); *New York v. Burger*, 482 U.S. 691, 107 S.Ct. 2636, 96 L.Ed.2d 601 (1987) (auto junkyard). The latter cases, however, introduced an additional three-part test: do the searches serve an important government purpose, are warrantless searches necessary to achieve that purpose, and does the statute authorizing the searches provide protections substituting for a warrant—providing notice of searches to the owner, limiting the scope of the search, and limiting the discretion of the inspecting officer.

When Congress enacted the Occupational Safety and Health Act in 1970, it provided broad powers to OSHA to inspect companies subject to its requirements in order to protect worker health and safety. In *Marshall v. Barlow's, Inc.*, 436 U.S. 307, 98 S.Ct. 1816, 56 L.Ed.2d 305 (1978), OSHA argued that industries involved in interstate commerce had long been subject to federal regulation, so the exception from the warrant requirement recognized in *Colonnade* and *Biswell* should likewise apply to OSHA inspections. The Court rejected the argument. Inasmuch as OSHA regulated virtually all industries in the United States, an exception applicable to inspections of those businesses would eviscerate the warrant requirement. Moreover, the Court was not convinced that a warrant requirement would

> impose serious burdens on the inspection system or the courts, [would] prevent inspections necessary to enforce the statute, or [would] make them less effective. In the first place, the great majority of businessmen can be expected in the normal course to consent to inspection without warrant....

In addition, there seemed to be no need for unannounced inspections, because OSHA had already provided by regulation that if a business refused entry, the inspector should not attempt a forced entry but return to his supervisor to determine the appropriate response, "including compulsory process, if necessary."

The following two problems address the impact of the Fourth Amendment on OSHA's authority to inspect workplaces. In addition, you will be asked to consider some of the practical implications of representing OSHA and the employer it seeks to inspect.

Problem 7–1: OSHA Inspection

Suppose that you are an OSHA attorney who has received a telephone call from Ms. Joyce Regan, a workplace inspector, assigned to the inspection of poultry factories. Tomorrow morning, Ms. Regan plans to visit the Ajax Poultry Co. She wants to know whether she needs to obtain a warrant before going to the factory, or whether she should just show up and ask for consent to search.

(a) How would you advise Ms. Regan?

(b) Now assume that you represent the Ajax Poultry Company rather than OSHA. You have received a telephone call from Ajax's President Mary Kay Zurk indicating that a Ms. Regan, an OSHA inspector, just "showed up" at Ajax's factory—unannounced and without a warrant. Apparently, OSHA's attorneys advised Ms. Regan to proceed without a warrant. Ms. Zurk wants to know whether she should allow the inspector to enter. She feels that her plant is in compliance with OSHA regulations, but an overzealous inspector could probably find a violation of one of OSHA's numerous regulations. How would you advise Ms. Zurk? What factors might encourage her to consent to the search? What factors might encourage her to refuse consent?

Problem 7–2: Another OSHA Inspection

OSHA officials attempted a warrantless inspection of an iron foundry in Coeur d'Alene, Idaho, owned and operated by Deets Iron Works (Deets). Herb Deets, principal owner and chief executive officer of the company, refused inspection, and OSHA aborted its plan. This pattern was repeated a year later.

Two years later, Mabel McCown, Acting Area Director of OSHA, forwarded a letter of inquiry to Deets. The letter detailed a variety of employee complaints, ranging from unsanitary restrooms to the presence of rats and snakes near the eating areas, to a lack of proper protective equipment for employees. In a strongly worded response, Deets denied the charges. OSHA did not attempt to inspect the premises.

The following year, OSHA received more employee complaints about Deets. OSHA's new Area Director, Carol King, again directed an inquiry letter to the company. Again, Deets fired off a combative response. This time he not only attacked the factual accuracy of the allegations but also challenged the very premise of the OSHA inspection system. "The result of all this is that I have wasted a bunch of my time and you have wasted a bunch of the taxpayer's money and nobody is any safer. This is the whole problem with OSHA. All you are doing is serving as a tool whereby disgruntled ex-employees who didn't get their unemployment benefits can make anonymous phone calls and cause trouble for business. It makes you look like fools and wastes everyone's time and money. If you want to do something for safety, why don't you try to help the employers by providing information about unsafe products and processes rather than running around like the Gestapo with our secret informants and star courts." Deets sent copies of the missive to his elected representatives in Washington.

(1) Assume Ms. King decides to seek a warrant to inspect all of Mr. Deets' foundry operation on the basis of the employees' complaints that she has received. What should the affidavit say? How would you assess the likelihood that the courts will enforce the warrant?

(2) Assume Mr. Deets' firm has been scheduled for inspection pursuant to OSHA's General Schedule System (GSS). (The details of this system are described in *In re Trinity Industries, Inc.*, 876 F.2d 1485 (11th Cir.1989), which appears in the problem materials below.) You are asked to write an affidavit to be signed by Ms. King to support the application for the warrant. What should the affidavit say? How can you draft the affidavit to respond to objections that Mr. Deets is likely to raise concerning the validity of the warrant? How would you assess the likelihood that the courts will enforce the warrant?

Problem Materials

TRINITY INDUSTRIES, INC. v. OSHRC

16 F.3d 1455 (6th Cir.1994).

BOYCE F. MARTIN, JR., CIRCUIT JUDGE.

[Trinity] Industries manufactures tanks and what are referred to as pressure vessels at its plant in Sharonville, Ohio. On February 23, 1988, a Trinity employee filed a formal complaint with the Occupational Safety and Health Administration, alleging that portable grinders and rollers used in the plant were improperly wired, that compressed gas cylinders were unsecured and not fitted with valve protection caps, and that oil-slick floors and stored materials impeded safe access to workplace aisles and passageways. After Trinity refused to grant OSHA permission to inspect the facility, the agency sought an administrative inspection warrant from a federal magistrate judge. In its warrant application, OSHA explained that the employee complaint it had received met the formality requirements of [the] Occupational Safety and Health Act of 1970, and that a special inspection was required under the terms of that section of the Act.

[After some litigation,] Trinity agreed to allow OSHA to review the company's safety and health records, and to conduct a comprehensive inspection if the records revealed an establishment lost workday injury rate of 4.2 or more. After calculating a lost workday injury rate of 13.6, OSHA safety specialists and industrial hygienists undertook two concurrent but independent comprehensive inspections of the Sharonville facility. Their recommendations resulted in the issuance of one set of health citations and one set of safety citations. Trinity challenged these citations in two separate administrative actions. Altogether, OSHA issued, and Trinity contested, five citations that alleged numerous violations of the Act. The penalties proposed by OSHA totaled almost $33,000.

[Trinity] contends that inspections of employers selected on the basis of specific evidence of existing violations, such as employee complaints, must be limited to the scope of the complaint, whereas inspections of employers selected on the basis of a reasonable administrative plan may be comprehensive in nature. [Since] OSHA initially selected Trinity for inspection solely on the basis of an employee complaint and request for special inspection, pursuant to Section 8(f) of the Act, the warrant issued should have limited the scope of both the physical inspection of the Sharonville worksite and of the records review to the allegations in the complaint. OSHA ..., Trinity maintains, is merely [attempting] to expand limited inspections into full-scope inspections. . . .

... In *Barlow's*, the Supreme Court held that warrants are required for administrative inspections under the Act. The Court also stated that probable cause justifying the issuance of a warrant for administrative purposes may be based either on "specific evidence of an existing violation" or "on a showing that 'reasonable legislative or administrative standards for conducting [an] inspection are satisfied with respect to a particular [establishment].' " Expounding on the second basis, the Court noted that a "warrant showing that a specific business has been chosen for an OSHA search on the basis of a general administrative plan for the enforcement of the Act derived from neutral sources [would] protect an employer's Fourth Amendment rights." Because administrative and legislative guidelines ensure that employers selected for inspection pursuant to neutral administrative plans have not been chosen simply for the purpose of harassment, courts have held that administrative plan searches may properly extend to the entire workplace. In the case of searches based on employee complaints, however, such safeguards are absent. Given the "increased danger of abuse of discretion and intrusiveness" presented by such searches, we agree with those circuits that have explicitly recognized that "a complaint inspection must bear an appropriate relationship to the violation alleged in the complaint."

The flaw in OSHA['s action] is that [b]y allowing an employee complaint to trigger an administrative plan search, OSHA attempts to authorize a full-scope inspection of an employer in the absence of the probable cause showing required by *Barlow's* for such an inspection. . . .

[W]e disagree with the company's contention that the same warrant improperly authorized OSHA to review all of Trinity's injury and illness records, rather than just those records related to the complaint that triggered the special inspection of the facility. First, as a practical matter, it would be difficult to discern which of these records are and are not "related to the complaint." [Second,] "[r]equiring that an employer produce for the Secretary's inspection records that by law he must keep for her use is hardly equivalent to undertaking a comprehensive plant inspection." [L]imiting the scope of a physical inspection of a worksite while also allowing review of all injury and illness records is consistent with the goals and provisions of the Act.

The proper procedure in cases such as this one [is] for the Secretary to secure a search warrant limited in scope to the employee complaint that triggers the inspection. If this limited search and a review of the employer's injury and illness records leads the Secretary to suspect that further physical investigation of the worksite is necessary, the Secretary should then apply for a second warrant based on these findings authorizing a full-scope inspection.

IN RE TRINITY INDUSTRIES, INC.

876 F.2d 1485 (11th Cir.1989).

COX, CIRCUIT JUDGE:

[F]ederal magistrates issued the Secretary of Labor (Secretary) two separate warrants, one authorizing a health and safety inspection of Trinity's Jacksonville, Florida plant, which manufactures propane gas cylinders, and the other, a safety inspection of Mosher's Birmingham, Alabama plant, which manufactures fabricated structural steel, for possible violations of the Occupational Safety and Health Act, 29 U.S.C. §§ 651–78 (1982) (the OSH Act). The warrants were not based on specific complaints; instead, they were issued pursuant to OSHA plans of programmed inspections.

Trinity and Mosher refused to permit the inspections. Thereafter, the Secretary petitioned the [courts] to hold Trinity and Mosher in civil contempt for failure to honor the warrants. [Under threat of contempt,] Mosher permitted the inspection and appealed. [Trinity refused to permit the inspection, and the] district court ordered Trinity to permit the inspection and imposed a $10,000 per day fine for each day that Trinity refused to do so. Trinity delayed the inspection for one day, incurred a $10,000 fine, and appealed the district court's order.

[On] appeal, Mosher and Trinity [contend] that the warrant applications in question did not contain sufficient information from which the magistrates could make a probable cause determination. . . .

[W]e initially must consider whether the federal magistrates acted on probable cause in issuing the warrants authorizing the inspections. If the magistrates did not so act, then the district courts should have quashed the warrants and dismissed the contempt petitions.

The starting point for any analysis of probable cause for OSHA administrative search warrants is *Marshall v. Barlow's, Inc.*, 436 U.S. 307 (1978), wherein the Supreme Court stated:

> For purposes of an administrative search such as this, probable cause justifying the issuance of a warrant may be based not only on specific evidence of an existing violation but also on a showing that "reasonable legislative or administrative standards for conducting [an] inspection are satisfied with respect to a particular [establish-

ment]." [A] warrant showing that a specific business has been chosen for an OSHA search on the basis of a general administrative plan for the enforcement of the Act derived from neutral sources such as, for example, dispersion of employees in various types of industries across a given area, and the desired frequency of searches in any of the lesser divisions of the area, would protect an employer's Fourth Amendment rights.

To determine whether a warrant application meets the *Barlow's* "administrative plan" criterion (as contrasted with the "specific evidence of a violation" criterion), the magistrate must apply a two-part test: First, the magistrate must determine that the plan pursuant to which the warrant is to be issued is based on specific, "neutral" criteria and, second, the magistrate must determine that the warrant application clearly and adequately establishes that the particular company was selected for inspection pursuant to an application of the plan's neutral criteria. In reviewing a magistrate's probable cause determination, this Court generally may consider only that evidence which was presented to the magistrates, which, in the case before this Court, consists of the warrant applications and supporting materials. Therefore, with the *Barlow's* test in mind, we must examine the applications in question.

The warrant applications involved here were virtually identical. Each contained a copy of the Secretary's administrative plan for programmed health and safety inspections and a sworn affidavit by an OSHA supervisor declaring that Mosher and Trinity were selected for safety and health inspections, respectively, pursuant to that plan. Additionally, the Trinity application was accompanied by a copy of [OSHA's] administrative plan for programmed health and safety inspections[], and a sworn affidavit by an OSHA supervisor declaring that Trinity had been selected for a safety inspection pursuant to that plan.

To enable a magistrate to determine whether the first prong of the *Barlow's* test has been met, the warrant application must contain adequate information from which the magistrate properly may assess the inspection plan's neutrality. "The adequacy determination is to be made by examining the inspection plan itself to ascertain that it contains the requisite neutral criteria," and "as a whole is susceptible of neutral nonarbitrary application." The court is not authorized to inquire into the facts which presaged formulation of the plan.

[OSHA's regulations for safety and health inspection plans], which are virtually identical, have received widespread acceptance by the courts. Each establishes a three-step, "worst-first" ranking system for inspecting companies in high-hazard industries for health and/or safety violations. Under the plans, the national OSHA office initially provides the area OSHA office with a statewide Industry Ranking Report, which ranks companies according to lost workday injury (LWDI) rates (for safety inspections) or potential exposure to hazardous substances (PEHS) (for health inspections) using a four-digit Standard Industrial Classification (SIC) Code. The industry with the highest LWDI or PEHS rate is ranked first. The national office also provides the area office with a list of companies for each SIC Code on the statewide Industry Ranking Report that are located within the area office's jurisdiction. Companies with ten or fewer employees are not shown on the list, and companies having a better LWDI rate than the national average for all private sector industries are not included on the list for safety inspections. The companies are listed by SIC Code, county, and size. Within each SIC Code, counties are listed alphabetically, and within each county, companies are listed according to size, with the largest company being listed first.

After receiving the statewide Industry Ranking Report from the national office, the area office examines the list for errors and makes appropriate additions or deletions. For safety inspections, any company that was inspected within the previous fiscal year is deleted from the list; for health inspections, however, any company that underwent a "substantially complete" health inspection within the current year or previous three fiscal years and had no serious violations cited is removed from the list. After changes are made to the list, all remaining institutions are numbered consecutively.

Finally, the area OSHA office compiles the inspection register. In so doing, the office calculates the number of companies on the register by doubling the number of programmed inspections projected for the fiscal year. Then, the inspection register is divided into two "cycles," with those companies listed on the first half of the list being grouped in one cycle, and those on the other half being grouped in the second cycle. Within an inspection cycle, companies are inspected in an order that makes most efficient use of OSHA's resources. With only limited exceptions, each inspection cycle must be completed before a new cycle is begun.

Mosher and Trinity strenuously assert that [OSHA's inspection plans] are unfair and engender discriminatory and selective enforcement. In our opinion, however, [the plans] are rational, neutral plans which satisfy the first prong of the *Barlow's* test. Clearly, each is calculated to result in an unbiased enforcement of the OSH Act and is intended and designed to protect the greatest number of employees who are exposed [to] the greatest on-the-job health and safety risks. For safety inspections, for instance, only those companies having a safety record below the national average for all private sector industries are ever inspected. Furthermore, for both health and safety inspections, companies are ranked on a "worst-first" basis so that companies in the most hazardous industries are inspected first. Within the "worst" industries, companies are ranked alphabetically, according to county. Conceivably, a company which is included in the "worst" industry ranking could escape inspection during its designated cycle if it is located in a county the name of which begins with a letter near the end of the alphabet. That fact, however, hardly justifies characterizing the plans as discriminatory.

After the alphabetical ranking is made, companies are ranked in descending order based on the number of employees, a step which obviously furthers the objective of protecting the greatest number of employees. Moreover, the process of dividing the total number of companies to be inspected into two groups or "cycles" is patently indiscriminatory. Finally, inspecting firms within a cycle in an order which makes most efficient use of OSHA's resources does not alter the plans' neutrality.

Ultimately, the plans may result in relatively frequent inspections of a select portion of all industries (the high-hazard sector); however, it is entirely reasonable for OSHA to concentrate on the most dangerous workplaces having the most employees at risk. In fact, that result is consistent with OSHA's objective of reducing safety and health risks in the workplace.

Having determined that the first prong of the *Barlow's* test was satisfied with respect to the OSHA plans in question, it is necessary to consider the second prong of the test: whether the warrant applications clearly and adequately establish that Mosher and Trinity were selected pursuant to the plans' specific, neutral criteria. Appellants contend that this prong of the *Barlow's* test was not satisfied because the applications in question did not contain adequate information from which the magistrates could determine how Mosher and Trinity were selected for inspection. More specifically, Mosher and Trinity contend that *Barlow's* requires the Secretary, in its warrant applications, to demonstrate affirmatively that the processes for selecting particular companies for inspection are reasonable, fair, and nondiscriminatory by appending encoded industry ranking reports and establishment lists to every warrant application. Without such documents, they maintain, the magistrate cannot determine how many businesses are subject to inspection, how frequently the selected businesses will be inspected, how many of Mosher and Trinity's direct competitors are exempted or excluded from OSHA review, and whether local additions to or deletions from the establishment lists were made arbitrarily.

[N]o other circuit requires OSHA to append such documents to its warrant applications. [Other] courts have held, and we agree, that in order to satisfy the second prong of the *Barlow's* test, the warrant application need only contain a description of the procedure used in selecting a particular company for inspection (*i.e.*, describe how the establishment lists and inspection registers in question were compiled and how a company was chosen for inspection from among those contained on the register).[4]

4. [The] *Barlow's* Court contemplated that proceedings to review OSHA warrant applications would be limited in scope and would not unduly consume judicial and administrative resources or exceed manageable proportions. An extended inquiry into the validity of the data underlying a particular administrative plan and proposed inspection would far exceed the bounds of the limited inquiry contemplated by *Barlow's*. [Second,] a magistrate is entitled to rely on [an] OSHA official's representation that selection was made in a nondiscriminatory manner, pursuant to a plan's neutral criteria.

In this case, each of the applications in question contains a sworn affidavit by an OSHA supervisor declaring that Mosher and Trinity were selected for inspections pursuant to OSHA's administrative plans for programmed inspections. Each affidavit contains a detailed description of how the plans were executed, including how the relevant establishment lists and inspection registers were developed and how Mosher and Trinity were chosen from the registers for inspection. The information provided was sufficient to enable the magistrates to conclude that Mosher and Trinity were selected by application of the plans' specific, neutral criteria.

Since both warrant applications satisfied the *Barlow's* test for probable cause, we conclude that the magistrates did not err in issuing the warrants authorizing the inspections of Mosher and Trinity, and the district courts acted within their discretion in holding Mosher and Trinity in civil contempt for failing to honor those warrants. . . .

Notes and Questions

1. In *Camara*, the Court indicated that an administrative agency could obtain a warrant even if it lacked probable cause that a particular individual or firm had violated a statute or regulation. This was true both for the general, area-wide, neutral searches, as well as the focused, complaint-based administrative searches. On what grounds did the Court relax the probable cause standard? Do you agree that administrative searches should take place under a more lenient constitutional rule than criminal searches?

2. In its most recent case dealing with administrative searches, *New York v. Burger*, 482 U.S. 691, 107 S.Ct. 2636, 96 L.Ed.2d 601 (1987), the Court seemed to muddy the water concerning the line between administrative and criminal searches. Burger ran an automobile junkyard, which was raided by New York police who suspected him of running a "chop shop," a place where stolen cars are dismantled for parts. They found stolen cars on his property, and he was convicted of possession of stolen property. He moved to suppress the evidence on the grounds that the search was unconstitutional. Under the New York Vehicle and Traffic Law, persons engaged in the business of vehicle dismantling were required to have a license and keep records of the vehicles coming into their possession. The law further provided that "[u]pon request of an agent of the commissioner or of any police officer and during his regular and usual business hours, a vehicle dismantler shall produce such records and permit said agent or police officer to examine them and any vehicles or parts of vehicles which are subject to the record keeping requirements." No warrant was required by the statute and none was obtained. New York defended its action on the grounds that it was an administrative search of a pervasively regulated business.

Using its tests for the exception to the administrative warrant requirement for pervasively regulated businesses, the Court concluded that the search was constitutional. To the claim that this was no "administrative" search at all, inasmuch as it was conducted by police officers and was intended to find evidence of criminal activity, the Court responded that there was no constitutional significance to the fact that police were used to make the inspections or that they might find evidence of crime in addition to evidence of regulatory violations (such as failure to have a license or keep appropriate records). "So long as a regulatory scheme is properly administrative, it is not rendered illegal by the fact that the inspecting officer has the power to arrest individuals for violations other than those created by the scheme itself."

2. REMEDIES FOR ILLEGAL INSPECTIONS

Even though *Camara* loosened the probable cause requirements for administrative searches, illegal inspections do occur. Sometimes, an agency obtains a warrant but the warrant was invalidly issued. In other cases, as in *Barlow's*, the agency searches without a warrant when one is required. Or, as sometimes happens, the police conduct an illegal search and give the results to administrative officials.

What remedies are available for police or administrative misconduct? To the extent that officials enter a home or business without authority, they may be liable in tort under state law (*e.g.*, trespass). They might also be liable under federal law. When federal, state, or local officials violate a citizen's Fourth Amendment right to be free from unreasonable searches and seizures, they can be sued under the Constitution itself, *Bivens v. Six Unknown Named Agents of the Federal Bureau of Narcotics*, 403 U.S. 388, 91 S.Ct. 1999, 29 L.Ed.2d 619 (1971) (petitioner entitled to sue federal officials for violating his Fourth Amendment rights), or under 42 U.S.C.A. § 1983 (authorizing suits against state officials who infringe citizens' "rights, privileges, or immunities secured by the Constitution and laws" of the United States).

Another potential remedy is the exclusionary rule. The federal courts have long prohibited federal prosecutors from using in a criminal case evidence seized in violation of a defendant's constitutional rights. *Weeks v. United States*, 232 U.S. 383, 34 S.Ct. 341, 58 L.Ed. 652 (1914). In *Mapp v. Ohio*, 367 U.S. 643, 81 S.Ct. 1684, 6 L.Ed.2d 1081 (1961), the Court extended this rule to state prosecutions. What was not clear was whether the exclusionary rule would be used to deny administrative agencies the use of information in administrative cases. The following two Supreme Court cases are typical of the Court's decisions not to extend the rule to administrative cases.

UNITED STATES v. JANIS
428 U.S. 433, 96 S.Ct. 3021, 49 L.Ed.2d 1046 (1976).

MR. JUSTICE BLACKMUN delivered the opinion of the Court.

This case presents an issue of the appropriateness of an extension of the judicially created exclusionary rule: Is evidence seized by a state criminal law enforcement officer in good faith, but nonetheless unconstitutionally, inadmissible in a civil proceeding by or against the United States?

[After searching an apartment, pursuant to a warrant, Los Angeles police officers arrested the occupants for conducting a bookmaking operation. They seized bookmaking records and turned them over to an agent of the Internal Revenue Service. Based on this information, the IRS made an assessment against the bookmakers for back taxes. After a judge ruled that the police search of the apartment was illegal because of defects in the warrant, the bookmakers argued the IRS claim should be dismissed because the agency's evidence had been obtained through the illegal actions of the Los Angeles police. Without this evidence, the IRS was unable to prove that the bookmakers owed back taxes.]

[In 1914, this] Court held that the Fourth Amendment alone may be the basis for excluding from a federal criminal trial evidence seized by a federal officer in violation solely of that Amendment. . . .

[The] "prime purpose" of the rule, if not the sole one, "is to deter future unlawful police conduct." Thus, "[i]n sum, the rule is a judicially created remedy designed to safeguard Fourth Amendment rights generally through its deterrent effect, rather than a personal constitutional right of the party aggrieved." And "[a]s with any remedial device, the application of the rule has been restricted to those areas where its remedial objectives are thought most efficaciously served."

In the complex and turbulent history of the rule, the Court never has applied it to exclude evidence from a civil proceeding, federal or state. . . .

[If] the exclusionary rule is the "strong medicine" that its proponents claim it to be, then its use in the situations in which it is now applied (resulting, for example, in this case in frustration of the Los Angeles police officers' good-faith duties as enforcers of the criminal laws) must be assumed to be a substantial and efficient deterrent. Assuming this efficacy, the additional marginal deterrence provided by forbidding a different sovereign from using the evidence in a civil proceeding surely does not outweigh the cost to society of extending the rule to that situation. If, on the other hand, the exclusionary rule does not result in appreciable deterrence, then, clearly, its use in the instant situation is unwarranted. Under either assumption, therefore, the extension of the rule is unjustified.

In short, we conclude that exclusion from federal civil proceedings of evidence unlawfully seized by a state criminal enforcement officer has not been shown to have a sufficient likelihood of deterring the conduct of the state police so that it outweighs the societal costs imposed by the exclusion. This Court, therefore, is not justified in so extending the exclusionary rule. . . .

MR. JUSTICE BRENNAN, with whom MR. JUSTICE MARSHALL concurs, dissenting.

[T]he exclusionary rule is a necessary and inherent constitutional ingredient of the protections of the Fourth Amendment. . . .

MR. JUSTICE STEWART, dissenting. . . .

[If] state police officials can effectively crack down on gambling law violators by the simple expedient of violating their constitutional rights and turning the illegally seized evidence over to Internal Revenue Service agents on the proverbial "silver platter," then the deterrent purpose of the exclusionary rule is wholly frustrated. "If, on the other hand, it is understood that the fruit of an unlawful search by state agents will be inadmissible in a federal trial, there can be no inducement to subterfuge and evasion with respect to federal-state cooperation in criminal investigation."

INS v. LOPEZ–MENDOZA

468 U.S. 1032, 104 S.Ct. 3479, 82 L.Ed.2d 778 (1984).

JUSTICE O'CONNOR announced the judgment of the Court and delivered the opinion of the Court with respect to Parts I, II, III, and IV, and an opinion with respect to Part V, in which JUSTICE BLACKMUN, JUSTICE POWELL, and JUSTICE REHNQUIST joined.

[An illegal alien was arrested unlawfully and made an admission that he was an illegal alien. In the deportation proceeding before the INS, he sought to have this admission excluded as the product of an illegal arrest.]

IV.

[H]ere, in contrast to *Janis*, the agency officials who effect the unlawful arrest are the same officials who subsequently bring the deportation action. . . .

Nonetheless, several other factors significantly reduce the likely deterrent value of the exclusionary rule in a civil deportation proceeding. First, regardless of how the arrest is effected, deportation will still be possible when evidence not derived directly from the arrest is sufficient to support deportation. [Since] the person and identity of the respondent are not themselves suppressible, the INS must prove only alienage, and that will sometimes be possible using evidence gathered independently of, or sufficiently attenuated from, the original arrest. . . .

The second factor is a practical one. In the course of a year the average INS agent arrests almost 500 illegal aliens. Over 97.5% apparently agree to voluntary deportation without a formal hearing. [In] these circumstances, the arresting officer is most unlikely to shape his conduct in anticipation of the exclusion of evidence at a formal deportation hearing.

Third, and perhaps most important, the INS has its own comprehensive scheme for deterring Fourth Amendment violations by its officers

. . .

Finally, the deterrent value of the exclusionary rule in deportation proceedings is undermined by the availability of alternative remedies for institutional practices by the INS that might violate Fourth Amendment rights [including declaratory relief].

[On] the other side of the scale, the social costs of applying the exclusionary rule in deportation proceedings are both unusual and significant. [Applying] the exclusionary rule requires the courts to close their eyes to ongoing violations of the law. This Court has never before accepted costs of this character in applying the exclusionary rule.

. . . Other factors also weigh against applying the exclusionary rule in deportation proceedings. The INS currently operates a deliberately simple deportation hearing system, streamlined to permit the quick resolution of very large numbers of deportation actions, and it is against this backdrop that the costs of the exclusionary must be assessed. [The] average immigration judge handles about six deportation hearings per day. Neither the hearing officers nor the attorneys participating in those hearings are likely to be well versed in the intricacies of Fourth Amendment law. The prospect of even occasional invocation of the exclusionary rule might significantly change and complicate the character of these proceedings. . . .

Finally, the INS advances the credible argument that applying the exclusionary rule to deportation proceedings might well result in the suppression of large amounts of information that had been obtained entirely lawfully. INS arrests occur in crowded and confused circumstances. [The] demand for a precise account of exactly what happened in each particular arrest would plainly preclude mass arrests, even when the INS is confronted, as it often is, with massed numbers of ascertainably illegal aliens, and even when the arrests can be and are conducted in full compliance with all Fourth Amendment requirements.

In these circumstances we are persuaded that the *Janis* balance between costs and benefits comes out against applying the exclusionary rule in civil deportation hearings held by the INS. . . .

V.

[Our] conclusions concerning the exclusionary rule's value might change, if there developed good reason to believe that Fourth Amendment violations by INS officers were widespread. Finally, we do not deal here with egregious violations of Fourth Amendment or other liberties that might transgress notions of fundamental fairness and undermine the probative value of the evidence obtained. At issue here is the exclusion of credible evidence gathered in connection with peaceful arrests by INS officers. We hold that evidence derived from such arrests need not be suppressed in an INS civil deportation hearing.

Problem 7–3: Exclusion of Illegally Obtained Evidence

Suppose that IRS investigators enter Grace Harlow's home in hopes of finding evidence of illegal gambling. Acting without a warrant even though one is required, they enter without knocking. When Harlow confronts the investigators, they beat and restrain her. Ultimately, the investigators uncover evidence of illegal gambling and seek to use that evidence against Harlow in a civil tax proceeding.

Suppose that you have been hired to represent Harlow, how can you distinguish *Janis* and *Lopez–Mendoza* and argue that the exclusionary rule should be applied to Harlow's case? If you were the IRS attorney, how might you respond?

C. RECORDKEEPING AND REPORTING REQUIREMENTS

Agencies require information from the public for a variety of purposes and in a variety of manners. Some information gathering is statistical in nature. For example, the Bureau of the Census in the Department of Commerce is responsible not only for the decennial census mandated by the Constitution but also for a number of more targeted censuses required by Congress to monitor the economy and social structure of the nation. The Energy Information Administration in the Department of Energy performs much the same role with respect to energy information, so that, among other things, it reports how much oil is imported into the United States and from where. Some information gathering by agencies constitutes monitoring of their regulatory programs. For instance, persons with pollution discharge permits under the Clean Water Act are required to submit monthly monitoring reports of their discharges to the permitting agency. Some information gathering involves agencies enforcing their programs by investigating to determine whether statutes or regulations have been violated or by gathering evidence to proceed against the violators. Probably the largest collection of information by the government involves tax reporting at all levels of government.

Just as there are many different types of information the government wants and reasons for wanting it, there are many different ways the government can obtain it. Recordkeeping requirements imposed on persons, as one system by which government may be able to generate information, are usually imposed by regulation. OSHA, for example, requires employers with eleven or more employees to "maintain in each establishment a log and summary of all recordable injuries and illnesses" and to provide access "for inspection and copying by any representative of the Secretary of Labor for the purpose of carrying out the provisions of the act." 29 C.F.R. §§ 1904.2(a)(1), 1904.7. Many reporting requirements likewise are imposed by regulation; some involve government required forms. Income tax returns filed by individuals, for instance, are prescribed by IRS regulations. Some reporting requirements, however, are not imposed by regulation but merely by letter or other communication from the agency.

If expressly provided by statute, agencies can issue subpoenas. Courts also have the power to issue subpoenas. Subpoenas are of two types: subpoenas ad testificandum and subpoenas duces tecum. The first requires the person to come and testify; the second requires a person to come and bring something with him, usually documents. Usually, but not always, subpoenas are used when an agency is investigating possible violations of its regulations or a law. A person receiving a subpoena has three options: she can comply with it; she can go to court and move to quash the subpoena; or she can ignore it. Historically, there was no penalty for ignoring a subpoena. The authority that sought the subpoena would then go to court to enforce the subpoena. Thus, the object of the subpoena could either initiate the court review or await the government's invocation of judicial enforcement. The object of the subpoena could then make its legal arguments for avoiding the subpoena. If the court enforced the subpoena, or failed to quash it, the object is bound to comply. Failure to comply at this point is punished by the government moving for contempt of court. Some modern statutes have begun to streamline the process by providing for a penalty for failure to comply with the original subpoena.

An agency's ability to obtain information depends both on its substantive authority as well as any limitations placed on that authority. Its substantive authority is always derived from statute; limitations may be found in statutes or the Constitution.

1. STATUTORY AUTHORITY AND LIMITATIONS

a. *Statutory Authority*

An agency must be able to find statutory authority for any reporting or recordkeeping requirements that it imposes on people. When the reporting or recordkeeping requirement is imposed by regulation, the agency need not show express authority for that requirement. Rather, like any regulation, the authority may be implied by the statute creating the regulatory program. If, however, the agency wishes to issue a subpoena or report order or simply to impose a reporting requirement by letter, the authority must be express. There is no implied authority to issue a subpoena. Moreover, statutes granting subpoena power contain their own limitations as to what may be subpoenaed. The FTC's subpoena authority is representative:

> For the purposes of this subchapter the Commission, or its duly authorized agent or agents, shall at all reasonable times have access to, for the purpose of examination, and the right to copy any documentary evidence of any person, partnership, or corporation being investigated or proceeded against; and the Commission shall have power to require by subpoena the attendance and testimony of

witnesses and the production of all such documentary evidence relating to any matter under investigation. . . .

15 U.S.C.A. § 49. The FTC can also compel reports subject to the following limitations:

> To require, by general or special orders, persons, partnerships, and corporations, engaged in or whose business affects commerce, excepting banks, savings and loan institutions . . ., Federal credit unions . . ., and common carriers . . . to file with the Commission in such form as the Commission may prescribe annual or special, or both annual and special, reports or answers in writing to specific questions, furnishing to the Commission such information as it may require as to the organization, business, conduct, practices, management, and relation to other corporations, partnerships, and individuals of the respective persons, partnerships, and corporations filing such reports or answers in writing.

Id. § 46(b).

b. *Administrative Procedure Act*

When an agency imposes a reporting or recordkeeping requirement by rule, the rulemaking requirements of the APA obviously apply. What if, however, an agency with clear statutory authority to collect information does not impose its reporting requirement by rule, but merely notifies the class of respondents that they are required to report to the agency regarding certain matters? Can this requirement be imposed without rulemaking? The definition of a rule, an "agency statement of general or particular applicability and future effect designed to implement . . . or prescribe law or policy . . .," would seem to include reporting requirements imposed pursuant to a statutory authorization. In *In re FTC Line of Business Report Litigation*, 595 F.2d 685 (D.C.Cir.1978), however, the D.C. Circuit held that information gathering was not required to be done by rulemaking. The case involved the FTC's attempt to gather basic industry data from 450 of the nation's largest domestic manufacturing concerns in a "Line of Business" (LB) survey and from over 1100 major domestic corporations in its Corporate Patterns Report (CPR). The purpose of the surveys was to establish a data bank on market structures that the FTC could use in antitrust enforcement, economic analysis, and policy planning. The court said:

> [T]he Administrative Procedure Act does not independently require rulemaking prior to the issuance of FTC informational report orders. The language and legislative history of the APA suggest a classification of agency activity into three basic categories: rulemaking, adjudication and investigation. The issuance of agency orders to compel the filing of informational reports was plainly regarded an investigative act by the drafters of the APA, not a rule or adjudication. . . . Investigative acts, specifically including report orders, are encompassed in Section 6(c) [555(c)] of the APA, which states "process, requirement of a report, inspection, or other investigative

act or demand may not be issued, made, or enforced except as authorized by law." Section 6(c) [manifestly] applies to the surveys in issue, which exact informational reports from selected corporations. Thus, that provisions's limitation that investigative orders "may not be issued, made, or enforced except as authorized by law" has direct bearing on this litigation. That phrase, however, simply refers to the statute authorizing the activity. In this case, the enabling statutory provision is Section 6(b) [§ 46(b) reproduced above] of the FTC Act, which [does] not impose rulemaking upon the FTC. Accordingly, the Commission is not obligated under the Administrative Procedure Act to pursue rulemaking proceedings prior to implementation of the LB and CPR programs.

The Federal Trade Commission Act (FTC Act) provides a clear basis of authority for the Commission to issue orders requiring corporations to submit informational reports to the FTC. . . .

[The] LB and CPR surveys, too, are "clearly investigatory in nature" and just as plainly exempt from the Administrative Procedure Act's compulsory rulemaking requirements. . . .

The Supreme Court denied certiorari in the case, and the D.C. Circuit's conclusion has been accepted ever since.

c. The Paperwork Reduction Act

When an agency wishes to impose a reporting or recordkeeping requirement on 10 or more persons, the Paperwork Reduction Act. 44 U.S.C.A. §§ 3501 *et seq.*, imposes substantive and procedural requirements on the agency. This law was briefly described in Chapter 2 because it applies to agency rules that impose reporting or recordkeeping requirements, but it applies to the imposition of such requirements whether or not by rulemaking. The statute regulates the "collection of information" by agencies, defined as "the obtaining, causing to be obtained, soliciting, or requiring the disclosure to third parties or the public, of facts or opinions by or for an agency, regardless of form or format" calling for answers from ten or more persons. 44 U.S.C.A. § 3502(3). Exempted from the Act, however, are collections of information during a federal criminal investigation, in the course of any judicial action to which the United States or an agency is a party, during any administrative action or investigation by an agency directed against specific persons, performed by intelligence agencies, or by compulsory process under the Antitrust Civil Process Act or Section 13 of the Federal Trade Commission Improvements Act.

The Act requires all agencies to establish offices to oversee the agencies' information collection activities. 44 U.S.C.A. § 3506(a)(2). This office is to review each proposed information collection requirement by the agency to ensure that it contains: an evaluation of the need for the collection of information; a functional description of the information to be collected; a plan for the collection of the information; a specific, objectively supported estimate of the burden the collection will impose on persons (measured in hours); a test of the collection of information through a pilot program, if appropriate; and a plan for the efficient and effective management and use of the information to be collected. 44 U.S.C.A. § 3506(c)(1). In addition, the office is to ensure that each collection: is inventoried, displays a control number and, if appropriate, an expiration date; indicates the collection is in accordance with the clearance requirements of the Act; and informs the person receiving the collection of information of—the reasons the information is being collected; the way such information is to be used; an estimate, to the extent practicable, of the burden of the collection; whether responses to the collection of information are voluntary, required to obtain a benefit, or mandatory; and the fact that an agency may not conduct or sponsor, and a person is not required to respond to, a collection of information unless it displays a valid control number. *Id.*

Having done this, if the collection is not done by rulemaking (in which case it must go through the rulemaking requirements of the APA), the office in the agency must provide notice in the Federal Register of the proposed collection requirement and allow 60 days for public comment. 44 U.S.C.A. § 3506(c)(2). After receiving the public comments and making such changes as are appropriate, the office must certify that the information collection requirement: (A) is necessary for the proper performance of the functions of the agency, including that the information has practical utility; (B) is not unnecessarily duplicative of information otherwise reasonably accessible to the agency; (C) reduces to the extent practicable and appropriate the burden on small entities, as defined under the Regulatory Flexibility Act, by establishing differing compliance or reporting requirements or timetables or an exemption from coverage of the collection of information, or any part thereof; (D) is written using plain, coherent, and unambiguous terminology and is understandable to those who are to respond; (E) is to be implemented in ways consistent and compatible, to the maximum extent practicable, with the existing reporting and recordkeeping practices of those who are to respond; (F) indicates for each recordkeeping requirement the length of time persons are required to maintain the records specified; (G) contains the requisite statements and information concerning the collection; (H) has been developed by an office that has planned and allocated resources for the efficient and effective management and use of the information to be collected, including the processing of the information in a manner which shall enhance, where appropriate, the utility of the information to agencies and the public; (I) uses effective and efficient statistical survey methodology appropriate to the purpose for which the information is to be collected; and (J) to the maximum extent practicable, uses information technology to reduce burden and improve data quality, agency efficiency and responsiveness to the public. 44 U.S.C.A. § 3506(3). In short, the agency is required to engage in an elaborate procedure designed to ensure that only important information collection activities are undertaken.

Even with these exhaustive procedures, the Act does not leave the decision to engage in a collection of information in the hands of the agency alone. The agency must submit its proposed information collection requirement to the Office of Information and Regulatory Affairs (OIRA) in OMB for its approval. 44 U.S.C.A. § 3507(a)(1)(C). When the agency submits the proposal to OIRA, it must make another Federal Register notice informing the public of the submission, and OIRA cannot make a decision on the proposal until the public has had 30 days in which to comment on the submission. If the information collection requirement is not contained in a rule, OIRA either approves or disapproves the collection within 60 days. 44 U.S.C.A. § 3507(c). If the information collection requirement is contained in the rule, OIRA comments on the proposed rule. 44 U.S.C.A. § 3507(d). When the agency issues the final rule, it must respond to OIRA's comments. *Id.* If OIRA finds that the agency's response to its comments are "unreasonable," OIRA may disapprove the final rule within 60 days of its promulgation. *Id.* Apparently, however, this power has never been exercised. The Act provides that the head of the agency can seek immediate approval from OIRA of a collection of information without going through the above procedures, if the agency head determines there is an emergency. 44 U.S.C.A. § 3507(j). The standard for OIRA's approval of a collection of information is OIRA's determination whether "the collection of information by the agency is necessary for the proper performance of the functions of the agency." 44 U.S.C.A. § 3508.

The Act specifically exempts from judicial review an OIRA decision to approve or not to disapprove a collection of information contained in an agency rule. 44 U.S.C.A. § 3507(d)(6). The negative implication from this is that an OIRA decision to *disapprove* a collection of information would be subject to judicial review under the APA. OIRA, however, rarely disapproves a collection, and there are no cases where persons have challenged disapprovals. Its strategy mirrors its powers under E.O. 12866, to comment on an agency's proposed collection, whether or not in a rule, and use its political influence with the agency to obtain the agency's agreement. It is an open question whether an OIRA approval or failure to disapprove a collection of information not in a rule would be subject to judicial review. It would seem that a failure to disapprove would be committed to agency discretion by law and therefore be immune from judicial review.

Independent regulatory agencies are authorized to override OIRA's disapproval of a collection of information by a majority vote of the members. 44 U.S.C.A. § 3507(f).

OIRA approvals cannot extend beyond three years, after which the collection must go through the process again. 44 U.S.C.A. § 3507(g), (h).

When OIRA approves a collection of information, it assigns a control number to the collection. 44 U.S.C.A. § 3507(a)(3). This control number must appear on the form or in the regulation or report order. In addition, agencies are required to include a notice on the form or in the regulation or report order to the effect that the absence of a control number excuses a person from having to comply with the collection requirement. If the document does not contain the control number or the notice, the Act prohibits penalizing any person "for failing to comply" with the collection requirements. 44 U.S.C.A. § 3512. The idea behind this "public protection" provision is to create a potent disincentive for agencies to ignore the Act's requirements. There have been a few cases in which persons have avoided penalties as a result of this provision, *see, e.g., United States v. Hatch*, 919 F.2d 1394 (9th Cir.1990) (miner could not be penalized for failing to file an approved operations plan with Forest Service where requirement did not have a control number). In most cases, however, courts have found the provision inapplicable. Primarily this is due to the fact that the reporting or recordkeeping requirement is imposed by statute, rather than by regulation, form, or report order. The cases are uniform that if a reporting requirement is imposed by statute, such as the requirement to file an income tax return, an agency's failure to include a control number on the regulation or form implementing the statute does not protect the person from penalties for failure to make the report required by the statute. Presumably, if the person filed the statutorily required information, but not on the form lacking the control number, the person would be protected from penalty, but that has never been the case. Moreover, the lack of a control number or notice on a form, regulation, or report order does not insulate the respondent from penalty if he files *false* information.

The following problem involves application of the above statutory materials.

Problem 7–4 Treasury Reporting Requirements

The Bank Secrecy Act of 1970 authorized the Secretary of the Treasury to impose recordkeeping and reporting requirements on banks and other financial institutions in this country. In passing the legislation, Congress was concerned about a serious and widespread use of foreign financial institutions, located in jurisdictions with strict laws of secrecy as to bank activity, for the purpose of violating or evading domestic criminal, tax, and regulatory enactments. Congress was also concerned about the maintenance of domestic records which "have a high degree of usefulness in criminal, tax, or regulatory investigations or proceedings." The Secretary was therefore authorized to require the reporting of what may be described as large domestic and international financial transactions in currency or its equivalent. The Act imposed civil and criminal penalties for willful violations of the recordkeeping and reporting requirements.

The Secretary the Treasury is thinking about requiring financial institutions to file reports with the Commissioner of Internal Revenue. These reports would detail each deposit, withdrawal, exchange of currency, or other payment or transfer "which involves a transaction in currency of more than $10,000." The Secretary plans to exempt from the reporting requirement certain intrabank transactions and "transactions with an established customer maintaining a deposit relationship (in amounts) commensurate with the customary conduct of the business, industry, or profession of the customer concerned." The Secretary plans to make some of the information available to other departments or agencies of the United States. The Secretary plans to grant exceptions to or grant exemptions from the requirements of the regulation.

Suppose that you are an attorney for the Treasury Department. Is the agency required to promulgate the recordkeeping and reporting requirements by rulemaking? Does the agency have to comply with the Paperwork Reduction Act? If so, what does it need to do? If no control number is on the reporting requirement, what effect will that have?

2. FOURTH AMENDMENT

In its early decisions, the United States Supreme Court interpreted the Fourth Amendment broadly to limit the power of administrative agencies to subpoena information. The leading case was *Federal Trade Commission v. American Tobacco Co.*, 264 U.S. 298, 44 S.Ct. 336, 68 L.Ed. 696 (1924), in which the FTC sought to investigate manufacturers and sellers of tobacco in order to determine whether they had unlawfully regulated the price at which their products were sold. As part of its investigation, the FTC subpoenaed the "records, contracts, memoranda and correspondence" of tobacco companies for inspection and copying. In an opinion written by Mr. Justice Holmes, the Court refused to enforce the subpoena because the FTC lacked "some ground" for "supposing" that the documents were evidence that the companies had violated the law.

In *Oklahoma Press Publishing Co. v. Walling*, 327 U.S. 186, 66 S.Ct. 494, 90 L.Ed. 614 (1946), however, the Court enforced a subpoena issued by the Wage and Hour Administrator despite the administrator's lack of probable cause. It held that probable cause was not necessary because neither the statute nor the Fourth Amendment required it. There was no Fourth Amendment requirement because an agency subpoena involves less of an invasion of privacy than an actual search. In response to the subpoena, the newspaper would bring the documents to the agency at its office. In addition, the Court balanced the newspaper's privacy interests against the interests of the government. The Court expressed concern that if probable cause were required, it "would stop much if not all of the investigation in the public interest at the threshold of the inquiry."

Instead of probable cause, the Court established the following test for administrative subpoenas:

> [T]he Fourth [Amendment] ... at most guards against abuse only by way of too much indefiniteness or breadth in the things required to be "particularly described," if also the inquiry is one the demanding agency is authorized by law to make and the materials specified

are relevant. The gist of the protection is in the requirement, expressed in terms, that the disclosure shall not be unreasonable.

... It is not necessary, as in the case of a warrant, that a specific charge or complaint of violation of law be pending or that the order be made pursuant to one.

In *United States v. Morton Salt Co.*, 338 U.S. 632, 70 S.Ct. 357, 94 L.Ed. 401 (1950), the Court extended *Oklahoma Press* to the compelled disclosure of information through required reports. The Commission had ordered Morton Salt and nineteen other salt producers to cease and desist from violations of the FTC Act and to file reports every 90 days to indicate their compliance with the order. In response to the company's claim that the FTC was engaged in a "fishing expedition," the Court responded:

> [Because] judicial power is reluctant if not unable to summon evidence until it is shown to be relevant to issues in litigation, it does not follow that an administrative agency charged with seeing that the laws are enforced may not have and exercise powers of original inquiry. It has a power of inquisition, if one chooses to call it that, which is not derived from the judicial function. It is more analogous to the Grand Jury, which does not depend on a case or controversy for power to get evidence but can investigate merely on suspicion that the law is being violated, or even just because it wants assurance that it is not. . . .
>
> Of course a government investigation into corporate matters may be of such a sweeping nature and so unrelated to the matter under inquiry as to exceed the investigatory power. But it is sufficient if the inquiry is within the authority of the agency, the demand is not too indefinite and the information sought is reasonably relevant.

The Court found that "[n]othing on the face of the Commission's order transgressed these bounds."

Notes and Questions

1. In *Oklahoma Press* and *Morton Salt*, the Court struck the balance between the government's need for disclosure and the individual's scope of privacy heavily in favor of the government. Because of these cases, the government's authority to compel the disclosure of information by a subpoena or required report is only broadly limited by the Fourth Amendment. Since most agencies have an expansive statutory mandate to compel the disclosure of documents or command the production of reports, they are usually able to obtain most of the information they seek.

What factors justify the Court's refusal to apply literally the Fourth Amendment? Is the Court's nonliteral approach justified because a subpoena or required report is a "constructive" search in the sense that the government does not actually enter a person's property? Is it justified because administrative enforcement would be nearly impossible if agencies had to have probable cause to investigate? Is it justified by other considerations? Consider the following conclusion:

> Ultimately, the public suffers the burdens of a broad investigatory power in order to gain its benefits. The realm of privacy has been reduced so that the efficacy of regulation can be improved. The relevant issue therefore is not whether there has been too little privacy, but whether there is too much regulation. Without information, regulation will not work. Hence, when the country chooses to regulate, its citizens will need to make the necessary trade-off in terms of their privacy.

RICHARD J. PIERCE, JR., SIDNEY A. SHAPIRO, PAUL R. VERKUIL, ADMINISTRATIVE LAW & PROCESS 420 (3d ed. 1999). Do you agree?

2.   The Fourth Amendment provides one sort of protection against government reporting requirements, but the Court has suggested that the constitutional Right to Privacy may provide another level of protection. *See* JOHN E. NOWAK & RONALD D. ROTUNDA, CONSTITUTIONAL LAW § 1430(b) (5th ed. 1995).

In *Whalen v. Roe*, 429 U.S. 589, 97 S.Ct. 869, 51 L.Ed.2d 64 (1977), for example, the Court considered a claim that a New York statute, which required physicians to submit copies of drug prescriptions to the state, constituted a violation of the right to privacy. The law was intended to assist the state in preventing drug users from obtaining prescriptions from more than one doctor, and to prevent doctors from over-prescribing, either by authorizing an excessive amount in one prescription or by giving one patient multiple prescriptions. Although the Court rejected plaintiffs' argument that the law's impact was sufficient to constitute an invasion of any right or liberty protected by the Fourteenth Amendment, it indicated that the right of privacy may limit the government's acquisition and use of information in some cases:

> [We] are not unaware of the threat to privacy implicit in the accumulation of vast amounts of personal information in computerized data banks or other massive government files. The collection of taxes, the distribution of welfare and social security benefits, the supervision of public health, the direction of our Armed Forces, and the enforcement of the criminal laws all require the orderly preservation of great quantities of information, much of which is personal in character and potentially embarrassing or harmful if disclosed. The right to collect and use such data for public purposes is typically accompanied by a concomitant statutory or regulatory duty to avoid unwarranted disclosures. Recognizing that in some circumstances that duty arguably has its roots in the Constitution, nevertheless New York's statutory scheme, and its implementing administrative procedures, evidence a proper concern with, and protection of, the individual's interest in privacy. . . .

New York's statutory scheme protected an individual's interest in privacy because, among other reasons, access to the information was highly restricted to a few state officials.

The right to privacy considered in *Whalen* has its origins in a line of decisions, the most famous of which is *Roe v. Wade*, 410 U.S. 113, 93 S.Ct. 705, 35 L.Ed.2d 147 (1973). The right of privacy recognized in these cases receives enhanced protection under the due process clauses of the Fifth and Fourteenth Amendments. It includes intimate personal matters in areas such as marriage, family, and procreation and child rearing, although its precise contours remain unclear.

Problem 7–5: FTC Subpoena

You represent Country Bob's, an automobile dealer, which has faxed to you the subpoena in the problem materials. Your client indicates that it would be expensive and time-consuming to comply with several of the specifications of the subpoena. Since the dealer has been in business for more than forty years, the list of current and former officers and employees will be difficult to construct and will be quite long. The company has the same difficulty with providing a list of customers whose cars were repossessed and resold. Finally, Mr. Boone, the owner, objects to providing the FTC with information about the assets of the company, such as the amount of money in its bank account and the property owned by the corporation.

You call a meeting of the attorneys in your firm who will work on this matter to discuss your strategy. Should you advise the client to comply with the subpoena, to authorize you to negotiate with the FTC concerning compliance, or to refuse compliance.

(1) What risks and burden does the client have in complying with the subpoena? Are there any advantages? Is it ever in the interest of a client to comply with an administrative subpoena?

(2) If the client follows the negotiation option, what would you negotiate with the Commission? Is it likely that the FTC staff would withdraw the subpoena? If not, what could you hope to obtain from such a meeting?

(3) What risks and burden does the client have in refusing to comply with the subpoena? Are there any advantages? What legal grounds do you have for resisting compliance with the subpoena? What counterarguments would you expect the FTC staff to make? How would you assess the likelihood that you would prevail for your client?

Problem Materials

Subpoena

UNITED STATES OF AMERICA
FEDERAL TRADE COMMISSION

To: Bob Boone
Country Bob's Automobile
Dealership
3000 Sunydale Rd., Phoenix,
Arizona

You are hereby required to appear before Jan Jones, Attorney and Examiner of the Federal Trade Commission, at the Federal Building, 200 Main Street, in the city of Phoenix, Arizona, on the 10th day of February, at 10:00 a.m. to testify in connection with the Federal Trade Commission's investigation of the automobile sales industry, pursuant to the Federal Trade Commission's Resolution dated Jan. 15, a copy of which is attached hereto and made a part hereof.

And you are hereby required to bring with you and produce at said time and place the following books, papers, and documents: See attached Definitions, Instructions, and Specifications.

Fail not at your peril.

In testimony whereof, the undersigned, an authorized official of the Federal Trade Commission, has caused the seal of said Federal Trade Commission to be affixed, and has hereunto set his hand at Phoenix, Arizona, this 18th day of January.

Roger Smith

Regional Director

DEFINITIONS AND INSTRUCTIONS

(a) For purposes of making return to the attached subpoena, the term "company" will mean Country Bob's Automobile Dealership, 3000 Sunydale Rd., Phoenix, Arizona.

(b) For purposes of making return to the attached subpoena, the term "documents" will mean the originals and all nonidentical copies (whether different from the originals by reason of notations made on such copies or otherwise) of all letters, telegrams, memoranda, books, contracts, records, reports, research papers, surveys, studies, medical articles and findings, tabulations, charts, computer printouts, disks, and files stored in computer memory, notes of interviews or communications and all other written information or materials of any nature whatsoever in the possession, custody, or control of the company, its officers, directors, employees, or agents.

(c) For the purpose of making return to the attached subpoena, the term "verified statement" will mean a written statement or list, the correctness and veracity of which have been certified by an appropriate company official.

(d) In the event that the same document is required to be submitted for more than one Specification, the company may at its option, refer to any document it has submitted in response hereto, rather than submitting the same document more than once.

(e) All documents submitted will be clearly and precisely identified as to the Specification(s) to which they are responsive.

SPECIFICATIONS

SPECIFICATION 1: Documents or, in lieu thereof, a verified statement which will show the date and state of Country Bob's incorporation.

SPECIFICATION 2: A copy of Country Bob's Articles of Incorporation and Bylaws.

SPECIFICATION 3: Documents or, in lieu thereof, a verified statement which will provide a list, with names, addresses, telephone numbers, and a description of duties, of each of Country Bob's current and former officers and employees, who held such positions from its date of incorporation.

SPECIFICATION 4: A copy of Country Bob's certified financial statements since its date of incorporation.

SPECIFICATION 5: Documents or, in lieu thereof, a verified statement which will show all assets owned by Country Bob's including, but not limited to, bank accounts, brokerage accounts, and property.

SPECIFICATION 6: Documents or, in lieu thereof, a verified statement which will provide a list, with names and addresses, and telephone numbers, of the owners of all automobiles resold by County Bob's after a default in payments for an automobile, the resale price of each automobile, and the amount of money refused to the buyer as a surplus.

UNITED STATES OF AMERICA
BEFORE THE FEDERAL TRADE COMMISSION

RESOLUTION DIRECTING USE OF COMPULSORY PROCESS IN A NONPUBLIC INVESTIGATION OF AUTOMOBILE SALES PRACTICES

File No. 13–135671

Nature and Scope of Investigation:

To investigate the advertising and marketing of automobiles for the purpose of determining whether unnamed persons, partnerships, or corporations, or others engaged in the advertising and marketing of automobiles have or are engaging in unfair or deceptive acts or practices in violation of Section 5 of the Federal Trade Commission Act, 15 U.S.C.A. § 45, as amended, including, but not limited to, the method used by car dealers of calculating the consumer surplus after the resale of automobiles which are repossessed. The investigation is also to determine whether Commission action to obtain redress of injury to consumers or others would be in the public interest.

The Federal Trade Commission hereby resolves and directs that any and all compulsory processes available to it be used in connection with this investigation.

Authority to Conduct Investigation: Sections 6, 9, and 10 of the Federal Trade Commission Act, 15 U.S.C.A. §§ 46, 49 and 50, as amended; FTC Procedures and Rules of Practice, 16 C.F.R. § 1.1 *et seq.* and supplements thereto.

By direction of the Commission

Susan O'Reilly
Secretary
Jan. 15.

FREESE v. FEDERAL DEPOSIT INSURANCE CORP.

837 F.Supp. 22 (D.N.H.1993).

LOUGHLIN, SENIOR DISTRICT JUDGE. . . .

On October 10, 1991, the Federal Deposit Insurance Corporation ("FDIC") was appointed receiver and liquidating agent for New Hampshire Savings Bank. On September 18, 1992, the FDIC issued an Order of Investigation. The purpose of the investigation was to determine whether any valid claims existed against the Bank's former officers and directors; whether sufficient assets existed to pursue any potential claims against them; and whether the FDIC should seek to freeze or attach any of their assets.

In connection with the investigation, the FDIC issued administrative subpoenas *duces tecum* on June 3, 1993, to [several persons who] were former officers and directors of the New Hampshire Savings Bank. The subpoenas were identical and sought extensive personal financial information in relation to the plaintiffs and their families for the five years preceding the date of the subpoenas. . . .

It is well settled that an agency subpoena is enforceable if the subpoena is issued for a proper purpose authorized by Congress, if the information sought is relevant to that purpose and is adequately described within the subpoena, and the statutory procedures have been followed in the subpoena's issuance. . . . An affidavit from a government official is sufficient to establish a prima facie showing that the requirements have been met.

The plaintiffs have not alleged that the subpoenas in this case were issued in violation of statutory procedure. Instead, the plaintiffs claim that the subpoenas were sought for improper purposes, that even if the court determined that the purposes were proper the information sought was not relevant to those purposes and that the subpoenas were issued in violation of the Fourth Amendment.

In the Order of Investigation, the FDIC has stated four purposes for which the subpoenas were issued. The FDIC seeks to determine whether (1) the former officers and directors of the New Hampshire Savings Bank may be liable as a result of any action or failure to act; (2) the pursuit of litigation against the plaintiffs would be cost effective; (3) the FDIC should seek to avoid any transfers made by the plaintiffs; and (4) the FDIC should seek an attachment of the plaintiffs' assets.

A determination of whether the pursuit of a civil suit against the plaintiffs would be cost effective is not a proper purpose to issue a subpoena. The FDIC may not freely peruse personal financial records in order to determine the party's financial ability to satisfy a judgment. Courts have routinely denied access to personal financial records in civil discovery reasoning that a party's ability to satisfy a judgment is irrelevant to the subject matter of the action. While the rules of civil discovery do not control an administrative subpoena, even the broad powers of the FDIC do not extend to an invasion of privacy.

The FDIC urges that even if determining the cost effectiveness of the litigation is not a proper purpose, the remaining articulated purposes are sufficient to justify the issuance of the subpoena. The FDIC asserts that subpoenas were necessary to determine whether the plaintiffs may be liable for any action or inaction as officers and directors of New Hampshire Savings Bank or whether the FDIC should freeze or avoid any transfer of the plaintiffs' assets. However, the FDIC fails to assert that there was even a suspicion of wrongdoing on the part of the plaintiffs.

In her affidavit, Emily E. Sommers, Senior Attorney in the Professional Liability Section of the FDIC, simply states that the information sought is relevant to the purposes for which the subpoenas were issued. On the basis of this bald statement the FDIC urges that there is a *prima facie* showing that the requirements necessary to the issuance of the subpoena were met. The FDIC claims that a review of all of the plaintiffs' and their spouses financial documents for the past five years is necessary to determine if there were any "suspicious accretions to wealth."

The FDIC has not offered a basis on which to assert that the plaintiffs may have been liable for any wrongdoing in their capacities as directors or officers of New Hampshire Savings Bank.

. . . The court does not intend to imply that the FDIC was required to establish a showing of probable or reasonable cause in order to support the enforcement of the subpoena. However, to allow the FDIC to conduct a fishing expedition through the plaintiffs' private papers in the hope that some evidence of wrongdoing will surface flies in the face of the spirit, if not the letter, of the Fourth Amendment.

Commenting further, this shotgun approach to the use of the subpoena powers in a hubristic manner infringes upon fundamental constitutional rights we are all entitled to, even losers. There has been some mitigation of the untoward situation presented by the facts in this case as most documents have been sealed. Albeit, individuals subject to the subpoena powers have incurred legal expenses, anxiety and trepidation in facing the shotgun method the defendant has used to expose putative violations of the law. . . .

ADAMS v. FEDERAL TRADE COMMISSION

296 F.2d 861 (8th Cir.1961).

MATTHES, CIRCUIT JUDGE.

[The FTC issued a complaint that alleged the Adams Dairy Company (Adams) and several grocery stores had engaged in a conspiracy to set prices in violation of the FTC Act. The hearing examiner issued six administrative subpoenas for various documents of the defendants. When Adams refused to comply, the Commission sought judicial enforcement of the subpoena. The circuit court reviewed the decision of the district court to deny enforcement of part or all of a number of specifications in the subpoena.]

While there is a suggestion by appellees that the specifications fail to properly specify the documents sought, their principal claim is that the subpoenas called for irrelevant material and that "they are unduly broad and burdensome and unreasonable in scope." In determining whether the Commission is entitled to enforcement in light of the standards or tests to be applied, we must lay the specifications alongside the complaints. In summary, the complaints charge Adams and the respective grocery companies (Kroger, Safeway and A & P) with maintaining a conspiracy in restraint of interstate trade in Missouri, Kansas, Illinois and Kentucky. Each complaint alleges, *inter alia*, that in furtherance of the conspiracy, the named respondents had pursued the policy and practice of fixing prices and coercing competitors into maintaining prices and price differentials; that the grocery companies had engaged in territorial price wars and price discriminations and had given preferential treatment to Adams; that Adams had subsidized the practices and policies of the grocery companies in certain areas by various methods, which are enumerated in detail. . . .

1. Books, records, etc., showing:

(a) types of products manufactured, processed, distributed, or sold from date of incorporation [January 1, 1940] to September 24, 1959;

(b) geographical areas in which each type of product in (a) was distributed and sold.

The district court enforced this provision but limited the time period, stating "the period subsequent to 1954 should be adequate." The Commission contends the data sought by this specification is necessary to determine the nature and scope of Adams' business and is relevant to the allegation that the companies are engaged in interstate commerce. The period between October 1, 1954, and September 24, 1959, should prove entirely adequate to establish the nature and scope of Adams' business and that they are engaged in interstate commerce, concerning which there should not be much dispute.

2. Copies of annual reports to stockholders and profit and loss statements from date of incorporation ... to September 24, 1959.

The district court refused to enforce this provision, stating that it was too broad in scope. However, since a conspiracy to fix prices is alleged to have existed 'for many years past' the material sought is relevant as it may disclose business relations with other companies and profit trends. [B]roadness alone is not sufficient justification to refuse enforcement of a subpoena so long as the material sought is relevant. It is readily apparent that many of the specifications of the subpoenas are broad in scope. However, when a conspiracy is alleged the search might take a broad sweep in order that information revealing the nature of the relationship between the alleged co-conspirators can be obtained.

3. Any documents or writings relating to securing or maintaining licenses and permits required by law from January 1, 1950, to September 24, 1959.

The district court refused enforcement of this provision, stating that it was unreasonable, arbitrary and too broad in scope.... The method of distributing dairy products, that is, whether by independent contractors or agents and employees of Adams, is, in our opinion, relevant to the issue of Adams' responsibility for the acts and conduct of these distributors of dairy products. The documents called for in this specification should be limited, however, to the period from October 1, 1954, to September 24, 1959.

4. Any writings pertaining to the establishment, initial operating, or incorporation of [Adams] prepared by [its] officers, representatives or agents; from date of incorporation ... to September 24, 1959.

The district court denied enforcement of this provision for the same reason relied upon in denying enforcement of Specification 3. Commission asserts that the conspiracy charged was initiated at or about the time of incorporation of Adams. The record discloses that in 1941 there was correspondence between Safeway and a bank in Kansas City relating to a contemplated loan to be made by the bank to "Mr. Adams." In view of this circumstance and the assertion by Commission that the conspiracy has existed for many years, the documents called for are reasonably relevant. Enforcement of this specification should be granted.

5. Any writings prepared by [Adams'] employees, etc., pertaining to the company's relations, dealings or business with: Kroger, Safeway, A & P, from date of incorporation ... to September 24, 1959.

The district court stated "If it (specification 5) were confined to the correspondence between the respondent and The Kroger Company, Safeway Stores, Inc. and The Great Atlantic and Pacific Tea Company, Inc. (it) would be a perfectly valid request." The remainder of the specification was in the court's opinion "entirely too broad." Recognizing that direct proof of a conspiracy generally is not available and that a conspiracy ordinarily is established by developing circumstances from various sources of information, we conclude that this specification should not be limited to correspondence by Adams....

8.   Books, records, etc., showing for the period October 1, 1954, to September 24, 1959:

(a) annual net sales of dairy products in gallons or pounds and dollars;

(b) monthly net sales in dollars and by quantities of each container size for each type of product sold directly or indirectly to Kroger, Safeway and A & P;

(c) locations where items in (b) were delivered and by whom.

While the court apparently approved Specification 8(a), it failed to specifically direct enforcement thereof. As to 8(b) and (c) the court entertained doubts as to "how the respondents could be required to comply * * *," stating that the records called for "would require a boxcar to contain them." In our view, the information called for in 8(b) and (c), while undoubtedly voluminous, may be revealing as to the effect of the alleged price was, price discriminations and other practices charged in the complaints. The court did not find that this data was irrelevant to the conspiracy charged. Enforcement should be granted.

13.   ... Books, records, etc., disclosing names of all distributors of [Adams'] products from date of incorporation to September 24, 1959, and showing following information for each distributor:

(a) last mailing address;

(b) date when started handling [Adams'] products;

(c) date when stopped handling these products;

(d) reason distributors stopped handling these products;

(e) all cities and towns in distributor's original route;

(f) changes and dates changes in routes were made;

(g) names and addresses of all local customers of distributors.

The district court refused to enforce this specification, claiming it was too broad in time, was unreasonable and irrelevant. We agree with the district court to the extent that the subpoena is too broad in time. The Commission's position is that the documents sought are relevant to the determination of whether the distributors were independent contractors; for the purpose of determining the distributors which operated in particular areas and for the purpose of obtaining information relating to specific price wars, price discriminations and sales below cost. The relationship between the distributors and Adams is the subject of other specifications. The Commission had limited other specifications concerning price wars, price discriminations and sales below cost to the period subsequent to October 1, 1954, (e.g. see Specification 8), and we see no reason why this request should not be so limited. The period prior to October 1, 1954, is not reasonably relevant to these allegations, particularly in view of the fact that the Commission itself has concentrated on activities subsequent to this time. Enforcement should be ordered for the period from October 1, 1954, to September 24, 1959. . . .

3. FIFTH AMENDMENT

In addition to Fourth Amendment constraints, government efforts to compel the disclosure of information are subject to the Fifth Amendment's protection against self-incrimination, which provides that no person "shall be compelled in any criminal case to be a witness against himself. . . ." U.S. CONST. Amend V. Despite its language, the Self–Incrimination Clause extends beyond criminal cases to any government compulsion to testify in a manner that would criminally incriminate the person testifying. Thus, neither courts, agencies, nor Congress can compel a person to testify in a way that incriminates that person, unless the person is given immunity from prosecution on that evidence. *See* 18 U.S.C.A. §§ 6002, 6003 (authorizing the Justice Department to seek a court order granting use immunity to witnesses before courts, agencies, and committees of Congress). Nevertheless, the Fifth Amendment offers only limited protection against administrative attempts to obtain documents, as opposed to oral testimony.

First, the Supreme Court determined years ago that "a corporation cannot resist production of [records] upon the ground of self-incrimination." *Wilson v. United States*, 221 U.S. 361, 31 S.Ct. 538, 55 L.Ed. 771 (1911). In *Hale v. Henkel*, 201 U.S. 43, 26 S.Ct. 370, 50 L.Ed. 652 (1906), the Court explained that whereas an "individual may stand upon his constitutional rights as a citizen," the "corporation is a creature of the state. . . ." For this reason, "[i]t would be a strange anomaly to hold that a state, having chartered a corporation to make use of certain franchises, could not, in the exercise of its sovereignty, inquire how these franchises had been employed, and whether they had been abused, and demand the production of the corporate books and papers for that purpose. . . ." Moreover, the Court has long made clear that unincorporated groups likewise are not protected by the Self–Incrimination Clause. In *United States v. White*, 322 U.S. 694, 64 S.Ct. 1248, 88 L.Ed. 1542 (1944), the Court held that an unincorporated labor union did not have a privilege against self-incrimination. The Court recognized that its earlier decisions had been based on the fact that corporations were charted by the government. In *White*, it held that the framers intended the privilege to extend only to *individuals* and not to organizations and other entities:

> Basically, the power to compel the production of the records of any organization, whether it be incorporated or not, arise out of the inherent and necessary power of the federal and state governments to enforce their laws, with the privilege against self-incrimination being limited to its historical function of protecting only the natural

individual from compulsory incrimination, through his own testimony or personal records.

See also Bellis v. United States, 417 U.S. 85, 94 S.Ct. 2179, 40 L.Ed.2d 678 (1974) (three person law firm had no right against self-incrimination).

Second, when the government seeks documents from a non-natural person, the natural person who must respond for the organization cannot claim a personal privilege for the organization's documents, even though those documents might incriminate the person.

[The person] held the corporate books subject to the corporate duty. If the corporation were guilty of misconduct, he could not withhold its books to save it; and if he were implicated in the violations of law, he could not withhold the books to protect himself from the effect of their disclosures.

Wilson v. United States, 221 U.S. 361, 31 S.Ct. 538, 55 L.Ed. 771 (1911).

Third, even when the documents sought are those of an individual (or sole proprietorship), the Fifth Amendment provides only little more protection. In *Shapiro v. United States*, 335 U.S. 1, 68 S.Ct. 1375, 92 L.Ed. 1787 (1948), the Court held that the privilege does not apply to so-called "required records." Mr. Shapiro's conviction for violation of wage and price regulations adopted during World War II was based in part on records that he was required by law to keep. The Court held there was no Fifth Amendment right because the records were "public" rather than "private" records. The records were "public" because the law required Shapiro to keep them "in order that there may be suitable information of transactions which are the appropriate subjects of government regulation and the enforcement of restrictions validly established." *See* Stephen Saltzburg, *In Honor of Bernard D. Meltzer, The Required Records Doctrine: Its Lessons for the Privilege Against Self–Incrimination*, 53 U. Chi. L. Rev. 6 (1986).

Fourth, even when records are not required to be kept by the government, the Court has indicated that requiring the production of already created documents is not self-incrimination within the meaning of the Fifth Amendment, because that amendment goes to compelled *testimony*, and compelling the production of already existing documents is not compelling testimony. *See United States v. Doe*, 465 U.S. 605, 104 S.Ct. 1237, 79 L.Ed.2d 552 (1984).

Nonetheless, there are situations where persons are, or may be, protected. In *Marchetti v. United States*, 390 U.S. 39, 88 S.Ct. 697, 19 L.Ed.2d 889 (1968), for example, Marchetti had been convicted of failing to register with the government as a person engaged in the business of accepting wagers (*i.e.*, being a bookie). He claimed that the requirement to so register compelled him to incriminate himself. The government claimed that the required records exception applied, but the Court disagreed.

Each of the three principal elements of the doctrine, as it is described in *Shapiro*, is absent from this situation. First, petitioner Marchetti was not, by the provisions now at issue, obliged to keep and preserve records "of the same kind as he has customarily kept"; he was required simply to provide information, unrelated to any records which he may have maintained, about his wagering activities. This requirement is not significantly different from a demand that he provide oral testimony. Second, whatever "public aspects" there were to the records at issue in *Shapiro*, there are none to the information demanded from Marchetti. The Government's anxiety to obtain information known to a private individual does not without more render that information public; if it did, no room would remain for the application of the constitutional privilege. Nor does it stamp information with a public character that the Government has formalized its demands in the attire of a statute; if this alone were sufficient, the constitutional privilege could be entirely abrogated by any Act of Congress. Third, the requirements at issue in *Shapiro* were imposed in "an essentially non-criminal and regulatory area of inquiry" while those here are directed at a "selective group inherently suspect of criminal activities." . . .

There also remains a question whether the rule of *Doe*, that requiring the production of already created documents does not involve compelled testimony as to their contents, applies to purely personal documents, such as a diary. Justice O'Connor, concurring in *Doe*, specifically addressed this issue to make "explicit . . . that the Fifth Amendment provides absolutely no protection for the contents of private papers of any kind." Justices Brennan and Marshall, however, wrote specifically to disagree with her, and the rest of the Court was silent on the matter. The lower courts appear to be badly split. *See* Anne Marie Demarco & Elisa Scott, *Confusion Among the Courts: Should the Contents of Personal Papers Be Privileged by the 5th Amendment Self–Incrimination Clause*, 9 St. John's J. Legal Comm. 219 (1993).

Finally, and most significantly, another way the Self–Incrimination Clause can protect a person from a demand for documents is when the mere act of producing the documents, as opposed to the contents of the documents, may incriminate the person producing the documents. Under traditional rules of evidence, as well as the Federal Rules of Evidence, documents, when offered for the truths asserted therein, are "hearsay" and, in the absence of one of the hearsay exceptions or exclusions, are not admissible in evidence. Several of the exceptions and exclusions rely upon showings that the documents come from a particular source. For example, if a diary contained statements confessing certain illegal activities, those statements might fall within the exclusion for "admissions against interest." However, in order to show that these fall within the exclusion, the government would need to show that the diary was in fact the diary of the person against whom it was to be used. Similarly, regularly kept business records are a hearsay exception. Again, however, to introduce these records into evidence, the government would need to show that they are in fact ordinary business records. If a person responds to a subpoena directing him to produce his diary or ordinary business records, the "act of production" of the documents may be evidence that they are responsive documents; that is, that the documents produced are in fact the documents sought. In this way, the government effectively compels a person to "testify" as to the documents' provenance through compelling the person to produce specific documents, and this "testimony" incriminates the person if the underlying documents contain incriminating information. Thus, even though a person does not have a privilege with respect to the contents of documents *per se*, the person may still have a Self–Incrimination Clause defense to production because the act of production itself may incriminate him. For example, in *United States v. Doe*, 465 U.S. 605, 104 S.Ct. 1237, 79 L.Ed.2d 552 (1984), while the court held the individual had no privilege against self-incrimination with respect to the contents of his personal tax records he was required to produce, the Court upheld the quashing of the subpoena because the courts below had found that his production of the documents would "tacitly [concede] the existence of the papers demanded and their possession or control by the taxpayer. It also would indicate the taxpayer's belief that the papers are those described in the subpoena," and this would constitute self-incrimination.

Problem 7–6 Subpoena of Company Records

You have long represented Karen Trowbridge. She founded a men's and ladies' clothing manufacturing concern. Until two years ago, the firm was a sole proprietorship, but it was so successful that she then had you incorporate the firm as Jodhpurs, Inc., a small closely held corporation of which Karen is the Chief Executive Officer. The concern is and has been subject to the Fair Labor Standards Act (FLSA), which among other things regulates the wages and hours of workers in industries affecting commerce. Karen has received a subpoena addressed to her from the Administrator of the Wage and Hour Division of the Department of Labor, the agency responsible for enforcing the FLSA. The subpoena requires her to appear and testify at a deposition and to bring with her copies of the company's personnel and wage and hour records for the past five years. She is concerned that there may be information contained in those records suggesting that the corporation has been employing child labor in violation of the FLSA. She asks you whether there is any way that she can avoid having to supply this information.

Problem Materials

Fair Labor Standards Act
29 U.S.C.A.

§ 209. Attendance of witnesses

For the purpose of any hearing or investigation provided for in this chapter, the provisions of sections 49 and 50 of Title 15 [the FTC's subpoena provisions] (relating to the attendance of witnesses and the production of books, papers, and documents), are made applicable to the jurisdiction, powers, and duties of the Administrator, the Secretary of Labor, and the industry committees.

§ 211. Collection of data

(a) Investigations and inspections

The Administrator or his designated representatives may investigate and gather data regarding the wages, hours, and other conditions and practices of employment in any industry subject to this chapter, and may enter and inspect such places and such records (and make such transcriptions thereof), question such employees, and investigate such facts, conditions, practices, or matters as he may deem necessary or appropriate to determine whether any person has violated any provision of this chapter, or which may aid in the enforcement of the provisions of this chapter. . . .

§ 212. Child labor provisions

(a) Restrictions on shipment of goods; prosecution; conviction

No producer, manufacturer, or dealer shall ship or deliver for shipment in commerce any goods produced in an establishment situated in the United States in or about which within thirty days prior to the removal of such goods therefrom any oppressive child labor has been employed. . . .

(c) Oppressive child labor

No employer shall employ any oppressive child labor in commerce or in the production of goods for commerce or in any enterprise engaged in commerce or in the production of goods for commerce.

(d) Proof of age

In order to carry out the objectives of this section, the Secretary may by regulation require employers to obtain from any employee proof of age.

§ 215. Prohibited acts; prima facie evidence

(a) After the expiration of one hundred and twenty days from June 25, 1938, it shall be unlawful for any person— . . .

(4) to violate any of the provisions of section 212 of this title. . . .

§ 216. Penalties

(a) Fines and imprisonment

Any person who willfully violates any of the provisions of section 215 of this title shall upon conviction thereof be subject to a fine of not more than $10,000, or to imprisonment for not more than six months, or both. No person shall be imprisoned under this subsection except for an offense committed after the conviction of such person for a prior offense under this subsection. . . .

(e) Civil penalties for child labor violations

Any person who violates the provisions of section 212 of this title, relating to child labor, or any regulation issued under that section, shall be subject to a civil penalty of not to exceed $10,000 for each employee who was the subject of such a violation.

BRASWELL v. UNITED STATES

487 U.S. 99, 108 S.Ct. 2284, 101 L.Ed.2d 98 (1988).

CHIEF JUSTICE REHNQUIST delivered the opinion of the Court.

. . . In August 1986, a federal grand jury issued a subpoena to "Randy Braswell, President Worldwide Machinery Sales Inc. [and] Worldwide Purchasing, Inc.," requiring petitioner to produce the books and records of the two corporations. . . . Petitioner moved to quash the subpoena, arguing that the act of producing the records would incriminate him in violation of his Fifth Amendment privilege against self-incrimination. . . .

There is no question but that the contents of the subpoenaed business records are not privileged. Similarly, petitioner asserts no self-incrimination claim on behalf of the corporations; it is well established that such artificial entities are not protected by the Fifth Amendment. Petitioner instead relies solely upon the argument that his act of producing the documents has independent testimonial significance, which would incriminate him individually, and that the Fifth Amendment prohibits Government compulsion of that act. . . .

In *Fisher v. United States*, 425 U.S. 391 (1976), the Court was presented with the question whether an attorney may resist a subpoena demanding that he produce tax records which had been entrusted to him by his client. . . . In analyzing the Fifth Amendment claim forwarded by the attorney, the Court considered whether the client-taxpayer would have had a valid Fifth Amendment claim had he retained the records and the subpoena been issued to him. . . . The Court [observed]:

> The act of producing evidence in response to a subpoena nevertheless has communicative aspects of its own, wholly aside from the contents of the papers produced. Compliance with the subpoena tacitly concedes the existence of the papers demanded and their possession or control by the taxpayer. It also would indicate the taxpayer's belief that the papers are those described in the subpoena. The elements of compulsion are clearly present, but the more difficult issues are whether the tacit averments of the taxpayer are both "testimonial" and "incriminating" for purposes of applying the Fifth Amendment. These questions perhaps do not lend themselves to categorical answers; their resolution may instead depend on the facts and circumstances of particular cases or classes thereof.

... Eight years later, in *United States v. Doe*, 465 U.S. 605 (1984), the Court revisited the question, this time in the context of a claim by a sole proprietor that the compelled production of business records would run afoul of the Fifth Amendment. ... The Court concluded that respondent had established a valid Fifth Amendment claim. It deferred to the lower courts, which had found that enforcing the subpoenas at issue would provide the Government valuable information: By producing the records, respondent would admit that the records existed, were in his possession, and were authentic.

Had petitioner conducted his business as a sole proprietorship, *Doe* would require that he be provided the opportunity to show that his act of production would entail testimonial self-incrimination. But petitioner has operated his business through the corporate form, and we have long recognized that, for purposes of the Fifth Amendment, corporations and other collective entities are treated differently from individuals. This doctrine—known as the collective entity rule—has a lengthy and distinguished pedigree. ...

The plain mandate of these decisions is that without regard to whether the subpoena is addressed to the corporation, or as here, to the individual in his capacity as a custodian, a corporate custodian such as petitioner may not resist a subpoena for corporate records on Fifth Amendment grounds. ...

The agency rationale undergirding the collective entity decisions, in which custodians asserted that production of entity records would incriminate them personally, survives. [T]he Court has consistently recognized that the custodian of corporate or entity records holds those documents in a representative rather than a personal capacity. Artificial entities such as corporations may act only through their agents, and a custodian's assumption of his representative capacity leads to certain obligations, including the duty to produce corporate records on proper demand by the Government. Under those circumstances, the custodian's act of production is not deemed a personal act, but rather an act of the corporation. Any claim of Fifth Amendment privilege asserted by the agent would be tantamount to a claim of privilege by the corporation—which of course possesses no such privilege. ...

Petitioner asserts that ... although the contents of a collective entity's records are unprivileged, a representative of a collective entity cannot be required to provide testimony about those records. It follows, according to petitioner, that ... because ... the act of production is potentially testimonial, such an act may not be compelled if it would tend to incriminate the representative personally. ...

Although a corporate custodian is not entitled to resist a subpoena on the ground that his act of production will be personally incriminating, we do think certain consequences flow from the fact that the custodian's act of production is one in his representative rather than personal capacity. Because the custodian acts as a representative, the act is deemed one of the corporation and not the individual. Therefore, the

Government concedes, as it must, that it may make no evidentiary use of the "individual act" against the individual. For example, in a criminal prosecution against the custodian, the Government may not introduce into evidence before the jury the fact that the subpoena was served upon and the corporation's documents were delivered by one particular individual, the custodian. The Government has the right, however, to use the corporation's act of production against the custodian. The Government may offer testimony—for example, from the process server who delivered the subpoena and from the individual who received the records—establishing that the corporation produced the records subpoenaed. The jury may draw from the corporation's act of production the conclusion that the records in question are authentic corporate records, which the corporation possessed, and which it produced in response to the subpoena. And if the defendant held a prominent position within the corporation that produced the records, the jury may, just as it would had someone else produced the documents, reasonably infer that he had possession of the documents or knowledge of their contents. Because the jury is not told that the defendant produced the records, any nexus between the defendant and the documents results solely from the corporation's act of production and other evidence in the case.[11]

Consistent with our precedent, the United States Court of Appeals for the Fifth Circuit ruled that petitioner could not resist the subpoena for corporate documents on the ground that the act of production might tend to incriminate him. The judgment is therefore affirmed.

[JUSTICES KENNEDY, BRENNAN, MARSHALL, and SCALIA dissented.]

SMITH v. RICHERT

35 F.3d 300 (7th Cir.1994).

POSNER, CHIEF JUDGE.

It used to be thought that if a person was required by the government to yield up an incriminating document, this was the equivalent of his being forced, in violation of the self-incrimination clause of the Fifth Amendment, to testify against himself. It was in this setting that the "required records" doctrine evolved. A person could not complain about being forced to yield up a document that he was required as a member of a regulated industry to keep and to grant the government free access to. His choice to enter such an industry was a voluntary one, and once in it he was required to abide by its rules. The compulsion to testify against

---

11. We reject the suggestion that the limitation on the evidentiary use of the custodian's act of production is the equivalent of constructive use immunity. . . . Rather, the limitation is a necessary concomitant of the notion that a corporate custodian acts as an agent and not an individual when he produces corporate records in response to a subpoena addressed to him in his representative capacity. We leave open the question whether the agency rationale supports compelling a custodian to produce corporate records when the custodian is able to establish, by showing for example that he is the sole employee and officer of the corporation, that the jury would inevitably conclude that he produced the records.

himself through the document came, therefore, from a lawful regulatory regime and, critically, from his voluntary decision to submit himself to it, rather than being exerted by government officers in aid of a criminal investigation or prosecution.

But then the Supreme Court decided that the compelled surrender of a self-incriminating document was not compulsion to testify unless the author had been forced to write the document. *United States v. Doe*, 465 U.S. 605 (1984). This change of view greatly reduced the significance of the required records doctrine. Now the government could compel the production of nonrequired records, because their creation, and the setting forth of potentially self-incriminating facts entailed by that creation, were the author's voluntary choice; the government had not made him give utterance to or record these facts, as it would have done had it forced him to testify or beaten a confession out of him. The only time the government needed the required-records doctrine any more was when the act of production was itself testimonial, that is, when it communicated knowledge possessed by the person making the production and was, therefore—but for the doctrine—protected by the Fifth Amendment from being compelled by the government. If a subpoena demanded all the documents possessed by the subpoenaed person concerning some subject, by producing them the person would be acknowledging that he possessed them and that they concerned the subject in question, and if this acknowledgment was self-incriminating he could not be forced to produce them. *United States v. Doe, supra*. But if the documents were required records the person could not resist the subpoena on this ground, for the only acknowledgment conveyed by compliance would be of the existence and applicability of the regulatory program that required him to maintain the records.

This thumbnail sketch of the evolution of self-incrimination doctrine relating to documents provides the background necessary for an understanding of the present case. The Indiana Department of Revenue believed that William Smith and his wife had not filed Indiana income tax returns for some years though required by law to do so. The Department served the Smiths with a subpoena duces tecum which commanded them to produce, for the years 1984 through 1988, "Books, accounts, Forms W–2, Forms 1099, Receipts, Invoices, Cancelled checks and any other records necessary to determine the Indiana Adjusted Gross Income Tax Liability of William E. and Beverly K. Smith, as required by" an Indiana statute which provides that any person subject to an Indiana tax "must keep books and records so that the [Department of Revenue] can determine the amount, if any, of the person's liability for that tax by reviewing those books and records." Smith refused on Fifth Amendment and other grounds to comply with the subpoena and was prosecuted for and convicted of failing to permit the examination of records that the Indiana statute required him to keep, a misdemeanor. His principal defense was that by complying with the subpoena and thus allowing such examination he would have been testifying against himself. His conviction was affirmed over Fifth Amendment. The court ruled that the records sought by the subpoena were required records and so could lawfully be compelled to be produced. Smith then applied for federal habeas corpus. . . .

A statute that merely requires a taxpayer to maintain records necessary to determine his liability for personal income tax is not within the scope of the required-records doctrine. . . . Despite the fears expressed by Justice Jackson, dissenting in *Shapiro*, a statute that required all Americans to keep a diary in which they recorded every arguably illegal act that they committed, or make a tape-recorded confession whenever they committed an illegal act, would not empower the authorities, under the aegis of the required-records doctrine, to compel the production of the diary or the tape. A statute that requires taxpayers to maintain records relating to an activity in which the government has a legitimate interest—whether our Orwellian hypothetical statute or a statute, federal or state, that requires taxpayers to maintain records required to document their tax liability—does not violate the self-incrimination clause of the Fifth Amendment (our hypothetical statute might of course violate other provisions of the Constitution). But this does not dispose of the question whether the compelled production of those records without a suitable grant of immunity would comport with the clause. The hypothetical case in which every individual is required to maintain a record of everything he does that interests the government is remote from the case of the individual who enters upon a regulated activity knowing that the maintenance of extensive records available for inspection by the regulatory agency is one of the conditions of engaging in the activity. The decision to become a taxpayer cannot be thought voluntary in the same sense. Almost anyone who works is a taxpayer, along with many who do not.

[T]he state points out that Smith is a farmer and cites Indiana statutes that the state contends require farmers to keep certain records. Now to begin with there is no evidence that Smith is a farmer, other than what little can be inferred from the testimony of the revenue agents that when they approached him about the documents they wanted he was "standing in a field." Not every field is on a farm, and not every person standing in a farmer's field is a farmer. But suppose Smith is a farmer. It is true that like most businesses nowadays farming is regulated to a considerable extent; but it is far from the usual conception of a regulated industry, such as electrical generation, local telephone service, or railroad transportation. We need not run this hare to the ground, however, since the statutes that the state has cited to us are addressed to persons who warehouse farm commodities, rather than to farmers, and since in any event the relation between Smith's occupation as a farmer and the subpoena is adventitious. Nothing in the subpoena identifies the records sought as records required by the state's agricultural statutes to be kept. On the contrary, the subpoena specifies the source of the requirement as the Indiana tax statute, which applies to every Indiana taxpayer, and Smith was neither charged with nor convicted of failure to keep or produce records required by any other statute....

A conclusion that the documents sought by the subpoena were not required records does not conclude the case. Smith could resist the production of nonrequired records only if the act of production would incriminate him, as by authenticating incriminating documents. Authentication is not the issue with the W–2's and 1099's, for ... they are forms prepared by third parties and mailed to the taxpayer, rather than prepared by himself. Even so, by producing them Smith would have acknowledged having received them, foreclosing any defense of nonwillfulness based on an argument that he had omitted the income shown on the form from his income tax return only because he had no record of receiving the income and had forgotten about it. Production in these circumstances would be testimonial and incriminating. And we point out that if the state did not want to use the act of production to incriminate Mr. Smith, it could have agreed not to disclose at any trial arising out of a prosecution of Smith for willful nonpayment of Indiana taxes that it had obtained the documents establishing Smith's tax liability from Smith himself, with all that that would have implied.

... Nor is ours a case like *Braswell v. United States*, 487 U.S. 99 (1988), where because the records were corporate rather than individual, the custodian could not resist their production on the ground of self-incrimination, since a corporation has no rights under the Fifth Amendment.... It is enough to point out that in a case in which the production of personal (not business) tax records ... would have testimonial force and incriminate the taxpayer, the principles of ... Doe establish that the required-records doctrine is inapplicable and that production is excused by the self-incrimination clause.

All this said, it is unlikely that the production of each and every one of the documents that Indiana sought from Smith would have incriminated him....

So it would be premature for us to decide that Smith is entitled to relief. But because the ground on which the state court relied, and, it appears, the district court as well—that all the documents sought by the subpoena were required records—is untenable and no alternative ground is adequately presented, the judgment of the district court must be reversed and the case remanded.

Notes and Questions

1. Justice Jackson objected in *Shapiro* that the majority permitted Congress to avoid the Fifth Amendment privilege by the simple expediency of passing a law to require someone to keep records that are incriminating. He warned, "If records merely because required to be kept by law *ipso facto* become public records, we are indeed living in glass houses." After *Marchetti*, is Justice Jackson's warning still valid? How did Judge Posner distinguish *Shapiro*?

2. If *Doe* says that compulsion to turn over already written documents does not implicate the Self–Incrimination Clause, because it does not compel testimony, what is the continuing importance of the Required Records doctrine from *Shapiro*? Is it, as Judge Posner says, that the "act of production" defense does not apply to required records? Why doesn't it?

3. Because the "act of production" theory of compelling incriminating testimony derives from use of the act of production to overcome hearsay objections, what is the status of the theory in administrative proceedings where hearsay is not excluded from evidence? Ordinarily, hearsay is not excluded from administrative adjudications; it is fully admissible, although its probative value may be diminished because it is hearsay. Thus, the government need not authenticate documents to have them considered by the agency in the adjudication. Here, the whole "act of production" could become an irrelevancy. Accordingly, even this remaining Fifth Amendment protection might be unavailing whenever the subpoena is for production and use in an administrative adjudication instead of in a judicial trial. This issue does not appear to have been considered by the courts yet.

D.   PARALLEL PROCEEDINGS

In some instances, when the government seeks information from companies or private individuals, it is pursuing both civil and criminal objectives. If the government is contemplating criminal charges, is it appropriate for it to use its civil powers to compel the disclosure of information? The following case indicates how the courts police parallel proceedings and the problem which follows tests the application of this judicial supervision.

SECURITIES AND EXCHANGE COMMISSION v. DRESSER INDUSTRIES, INC.

628 F.2d 1368 (D.C.Cir.1980).

J. Skelly Wright, Chief Judge:

[The] principal issue facing this en banc court is whether Dresser is entitled to special protection against this SEC subpoena because of a parallel investigation into the same questionable foreign payments now being conducted by a federal grand jury under the guidance of the United States Department of Justice (Justice)....

[After revelations in 1973 that United States companies had used corporate funds to bribe foreign officials, the SEC investigated whether Dresser had falsified its financial records to hide such payments from public view. The SEC has the regulatory responsibility to ensure the completeness and accuracy of corporate financial reporting which underlies the purchase of securities. At about the same time, the Department of Justice was also investigating the possibility of criminal violations arising from illegal foreign payments. Justice had requested and received information from the SEC that Dresser had submitted voluntarily to the agency. After considering this information, Justice brought the matter before a grand jury in the District of Columbia. Both the SEC and the grand jury issued subpoenas seeking information from Dresser. Dresser appealed the decision of the District Court to enforce the SEC subpoena.]

The civil and regulatory laws of the United States frequently overlap with the criminal laws, creating the possibility of parallel civil and criminal proceedings, either successive or simultaneous. In the absence of substantial prejudice to the rights of the parties involved, such parallel proceedings are unobjectionable under our jurisprudence. . . .

The Constitution [does] not ordinarily require a stay of civil proceedings pending the outcome of criminal proceedings. Nevertheless, a court may decide in its discretion to stay civil proceedings, postpone civil discovery, or impose protective orders and conditions "when the interests of justice seem to require such action, sometimes at the request of the prosecution, [sometimes] at the request of the defense[.]" The court must make such determinations in the light of the particular circumstances of the case.

Other than where there is specific evidence of agency bad faith or malicious governmental tactics, the strongest case for deferring civil proceedings until after completion of criminal proceedings is where a party under indictment for a serious offense is required to defend a civil or administrative action involving the same matter. The noncriminal proceeding, if not deferred, might undermine the party's Fifth Amendment privilege against self-incrimination, expand rights of criminal discovery beyond the limits of Federal Rule of Criminal Procedure 16(b), expose the basis of the defense to the prosecution in advance of criminal trial, or otherwise prejudice the case. If delay of the noncriminal proceeding would not seriously injure the public interest, a court may be justified in deferring it. [H]owever, the courts may adequately protect the government and the private party by merely deferring civil discovery or entering an appropriate protective order. The case at bar is a far weaker one for staying the administrative investigation. No indictment has been returned; no Fifth Amendment privilege is threatened; Rule 16(b) has not come into effect; and the SEC subpoena does not require Dresser to reveal the basis for its defense. . . .

Effective enforcement of the securities laws requires that the SEC and Justice be able to investigate possible violations simultaneously. Dissemination of false or misleading information by companies to members of the investing public may distort the efficient workings of the securities markets and injure investors who rely on the accuracy and completeness of the company's public disclosures. If the SEC suspects that a company has violated the securities laws, it must be able to respond quickly: it must be able to obtain relevant information concerning the alleged violation and to seek prompt judicial redress if necessary. Similarly, Justice must act quickly if it suspects that the laws have been broken. Grand jury investigations take time, as do criminal prosecutions. If Justice moves too slowly the statute of limitations may run, witnesses may die or move away, memories may fade, or enforcement resources may be diverted. The SEC cannot always wait for Justice to complete the criminal proceedings if it is to obtain the necessary prompt civil remedy; neither can Justice always await the conclusion of the civil proceeding without endangering its criminal case. Thus we should not block parallel investigations by these agencies in the absence of "special circumstances" in which the nature of the proceedings demonstrably prejudices substantial rights of the investigated party or of the government.

Problem 7–7: State Civil and Criminal Enforcement

Kentucky's Natural Resources and Environmental Protection Cabinet (Cabinet), which has responsibility for enforcing state and some federal environmental laws, brings a civil action against the Steel Corporation (Steel) for environmental violations. The Cabinet contends that Steel discharged waste water without a permit as required by federal and state law. Simultaneously, the Cabinet's Crimes Work Group is investigating Steel for criminal violations with regard to the discharge. Several of Steel's employees have knowledge of the company's actions relating to the violation, but all refuse to testify on its behalf for fear that they may incriminate themselves. Steel claims that it is unable to defend itself in the civil proceeding and requests a stay of the proceeding.

If you represent Steel, what arguments can you make on its behalf? As the attorney for Kentucky, how would you respond? How would you predict the court will rule on Steel's motion to stay the civil proceeding?

Problem Materials

UNITED STATES v. KORDEL

397 U.S. 1, 90 S.Ct. 763, 25 L.Ed.2d 1 (1970).

MR. JUSTICE STEWART delivered the opinion of the Court.

The respondents are the president and vice president, respectively, of Detroit Vital Foods, Inc. They were convicted in the United States District Court for the Eastern District of Michigan, along with the corporation, for violations of the Federal Food, Drug, and Cosmetic Act [FDC Act]. The Court of Appeals for the Sixth Circuit reversed the respondent's convictions on the ground that the Government's use of interrogatories to obtain evidence from the respondents in a nearly contemporaneous civil condemnation proceeding operated to violate their Fifth Amendment privilege against compulsory self-incrimination. We granted certiorari to consider the questions raised by the Government's invocation of simultaneous civil and criminal proceedings in the enforcement of federal law.

[In June, 1960, the General Counsel of FDA requested the United States Attorney for the Eastern District of Michigan to file a law suit in district court to seize two products manufactured by Detroit Vital Foods because the sale of the products was in violation of the FDC Act. The U.S. Attorney then filed interrogatories which the company was required to answer under the Federal Rules of Civil Procedure. Ten days later, the government notified Vital Foods pursuant to § 305 of the FDC Act that it was the subject of a contemplated criminal proceeding. Vital Food's attorney asked the district court] to stay further proceedings in the civil action or, in the alternative, to extend the time to answer the interrogatories until after disposition of the criminal proceeding signaled by the § 305 notice. The motion was accompanied by the affidavit of counsel. The moving papers urged the District Court to act under Rule 33 "in the interest of substantial justice" and as a "balancing of hardship and equities of the respective [parties]." Permitting the Government to obtain proof of violations of the Act by resort to civil discovery procedures, the movant urged, would be "improper" and would "work a grave injustice against the claimant"; it would also enable the Government to have pretrial discovery of the respondents' defenses to future criminal charges. Counsel expressly disavowed any "issue of a self-incrimination privilege in favor of the claimant corporation." And nowhere in the moving papers did counsel raise a claim of the Fifth Amendment privilege against compulsory self-incrimination with respect to the respondents.

On June 21, 1961, the District Court denied the motion upon finding that the corporation had failed to demonstrate that substantial prejudice and harm would result from being required to respond to the interrogatories. The court reasoned that the § 305 notice did not conclusively indicate the Government would institute a criminal proceeding, that six to 12 months could elapse from the service of the statutory notice to initiation of a criminal prosecution, and that the Government could obtain data for a prosecution from the testimony in the civil action or by subpoenaing the books and records of the corporation. Accordingly, the court concluded, the interests of justice did not require that the Government be denied the information it wanted simply because it had sought it by way of civil-discovery procedures. On September 5, 1961, in compliance with the court's directive, the corporation, through the respondent Feldten, answered the Government's interrogatories.

[After the District Court's order, but before receipt of the answers to the interrogatories, the FDA staff recommended a criminal prosecution and FDA subsequently requested the Department of Justice to institute a criminal proceeding.] The civil case, still pending in the District Court, proceeded to settlement by way of a consent decree in November 1962, and eight months later the Government obtained the indictment underlying the present judgments of conviction.

I

[W]e assume that the information Feldten supplied the Government in his answers to the interrogatories, if not necessary to the proof of the Government's case in the criminal prosecution, as the Court of Appeals thought, at least provided evidence or leads useful to the Government. However, [the] Government did not act in bad faith in filing the interrogatories. Rather, the testimony before the trial court demonstrated that the Division of Regulatory Management regularly prepares such interrogatories upon the receipt of claimants' answers to civil libels, and files them in over three-fourths of such cases, to hasten their disposition by securing admissions and laying the foundation for summary judgments.

The Court of Appeals thought the answers to the interrogatories were involuntarily given. The District Judge's order denying the corporation's motion to defer the answers to the interrogatories, reasoned the court, left the respondents with three choices: they could have refused to answer, thereby forfeiting the corporation's property that was the subject of the libel; they could have given false answers to the interrogatories, thereby subjecting themselves to the risk of a prosecution for perjury; or they could have done just what they did—disclose the requested information, thereby supplying the Government with evidence and leads helpful in securing their indictment and conviction.

In this analysis we think the Court of Appeals erred. For Feldten need not have answered the interrogatories. Without question he could have invoked his Fifth Amendment privilege against compulsory self-incrimination. Surely Feldten was not barred from asserting his privilege simply because the corporation had no privilege of its own, or because the proceeding in which the Government sought information was civil rather than criminal in character.

To be sure, service of the interrogatories obliged the corporation to "appoint an agent who could, without fear of self-incrimination, furnish such requested information as was available to the corporation." The corporation could not satisfy its obligation under Rule 33 simply by pointing to an agent about to invoke his constitutional privilege.... Such a result would effectively permit the corporation to assert on its own behalf the personal privilege of its individual agents.

The respondents press upon us the situation where no one can answer the interrogatories addressed to the corporation without subjecting himself to a "real and appreciable" risk of self-incrimination. For present purposes we may assume that in such a case the appropriate remedy would be a protective order under Rule 30(b), postponing civil discovery until termination of the criminal action. But we need not decide this troublesome question. For the record before us makes clear that even though the respondents had the burden of showing that the Government's interrogatories were improper, they never even asserted, let alone demonstrated, that there was no authorized person who could answer the interrogatories without the possibility of compulsory self-incrimination....

II

The respondents urge that even if the Government's conduct did not violate their Fifth Amendment privilege against compulsory self-incrimination, it nonetheless reflected such unfairness and want of consideration for justice as independently to require the reversal of their convictions. On the record before us, we cannot agree that the respondents have made out either a violation of due process or a departure from proper standards in the administration of justice requiring the exercise of our supervisory power. The public interest in protecting consumers throughout the Nation from misbranded drugs requires prompt action by the agency charged with responsibility for administration of the federal food and drug laws. But a rational decision whether to proceed criminally against those responsible for the misbranding may have to await consideration of a fuller record than that before the agency at the time of the civil seizure of the offending products. It would stultify enforcement of federal law to require a governmental agency such as the FDA invariably to choose either to forgo recommendation of a criminal prosecution once it seeks civil relief, or to defer civil proceedings pending the ultimate outcome of a criminal trial.

We do not deal here with a case where the Government has brought a civil action solely to obtain evidence for its criminal prosecution or has failed to advise the defendant in its civil proceeding that it contemplates his criminal prosecution; nor with a case where the defendant is without counsel or reasonably fears prejudice from adverse pretrial publicity or other unfair injury; nor with any other special circumstances that might suggest the unconstitutionality or even the impropriety of this criminal prosecution.

Overturning these convictions would be tantamount to the adoption of a rule that the Government's use of interrogatories directed against a corporate defendant in the ordinary course of a civil proceeding would always immunize the corporation's officers from subsequent criminal prosecution. . . .

UNITED STATES v. LASALLE NATIONAL BANK

437 U.S. 298, 98 S.Ct. 2357, 57 L.Ed.2d 221 (1978).

MR. JUSTICE BLACKMUN delivered the opinion of the Court.

[The Internal Revenue Service (IRS or Service) assigned John Olivero, a special agent with the Intelligence Division of the Chicago District of the Internal Revenue Service, to investigate the tax liability of John Gattuso for his taxable years 1970–1972. In order to determine the accuracy of Gattuso's income reports, Olivero issued summons (*i.e.,* subpoenas) for Gattuso's bank records to two banks. Section 7602 authorizes the Service to examine books, papers, and records "[f]or the purpose of ascertaining the correctness of any return, making a return where none has been made, determining the liability of nay person for any internal revenue tax. . . ." When the banks refused to comply, the IRS sought enforcement in the appropriate district court. Although Olivero testified that he had not determined whether criminal charges were justified and had not many any report or recommendation about the case to his superiors, Gattuso's lawyer insisted that Olivero's investigation was "purely criminal." The district court agreed and held that the IRS had improperly sought to pursue a civil investigation to obtain evidence for a criminal proceeding. The Court of Appeals affirmed.]

The present case requires us to examine the limits of the good faith use of an Internal Revenue summons issued under § 7602. . . .

The legislative history of the [Internal Revenue] Code supports the conclusion that Congress intended to design a system with interrelated criminal and civil elements. . . .

In short, Congress has not categorized tax fraud investigations in civil and criminal components. Any limitation on the good-faith use of an Internal Revenue summons must reflect this statutory purpose.

[T]he primary limitation on the use of a summons occurs upon the recommendation of criminal prosecution to the Department of Justice. Only at that point do the criminal and civil aspects of a tax fraud case begin to diverge. We recognize, of course, that even upon recommendation to the Justice Department, the civil and criminal elements do not separate completely. The Government does not sacrifice its interest in unpaid taxes just because a criminal prosecution begins. Logically, then, the IRS could use its summons authority under § 7602 to uncover information about the tax liability created by a fraud regardless of the status of the criminal case. But the rule forbidding such is a prophylactic intended to safeguard the following policy interests.

A referral to the Justice Department permits criminal litigation to proceed. The IRS cannot try its own prosecutions. Such authority is reserved to the Department of Justice and, more particularly, to the United States Attorneys. Nothing in § 7602 or its legislative history suggests that Congress intended the summons authority to broaden the Justice Department's right of criminal litigation discovery or to infringe on the role of the grand jury as a principal tool of criminal accusation. . . .

Prior to a recommendation for prosecution to the Department of Justice, the IRS must use its summons authority in good faith. [In *United States v. Powell*, 379 U.S. 48, 57–58 (1964)], the Court announced several elements of a good-faith exercise:

> "[The Service] must show that the investigation will be conducted pursuant to a legitimate purpose, that the inquiry may be relevant to the purpose, that the information sought is not already within the Commissioner's possession, and that the administrative steps required by the Code have been [followed]. [A] court may not permit its process to be abused. Such an abuse would take place if the summons had been issued for an improper purpose, such as to harass the taxpayer or to put pressure on him to settle a collateral dispute, or for any other purpose reflecting on the good faith of the particular investigation."

A number of the Courts of Appeals, including the Seventh Circuit in this case, have said that another improper purpose, which the Service may not pursue in good faith with a summons, is to gather evidence solely for a criminal investigation. . . .

In this case, respondents submit that such a departure did indeed occur because Special Agent Olivero was interested only in gathering evidence for a criminal prosecution. We disagree. The institutional responsibility of the Service to calculate and to collect civil fraud penalties and fraudulently reported or unreported taxes is not necessarily overturned by a single agent who attempts to build a criminal case. The review process over and above his conclusions is multilayered and thorough. Apart from the control of his immediate supervisor, the agent's final recommendation is [subject to review by several offices and officials of the IRS]. At any of the various stages, the Service can abandon the criminal prosecution, can decide instead to assert a civil penalty, or can pursue both goals. While the special agent is an important actor in the process, his motivation is hardly dispositive.

It should also be noted that the layers of review provide the taxpayer with substantial protection against the hasty or overzealous judgment of the special agent. The taxpayer may obtain a conference with the district Intelligence Division officials upon request or whenever the chief of the Division determines that a conference would be in the best interests of the Government. If prosecution has been recommended, the chief notifies the taxpayer of the referral to the Regional Counsel.

[W]e [previously have] refused to draw the line between permissible civil and impermissible criminal purposes at the entrance of the special agent into the investigation, [and] we cannot draw it on the basis of the agent's personal intent. To do so would unnecessarily frustrate the enforcement of the tax laws by restricting the use of the summons according to the motivation of a single agent without regard to the enforcement policy of the Service as an institution. Furthermore, the inquiry into the criminal enforcement objectives of the agent would delay summons enforcement proceedings while parties clash over, and judges grapple with, the thought processes of each investigator. This obviously is undesirable and unrewarding. As a result, the question whether an investigation has solely criminal purposes must be answered only by an examination of the institutional posture of the IRS. . . .

Without doubt, this burden is a heavy one. Because criminal and civil fraud liabilities are coterminous, the Service rarely will be found to have acted in bad faith by pursuing the former. On the other hand, we cannot abandon this aspect of the good-faith inquiry altogether. We shall not countenance delay in submitting a recommendation to the Justice Department when there is an institutional commitment to make the referral and the Service merely would like to gather additional evidence for the prosecution. Such a delay would be tantamount to the use of the summons authority after the recommendation and would permit the Government to expand its criminal discovery rights. Similarly, the good-faith standard will not permit the IRS to become an information-gathering agency for other departments, including the Department of Justice, regardless of the status of criminal cases.

In summary, then, several requirements emerge for the enforcement of an IRS summons. First, the summons must be issued before the Service recommends to the Department of Justice that a criminal prosecution, which reasonably would relate to the subject matter of the summons, be undertaken. Second, the Service at all times must use the summons authority in good-faith pursuit of the congressionally authorized purposes of § 7602. . . .

On the record before us, respondents have not demonstrated sufficient justification to preclude enforcement of the IRS summonses. No recommendation to the Justice Department for criminal prosecution has been made. Of the *Powell* criteria, respondents challenge only one aspect of the Service's showing: They suggest that Olivero already may possess the evidence requested in the summonses. . . . Finally, the District Court . . . failed to consider whether the Service in an institutional sense had abandoned its pursuit of Gattuso's civil tax liability. The Court of Appeals did not require that inquiry. On the record presently developed, we cannot conclude that such an abandonment has occurred. . . .

Mr. Justice Stewart, with whom the Chief Justice, Mr. Justice Rehnquist, and Mr. Justice Stevens join, dissenting.

[The] Court concedes that the task of establishing the "purpose" of an individual agent is "undesirable and unrewarding." Yet the burden it imposes today—to discover the "institutional good faith" of the entire Internal Revenue Service—is, in my view, even less desirable and less rewarding. The elusiveness of "institutional good faith" as described by the Court can produce little but endless discovery proceedings and ultimate frustration of the fair administration of the Internal Revenue Code. In short, I fear that the Court's new criteria will prove wholly unworkable.

Notes and Questions

1. Are the existing rules adequate to protect companies and individuals who are subject to parallel proceedings? How likely is it that the government will acquire information in a civil proceeding that will be used later in a criminal proceeding? Should individuals be protected from the possibility? Why or why not?

2. As an administrative law practitioner, should you represent a client once it becomes known that the client is subject to both a civil and criminal proceeding? Do you have a professional or ethical obligation to advise the client to hire a lawyer with experience in criminal law? Why or why not?

Chapter 8

PUBLIC ACCESS TO AGENCY PROCESSES

Democratic government (or more accurately a republican form of government) requires the electorate to have sufficient information to make informed choices between candidates. This in turn implies that government processes and action are public, so that relevant information can be obtained. The Constitution itself mandates certain information and processes be public. For example, Article I, Section 4, clause 3, requires each house to keep and publish from time to time a journal of its proceedings, which must include a record of any Presidential vetoes and "the names of the persons voting for and against" bills in the houses. *See* Article I, Section 7, clause 2. Article I, Section 9, clause 7 requires a public accounting of receipts and expenditures of the United States. The Sixth Amendment guarantees the right to a public trial in criminal prosecutions.

At the same time, the Constitution also recognizes that government processes may need to be kept confidential and not open to the public in certain situations. For instance, the requirement for both houses to publish a journal provides an exception for "such parts as may in their judgment require secrecy." Moreover, the Constitution itself was drafted by the "Founding Fathers" under an injunction of secrecy until the final product had been agreed upon. As the principal historian of the Convention wrote: "it was considered important that the delegates should be protected from criticism, and that their discussions should be free from the pressure of public opinion." MAX FARRAND, THE FRAMING OF THE CONSTITUTION OF THE UNITED STATES 58 (1913).* Similarly, the Supreme Court unanimously agreed in *United States v. Nixon*, 418 U.S. 683, 94 S.Ct. 3090, 41 L.Ed.2d 1039 (1974), that the confidentiality of the President's conversations and correspondence was a privilege "fundamental to the operation of Government and inextricably rooted in the

---

* An anecdote is told that George Washington, President of the Convention, found a copy of a draft proposition that a member had dropped on the floor. "Washington arose from his seat and reprimanded the member for his carelessness. 'I must entreat Gentlemen to be more careful, least our transactions get into the News Paper, and disturb the public repose by premature speculations.' " *Id.* at 65.

separation of powers under the Constitution." Thus, the foundation of our government recognizes two themes—one supporting public access to government decisionmaking and one supporting confidentiality in government decisionmaking.

Until relatively recently the theme of confidentiality clearly had the upper hand. Politics, whether congressional or executive, was characterized by the paradigmatic "deal made in a smoke-filled room." Indeed, government regulations were not even published until well into the New Deal. The original APA reflected the practice of the time by requiring agencies to publish their procedures, organization, substantive rules, and statements of general policy or interpretations adopted for the guidance of the public. In addition, agencies either had to publish or make available for public inspection "final opinions and orders in the adjudication of cases" and all rules. Finally, other "matters of official record" were to "be made available to persons properly and directly concerned...." Generally speaking, government business was viewed as the business of government.

The 1960s constituted a cultural divide in many ways, and one of those ways was in the growth of the media and in particular an increased interest in "investigative journalism." Media interests pressed for legislation that would open up the decision making processes of agencies. From all of this sprang the first Freedom of Information Act in 1966, which created a new right of access to government information. In 1974, coincident with the Watergate scandals, Congress passed amendments significantly strengthening that right. In 1972, Congress passed the Federal Advisory Committee Act, regulating the operation of agency and presidential advisory committees, a perceived inside track for traditional business groups to unduly influence agency action. In 1976, Congress passed the Government in the Sunshine Act, intended to open up the decisionmaking process of independent regulatory agencies to public scrutiny.

A. THE FREEDOM OF INFORMATION ACT (FOIA)

Today, section 552 of the APA is generally referred to as the Freedom of Information Act (FOIA). Paragraphs (a)(1) and (2) generally continue the requirements of the original APA with a few changes. The major change is to add administrative staff manuals and statements of policy or interpretation that had not been published in the Federal Register to the materials that agencies must make available for inspection and copying. Moreover, agencies are required to create indexes to all the material required to be published or made available. As a result of recent amendments, agencies in the future will be required to make these materials available electronically. Agencies generally have not rigorously adhered to all of these requirements. For example, a study by the General Accounting Office in 1986 found widespread agency failure to index adjudicatory decisions. *See* GAO, FREEDOM OF INFORMATION ACT: NONCOMPLIANCE WITH AFFIRMATIVE DISCLOSURE PROVISIONS (1986). Paragraph (a)(2) specifically provides that agency adjudicatory decisions cannot be used as precedent against a person unless they have been indexed and made available to the public (or the person has actual notice). Agencies, led by the Social Security Administration, whose Office of Hearings and Appeals issues over a quarter million decisions annually, have interpreted this provision to mean that they need not index any decisions they do not intend to use as precedent. While this interpretation is difficult to square with the statutory language, and the one court to address the issue disagreed with the interpretation, *see National Prison Project v. Sigler*, 390 F.Supp. 789 (1975), the practical effects of requiring indexing for all adjudicatory decisions (estimated at $10 million for Social Security alone), especially in light of the modern practice not to publish even appellate judicial decisions that are not intended to have precedential effect, perhaps suggest statutory modification is in order.

When people think about the Freedom of Information Act, they usually think of section 552(a)(3), which requires that agencies, "upon any request for records which reasonably describes such records and is made in accordance with published rules stating the time, place, fees (if any), and procedures to be followed, shall make the records promptly available to any person." Section 552(b) then provides nine specific exemptions from this general requirement. Roughly stated, they are:

1. Classified information;

2. Internal agency personnel rules and practices;

3. Information specifically exempted from disclosure by statute;

4. Private commercial or trade secret information;

5. Inter-agency or intra-agency privileged communications;

6. Personnel, medical, or similar files the disclosure of which would constitute a clearly unwarranted invasion of privacy;

7. Information compiled for law enforcement purposes;

8. Information related to reports for or by an agency involved in regulating financial institutions; and

9. Geological information concerning wells.

While this might seem a long list of exceptions, courts have construed the exceptions relatively strictly, in accordance with the FOIA's legislative intent to further government disclosure. Moreover, even if a record contains exempt material, if it also contains "any reasonably segregable portion" that is not exempt under these nine exceptions, the FOIA requires that portion to be provided after deletion of the exempt portions.

1. FOIA TIME LIMITS

The FOIA requires an agency receiving a proper request for records to determine within 20 working days whether to comply with the request. *See* 5 U.S.C.A. § 552(a)(6)(A)(i). If it denies the request, it must explain why and inform the person of any internal appeal opportunities. If a person seeks such an appeal, the agency has 20 working days to decide the case. Both of these time limits can be extended for a maximum of ten days each "in unusual circumstances." 5 U.S.C.A. § 552(a)(6)(B)(i). "Unusual circumstances" is defined narrowly to mean when the facility housing the records is physically separated from the facility receiving the request, there is a need for consultation with another agency, or there is a need to search and examine a "voluminous amount of separate and distinct records which are demanded in a single request." As a practical matter, agencies rarely comply within the required time frame. Certainly any difficult request will require a longer period, especially if the records must be reviewed as possibly exempt. If the agency fails to meet the deadlines, the requester may treat the failure as a denial and seek judicial review. 5 U.S.C.A. § 552(a)(6)(C). A court may allow the agency additional time if it can show that "exceptional circumstances exist and that the agency is exercising due diligence in responding to the request." Generally speaking, courts were not strict in applying the exceptional circumstances standard. *See, e.g., Open America v. Watergate Special Prosecution Force*, 547 F.2d 605 (D.C.Cir. 1976). Agencies often have substantial FOI request backlogs that preclude timely determinations. Consequently, courts, recognizing the impossibility of ordering agencies to comply in a particular time, accepted the creation of "first-in, first-out" processing systems as evidence of due diligence. Agencies in these situations normally notified the requester that the request had been logged into the system within the statutory 10–day period, but an actual determination on the request might wait a long time. Some requests to the FBI have taken years.

Concerned about systemic delays, Congress amended the FOIA in 1996 (effective in October 1997) attempting to mitigate the problem. One change was to allow the agency to adopt multi-track processing of requests, so that easy requests do not have to wait in line behind difficult requests. In addition, agencies are required to give expedited processing when there is urgency to inform the public about some government activity. The amendments also provide that when the agency receives a request that would take longer than the allowable time, it is to notify the requester and allow the person an opportunity to narrow the request, thereby enabling compliance within a shorter period. If the person refuses to narrow the request, the agency can treat that as a factor in determining whether "exceptional circumstances" exist—allowing for delays. Thus, persons will be able to decide if they want more voluminous information but have to wait longer for it, or receive more limited information in a faster time frame. At the same time, the amendments preclude a determination that "exceptional circumstances" exist if the delay results from a "predictable agency workload of requests," unless the agency is making "reasonable progress in reducing its backlog of pending requests." There is some indication that these amendments may marginally reduce agency delay, but it continues to be true that the vast majority of FOIA requests take longer than the statutory maximum length.

2. FOIA FEES

The cost of the FOIA has been estimated at $50 to $200 million per year, but Congress originally believed it would involve little cost. Cost estimates made during the 1974 amendments indicated the entire cost to the government in 1976 would be $100,000. The cost to the FBI alone that year was over $2.5 million. *See Open America v. Watergate Special Prosecution Force*, 547 F.2d 605 (D.C.Cir.1976). Cost was not the only surprise in its application. Originally, it was thought that newspaper reporters and public interest groups would be the primary requesters. In fact, the vast majority of FOI requesters are private businesses or their lawyers, generally seeking information on their competitors. In 1981, one estimate was that only five percent of FOIA requests came from journalists, scholars, and authors combined. The rest came from businessmen or their representatives. A study made of the experience of the Food and Drug Administration revealed that one percent of the requests came from the press and one percent came from public interest groups. The rest came from businesses, directly or indirectly. The FDA estimated that in 1981 its costs in implementing the FOIA were almost $3.5 million.

Although the original FOIA in 1966 had authorized agencies to impose "fair and equitable charges" on persons making requests, Congress limited this authority in the 1974 amendments under the belief that persons were being deterred from making requests by excessive fee schedules. Over the next decade, with the explosion in FOIA requests, commentators began to express concern that the limitation on fees provided an unnecessary subsidy to persons making requests, especially those making them for commercial purposes. This had two adverse effects: first, the government was deprived of the money necessary to implement FOIA, and second, the artificially low cost of making requests resulted in more requests being made than should have been. Consequently, in 1986 Congress made major revisions to the fee provisions to try to more closely recapture the cost of FOIA, at least for commercial requesters.

Now, agencies may charge fees to recover the direct costs of search, duplication, and review associated with commercial requests. 5 U.S.C.A. § 552(a)(4)(A). Review costs, however, are not to include any costs associated with "resolving issues of law or policy" that may be raised in the course of the review. In other words, if the agency employee first identifying the documents determines that they raise issues of law or policy in terms of whether they fit within an exception, this time is covered by the fee schedule, but the time spent by others to resolve those issues is not. If the request is for non-commercial uses and is made by a representative of the news media, or by an educational or non-commercial scientific organization for scholarly or scientific research, the agency can assess only reasonable duplicating fees. If a request does not fall into either the commercial or scholarly/news categories, the agency can charge for search and duplication, but not review. If "disclosure of the information is in the public interest because it is likely to contribute significantly to public understanding of the operations or activities of the government and is not primarily in the commercial interest of the requester," the fees in the regulations are to be waived or reduced. Agencies are not to charge any fee for the first two hours of search time and the first 100 pages of duplication for any non-commercial request, or if the cost of collecting the fee would exceed the amount of the fee.

3. JUDICIAL REVIEW UNDER THE FOIA

If an agency denies an FOIA request, the requester may seek judicial review under the FOIA itself, 5 U.S.C.A. § 552(a)(4)(B), not Section 706 of the APA. There are important differences between review under this provision and under Section 706. First, the defendant agency, not the plaintiff requester, has the burden of proof to justify its action. Second, the court determines the case de novo; it is not limited to reviewing the agency record, and it is not to defer to the agency's decision.* Third, the FOIA authorizes reasonable attorneys fees and costs if the plaintiff substantially prevails. If the court overturns the agency denial and believes that the agency acted arbitrarily or capriciously in denying the request, it may issue a written finding to that effect, which triggers a requirement for the Special Counsel of the Merit System Protection Board to initiate a proceeding to determine whether disciplinary action against the offending employees is warranted. 5 U.S.C.A. § 552(a)(4)(F). As of 1994, however, only one court had ever made such a written finding, *see Holly v. Acree*, 72 F.R.D. 115 (D.D.C.1976), *aff'd sub nom. Holly v. Chasen*, 569 F.2d 160 (D.C.Cir.1977), and no disciplinary action was taken.

As has been discussed in an earlier chapter, the Justice Department generally is responsible for all litigation involving the federal government, including FOIA litigation. The Department, however, does not view itself merely as the lawyer for a client agency (*i.e.*, the agency that denied an FOIA request and is being sued). Rather, it views its role as coordinating the litigation of the entire executive branch. In this role, Justice may refuse to defend an agency, if it believes that the facts or law do not support the agency's position. Thus, Justice's control of litigation can substantively affect agency practice under the FOIA. In 1977, the Attorney General under President Jimmy Carter issued a memorandum to heads of departments and agencies announcing that henceforth the Justice Department would not defend FOIA denials by agencies, even if the records were within an FOIA exemption, unless the agency made an additional finding that release of the records would be contrary to the public interest. This was done both in spirit of openness and to reduce

* If the challenge relates to a denial of a waiver of fees, the FOIA provides that the court is to determine the matter de novo, but the review is limited to the record before the agency. In addition, judicial review of a denial of a request for "expedited processing" is also limited to the agency record.

the litigation backlog at Justice. As a result, agencies were more likely to release information. In 1981, the Attorney General under President Ronald Reagan rescinded this memorandum, indicating that Justice would defend agencies whenever an FOIA exemption applied. Then, in 1994, Attorney General Reno, under President Bill Clinton, rescinded the Reagan-era policy, and issued a new memorandum equivalent to the one under President Carter.

4. THE FOIA REQUEST

The FOIA refers to requests by "any person." This broad language has been enforced by the courts to require agencies to respond to requests by foreign citizens, corporations, and governments, *see Stone v. Export–Import Bank of the U.S.*, 552 F.2d 132 (5th Cir.1977), illegal aliens, *see Doherty v. U.S. Department of Justice*, 596 F.Supp. 423 (S.D.N.Y.1984), non-resident aliens, *see DeLaurentiis v. Haig*, 528 F.Supp. 601 (E.D.Pa.1981), *affirmed* 686 F.2d 192 (3d Cir.1982), and prison inmates, *see, e.g., Cox v. U.S. Department of Justice*, 576 F.2d 1302 (8th Cir.1978). The exception that proves the rule was the refusal of courts to enforce the FOIA in favor of a fugitive from justice seeking law enforcement records, *see Doyle v. U.S. Department of Justice*, 494 F.Supp. 842 (D.D.C.1980), *affirmed* 668 F.2d 1365 (D.C.Cir.1981). Equally important is that the person need not show any need for the records. Idle curiosity, a desire to harass the agency, or a wish to save the world are all equally irrelevant to the basic right to disclosure. The purpose of the request, while not relevant to the basic right to disclosure, is relevant, as noted above, to what fees may be charged and whether expedited processing is appropriate. Moreover, as we will see, the purpose of the request in some circumstances may be relevant to whether one of the exemptions applies. Finally, because agencies and courts are made up of human actors, they are more likely to be sympathetic or responsive to requests that appear to be substantially justified.

The request must "reasonably describe" the records sought. The legislative history stated that this meant that "a professional employee of the agency who was familiar with the subject area of the request [would be able] to locate the record with a reasonable amount of effort." A requester is more likely to obtain a positive response the more specifically records are described, but at the same time, the more specific the request, the more likely that there are records the requester would be interested in but which fall outside the bounds of the request. Thus, a request often will include both specific requests and a more generic request for records pertaining to the same subject matter as the specifically requested records. The "reasonably described" requirement is sometimes used by courts to relieve agencies from excessively burdensome requests. For example, a request for all agency records containing the requester's name certainly describes the documents quite specifically, but except to the extent that the records are filed (or retrievable) by the requester's name, the agency would have to search all of its files to see if any of them referred to the requester. *See Keese v. United States*, 632 F.Supp. 85 (S.D.Tex.1985) (request not reasonably specific).

The FOIA also requires requests to be made in accordance with any published agency rules. Virtually every agency currently has rules directing persons where and in what form to make FOIA requests. It is important to attend to these. These rules also specify the fees the agency charges, the standards for waiver requests, and any requirements for pre-payment.

There is no term "agency records" in the FOIA, but the Court has held that agencies must only respond to requests for "agency records." Agency is specifically defined in section 552 to expand the general meaning of "agency" under the APA to include government corporations and the Executive Office of the President. Precisely what is a government corporation for purposes of FOIA is not entirely clear. Apparently, the mere fact that the corporation is incorporated under federal law is insufficient. *See Irwin Memorial v. American Nat'l Red Cross*, 640 F.2d 1051 (9th Cir.1981) (Red Cross not an "agency" under FOIA). Also, the mere fact that a corporation receives federal funding does not bring it under FOIA. *See, e.g., Forsham v. Harris*, 445 U.S. 169, 100 S.Ct. 977, 63 L.Ed.2d 293 (1980) (Corporation for Public Broadcasting not an "agency" under FOIA). Thus, some combination of federal chartering and federal funding and federal control is necessary. *See, e.g., Rocap v. Indiek*, 539 F.2d 174 (D.C.Cir.1976) (Federal Home Loan Mortgage Corporation is an "agency" for FOIA). The reference to the Executive Office of the President was not intended to include within FOIA either the President, his immediate staff (*e.g.*, the White House Counsel, the National Security Advisor), or those entities whose only function is to advise the President. Thus, the Office of Management and Budget, the Office of Science and Technology, and the Council on Environmental Quality, all of which have statutory duties assigned to them in addition to advising the President, have been held covered by FOIA, while the Council of Economic Advisors, whose only function is to advise the President, has been held outside the FOIA.

In order for a record to be an "agency record," the agency must actually possess the record in question. Even if the agency may legally own the record, but it is not in the agency's possession, the agency is not required to produce the record. *See Kissinger v. Reporters Committee for the Freedom of the Press*, 445 U.S. 136, 100 S.Ct. 960, 63 L.Ed.2d 267 (1980) (because the Secretary of State's telephone notes had been taken from the State Department before the FOI request was made, the agency had neither custody nor control to enable it to produce the information). At the same time, custody or control by itself may not be enough. *Id.* (telephone records of National Security Advisor to the President were not "agency records" of the State Department even if he brought them with him to the Department of State).

Problem 8–1 Agency Records

The Washington Post has received a tip that Assistant Secretary Black of the Department of Commerce has been maintaining a diary over the past two years. According to this tip, the diary contains an expansive recitation of the events of each day and Secretary Black's reaction to them and plans for the future. Apparently, Secretary Black dictates the diary during the day on a portable recorder, usually in his office, and concludes it at the end of the day at home. The next morning he gives the tape to his secretary to transcribe; he edits the draft transcription and has it typed in final. It is then filed in the filing cabinet in his office under the heading, "diary." The Post has heard rumors that Secretary Black has engaged in sexual harassment of several of his office staff, and it believes that there might be indications of it in his "diary." The Post would like to know whether they can obtain these records under the FOIA. Your boss, counsel for the Post, would like you to answer the preliminary question whether the "diary" constitutes agency records.

Problem Materials

THE BUREAU OF NATIONAL AFFAIRS, INC. v. UNITED STATES DEPARTMENT OF JUSTICE

742 F.2d 1484 (D.C.Cir.1984).

MIKVA, J.:

In these cases we are asked to decide a novel question concerning the scope of the Freedom of Information Act (FOIA or the Act): whether appointment calendars, phone logs and daily agendas of government officials are "agency records" subject to disclosure under FOIA. We conclude that appointment materials that are created solely for an individual's convenience, that contain a mix of personal and business entries, and that may be disposed of at the individual's discretion are not "agency records" under FOIA. . . .

. . . In 1981, the Bureau of National Affairs (BNA) filed a FOIA request with the Department of Justice (DOJ or the Justice Department) for all records of appointments and meetings between William Baxter, then Assistant Attorney General for Antitrust, and all parties outside the Justice Department. DOJ denied BNA's request on the ground that the materials were not "agency records" subject to disclosure under FOIA. . . .

The Environmental Defense Fund (EDF) requested the Office of Management and Budget (OMB) to disclose several categories of documents relating to the Environmental Protection Agency's (EPA) implementation of federal hazardous waste laws, particularly the 1980 Superfund legislation. OMB denied the request in part. . . .

Among the records requested by EDF were the appointment calendars and telephone logs of six OMB officials. . . .

Both DOJ and OMB claim that appointment materials are not "agency records" within the meaning of section 552(a)(4)(B) of FOIA.... Unless the calendars, agendas, and logs sought by BNA and EDF are "agency records" the district court lacks jurisdiction over their claims.

Neither the language of the statute nor the legislative history provides much guidance in fleshing out the meaning of the term "agency records." "As has often been remarked, the Freedom of Information Act, for all its attention to the treatment of 'agency records,' never defines that crucial phrase." Moreover, "the legislative history yields insignificant insight into Congress' conception of the sorts of materials the Act covers."

Nor does the case law indicate whether the appointment materials in these cases are "agency records." Most opinions in this circuit and elsewhere that focus on the meaning of the term "agency records" involved records that were created originally by entities exempt from FOIA's coverage and that later were transferred to a FOIA agency. The issue in those cases is whether a FOIA agency has "obtained" a record concededly "created" elsewhere. The instant cases, however, present a totally different issue: under what circumstances can an individual's creation of a record be attributed to the agency, thereby making the material an "agency record" disclosable under FOIA, rather than personal material not covered by the Act? We turn to the case law to find the principles that should guide us in our analysis.

1. Judicial interpretation of the term "agency records"

The Supreme Court has elaborated on the meaning of the term "agency records".... Thus, in determining whether the documents were "agency records" under FOIA, the Court focused on several factors: whether the documents were (1) in the agency's control; (2) generated within the agency; (3) placed into the agency's files; and (4) used by the agency "for any purpose." ...

The government argues that we rejected a use test for determining whether a document is an "agency record" in *McGehee v. Central Intelligence Agency*. In *McGehee*, a relative of three victims who died at "People's Temple" in Jonestown, Guyana, filed a FOIA request with the Central Intelligence Agency (CIA) for documents relating to various aspects of the community led by Jim Jones. One of the issues on appeal was whether the documents obtained by the CIA from the State Department and the Federal Bureau of Investigation were "agency records" of the CIA. We concluded that they were. In prior cases, this court and others had held that, where documents originate within the Congress, the judiciary, and FOIA-exempt executive agencies, sometimes "special policy considerations militate against a rule compelling disclosure of [such] records ... merely because such documents happen to come into the possession of an agency." Where the originating agency, however, is also covered by FOIA—as was the case in McGehee—we held that transfer of such documents to another FOIA agency did not alter their status as "agency records." Otherwise, agencies could shield themselves from FOIA by transferring documents to a different government department. We therefore concluded that "all records in an agency's possession, whether created by the agency itself or by other bodies covered by the Act, constitute agency records."

Here, reliance solely on a possession or control test could be the more restrictive approach. An "agency" may choose not to assert any control over a particular document, but an employee who created that document for the express purpose of enabling him to perform his duties certainly retains possession and control over the document. The issue is not simply whether the agency as an institution has taken steps to "obtain" the document. Rather, the question presented by these cases is whether, when an employee creates a document, that creation can be attributed to the agency under FOIA.

Under the case law, it is clear that, at least in some circumstances, the agency's use of a document is relevant for determining its status as an "agency record." Where, as here, a document is created by an agency employee, consideration of whether and to what extent that employee used the document to conduct agency business is highly relevant for determining whether that document is an "agency record" within the meaning of FOIA. Use alone, however, is not dispositive; the other factors mentioned in *Kissinger* must also be considered: whether the document is in the agency's control, was generated within the agency, and has been placed into the agency's files. Our inquiry must therefore focus on the totality of the circumstances surrounding the creation, maintenance, and use of the document to determine whether the document is in fact an "agency record" and not an employee's record that happens to be located physically within an agency.

In particular, the statute cannot be extended to sweep into FOIA's reach personal papers that may "relate to" an employee's work—such as a personal diary containing an individual's private reflections on his or her work—but which the individual does not rely upon to perform his or her duties. In this regard, use of the documents by employees other than the author is an important consideration. An inquiry is therefore required into the purpose for which the document was created, the actual use of the document, and the extent to which the creator of the document and other employees acting within the scope of their employment relied upon the document to carry out the business of the agency.

In adopting this analysis, we reject the government's invitation to hold that the treatment of documents for disposal and retention purposes under the various federal records management statutes determines their status under FOIA. Those statutes prescribe how federal agencies are to create, dispose of, and otherwise manage documents and other material. See, e.g., Federal Records Act of 1950, 44 U.S.C. § 2901 et seq.; Records Disposal Act, 44 U.S.C. § 3301 et seq. However tempting such a "bright line" test may be, it cannot be used as the divining rod for the meaning of "agency records" under FOIA. . . .

The government would have us ... rely solely on the agencies' treatment of the documents under their records disposal regulations and policies to determine the status of those documents under FOIA. Rigid adherence to the records disposal regulations to determine the status of a document under FOIA, however, would contradict the policy of disclosure underlying FOIA. Although an agency's treatment of documents for preservation purposes may provide some guidance to a court, an agency should not be able to alter its disposal regulations to avoid the requirements of FOIA. . . .

2. Appointment materials as "agency records"

Three categories of appointment materials are sought in these cases: yellow telephone message slips; appointment calendars; and daily agendas indicating Mr. Baxter's schedule that were distributed to staff within the Antitrust Division of the Justice Department. All of these materials share three common attributes that are relevant for our analysis. First, all of these materials were "generated" within the agencies. They were prepared on government time, at government expense and with government materials, including the blank appointment calendars themselves. In several cases, the officials' personal secretaries maintained the appointment records as part of their official agency duties. Second, the materials have not been placed into agency files. Third, both DOJ and OMB permit their employees to dispose of these "non-record materials" at their discretion. Thus, the agencies have not sought to exercise any institutional control over appointment documents, although they could do so under the applicable statute and regulations. The government argues that this indicates that the agencies have not "obtained" the documents from their individual employees. In the context of these cases, however, the question is whether the employee's creation of the documents can be attributed to the agency for the purposes of FOIA, regardless of whether the agency requires employees to retain the documents. The government is correct, however, in one respect. Because FOIA does not require an agency to create or obtain a record, so long as the records disposal regulations permit destruction of "non-record materials" at the discretion of an agency or agency employee, documents will be available under FOIA solely based on whether an individual has chosen to keep those documents.

We now turn to the three categories of documents to analyze, in particular, how the documents are used within the agency.

A. TELEPHONE MESSAGE SLIPS

EDF requested the telephone logs of certain OMB officials. No such logs existed, but one OMB official kept his yellow telephone message slips for short periods of time and disposed of them intermittently on a haphazard basis. The official indicated that the slips "contain[ed] no substantive information." Presumably they indicated the name of the caller, the date and time of the call and, possibly, a telephone number where the caller could be reached. The purpose of creating these documents was to inform the official of any calls he had received while he was away from his office. The slips do not indicate why the call was made and, most importantly, whether the call was personal or related to official agency business.

It is clear that these slips are not "agency records" within the meaning of FOIA. No substantive information is contained in them. No one but the official for whom the messages were taken used the telephone slips in any way. And, in many cases, there might be no way for the official to segregate personal from business calls.

B. DAILY AGENDAS

Mr. Baxter's secretary at DOJ created daily agendas indicating Mr. Baxter's schedule. She circulated these agendas to certain members of Mr. Baxter's staff. Although the staff threw out the agendas regularly, Mr. Baxter's secretary maintained copies in her desk, apparently in the absence of any instructions to the contrary. The purpose of the agendas was to inform the staff of Mr. Baxter's availability; they facilitated the day-to-day operations of the Antitrust Division.

Unlike the telephone slips, the daily agendas are "agency records" within the meaning of FOIA. They were created for the express purpose of facilitating the daily activities of the Antitrust Division. Even though the agendas reflected personal appointments, they were circulated to the staff for a business purpose. The agency can segregate out any notations that refer to purely personal matters. The daily agendas, unlike the appointment calendars, were not created for Mr. Baxter's personal convenience, but for the convenience of his staff in their conduct of official business.

C. APPOINTMENT CALENDARS

The appointment calendars are the most difficult to categorize. The purpose of the calendars was to facilitate the individuals' performance of their official duties and to organize both their business and personal activities. Unlike the telephone slips, the calendars often gave some indication of the topic of a particular meeting, as well as the location and identity of the participants. Furthermore, it would be much easier to segregate the personal appointments from the business appointments than it would be with the case of a telephone message. In the case of Mr. Baxter and at least one OMB official, immediate staff had access to the calendars to determine the officials' availability. In that sense, the calendars were similar to the daily agendas.

We conclude, however, that these particular appointment calendars are not "agency records." They are distinguishable from the daily agendas in two important respects. First, they were not distributed to other employees, but were retained solely for the convenience of the individual officials. Second, the daily agendas were created by Mr. Baxter's secretary for the express purpose of informing other staff of Mr. Baxter's whereabouts during the course of a business day so that they could determine Mr. Baxter's availability for meetings. Thus the daily agendas were created for the purpose of conducting agency business. In contrast, the appointment calendars were created for the personal convenience of individual officials so that they could organize both their personal and business appointments.

The inclusion of personal items in the appointment calendars buttresses the conclusion that the calendars were created for the personal convenience of the individual employees, not for an official agency purpose. The inclusion of personal information does not, by itself, take material outside the ambit of FOIA, for personal information can be redacted from the copies of documents disclosed to a FOIA requester. But the presence of such information may be relevant in determining the author's intended use of the documents at the time he or she created them. Here, the appointment calendars were created for the personal convenience of individual officials in organizing both their personal and business appointments. Neither OMB nor DOJ required its employees to maintain such calendars. FOIA's reach does not extend to such personalized documents absent some showing that the agency itself exercised control over or possession of the documents. In contrast, the daily agendas were created and distributed to staff solely for their use in determining Mr. Baxter's availability for meetings. The personal information contained in the agendas is identical to that found in Mr. Baxter's appointment calendars and may be redacted from the copies made available to BNA.

We hold that, with the exception of the daily agendas that were distributed within the Antitrust Division, the appointment materials requested by EDF and BNA are not "agency records" within the meaning of FOIA. Our conclusion might be different if the agencies had exercised any control over the materials or if the documents had been created solely for the purpose of conducting official agency business. On the facts presented here, however, these documents are not "agency records." . . .

UNITED STATES DEPARTMENT OF JUSTICE v. TAX ANALYSTS

492 U.S. 136, 109 S.Ct. 2841, 106 L.Ed.2d 112 (1989).

Marshall, J.:

The question presented is whether the Freedom of Information Act (FOIA or Act) requires the United States Department of Justice (Department) to make available copies of district court decisions that it receives in the course of litigating tax cases on behalf of the Federal Government. We hold that it does.

I

The Department's Tax Division represents the Federal Government in nearly all civil tax cases in the district courts, the courts of appeals, and the Claims Court. Because it represents a party in litigation, the Tax Division receives copies of all opinions and orders issued by these courts in such cases. Copies of these decisions are made for the Tax Division's staff attorneys. The original documents are sent to the official files kept by the Department. . . .

Respondent Tax Analysts publishes a weekly magazine, Tax Notes, which reports on legislative, judicial, and regulatory developments in the field of federal taxation to a readership largely composed of tax attorneys, accountants, and economists. As one of its regular features, Tax Notes provides summaries of recent federal-court decisions on tax issues. To supplement the magazine, Tax Analysts provides full texts of these decisions in microfiche form. Tax Analysts also publishes Tax Notes Today, a daily electronic data base that includes summaries and full texts of recent federal-court tax decisions.

In late July 1979, Tax Analysts filed a FOIA request in which it asked the Department to make available all district court tax opinions and final orders received by the Tax Division earlier that month. The Department denied the request on the ground that these decisions were not Tax Division records.

II

In enacting the FOIA 23 years ago, Congress sought " 'to open agency action to the light of public scrutiny.' " Congress did so by requiring agencies to adhere to " 'a general philosophy of full agency disclosure.' " Congress believed that this philosophy, put into practice, would help "ensure an informed citizenry, vital to the functioning of a democratic society."

The FOIA confers jurisdiction on the district courts "to enjoin the agency from withholding agency records and to order the production of any agency records improperly withheld." Under this provision, "federal jurisdiction is dependent on a showing that an agency has (1) 'improperly' (2) 'withheld' (3) 'agency records.' " Unless each of these criteria is met, a district court lacks jurisdiction to devise remedies to force an agency to comply with the FOIA's disclosure requirements.[3] . . .

A

In this case, all three jurisdictional terms are at issue. Although these terms are defined neither in the Act nor in its legislative history, we do not write on a clean slate. Nine terms ago we decided three cases that explicated the meanings of these partially overlapping terms. *Kissinger v. Reporters Committee for Freedom of Press*; *Forsham v. Harris*, 445 U.S. 169 (1980); *GTE Sylvania, Inc. v. Consumers Union of United*

---

3. The burden is on the agency to demonstrate, not the requester to disprove, that the materials sought are not "agency records" or have not been "improperly" "withheld." See S.Rep. No. 813, 89th Cong., 2nd Sess., 8 (1965) ("Placing the burden of proof upon the agency puts the task of justifying the withholding on the only party able to explain it"); H.R.Rep. No. 1497, 89th Cong., 2d Sess., 9 (1966), U.S.Code Cong. & Admin.News 1966, pp. 2418, 2426 (same).

States, Inc., 445 U.S. 375 (1980). These decisions form the basis of our analysis of Tax Analysts' requests.

We consider first whether the district court decisions at issue are "agency records," a term elaborated upon both in *Kissinger* and in *Forsham. Kissinger* involved three separate FOIA requests for written summaries of telephone conversations in which Henry Kissinger had participated when he served as Assistant to the President for National Security Affairs from 1969 to 1975, and as Secretary of State from 1973 to 1977. Only one of these requests—for summaries of specific conversations that Kissinger had had during his tenure as National Security Adviser—raised the "agency records" issue. At the time of this request, these summaries were stored in Kissinger's office at the State Department in his personal files. We first concluded that the summaries were not "agency records" at the time they were made because the FOIA does not include the Office of the President in its definition of "agency." We further held that these documents did not acquire the status of "agency records" when they were removed from the White House and transported to Kissinger's office at the State Department, a FOIA-covered agency: "We simply decline to hold that the physical location of the notes of telephone conversations renders them 'agency records.' The papers were not in the control of the State Department at any time. They were not generated in the State Department. They never entered the State Department's files, and they were not used by the Department for any purpose. If mere physical location of papers and materials could confer status as an 'agency record' Kissinger's personal books, speeches, and all other memorabilia stored in his office would have been agency records subject to disclosure under the FOIA."

Forsham, in turn, involved a request for raw data that formed the basis of a study conducted by a private medical research organization. Although the study had been funded through federal agency grants, the data never passed into the hands of the agencies that provided the funding, but instead was produced and possessed at all times by the private organization. We recognized that "[r]ecords of a nonagency certainly could become records of an agency as well," but the fact that the study was financially supported by a FOIA-covered agency did not transform the source material into "agency records." Nor did the agencies' right of access to the materials under federal regulations change this result. As we explained, "the FOIA applies to records which have been in fact obtained, and not to records which merely could have been obtained."

Two requirements emerge from *Kissinger* and *Forsham,* each of which must be satisfied for requested materials to qualify as "agency records." First, an agency must "either create or obtain" the requested materials "as a prerequisite to its becoming an 'agency record' within the meaning of the FOIA." In performing their official duties, agencies routinely avail themselves of studies, trade journal reports, and other materials produced outside the agencies both by private and governmental organizations. To restrict the term "agency records" to materials generated internally would frustrate Congress' desire to put within public reach the information available to an agency in its decision-making processes. As we noted in *Forsham*, "The legislative history of the FOIA abounds with ... references to records acquired by an agency."

Second, the agency must be in control of the requested materials at the time the FOIA request is made. By control we mean that the materials have come into the agency's possession in the legitimate conduct of its official duties. This requirement accords with *Kissinger*'s teaching that the term "agency records" is not so broad as to include personal materials in an employee's possession, even though the materials may be physically located at the agency. This requirement is suggested by *Forsham* as well, where we looked to the definition of agency records in the Records Disposal Act. Under that definition, agency records include "all books, papers, maps, photographs, machine readable materials, or other documentary materials, regardless of physical form or characteristics, made or received by an agency of the United States Government under Federal law or in connection with the transaction of public business...."[5] ...

Applying these requirements here, we conclude that the requested district court decisions constitute "agency records." First, it is undisputed that the Department has obtained these documents from the district courts. This is not a case like *Forsham*, where the materials never in fact had been received by the agency. The Department contends that a district court is not an "agency" under the FOIA, but this truism is beside the point. The relevant issue is whether an agency covered by the FOIA has "create[d] or obtaine[d]" the materials sought, not whether the organization from which the documents originated is itself covered by the FOIA.

Second, the Department clearly controls the district court decisions that Tax Analysts seeks. Each of Tax Analysts' FOIA requests referred to district court decisions in the agency's possession at the time the requests were made.... Furthermore, the court decisions at issue are obviously not personal papers of agency employees....

JUSTICE BLACKMUN, dissenting.

... Respondent Tax Analysts, although apparently a nonprofit organization for federal income tax purposes, is in business and in that sense is a commercial enterprise. It sells summaries of these opinions and supplies full texts to major electronic data bases. The result of its now-

---

5. In *GTE Sylvania, Inc. v. Consumers Union of United States, Inc.*, 445 U.S. 375 (1980), we noted that Congress intended the FOIA to prevent agencies from refusing to disclose, among other things, agency telephone directories and the names of agency employees. We are confident, however, that requests for documents of this type will be relatively infrequent. Common sense suggests that a person seeking such documents or materials housed in an agency library typically will find it easier to repair to the Library of Congress, or to the nearest public library, rather than to invoke the FOIA's disclosure mechanisms. To the extent such requests are made, the fact that the FOIA allows agencies to recoup the costs of processing requests from the requester may discourage recourse to the FOIA where materials are readily available elsewhere.

successful effort in this litigation is to impose the cost of obtaining the court orders and opinions upon the Government and thus upon taxpayers generally. There is no question that this material is available elsewhere. But it is quicker and more convenient, and less "frustrat[ing]," for respondent to have the Department do the work and search its files and produce the items than it is to apply to the respective court clerks.

This, I feel, is almost a gross misuse of the FOIA. What respondent demands, and what the Court permits, adds nothing whatsoever to public knowledge of Government operations. That, I had thought, and the majority acknowledges, was the real purpose of the FOIA and the spirit in which the statute has been interpreted thus far. I also sense, I believe not unwarrantedly, a distinct lack of enthusiasm on the part of the majority for the result it reaches in this case.

If, as I surmise, the Court's decision today is outside the intent of Congress in enacting the statute, Congress perhaps will rectify the decision forthwith and will give everyone concerned needed guidelines for the administration and interpretation of this somewhat opaque.

Notes and Questions

1. In *Bureau of National Affairs*, the court indicates that the status of documents under federal records management statutes should not be determinative of whether the documents are "agency records" for FOIA purposes. It concedes that the documents involved in that case were "non-record documents" under those statutes and, therefore, were not required to be maintained and could have been destroyed, consistent with agency regulations, by the employee creating them. If this is so, how would it "contradict the policy of disclosure underlying FOIA" to consider these documents not agency records? Could the employee destroy the documents upon receiving the FOIA request? In *Tax Analysts*, the Court says that its decision is consistent with its decision in *Forsham*, where it looked to the federal Records Disposal Act for guidance as to what an agency record was. Is *Bureau of National Affairs* still good law?

2. In *Bureau of National Affairs*, the court read the Supreme Court cases to implicate four factors in determining whether a document was an agency record. In *Tax Analysts*, the Court only mentions two—control and possession.

3. In *Tax Analysts*, the Court rejected all arguments that merely because the tax opinions were otherwise publicly available from the courts of record the opinions should not be considered agency records when they were in the possession and control of the Department of Justice. What about Justice Blackmun's point that this means that the taxpayer is subsidizing a commercial enterprise? Is the majority correct that Justice can charge fees to cover the cost?

4. Until recently, a major issue with respect to agency records was the treatment of electronic or computer "records." The FOIA was originally written with paper records in mind, and much computer information did not fit well within that framework. In 1996, however, Congress amended the FOIA to provide specifically for electronic records. As a result, a requester can now request that searches for records include electronic records and that electronic records be produced in electronic format.

5. FOIA EXEMPTIONS

As noted earlier, there are nine specified exemptions from the FOIA. Subsection (b) begins by saying that the FOIA does not apply to "matters" within the exemptions. If a record contains both exempt and non-exempt matters, there is no requirement to disclose the exempt matters, but it does not mean that the record is itself necessarily exempt. The last sentence of the subsection requires "reasonably segregable portions of a record" to be disclosed after deletion of exempt portions. In deciding what is "reasonably" segregable, courts generally consider whether the non-exempt portions would still be intelligible and the extent of the burden in editing or segregating the non-exempt material.

The most common form of litigation under the FOIA denial is a challenge to an agency's determination that certain records are exempt under one or more of the FOIA exemptions. Most of those exemptions depend upon the content of those records falling within the terms of the exemption, but, of course, the plaintiff/requester has not seen the records, so it is difficult for the plaintiff to dispute the agency's claim. To provide the plaintiff with some helpful information in this regard and to ease the burden on the court in its determinations, the D.C. Circuit, since followed by virtually all the circuits, adopted a discovery rule for FOIA cases that requires agencies to provide the court and plaintiff with an itemized "index" of the withheld records (normally called a "Vaughn index" after the case that created the requirement). *See Vaughn v. Rosen,* 484 F.2d 820 (D.C.Cir.1973). The index must contain a description of each document or withheld portion and a detailed justification of the agency's grounds for withholding, specifying which exemptions apply to each record or portion withheld.

a. Classified Information

The first exemption and a common exemption invoked by agencies concerns classified, national security information. Most classified, national security information (typically Top Secret, Secret, or Confidential information) is classified pursuant to an executive order, not pursuant to statute. The grounds and procedures for classifying information are specified in the executive order, but they change from President to President. The FOIA does not limit the President's discretion in determining what kind of information should be classified; it exempts any matters authorized to be classified by an executive order and properly classified under an order. A matter can even be classified after an FOIA request is made.

A particular problem may arise when merely acknowledging the existence of a document may disclose national security information. The FOIA requires agencies to respond to an FOIA request by either complying or explaining why it is not providing the document. Usually this means explaining which exemption applies. Imagine, however, that someone asks for a record concerning a particular intelligence operation, the existence of which is supposed to be secret. If the agency responds by denying the request on the ground that the matters are properly classified, the requester at least has confirmation that the operation exists. If the agency responds falsely, by denying the records exist, that would be illegal. This problem first came to attention when a person sought CIA records concerning the Glomar Explorer. *See Phillippi v. CIA*, 546 F.2d 1009 (D.C.Cir.1976). In fact, the Glomar Explorer was a ship the CIA had built and used to try to raise a sunken Soviet submarine from the floor of the ocean. The cover story to explain what the ship was doing was that the Hughes Corporation was using it to mine manganese nodules from the ocean floor. If the cover story was true, the CIA would not have had any records about the ship. The CIA made what has now come to be called a "Glomar denial," denying the FOIA request on the grounds that it could neither confirm nor deny the existence of any such records. This type of denial ultimately was accepted, if confirming the existence of such records would itself disclose classified information.

While an invocation of the exemption for classified information is subject to the same de novo judicial review as other exemptions to determine whether it is properly invoked, as a practical matter courts are extremely reluctant to substitute their judgment as to whether information would harm the national security.

b. Internal Personnel Rules

FOIA's second exemption is for matters "related solely to the internal personnel rules and practices of an agency." In the sole Supreme Court decision under this exemption, the Court held that the case summaries of the Air Force Academy's disciplinary proceedings did not fall within this exemption. Although these summaries were clearly "internal personnel" documents, the Court found that the public interest in the integrity of the Air Force's disciplinary system meant that the records were of more than internal significance and therefore were not "solely" related to internal personnel rules. In essence, the Court found that the exemption only applied to trivial, internal matters in "which the public could not reasonably be expected to have an interest." Because the case did not present the issue, the Court left open whether there might be some internal personnel rules which, although having some public interest, should be exempt because release might interfere with proper agency functioning. Subsequent case law has recognized an exemption for internal personnel manuals, where disclosure might lead to circumventing the agency's regulations or practices. *See, e.g., Crooker v. BATF*, 670 F.2d 1051 (D.C.Cir.1981) (*en banc*) (BATF training manual concerning surveillance techniques exempt); *NTEU v. U.S. Customs Service*, 802 F.2d 525 (D.C.Cir.1986) (personnel manual used in selecting personnel for promotion exempt); *Dirksen v. U.S. Dept. of HHS*, 803 F.2d 1456 (9th Cir.1986) (Medicare claims processing guidelines exempt); *Schiller v. NLRB*, 964 F.2d 1205 (D.C.Cir.1992) (guidelines on implementing Equal Access to Justice Act exempt). This has resulted in what has become known as "Low 2 exemptions" and "High 2 exemptions." The former are trivial internal personnel matters that are exempt, and the latter are the internal personnel matters which if released would interfere with proper agency functioning.

Because the application of exemption 2 can to a certain extent depend upon the value to the public of the information being disclosed, this exemption creates an exception to the general rule under the FOIA that the requester's desire for the information is irrelevant to the requirement to disclose.

c. *Specifically Exempted by Statute*

Not surprisingly, there are a number of statutes that by their terms try to maintain the confidentiality of information in the government's possession. For example, raw census information is prohibited from being used for other than statistical purposes. To overcome a Supreme Court decision, *Administrator, FAA v. Robertson*, 422 U.S. 255, 95 S.Ct. 2140, 45 L.Ed.2d 164 (1975), interpreting the earlier version of exemption three, Congress required that statutes that exempt disclosure must do so absolutely (with no room for agency discretion) or must provide particular criteria for withholding or particular types of information to be withheld. For a list of statutes that satisfy these criteria and of those that do not, *see* Litigation under the Federal Open Government Laws, 20th ed., 66–74 (Allan Adler, Ed. 1997).

d. *Confidential Business Information*

Exemption 4 applies to trade secrets and commercial or financial information if it is obtained from a person and is either privileged or confidential. There is some dispute as to what is a "trade secret." Some courts have indicated that the definition of the Restatement of Torts is appropriate; other courts, and notably the D.C. Circuit, have opted for a narrower definition. *See Public Citizen Health Research Group v. FDA*, 704 F.2d 1280 (D.C.Cir.1983). Both require the information to be commercially valuable, used in one's business, and maintained by the company in secrecy; the D.C. Circuit would further require that the information relate directly to the production process. Even if something is not a trade secret, however, it may still qualify as "commercial" or "financial" information, which the courts have said have their ordinary meaning.

In order to be exempt as "commercial" or "financial" information, the information must have been obtained from a person, not generated by the government itself, but the person that provided the information need not be the person to whom the information relates. Whether information is "privileged" is determined from the Constitution, statute, or common law. More commonly, the claim is that the information is "confidential."

Problem 8–2 What Information is "Confidential"?

Under the Department of Energy Organization Act, the Energy Information Administration is authorized to collect general energy statistics to inform the government about energy trends and developments. It requires some information to be submitted under threat of penalty for failure to report; other information it obtains from voluntary submissions pursuant to requests for assistance. A monthly refinery capacity utilization report obtained from the seven major oil companies is an example of voluntarily-obtained information. This information is then used to report aggregate refinery capacity utilization.

A commercial reporting service seeks the reports made by each of the major oil companies; it wishes to report each company's refinery capacity utilization. The EIA asks the General Counsel's office whether this information is required to be disclosed under the FOIA. The General Counsel asks you. You note that the companies have stamped the reports "confidential."

Problem Materials

NATIONAL PARKS AND CONSERVATION ASSOCIATION v. MORTON

498 F.2d 765 (D.C.Cir.1974).

TAMM, J.:

Appellant brought this action under the Freedom of Information Act, seeking to enjoin officials of the Department of the Interior from refusing to permit inspection and copying of certain agency records concerning concessions operated in the national parks. The district court granted summary judgment for the defendant on the ground that the information sought is exempt from disclosure under section 552(b)(4) of the Act which states:

(b) This section does not apply to matters that are—

(4) trade secrets and commercial or financial information obtained from a person and privileged or confidential. . . .

In order to bring a matter (other than a trade secret) within this exemption, it must be shown that the information is (a) commercial or financial, (b) obtained from a person, and (c) privileged or confidential. Since the parties agree that the matter in question is financial information obtained from a person and that it is not privileged, the only issue on appeal is whether the information is "confidential" within the meaning of the exemption.

Unfortunately, the statute contains no definition of the word "confidential." In the past, our decisions concerning this exemption have been guided by the following passage from the Senate Report, particularly the italicized portion:

> This exception is necessary to protect the confidentiality of information which is obtained by the Government through questionnaires or other inquiries, *but which would customarily not be released to the public by the person from whom it was obtained.*

We have made it clear, however, that the test for confidentiality is an objective one. Whether particular information would customarily be disclosed to the public by the person from whom it was obtained is not the only relevant inquiry in determining whether that information is "confidential" for purposes of section 552(b)(4). A court must also be satisfied that non-disclosure is justified by the legislative purpose which underlies the exemption. Our first task, therefore, is to ascertain the ends which Congress sought to attain in enacting the exemption for "commercial or financial" information.

In general, the various exemptions included in the statute serve two interests—that of the Government in efficient operation and that of persons supplying certain kinds of information in maintaining its secrecy. The exemption with which we are presently concerned has a dual purpose. It is intended to protect interests of both the Government and the individual.

The "financial information" exemption recognizes the need of government policymakers to have access to commercial and financial data. Unless persons having necessary information can be assured that it will remain confidential, they may decline to cooperate with officials and the ability of the Government to make intelligent, well informed decisions will be impaired. This concern finds expression in the legislative history as well as the case law. . . . As the Senate Report explains:

> This exception is necessary to protect the confidentiality of information which is obtained by the Government through questionnaires or other inquires. . . . It would also include information which is given to an agency in confidence, since a citizen must be able to confide in his Government. Moreover, where the Government has obligated itself in good faith not to disclose documents or information which it receives, it should be able to honor such obligations.

> . . . Apart from encouraging cooperation with the Government by persons having information useful to officials, section 552(b)(4) serves another distinct but equally important purpose. It protects persons who submit financial or commercial data to government agencies from the competitive disadvantages which would result from its publication. . . . [The legislative] history firmly supports the inference that section 552(b)(4) is intended for the benefit of persons who supply information as well as the agencies which gather it. . . .

To summarize, commercial or financial matter is "confidential" for purposes of the exemption if disclosure of the information is likely to have either of the following effects: (1) to impair the Government's ability to obtain necessary information in the future; or (2) to cause substantial harm to the competitive position of the person from whom the information was obtained.

The financial information sought by appellant consists of audits conducted upon the books of companies operating concessions in national parks, annual financial statements filed by the concessioners with the National Park Service and other financial information. The district court concluded that this information was of the kind "that would not generally be made available for public perusal." While we discern no error in this finding, we do not think that, by itself, it supports application of the financial information exemption. The district court must also inquire into the possibility that disclosure will harm legitimate private or governmental interests in secrecy.

On the record before us the Government has no apparent interest in preventing disclosure of the matter in question. Some, if not all, of the information is supplied to the Park Service pursuant to statute. Whether supplied pursuant to statute, regulation or some less formal mandate, however, it is clear that disclosure of this material to the Park Service is a mandatory condition of the concessioners' right to operate in national parks. Since the concessioners are *required* to provide this financial information to the government, there is presumably no danger that public disclosure will impair the ability of the Government to obtain this information in the future.

As we have already explained, however, section 552(b)(4) may be applicable even though the Government itself has no interest in keeping the information secret. The exemption may be invoked for the benefit of the person who has provided commercial or financial information if it can be shown that public disclosure is likely to cause substantial harm to his competitive position. Appellant argues that such a showing cannot be made in this case because the concessioners are monopolists, protected from competition during the term of their contracts and enjoying a statutory preference over other bidders at renewal time. In other words, appellant argues that disclosure cannot impair the concessioners' competitive position because they have no competition. While this argument is very compelling, we are reluctant to accept it without first providing appellee the opportunity to develop a fuller record in the district court. It might be shown, for example, that disclosure of information about concession activities will injure the concessioner's competitive position in a nonconcession enterprise. In that case disclosure would be improper. This matter is therefore remanded to the district court for the purpose of determining whether public disclosure of the information in question poses the likelihood of substantial harm to the competitive positions of the parties from whom it has been obtained. . . .

CRITICAL MASS ENERGY PROJECT v. NUCLEAR REGULATORY COMMISSION

975 F.2d 871 (D.C.Cir.1992) (*en banc*).

BUCKLEY, J.:

Appellant seeks the release of certain reports that have been provided to the Nuclear Regulatory Commission by the Institute of Nuclear Power Operations on the understanding that they will be treated as confidential. In granting the petition to rehear the case en banc, we agreed to reconsider a seventeen-year-old decision, *National Parks and Conservation Ass'n v. Morton*, in which we established a two-part test for determining when financial or commercial information in the Government's possession is to be treated as confidential under Exemption 4 of the Freedom of Information Act. We reaffirm the test but confine it to information that persons are required to provide the Government. We hold that where, as here, the information sought is given to the Government voluntarily, it will be treated as confidential under Exemption 4 if it is of a kind that the provider would not customarily make available to the public.

. . . This case involves a dispute between Critical Mass Energy Project ("CMEP") and the Nuclear Regulatory Commission ("NRC") over access to safety reports prepared by the Institute for Nuclear Power Operations ("INPO") and voluntarily transmitted to the NRC on the condition that the agency will not release the information to other parties without INPO's consent. INPO was formed after the 1979 Three Mile Island accident to promote safety and reliability in the operation of nuclear power plants. INPO is a nonprofit corporation whose membership includes all operators of nuclear power plants in the United States.

One of INPO's principal programs is the Significant Event Evaluation and Information Network ("SEE–IN"), a system for collecting, analyzing, and distributing information concerning the construction and operation of nuclear facilities. Compilation of these reports requires the solicitation of candid comments and evaluations from nuclear power plant employees. The reports are distributed on a voluntary basis to INPO members, certain other participants in the nuclear industry, and the NRC pursuant to the explicit understanding that they are not to be disclosed to additional persons without INPO's consent.

In 1984, CMEP asked the NRC, pursuant to FOIA, to provide it with copies of the INPO reports. The NRC denied the request, finding that they contained confidential commercial information and were therefore protected from disclosure by Exemption 4. CMEP then brought suit in district court challenging the NRC's determination. . . .

In challenging the definition of "confidential" presented in *National Parks*, the NRC and INPO ask us to set aside circuit precedent of almost twenty years' standing. In obedience to the principle of stare decisis, we reaffirm the definition but correct some misunderstandings as to its scope and application.

. . . Circuit courts of appeal, of course, play a different role in the federal system than the Supreme Court, and this is reflected in certain differences in the manner in which the principle of stare decisis is applied to circuit precedent. Thus, in addition to considering the factors [applicable to the Supreme Court's treatment of precedent], a circuit court may reexamine its own established interpretation of a statute if it finds that other circuits have persuasively argued a contrary construction. An en banc court may also set aside its own precedent if, on reexamination of an earlier decision, it decides that the panel's holding on an important question of law was fundamentally flawed.

Appellees NRC and INPO have failed to demonstrate any of the considerations that would justify our overturning the *National Parks* test. We note, first, the widespread acceptance of *National Parks* by other circuits. To date, seven have adopted its test of confidentiality; none has rejected it. Far from being overtaken by the tide of recent judicial developments, *National Parks*, it seems, has ridden its crest.

Nor have appellees pointed to any subsequent action in Congress that would tend to "remove[ ] or weaken[ ] the conceptual underpinnings" of *National Parks*. To the contrary, Congress has taken cognizance of the case in enacting subsequent legislation.

Finally, we find that *National Parks* has not proven so "unworkable" in practice as to constitute a "positive detriment to coherence and consistency in the law" or a "direct obstacle to the realization of important objectives embodied in other laws." Nor has there been a showing that the test, as applied in *National Parks*, will frustrate Congress's purposes in enacting Exemption 4. Appellees argue, nevertheless, that the decision has proven unworkable in its everyday application by agencies and the courts. They suggest that the impracticability of the "governmental impairment" prong is evidenced by the history of this case.

While these decisions illustrate the difficulties that can arise wherever judicial lines are drawn, they fall short of demonstrating that *National Parks* is so flawed that we would be justified in setting it aside. Moreover, we believe that the categorical rule we announce today will greatly simplify the application of Exemption 4 in a significant number of cases.

Having examined these and other arguments in favor of overturning *National Parks*, we conclude that none justifies the abandonment of so well established a precedent.

The *National Parks* two-part test was presented as a summary of its discussion of Exemption 4. The test must therefore be read in a manner consistent with the observations and conclusions that preceded it. . . .

In summarizing these various purposes and justifications, we formulated the now familiar two-part test that defined as "confidential" any financial or commercial information whose disclosure would be likely either "(1) to impair the Government's ability to obtain necessary information in the future; or (2) to cause substantial harm to the competitive position of the person from whom the information was obtained." In applying this test to the facts of *National Parks*, we held that because the concessioners [were] required to provide this financial information . . . , there is presumably no danger that public disclosure will impair the ability of the Government to obtain this information in the future. Then, because the record was incomplete as to the competitive harm that might be suffered by the concessioners on the release of the information, we remanded for further findings on that question.

While we indicated that the governmental interest is unlikely to be implicated where the production of information is compelled, we have since pointed out that there are circumstances in which disclosure could affect the reliability of such data. See Washington Post Co. v. HHS, 690 F.2d 252, 268–69 (D.C.Cir.1982) (possible effect of disclosure on accuracy of statements filed by consultants). Thus, when dealing with a FOIA request for information the provider is required to supply, the governmental impact inquiry will focus on the possible effect of disclosure on its quality.

When a FOIA request is made for information that is furnished on a voluntary basis, however, we have identified a different aspect of the governmental interest in securing confidential information. [T]he purpose served by the exemption in such instances is that of "encouraging cooperation with the Government by persons having information useful to officials." Moreover, we have taken note of the probable consequences of a breach of confidence by the Government: Unless persons having necessary information can be assured that it will remain confidential, they may decline to cooperate with officials[,] and the ability of the Government to make intelligent, well informed decisions will be impaired. Thus, when information is obtained under duress, the Government's interest is in ensuring its continued reliability; when that information is volunteered, the Government's interest is in ensuring its continued availability.

A distinction between voluntary and compelled information must also be made when applying the "competitive injury" prong. In the latter case, there is a presumption that the Government's interest is not threatened by disclosure because it secures the information by mandate; and as the harm to the private interest (commercial disadvantage) is the only factor weighing against FOIA's presumption of disclosure, that interest must be significant. Where, however, the information is provided to the Government voluntarily, the presumption is that its interest will be threatened by disclosure as the persons whose confidences have been betrayed will, in all likelihood, refuse further cooperation. In those cases, the private interest served by Exemption 4 is the protection of information that, for whatever reason, "would customarily not be released to the public by the person from whom it was obtained" . . . .

It should be evident from this review that the two interests identified in the *National Parks* test are not exclusive. [W]e note that ... the exemption also protects a governmental interest in administrative efficiency and effectiveness. And today, of course, we recognize a private interest in preserving the confidentiality of information that is provided the Government on a voluntary basis. We offer no opinion as to whether any other governmental or private interest might also fall within the exemption's protection.

The Supreme Court has encouraged the development of categorical rules whenever a particular set of facts will lead to a generally predictable application of FOIA....

The circumstances of this case lend themselves to categorical treatment. It is a matter of common sense that the disclosure of information the Government has secured from voluntary sources on a confidential basis will both jeopardize its continuing ability to secure such data on a cooperative basis and injure the provider's interest in preventing its unauthorized release. Accordingly, while we reaffirm the *National Parks* test for determining the confidentiality of information submitted under compulsion, we conclude that financial or commercial information provided to the Government on a voluntary basis is "confidential" for the purpose of Exemption 4 if it is of a kind that would customarily not be released to the public by the person from whom it was obtained.

We make three observations about this test. First, it is objective. As is the case with any claim under FOIA, the agency invoking Exemption 4 must meet the burden of proving the provider's custom. Second, we know of no case considered by this court in the past ... that would have been decided differently had this test been applied. Finally, in defining the limits of the *National Parks* confidentiality test, we do not repudiate any part of our holding in that case. A respect for stare decisis does not require the most expansive application of principles enunciated in a prior decision....

Applying this rule to the INPO reports, we agree with the district court's conclusion that the information they contain is commercial in nature; that the reports are provided to the NRC on a voluntary basis; and that INPO does not customarily release such information to the public. On the basis of these findings, we hold that the INPO reports are confidential within the meaning of Exemption 4 and therefore protected from disclosure.

CMEP asserts that the test we announce today may lead government agencies and industry to conspire to keep information from the public by agreeing to the voluntary submission of information that the agency has the power to compel....

We know of no provision in FOIA that obliges agencies to exercise their regulatory authority in a manner that will maximize the amount of information that will be made available to the public through that Act. Nor do we see any reason to interfere with the NRC's exercise of its own discretion in determining how it can best secure the information it needs. So long as that information is provided voluntarily, and so long as it is of a kind that INPO customarily withholds from the public, it must be treated as confidential. . . .

RUTH BADER GINSBURG, CIRCUIT JUDGE, joined by MIKVA, CHIEF JUDGE, WALD and HARRY T. EDWARDS, CIRCUIT JUDGES, dissenting from the court's opinion:

. . . I would preserve our *National Parks* precedent.

The court, instead, removes from the governance of *National Parks* all cases in which commercial or financial information is given to the Government voluntarily. The cutback substantially revises the law of this circuit and diminishes as well sister circuit case law patterned on our *National Parks* decision. Stare decisis, though protractedly addressed, has not been appropriately observed in today's decision. Nor has the guiding purpose of the Freedom of Information Act (FOIA)—to shed light on an agency's performance of its statutory duties—been well served by the en banc disposition. I therefore dissent from the court's FOIA and precedent unsettling judgment and opinion.

Under the test announced today, "financial or commercial information provided to the Government on a voluntary basis is 'confidential' for the purpose of Exemption 4 if it is of a kind that would customarily not be released to the public by the person from whom it was obtained." No longer is it necessary to show in each case "how disclosure will significantly harm some relevant private or governmental interest." Henceforth, in this circuit, it will do for an agency official to agree with the submitter's ascription of confidential status to the information. There will be no objective check on, no judicial review alert to, "the temptation of government and business officials to follow the path of least resistance and say 'confidential' whenever they seek to satisfy the government's vast information needs." Under the regime replacing *National Parks*, "the exemption [will] expand beyond what Congress intended." But the court sees virtue in a categorical rule, and such rules do have a place in FOIA's domain.

A categorical approach, however, is not in order across the board under FOIA, without regard to the character of the information requested. Such an automatic approach is not suitable for judging the wide range of cases presenting contests under exemption 4. That was Judge Tamm's essential point in *National Parks*.

The *National Parks* formulation fits the congressional design better than the virtual abandonment of federal court scrutiny approved by the court today for Government withholding of commercial or financial materials submitted voluntarily. For that reason, I dissent from the court's decision to overrule, in significant measure, our *National Parks* precedent.

e. Inter– or Intra–Agency Memoranda

The fifth exemption is one of the most commonly invoked FOIA exemptions, yet its language is opaque. It exempts inter-agency or intra-agency memoranda and letters "which would not be available by law to a party other than an agency in litigation with the agency." The legislative history is much more illuminating, stating that the exemption was intended to incorporate the government's common law privilege from discovery in litigation. The Supreme Court has recognized five such privileges: executive privileged material, attorney work-product, attorney-client confidential communications, confidential commercial information of the government itself, and factual statements made to air crash investigators. The executive privilege, discussed in the context of the President in *United States v. Nixon*, 418 U.S. 683, 94 S.Ct. 3090, 41 L.Ed.2d 1039 (1974), is intended to protect open and frank advice and recommendations from government employees to their superiors so that government officials will receive the fullest and most candid advice. Executive privileged material relates to pre-decisional documents, rather than decisional documents. Documents that reflect or direct a decision to be made are decisional documents. Thus, documents from superiors to subordinates do not qualify, because these direct a decision, rather than make recommendations. Even a pre-decisional advice document can become a decisional document if it is cited or incorporated by reference in a decisional document.

Because the essence of the executive privilege is protecting the integrity of the decisionmaking process, a number of types of documents that do not obviously appear to be advice and recommendations to superiors are still considered to qualify. For example, summaries of information provided for a decisionmaker, even though all the information is factual, have been considered part of the deliberative process, because the person making the summary is judging what is important and what is not important to be included in the summary to the decisionmaker. Also, drafts of documents are considered part of the deliberative process. Even factual information concerning the deliberative process has been held privileged. *See Wolfe v. Department of HHS*, 839 F.2d 768 (D.C.Cir.1988) (*en banc*) (upholding exemption 5 claim for agency's Regulations Log, which listed dates and determinations with respect to proposed rulemakings).

Exemption 5 only applies to inter-and intra-agency documents, but again focusing on the deliberative process, courts have used a functional rather than literal interpretation of these terms to include documents from persons participating in the decisionmaking process, such as advisory committees, consultants, and contractors. In each of these cases, the outsider had a formal relationship with the agency that reasonably could be said to bring them within the agency for purposes of the exemption.

If documents that would have qualified for exemption 5 have been released to third-parties, the privilege is generally considered waived.

f. Personal Privacy

Exemption 6 protects "personnel and medical files and similar files the disclosure of which would constitute a clearly unwarranted invasion of privacy." The Supreme Court has given a broad reading to the nature of the files subject to this exception, finding that they refer to "detailed government records on an individual which can be identified as applying to that individual." *U.S. Dept. of State v. Washington Post Co.*, 456 U.S. 595, 102 S.Ct. 1957, 72 L.Ed.2d 358 (1982). But this is only half of this analysis, because the question then is whether disclosure of the record would constitute "a clearly unwarranted invasion of privacy." This requires a balancing between the public interest in disclosing the information and the private interest in maintaining confidentiality. Thus, records that contain "personal" or "intimate details" of a person's life would require a very strong public interest to justify a determination that the invasion is warranted. Where the information is not obviously personal or intimate, there is less likelihood of the disclosure constituting an unwarranted invasion of privacy. If, however, the information could be used to harm the person about whom the information relates, the balance would shift in favor of privacy. *See, e.g., U.S. Department of State v. Ray*, 502 U.S. 164, 112 S.Ct. 541, 116 L.Ed.2d 526 (1991) (reports of interviews with persons who unsuccessfully sought to immigrate to the United States from Haiti within exemption). Often, however, records can be disclosed by deleting identifiable information, thereby protecting the privacy interest.

The case law has established that only individuals have a privacy interest under exemption 6, not corporations or business associations. Case law also generally has concluded that a person's privacy interest lapses upon the person's death. However, surviving family members may have a cognizable privacy interest. *See, e.g., New York Times Co. v. National Aeronautics and Space Administration.*, 920 F.2d 1002 (D.C.Cir.1990) (families of Challenger's crew had privacy interest in voice tapes of crew's last words).

The Supreme Court in *Department of Air Force v. Rose*, 425 U.S. 352, 96 S.Ct. 1592, 48 L.Ed.2d 11 (1976) described the public interest in disclosure as "open[ing] agency action to the light of public scrutiny." In *U.S. Dept. of Defense v. FLRA*, 510 U.S. 487, 114 S.Ct. 1006, 127 L.Ed.2d 325 (1994), the Court said that "the only relevant 'public interest in disclosure' . . . is 'contribut[ing] significantly to public understanding of the operations or activities of the government.' " Obviously, requests for information related to alleged misbehavior of the government would have "high" public interest consideration, whereas mere commercial interests are likely to have little or none. *See, e.g., Wine Hobby USA, Inc. v. U.S. IRS*, 502 F.2d 133 (3d Cir.1974) (names and addresses of amateur wine makers protected from disclosure to organization for commercial mailing).

The need to balance the public interest in disclosure against the privacy interest that would be affected might be seen to lead to consideration of the particular requester and his purposes for the information. The Supreme Court rejected this idea, which had been accepted by some circuits, in *U.S. Dept. of Defense v. FLRA*, 510 U.S. 487, 496, 114 S.Ct.

1006, 1013, 127 L.Ed.2d 325 (1994). The information is either affected with the public interest, or it is not.

g. *Law Enforcement Records*

In its original 1966 formulation, exemption 7 generally exempted "investigatory files compiled for law enforcement purposes." This was interpreted to require positive answers to two questions: was the nature of the file in which the record sought was found investigatory and had the file been compiled for law enforcement purposes. The result was that old, no longer current files remained exempt even though no further enforcement proceedings would occur or would be harmed by disclosure. In 1974, Congress amended exemption 7 to narrow its coverage, exempting investigatory records compiled for law enforcement purposes, but only if the record would cause one of six specified harms—interfere with enforcement proceedings, deprive a person of a fair trial, constitute an unwarranted invasion of privacy, disclose the identity of a confidential source (for law enforcement or national security investigations there was an irrebuttable presumption that confidential information supplied solely by a confidential source would disclose the source's identity), disclose confidential investigative techniques and procedures, or endanger the life or safety of law enforcement personnel. In 1986, Congress again amended the exemption, this time to broaden its reach in several ways. First, the amendment eliminated the requirement that the records be investigatory records. Second, the likelihood that disclosure would result in one of the specified harms was reduced from "would" occur to "could reasonably be expected" to occur. Third, confidential sources were defined to include any person, any private institution, or any state, local, or foreign agency that furnishes information on a confidential basis. Fourth, the presumption that information from a confidential source would identify the source was extended to any information provided by the confidential source, not just "confidential" information provided "solely" by the source. Fifth, the amendment broadened the range of documents that would constitute harm to law enforcement investigative techniques, practices, or guidelines. Sixth, endangering the life or safety or any person, not just law enforcement personnel, qualified for the exemption.

The basic requirement that the record have been compiled for law enforcement purposes has been construed to include information originally collected for a non-law enforcement purpose, but later compiled into a record for law enforcement purposes. *See John Doe Agency v. John Doe Corp.*, 493 U.S. 146, 110 S.Ct. 471, 107 L.Ed.2d 462 (1989). "Law enforcement" includes criminal, civil, and administrative enforcement activities.

The D.C. Circuit's decision in *Critical Mass Energy Project v. NRC*, which you read above, mentioned that categorical rules have their place in FOIA law. Attempts to create categorical rules have been particularly prevalent in applying the six harms that trigger exemption 7. Thus, in applying the "unwarranted invasion of privacy" aspect of harm, the

Court said, "as a categorical matter ... a third party's request for law enforcement records or information about a private citizen can reasonably be expected to invade that citizen's privacy, and that when the request seeks no 'official information' about a government agency, but merely records that the government happens to be storing, the invasion of privacy is 'unwarranted.'" *U.S. Department of Justice v. Reporters Committee for Freedom of the Press*, 489 U.S. 749, 109 S.Ct. 1468, 103 L.Ed.2d 774 (1989). Nevertheless, the Court rejected a categorical rule established by several circuits that any person who provides information to the FBI in an law enforcement investigation is a confidential source, although the Court was willing to accept categorically that paid informants are confidential sources. *See U.S. Dept. of Justice v. Landano*, 508 U.S. 165, 113 S.Ct. 2014, 124 L.Ed.2d 84 (1993).

h. *Financial Institution Records and Oil Well Data*

Exemptions 8 and 9 have not received much attention. The purpose of exemption 8 is to protect the information about financial institutions which the government collects in the course of its regulatory functions; this is to protect both the institutions and the effectiveness of the regulatory relationship between the government and the institutions. One not fully resolved issue is what constitutes a "financial institution." *See, e.g., Public Citizen v. Farm Credit Administration*, 938 F.2d 290 (D.C.Cir.1991).

6. REVERSE FOIA SUITS

As should be evident from the prior discussion, private persons or organizations about whom the government has information may have a very strong interest in whether the government releases information requested by someone. As indicated above, one administration may view the importance of withholding information much more importantly than another, and the Department of Justice's unwillingness to defend FOIA lawsuits except in certain situations may also affect an agency's willingness to invoke an exemption. The question arises then, what recourse is there for the person to whom the information relates to influence or object to the government's release of information pursuant to an FOIA request.

Problem 8–3 Agency Responsibilities

In Problem 8–2, as an attorney for the Department of Energy, you probably determined that the information was likely to be exempt under exemption 4. Nevertheless, you are aware of the Attorney General's policy statement that Justice will not defend agencies in FOIA suits unless the agency determines that release of the exempt information would be contrary to the public interest. You are doubtful that this is the case. In any case, you wonder what, if anything, you need to do if you decide to release the information.

Problem Materials

EXECUTIVE ORDER 12600
PREDISCLOSURE NOTIFICATION PROCEDURES
FOR CONFIDENTIAL COMMERCIAL INFORMATION

52 FR 23781 (1987).

By the authority vested in me as President by the Constitution and statutes of the United States of America, and in order to provide predisclosure notification procedures under the Freedom of Information Act concerning confidential commercial information, and to make existing agency notification provisions more uniform, it is hereby ordered as follows:

Section 1. The head of each Executive department and agency subject to the Freedom of Information Act shall, to the extent permitted by law, establish procedures to notify submitters of records containing confidential commercial information as described in section 3 of this Order, when those records are requested under the Freedom of Information Act (FOIA), 5 U.S.C. 552, as amended, if after reviewing the request, the responsive records, and any appeal by the requester, the department or agency determines that it may be required to disclose the records. Such notice requires that an agency use good-faith efforts to advise submitters of confidential commercial information of the procedures established under this Order. Further, where notification of a voluminous number of submitters is required, such notification may be accomplished by posting or publishing the notice in a place reasonably calculated to accomplish notification.

Sec. 2. For purposes of this Order, the following definitions apply:

(a) "Confidential commercial information" means records provided to the government by a submitter that arguably contain material exempt from release under Exemption 4 of the Freedom of Information Act, 5 U.S.C. 552(b)(4), because disclosure could reasonably be expected to cause substantial competitive harm.

(b) "Submitter" means any person or entity who provides confidential commercial information to the government. The term "submitter" includes, but is not limited to, corporations, state governments, and foreign governments.

Sec. 3. . . .

(b) For confidential commercial information submitted on or after January 1, 1988, the head of each Executive department or agency shall, to the extent permitted by law, establish procedures to permit submitters of confidential commercial information to designate, at the time the information is submitted to the Federal government or a reasonable time thereafter, any information the disclosure of which the submitter claims could reasonably be expected to cause substantial competitive harm.

Such agency procedures may provide for the expiration, after a specified period of time or changes in circumstances, of designations of competitive harm made by submitters. Additionally, such procedures may permit the agency to designate specific classes of information that will be treated by the agency as if the information had been so designated by the submitter. The head of each Executive department or agency shall, to the extent permitted by law, provide the submitter notice in accordance with section 1 of this Order whenever the department or agency determines that it may be required to disclose records:

(i) designated pursuant to this subsection; or

(ii) the disclosure of which the department or agency has reason to believe could reasonably be expected to cause substantial competitive harm.

Sec. 4. When notification is made pursuant to section 1, each agency's procedures shall, to the extent permitted by law, afford the submitter a reasonable period of time in which the submitter or its designee may object to the disclosure of any specified portion of the information and to state all grounds upon which disclosure is opposed.

Sec. 5. Each agency shall give careful consideration to all such specified grounds for nondisclosure prior to making an administrative determination of the issue. In all instances when the agency determines to disclose the requested records, its procedures shall provide that the agency give the submitter a written statement briefly explaining why the submitter's objections are not sustained. Such statement shall, to the extent permitted by law, be provided a reasonable number of days prior to a specified disclosure date.

Sec. 6. Whenever a FOIA requester brings suit seeking to compel disclosure of confidential commercial information, each agency's procedures shall require that the submitter be promptly notified.

Sec. 7. The designation and notification procedures required by this Order shall be established by regulations, after notice and public comment. If similar procedures or regulations already exist, they should be reviewed for conformity and revised where necessary. Existing procedures or regulations need not be modified if they are in compliance with this Order.

.   .   .

Sec. 9. Whenever an agency notifies a submitter that it may be required to disclose information pursuant to section 1 of this Order, the agency shall also notify the requester that notice and an opportunity to comment are being provided the submitter. Whenever an agency notifies a submitter of a final decision pursuant to section 5 of this Order, the agency shall also notify the requester.

Sec. 10. This Order is intended only to improve the internal management of the Federal government, and is not intended to create any right or benefit, substantive or procedural, enforceable at law by a party against the United States, its agencies, its officers, or any person.

Code of Federal Regulations
Title 10—Energy
Chapter X—Department of Energy (General Provisions)
Part 1004—Freedom of Information

§ 1004.11 Handling information of a private business, foreign government, or an international organization.

(a) Whenever a document submitted to the DOE contains information which may be exempt from public disclosure, it will be handled in accordance with the procedures in this section. While the DOE is responsible for making the final determination with regard to the disclosure or nondisclosure of information contained in requested documents, the DOE will consider the submitter's views (as that term is defined in this section) in making its determination. Nothing in this section will preclude the submission of a submitter's views at the time of the submission of the document to which the views relate, or at any other time.

(b) When the DOE may determine, in the course of responding to a Freedom of Information request, not to release information submitted to the DOE (as described in paragraph (a) of this section, and contained in a requested document) without seeking any or further submitter's views, no notice will be given the submitter.

(c) When the DOE, in the course of responding to a Freedom of Information request, cannot make the determination described in paragraph (b) of this section without having for consideration the submitter's views, the submitter shall be promptly notified and provided an opportunity to submit his views on whether information contained in the requested document (1) is exempt from the mandatory public disclosure requirements of the Freedom of Information Act, (2) contains information referred to in 18 U.S.C. 1905, or (3) is otherwise exempt by law from public disclosure. The DOE will make its own determinations as to whether any information is exempt from disclosure. Notice of a determination by the DOE that a claim of exemption made pursuant to this paragraph is being denied will be given to a person making such a claim no less than seven (7) calendar days prior to intended public disclosure of the information in question. For purposes of this section, notice is deemed to be given when mailed to the submitter at the submitter's last known address....

(e) Notwithstanding any other provision of this section, DOE offices may require a person submitting documents containing information that may be exempt by law from mandatory disclosure to (1) submit copies of each document from which information claimed to be confidential has been deleted or (2) require that the submitter's views be otherwise made known at the time of the submission. Notice of a determination by the DOE that a claim of exemption is being denied will be given to a person making such a claim no less than seven (7) calendar days prior to intended public disclosure of the information in question. For purposes of this section, notice is deemed to be given when mailed to the submitter at the submitter's last known address....

(g) When the DOE, in the course of responding to a Freedom of Information request, determines that information exempt from the mandatory public disclosure requirements of the Freedom of Information Act is to be released in accordance with § 1004.1 [stating that DOE may disclose exempt material if it is in the public interest], the DOE will notify the submitter of the intended discretionary release no less than seven (7) days prior to intended public disclosure of the information in question.

(h) As used in this section, the term "submitter's views" means, with regard to a document submitted to the DOE, an item-by-item indication, with accompanying explanation, addressing whether the submitter considers the information contained in the document to be exempt from the mandatory public disclosure requirements of the Freedom of Information Act, to be information referred to in 18 U.S.C. 1905, or to be otherwise exempt by law from mandatory public disclosure. The accompanying explanation shall specify the justification for nondisclosure of any information under consideration. If the submitter states that the information comes within the exemption in 5 U.S.C. 552(b)(4) for trade secrets and commercial or financial information, the submitter shall include a statement specifying why such information is privileged or confidential and, where appropriate, shall address the criteria in paragraph (f) of this section. In all cases, the submitter shall address the question of whether or not discretionary disclosure would be in the public interest.

Notes and Questions

1. What is the authority for the President's Executive Order? Inasmuch as the FOIA contains strict timetables for agency responses to FOIA requests, timetables that surely could not be met if submitters of the information requested are notified and given an opportunity to provide their comments on possible release, does the Order or the DOE regulation violate the FOIA?

2. Under the DOE regulation, if the submitter wanted to obtain an oral hearing before the agency, could it get one?

Problem 8–4 Reverse FOIA

The Department of Energy has decided to release the individual oil company refinery utilization reports despite its determination that the reports are exempt from the disclosure requirements of the FOIA. DOE gives notice to each of the oil companies of its intent. Exxon is upset and contacts its Washington lawyers to stop the release. Your firm pushes the file at you and says, "go to it."

Problem Materials

CHRYSLER CORPORATION v. BROWN

441 U.S. 281, 99 S.Ct. 1705, 60 L.Ed.2d 208 (1979).

REHNQUIST, J.:

... This case belongs to a class that has been popularly denominated "reverse–FOIA" suits. The Chrysler Corp. (hereinafter Chrysler) seeks to enjoin agency disclosure on the grounds that it is inconsistent with the FOIA and 18 U.S.C. § 1905, a criminal statute with origins in the 19th century that proscribes disclosure of certain classes of business and personal information. . . .

[Chrysler, as a government contractor with the Defense Logistics Agency (DLA), was required by the Department of Labor's Office of Federal Contract Compliance Programs (OFCCP), pursuant to EO 11246, to provide reports about its affirmative action programs and the general composition of its workforce.] Regulations promulgated by the Secretary of Labor provide for public disclosure of information from records of the OFCCP and its compliance agencies. Those regulations state that notwithstanding exemption from mandatory disclosure under the FOIA, "records obtained or generated pursuant to Executive Order 11246 (as amended) . . . shall be made available for inspection and copying . . . if it is determined that the requested inspection or copying furthers the public interest and does not impede any of the functions of the OFCC[P] except in the case of records disclosure of which is prohibited by law."

It is the voluntary disclosure contemplated by this regulation, over and above that mandated by the FOIA, which is the gravamen of Chrysler's complaint in this case.

This controversy began on May 14, 1975, when the DLA informed Chrysler that third parties had made an FOIA request for disclosure of the 1974 Affirmative Action Program for Chrysler's Newark, Del., assembly plant. . . . Nine days later, Chrysler objected to release of the requested information. . . . DLA responded the following week that it had determined that the requested material was subject to disclosure under the FOIA and the OFCCP disclosure rules, and that both documents would be released five days later.

On the day the documents were to be released Chrysler filed a complaint in the United States District Court for Delaware seeking to enjoin release of the Newark documents. The District Court granted a temporary restraining order barring disclosure of the Newark documents. . . .

Chrysler made [two] arguments in support of its prayer for an injunction: that disclosure was barred by the FOIA; that it was inconsistent with 18 U.S.C. § 1905. . . .

... In contending that the FOIA bars disclosure of the requested equal employment opportunity information, Chrysler relies on the Act's nine exemptions and argues that they require an agency to withhold exempted material. In this case it relies specifically on Exemption 4.... Chrysler contends that the nine exemptions in general, and Exemption 4 in particular, reflect a sensitivity to the privacy interests of private individuals and nongovernmental entities. That contention may be conceded without inexorably requiring the conclusion that the exemptions impose affirmative duties on an agency to withhold information sought. In fact, that conclusion is not supported by the language, logic, or history of the Act.

The organization of the Act is straightforward. Subsection (a), places a general obligation on the agency to make information available to the public and sets out specific modes of disclosure for certain classes of information. Subsection (b), which lists the exemptions, simply states that the specified material is not subject to the disclosure obligations set out in subsection (a). By its terms, subsection (b) demarcates the agency's obligation to disclose; it does not foreclose disclosure.

That the FOIA is exclusively a disclosure statute is, perhaps, demonstrated most convincingly by examining its provision for judicial relief. Subsection (a)(4)(B) gives federal district courts "jurisdiction to enjoin the agency from withholding agency records and to order the production of any agency records improperly withheld from the complainant." That provision does not give the authority to bar disclosure, and thus fortifies our belief that Chrysler, and courts which have shared its view, have incorrectly interpreted the exemption provisions of the FOIA....

Enlarged access to governmental information undoubtedly cuts against the privacy concerns of nongovernmental entities, and as a matter of policy some balancing and accommodation may well be desirable. We simply hold here that Congress did not design the FOIA exemptions to be mandatory bars to disclosure....

We therefore conclude that Congress did not limit an agency's discretion to disclose information when it enacted the FOIA. It necessarily follows that the Act does not afford Chrysler any right to enjoin agency disclosure.

Chrysler contends, however, that even if its suit for injunctive relief cannot be based on the FOIA, such an action can be premised on the Trade Secrets Act, 18 U.S.C. § 1905. The Act provides: "Whoever, being an officer or employee of the United States or of any department or agency thereof, publishes, divulges, discloses, or makes known in any manner or to any extent not authorized by law any information coming to him in the course of his employment or official duties or by reason of any examination or investigation made by, or return, report or record made to or filed with, such department or agency or officer or employee thereof, which information concerns or relates to the trade secrets, processes, operations, style of work, or apparatus, or to the identity, confidential statistical data, amount or source of any income, profits, losses, or expenditures of any person, firm, partnership, corporation, or association; or permits any income return or copy thereof or any book containing any abstract or particulars thereof to be seen or examined by any person except as provided by law; shall be fined not more than $1,000, or imprisoned not more than one year, or both; and shall be removed from office or employment." There are necessarily two parts to Chrysler's argument: that § 1905 is applicable to the type of disclosure threatened in this case, and that it affords Chrysler a private right of action to obtain injunctive relief.

The Court of Appeals held that § 1905 was not applicable to the agency disclosure at issue here because such disclosure was "authorized by law" within the meaning of the Act. The court found the source of that authorization to be the OFCCP regulations that DLA relied on. . . . Chrysler contends here that these agency regulations are not "law" within the meaning of § 1905.

It has been established in a variety of contexts that properly promulgated, substantive agency regulations have the "force and effect of law." This doctrine is so well established that agency regulations implementing federal statutes have been held to pre-empt state law under the Supremacy Clause. It would therefore take a clear showing of contrary legislative intent before the phrase "authorized by law" in § 1905 could be held to have a narrower ambit than the traditional understanding. . . .

In order for a regulation to have the "force and effect of law," it must have certain substantive characteristics and be the product of certain procedural requisites. The central distinction among agency regulations found in the APA is that between "substantive rules" on the one hand and "interpretative rules, general statements of policy, or rules of agency organization, procedure, or practice" on the other. A "substantive rule" is not defined in the APA, and other authoritative sources essentially offer definitions by negative inference. But in [an earlier case] we noted a characteristic inherent in the concept of a "substantive rule." We described a substantive rule—or a "legislative-type rule"—as one "affecting individual rights and obligations." This characteristic is an important touchstone for distinguishing those rules that may be "binding" or have the "force of law."

That an agency regulation is "substantive," however, does not by itself give it the "force and effect of law." The legislative power of the United States is vested in the Congress, and the exercise of quasi-legislative authority by governmental departments and agencies must be rooted in a grant of such power by the Congress and subject to limitations which that body imposes. As this Court [has] noted . . . : "Legislative, or substantive, regulations are 'issued by an agency pursuant to statutory authority and . . . implement the statute, as, for example, the proxy rules issued by the Securities and Exchange Commission. . . . Such rules have the force and effect of law.' "

Likewise the promulgation of these regulations must conform with any procedural requirements imposed by Congress. For agency discretion is limited not only by substantive, statutory grants of authority, but also by the procedural requirements which "assure fairness and mature consideration of rules of general application." The pertinent procedural limitations in this case are those found in the APA.

The regulations relied on by the respondents in this case as providing "authoriz[ation] by law" within the meaning of § 1905 certainly affect individual rights and obligations; they govern the public's right to information in records obtained under Executive Order 11246 and the confidentiality rights of those who submit information to OFCCP and its compliance agencies. It is a much closer question, however, whether they are the product of a congressional grant of legislative authority.

. . . Since materials that are exempt from disclosure under the FOIA are by virtue of Part II of this opinion outside the ambit of that Act, the Government cannot rely on the FOIA as congressional authorization for disclosure regulations that permit the release of information within the Act's nine exemptions. . . .

The respondents argue, however, that even if these regulations do not have the force of law by virtue of [the FOIA], an explicit grant of legislative authority for such regulations can be found in 5 U.S.C. § 301, commonly referred to as the "housekeeping statute." It provides: "The head of an Executive department or military department may prescribe regulations for the government of his department, the conduct of its employees, the distribution and performance of its business, and the custody, use, and preservation of its records, papers, and property. This section does not authorize withholding information from the public or limiting the availability of records to the public." The antecedents of § 301 go back to the beginning of the Republic, when statutes were enacted to give heads of early Government departments authority to govern internal departmental affairs. Those laws were consolidated into one statute in 1874 and the current version of the statute was enacted in 1958.

Given this long and relatively uncontroversial history, and the terms of the statute itself, it seems to be simply a grant of authority to the agency to regulate its own affairs. What is clear from the legislative history of the 1958 amendment to § 301 is that this section was not intended to provide authority for limiting the scope of § 1905.[40]

. . . There is also a procedural defect in the OFCCP disclosure regulations which precludes courts from affording them the force and effect of law. That defect is a lack of strict compliance with the APA. . . . Certainly regulations subject to the APA cannot be afforded the "force

40. This does not mean, of course, that disclosure regulations promulgated on the basis of § 301 are "in excess of statutory jurisdiction, authority, or limitations" for purposes of § 10(e)(B)(3) of the APA, 5 U.S.C. § 706(2)(C). It simply means that disclosure pursuant to them is not "authorized by law" within the meaning of § 1905.

and effect of law" if not promulgated pursuant to the statutory procedural minimum found in that Act.

Section 4 of the APA, 5 U.S.C. § 553, specifies that an agency shall afford interested persons general notice of proposed rulemaking and an opportunity to comment before a substantive rule is promulgated.... [OFCCP had adopted the regulations without notice and comment, calling them interpretive rules.] We need not decide whether these regulations are properly characterized as "interpretative rules." It is enough that such regulations are not properly promulgated as substantive rules, and therefore not the product of procedures which Congress prescribed as necessary prerequisites to giving a regulation the binding effect of law. An interpretative regulation or general statement of agency policy cannot be the "authoriz[ation] by law" required by § 1905....

We reject, however, Chrysler's contention that the Trade Secrets Act affords a private right of action to enjoin disclosure in violation of the statute. Nothing in § 1905 prompts such an inference.... As our review of the legislative history of § 1905—or lack of same—might suggest, there is no indication of legislative intent to create a private right of action. Most importantly, a private right of action under § 1905 is not "necessary to make effective the congressional purpose," for we find that review of DLA's decision to disclose Chrysler's employment data is available under the APA.

While Chrysler may not avail itself of any violations of the provisions of § 1905 in a separate cause of action, any such violations may have a dispositive effect on the outcome of judicial review of agency action pursuant to § 10 of the APA. Section 10(a) of the APA provides that "[a] person suffering legal wrong because of agency action, or adversely affected or aggrieved by agency action ..., is entitled to judicial review thereof." 5 U.S.C. § 702.... [The Court remanded the case to the Court of Appeals to determine whether the information to be disclosed fell within the terms of § 1905.]

Notes and Questions

1. *Chrysler* did not fully resolve what the standard of review should be in a reverse-FOIA suit. Because the suit is pursuant to the APA, section 706 applies, but is this a case for de novo review under section 706? In *Chrysler* itself the Court said that the issue left in the case was whether the actual information sought was subject to 18 U.S.C.A. § 1905 and that such an issue would not normally require a de novo determination. This would suggest that the court below would be reviewing the agency's record of decision on the issue, but what if the agency had no particular record? Would the agency's decision be considered an application of law to facts? Does it matter whether the law being applied, usually 18 U.S.C.A. § 1905, is a criminal statute for which no particular agency is responsible for interpreting or applying?

2. The Court in *Chrysler* did not decide whether exemption 4 and section 1905 were co-extensive, although in a footnote it suggested that

in most cases they probably would be. It said, however, that it might be theoretically possible for information to be outside exemption 4 (and therefore required to be released under the FOIA) but within section 1905 (and therefore prohibited from release unless "in accordance with law"). In this circumstance, the Court said the FOIA "might" provide the necessary authorization of law. What do you think? Both the Ninth and D.C. Circuits have held that anything within section 1905 is also within exemption 4. *See CNA Financial Corp. v. Donovan,* 830 F.2d 1132 (D.C.Cir.1987); *Dowty Decoto, Inc. v. Department of the Navy,* 883 F.2d 774 (9th Cir.1989).

3. If the agency decides to withhold the information, and the requester sues under the FOIA for release, what can the submitter do at that point? Presumably the submitter could try to intervene in the FOIA suit, but that by itself would only resolve whether the agency was required (as opposed to permitted) to release the information. The submitter could try to sue the agency in a separate action to enjoin the agency from releasing the information. Could one court hold that the FOIA required the agency to release the information and another court hold that section 1905 precluded the release of the information?

4. Most reverse-FOIA litigation involves commercial information, but there is no particular reason why it cannot occur with respect to personal information as well. *See, e.g., NOW, Washington, D.C. Chapter v. Social Security Administration,* 736 F.2d 727 (D.C.Cir.1984). Obviously, 18 U.S.C.A. § 1905 would not be available; what statutes might be? Why do you suppose reverse-FOIA cases involving personal privacy are so few?

B. THE FEDERAL ADVISORY COMMITTEE ACT

In 1972, Congress passed the Federal Advisory Committee Act, 5 U.S.C.A. §§ 1–15, which imposes limitations on the executive branch use for advice of committees that include private persons. Unlike the Freedom of Information Act, which has been used successfully by citizens all over the nation, even if its use is dominated by businesses and their lawyers, FACA has remained largely an "inside the Beltway" law. Only recently has its potential power to provide public access and accountability, and alternatively to stymie government action, been tested.

Committees to advise the President or others in the Executive Branch have been around nearly as long as the Republic. Nevertheless, there is a common understanding that the great growth of advisory committees occurred after World War II, generally in response to the increased government regulation occasioned by the New Deal and perhaps by increased government and industry cooperation during the war. This growth naturally inspired some concerns. Initially, the concerns involved antitrust problems that might arise from collusion within advisory groups composed of business members. The response was the issuance of Guidelines by the Justice Department in 1950.

These Guidelines were recommendatory, not mandatory, and apparently were largely ignored. As a result, legislation was introduced in Congress in 1957 to make the Guidelines mandatory. While the House passed the bill, the Senate preferred to rely on executive oversight. In 1959, the Bureau of Budget issued a directive that essentially restated the Justice Guidelines. In 1962 President Kennedy issued Executive Order 11007, which again in large part continued the Justice Guidelines. The Order, like the BoB directive and Justice Guidelines before it, did not apply to Presidential advisory committees.

Advisory committee issues then lay dormant until 1970 when the Government Operations Committees in both the House and Senate held investigatory hearings. In the House, the initial focus was on "the alleged duplicativeness, wasteful expenditures, and limited impact of Presidential Advisory Committees." Later, the committee expanded its inquiry to include all advisory committees. In the Senate, the focus was on the alleged undue influence by industry acting through advisory committees on certain agency programs. After passage of separate bills by each house, a conference committee reported a bill that passed both houses.

FACA reflects the concerns expressed by the committees that considered the various bills. A general concern was with government waste. The sheer number of committees, estimated at the time as being approximately 3,000, gave reason to believe that many were unnecessary. Moreover, Presidential committees were noted for costing substantial amounts for products that often were little more than paperweights. Accordingly, as the Supreme Court noted in *Public Citizen v. U.S. Department of Justice*, 491 U.S. 440, 109 S.Ct. 2558, 105 L.Ed.2d 377 (1989), "FACA was born of a desire to assess the need for the 'numerous committees, boards, commissions, councils, and similar groups which have been established to advise officers and agencies in the executive branch of the Federal Government.'" Thus, much of FACA is aimed at monitoring the number and expenses of advisory committees and reducing their number. FACA also creates substantial bureaucratic hurdles to the creation of new advisory committees. It requires that no new advisory committee be established unless the President or statute specifically authorizes its creation or the head of an agency determines "as a matter of formal record, . . . after consultation with the Administrator, . . . [that such establishment is] in the public interest in connection with the performance of duties imposed on that agency by law." To assure that new advisory committees meet these standards, FACA prohibits any advisory committee from meeting or taking any action until its charter has been filed with the Administrator, for Presidential advisory committees, or with the head of the agency to which the committee will report and the standing committees of the House and Senate with jurisdiction over the agency. The charter must contain the advisory committee's title, its purpose, the time necessary to carry out that purpose, the agency or official to whom it reports and who is responsible for providing necessary support, the duties for which the committee is responsible, the estimated annual cost and number and frequency of meetings, the termination date, and the date the charter is filed. FACA sets a two-year limit for all advisory committees, except those created by statute with a different period, but it allows the President or agency head to extend a committee for an additional two years. There is no limit on the number of two-year extensions that may be granted to a committee. Advisory committees that are extended, including statutory advisory committees, must file new charters.

Reducing government waste was not Congress's only concern. At least of equal importance was a concern that special interests had captured advisory committees and were having undue influence on public programs. The particular target of the initial Senate hearings in 1970 had been the Advisory Council on Federal Reports and its sub-groups. The Bureau of the Budget had created that advisory committee to advise it with respect to the implementation of the Federal Reports Act of 1942, a predecessor of the Paperwork Reduction Act. In response to complaints concerning unnecessary and burdensome government reporting and recordkeeping requirements, Congress provided in the Federal Reports Act that the BoB would review and approve proposed agency requests for information from the private sector. The BoB asked five leading national business organizations to name representatives to a group, the Advisory Council on Federal Reports, upon which it could call for advice on proposed federal reporting and recordkeeping requirements. The Council formed standing committees concerned with particular industries and consisting of representatives of those industries. This relationship was criticized by legislators "as 'one-sided,' providing advice to the government only from representatives of 'big businesses' and with the power 'to withhold from the public information which it has the right to know....' " Nor was the Advisory Council on Federal Reports the only example.

Professor William Rodgers made a study of the National Industrial Pollution Control Council, an advisory committee created by President Nixon to "allow businessmen to communicate regularly with the President, the Council on Environmental Quality and other governmental officials and private organizations which are working to improve the quality of our environment." Professor Rodgers' study concluded that the Council's contribution to two environmental initiatives was to supply "invaluable inside-track opportunities for those who would redirect governmental policy...."

Two different aspects of advisory committee practice contributed to the potential of undue influence. First was the limited membership, designed to reflect one point of view. E.O. 11007, for example, had expressly approved of industry advisory groups, defined as a group "composed predominantly of members or representatives of a single industry or group of related industries, or of any subdivision of a single industry made on a geographic, service or product basis." Second was the relative secrecy in which advisory groups operated. Neither the

Justice Guidelines nor E.O. 11007 required committee meetings to be open to the public.

FACA addressed these perceived problems in several ways. Responding to the concern that advisory committees only reflected the views of particular interests, FACA required that the membership of advisory committees be "fairly balanced in terms of the points of view represented and the functions to be performed by the advisory committee." No longer would advisory committees be industry advisory committees.

FACA attempted to address the concern of advisory committees becoming the tail that wags the agency dog by requiring that no advisory committee meeting occur "except with the approval of, or with the advance approval of, a designated officer or employee of the Federal Government, and [except for Presidential advisory committees] with an agenda approved by such officer or employee." Moreover, no meeting can occur without the presence of a designated federal officer or employee, and the officer or employee is authorized to adjourn the meeting at any time "he determines it to be in the public interest."

FACA's response to the secrecy concern reflects the culture of the time, midway between the passage of the Freedom of Information Act and the Government in the Sunshine Act. Section 10 of FACA begins by requiring that "[e]ach advisory committee meeting shall be open to the public." In order to make this requirement meaningful, "timely notice" of meetings must be published in the Federal Register, and the Administrator is to prescribe rules for other types of public notice. Moreover, the public is entitled to participate in the meeting by appearing before and filing statements with the committee. FACA requires that committees keep "detailed minutes of each meeting," the accuracy of which the chair of the committee must certify, and which must contain "a record of the persons present, a complete and accurate description of matter discussed and conclusions reached, and copies of all reports received, issued, or approved by the advisory committee." These are available for public inspection and copying at the offices of the advisory committee or agency, unless they are subject to one of the exceptions from public release contained in the Freedom of Information Act.

The above requirements for the creation and operation of advisory committees involve a substantial burden for agencies and advisory committees. It is not surprising, therefore, that agencies seeking advice from outside groups and outside groups desiring to provide advice to agencies may wish to avoid its strictures. Their ability to do so usually depends upon the definition of an "advisory committee" under FACA. Section 3(2) defines the term as follows:

> any committee, board, commission, council, conference, panel, task force, or other similar group, or any subcommittee or other subgroup thereof . . ., which is
>
> (A) established by statute or reorganization plan, or
>
> (B) established or utilized by the President, or

(C) established or utilized by one or more agencies,

in the interest of obtaining advice or recommendations for the President or one or more agencies or officers of the Federal Government. . . .

The definition then excludes a number of specific advisory committees as well as any committee composed wholly of full-time Federal employees.

This definition and its application to various entities under various circumstances have occasioned the vast bulk of litigation under FACA, including the one Supreme Court case involving FACA.

That case, *Public Citizen v. U.S. Department of Justice*, involved the American Bar Association's Standing Committee on the Federal Judiciary. Presidents of the United States for years had provided that committee the names of potential nominees for appointment as federal judges. The committee then had reviewed the nominee's record and reported whether, in its view, the nominee was highly qualified, qualified, or not qualified for the position. These recommendations were perceived as highly influential in the process of appointment of judges. The committee, however, had never considered itself subject to FACA, despite the fact that it seemed to be "utilized by the President . . . in the interest of obtaining advice or recommendations for the President. . . ." Public Citizen, a public interest lobbying group, brought suit alleging violation of FACA when the committee would not allow Public Citizen to attend its meetings.

PUBLIC CITIZEN v. U.S. DEPARTMENT OF JUSTICE

491 U.S. 440, 109 S.Ct. 2558, 105 L.Ed.2d 377 (1989).

BRENNAN, J.:

. . . There is no doubt that the Executive makes use of the ABA Committee, and thus "utilizes" it in one common sense of the term. . . . "Utilize"[, however,] is a woolly verb, its contours left undefined by the statute itself. Read unqualifiedly, it would extend FACA's requirements to any group of two or more persons, or at least any formal organization, from which the President or an Executive agency seeks advice. We are convinced that Congress did not intend that result. . . .

Nor can Congress have meant—as a straightforward reading of "utilize" would appear to require—that all of FACA's restrictions apply if a President consults with his own political party before picking his Cabinet. . . .

Where the literal reading of a statutory term would "compel an odd result," we must search for other evidence of congressional intent to lend the term its proper scope. . . .

Consideration of FACA's purposes and origins in determining whether the term "utilized" was meant to apply to the Justice Department's use of the ABA Committee is particularly appropriate here, given the importance we have consistently attached to interpreting statutes to avoid deciding difficult constitutional questions where the text fairly admits of a less problematic construction. . . .

. . . FACA's principal purpose was to enhance the public accountability of advisory committees established by the Executive Branch and to reduce wasteful expenditures on them. That purpose could be accomplished, however, without expanding the coverage of Executive Order No. 11007 to include privately organized committees that received no federal funds. Indeed, there is considerable evidence that Congress sought nothing more than stricter compliance with reporting and other requirements—which were made more stringent—by advisory committees already covered by the Order and similar treatment of a small class of publicly funded groups created by the President.

The House bill which in its amended form became FACA applied exclusively to advisory committees "established" by statute or by the Executive, whether by a federal agency or by the President himself. . . .

Paralleling the initial House bill, the Senate bill that grew into FACA defined "advisory committee" as one "established or organized" by statute, the President, or an Executive agency. Like the House Report, the accompanying Senate Report stated that the phrase "established or organized" was to be understood in its "most liberal sense, so that when an officer brings together a group by formal or informal means, by contract or other arrangement, and whether or not Federal money is expended, to obtain advice and information, such group is covered by the provisions of this bill." While the Report manifested a clear intent not to restrict FACA's coverage to advisory committees funded by the Federal Government, it did not indicate any desire to bring all private advisory committees within FACA's terms. . . . Given the prominence of the ABA Committee's role and its familiarity to Members of Congress, its omission from the list of groups formed and maintained by private initiative to offer advice with respect to the President's nomination of Government officials is telling. If the examples offered by the Senate Committee on Government Operations are representative, as seems fair to surmise, then there is little reason to think that there was any support, at least at the committee stage, for going beyond the terms of Executive Order No. 11007 to regulate comprehensively the workings of the ABA Committee.

It is true that the final version of FACA approved by both Houses employed the phrase "established or utilized," and that this phrase is more capacious than the word "established" or the phrase "established or organized." But its genesis suggests that it was not intended to go much beyond those narrower formulations. The words "or utilized" were added by the Conference Committee to the definition included in the House bill. . . . The Conference Report offered no indication that the modification was significant, let alone that it would substantially broaden FACA's application by sweeping within its terms a vast number of private groups, such as the Republican National Committee, not formed at the behest of the Executive or by quasi-public organizations whose opinions the Federal Government sometimes solicits.... The phrase "or utilized" therefore appears to have been added simply to clarify that FACA applies to advisory committees established by the Federal Government in a generous sense of that term, encompassing groups formed indirectly by quasi-public organizations such as the National Academy of Sciences "for" public agencies as well as "by" such agencies themselves....

In sum, a literalistic reading of § 3(2) would bring the Justice Department's advisory relationship with the ABA Committee within FACA's terms, particularly given FACA's objective of opening many advisory relationships to public scrutiny except in certain narrowly defined situations. A literalistic reading, however, would catch far more groups and consulting arrangements than Congress could conceivably have intended. And the careful review which this interpretive difficulty warrants of earlier efforts to regulate federal advisory committees and the circumstances surrounding FACA's adoption strongly suggests that FACA's definition of "advisory committee" was not meant to encompass the ABA Committee's relationship with the Justice Department. That relationship seems not to have been within the contemplation of Executive Order No. 11007. And FACA's legislative history does not display an intent to widen the Order's application to encircle it. Weighing the deliberately inclusive statutory language against other evidence of congressional intent, it seems to us a close question whether FACA should be construed to apply to the ABA Committee, although on the whole we are fairly confident it should not. There is, however, one additional consideration which, in our view, tips the balance decisively against FACA's application.

"When the validity of an act of the Congress is drawn in question, and even if a serious doubt of constitutionality is raised, it is a cardinal principle that this Court will first ascertain whether a construction of the statute is fairly possible by which the question may be avoided." It has long been an axiom of statutory interpretation that "where an otherwise acceptable construction of a statute would raise serious constitutional problems, the Court will construe the statute to avoid such problems unless such construction is plainly contrary to the intent of Congress."

That construing FACA to apply to the Justice Department's consultations with the ABA Committee would present formidable constitutional difficulties is undeniable. The District Court declared FACA unconstitutional insofar as it applied to those consultations, because it concluded that FACA, so applied, infringed unduly on the President's Article II power to nominate federal judges and violated the doctrine of separation of powers. Whether or not the court's conclusion was correct, there is no gainsaying the seriousness of these constitutional challenges.... Where the competing arguments based on FACA's text and legislative history, though both plausible, tend to show that Congress did not desire FACA to apply to the Justice Department's confidential solicitation of the ABA

Committee's views on prospective judicial nominees, sound sense counsels adherence to our rule of caution. Our unwillingness to resolve important constitutional questions unnecessarily thus solidifies our conviction that FACA is inapplicable.

JUSTICE KENNEDY, with whom THE CHIEF JUSTICE and JUSTICE O'CONNOR join, concurring in the judgment.

[Justice Kennedy construed FACA to apply to the ABA committee, but as so applied he found that FACA unconstitutionally interfered with the President's authority under the Appointments Clause.]

Problem 8–5 Dealing with FACA

The United States Customs Service would like to improve its job of detecting import violations without impeding, and perhaps reducing existing barriers to, the free flow of foreign commerce. It believes that by talking to importers, shippers, and carriers in the trade it will be able to find ways to improve its performance in a way least burdensome to the industry. The Commissioner of the Customs Service asks his policy office to identify some key players in the industry who might be invited to a series of meetings to discuss possible initiatives and ideas. Someone, however, mentions the Federal Advisory Committee Act as a possible stumbling block. The Commissioner is perturbed at this interference, but he is persuaded to consult with his Chief Counsel on the matter. The Chief Counsel asks you to explore possible ways to accommodate the Commissioner's desires without having to charter a federal advisory committee.

Problem Materials

UNITED STATES CODE ANNOTATED
TITLE 5. GOVERNMENT ORGANIZATION AND EMPLOYEES
APPENDIX 2. FEDERAL ADVISORY COMMITTEE ACT

§ 3. Definitions

For the purpose of this Act—

(1) The term "Administrator" means the Administrator of General Services.

(2) The term "advisory committee" means any committee, board, commission, council, conference, panel, task force, or other similar group, or any subcommittee or other subgroup thereof (hereafter in this paragraph referred to as "committee"), which is—

(A) established by statute or reorganization plan, or

(B) established or utilized by the President, or

(C) established or utilized by one or more agencies,

in the interest of obtaining advice or recommendations for the President or one or more agencies or officers of the Federal Government, except that such term excludes (i) the Advisory Commission on Intergovernmental Relations, (ii) the Commission on Government Procurement, and (iii) any committee which is composed wholly of full-time officers or employees of the Federal Government.

(3) The term "agency" has the same meaning as in section 551(1) of Title 5.

CODE OF FEDERAL REGULATIONS
TITLE 41—PUBLIC CONTRACTS AND PROPERTY MANAGEMENT
SUBTITLE C—FEDERAL PROPERTY MANAGEMENT REGULATIONS SYSTEM
CHAPTER 101—FEDERAL PROPERTY MANAGEMENT REGULATIONS
SUBCHAPTER A—GENERAL
PART 101–6—MISCELLANEOUS REGULATIONS
SUBPART 101–6.10—FEDERAL ADVISORY COMMITTEE MANAGEMENT

§ 101–6.1003   Definitions.

"Act" means the Federal Advisory Committee Act, as amended, 5 U.S.C., App.

"Administrator" means the Administrator of General Services.

"Advisory committee" subject to the Act means any committee, board, commission, council, conference, panel, task force, or other similar group, or any subcommittee or other subgroup thereof, which is established by statute, or established or utilized by the President or any agency official for the purpose of obtaining advice or recommendations on issues or policies which are within the scope of his or her responsibilities.

"Agency" has the same meaning as in section 551(1) of Title 5 of the United States Code.

"Committee member" means an individual who serves by appointment on an advisory committee and has the full right and obligation to participate in the activities of the committee, including voting on committee recommendations.

"Presidential advisory committee" means any advisory committee which advises the President. It may be established by the President or by the Congress, or used by the President in the interest of obtaining advice or recommendations for the President. "Independent Presidential advisory committee" means any Presidential advisory committee not assigned by the President, or the President's delegate, or by the Congress in law, to an agency for administrative and other support and for which the Administrator of General Services may provide administrative and other support on a reimbursable basis.

"Staff member" means any individual who serves in a support capacity to an advisory committee.

"Utilized" (or "used"), as referenced in the definition of "Advisory committee" in this section, means a committee or other group composed in whole or in part of other than full-time officers or employees of the Federal Government with an established existence outside the agency seeking its advice which the President or agency official(s) adopts, such as through institutional arrangements, as a preferred source from which to obtain advice or recommendations on a specific issue or policy within the scope of his or her responsibilities in the same manner as that individual would obtain advice or recommendations from an established advisory committee.

§ 101–6.1004   Examples of advisory meetings or groups not covered by the Act or this subpart.

The following are examples of advisory meetings or groups not covered by the Act or this subpart;

(a) Any committee composed wholly of full-time officers or employees of the Federal Government;

. . .

(f) Any local civic group whose primary function is that of rendering a public service with respect to a Federal program, or any State or local committee, council, board, commission, or similar group established to advise or make recommendations to State or local officials or agencies;

(g) Any committee which is established to perform primarily operational as opposed to advisory functions. Operational functions are those specifically provided by law, such as making or implementing Government decisions or policy. An operational committee may be covered by the Act if it becomes primarily advisory in nature. It is the responsibility of the administering agency to determine whether such a committee is primarily operational. If so, it would not fall under the requirements of the Act and this Subpart, but would continue to be regulated under relevant laws, subject to the direction of the President and the review of the appropriate legislative committees;

(h) Any meeting initiated by the President or one or more Federal official(s) for the purpose of obtaining advice or recommendations from one individual;

(i) Any meeting initiated by a Federal official(s) with more than one individual for the purpose of obtaining the advice of individual attendees and not for the purpose of utilizing the group to obtain consensus advice or recommendations. However, agencies should be aware that such a group would be covered by the Act when an agency accepts the group's deliberations as a source of consensus advice or recommendations;

(j) Any meeting initiated by a group with the President or one or more Federal official(s) for the purpose of expressing the group's view, provided that the President or Federal official(s) does not use the group recurrently as a preferred source of advice or recommendations;

(k) Meetings of two or more advisory committee or subcommittee members convened solely to gather information or conduct research for a chartered advisory committee, to analyze relevant issues and facts, or to draft proposed position papers for deliberation by the advisory committee or a subcommittee of the advisory committee; or

(*l*) Any meeting with a group initiated by the President or one or more Federal official(s) for the purpose of exchanging facts or information.

NORTHWEST FOREST RESOURCE COUNCIL v. ESPY

846 F.Supp. 1009 (D.D.C.1994).

JACKSON, DISTRICT JUDGE.

. . . This case arises upon yet another attempt by the Executive Branch to escape the toils of FACA in formulating the current Administration's policy for the future of over 24 million acres of federally owned forest lands in the states of Oregon and Washington. The plaintiff Northwest Forest Resource Council ("NFRC") is a not-for-profit association incorporated in Oregon representing the interests of the timber and other forest products industries in the two states. Defendants are the U.S. Secretaries of Agriculture and Interior, a group of individuals comprising the object of this suit, an entity known as the Forest Ecosystem Management Assessment Team ("FEMAT"), and FEMAT's chairman, a research wildlife biologist with the U.S. Forest Service.

Plaintiff alleges that, as convened and employed by the President, FEMAT constituted an "advisory committee" within the contemplation of FACA which, if so, then entitled NFRC (and the public generally) to certain rights to be (or to have been) privy to and to have participated in FEMAT's proceedings. . . .

Defendants respond that, for various reasons, FEMAT was never conceived, nor did it function, as an "advisory committee" under FACA, and, were this Court to find it so, then FACA itself must be deemed an unconstitutional invasion of the executive privilege for communications necessary to his exercise of the powers entrusted by the Constitution to the President. . . .

The material facts are of record and are not genuinely in dispute. On April 2, 1993, President Clinton, Vice President Gore, and other government officials (including the defendant Secretaries) attended a day-long "forest conference" in Portland, Oregon, to address the long-standing controversy between environmentalists and the forest products industry over the uses to be made of federal forest lands. At the conclusion of the conference, . . . Katie McGinty, Director of the White House Office of Environmental Policy, in the Executive Office of the

President, established an inter-agency group called the Forest Conference Executive Committee ("Executive Committee") to direct and supervise the work of FEMAT, which was then already in the formative stages. The Executive Committee instructed FEMAT to identify management alternatives, employing an "ecosystem" approach, to attain the "greatest economic and social contribution from the forests."

FEMAT was composed of six subteams whose participants admittedly included private contractors paid with federal funds. FEMAT also established 14 advisory subgroups to provide it with biological impact assessments on various forms of plant and animal life. Altogether somewhere between 600 and 700 people contributed in some way to FEMAT's work.... At least five of those people, defendants also concede, were not regular federal employees. They were ... full-time faculty members at Oregon State University [and] the University of Washington. None of those professors took leaves of absence from their institutions while working for FEMAT; all continued to receive their full faculty paychecks, and they or their universities were paid varying sums by the federal government....

The defendants first argue that FEMAT was simply not an "advisory committee" or not the sort of "advisory committee" with which FACA is concerned. But FACA itself defines an "advisory committee" to which it applies as "any committee, board, commission, council, conference, panel, task force, or other similar group, or any subcommittee or subgroup thereof" that is "established or utilized" by the President or an agency "in the interest of obtaining advice or recommendations for the President or one or more agencies or officers of the Federal government."

By any fair interpretation of the facts and certainly by a literal reading of the statutory definition, FEMAT was an "advisory committee" within the contemplation of FACA in form and function, unless elsewhere excepted in the statute. It was a consultative assembly of knowledgeable persons for a specific purpose; calling it a "team" does not alter its nature. It was both "established" and "utilized" by the President for his guidance in devising a forest management policy. And it did render him "advice" and "recommendations" which he accepted and followed.

Elsewhere in the statute, however, conclaves identical to FEMAT are excluded from the status of being "advisory committees," and exempted from any obligations as such, if, but only if, they are "composed wholly of full-time officers or employees of the Federal Government." In other words, FACA does not apply if all of the people assembled to advise the President are already in government service....

In attempting to stretch the language of FACA's exception for committees "composed wholly of full-time officers or employees of the federal government" to reach FEMAT, however, the defendants take the concept of being in federal service to a meaningless extreme. They submit that the five outsiders, the professors who contributed to the work of FEMAT (and the only contributors they will concede to have been "members" of it) should still be regarded as "officers or employees of the federal government" within the meaning of the exception, because, as faculty at state universities, they were "state employees," and as such could have been "assigned," under an unrelated statute to engage in the performance of a federal function had it occurred to anyone that it might be necessary. But the presence of state employees on an advisory panel has ... not saved such panels from FACA in the past. Moreover, none of the five professors were ever officially assigned federal duties, and none of the formalities that would be expected to attend such assignments were ever observed.

Even if the Court were to find that the state university professors were "federal employees," they would not qualify as being "full-time" unless, as the defendants propose, they be given credit for full-time work because they each averaged over 40 hours per week for FEMAT during its existence. But the exception for "full-time officers and employees" only supports the purposes of FACA if the term as used in FACA is interpreted as drawing a distinction between regular civil servants and outsiders or hybrids; it clearly has no place in FACA as a wage-and-hour rule. As the AAPS court noted, "FACA would be rather easy to avoid if an agency could simply appoint 10 private citizens as special government employees for two days, and then have the committee receive the section 3(2) exemption as a body composed of full-time government employees."

The defendants next argue that FEMAT was not an "advisory committee" because it made only a "technical assessment" of various management options, but did not provide "policy advice." The Court finds, however, that FEMAT absolutely did render policy advice to the President. FEMAT's mandate was to develop and analyze the effects of alternative ecosystem management policy options for presentation to the Administration, and it did so. The Administration considered, so far as is shown, only the work of FEMAT in selecting a policy to implement, and chose one of the options FEMAT proposed. FEMAT directly influenced the President's ultimate policy decision.

Moreover, there is nothing in the statutory language or case law to support the defendants' assertion that FACA should not apply to "advisory committees" consisting only of technicians who supply the decisionmakers with data. To the contrary, several courts have applied FACA in just such circumstances. See *Public Citizen v. National Advisory Committee on Microbiological Criteria for Foods*, 886 F.2d 419 (D.C.Cir.1989) (FACA applied to committee to develop microbiological criteria by which the safety and wholesomeness of food could be assessed); *National Nutritional Foods Ass'n v. Califano*, 603 F.2d 327 (2d Cir.1979) (single meeting of five experts in the field of obesity research was subject to FACA)....

The defendants argue that if, as the Court has found, FEMAT was an "advisory committee" under FACA whose advice was integral to the Administration's decision to adopt the Forest Plan, the application of

FACA to the FEMAT proceedings would transgress the constitutional doctrine of the separation of powers, thus rendering it inevitable that the Court must declare the statute unconstitutional as applied.

Both the Supreme Court majority in *Public Citizen* and the D.C. Circuit majority in *AAPS* were able, by adroit semantics and near-clairvoyant discernment of legislative intent, to avoid that drastic result in the circumstances of those cases, but not, however, without difficulty, and in doing so incurred stern disapprobation from concurring brethren who were less squeamish. . . .

This Court has, however, rejected the opportunities offered by defendants to engage in similar creative statutory construction and interpretation, and no others have manifested themselves spontaneously. . . . [Consequently, the court declares that FEMAT was an advisory committee and its use violated FACA.]

Notes and Questions

1. President Clinton attempted to use groups like the FEMAT for a number of presidential initiatives. Another one involved President Clinton's Task Force on National Health Care Reform, all of whose members were full time officers and employees of the federal government except the chairperson, President Clinton's wife, Hillary Clinton. Groups opposed to health care reform challenged the Task Force as an advisory committee that did not comply with FACA. The D.C. Circuit decided that the First Lady, although not recognized by statute as such, should be considered a full time employee of the federal government for FACA purposes. *See Association of Am. Physicians and Surgeons v. Clinton*, 997 F.2d 898 (D.C.Cir.1993). Judge Buckley concurred in the judgement on the grounds that, while in his view the President's wife could not be considered a government employee, to apply FACA to require this group's deliberations to be open to the public would be an unconstitutional interference with the President's power to seek advice and counsel.

2. As discussed in Chapter 2, both Congress and the President are supportive of negotiated rulemaking. At the same time, FACA imposes barriers to the use of advisory committees, which are the entities that negotiate rulemakings. Ironically, the intent of FACA to limit the number of advisory committees was embraced wholeheartedly by the Clinton Administration, so that it established strict limits on agencies creating new advisory committees, at the same time that the President issued a memorandum to agencies calling upon them to use negotiated rulemaking. OMB, overseeing the President's numerical limit on advisory committees, actually disapproved the creation of some advisory committees agencies were going to create to do negotiated rulemaking. This points up the fact that sometimes one reform runs afoul of another.

3. Normally, courts have not been willing to enjoin agencies from using information or recommendations generated by an advisory com-

mittee in violation of the Act or to invalidate agency action based upon such information or recommendations. Usually, courts have merely required the information generated by the committee to be made public, although they have reserved the right to enjoin agency action in an appropriate case "if the unavailability of an injunctive remedy would effectively render FACA a nullity." *California Forestry Ass'n v. United States Forest Service*, 102 F.3d 609 (D.C.Cir.1996). *Accord Cargill, Inc. v. United States*, 173 F.3d 323 (5th Cir.1999). The Eleventh Circuit in *Alabama-Tombigbee Rivers v. Department of Interior*, 26 F.3d 1103 (11th Cir.1994), however, stated that "to allow the government to use the product of a tainted procedure would circumvent the very policy that serves as the foundation of the Act." Only injunctive relief "carries sufficient remedial effect to ensure future compliance with the FACA's clear requirements," the court said, enjoining the Fish and Wildlife Service from using any of the information generated by the group as a basis for listing the Alabama Sturgeon as an endangered species.

C. THE GOVERNMENT IN THE SUNSHINE ACT

The Government in the Sunshine Act, 5 U.S.C.A. § 552b, passed in 1976, was the third of the open government statutes, and it sprang from the same beliefs as the earlier laws. As the Senate Report said, the Sunshine Act was "founded on the proposition that the government should conduct the public's business in public." It reflected a belief that "[b]y requiring important decisions to be made openly, [the law] will create better understanding of agency decisions." Consequently, the fundamental requirement of the Sunshine Act is that "every portion of every meeting of an agency shall be open to public observation." 5 U.S.C.A. § 552b(b).

An initial limitation of this broad pronouncement is the definition of "agency." 5 U.S.C.A. § 552b(a)(1). Unlike the FOIA, the Sunshine Act only applies to agencies "headed by a collegial body composed of two or more individual members, a majority of whom are appointed to such position by the President with the advice and consent of the Senate, and any subdivision thereof authorized to act on behalf of the agency." In other words, only multi-member independent regulatory agencies, such as the FCC, FTC, SEC, etc., are subject to the Sunshine Act.

A second limitation on the broad requirement for open meetings is the definition of "meeting." 5 U.S.C.A. § 552b(a)(2). In order for the Sunshine Act to apply there must be a meeting of at least a quorum of the members of the agency required to take action. In addition, the meeting must involve "deliberations" that "determine or result in the joint conduct or disposition of official agency business."

Finally, like the FOIA, the open meeting requirement is subject to certain subject matter exceptions. Where the agency determines that the public interest requires a meeting to be closed, because an open meeting would likely disclose one of ten different specified types of information, then a meeting or portion thereof may be closed. 5 U.S.C.A. § 552b(c). Seven of the ten specified types of information are patterned after exemptions in the FOIA and are interpreted similarly. These are the exemptions for national defense and classified information, for internal personnel rules, for matters specifically exempted by statute, for trade secrets and privileged or confidential commercial or financial information, for information that would unwarrantedly invade a person's privacy, for investigatory records compiled for law enforcement purposes, and for information related to reports prepared by or for an agency regulating financial institutions. 5 U.S.C.A. § 552b(c)(1)–(4), (6)–(8). The three new exemptions involve: first, "accusing any person of a crime, or formally censuring any person"; second, in the case of agencies regulating currencies, securities, or commodities, information the disclosure of which would likely lead to significant financial speculation or significantly endanger the stability of any financial institution, or in the case of any agency, information the disclosure of which would be likely to significantly frustrate implementation of a proposed agency action; and third, information relating to an agency's issuance of a subpoena, participation in a civil action, or the conduct of a formal agency adjudication. 5 U.S.C.A. § 552b(c)(5), (9), (10). The latter two of these have been subject to some litigation.

In order to give effect to the requirement for open meetings, the Sunshine Act requires agencies to give at least seven days notice of a meeting's subject matter, time, place, and whether the meeting will be open or closed. 5 U.S.C.A. § 552b(e)(1). Notice must be published in the Federal Register. Agencies must maintain minutes or transcripts of meetings, whether they are open or closed. 5 U.S.C.A. § 552b(f)(1).

Problem 8–6 Dealing with the Sunshine Act

Many agencies subject to the Sunshine Act believe its requirements inhibit collegial decision making—one of the putative benefits of a multi-member agency. Some of the reasons for this would be: concern that providing initial views publicly, without sufficient thought and information, may harm the public interest by creating confusion or uncertainty; a desire on the part of members to speak with a uniform voice on matters of importance; reluctance of an agency member to embarrass another agency member or himself through tentative, inadvertent, argumentative, or exaggerated statements; and a concern that a member's statements may be presented out of context by the media or agency critics. Moreover, the notice requirements stifle the ability of the members to respond to changing events by considering issues not noticed in the meeting notice.

You work for a public interest group that monitors actions of the Federal Communications Commission. Your organization learns that the five members of the FCC are using various means to deliberate behind closed doors prior to formal meetings, so that the actual Sunshine Act meetings are sterile affairs with the members giving canned speeches and adopting policies that have clearly been discussed and debated prior to the open meeting.

Through inquiries to staff and commissioners, your organization discovers that the following techniques have been used to achieve members' consensus before holding open meetings.

1.　The Chairman initiates conference calls involving all the members.

2.　The Chairman calls and speaks to each member individually, making suggestions and representing what others have said, and inviting the recipient to call the other member if there is any question. Only two members talk on the phone at a time.

3.　Members discuss upcoming business in groups of two.

4.　Members have their staff persons meet as a group and discuss matters and then bring them back to the individual members, who then give their staffs further instructions, and the staff persons then go and discuss the matters further in a group.

5.　All the members meet together and discuss matters that will be the subject of future Sunshine Act meetings. However, the members do not take any votes or commit to taking any particular positions at the open meeting. Nonetheless, there is a full and frank discussion of the issues involved in the various matters.

Assess which are violative of the Sunshine Act.

Problem Materials

FEDERAL COMMUNICATIONS COMMISSION v. ITT WORLD COMMUNICATIONS, INC.

466 U.S. 463, 104 S.Ct. 1936, 80 L.Ed.2d 480 (1984).

JUSTICE POWELL delivered the opinion of the Court.

The Government in the Sunshine Act, 5 U.S.C. § 552b, mandates that federal agencies hold their meetings in public. This case requires us to consider whether the Act applies to informal international conferences attended by members of the Federal Communications Commission....

Members of petitioner Federal Communications Commission (FCC) participate with their European and Canadian counterparts in what is referred to as the Consultative Process. This is a series of conferences intended to facilitate joint planning of telecommunications facilities through an exchange of information on regulatory policies. At the time of the conferences at issue in the present case, only three American corporations—respondents ITT World Communications, Inc. (IT), and RCA Global Communications, Inc., and Western Union International—provided overseas record telecommunications services. Although the FCC had approved entry into the market by other competitors, European regulators had been reluctant to do so. The FCC therefore added the topic of new carriers and services to the agenda of the Consultative Process, in the hope that exchange of information might persuade the European nations to cooperate with the FCC's policy of encouraging competition in the provision of telecommunications services.

Respondents, opposing the entry of new competitors, initiated this litigation. First, respondents filed a rulemaking petition with the FCC concerning the Consultative Process meetings. The petition ... contended that the Sunshine Act required the Consultative Process sessions, as "meetings" of the FCC, to be held in public. See 5 U.S.C. § 552b(b). The FCC denied the rulemaking petition, and respondents filed an appeal in the Court of Appeals for the District of Columbia Circuit.

[T]he Court of Appeals held that the FCC had erred in concluding that the Sunshine Act did not apply to the Consultative Process sessions. . . .

We granted certiorari, to decide ... whether the Sunshine Act applies to sessions of the Consultative Process. We reverse. . . .

The Sunshine Act, 5 U.S.C. § 552b(b), requires that "meetings of an agency" be open to the public. Section 552b(a)(2) defines "meetings" as "the deliberations of at least the number of individual agency members required to take action on behalf of the agency where such deliberations determine or result in the joint conduct or disposition of official agency business." Under these provisions, the Sunshine Act does not require that Consultative Process sessions be held in public, as the participation by FCC members in these sessions constitutes neither a "meeting" as defined by § 522b(a)(2) nor a meeting "of the agency" as provided by § 552b(b).

Congress in drafting the Act's definition of "meeting" recognized that the administrative process cannot be conducted entirely in the public eye. "[I]nformal background discussions [that] clarify issues and expose varying views" are a necessary part of an agency's work. The Act's procedural requirements effectively would prevent such discussions and thereby impair normal agency operations without achieving significant public benefit.[7] Section 552b(a)(2) therefore limits the Act's application to "where at least a quorum of the agency's members ... conduct or dispose of official agency business."

Three Commissioners, the number who attended the Consultative Process sessions, did not constitute a quorum of the seven-member

---

7. The evolution of the statutory language reflects the congressional intent precisely to define the limited scope of the statute's requirements. For example, the Senate substituted the term "deliberations" for the previously proposed terms—"assembly or simultaneous communication" or "gathering"—in order to "exclude many discussions which are informal in nature."

Similarly, earlier versions of the Act had applied to any agency discussions that "concer[n] the joint conduct or disposition of agency business." The Act now applies only to deliberations that "determine or result in" the conduct of "official agency business." The intent of the revision clearly was to permit preliminary discussion among agency members.

Commission.[8] The three members were, however, a quorum of the Telecommunications Committee. That Committee is a "subdivision . . . authorized to act on behalf of the agency." The Commission had delegated to the Committee the power to approve applications for common carrier certification. The Sunshine Act applies to such a subdivision as well as to an entire agency.

It does not appear, however, that the Telecommunications Committee engaged at these sessions in "deliberations [that] determine or result in the joint conduct or disposition of official agency business." This statutory language contemplates discussions that "effectively predetermine official actions." Such discussions must be "sufficiently focused on discrete proposals or issues as to cause or be likely to cause the individual participating members to form reasonably firm positions regarding matters pending or likely to arise before the agency." R. Berg & S. Klitzman, An Interpretive Guide to the Government in the Sunshine Act 9 (1978) (hereinafter Interpretive Guide). On the cross-motions for summary judgment, however, respondents alleged neither that the Committee formally acted upon applications for certification at the Consultative Process sessions nor that those sessions resulted in firm positions on particular matters pending or likely to arise before the Committee. Rather, the sessions provided general background information to the Commissioners and permitted them to engage with their foreign counterparts in an exchange of views by which decisions already reached by the Commission could be implemented. As we have noted, Congress did not intend the Sunshine Act to encompass such discussions.

The Court of Appeals did not reach a contrary result by finding that the Commissioners were deliberating upon matters within their formally delegated authority. Rather, that court inferred from the members' attendance at the sessions an undisclosed authority, not formally delegated, to engage in discussions on behalf of the Commission. The court then concluded that these discussions were deliberations that resulted in the conduct of official agency business, as the discussions "play[ed] an integral role in the Commission's policymaking processes."

We view the Act differently. It applies only where a subdivision of the agency deliberates upon matters that are within that subdivision's formally delegated authority to take official action for the agency. Under the reasoning of the Court of Appeals, any group of members who exchange views or gathered information on agency business apparently could be viewed as a "subdivision . . . authorized to act on behalf of the agency." The term "subdivision" itself indicates agency members who have been authorized to exercise formally delegated authority. Moreover, the more expansive view of the term "subdivision" adopted by the Court of Appeals would require public attendance at a host of informal conversations of the type Congress understood to be necessary for the effective conduct of agency business. In any event, it is clear that the Sunshine

8. Since the Consultative Process sessions at issue here, held in October 1979, the Commission's membership has been reduced to five.

Act does not extend to deliberations of a quorum of the subdivision upon matters not within the subdivision's formally delegated authority. Such deliberations lawfully could not "determine or result in the joint conduct or disposition of official agency business" within the meaning of the Act. As the Telecommunications Committee at the Consultative Process sessions did not consider or act upon applications for common carrier certification—its only formally delegated authority—we conclude that the sessions were not "meetings" within the meaning of the Sunshine Act.

Notes and Questions

1. In *Hunt v. NRC*, 611 F.2d 332 (10th Cir.1979), the issue was whether the Nuclear Regulatory Commission's Nuclear Reactor Safety Board was a "subdivision" of the Commission for purposes of the Sunshine Act. The court held that an entity had to be a subdivision of the collegial body itself, not just a subdivision of the agency, in order to be covered by the Sunshine Act.

2. Strict interpretation of the exemptions justifying closing meetings has increased the desire to find ways around the Act. For example, multi-member agencies may want to discuss negotiating strategies, but the D.C. Circuit restrictively interpreted exemption 9, which permits closed meetings to prevent premature disclosure of information likely to frustrate implementation of proposed agency action, so as not to authorize the Nuclear Regulatory Commission to close its meetings to prevent premature disclosure to OMB of its budget bargaining positions. Moreover, the court went further and suggested that this exemption would apply only where the disclosure "would permit either financial gain at government expense or circumvention of agency regulation." *Common Cause v. NRC*, 674 F.2d 921 (D.C.Cir.1982).

3. Like the Freedom of Information Act, the Sunshine Act provides specific authority for judicial enforcement of its provisions. 5 U.S.C.A. § 552b(h). Also like the FOIA, the Sunshine Act places the burden on the defendant agency to justify its actions and provides for attorneys fees and litigation costs. The enforcement provision, however, specifically does *not* authorize a court to set aside, enjoin, or invalidate agency action because it was taken during an agency meeting in violation of the Sunshine Act. 5 U.S.C.A. § 552b(h)(2).

4. Concern that the Sunshine Act was not achieving its purposes while impeding collegial discussions among members of multi-member agencies led a special committee created by the Administrative Conference of the United States to recommend a trial experiment of allowing agencies to hold closed meetings subject to the requirement of a detailed summary of the meeting to be made public after the meeting. *See* Randolph May, *Taming the Sunshine Act*, LEGAL TIMES (February 5, 1996). Would you favor this reform?

Chapter 9

ATTORNEYS FEES

A. INTRODUCTION

The practice of law would not exist unless attorneys could receive suitable compensation for their work. This is no less true for the practice of administrative law. Traditionally, in the United States, courts have followed the so-called "American rule" for payment of attorneys fees. *See Alyeska Pipeline Service Co. v. Wilderness Society*, 421 U.S. 240, 95 S.Ct. 1612, 44 L.Ed.2d 141 (1975). Under this rule, each party in a case generally must bear its own legal expenses. In most of the rest of the world, the prevailing party in a case recovers its attorneys fees from the losing party. This practice in other countries puts a premium on winning and has the tendency to discourage litigation, because potential plaintiffs not only have the opportunity to win money, they also have the risk of losing money. Thus, many "tort reform" proposals involve elimination or modification of the American rule. At the same time, elimination of the American rule can benefit plaintiffs in a number of circumstances. For example, if a plaintiff is not wealthy and is not seeking a monetary judgement (from which a contingency fee could be paid), he might not be able to bring the suit because of the inability to hire counsel.

In administrative law, one of the parties to a lawsuit will almost invariably be the government. The government attorneys, of course, are paid a salary without regard to whether they win or lose cases and without regard to how much time is spent on a case. Their salaries are paid by tax dollars.

In suits against the government, the private law firm may be paid by a client in one of several ways. When the plaintiff seeks a monetary recovery, a contingency fee is widely used to pay the attorney. The attorney agrees to represent the plaintiff for a percentage of the ultimate monetary recovery; if the attorney loses, the plaintiff owes him nothing. Attorneys representing defendants and attorneys representing plaintiffs in non-monetary recovery cases normally have agreements with their clients for payment based upon an hourly fee. The more hours the attorney works, the more he gets paid. Finally, many types of services are handled for a fixed fee. This is more common in non-litigation situations.

Suits challenging a loss of government benefits, such as veterans or social security disability benefits, because they seek in essence a monetary recovery, are often handled on a contingency fee basis. However, traditionally, Congress has been hostile to contingency fees in benefits suits. Whether the fear is that attorneys will deprive the beneficiaries of funds they need or that contingency fees will make challenges more likely, Congress has often placed limits on attorneys fees received in benefits litigation. In *Walters v. National Association of Radiation Survivors*, 473 U.S. 305, 105 S.Ct. 3180, 87 L.Ed.2d 220 (1985), for example, the Court reviewed legislation enacted during the Civil War that limited to $10 the amount that an attorney could receive for representing a veteran seeking benefits. This limitation remained the law until 1988, when it was amended to limit the fee to 20% of the past due benefits award. *See* 38 U.S.C.A. § 5904(d). However, the past due benefits at stake in benefits litigation are usually relatively small, so that attorneys may be unwilling to take them on as contingency fee cases. The real benefit to the client may be a timely reinstatement of monthly payments, rather than a large cash award for past due amounts.

If a private litigant does not seek a monetary judgement against the government, the costs of litigation, including the attorneys fees, are likely to preclude a lawsuit by all but the most wealthy. When the private litigant is not a plaintiff, but a defendant, in a civil suit brought by the government, the situation is even worse, because the only way to avoid substantial legal expenses is to concede to the government.

Even under the American rule there is an exception where a party engages in bad faith litigation. Courts have inherent power to protect the integrity of litigation before them by using an award of attorney fees to punish bad faith, vexatious, wanton, or oppressive conduct in litigation. This exception focuses on the party's conduct in the litigation, not the nature of its underlying claims or defenses, and generally requires egregious and willful conduct. *See Chambers v. NASCO*, 501 U.S. 32, 111 S.Ct. 2123, 115 L.Ed.2d 27 (1991). Because governments enjoy sovereign immunity from suit, however, they may be insulated even from this exception under the common law.

In response to some of the concerns with the American rule, Congress has from time-to-time passed special fee shifting statutes, usually relating to a particular substantive area of law where Congress wanted to encourage, or at least not discourage, particular types of lawsuits. There are more than 100 federal statutory provisions for attorneys fees, and litigation over attorneys fees accounts for a substantial portion of federal civil litigation.

The desire to encourage certain types of lawsuits is most apparent in citizen suit provisions found in many environmental laws. *See, e.g.,* 16 U.S.C.A. § 1540(g) (ESA); 30 U.S.C. § 1270 (Surface Mining Control and Reclamation Act); 33 U.S.C.A. § 1365 (CWA); 33 U.S.C.A. § 1415(g)

(Ocean Dumping Act); 42 U.S.C.A. § 300j–8 (Safe Drinking Water Act); 42 U.S.C.A. § 6972 (RCRA); 42 U.S.C.A. § 7604 (CAA); 42 U.S.C.A. § 9659 (CERCLA). These citizen suit provisions typically contain specific authorization to award costs (including attorney fees) to "any prevailing or substantially prevailing party, whenever the court determines such an award is appropriate." One need not prevail overall to be a substantially prevailing party, nor need one receive a final judgment from a court when the litigation is settled favorably to the plaintiff. In citizen suit cases, it is generally understood that the plaintiff to collect must have served the public interest by furthering the proper implementation of the statute. *See, e.g., Sierra Club v. EPA*, 769 F.2d 796 (D.C.Cir.1985). While usually these citizen suit cases are brought against polluters, or their equivalents, the provisions also provide for suits against the agency responsible for implementing the law, if the agency fails to perform a non-discretionary duty. Absent the citizen suit provisions, this latter type of case could be brought under the APA.

In 1975 Congress amended the Voting Rights Act of 1965 to include an attorneys fee provision, 42 U.S.C.A. § 1973*l*(e), allowing to "the prevailing party, other than the United States, a reasonable attorney's fee as part of the costs." Similarly, in 1976 Congress enacted the Civil Rights Attorney's Fees Awards Act, 42 U.S.C.A. 1988, to generally authorize attorney fees to prevailing parties in civil rights litigation. More pertinent to administrative law is the attorneys fees provision of the Freedom of Information Act, 5 U.S.C.A. § 552(a)(4)(E), which authorizes costs and "reasonable attorney fees" "reasonably incurred" to a plaintiff who "substantially prevailed." As in the citizen suit provisions, one need not be totally victorious to be considered a prevailing party. Generally, a plaintiff is a prevailing party if he succeeds "on any significant issue in litigation which achieves some of the benefit the parties sought in bringing suit." *Hensley v. Eckerhart*, 461 U.S. 424, 103 S.Ct. 1933, 76 L.Ed.2d 40 (1983). However, the degree of success may affect the amount of the award.

B. EQUAL ACCESS TO JUSTICE ACT

The Equal Access to Justice Act (EAJA), passed as a temporary measure in 1980, was amended and made permanent in 1985. Unlike most attorneys fees provisions, which are limited to a particular substantive law, the EAJA applies broadly to any non-tort action against the United States, as well as to some agency adjudications. *See* 5 U.S.C.A. § 504; 28 U.S.C.A. § 2412. Thus, it includes ordinary APA judicial review cases and formal APA adjudications where the government is represented by an attorney.

1. ELIGIBILITY

The original motivation for the EAJA was a concern that small businesses and individuals of modest means would be disabled from challenging unreasonable government action because of the prohibitive costs of litigation, especially attorneys fees. Over time, the concept of small business and modest means has been expanded, but the EAJA still limits its awards to individual plaintiffs with a net worth of $2 million or less, businesses with fewer than 500 employees and a net worth less than $7 million, tax-exempt charitable organizations, or any other organization that would qualify as a "small entity" under the Regulatory Flexibility Act (primarily this would extend the EAJA to small governments as well). 5 U.S.C.A. § 504(b)(1)(B); 28 U.S.C.A. § 2412(d)(2)(B).

In addition to the costs and fees for court cases, the EAJA extends by its terms to three different types of adversarial adjudicatory action: a formal adjudication under the APA at which the government is represented by counsel (but not ratemaking or the grant or renewal of a license); an appeal of a government contract dispute;[1] and administrative penalty proceedings under the Program Fraud Civil Remedies Act (31 U.S.C.A. Chapter 38). As noted, the government must be represented by counsel in these administrative proceedings in order to trigger EAJA coverage, because the purpose of the Act was to level the playing field, not to subsidize a private litigant's advantage. In these types of cases, the adjudicative officer "shall" award attorneys fees to a prevailing party other than the United States "unless the adjudicative officer of the agency finds that the position of the agency was substantially justified or that special circumstances make the award unjust." 5 U.S.C.A. § 504(a)(1).

The judicial portion of the EAJA first provides for an award of costs (but not including attorneys fees) to any eligible prevailing party without a further showing. It then waives sovereign immunity, so that exceptions to the American rule will apply to the government on the same basis as to other parties. Finally, it authorizes payment of attorneys fees to "a prevailing party other than the United States," unless the court finds that "the position of the United States was substantially justified or that special circumstances make an award unjust."

The concept of limiting awards to a "prevailing party" is common in the attorneys fees statutes, and the meaning under one statute should be the same as under another. The concept in the EAJA that a prevailing party is entitled to a fee award unless the government's position is "substantially justified" is relatively unusual and subject to some interpretation. It is clear that the burden is on the government to establish that its position was substantially justified. Moreover, an amendment in

---

1. The Contract Disputes Act of 1978 (41 U.S.C.A. §§ 601–613) created an administrative procedure to govern government contract disputes. A person with a government contract who has a dispute with an agency over the contract makes a claim to the contracting officer. If the officer denies the claim, the person may appeal that denial to the Board of Contract Appeals for that agency or may sue in the United States Court of Federal Claims. Each board consists of three administrative judges (not ALJs) who hear the case *de novo* under what are supposed to be informal procedures. An adverse decision of the Board may be appealed to the Court of Appeals for the Federal Circuit, where it is reviewed on a substantial evidence basis. There is a substantial legal practice involved in Board of Contract Appeals cases, but it is usually considered a part of Government Contract practice, rather than general federal or administrative litigation.

1985 clarified that the "position of the United States" includes both its position in the litigation and its position that made the litigation necessary (that is, the justification for the underlying government action). 5 U.S.C.A. § 504(b)(1)(E); 28 U.S.C.A. § 2412(d)(2)(D). The leading case defining substantial justification follows:

PIERCE v. UNDERWOOD

487 U.S. 552, 108 S.Ct. 2541, 101 L.Ed.2d 490 (1988).

JUSTICE SCALIA delivered the opinion of the Court.

Respondents settled their lawsuit against one of petitioner's predecessors as the Secretary of Housing and Urban Development, and were awarded attorney's fees after the court found that the position taken by the Secretary was not "substantially justified" within the meaning of the Equal Access to Justice Act (EAJA).... We granted certiorari to resolve a conflict in the Courts of Appeals over important questions concerning the interpretation of the EAJA.

[Our first issue is] the meaning of the phrase "substantially justified" in 28 U.S.C. § 2412(d)(1)(A). The Court of Appeals, following Ninth Circuit precedent, held that the Government's position was "substantially justified" if it "had a reasonable basis both in law and in fact. "... In this petition, the Government urges us to hold that "substantially justified" means that its litigating position must have had "some substance and a fair possibility of success." Respondents, on the other hand, contend that the phrase imports something more than "a simple reasonableness standard." ...

In addressing this issue, we make clear at the outset that we do not think it appropriate to substitute for the formula that Congress has adopted any judicially crafted revision of it—whether that be "reasonable basis in both law and fact" or anything else. "Substantially justified" is the test the statute prescribes, and the issue should be framed in those terms. That being said, there is nevertheless an obvious need to elaborate upon the meaning of the phrase. The broad range of interpretations described above is attributable to the fact that the word "substantial" can have two quite different—indeed, almost contrary—connotations. On the one hand, it can mean "[c]onsiderable in amount, value, or the like; large," Webster's New International Dictionary 2514 (2d ed. 1945)—as, for example, in the statement, "He won the election by a substantial majority." On the other hand, it can mean "[t]hat is such in substance or in the main,"—as, for example, in the statement, "What he said was substantially true." Depending upon which connotation one selects, "substantially justified" is susceptible of interpretations ranging from the Government's to the respondents'.

We are not, however, dealing with a field of law that provides no guidance in this matter. Judicial review of agency action, the field at issue here, regularly proceeds under the rubric of "substantial evidence" set forth in the Administrative Procedure Act. That phrase does not mean a large or considerable amount of evidence, but rather "such relevant evidence as a reasonable mind might accept as adequate to support a conclusion." In an area related to the present case in another way, the test for avoiding the imposition of attorney's fees for resisting discovery in district court is whether the resistance was "substantially justified," Fed.Rules Civ.Proc. 37(a)(4) and (b)(2)(E). To our knowledge, that has never been described as meaning "justified to a high degree," but rather has been said to be satisfied if there is a "genuine dispute," or "if reasonable people could differ as to [the appropriateness of the contested action]."

We are of the view, therefore, that as between the two commonly used connotations of the word "substantially," the one most naturally conveyed by the phrase before us here is not "justified to a high degree," but rather "justified in substance or in the main"—that is, justified to a degree that could satisfy a reasonable person. That is no different from the "reasonable basis both in law and fact" formulation adopted by the Ninth Circuit and the vast majority of other Courts of Appeals that have addressed this issue. To be "substantially justified" means, of course, more than merely undeserving of sanctions for frivolousness; that is assuredly not the standard for Government litigation of which a reasonable person would approve. . . .

We reach, at last, the merits of whether the District Court abused its discretion in finding that the Government's position was not "substantially justified." Both parties argue that for purposes of this inquiry courts should rely on "objective indicia" such as the terms of a settlement agreement, the stage in the proceedings at which the merits were decided, and the views of other courts on the merits. This, they suggest, can avoid the time-consuming and possibly inexact process of assessing the strength of the Government's position. While we do not disagree that objective indicia can be relevant, we do not think they provide a conclusive answer, in either direction, for the present case.

Respondents contend that the lack of substantial justification for the Government's position was demonstrated by its willingness to settle the litigation on unfavorable terms. Other factors, however, might explain the settlement equally well—for example, a change in substantive policy instituted by a new administration. The unfavorable terms of a settlement agreement, without inquiry into the reasons for settlement, cannot conclusively establish the weakness of the Government's position. To hold otherwise would not only distort the truth but penalize and thereby discourage useful settlements.

Respondents further contend that the weakness of the Government's position is established by the objective fact that the merits were decided at the pleadings stage. We disagree. At least where, as here, the dispute centers upon questions of law rather than fact, summary disposition proves only that the district judge was efficient.

Both parties rely upon the objective indicia consisting of the views expressed by other courts on the merits of the Government's position.

Obviously, the fact that one other court agreed or disagreed with the Government does not establish whether its position was substantially justified. Conceivably, the Government could take a position that is not substantially justified, yet win; even more likely, it could take a position that is substantially justified, yet lose. Nevertheless, a string of losses can be indicative; and even more so a string of successes....

We turn, then, to the actual merits of the Government's litigating position. [The Court summarized the parties' differing characterizations of the Government's litigating position and then stated without further analysis:] We cannot say that this description commands the conclusion that the Government's position was substantially justified. Accordingly, we affirm the Ninth Circuit's holding that the District Judge did not abuse his discretion when he found it was not.

Problem 9–1 Substantially Justified?

Recall the case of Ricardo Davila–Bardales from Chapter 3 (*see* Problem Materials for Problem 3–9). Although the applicable Immigration and Naturalization Service regulations prohibited Immigration Judges from accepting admissions of deportability from an unrepresented party under the age of 16, unless the minor was accompanied by an adult guardian, relative, or a friend, the Immigration Judge asked the then–15–year–old Davila–Bardales whether it was true that he was a Peruvian national who had illegally entered the United States. Davila–Bardales, unrepresented and unaccompanied by any adult, answered in the affirmative. In addition, the Immigration Judge entered into evidence a form filled out by INS officers attributing like admissions to Davila–Bardales when he was apprehended, and the Immigration Judge also obtained an admission in the hearing that the statements in the form were true.

Davila–Bardales appealed his deportation order on the ground that his admissions and the form could not be used in evidence against him. The INS acknowledged that his verbal admission of deportability in the hearing could not be used against him, but it defended the validity of the deportation order on the ground that the regulation only referred to admissions in immigration hearings; it did not refer to admissions made in interviews by INS officers or the admission of such evidence in the hearing. The Board of Immigration Appeals affirmed the Immigration Judge's order, but the First Circuit vacated the decision and remanded the case for further proceedings. The basis of the court's decision was that the BIA had issued inconsistent decisions regarding the admission of such forms when unrepresented and unaccompanied juveniles made admissions under INS officers' interrogations. The BIA had not adequately articulated an explanation for how these decisions might be reconciled or justified. On remand, it did not rule out the possibility that the INS might still uphold the deportation order if it articulated sufficient reasons distinguishing or explaining the inconsistent decisions.

If you were Davila–Bardales' lawyer, do you think you can get attorneys fees for the litigation in the First Circuit?

Problem Materials

MARTINEZ v. SECRETARY OF HEALTH & HUMAN SERVICES

815 F.2d 1381 (10th Cir.1987).

Per Curiam.

The issue in this case is whether the plaintiff is entitled to attorney's fees and expenses as a prevailing party under the Equal Access to Justice Act (EAJA)....

I

Plaintiff was injured in a work accident in 1978. Sometime thereafter, he began receiving disability benefits under the Social Security Act. A continuing disability investigation led to the cessation of plaintiff's disability benefits in 1981. The termination of benefits was upheld after a hearing before an Administrative Law Judge. Plaintiff's request for review of the hearing decision was denied by the Appeals Council in mid–1983.... Plaintiff sought judicial review of the Secretary's decision.

Plaintiff argued in district court that ... termination of disability benefits requires evidence that the claimant's medical condition has improved.... The Secretary asserted that the medical improvement test was not applicable, and that the claimant had the burden to prove that he or she was still disabled, which plaintiff had not proven.

On August 10, 1984, [in a wholly unrelated case,] this court held that Social Security disability benefits cannot be discontinued without a finding that the claimant's condition has improved and that failure to apply the correct legal standard is, by itself, sufficient to command reversal of a termination case. Based on [this case], the district court, on October 5, 1984, sua sponte reversed plaintiff's termination and directed the Secretary to reinstate plaintiff's benefits.

As the prevailing party below, plaintiff applied for attorney's fees and expenses under [the EAJA], arguing that the agency's position, both in the decision to terminate plaintiff's benefits and in the civil action, was not substantially justified and was taken in bad faith. Plaintiff argued that [this court had decided this issue in 1981 in an unpublished decision, in which] we adopted the medical improvement standard in this court and thereby made defendant's position both at the administrative level and in this litigation "substantially unjustified." The Secretary responded to the motion by arguing that the medical improvement standard had not yet been adopted by the agency or in this circuit at the time of the termination decision or at the time this action was brought.

The Secretary argued that the medical improvement standard was not adopted in this circuit until [the decision in] 1984—the decision which, of course, led to the district court's reversal of the Secretary's decision in this case.... The Secretary concluded that, because [that case] had not been decided at the time of the initial administrative decision or the court action [in this case], there was no basis for attorney's fees under [the EAJA]. The district court agreed with the Secretary and denied plaintiff's motion for attorney's fees and expenses.

II

... We agree with the district court's conclusion that the Secretary's position at trial was substantially justified. Martinez filed this action in district court on July 15, 1983. As the district court noted, at that time several circuits had adopted the medical improvement standard.

The state of the law in our circuit, however, was less certain. On January 8, 1981, in an unpublished decision, we strongly intimated that we too would follow the medical improvement standard. But that decision was subject to varying interpretations by district courts within our circuit. For example, as the district court here noted, "six months before this civil action was filed, this court [in a similar case] failed to adopt an improvement standard and held that the decision of the Secretary should be upheld if supported by substantial evidence." [Moreover, another district court in this circuit reached the same conclusion in 1984.] To add to the confusion, however, on August 16, 1983, another judge in the district of Colorado held that our [unpublished] decision ... represented an "unequivocal" adoption of the medical improvement standard.[1]

"For purposes of the EAJA, the more clearly established are the governing norms, and the more clearly they dictate a result in favor of the private litigant, the less 'justified' it is for the government to pursue or persist in litigation." Conversely, if the governing law is unclear or in flux, it is more likely that the government's position will be substantially justified. In light of the contrary district court interpretations of [our unpublished decision], we hold that the Secretary had substantial reason to press its view of the proper standard on the district court. We recognize that in [our 1984 decision] we stated that we had "adopted" the medical improvement standard in [the earlier unpublished decision]. But prior to [the 1984 decision], the import of [the earlier unpublished decision] was far from clear....

McKay Circuit Judge, dissents because he believes that the government's position was not substantially justified in this case.

FRIENDS OF THE BOUNDARY WATERS WILDERNESS v. THOMAS
53 F.3d 881 (8th Cir.1995).

John R. Gibson, Senior Circuit Judge.

The Friends of the Boundary Waters Wilderness' efforts to recover attorney's fees incurred in litigation over the management of the Superior National Forest in Minnesota have produced this appeal....

1. [Nevertheless,] the district court ... denied the prevailing plaintiff's request for attorney fees, finding that the government's position was substantially justified. That the same court could find that we had un-equivocally adopted the medical improvement standard and yet conclude that a challenge to this standard was justified, further demonstrates that this issue was not entirely settled within this circuit.

The Boundary Waters Canoe Wilderness Area located in northeastern Minnesota consists of some 1,075,000 acres of streams, lakes, and forests. In 1978, Congress passed the Boundary Waters Canoe Area Wilderness Act. Section 4(g) of the Act states:

> Nothing in this Act shall be deemed to require the termination of existing operation of motor vehicles to assist in the transport of boats across the [Prairie Portage, Four Mile Portage, and the Trout Lake Portage] during the period ending January 1, 1984. Following said date, unless the Secretary determines that there is no feasible nonmotorized means of transporting boats across the portages listed above, he shall terminate all such motorized use of each portage listed above.

In June 1986, the Forest Service completed the Plan for the Superior National Forest authorizing the continued motorized operation of Prairie Portage, Four Mile Portage, and Trout Lake Portage. The Plan concluded that the portages should remain open to motorized operation because it was not "feasible" to use nonmotorized portage wheels to move the boats across the portages.

The Friends brought an administrative appeal challenging the continued use of the motorized portages. [The Chief of the United States Forest Service (Chief) ordered a feasibility study to be made.] After the feasibility study was completed, the Chief considered the results and determined that though portaging by nonmotorized means could be done, it was not feasible in light of the risks to health and safety of the portagers. The Chief ruled that all three motorized portages should remain open indefinitely.

The Friends then filed suit challenging the Chief's decision. The district court held that the Wilderness Area Act was ambiguous and that the Chief's determination was a reasonable interpretation of the Act. The Friends appealed, and we reversed. We held that the language of the Act was unambiguous, and that the Chief's interpretation was contrary to the proper definition of the term "feasible." [Judge Magill dissented.]

[T]he Friends applied for $72,973.68 in costs and attorney's fees under the Equal Access to Justice Act. The district court denied the Friends' request for attorney's fees, reasoning that Congress' silence as to what it meant by "feasible," made it impossible to conclude that the Secretary's interpretation was not substantially justified, even though this court found it to be erroneous. In reaching this conclusion, the district court relied upon its earlier opinion as well as Judge Magill's dissent. . . .

The Friends contend that the district court abused its discretion when it concluded that the Chief's position on the portage issue was substantially justified and that the Friends were not entitled to attorney's fees under the EAJA. We reverse a district court decision not to award fees under the EAJA only for an abuse of discretion.

The EAJA provides that "a court shall award to a prevailing party other than the United States fees and other expenses, ... unless the court finds that the position of the United States was substantially justified or that special circumstances make an award unjust." The Chief bears the burden of proving that his position is substantially justified. In order for the Chief to prevail he must show that his position was "clearly reasonable, well founded in law and fact, solid though not necessarily correct." *See Pierce v. Underwood*, 487 U.S. 552 (1988) (in order for the government's position to be substantially justified it must be "justified to a degree that could satisfy a reasonable person" and have a "reasonable basis both in law and fact."). The Chief has failed to meet this burden and the district court abused its discretion in concluding that the Chief was substantially justified.

In concluding that the Chief's position was substantially justified, the district court relied too heavily upon its original opinion and Judge Magill's dissent from our decision reversing that opinion. The most powerful indicator of the reasonableness of an ultimately rejected position is a decision on the merits and the rationale which supports that decision. The views of the district court and dissenting judges are properly considered when conducting this inquiry. However, in the present case, our conclusion that the Chief's position was plainly contrary to existing law counsels so strongly against the conclusion that the Chief's position was substantially justified that it must determine the outcome.

An examination of this court's reasoning in rejecting the Chief's interpretation of the statute demonstrates that the Chief's position was not substantially justified. The Chief contended that "feasible," as the term was used in the statute, meant "reasonable," "practicable," or "likely," and relied heavily on the findings of the study with respect to safety and health of the portagers. However, we held that "[i]n applying the clearly expressed intent of Congress, we can only conclude that 'feasible' means 'capable of being done' or 'physically possible,' and as a matter of law the Chief erred in ordering that the portages remain open." We concluded that the Supreme Court had considered the definition of feasible on two previous occasions and that "the Chief's definition of 'feasible' was overly restrictive and contrary to clear congressional intent and the plain meaning of the word 'feasible.' " We cannot hold the Chief's position to be "clearly reasonable" or "well founded in law and fact," in light of our unequivocal rejection of the Chief's position as being contrary to existing law and clear congressional intent.

It is also significant that the Chief originally interpreted the statute in a manner consistent with our holding. The Chief first determined that "feasible" meant "possible," not "ideal" or "most practical," but later revised his interpretation. The Friends contend that the Chief's reversal of policy was the result of political influence. However, the Chief asserts that he did not reverse policy but merely "refined his definition of 'feasible' in light of the factual findings in the Portage Report." Accepting the Chief's explanation as to why he abandoned his original interpretation, we still conclude that he was not substantially justified in doing so. The question before the Chief was one of statutory interpretation, and should not have turned upon the outcome and findings of the feasibility study, but rather existing law and congressional intention. Therefore, we hold that the district court abused its discretion in concluding that the Chief was substantially justified. . . .

Notes and Questions

1. Section 504, relating to EAJA attorneys fees for administrative adversary adjudications, refers to "adjudication under section 554" of the APA. While this clearly encompasses adjudication required to conform to section 554, the question arose whether adjudication that merely replicated the procedures of section 554 also would qualify. In particular, the question arose with respect to immigration hearings that essentially duplicate section 554 hearings, even if they are not subject to section 554 (and consequently do not have ALJs as presiding officers). The Supreme Court, interpreting the statute strictly, held that only hearings required to be conducted pursuant to section 554 qualified for EAJA attorneys fees. *Ardestani v. I.N.S.*, 502 U.S. 129, 112 S.Ct. 515, 116 L.Ed.2d 496 (1991). Accordingly, in Problem 9–1, Davila–Bardales cannot obtain attorneys fees under 5 U.S.C.A. § 504 for the litigation before the BIA or INS. Once he appeals the BIA's decision to court, however, the EAJA fees are governed by 28 U.S.C.A. § 2412.

2. Note that in *Pierce* the Court made clear that appellate court review of district court determinations as to the substantial justification for the government's position is to be made on the basis of "abuse of discretion." This, in effect, gives substantial leeway to district judges in making this determination. Of course, errors of law constitute an abuse of discretion, so if a court of appeals can characterize the district court's decision as an error of law, it can easily reverse the lower court's opinion.

3. A large number of EAJA fees arise out of Social Security Disability litigation. Under the section of the law providing for judicial review of disability denials, 42 U.S.C.A. § 405(g), district courts can make "sentence four" decisions (referring to the fourth sentence of the section) affirming, modifying, or reversing the final decision of the Commissioner of Social Security, with or without remanding the case to Social Security. If a district court set aside a decision denying a disability benefit and remanded the case to Social Security for proceedings consistent with the decision, it would not yet be clear whether the plaintiff would ultimately succeed in obtaining the benefit. Perhaps Social Securi-

ty applied the wrong legal standard but applying the correct one will still lead to a denial. Nevertheless, the plaintiff is a prevailing party in the judicial litigation; he obtained what he sought, which was to overturn the denial. *See Shalala v. Schaefer*, 509 U.S. 292, 113 S.Ct. 2625, 125 L.Ed.2d 239 (1993). On the other hand, section 405(g) provides in its sixth sentence for remands to Social Security if the Commissioner moves for a remand to take additional evidence. In this circumstance, the court does not issue any final order upon remand, but instead retains jurisdiction of the case. Because there is no final order, the plaintiff is not yet a prevailing party. *See generally Melkonyan v. Sullivan*, 501 U.S. 89, 111 S.Ct. 2157, 115 L.Ed.2d 78 (1991). Accordingly, if the plaintiff loses on remand to the Commissioner (and, if appealed, the decision is sustained by the courts), the plaintiff will not qualify as a prevailing party at any stage in the judicial proceedings, because no final decision of a court would have given the plaintiff what he wanted. On the other hand, if the plaintiff wins on remand, the plaintiff qualifies for EAJA fees under 28 U.S.C.A. § 2412 not only for the district court litigation, but also for the proceedings before the Social Security Administration upon remand. The plaintiff is entitled to an award because the action before Social Security upon remand is, in a sense, a continuation of the court action, given the court's continuing jurisdiction. *Id. See also Sullivan v. Hudson*, 490 U.S. 877, 109 S.Ct. 2248, 104 L.Ed.2d 941 (1989).

4. A recurring practical problem for attorneys seeking fees under the EAJA is the short time period in which a fee request, including an itemized statement of time expended, must be filed: within 30 days of final judgment in a court or final disposition in an adjudicative proceeding. Since a "final judgment" is defined as a judgment that is final and not appealable, 28 U.S.C.A. § 2412(d)(2)(G), when a judgment is appealable, the date of the final judgment occurs when the time for appeal expires. If a judgment is not appealable, such as when there is a judgment upon settlement, the final judgment occurs on the date of the judgment. When a district court makes a "sentence four" remand, the "final judgment" is the date when the court decision can no longer be appealed. The action is not considered still open despite the fact that the agency is still dealing with the case. *See Melkonyan v. Sullivan*, 501 U.S. 89, 111 S.Ct. 2157, 115 L.Ed.2d 78 (1991). In a "sentence six" remand, however, because the court retains jurisdiction, there is no final judgment until the case has returned to the district court, and it has entered a final order. *Id.* There is no equivalent definition in the statute of a "final disposition in an adjudicative proceeding," so the appealability of an adjudicative decision to a court does not appear to toll the 30–day period. Because the EAJA represents a waiver of sovereign immunity, its limitations are strictly construed. It is unclear whether an incomplete fee request suffers this jurisdictional defect, or whether, if the request is sufficient to give notice to the government and court, it can be supplemented after the 30–day period. *See Dunn v. United States*, 775 F.2d 99 (3d Cir.1985) (where request was filed in a timely manner but did not

contain the itemized statement required by the statute, this information could be supplied later).

5. Organizations (other than charitable organizations) must meet the net worth and number-of-employees limitations in the EAJA provisions. What happens when an organization is a membership association—do the limitations apply to the organization or its members? In *Love v. Reilly*, 924 F.2d 1492 (9th Cir.1991), the court held that the Northwest Food Processors Association qualified for attorneys fees because it exceeded neither the net worth nor number-of-employees limitations, even if some of its member corporations did and even if they were beneficiaries of the litigation. The member corporations were not liable for the association's attorneys fees and did not direct the litigation. *Accord: National Ass'n of Manufacturers v. Department of Labor*, 159 F.3d 597 (D.C.Cir.1998).

6. Often lawsuits are brought by a number of plaintiffs, all of whom are represented by the same attorney. What if only one of the plaintiffs qualifies for attorneys fees under the EAJA; can all the attorneys' time be counted against that one plaintiff on the grounds that the same amount of work would have been done had there been only one plaintiff? The answer is not clear, but the government has argued in some cases that the attorneys fees should be disallowed or decreased on the grounds that "special circumstances make an award unjust."

7. In 1996 Congress amended the EAJA to extend its attorneys fees provision to situations where the government, in enforcing a regulatory requirement, makes a "demand" "substantially in excess of the decision of the adjudicative officer" that "is unreasonable when compared with such decision, under the facts and circumstances of the case." 5 U.S.C.A. § 504(a)(4). Similar language was added to address judicial enforcement cases. 28 U.S.C.A. § 2412(d)(1)(D). This was aimed at countering a perceived sense that agencies place large demands in their enforcement complaints to extort compliance or settlement from defendants. Whether there is reality behind this perception is not yet clear.

2. AMOUNT OF AWARD

If a person qualifies for attorneys fees under the EAJA, the agency or court is to base the fees on "prevailing market rates for the kind and quality of the services furnished, except that an attorney fee cannot exceed $125 per hour," unless the court [or agency by regulation] determines that an increase in the cost of living or a special factor, such as the limited availability of qualified attorneys for the proceedings involved, justifies a higher fee. 28 U.S.C.A. § 2412(d)(2)(A)(ii); 5 U.S.C.A. § 504(b)(1)(A)(ii). Until amended in 1996, the ceiling was $75 per hour, and requests for enhancements to the fee amount were routine. What was considered a "special factor" was subject to substantial disagreement. In *Pierce v. Underwood*, part of which you read above, the Court also addressed this issue.

PIERCE v. UNDERWOOD

487 U.S. 552, 108 S.Ct. 2541, 101 L.Ed.2d 490 (1988).

JUSTICE SCALIA delivered the opinion of the Court.

The final issue before us is whether the amount of the attorney's fees award was proper.... In allowing fees at a rate in excess of the $75 cap (adjusted for inflation), the District Court relied upon some circumstances that arguably come within the single example of a "special factor" described in the statute, "the limited availability of qualified attorneys for the proceedings involved." We turn first to the meaning of that provision.

If "the limited availability of qualified attorneys for the proceedings involved" meant merely that lawyers skilled and experienced enough to try the case are in short supply, it would effectively eliminate the $75 cap—since the "prevailing market rates for the kind and quality of the services furnished" are obviously determined by the relative supply of that kind and quality of services. "Limited availability" so interpreted would not be a "special factor," but a factor virtually always present when services with a market rate of more than $75 have been provided.... If that is to be so, the exception for "limited availability of qualified attorneys for the proceedings involved" must refer to attorneys "qualified for the proceedings" in some specialized sense, rather than just in their general legal competence. We think it refers to attorneys having some distinctive knowledge or specialized skill needful for the litigation in question—as opposed to an extraordinary level of the general lawyerly knowledge and ability useful in all litigation. Examples of the former would be an identifiable practice specialty such as patent law, or knowledge of foreign law or language. Where such qualifications are necessary and can be obtained only at rates in excess of the $75 cap, reimbursement above that limit is allowed.

For the same reason of the need to preserve the intended effectiveness of the $75 cap, we think the other "special factors" envisioned by the exception must be such as are not of broad and general application. We need not specify what they might be, but they include nothing relied upon by the District Court in this case. The "novelty and difficulty of issues," "the undesirability of the case," the "work and ability of counsel," and "the results obtained" are factors applicable to a broad spectrum of litigation; they are little more than routine reasons why market rates are what they are. The factor of "customary fees and awards in other cases," is even worse; it is not even a routine reason for market rates, but rather a description of market rates. It was an abuse of discretion for the District Court to rely on these factors.

The final factor considered by the District Court, "the contingent nature of the fee," is also too generally applicable to be regarded as a "special" reason for exceeding the statutory cap....

We conclude, therefore, that none of the reasons relied upon by the District Court to increase the rate of reimbursement above the statutory was a "special factor."

Problem 9–2 What are special factors?

You have recently represented a small food processing company in Boston, Massachusetts, successfully appealing an EPA permit condition under the Clean Water Act to the First Circuit. You do not believe that EPA was substantially justified in imposing the permit condition, and you will request attorneys fees under the EAJA. You specialize in representing companies in the New England area that are regulated by EPA under the Clean Water Act, you have developed a substantial practice in that field and you are recognized by companies and EPA as one of the leading practitioners of Clean Water Act law in New England. As might be imagined, there are few, if any, attorneys willing to represent businesses before EPA for $125 per hour. The market fee for that kind of attorney service is $175–200 per hour. What kind of information and arguments do you need to put into your fee petition, if you want to request the market-level fee? What do you think are your chances of obtaining it?

Problem Materials

PIRUS v. BOWEN

869 F.2d 536 (9th Cir.1989).

WILLIAM A. NORRIS, CIRCUIT JUDGE:

Appellant Sidell Pirus brought a class action against the Secretary of the Department of Health and Human Services, challenging the Secretary's decision to deny social security benefits to her and the class she represented. After the district court granted Pirus' motion for summary judgment, Pirus petitioned the court for attorney's fees under the Equal Access to Justice Act. The district court granted Pirus' petition, holding that the Secretary's original decision to deny benefits to the class and then to defend that position through litigation was not "substantially justified" within the meaning of the EAJA. The court also determined that "special factors" justified awarding fees in excess of the $75 per hour cap mandated by the Act. The government challenges ... the fee enhancement. We affirm the district court. . . .

The final issue before us is whether the amount of the fee award was proper. The EAJA provides that attorney's fees "shall be based upon prevailing market rates for the kind and quality of the services furnished," but "shall not be awarded in excess of $75 per hour unless the court determines that an increase in the cost of living or a special factor, such as the limited availability of qualified attorneys for the proceedings involved, justifies a higher fee." The district court awarded fees in excess of the $75 per hour statutory cap. . . . Part of the increase . . . was attributable to the presence of several "special factors." First, Pirus' attorneys were expert in the field of social security law. Second, the court found that there were no lawyers in the community willing to undertake this case at the statutory rate. Finally, the court noted that Pirus' lawyers were uniquely situated to handle her case because of their recent experience litigating a similar case, ... all the way to the Supreme Court.... We review the district court's decision to award fees in excess of the statutory cap for abuse of discretion.

In *Underwood*, the Supreme Court considered what Congress meant by a "special factor" that would justify fees at an hourly rate higher than $75. The "special factor" suggested by Congress as an example—"the limited availability of qualified attorneys for the proceedings involved"—received considerable attention. In this regard, the Court concluded that it is not enough to simply say that "lawyers skilled and experienced enough to try the case are in short supply." ... Congress instead intended for courts to deviate from the statutory cap only if there was limited availability of "attorneys having some distinctive knowledge or specialized skill needful for the litigation in question." As examples of the type of lawyers who possess the distinctive knowledge or skill that would justify deviation from the $75 cap, the Court described lawyers who have "an identifiable practice specialty such as patent law," or those who have knowledge of "foreign law or language." "Where such qualifications are necessary, and can be obtained only at rates in excess of the $75 cap, reimbursement above the limit is allowed."

The Court in *Underwood* thus recognized that lawyers who develop a practice specialty acquire distinctive knowledge and skills which may be necessary to a particular case. Although patent law was the only specialty identified by the Court, there is no reason to believe the Court intended the universe of such specialties to be limited to patent law alone. In the instant case, Pirus' attorneys had developed a practice specialty in social security law. Having litigated various class actions challenging provisions of the Act, they had extensive knowledge of the Act, its legislative history, and the development of the Social Security Administration's regulations. The expertise and skills that they developed are in many ways akin to those developed by a patent lawyer: expertise with a complex statutory scheme; familiarity and credibility with a particular agency; and understanding of the needs of a particular class of clients—in this case, the elderly—and of how those needs could best be met under the existing statute and regulations.

It is not enough, however, that the attorney possess distinctive knowledge and skills. Those qualifications warrant additional fees only if they are in some way needed in the litigation and cannot be obtained elsewhere at the statutory rate. In this case the district court ruled that the special expertise of the attorneys was necessary because the litigation involved a highly complex area of the Social Security Act, with which plaintiff's attorneys had already developed familiarity and expertise. The court noted that Pirus' class action was no routine disability case; it required substantial knowledge of the legislative history of the "widow's insurance" provisions of the Act. The court also found, as *Underwood* requires, that these skills could not be obtained at the statutory rate; indeed, the court determined that there were no lawyers in the Los Angeles area besides Pirus' attorneys who possessed the skills necessary to the case who would take the case for $75 an hour.

CHYNOWETH v. SULLIVAN

920 F.2d 648 (10th Cir.1990).

BALDOCK, CIRCUIT JUDGE.

Plaintiff-appellant Mary Chynoweth appeals from a district court ruling denying her request to exceed the $75 per hour cap on attorney's fees awarded to her pursuant to the Equal Access to Justice Act (EAJA). Plaintiff argues that her attorney's expertise in Social Security disability law constituted a "special factor" ... warranting a departure from the statutory rate....

Plaintiff petitioned the district court for attorney's fees of $130 per hour pursuant to the Equal Access to Justice Act. Plaintiff's counsel indicated that he was a specialist in Social Security benefits law and had litigated many cases in federal court involving disability benefits. Plaintiff produced affidavits from several attorneys attesting that there were few lawyers in plaintiff's vicinity willing to handle Social Security disability cases and that $130 per hour was a reasonable fee for such services.

The district court found that the Secretary's denial of plaintiff's disability benefits was not substantially justified and consequently held that plaintiff was entitled to attorney's fees under EAJA. Exercising its discretion, the court increased the EAJA hourly rate of $75 to $96.75 to allow for cost-of-living increases. However, the district concluded that, based on *Pierce v. Underwood*, counsel's expertise in Social Security benefits law did not constitute a "special factor" ... justifying an additional increase in the $75 rate.

... EAJA mandates that attorney's fees awarded "be based upon prevailing market rates for the kind and quality of the services furnished," but "shall not be awarded in excess of $75 per hour unless the court determines that an increase in the cost of living or a special factor, such as the limited availability of qualified attorneys for the proceedings involved, justifies a higher fee." ...

Plaintiff argues that Social Security benefits law comprises a specialized practice area warranting payment in excess of the $75 rate. We disagree. "Incomparable expertise, standing alone, will not justify the higher rate." Rather, the statutory cap may be exceeded only in the "unusual situation" where the legal services rendered require specialized training and expertise unattainable by a competent attorney through a diligent study of the governing legal principles. The law contains a myriad of practice areas; no attorney can be expected to master all areas at once. Yet merely because some scholarly effort and professional experience is required to attain proficiency in a particular practice area does not automatically require enhancement of the EAJA rate. Although Social Security benefits law involves a complex statutory and regulatory framework, the field is not beyond the grasp of a competent practicing attorney with access to a law library and the other accoutrements of modern legal practice.

In arguing that Social Security benefits law comprises a specialized practice area subject to enhancement of the EAJA rate, plaintiff places primary reliance upon *Pirus v. Bowen*. In *Pirus*, the district court found that plaintiff's class action against the Secretary was "no routine disability case" and that no attorney in the Los Angeles area capable of handling the case would take it for $75 per hour. Because the Ninth Circuit could not say that the district court's findings were clearly erroneous, it held that the court had not abused its discretion by awarding fees in excess of the statutory cap. In contrast, the district court in the instant case made no findings that plaintiff's action was a particularly difficult disability case or that she would be unable to obtain competent representation at $96.75 per hour.... We therefore find *Pirus* ... distinguishable.

RAINES v. SHALALA

44 F.3d 1355 (7th Cir.1995).

RIPPLE, CIRCUIT JUDGE.

After William Raines won entitlement to social security disability benefits and supplemental security income, the district court awarded him attorney fees and expenses under the Equal Access to Justice Act ("EAJA"). The Secretary of Health and Human Services ("Secretary") appeals that award. She challenges ... the district court's decision that a special factor justified enhancement of the award.... For the following reasons, we reverse the district court's judgment and remand the case for further proceedings consistent with this opinion.

... Mr. Raines' petition requested $175.00 per hour for attorney fees. The petition claimed that this hourly rate was the prevailing market rate for this type of litigation because of the limited availability of qualified social security lawyers....

At the outset of its consideration of the fee petition, the district court noted that, in *Pierce v. Underwood*, the Supreme Court had stated that the exception to the $75.00 statutory cap for attorneys "qualified in the proceedings" referred to qualifications "in some specialized sense, rather than in general legal competence." Therefore, it was necessary that the attorney possess "some distinctive knowledge or specialized skill needful for the litigation in question—as opposed to an extraordinary level of general lawyerly knowledge and ability useful in all litigation." It also noted that the Ninth Circuit had applied the special factor concept of *Pierce* to lawyers who have an expertise in the area of social security law in *Pirus v. Bowen*. Employing these two cases as its decisional matrix, the court then examined the facts of this case to determine whether such an enhancement was appropriate. It found that Frederick J. Daley, Mr. Raines' attorney, possessed an expertise in the area of social security law.... Additionally, noted the district court, his law firm had litigated numerous social security cases before the Seventh Circuit and district courts. The court also found that "there is limited availability of attorneys in Chicago who are both experienced in Social Security law and willing to take a case such as Raines' for less than the prevailing rate." Finally, the court determined that the case involved complex issues requiring "more than just routine lawyering skills available from the general bar." On the basis of these findings, the court held that Mr. Raines' attorney met the criteria for awarding the special factor market fee. It summarized those factors as follows: 1) expertise with a complex statutory scheme; 2) familiarity and credibility with a particular agency; and 3) understanding the needs of a particular class of clients....

The Secretary has not objected to a fee award for Mr. Raines' counsel; in fact, she expressly has agreed that a cost of living adjustment to the $75.00 hourly rate was appropriate. Nor has the Secretary contested the district court's conclusion that plaintiff's counsel is skilled in social security law. The Secretary's submission on appeal is more precisely tailored: that the district court erred in enhancing the attorney fees on the basis that social security benefits law constitutes a "specialized" practice for EAJA purposes. In support of her position, the Secretary points out that, if such practice specialties routinely are recognized as "special factors," fee awards that are actually subject to the statutory cap imposed by Congress would be rare. The Secretary urges that we adopt the views of the Courts of Appeals for the District of Columbia and Tenth Circuits, which require skills or expertise above and beyond an attorney's knowledge of a particular area of the law. *See Chynoweth v. Sullivan* (holding that a social security specialist does not, solely by virtue of that expertise, fall under the "special factor" exception); *Waterman S.S. Corp. v. Maritime Subsidy Bd.*, 901 F.2d 1119, 1124 (D.C.Cir.1990) (noting that the two specialties listed as examples in *Pierce* require "technical or other education outside the field of American law"). In short, the Secretary submits that we should conclude that a specialization in social security law does not constitute a special factor justifying an enhanced award....

The EAJA "is not designed to reimburse reasonable fees without limit." ... Because the Supreme Court elucidated the meaning of "special factor" in *Pierce*, our analysis must begin with that case. The Justices explained that the higher fee could not be based simply on the limited availability of qualified attorneys. Rather, the Court held that an enhancement of the hourly rate could be justified under the exception if the availability of qualified attorneys is limited and if the nature of the case makes it necessary to retain the services of attorneys qualified in "some specialized sense, rather than just in their general legal competence." ... The Court suggested that the distinctive knowledge and skill are exemplified by an "identifiable practice specialty such as patent law, or knowledge of foreign law or language." It then concluded that reimbursement above the $75.00 ceiling is allowed when "such qualifications are necessary and can be obtained only at rates in excess of the $75 cap."

We think that the directive of the Supreme Court in *Pierce* makes clear that the special skill requirement of the statute can be defined in terms of either an identifiable practice specialty not easily acquired by a reasonably competent attorney or special non-legal skills such as knowledge of a foreign language. To the extent that the Secretary's submission can be read as defining "special skill" only in the latter terms, she invites us to adopt too narrow, or at least too rigid, a definition.[8] Indeed, often these two elements will be inextricably intertwined. Rather, we believe that *Pierce* directs the courts to recognize that certain practice areas require more advanced and specialized legal skills than those possessed or easily acquired by most members of the bar. In our view, *Pierce* acknowledges that there will be cases in which such specialized training will be necessary. Nevertheless, we believe that such cases will be the exceptional situation and that, by providing for the "specialized case," Congress did indeed contemplate such a situation. A "specialized case" cannot be defined, however, in terms of broad generalizations such as the "novelty and the difficulty of issues," "the undesirability of the case" or the "results obtained."

In any event, we agree with our colleagues in the Eighth and Tenth Circuits that the area of social security law cannot in itself be considered such a specialized area of law practice as to warrant, as a general rule, payment in excess of the $75.00 rate. *Stockton v. Shalala*, 36 F.3d 49, 50 (8th Cir.1994); *Chynoweth v. Sullivan*. [T]o the extent that *Pirus* may be read as holding that social security cases are always a matter of specialization for purposes of the EAJA, we find ourselves in respectful disagreement.[9] Rather, the appropriate inquiry is whether the individual case presents such an " 'unusual' " situation that it requires someone of "specialized training and expertise unattainable by a competent attorney through a diligent study of the governing legal principles." ...

We believe that the district court began its analysis on the right foot when it stated that social security cases are not automatically entitled to the enhancement of fees. The district court made a specific assessment

---

8. We note that the District of Columbia Circuit has characterized the two examples given in *Pierce*, patent law and foreign language ability, as both requiring "technical or other education outside the field of American law." We do not read this dictum ... to be intended as an all-inclusive description of the exception.

9. The Ninth Circuit has also stated that environmental litigation may "constitute 'an identifiable practice specialty,' and that an attorney's prior insecticide litigation experience, coupled with his experience in obtaining federal preliminary injunc-

tions," may qualify as " 'distinctive knowledge' under Pirus." But in both cases the court remanded the fees decision to the district court, without awarding enhanced fees, because the appellants had not established another requisite element of the *Pierce* criteria for the special factor exception. Judge Wallace, concurring in part and dissenting in part, stated that "the Supreme Court's language in *Pierce* convinces me that such a broad legal field [as environmental litigation] cannot qualify as a specialized practice area warranting payment in excess of $75 an hour."

that "the issues present in Mr. Raines' case were complex and required more than just routine lawyering skills available from the general bar." In the district court's view, "[f]or Raines to receive effective representation, he needed counsel with intimate knowledge of the Social Security Act and how benefits under the Act relate to other entitlement programs impacting on areas of his life which are vital to his well-being." In short, the district court concluded that the plaintiff had made an adequate case that "distinctive knowledge or specialized skill" was "needful for the litigation in question." It is this determination that must now be scrutinized to determine whether the decision of the district court ought to stand.

Our reading of *Pierce* convinces us that the district court employed too lenient a test to determine that a special factor enhancement was justified. We do not question the proficiency of Mr. Raines' attorney in the area of social security benefits law. However, we believe that the specialized skills described by the district court do not constitute the sort of expertise that is unattainable by a competent attorney who has diligently accomplished the legal work necessary in this case. We also believe that the district court erroneously determined that Mr. Raines' case was so complex that it necessarily required extraordinary lawyering skills. Our review of the record convinces us that this case cannot be characterized as requiring specialized skills on the part of the attorney. Indeed, the principal issues ... are issues that arise not infrequently in disability litigation. The attorney's appreciation of the interrelationship of disability benefits and supplemental security income was also a matter that was not beyond the ability of the diligent practitioner.

Accordingly, we believe that the district court should not have permitted the enhancement of the fee award on the ground that this case required "distinctive knowledge or specialized skill." Because we do not believe that the district court's decision was among those options from which one could have expected the court to choose on the basis of this record, we cannot let its judgment stand even under a deferential standard of review.

Notes and Questions

1. The EAJA also authorizes enhancement of the fee limit in light of increases in the cost of living. Prior to the recent increase from $75 to $125, the cost of living increase allowance was a potentially significant escalator. The cost of living increase is calculated by reference to the general increase in the Consumer Price Index since the last amendment to the fee limitation amount. *See Dewalt v. Sullivan*, 963 F.2d 27 (3d Cir.1992).

2. Courts have also held that agency "bad faith" is grounds for an enhanced fee award. *See Brown v. Sullivan*, 916 F.2d 492, 495–496 (9th Cir.1990).

3. All of the cases in this section involve attempts to obtain a fee enhancement for representation in a court case under 28 U.S.C. § 2412.

The determination of whether to grant an enhancement is made by the district court judge, subject to review on appeal for abuse of discretion (or legal error). However, when a person seeks enhancement of a fee for representation in a formal adjudication, the determination of the standard for and the amount of enhancement *must* be contained in an agency regulation; it is not a matter for judicial determination. *See Mendenhall v. National Transportation Safety Board*, 213 F.3d 464 (9th Cir.2000).

4.   If you can obtain attorneys fees for the cost of litigating against the government when the government's position is not substantially justified, can you obtain attorneys fees for the time spent in collecting the attorneys fees? For example, what if the government opposes your fee request, forcing you to litigate to collect? Obviously, if you lose that litigation, you do not collect, but if you win, can you collect attorneys fees *for the litigation to collect the fees*? And if so, does the government have a defense that its opposition *to your fee request*, as opposed to its defense of its original action, was substantially justified. In *Commissioner v. Jean*, 496 U.S. 154, 110 S.Ct. 2316, 110 L.Ed.2d 134 (1990), the government contested the award and amount of attorneys fees to the plaintiff made by the district court. The court of appeals upheld the award but remanded for calculation of the amount. The plaintiff thereafter sought attorneys fees for the fee litigation as well, but the government maintained that its opposition to the attorneys fees was substantially justified, in light of the court of appeals' remand for calculation of the amount. The Supreme Court rejected the government's argument, holding that so long as the plaintiff is eligible for attorneys fees in the underlying case, the plaintiff is presumptively eligible for attorneys fees in the fee litigation. The district court continues to have significant discretion to determine the amount of the fee award in light of all the facts and circumstances.

Index

†